PREFACE

JESUS WAS A JEW

Jesus was a Jew.

Jesus was not a Christian.

THE GOSPELS

Having lived in a nation which is predominately Christian, I became aware at an early age that most Christians, although they know of the origins of Jesus, somehow relegate his Jewishness into a far away dark corner of his past to the point that it is as if it never existed and all but obscured by 2,000 years of editing. The attitude is usually something like, *"yes, he was Jewish, but..."*. This same attitude can be said of the Jewish people who have many different understandings regarding Jesus the Jew.

Most of this comes about through the way the Gospels have been translated and have come down to us in what ever language one chooses. But it also is a direct result of doctrine, prejudice, ignorance and in some cases anti-Semitic dogma from an early period in church history after there were no more Jews in it's ranks and when it was being *codified* into a *religion* devoid of it's Jewish origin. It had begun by Jewish followers who kept the Law, but it became a new Gentile *religion* based on the life of a Jewish martyr, and without any Jewish presence, character or soul. It had taken on a life of it's own and metastasized into a global phenomenon totally cut off from it's mooring in the Law of Moses, devoid of it's origin based on Commandments.

JEWS AND CHRISTIANS

In putting my thoughts together to write this book, it became apparent to me early on that it would have to be geared towards the Jewish reader, although to the Christian, much can be learned regarding the historical time of Jesus. This is especially true if the reader is unfamiliar with the Law which dominates much of the discussion within the four Gospels. For his entire ministry revolved around the interpretation and application of the Law of Moses. From the time that Jesus was born and circumcised according to the Law of Moses, until his eventual sentencing to death for *"blasphemy"* by the Priests according to their interpretation of the Law of Moses, the Law of Moses dominated his existence. The Gospels are a discussion of this Law.

For this reason, the Law of Moses, it's Commandments, Statutes and Ordinances as discussed and debated by the Pharisees, Scribes, Sadducee and Priests with Jesus are analyzed. For whether Jesus was the "*son of David*", "*savior*", or the "*anointed*" son of God, it is within the Law of Moses and the Prophets which will attest to it's truth. And it is within this context that understanding what all of the "*fuss*" was about regarding who and what Jesus was to the Jewish people of his day is discussed. Also, it will expose the reader not familiar with the Law to some of the legal issues they debated.

As many Jewish people and most Gentile people do not know the Law of Moses and it was the Law of Moses which dominated the life story of Jesus, undertaking a brief discussion of the Law as it applied to the situation in his life is imperative if the events which eventually took his life are to have any real meaning. This book is by no means a complete work on the subject nor was it meant to be a scholarly work. Only the main *legal issues* are looked at, for the discussion on these points is in no way exhausted in this book.

Additionally, this is not meant to be a comment on whether he or the Pharisees or Priests were correct, but that it was the Law of Moses in many respects which was the central, behind the scenes player and in most respects (other than GOD HIMSELF) the catalyst for the events which unfolded.

The many discussions between Jesus and his fellow Jews, the Pharisees, Priests as well as others in the Gospels, are an education in the ancient Law of Moses as it was understood and practiced during his life time. But these discussions only have any real meaning if the Law of Moses is understood well enough that the discussions between Jesus and others make sense from the perspective of the "*Law*" itself. For it was the Law they were debating.

This is also true with respect to how the sons of Israel related to those peoples around them who they viewed as "*different*". Whether they were Roman, Samaritan, Greek or Canaanite, from the Jewish perspective, and from the Law, these people were viewed separately. They were not the sons of GOD nor were they under the SEED Covenant of Abraham nor the Law Covenant of Sinai according to their Covenant with GOD. Samaritans were not only thought of as heretics but were no longer even thought of as being of the SEED of Abraham by the majority of the Jewish people in Israel. They were considered "*unclean*" and their land was avoided by most Jews.

WORDS IN THE GOSPELS

My approach has been to concentrate only on the words spoken by Jesus as much as possible and the quotes he gives from the Law of Moses including the words of the Prophets either given or referenced within the four Gospels. The rest of the Christian Bible was not part of this book for a very simple reason. The four Gospels are the basis for all of what follows. Understanding the basis of what was originally considered in the beginning, just another Jewish sect by it's people, is the key to understanding all of which followed. Indeed, Jewish believers in Jesus continued living as Jews and even went to synagogue with other fellow Jews and debated the Law. Whether as a believer or as a non-believer, the history and growth of Christianity is already fairly well documented. So it is the words of Jesus which concerns this book.

The teachings of Jesus changed drastically as it went from Jesus in the holy land itself, to his Jewish

JESUS the JEW

JESUS the JEW

SON of the SEED of Abraham

Mika'el ben David

In Memory of:

David R. Friedman and Ronald F. Friedman

My brothers, thou hast been unto me more than the rising of the sun and the perfume of love; gracious hast thy kindness been unto me beyond my soul. I miss thee in the depth of my heart; always, will I never forget thy affection nor thy love.

Mika'el ben David

OTHER BOOKS BY THIS AUTHOR
(http://www.wix.com/mikaelll/seed-covenant)

TABLE OF CONTENTS

followers teaching to other Jews, and later to Paul who with his radical understanding brought it onto the world stage. Finally, after the Jews were no longer the leaders of the movement and faded from sight, it took yet another radical turn as it was established as the new religion of the Gentiles of western civilization becoming it's new foundation stone.

Whether one wants to put a time line on this event or not, it came about roughly when the Roman Emperor Constantine converted and afterward convened the Council of Nicaea in 325 which all but put the final nail in Jesus as a Jew. For the council and subsequent councils slowly made Christianity into a religion devoid of any connection to the Law of Moses, Israel or the Jewish people, and beginning with the influence of Emperor Constantine the Jewish people became more and more the stereotypical *"Judas"* rather than the family and the people of Jesus who spread his word.

As a Jew trying to make sense of some of the discussions between Jesus and the different groups whom he dealt with, knowing better the argument pertaining to the Law which they were debating becomes imperative. For it is the Law which was not only discussed, debated and taught, it was the *"Law"* which was used to condemn Jesus to death for the act of *"blasphemy"*. The *"Law"* is the central character other than Jesus. For more than anything else, it represents YHWH and may be considered the central player in the saga.

Jesus came into the world and as an infant and was circumcised according to the Law of Moses. For the rest of his life, it was this Law which dominated his entire existence all the way up until, and including the Priests using the Law to condemn him to death. From cradle to grave, and all in between, it was the Law which was center stage in his life. Without the Law of Moses, Jesus would have no reason to exist. For by his own words, it was the Commandments of the Law for which he came to fulfill.

Additionally, the Law of Moses reflected not only the religious, but the cultural, social and even the political period in which he lived. With few exceptions, the Law of Moses permeated just about every aspect of daily life.

Because so much of the material is regarding the Law of Moses which Israel lived under and which Jesus was a part of, to read the Gospels with no understanding of these discussions leaves one at a sever disadvantage. This is especially true for the Jewish reader, but also it is very important for the Christian who may not understand what was such a big deal with the Jews regarding such things as Jesus saying he had a *"new commandment"*, or emphasizing his own *name* and declaring himself the *"messiah"*, or what he had to say about *divorce, swearing, "kashrut"*, *hating* one's father and mother, bringing *division, fornication* and *adultery, healing* or *plucking* corn on Shabbat and other issues which seemingly challenged the Law of Moses.

Not only did he seemingly challenged the Law of Moses, but he also became a threat to most if not all of the establishment, including the Pharisees, Temple Priests and even the Romans. For the Christian to fully appreciate the situation in which Jesus lived, he must understand the complexity of the legal rhythm of his time. The Law of Moses was everything. This was true for the Priests, the Pharisees, Sadducee the Herodians and even the Zealots who saw briefly in Jesus the *"messiah"* who would immediately restore the throne of David and rid Israel of the foreign Roman occupiers.

During this time period Greek Hellenism was still prevalent amongst the people. But competing with Hellenization and the Law of Moses was also Roman Law which dominated every other aspect of life and at times overruled religious Law. With this came the many competing Jewish sects, especially the Pharisees with their own competing system of *"synagogues"* and their *"oral law"* verses the Priests, written Law of Moses, (Safer Torah) and the Temple. The Pharisaic *"oral law"* was a creation by the Pharisees which was neither accepted by nor taught by the Temple Priests. This so called *"oral law"* created by the rabbis will be discussed much, because of it's corrosive affect on the Jewish people to understand their own Law as given to Moses and because Jesus harangued the Pharisees for their *"traditions"* per their *"oral law"*. Because the Pharisees are such a big part of the discussion in the life of Jesus, the fact that they were so heavily influenced by their own oral traditions created by their rabbis, plays a disproportionate part in the Gospels.

Another aspect for the Christian reader, of whom many if not most disregard the first half of their bible which they call the *"Old Testament"*, as being not much more than interesting stories of an ancient people with a few eternal moral lessons, is that it is much, much more than what it appears to be on the surface. It is considerably more than the sum of it's parts. Many Christians believe the Law itself as being little more than a dead relic of the past. The discussion of certain points of *"Law"* which were debated in the Gospels will hopefully dispel any notion that the Jews were just cold heartless followers of an ancient legal code which blinded them to seeing in Jesus their long awaited *"messiah"*. It was nothing so simple.

The fear of GOD and HIS words regarding what HE would do to Israel for going after other *"gods"* or for being deceived by *"false prophets"* was a very real and legitimate fear. It was written into the Law and warned by GOD'S prophets often for Israel to be careful and not stray from YHWH.

There was much more going on in the story of Jesus as Jesus was seen by his fellow Jews through the *"Law"* and the *"Prophets"* in everything he said and did. His every word and action was weighed against what was known, rightly or wrongly by those who heard and saw him, as they applied to the Laws and words of the prophets by which Jewish people lived and was a considerably more complex situation for these ancient people living under the Law of Moses than many of today's *"armchair"* moralists give them credit for.

The *"curses"* from GOD regarding *what would happen to Israel* for going *astray* take up much scripture throughout all of TaNaKh. The many examples of active curses provide proof that fear of GOD was / is a legitimate emotion.

For most Christians see in the Hebrew Bible only the moral stories, miracles poetry and what they interpret as a dead legal code of Law, rather than a living Eternal Covenant between YHWH and HIS people Israel. Largely because of this, they fail to comprehend in the discussions between Jesus, the Pharisees, Priests and others the seriousness of their arguments as they relate to their Eternal Covenant with GOD and it's Law. It is precisely because to many believers in Jesus, that they believe the Covenant YHWH made with Israel and HIS *"Law"* is *"dead"*, that they ignore everything about it which the Hebrew Bible says is *"eternal, everlasting, for ever"* and still in force.

But perhaps more importantly, because they either were not born under the Law, do not live under the Law, do not know or understand the Law, nor have the fear of GOD which one possesses by really living by HIS Law, they are not able to fully comprehend much of what they profess to believe in. I say this not as a criticism, but as a fact after having spent years in discussion and debating with believers in Jesus regarding their faith.

Largely because nothing is at stake for the Gentile believer and there is nothing to lose or give up by believing in Jesus, the details of the Law of Moses are not only not important and boring, they are considered irrelevant. When saying that they have nothing to *"give up"*, I am speaking of the 3,500 years of relationship the Jewish people have enjoyed with YHWH their GOD, and how believing in Jesus could jeopardize this forever.

According to most Christian doctrine, the Covenant at Sinai which gave Israel the Law, is considered dead and void, having been replaced by *"grace"* by the *"blood of Jesus"* .This, is the crux of the problem of accepting Jesus for the Jew. For the Jewish person is being asked to give up something (the Law) that he and his family have lived and died by for almost 3,500 years since receiving it at Sinai. For it is not just the Law, but the name of *"YHWH"* their GOD which is at the core of their own belief, even if they can no longer pronounce it. YHWH has been the family God for more than 3,500 years since Abraham. YHWH is the one and only GOD. Israel is HIS people.

Another aspect exists as well. There is another binding, eternal, preexisting Covenant between YHWH and Israel made before the Law of Moses given at Sinai. The Covenant of Abraham is still in force, without the Law of Moses. This SEED Covenant of Abraham too was made with YHWH GOD.

In many respects, for the Jewish person to accept and believe in the name of *"Jesus"*, he is faced with the dilemma of a conflict of *that* name and with the name of *"YHWH"* his GOD. For there is a curse regarding other names of *"gods"*. And according to the Gospels, Jesus was considered as *"god"*. Catholics call Mary the mother of Jesus, *"mother of god"*. Additionally, the Jewish believer is faced with the conflict of what to do regarding the *"Law"*. What is he to do regarding the *"Law"*. For it has curses associated with it if it is not kept and adhered to. For the Law is eternal and must be kept. Jesus said himself that the Commandments must be kept. This topic is discussed much.

To the Gentile, these fears, anxieties and threats regarding being cut off from one's people and from one's GOD are non-existent. I speak of a threat from GOD YHWH HIMSELF, not for example, of the father of a Gentile who objects to a son becoming an Israelite, and putting himself under the Law of Moses. Or a young woman who wants to *"convert"* to Rabbinic Judaism in order to marry a Jew. These are issues of a different nature and not life threatening changes as exist in the Hebrew Bible which begin with, *"Thus saith YHWH....."*. For it is like comparing *"apples and oranges"*. For a Jewish person to abandon or forsake YHWH and HIS Law, he is risking all.

JEWS AND THE CHRISTIAN BIBLE

For the Jew who is trying to make sense of the Christian Bible, it is imperative to know the basis of the Law of Moses well enough to follow the discussions and teachings given by Jesus the Jew. For the Jewish person reading the Christian Bible must understand that the story of Jesus is part of his own story. It is part of the history of the Jewish people, whatever one chooses to believe. As a nonbeliever, and as a Jew, I wanted to know myself as best I could, what transpired in the tiny kingdom of Israel 2,000 years ago which fundamentally changed the world. For today, there are estimates of 2.2 billion Christians in the world who follow Jesus, a sum I will repeat.

But mostly, it is a book attempting to analyze how his coreligionists may have regarded Jesus, how they saw Jesus and his actions and his words, and understood him according to the Law of Moses, through the eyes of those who lived according to it's Statutes and Ordinances. How did the Jewish people see Jesus through Jewish eyes? And perhaps more importantly, why the overwhelming majority of the Jewish people rejected him as their messiah during his life time. What does the Law and the Prophets actually say about an anointed savior, *"messiah"*? Did Jesus really *"fulfill"* prophesy about himself as *"messiah"*? What do the prophets actually say?

I am not attempting to pass judgment on how the Priests and Pharisees understood and applied the Law, but how they and others saw Jesus in light of their understanding of their Law. How did it affect their view of him?

WHAT

This book is not so much about *who* Jesus was, but is about *what* he was as a man, as a member of his tribe of people and as a historical figure during the time in which he lived within his historical setting. What was Jesus as a Jew?

It is about a religious man steeped in the words of the Law of GOD as written by Moses and the ancient Prophets of his people. This book is about what Jesus was in relation to the Safer Torah, the Law of YHWH and the Prophets as given to Moses for Israel his people to worship HIM and to live by.

Jesus the Jew, is about Jesus the historical figure and how he and his life relate to the words of the prophets and the Law under which he and the Kingdom of Israel attempted to live during desperate times.

The focus of the book is on the very small world in which Jesus lived and the people he interacted with during trying circumstances 2,000 years ago, not on the wider world few of Jesus as he is thought of today as a religious figure for which he has become known. Whether Jesus was or was not the "*messiah*" of Israel is a question for the reader to answer for himself and is not the focus of this book. But rather, how did he fit into what was the dynamic which was the Jewish world that he lived in 2,000 years ago? How was he seen by Jews?

My aim is to look into the reason why most of the Jewish people of his time rejected such claims made either by himself or made by others. For this purpose, I view his words and actions from the perspective of someone living according to the Law of Moses. For it was this Law by which he was judged. For Jesus was under the Law, the Pharisees, Scribes and Priests were under the Law. And the rest of the Jewish people of Israel were under the Law, as is this author. It is in this context that the Gospels are analyzed and discussed.

This will be done primarily by analyzing the words of Jesus in the Gospels and comparing them against the words of YHWH and HIS Prophets. As it was primarily the Law of Moses which was the central theme during his ministry, it is the Law of Moses which is reviewed.

The culture of ancient Israel, it's religion and political situation is observed and discussed with the idea that Jesus did not just appear out of no where. By this point in the history of the Jewish people, if GOD was going to send a "*messiah*", it could not have been a better time to offer relief to HIS people by what ever method that HE deemed appropriate. But by the same token, if YHWH was going to send a Prophet to "*proof*" Israel, as HE seemed to indicate that HE would, it was an ideal time as well.

The time in which he lived was by far, the most corrupt in the history of the Jewish people. I say this often, having studied the other periods of Israel relentlessly, there simply is no comparison. This is saying quite allot when compared to the first Kingdom of Israel before their exile by the Assyrians and that of the Kingdom of Judah before their own exile to Babylon. But these pale in comparison to the religious, political, and cultural sickness which existed just prior to, during and after the time of Jesus. The depth and scale of the political, religious and personal blood letting during a period lasting over several hundred years was truly appalling.

Perhaps more than any other act of debauchery, is the gift to the daughter of Herodias by Herod of the head of John the Baptist on a platter, as a reward for her dance. This single event more than any other seems to sum up the decadence of this period. Especially in that Herod considered John a Prophet.

Something very profound appeared to have occurred when the Kingdom of Judah was exiled to Babylon and the Temple of YHWH was destroyed. When the Jewish people returned, they never seemed to be able to return to the level of the fear of GOD and of the *"holiness"* once known by the people.

Leviticus 11:45, (45) For I am YHWH that brought you up out of the land of Egypt, to be your God; ye shall therefore be holy, for I am holy.

From the time of Israel's last Prophets around the period of Ezra and Nehemiah, and the wars against the Greeks by the Maccabees, to the final destruction of the rebuilt Temple of YHWH by the Romans in 70 CE, the people appeared to have lost something very tangible. There was a gradual decline in the level of *"holiness"* of the people for many and various reasons. There *"connectedness"* to their GOD YHWH appeared to have undergone a fundamental change beginning in Babylon while their Temple was destroyed. It seems to have been a kind of graduated diminishing of spiritual awareness and sanctification of the people occurring from generation to generation.

Most of this was due mainly to hundreds of years of increasing corruptness on the part of the leaders both religious and secular as well as the confusion of so many different and opposing interpretations of the Law. The exposure to Babylonian and then Greek and finally Roman culture had a devastatingly negative impact also, affecting every aspect of life while a conquered people.

These and related topics are looked at with the understanding of how Jesus would have been viewed by a desperate people with a long memory and who were waiting and looking to their GOD for relief.

WHO

There is no way the subject of *who* many people thought Jesus was as a religious figure cannot be discussed, although it is not the main focus. For it would be impossible to separate *what* he was as a Jew from *who* he was *perceived* to be as a Jew, at least in the eyes of his people during the time in which he lived. There is too much of his life either directly or indirectly effected by the Law or the Prophets and prophesy attributed to Jesus assumed to be fulfilled during his lifetime to ignore. Additionally, there is too much of his life and words directly challenging the power structure which existed during his short stay to disregard. These issues are addressed to determine where and how his life and his death come together with the Law and biblical prophesy scriptures in TaNaKh as well as those referenced in the Gospels.

Therefore, where his actions and /or his words appear to directly contradict or question the Law of Moses in the Hebrew Bible, these issues are discussed within that context. Additionally, when and where either his life, actions, or words intersect with those of the Law or Prophets, these too are discussed.

Having said this, my approach is to *assume* that all of what was written in the four Gospels is accurate.

That the many prophetic quotes in the Gospels from the Hebrew Bible that are used to show how he was *"messiah, son of David"*, do speak of *"him"*. And how his life, his words and actions, stack up against these *"prophecies"* which according to the Gospels were *"fulfilled"*.

Once again, the purpose here is not to either prove or disprove that Jesus was the *"messiah"*, although I have little doubt but that my own prejudices from time to time will be evident, but to take as much of an objective view as is possible to try to understand both he and his words within *"context"*.

Again, *"context"* here meaning, Israel under foreign Roman occupation and rule 2,000 years ago, during an extremely corrupt religious, political and historical period, the Law of Moses as it relates to Jesus and the words, actions and prophesies regarding Jesus as *"messiah"*. And *who* and *what* were the Jews expecting as *"messiah"?* What does the ancient Hebrew text itself actually say about *"a"* messiah or *"the"* messiah? How was Jesus viewed within the context of a Jew living in a kingdom under the Law of Moses by other Jews living under the Law of Moses and it's commandments?

As Jesus was and still is, such a very divisive figure within the Jewish community, what a Jewish person knows or understands about his own Law as given to Israel by the Prophet Moses as well as the words of other Prophets, can help significantly in understanding where that individual fits into the story of the Jew called Jesus and how he was seen by his own people at the time in which he lived. For it was through the Law then, and through the Law now, that his words and actions must be approached.

GOSPELS

The main source material for this subject is the four Christian Gospels in the Christian Bible, also called the *"New Testament"*. The books of Matthew, Mark, Luke and John are used. Specifically, the focus in these four books is on the words of Jesus himself and the words of the Prophets given either by himself or by others in the Gospels which are said to refer to him. His own words as opposed to what others have said or what was reported about him by others is what is discussed. For his words form the basis of Christianity.

This last point is extremely important. As I am using only the four Gospels, none of the rest of the Christian Bible, especially the writings of the former Pharisee Paul are taken into account or used. The emphasis is on the words and actions of Jesus as compared to the Law of Moses and the Prophets.

The reason for this is that it keeps the emphasis on Jesus himself and not on the rest of the Christian Bible and other later developments as those words were written about events and issues which took place after his death. The former Pharisee Saul (Paul) and other writers are not used as I am only interested in the actual words and actions of Jesus himself for my purpose, for it was his own words and actions which got him crucified.

Additionally, I have also reviewed the prophesies quoted or referenced in these Gospels of Israel's prophets which purport to show how Jesus either fulfilled a scripture either by an action, or as a prophesy as the *"messiah"* or, which allude to Jesus in some way as fulfilling some other scripture because of something he said or did. There are many such prophesies mentioned.

Again, my purpose is not to attempt to prove or to disprove who he was, but to look at him as a Jewish man, about a Jewish man, who lived and died 2,000 years ago as a Jewish man in a Jewish world living under the Law of Moses. But also to look at the many scriptures from the Hebrew Bible to try to understand why so many of his coreligionists were not convinced enough to accept him as their *"messiah"* during and immediately after his life. This is said acknowledging that many did believe on him, according to the Gospels.

WHAT LAW WAS BEING DISCUSSED

Additionally, as the life and death of Jesus was within the confines of life under the Law, these Laws of Moses are analyzed to see what was being discussed and why. Not all of the legal issues will be looked at, but the majority of the larger issues of which the Jewish people lived by and for which Jesus was accused of desecrating, breaking, ignoring, or violating are discussed. His teachings will be viewed according to the Law in the Safer   Torah, the written Law of YHWH. And as the Law of Moses, it's Statutes, Commandments, and Ordinances are *"technical"* in nature in both their understanding and application, the details of some of them are viewed to expose them to light unseen by most Christian believers and no doubt to many Jewish readers.

For it must be remembered that Israel was under a Covenant with GOD (oath, agreement, contract) of the *"Law"* given at Sinai. In very simple terms, Israel was under a *"legally binding contract"* with their GOD YHWH. It remains a very serious *agreement* made between GOD and man, between YHWH and Israel HIS people. It was taken seriously by most of Israel, regardless of how they understood all of it's Commandments. The discussions between Jesus and the Pharisees, Priests and Scribes was not just a debate over points of Law but was a discussion about an Eternal Covenant made between an entire people called Israel, and the one and only GOD YHWH. YHWH, who was their GOD, their Father and their Savior.

CONTEXT

Under these circumstances, how was Jesus viewed by his contemporaries?The reader needs to keep in mind that the current year of this planet, and the world that we live in, and the world and time period in which Jesus the Jew lived, are literally worlds apart. It must be recalled that in ancient Israel, even next door to their own neighbors (Egyptians, Philistines, Moabites, etc.), Israel was a vastly different people, culture and religion in most respects. To a casual observer from the outside, they may have appeared the same, but they were not. Israel had a life rhythm all of it's own, dictated by GOD.

Some of the topics discussed are those which go directly to the heart of *what* Jesus was. It is within this understanding that Jesus the Jew must be viewed. Thus from the outset, Jesus was a circumcised Jewish male descendant of the SEED Covenant of Abraham, of the kingdom of Israel, of the tribe of Judah, who lived under the Law Covenant of Sinai.

Accordingly, he would have worshiped the one and only GOD of Israel whose name is **"YHWH"** (*Yood-Heh-Vav-Heh*). During his life time, the name of YHWH was still known and pronounced, for it was only later that the rabbis as part of their new religion forbid the utterance of GOD'S holy name. Previously, it's pronunciation was always a part of the ancient religion of Israel as YHWH had told Israel to swear only by HIS name, *"YHWH"*.

Jesus was a Jewish man who lived an observant life based on the Temple of YHWH and it's priests and the daily sacrificial offering. There was no such thing as *"Rabbinic Judaism"* or *"oral law"* as the Temple of YHWH with it's priests still stood and was the **only** religion of Israel. Jesus was neither a *"rabbi"* nor a Pharisee, a Scribe, Herodian or a Sadducee. Jesus was neither an Essene nor a Sicarii or a *"Jewish Zealot"*, bent on throwing off the Roman yoke. Jesus was not a *"Christian"*. They did not exist. Jewish was a ***"Jew"***.

Jesus was an observant Jew who grew up worshiping the GOD YHWH of Israel and living according to HIS Law. This would have included making the appropriate Temple of YHWH sacrifices and offerings in their season.

Jesus did *appear* to be *"radical"* to many, especially to the Pharisees whose own *"traditions"* clouded their vision considerably when it came to the Law. And to the Priests who no doubt looked on this man from Nazareth somewhat differently than the Pharisees as a threat to their livelihood. There were others as well who would have definitely thought that some of his ideas were radical and therefore a threat, not only to the Temple and the priesthood, but to their precarious relationship with the Roman occupiers by disrupting their lives.

All of the major players in this saga were either challenged or threatened by Jesus for different reasons. The Romans occupiers who wanted to keep the peace and collect their taxes, the corrupt Temple Priests whose authority felt threatened and the misguided Pharisees who Jesus ridiculed, or the Zealots who wanted a military leader all had their own reasons to fear, hate, feel challenged, threatened or let down by Jesus. His presence made allot of different people feel similarly uncomfortable. He was a problem to them all and no doubt when he was crucified, many sighed a sigh of relief.

As stated above, on the other hand Jesus was not seen as radical enough by some who wanted him to lead Israel out from under the Roman yoke in a more physical way and reestablish the Kingdom of Israel as their *"messiah"* with force and without any foreign overseer. These *"zealots"* were looking more for a man with a sword, than with *"loaves and fishes"*.

Jesus was a man who practiced a form of worship based on the Law of Moses and the Temple of YHWH, the priesthood and sacrificial offerings and who kept the holy festivals of his GOD YHWH.

'HOUSE OF ISRAEL'

Jesus was a Jewish man who spent his entire existence within walking distance of the place where he was born. This fact is often mentioned by historians as well as the fact of the relatively short period he taught. The number of Christian's in the world today is quite remarkable when this is taken into consideration. For Jesus only preached for three years according to most accounts. His entire focus and his audience was to Israel and his fellow Jews. He said he came for *"Israel"*, and repeated this several times.

"I am not sent but unto the Lost Sheep of the House of Israel"

This topic will be revisited often, as it is a key piece of information in attempting to understand *what message*, and to *whom* his *"message"* was for.

When speaking these lines, Jesus had been approached by a Gentile woman. His response to her was that he had *"but"*, **(only)** come for the lost sheep of the house of Israel. *"Bnei Israel"* is more accurately translated as *"Sons of Israel"*, but in a very literal sense also means *"SEED"* of Israel. As it is the male offspring of Jacob being referred to, his *"sons"*, ie. **"Israel"** is the subject. He says this several different times in various ways throughout the Gospels. So who was Israel? Who was Jesus referring to? Who was he referring to by *"the lost sheep of the house of Israel"?* (Matthew 15:24)

When Jesus was addressing any other than *"Israel"*, it is noted as such in the Gospels, such as with the quote above or with the Samaritan woman or the Roman centurion. For in the Gospels, there is a very clear distinction made between the Jews of Israel, and the *"Gentiles"*. Whenever his focus audience was altered it was a matter of exception, not of rule. For instance, Jesus occasionally *healed* or *preached* to *"Gentiles"*. But the reader only knows this because the author makes it a point in the story to identify the *"Gentile"*. Nevertheless he made it clear himself, that it was to Israel he came for. For it was the *"salvation"* of Israel that he preached, not healing of the flesh.

In the Gospels, unless otherwise noted, the subject audience is always the Jews of Israel. Although for reasons which will be discussed and analyzed later, even when the audience is obviously Jewish, such as when Jesus was confronted by the Pharisees or the Priests or when mentioning the feasts of Israel, the authors of the Gospels will routinely identify them as being of *"the Jews"*. It is a profound oddity which is looked at and discussed in depth.

Jesus spoke to the remnant of Israel as represented by the Jewish people. Jesus spoke to a Jewish audience, about a Jewish GOD, in a Jewish kingdom called Israel, about the Jewish Law (Law of Moses), and Jewish prophesy (Prophets of Israel), spoken and written down by Jewish prophets (Prophets of Israel), and he was referred to as the Jewish *"anointed"* *(messiah)* one who would be the salvation of *"Israel",* the people of GOD. The followers of Jesus were Jewish, his protagonists were Jewish and his concern his whole life was for the remnant of the SEED of Abraham as represented by his own Jewish people, and for the *"lost sheep of the House of Israel"*. For as shall be explained, his own Jewish people were only part of the *"lost sheep of the House of Israel"*.

TRANSLATIONS
TRANSLATIONS of TRANSLATIONS

Unlike the study of the Hebrew Bible, where the original text can be researched in it's original Hebrew language, the Christian Bible does not have an original Hebrew or Aramaic text to use as a standard which would allow for a more precise study of the words. This is assuming that it was indeed written originally in a language other than Greek. Today, there is either Greek, Coptic, Ethiopic or parts of Aramaic scraps of scripture, pieces of several manuscripts put together or something else which exist which make up the bulk of the oldest texts. It is from these scraps of texts and codices that the oldest examples of the Gospels exist. Understanding or misunderstanding a poorly translated text is, and has always been, a real possibility as there is *no original* complete Christian Bible in any Semitic language that can be used as a foundation or standard for research or for anything else.

This is important because the Law of Moses is a technical document. As best that can be determined, the oldest known complete Gospel texts are written in Greek. As the possibility exists that the original Gospels may have been in Greek, as the Greek language and culture were the international language (lingua franca) of it's day, much as English is in our time, this is a distinct possibility. However, most scholars seem to agree that there were at least some original Gospel texts written in a Semitic language now apparently lost.

The topic of *translation* cannot be emphasized enough and is revisited often, especially because the Law as stated above is by nature a legal code and is, *"technical"*. It was the technical points of the Law discussed in the Gospels.

HEBREW / ARAMAIC / GREEK

Today, there is evidence which exists that there were originally some Semitic texts in existence from which some of the earliest Greek translation of the Christian Bible was made, or at least parts of it were translated from. If this is true, there no longer exist any Semitic text, Hebrew or Aramaic from these originals. These earliest Greek translations form the basis for most all other translations of the Christian Bible. If however, there was an original Hebrew / Aramaic copy of the Gospels, then in theory for example, the English copy of the Christian Bible, is an English copy of a Greek copy of an original Semitic text of the Christian Bible which no longer exists. It is a copy of a copy.

Understanding this is critical because the very basis of the story of Jesus, his words regarding GOD and the Law, the accusations against him, his trial and execution were all based on the Law of Moses. It is as if we are to understand the story told of someone who is accused of a crime, tried and then sentenced to death based on incomplete information and based on a legal code of Law not fully detailed in the story. This, after 2,000 years of filtered hearsay, third party rumor and much editing and redacting of the physical evidence. The entire life and death of Jesus can be understood in this light. This is why the Greek translation of his words and actions and the charge of "*blasphemy*" leveled against him are so devastating. For as the Law is technical, to understand the story of Jesus based on a legal code of Law which is at best not fully explained in the Gospels, makes really understanding the complete truth of what all happened 2,000 years ago nearly impossible.

With this said, because so much of what occurred in the Gospels was legal and "*technical*", the story of Jesus and his life becomes all the more difficult, as an original translation as it was originally written in his language does not exist to be studied. It becomes especially difficult because so much of the discussion between Jesus, the rabbis and the Priests was "*technical*" in nature regarding points of Law. An original Semitic text written by a Jew under the Law would have allowed for a better rendering of the words and events which took place because the scribe would have been more sensitive to the importance of the Law and his choice of words used than anyone else. This will become more obvious as the Gospels are analyzed

LANGUAGE

Aramaic was learned in Babylon and largely replaced spoken Hebrew during the 70 year exile and was brought back with the returning Jews along with a new Aramaic alphabet. But there is biblical evidence that Aramaic was easily understood by Israel long before their exile to Babylon as Hebrew and Aramaic are two very closely related Semitic languages, much more so than the Semitic languages of Hebrew and Arabic.

Then at least, Aramaic was probably the closest Semitic language to ancient Hebrew that existed. Most of these people, the Phoenicians, Ammonites and Moabites and others, seemed to have been able to understand one another as well. To get back to the point, Aramaic, with allot of Hebrew, appeared to have been the spoken vernacular of his day and the language of Jesus.

It is interesting to note that when Jesus was crucified, Pilate had the sign made saying, *"This is the King of the Jews"* written in *Hebrew, Greek* and *Latin*. So apparently the Greek language was still read and or spoken commonly enough to justify using Greek with Hebrew and Latin for the sign (Luke 23:38). The Greeks and especially Greek culture existed for several generations prior to the time of Jesus but still existed during his time.

That one of the translations on the sign was in Greek is significant. Which meant that there were still significant enough numbers of Greeks and other Greek reading people in Israel to justify using Greek on the sign. And we are aware that Greeks still existed in Israel as according to the Gospel of John (12:20-23), certain Greeks came to worship at the feast and inquired of Jesus. And we also know from other scriptures in the Gospels that people who were still identified as Greeks existed in Israel. So, it would not be too far fetched to think that the original four Gospels may not all have been in either Hebrew, Aramaic or Greek, but possibly more than one language.

TEXTS & TEXTS

In this book, the 1611 King James Version of the Christian Bible is used along with the 1917 Jewish Publication Society (JPS) translation according to the original Masoretic Text and the original Hebrew itself. I have read that the 1917 JPS translation of the Hebrew Scriptures was largely based on this earlier 1611 King James Version translation of the Hebrew text into English. The 1917 JPS is better than the newer 1999-2000 JPS, although it is not a perfect translation and often takes very politically correct liberties with the Hebrew scriptures, even for 100 years ago.

The 1611 English translation of the Hebrew Bible too, was based on an earlier 1525 English translation called the *"Mikraot Gedolot"* but generally referred to as the *"Rabbinic Bible"*. The King James Version itself relied heavily on the *"Textus Receptus"* which is a printing of the Greek New Testament by Desiderius Erasmus. Additionally, it is estimated that approximately 80% of the King James Version was based on the earlier *"Tyndale Bible"* translation.

Given this, the Tyndale translation of all of the Christian Bible and about half of the Hebrew Bible, as it was never completed, was also based on the earlier Martin Luther German translation of the Latin Vulgate, the Erasmus Greek New Testament and the Erasmus Latin New Testament. For the Hebrew part of his bible, the Hebrew Pentateuch, possibly the Septuagint and the Polyglot Bible were used. The Polyglot Bible, also called the Complutensian Polyglot Bible, refers to the printing of the Greek New Testament, Septuagint and the Targum Onkelos.

The Coptic Bible would probably have been a better source for ancient scripture translation than the use of the Latin Vulgate, for both the Hebrew Bible and the Christian Bible. Given the source of the Alexandrian Greek Version (Septuagint) and the Coptic New Testament translation from Greek as early as the second century, their value would have been much greater than that of the Latin Vulgate which was not penned until two centuries later. As most if not all of the Latin Vulgate was translated by Saint Jerome from both the Greek New Testament and the Septuagint, it would make the Coptic Bible one less translation of a translation from the original and therefore of more value.

CUSTOMIZING

In some translations of both the Hebrew text and the older Christian text, *"adjustments"*, (*"Christological" interpretation*) were made to conform to existing Christian beliefs or doctrines which better reflected the officially accepted church theology.

Both the Septuagint, an earlier Greek translation of the Hebrew Bible, and the Latin Vulgate were assessed in the translation of the King James Version as well as other sources. However, when the written word in the original Hebrew text or the Greek or Latin in anyway either contradicted or did not fully support the English translation, especially with regard to the words of the prophets (as they relate to Jesus), "*adjustments*" were made to the Christian Bible translation to make them better "*agree*".

By their "*choice*" of certain words or phrases over other words or phrases, they were "*synchronized*" in a manner of speaking. The consistent reference made to *"the Jews"* throughout all four of the Gospels is a case in point. It goes without saying that there were certain translators who may have had their own "*agenda*" as well, which effected their work and there is evidence this did occur. This is true of translations by Rabbinic scholars as well as Christian scholars. Everyone is unconsciously or consciously influenced by their own religious dogma. And some scribes were possibly just dishonest.

Compare in the King James Bible Matthew 12:18-21 which is supposed to be quoting from Isaiah 42:1-4. The last line has been *rewritten* completely.

Matthew 12:21, (21) ***And in his name shall the Gentiles trust.***

Isaiah 42:4, (4)...... ***and the isles shall wait for his Law.***

I speak of this more in detail elsewhere, but as a point to be made concerning scripture bias, and agenda in translation, both of these scriptures were copied from the same 1611 King James Bible supposedly quoting from the same Hebrew text. Yet, no matter how hard one tries, there is no way that the last sentence of verse Matthew twenty-one can be translated from Hebrew as, "*And in his name shall the Gentiles trust.* " from "*and the isles shall wait for his Law*" and is clearly an example of one of the Gospel writers or a later scribe, altering the text to fit a doctrinal belief. One might suspect that neither GOD nor HIS Prophet Isaiah would be very amused by this action.

Words chosen in English when translating from the Greek would often be weighed as to it's "*agree*" value. Sometimes words which were more in "*sync*" with their doctrine, instead of words which were either more vague, or did not agree and even possibly contradicted would be used. Thus today, not having a Christian Bible text as a source in it's original language presents the religious person or scholar with a very real dilemma, at least with regard to the Christian Bible and not being able to study it in a Semitic language. As shall be discussed more later, it is critical, precisely because the Christian Bible from beginning to end deals with the "*technical"* issues of the Law.

Even the best translation is at best a "*translation*". And quite often, that translation is a translation of a translation, or worse. The idea here is, that whenever translations are used, sometimes something is going to go missing, and sometimes that "*something*" that goes missing may be the *facts*, which are reflective of the *truth* itself. It was the "*technical*" Statutes of the Law which was used to condemn Jesus based on his own words and actions.

This is why an English, a Greek, a Latin or an Ethiopic translation of the accusations against Jesus and his trial based on the technical legal code of Law from the ancient Hebrew text of the Law of Moses is a serious impediment to understanding the facts of what actually occurred. Even if all of the translations are 100% accurate and without prejudice, dogma or doctrine and without any religious agenda, it is difficult to know the truth.

To customize an old saying, *"the truth is in the details"*. And the details concerning his life are obscure. In writing about Jewish history, sometimes the truth becomes blurred by tradition, myth and translation. And contrary to what some may think or choose to believe, writing about the life of Jesus is writing about Jewish history. Jesus the Jew was one of Israel's own. It was the details of the Law by which he lived and that condemned him to die. Details are important.

Whatever one may think of Jesus, who he was or what he was, he was a circumcised SEED of Abraham and was part of the Eternal Covenant with GOD. He was part of Israel then and now. Whether one chooses to accept this or not is a matter for them to decide. But Jesus, if nothing else, belonged to Israel. He is one of Israel's own sons.

This book is not meant to be an academic work to be found collecting dust somewhere within the galleys of academia. It is nothing of the kind. It is a small attempt to see Jesus as the Jew that he was, not what he has become.

Additionally, for the Jewish person who does not know, does not understand or is confused about Jesus the Jew, especially today with the Messianic movement, this may be a start for them to *"search the scriptures"* (Hebrew Bible) and see that they have *"everlasting salvation"* in YHWH their GOD.

Finally, this book is an attempt to separate out tradition and myth from the text and expose a bit more of the facts. Hopefully these facts will shed more light on the truth. Facts of the Law are reviewed for a clearer truth of what happened 2,000 year ago in the place called *"Israel"*.

ACKNOWLEDGMENTS

The Holy Scriptures According to the Masoretic Text
The Holy Scriptures According to the Masoretic Text (Hebrew) and the
Jewish Publication Society of America (JPS) 1917 English Translation ,
Philadelphia, The Jewish Publication Society of America, 1955.

The Five Books of Moses, A New Translation with Introductions,
Commentary, and Notes by Everett Fox, Schocken Books, New York. By
Everett Fox, 1983, 1986, 1990, 1995.

The Five Books of Moses, A Translation with Commentary, W.W. Norton
& Company, New York, London, by Robert Alter, 2004.

Brown-Driver Briggs Hebrew and English Lexicon, Francis Brown, S.R
Brown, Charles A. Briggs, Henderson Publishers, 2003.

The New Complete Works of Josephus, Translated by William Whiston and
Commentary by Paul L. Maier, Kregel Publications, 1999.

Young's Literal Translation of the Holy Bible, translated by Robert
Young,Greater Truth Publishers 2004, (based on 1898 3rd edition of
Young's Literal Translation of the Holy Bible)

The Holy Bible, The King James Version of the Bible; 1611, Zondervan
Publishing House

Septuagint, Greek Interlinear Translation of the Hebrew Bible

INTRODUCTION

Most people have a general idea of the historical figure of Jesus or at least have a vague idea of his life and death. This is generally true of people who are not religious in any sense of the word nor who are Christian.

This idea of Jesus usually takes the form of a religious person in ancient Israel who in a fashion, challenged the existing powers that ruled during his life time, and who paid for it by his being nailed to a Roman cross, becoming a religious martyr in the process.

To some, Jesus was the promised "*messiah*" sent by GOD to His people Israel who rejected him, and who willingly gave his life for all of mankind as part of GOD'S divine plan for salvation of the world. Thus by his martyrdom, Jesus became the central figure in the religion which was built around his brief three year stint as a preacher / teacher and is based on his name.

But very few Christians or Jews for that matter, think of Jesus as a "*Jew*" even though they know that he was "*Jewish*". Yet, Jesus lived his entire life as a "*Jew*". He was born a "*Jew*", circumcised on the eight day and died as a "*Jew*" with the words of King David on his lips, having spent his entire life living according to the Law of YHWH as given to the Prophet Moses, as a "*Jew*". Whether he lived by the *Law* according to some of those people of his time is a matter of degree not of kind. He was an observant Jew of his day.

His life and how the existing circumstances in which he was born and during the time he lived are discussed, as Jesus did not live in a vacuum. His "*ministry*" would have had far less meaning, and perhaps would not have been as possible at any other time. For his time was unique. For many of the elements which existed during the time of Jesus existed before him, but not all of them at once.

There have been many times during the history of the people of Israel when GOD'S prophets were sent to them because of their behavior. For the outside forces which interacted with the kingdoms of both Israel and of Judah, whether Aramean, Assyrian, Egyptian, Philistine, Ethiopian, Babylonian, Persian, Greek or Roman, they and their actions were a direct reflection of Israel and Judah's relationship with YHWH their Father.

The Roman period of Israel, during the reign of Herod and later, was a time unlike any other in the history of ancient Israel. Knowing what led up to this period in Israel's long history, as well as the period of Herod itself, will facilitate understanding Jesus as a religious Jew living under the Roman yoke and the immense pressures which existed within his small world.

There were many different political, religious, cultural and historical events all happening simultaneously as the Jew Jesus, grew up in his small kingdom dominated by a foreign power.

Before a discussion of Jesus can begin however, a brief overview of the events leading up to his life. For understanding Jesus the Jew and his words necessitates an understanding of his world and what he was talking about. For much reference in the Gospels is made of Israel's past and the words of Moses and their prophets, many whose words are used to give weight to Jesus as the expected "*messiah*". As these prophets lived at a time long before Jesus, they and the words which are quoted in the Gospels which are said to speak of Jesus are discussed, as the example in Matthew12 already quoted. Only the *Five Books of Moses* are referred to as the *Safer Torah* or the *Law of Moses, Law of YHWH,* the *Torah* or just the *Law*. The entire Hebrew Bible is generally referred to as *TaNaKh* or simply, *"Hebrew Bible"*.

A brief retelling of the period prior to the first two temples and the two Temple periods leading up to the life of Jesus will begin this book, for it is necessary as so much of what Jesus said and did was a direct reflection or result of what came before him and according to his own words, was why he came to save his people Israel. It sets a very important stage for his ministry.

TRIBES

Ancient Israel consisted of thirteen tribes. When the ten northern tribes which made up Israel, went into exile, the tribes of Judah, Benjamin and Levi remained in the southern Kingdom of Judah. This is why "*Jews*" are called "*Jews*". However, in actuality not all "*Jews*" are of the tribe of Judah, but may be either of Benjamin or Levi, or any one of the other "*lost*" tribes, as many from the north came south, took refuge, and lived under the kings of the house of David and remained close to their ancient Temple of YHWH. There is considerable scriptural evidence of this in TaNaKh. However, these remnants from the north were a distinct minority, for the southern Kingdom of Judah consisted primarily of the tribes of Judah, Benjamin and Levi.

According to Hebrew scripture, for a long time after the northern tribes had been destroyed, the remaining peoples from the southern kingdom after their exile to Babylon were referred to as *"Judah and Benjamin"*. For these two **royal** tribes along with Levi remained together and returned together.

Unless otherwise stated, whenever reference is made to "*Israel*", or Jews / Jewish people, I am taking into account that today's Jewish people, as they were during the time of Jesus, represent the remnant of all the people from all of the ancient tribes of Israel as well as including both of the tribes of Benjamin and the tribe of Levi. Within Judah was the Royal House of David. Benjamin represents the Royal House of Saul. Levi remained the servant tribe to YHWH and of the Temple Priests, the Cohanim, after the split of the northern and southern kingdoms. So in this context, "*Jews*" and "*Israel*" are synonymous as the Jewish people today represent the remnant of all Israel.

YESTERDAY JEWS AND TODAY JEWS

Today, the terms "*Jew*" and "*Israel*" are often used interchangeably, but this was not always so. "*Jew*" use to refer to the people of the tribe of Judah from the south of the kingdom, and "*Israel*" use to refer to "*Jacob*" and Jacob's sons, and later to all of the people of Israel of the tribes named after his sons, including the people of the tribe of Judah. Later "*Israel*" referred to only the northern Kingdom of Israel, also called at times "*Samaria*" and even referred to poetically at times as "*Ephraim*" and "*Joseph*". It is most helpful to know which time or period is being referred to as sometimes these names have different meanings depending on what era is being discussed.

By way of example, "*Israel*" during the time of King Saul, meant all of the tribes, north and south as one unified kingdom. There was a total of thirteen tribes (Joseph was Ephraim & Manasseh). The term

"*Judah*" was both the name of a southern tribe and a physical or geographical area located in the south. Upon the death of King Saul, the tribes divided. "*Israel*" meant all of the tribes of Israel in the north dominated by "*Benjamin*" but without "*Judah*" who was not included. At that time, "*Judah*" meant only "*Judah*".

There was a civil war between the two (Israel & Judah). And "*Judah*"during this same time period meant the tribe of "*Judah*" and the brief seven year Kingdom of "*Judah*" with David as King.

After the civil war between the northern tribes of the Kingdom of "*Israel*" and the southern tribe of the Kingdom of "*Judah*", the two kingdoms were once again reunited as one unified "*Israel*" under King David as when Saul was king. "*Judah*" reverted back to being a geographical designation and the name of a tribe. "*Israel*" once again represented all of the thirteen tribes.

During the beginning of the reign of King Solomon's son King Rehoboam, the united kingdom of all of the tribes of "*Israel*" split up again, but this time tribal loyalties were different. The ten tribes of the north including Ephraim, Manasseh, Issachar, Zebulun, Gad, Dan, Asher, Reuben, Simeon and Naphtali made up the northern Kingdom of "*Israel*". Just to make things more confusing, the northern Kingdom of "*Israel*" was also referred to as "*Samaria*". Later, when the Assyrians destroyed the northern kingdom of Israel, they are often referred to as the "*ten lost tribes*".

The southern Kingdom of "*Judah'* consisted of the tribes of "*Judah*", *Benjamin* and *Levi*, and was often referred to as ***Judah and Benjamin***. As already mentioned, later many refugees fleeing the Assyrians from the northern tribes would join with southern Kingdom of "*Judah*". Nevertheless, "*Judah*", during this time period, refers to the southern Kingdom of "*Judah*".

There are several more changes which could be mentioned such as the Kingdom of "*Israel*" during the time of Jesus, which consisted primarily of the tribe of "*Judah*" *Benjamin* and *Levi* and remnants of the others including the *Idumeans*. In the north, what had been "*Israel*" was now referred to as "*Samaria*" which was a mixture of ancient Israelites and Assyrians brought in. Or today, the State of "*Israel*" consists of the same three tribes plus remnants of the others. Today the nation of "*Israel*" is called the "*Jewish*" State. In the northern area of what was once the center of what was "*Samaria*", lives the remnants of the people called "*Samaritans*". Today's Jewish people in "*Israel*" consists in many ways the same genetic make up as during the time of Jesus.

I have been a historian my entire life in one capacity or another. As such, I try to be very careful in the names I use and I take great offense in the misapplication of names, titles, attributes, appellations or descriptions etc. It is for this reason that I attempt to be consistent when referring to people. I always try to be precise. I may not always succeed, but I make as much of an effort as possible at getting it right.

The Jewish people are often the worse offenders in this area. For example, Abraham was not a "*Jew*", or "*the first Jew*" although you will hear the "*rabbis*" say this often. Abraham was the father of Isaac, who was the father of Jacob (called Israel), who was the father of twelve sons, one whose name is "*Judah*". It is from the great grandson of Abraham that the name "*Jew*" and "*Jewish*" originates. Not only was Abraham not a descendant of Judah, his great grandson, but he is referred to as the "*wandering Aramean*" in the Hebrew Bible. Abraham, as was his siblings in Haran, called an "*Aramean*".

The point is to call things according to what they are in TaNhKh and not to take liberties with the facts or to confuse them. Abraham was not a "*Jew*".

I understand as well that when the rabbis say that Abraham was a "*Jew*", that they most often are referring to his "*religion*". Well, if they are saying that Abraham was as one of _them_, as in "*Judaism*", here too they would be very wrong. The GOD YHWH which Abraham worshiped and the Law of Moses which was not given yet, and finally what the rabbis refer to as "*Rabbinic Judaism*" created by themselves, are two radically different "*religions*" to use this term. Abraham in no way was a "*Jew*" either by *pedigree* or *religion*.

Deuteronomy 26:5 (5) And thou shalt speak and say before YHWH thy God: '_A wandering Aramean was my father_, and he went down into Egypt, and sojourned there, few in number; and he became there a nation, great, mighty, and populous.

Like the rest of the male offspring of Terah the father of Abraham, Abraham is referred to as an "*Aramean*", as Laban, and Bethuel from Paddan-aram.

Genesis 25:20, (20) And Isaac was forty years old when he took Rebekah, the daughter of _Bethuel the Aramean_, of Paddan-aram, the sister of _Laban the Aramean_, to be his wife.

Both the son and grandson of Nahor, Abraham's brother, are referred to here as being "*the Aramean*", as they are elsewhere. Abraham was in fact, an "*Aramean*". None of Abraham's sons born in the land of Canaan are ever referred to by this name. YHWH, when he had first contacted Abraham refers to his (Abraham's) "*country*", thy "*kindred*", and thy "*fathers house*".

Additionally, when Abraham sent his servant to find a wife for Isaac, his servant was sent to "*my country*", to "*my kindred*". Abraham's servant was sent to "*Aram-naharaim*". Which roughly translates as "*Aram-rivers-garden*" or "*Aram-garden-(of) rivers*". "*Aram*" can represent the land and / or the people. When one thinks of the very fertile and well watered land between the Tigris and Euphrates Rivers, this would be an appropriate name. The Greeks called this land "*Mesopotamia*" (land between rivers).

When YHWH spoke with Abraham, to emphasize that it is to a ***different*** country to which Abraham is to go to and to ultimately inherit, YHWH tells Abraham to go "*into the land that I will show thee*" (Genesis 12:1). The idea here is, that Abraham the "*Aramean*" was told by GOD to leave "*his*" land and go to a different _land_. Abraham was an "*Aramean*" going to "*Canaan*".

Genesis 12:1, (1) Now YHWH said unto Abram: 'Get thee out of _thy country_, and from _thy kindred_, and from _thy father's_ house, _unto the land that I will show thee._

Abraham was an "*Aramean*". He was to leave "*Aram*" behind him and to travel to a distant land of Canaan etc. Abraham was ***not*** a "*Jew*". Abraham worshiped and served only his GOD "*YHWH*", not some long dead "*rebbe*" who made up a rule about which shoe to put on first. Abraham was ***not*** a "*Jew*" in any sense of the word.

ARABS – MUSLIMS - ISHMAELITES

Additionally, all Arabs and / or Muslims are not from Ishmael or "*Ishmaelites*" although many are. There were many, many, tribes, peoples and kingdoms in and around Abraham, Isaac and Jacob, long before Ishmael was conceived. Do the math. In addition, all Arabs are not Muslim, and all Muslims are not Arab. Yet, people consistently use these terms interchangeably as if they were synonymous. They are not.

And as I discussed earlier, not all people called *"Jews"* are actually *Jews*. Levites and Cohanim for example, are not technically Jews, although we call them Jews. They are from the priestly tribe of *"Levi"*. They are *"Levites"* from the tribe of *"Levi"* as *"Jews"* are from the tribe of *"Judah"*. Both are of *"Israel"*, sons of Jacob. Although today, anyone who once was of *"Israel"* and is part of the Covenant of YHWH, are today called *"Jews"*. As already mentioned, the Jewish people today are technically made up mostly of three tribes, Judah, Benjamin and Levi, remnants of the Kingdom of Judah.

The point here, if dealing with the Middle East and either the people, culture, history or religion that originate from this area, it is necessary to have a firm foundation under your feet. And when it comes to without a doubt, the most complicated place on the planet, with without a doubt the most complicated problems on the planet, it helps to get ones *"facts"* correct, or at least exhaust one's attempts trying. The area has an extremely long and fascinating history. Many of today's problems can be traced back to the *"don't confuse me with the facts"* attitude which is prevalent amongst a large proportion of the people, especially the Arabs, but exists as well in the west. Either call it what it is or at least know the difference or make an effort.

This brings us back to the topic of the *"Law"*. So much of the Gospels have to do with the Law of Moses, that the *"technical"* facts of what Jesus actually said, or really did, verses the *"technical"* Statutes written in the Law, make getting at the truth much more complicated than what it might seem. It was the *"technicality"* of the Law, which sentenced Jesus to death based on what he is reputed to either have said or did. This, is why the facts are important.

STYLE

Briefly, my style of writing is less than the standard fodder for this type of book. It is not, nor was it meant to be, a scholarly undertaking. I use many scriptural examples and often repeat them in other places to make a point. These many quotes were checked, but it may be that one or two have the wrong reference book or number. If so, please forgive and read for content. Mostly, as the Law of YHWH is being defended, it is HIS word which can most easily defend against the words in the Gospels which contradict the words of YHWH and HIS Law. For this reason, I make liberal use of quotes from the Law, Prophets and Writings in this book. My writing style is repetitious, often redundant and not politically correct. No doubt there are both grammatical and spelling mistakes, so read for content.

As to the the meat of the book, I have tried to be as objective as I could, keeping with the words of Jesus and the Law and Prophets to bring to the surface what I see as being hidden beneath. Because there is no original Semitic text to go to in researching the Gospels, some of the larger issues, for example the use of the name *"YHWH"* was not resolvable. The Greek copy of the Gospels is an inexact translation to work from as it often obscures what the original may have been because it is by it's nature, a *"translation"*. Or at least it is assumed not to be the original text. As it is all we have to work from, it really does not matter.

Having said this, there is ample evidence that both Greeks and Greek speaking, reading and writing people still existed in large enough numbers in Israel so that at least several of the Gospels may have been originally written in Greek. However, even if this was the case, it does not help solve such serious issues for example regarding the name *"YHWH"*, and if Jesus ever uttered it. For to a Jewish listener of

Jesus, this would have been of profound importance but not to a non Jewish Greek writer. Nor does it answer the issue regarding the constant use of term *"the Jews"* when referring to the people in the Gospels as if they were something being observed under a microscope lens by an alien species.

The Greek scribes would not have been sensitive to certain words such as *"YHWH"* verses *"Lord"* when translating, which would have had a profound affect on the meaning of the text to a Jewish audience. And indeed, this very issue will be discussed because of the translation of at least one example of the name of GOD *"YHWH"* in the Shema which is known to exist, which opens up many other similar possibilities which are examined.

'HEBERW SCRIPTURE'

The reader may sense from the many quotes from the Hebrew Bible that this writer is totally captivated by the word of GOD. The truth is, that this writer is in love with the word of YHWH our GOD, as it is the purest truth available to man given and left to us by the most holy creator of all heaven and earth. The word of GOD quite simply put, is the most divine and holy possession given to man by the Almighty GOD YHWH. It is our most treasured possession whether we are aware of it or not. For man to ignore such a gift from GOD, he so does at his own peril. The Law of Moses is the most precious thing on this earth. The word of GOD is mans true hope.

THE NAME

The name of *"YHWH"* and that of *"Jesus"* are discussed often, primarily because of the contrast between what YHWH said about HIMSELF and HIS own name, and later what Jesus said about his own name. I make quite allot about their words concerning their names. There is an extremely good reason for this as the reader will discover. Additionally, many scriptures from the Hebrew text will be given referencing the many things which YHWH GOD and HIS prophets had to say about HIS holy name. Some are repeated more than once. What YHWH had to say about HIS holy name could fill an entire book. One might even say that it does fill many books.

Some Hebrew words are written phonetically to explain their meaning. An earlier attempt to use Hebrew script proved unsuccessful and was dropped.

'THE LOST SHEEP OF THE HOUSE OF ISRAEL'

The purpose of the ministry of Jesus is written about much, primarily because there is an entire religion today which is built around what is believed to be the reason that he came to Israel in the first place. Jesus stated several times who he came for and why. Additionally, he stated what Israel was to do. Jesus came for Israel and preached keeping the Commandments of the Law.

THE AUTHOR

As mentioned, neither myself nor my writing style are *"politically correct"*. I make no apologies, I am what I am, and it is what it is and all grammatical and other mistakes are my own. I made an attempt to catch all of my errors. I may have missed one or two. Ignore the errors, and read for content.

Disclaimer: I am an observant Jew who follows only the Laws contained within the Safer Torah. I follow no *"rabbi"* nor believe that such a thing exists in the Safer Torah, nor at all. Nor do I believe in any authority but GOD *"YHWH"*. Additionally, I make no attempt to hide my complete disdain for the alleged *"oral law"*, but not those who keep it. For they are of the blessed SEED of Abraham and we are brothers. The so called *"oral law"* does not exist. Without a doubt, it is some of the most intellectually deficient nonsense on the face of the planet. But what is really the reason this silliness is looked at by this writer in such low esteem, is because as a historian, I am more than a little aware of the damage it has caused the Jewish people for the greater part of the last 2,000 years. It has been very detrimental.

The only *"Laws"* that I recognize are those given by GOD YHWH to HIS Prophet Moses written down in the Safer Torah (Five Books of Moses). The only *"holy books"* which I recognize are those within the Hebrew Bible referred to as TaNaKh (Five Books of Moses, Prophets, Writings), the inspired word of YHWH GOD, written by the hand of HIS prophets for HIS people Israel.

Additionally, as I am not a *"Christian"*, I do not call the Christian Bible the *"New Testament"* as this term for the Christian Bible infers a negative connotation upon the Hebrew Bible and implies that the Covenant of YHWH with Israel, and the Law of Moses is *"old"* or is somehow *"less"* than it is. As I do not personally believe that the Christian Bible is a *"New Testament"* (New Covenant), I therefore do not refer to the Hebrew Bible as the *"Old Testament"*. As a practicing Jew there is but one *"Bible"* (inspired word of GOD) and one truth and one GOD *"YHWH"* who is **"ONE"**. This would be the same GOD which Jesus grew up with as the GOD of Israel whom he is reputed to have worshiped. Only in TaNaKh is it written *"thus saith YHWH"*. Not in the Talmud and not the Christian Bible is this written. In this book, *"Christian Bible"* generally refers only to the *"New Testament"*.

GOD YHWH the Father, is the same GOD which the Jew Jesus professed to worship, to pray to and whose Laws he professed to live by. It is the reason why he was circumcised on the eighth day of his life. Yet he was man. As YHWH is the GOD of Israel, it makes the reconciliation of GOD'S name and that of Jesus a problem. It is as if one were trying to put two pegs into the same hole at the same time.

YHWH the GOD of Israel is the GOD in whom Jesus professed to worship, and as with all of Israel whose name of *"YHWH"* is on him, Jesus was a son of GOD as are all of the circumcised male SEED descendants of Israel (Jacob). As a first born son, Jesus would have had an even higher status amongst his own people and with GOD. Jesus whoever he was, was a son of Jacob. Jesus said to keep the Commandments of GOD if Israel wants to enter eternal life. For it was eternal life which he preached to Israel. As it was the Law of Moses which Jesus lived under and said to keep, *"but if thou wilt enter into life, keep the Commandments"*, there is no contradiction with keeping the Law.

'LORD AND GOD'

There are issues regarding Jesus being referred to as *"Lord and God"*, having *"new"* commandments and his interpretation on existing Law (divorce swearing) which are causes for concern and are addressed. However, there is agreement with some of the other things he said. Additionally, as Jesus stated on several occasions making his feelings as to whom his message was directed known, I have no problem with much of what he had to say in this regard. For example, in his words regarding going only *'to the lost sheep of the House of Israel'*, and when sending out his disciples, telling them to avoid the Gentiles, he was being consistent, unlike much later Christian doctrine.

As I make clear, I am convinced that much of his words regarding who he was addressing, as well as who he was sending his disciples to preach to have been either misunderstood, misapplied, misinterpreted, misconstrued or mistranslated by the filtering process of the many hands used in the *"editing"* of the original texts, long before there final resting place on calf skin.

As a nonbeliever, it is within the context of the *"Law"* that I view his words and actions. Jesus was a Jew, preaching to the Jewish people, and to the *"lost sheep"*, the sons, the remnant of Israel, *"Bnei Israel"*. It was to Israel to whom his message was directed, and it is within this context that this author understands his message and which the Gospels are viewed in their entirety.

I have tried to be as objective as I could. But the reader must understand and appreciate the place from which this writer writes as well. As an observant Jew, it is the Law of YHWH which is the basis for most all of my thought. That today the words and life of Jesus are the basis for a third of the worlds population is not taken lightly either. With this in mind, my approach at understanding Jesus is through the **Law of Moses** which was his and all of Israel's *"life"*. This was done by assessing the *Law* as it relates to Jesus.

The *"**Law**"* which I speak of is the Law of Moses as taught and practiced 2,000 years ago by the Levites and Temple Priests and Israel, NOT today's perverted *"Rabbinic Judaism"* which is in no way reflective of GOD'S Law. This is important to keep in mind as they are two very distinct *"religions"*.

As a non believer from the Jewish perspective, my hope is that I have at least shed some light on the life of Jesus in his time, and some of the legal issues concerning the Law which was the basis for so much of his ministry, and for which in the end he was condemned by his own people.

Finally, an attempt was made to better understand how an observant Jew who lived 2,000 years ago upon seeing what transpired during the ministry of Jesus, was to make of his fellow Jew per the Law under which they both lived. How did they translate or understand Jesus's words according to the Law of Moses. How was he viewed through the eyes of a fellow Jew during his lifetime?

CHAPTER ONE

FIRST TEMPLE OF YHWH

When YHWH had originally made HIS ***SEED Covenant*** with Abraham, HE ***did not do everything immediately. But GOD did have a plan for his SEED.***

'AND YHWH APPEARED UNTO ABRAHAM'

There was not enough of Abraham's SEED to occupy the land that was promised, *"And YHWH appeared unto Abram, and said: 'Unto thy SEED will I give this land'."* Abraham's "***SEED***" was to go down to Egypt and become slaves for more than 400 years, then be freed, receive the Law and wander for another 40 years in the desert being led by Moses. Only then did they cross into the Promised Land being led by Joshua and live for the next 100-200 years. Eventually they asked for a king so they could be like their neighbors. Their first king Saul, did not work out so good, but David turned out to be a pretty good king with his SEED lasting for about twenty more generations on his throne. This is the really short version of the events of Israel leading up to the first Temple of YHWH being built.

FIRST TEMPLE OF YHWH

As King, David united the tribes and with GOD'S help, YHWH chose the place where HE would put HIS name. It is this place on Mount Moriah in Jerusalem, today's Temple Mount, where Solomon as King, built the first Temple of YHWH. The *"Mishkan"* was replaced by a permanent home, the Temple of YHWH.

SOLOMON'S TEMPLE

In approximately 968 BCE of the reign of King Solomon (961 BCE – 931 BCE), the Temple of YHWH was completed. Seven years in the making, it's beauty when recalled by it's priests after later being destroyed, was enough to make them weep. The best craftsmen and materials from Israel and the surrounding kingdoms had been used to construct the Temple of YHWH (HaHakl YHWH) according to plans given by GOD to King David. The amount of gold, silver, brass, cedar and other materials used was astounding.

After the wise King Solomon died, his not so intelligent son Rehoboam inherited the throne but without his father's wisdom. The Kingdom of Israel split back into the northern Kingdom of Israel, and the southern Kingdom of Judah. The northern Kingdom of Israel would slowly disintegrate, being picked apart by it's neighbors. First the Arameans killed and stole their land, and then the Assyrians finally destroyed them.

NORTHERN KINGDOM OF ISRAEL

ARAMEANS

'In those days YHWH began to cut Israel short'

Through Israel's many Prophets, YHWH warned them what HE would do to them if they did not keep HIS Law. But they went astray. YHWH chipped away at Israel piece meal, as HE allowed Israel's neighbors to conquer them.

The northern Kingdom of Israel steadily became weaker with time through their idolatress practices. The weaker they became, the more that they were invaded by their neighbors and lost their lands, their people and freedom.

Even with all that they were doing, YHWH their GOD, never gave up on them, knowing full well what would become of them. In a strange way, YHWH practiced what might be called *"due diligence"* as HE continued to send HIS prophets to Israel, even knowing what the eventual outcome would be. This is an example of GOD'S mercy. He sent them prophet after prophet, *"betimes and often"* to warn them, beseeching them to *"return"*. In addition, YHWH was allowing Israel's neighbors to pick them apart. In hope perhaps, that they would get the message and *"return"*. They didn't.

There is actual evidence that many from the north did come south during the major festivals of YHWH when the males were required to present themselves before YHWH. Many remained in the south in Judah as well before and after the fall of the northern Kingdom of Israel.

But the majority of Israel were too far removed both physically and spiritually from YHWH'S Holy Temple in Jerusalem and the Law to obey GOD'S prophets. Some, however did return. Some had remained as they had been living in the south all along for various reasons such as commerce.

The northern Kingdom of Israel was often referred to a *"Samaria"*, named after *"Shemer"*, the original owner of the hill on which the city of Samaria was built by King Omri (I Kings 16:23-24).

But Israel's neighbors, first King Hazael of Aram *"smote"* those lands east of the Jordan which belonged to three of Israel's tribes. YHWH has always been merciful, albeit, in very subtle ways. The loss of those lands east of the Jordan should have been a message to all of Israel west of the Jordan, a *"wake up call"*. But they were not paying attention. Later this would repeat itself more than once. King Hazael would go up against the southern Kingdom of Judah as well, leaving with much *"booty"*.

II Kings 10:32-33, (32) <u>In those days YHWH began to cut Israel short</u>; and Hazael smote them in all the borders of Israel: (33) <u>from the Jordan eastward,</u> all the land of Gilead, the Gadites, and the Reubenites, and the Manassites, from Aroer, which is by the valley of Arnon, even Gilead and Bashan.

ASSYERIANS

After the Arameans, the Assryians ascended to power. They too began to pick apart Israel as they sensed the weakling people to their south. With their first foray into Israel, King Tiglath-pileser invaded the northern parts of the land, and carried away captive most of the inhabitants of the tribe of Naphtali. All the while, YHWH continued to send them prophets to *"return"*.

II Kings 15:29, (29) In the days of Pekah king of Israel came Tiglath-pileser king of Assyria, and took Ijon, and Abel-beth-maacah, and Janoah, and Kedesh, and Hazor, and Gilead, and Galilee, <u>all the land of Naphtali; and he carried them captive to Assyria</u>.

Eventually, it would be Shalmaneser King of Assyria who would destroy the northern Kingdom of Israel, taking most of the people away captive. And as was the custom of conquering armies, he replaced most of the inhabitants with other peoples from his empire. But as scripture indicates, far from all of Israel were taken away and some of their priests were returned.

YHWH describes HIS actions and how HE was justified in allowing Israel to be destroyed because of their repeated *"evil ways"*, and by ignoring HIS prophets that HE sent to warn them.

'AND WROUGHT WICKED THINGS TO PROVOKE YHWH'

II Kings 17:6, (6) In the ninth year of Hoshea, <u>the king of Assyria took Samaria, and carried Israel away unto Assyria</u>, and placed them in Halah, and in Habor, on the river of Gozan, and in the cities of the Medes.

The Assyrians, as was the ancient practice of the time for many of the nations, brought people from their land and replaced the Israelites whom they removed to Assyria. Not all of Israel was removed. The poorest of the land were generally left to till the fields and maintain the vineyards and crops for the new landlords. But the majority of the people, especially the ruling class, nobles and merchants etc., were removed and replaced. Few were left.

The reason the poorest were generally left behind is that it was they who provided the wheat and barley, the grapes for wine and oil for lamps, the wool for clothes and other necessities. As poor people, bringing them back to Assyria would have been more of a burden than an asset. So some were left.

Some historians using ancient Assyrian inscriptions, ascribe the destruction of Israel to the Assyrian King Sargon II not to **Shalmaneser** King of Assyria. Unless they were one and the same king, which here it is doubtful. A king of Assyria by whatever name, destroyed what was left of Israel. Depending on how one wishes to interpret it, possibly more than one destruction occurred. But in the final analysis it really is unimportant as Israel was destroyed.

II Kings 17:24, (24) <u>And the king of Assyria brought men from Babylon, and from Cuthah, and from Avva, and from Hamath and Sepharvaim, <u>and placed them in the cities of Samaria instead of the sons of Israel</u>; and they possessed Samaria, and dwelt in the cities thereof.

Which of these two kings actually gets credit for the northern Kingdom of Israel's final destruction is far less important than that Israel was allowed to be destroyed in the first place and why. Approximately one hundred and thirty five years later, it would be the turn of the southern Kingdom of Judah to be destroyed. Although unlike the northern kingdom GOD'S plan was to return them to their land and reestablish them after their exile to Babylon.

Returning to the northern kingdom, the entire story of the long suicidal slide to self destruction of the northern Kingdom of Israel can be read in the Hebrew Bible in the First and Second Book of Kings (II Kings 17:1-41) as well as in the Prophets and Second Chronicles as well as references are made to Samaria in both of the Books of Ezra and Nehemiah and in the Prophets.

In Chapter 17 of II Kings, GOD lays out HIS reason in detail, a strong case against Israel *why* HE was destroying Israel *"and they went after things of nought, and became nought"*. They left GOD and HIS blessings for nothing.

After the exile of Israel to Assyria, the king of Assyria returned one of the *priest* whom they had carried away to teach the people how to worship *"the GOD of the land"*. Apparently others followed. This is even born out today, as Y-DNA evidence of three of the four Priestly family lines of the Samaritan Priests, the *"Cohanim"*, have the Cohen Modal Haplotype (CMH) just as those Cohanim of today's Jewish descendants carry this unique priestly gene.

According to the scripture, these people *"feared YHWH, and served their own gods"*. The descendants of these people are the *"Samaritans"* spoken of in the Christian Bible. Most of them appear to have been from the empire of Assyria and also remnants of Israel left behind or who returned from hiding.

It bears to keep this in mind, as the population prior to their exile by the Assyrians, was made up of Israelites from the sons of Jacob. Now they were a mixed people from the two kingdoms of Israel and Assyria.

Now it will be Judah's turn. The Kingdom of Judah lasted longer, but it too eventually succumbed to their own self inflicted wound, and can be read in First and Second Kings and in II Chronicles and in the Prophets.

SOUTHERN KINGDOM OF JUDAH

BABYLONIANS

So now after the destruction of the northern Kingdom of Israel, fast forward about 135 years to the destruction of the southern Kingdom of Judah by the Babylonians. They were taken to Babylon but later after Babylon was defeated by the Persians, the Jews were allowed to return to Israel after 70 years and reestablish their Temple. When the Persians were later defeated by the Greeks, the Jews fought against the Greeks and won a short lived independence as *"Israel"*. This was accomplished by the Maccabees who reestablished the kingdom of Israel. But this independence was not very *"independent"* for very long.

Eventually, the Romans would dominate the area and make Israel a vassal state. The Maccabees, also known as the *"Hasmoneans"* was a priestly family. Contrary to their own history and GOD'S oath to Aaron and to David they would eventually become both the High Priest and the *"King"* of Israel. However, they were neither of the right linage of priests to be High Priest, nor were they of the SEED of David to be king. They had neither the right pedigree for the priesthood (Zadok) nor for the throne. And holding both of these positions of power was not *"kosher"*. They were exceedingly corrupt and their close association with the Idumaeans and Romans only helped a bad situation become worse. It was into this situation which Jesus would be born.

GETTING RE-ESTABLISHED

The history of the reestablishment of "*Israel*" after the return of Judah from exile in Babylon and how the Jew Jesus fits into the narrative is all too important to overlook. What became known as the "*Samaritans*" **after** the exile of the northern Kingdom of Israel and it's ten tribes, plays a major part in the ministry of Jesus. For Jesus spent most all of his ministry in the northern half of Israel, in what was the territorial lands of the ten northern tribes. This area included what was also called "*Samaria*". But this was a different "*Samaria*" than that which existed during the time of it's corrupt kings from Jeroboam to Hoshea (931 BCE-722 BCE), prior to their exile.

It was the demise of the original inhabitants of Samaria, before their exile, that is central to understanding why the ministry of a Jew such as Jesus, would be necessary in the first place. For Jesus said on several occasions that it was only to the "*lost sheep of the House of Israel*" for which he came. This will be repeated often as it is important. Then it becomes the question of, *"who are the lost sheep of the House of Israel"?* The answer may come in something Jesus said to the Samaritan woman at the well. *"Ye worship ye know not what: we know what we worship: **for salvation is of the Jews**".*

In responding to the Samaritan woman, Jesus was alluding to several things here. The first was that the Samaritans did not accept Jerusalem as the place where GOD YHWH put HIS name. They worshiped at Mount Gerizim in Samaria. Additionally, the *"religion"* of the Samaritans, although they worshiped "*YHWH*", was corrupt. But he was also making a statement regarding his tribe, that the salvation of Israel would come from the tribe of Judah. Many of the ancient people of the northern tribes of Israel still existed but were spread out over many "*nations*". Israel was scattered far and wide.
It was to these nations which Jesus seemed to be directing his own disciples to go and find these "*lost sheep of the House of Israel"*. Finally, neither do the Samaritans accept the House of David as being the *Royal House* of Israel.

CHAPTER TWO

SECOND TEMPLE OF YHWH

RETURN OF THE EXILES

In the Hebrew Bible, the two books of Ezra and Nehemiah are excellent for giving the reader a sense of what the returning Jews faced when confronted with the rebuilding of the Temple of YHWH as well as all of the other many obstacles thrown into their path by their many adversaries. The recounting of these events is important for understanding just how dire the circumstances were for the returning Jews from what had been Babylon.

The *"obstacles"* were not just physical and financial problems, but they were emotional as well. Add to this the hostility of the Samaritans and others, it was an up hill climb all of the way to rebuild and inaugurate the Temple.

From Ezra and Nehemiah there is a real sense of how much the returning Jews understood just how much they had displeased their GOD YHWH, and how serious and dedicated they had to be to correct their past mistake. These people worked very, very hard with little but their hands, a strong back and their fear of GOD to rebuild a city, it's walls and the Temple of GOD. For anyone who has never put away his wife and /or children for a religious Law, the unimaginable amount of pain and effort it took to recapture their lost world, is impossible to know. For some of the events which took place are truly astounding. These were very special people who understood clearly what was at stake and had comprehended the importance of their mission.

Eventually, the Temple of YHWH was rebuilt to resemble somewhat the ancient Temple that they had known. To most who remembered the Temple of YHWH which Solomon had built, *"resemble"* may be too strong a word. Nevertheless, the Second Temple was built on the ruins of the First Temple on the mount in Jerusalem upon the return of the Jews from exile in Babylon.

Not to get too far ahead of the story, but as mentioned, many historians claim that later during the Roman period, it was Herod who built the *"Second Temple"*. What Herod had actually done was to completely renovate and expand the existing Second Temple of YHWH and expand the Temple Mount area. He renovated what the exiled Jews of Babylon had built, until it completely overshadowed what had been there before. So, *"Herod's Temple"* was the Second Temple **renovated**, he did not build a Second Temple. Or if one insists that he did build a Temple, it would have been a *"Third Temple"*.

The Second Temple existed before, during, and after his reign as *"king"*. Additionally, today's *"Western Wall"* itself is the <u>*retaining wall*</u> built by Herod to hold the many tons of fill dirt used to expand the Temple Mount area. It is not part of the Temple, but the wall around of the mount itself.

"Herod's" Temple (49 BCE-1 BCE) renovation / construction was begun before Jesus was born by renovating or replacing the earlier humble structure constructed by the returning exiles or adding to it.

The exiles had been poor, so their Second Temple no doubt was modest in comparison to that of King Solomon it had replaced, and what Herod ended up building over it.

As Herod had plenty of wealth to use in his own building endeavor, what was accomplished by all of his money in the eyes of many, constituted a completely new Temple of YHWH. So why did they not just call it the *"Third Temple"* and not the *"Second Temple"* instead?

But long before Herod, the returning Jews had many problems to overcome. There were other serious issues they had to deal with, not the least was that of intermarriage of Israel with the Babylonians while in Babylon, especially the descendants of priests of the tribe of Levi. Because the ancient patriarchal society of Israel was *"patrilineal"* (identity was determined by the father), and the priests could only marry *"Israel"*, many who married Babylonians were not found in the *"Book of Genealogy"*, and many could not determine if they were *"of Israel"*, or if they were qualified for the priesthood.

For the priests, if they were a Cohen and had a foreign wife, they were disqualified. Additionally, if they were the offspring of the union of a Cohen and a Babylonian *"babe"*, they were disqualified. Most of the intermarriage appears to have been the taking of foreign wives by the Jewish men including those from all of the other tribes which made up *"Judah"*, especially *Levi*. Of interest, even this many generations after the split up of the tribes from the time of King Rehoboam, the people still referred to itself as *"Judah and Benjamin"* upon the return from exile during the time of Ezra and Nehemiah. Individual tribal identity still existed and was strong amongst Jacob's sons.

It must be noted that if daughters of Israel married Babylonian men, it would not have brought about either a serious debate nor a crisis such as with that of the males. As the genealogy of Israel was *"patrilineal"*, and *"pedigree"* was from father to son, it would not have been much of an issue for most of Israel as inheritance, kingship and priesthood were patrilineal. It was a problem for the Priests who could only marry daughters of *"Israel"*.

Ezra 2:59, (59) And these were they that went up from Tel-melah, Tel-harsa, Cherub, Addan, and Immer; but they could not tell their fathers' houses, and their SEED, whether they were of Israel:

Ezra 2:62, (62) These sought their register, that is, the genealogy, but it was not found; therefore were they deemed polluted and put from the priesthood.

A person's pedigree was determined through the SEED of their fathers house.

It is important to note here how extremely important *"SEED"* is regarding Israel. This is no less true today than it was 2,000-3,000 years ago. Some of the people could not tell if they were of *"Israel"* because they could not tell the *"SEED"* of their father. For they needed to know the *"SEED"* of their father in order to determine if they were *"of Israel"*. As it was through the *"SEED"* of the father that all of Israel determined their pedigree, genealogy, family, house, clan, tribe and people. It's true today according to Safer Torah.

As touched on earlier, the issue was so serious, that many, at least the *"sons of the priests"* took a solemn oath to put away their wives and apparently those who had children by their foreign wives as well.

Ezra 10:19, 44, (19) And they gave their hand that they would put away their wives; and being guilty, they offered a ram of the flock for their guilt...(44) All these had taken foreign wives; and some of

them had wives by whom they had children.

To have left the fleshpots of Babylon and return to the land of their ancestors, a destroyed kingdom far away, took a supreme act of faith. Many were not able to bring themselves to leave, and a remnant of their descendants remain their until this day (Iran/Iraq). It was an incredible feat of perseverance for these returning exiles who dedicated themselves to obeying the Law of the GOD of their forefathers, to rebuild the Temple of YHWH, restore the wall surrounding Jerusalem and honoring HIS Shabbat. They were true Zionists in the very literal meaning of the word. While they were doing all of theses things, they had to fend off Arabians, Ammonites, Ashdodites, Horonites and Samaritans who were constantly conspiring against them ever bit of the way.

Regardless, amidst all of the drama, the trauma and intrigue, during the sixth year of the reign of King Darius II of Persia, the house of GOD, the Second Temple of YHWH was completed and remained until destroyed by Rome.

GREEKS

Well, the Persians treated the Jewish people pretty good, especially when compared with some of the other kingdoms and empires. As a matter of fact, the Jewish people have seldom been treated as well to this day, with a few exceptions, as when they were part of the Persian Empire. But this period of good will would eventually come to an end with the rise of a Macedonian king by the name of Alexander.

It is said that the Greek Empire under Alexander was good to the Jewish people as well. At least while he was alive. But he died suddenly mysteriously and so his personal good will was short lived. Many Jewish people still have no problem naming their children "_Alexander_". He died young at the age of 32, so what may have been we may never know. Many historians, as does this author, believe that he was poisoned by his own generals or possibly by Cassander son of Antipater.

Before his death, while Alexander and his generals were busy conquering most of the civilized world, the Jews were still rebuilding their ancient city and it's Temple by decree from the Persians who were losing their empire now to the Greeks.

ANOTHER LANDLORD

The Greeks, lead by Alexander III of Macedon, better known as Alexander the Great, conquered Persia around 330 BCE. Aside from being considered by many as the most successful general to ever lead an army into battle, Alexander's most lasting legacy may have been the Greek culture he left behind his wake. This was to become a major point of contention during the next few hundred years with the Jewish people. The Greek culture, originally spread by Greek colonies begun throughout the Empire, was a cultural war against the defeated peoples every bit as threatening as was the sword.

"_Hellenism_" was so powerful that the centers of Greek culture were no longer in Greece proper, but in Alexandria and Antioch, the respective capitols of Ptolemy Egypt and Seleucid Syria, two of the four kingdoms which his generals ended up with after the mysterious death of Alexander.

Whether or not it was a planned assault on other cultures, the effect was devastating to the Jews. "_Hellenism_" whether "_de-facto_"or "_de-jure_", had the same effect on the Jewish people as any war. In many ways it was worse, as it pitted "_Hellenistic Jews_" against the Law of YHWH and those Jews who feared GOD. It threatened their very existence every bit as the Babylonians.

After the death of Alexander in 323 BCE, the Macedonian Empire broke up amongst his generals. Four kingdoms developed from what was a very large empire. The Jews were caught between the Ptolemaic Kingdom of Egypt and the Seleucid Kingdom of Syria. These two kingdoms were arguably the largest and most powerful of the four. The other two kingdoms were the Cassander Kingdom and the Lysimachus Kingdom in Asia Minor.

A large part of what essentially had been Judea before exile, became part of the Seleucid Kingdom of Syria. Things went rapidly down hill for the Jewish people. Eventually a rebellion would brake out beginning with a priestly family which spread throughout all of Judea. The details of that rebellion are not as important as understanding the idea of one culture imposing it's own culture on a subjugated people. Or put another way, a pagan culture clashing with the one and only GOD *"YHWH"* and HIS people, Israel.

In 167 BCE the Seleucid King Antiochus IV Epiphanes outlawed Jewish sacrifice and Jewish feasts, forbid the circumcision of Jewish males, the Holy Temple of YHWH was desecrated with a statue of the Greek god Zeus, and sacrificial alters were erected and impure animals were sacrificed. A revolt by the Jews could not be far behind these measures.

MACCABEES

The story of the Maccabees is an extremely important part of Jewish history. Their story is of heroic proportions but it is also a sad story of how a people lost their way. The steady Hellenization process amongst the Jewish population and it's practitioners, supported much of the Seleucid king's policies and dictates. But underneath was a rebellion waiting for a spark to set it off. This came about with a Priest by the name of Mattathias the Hasmonean. He and his sons and their followers rebelled and eventually defeated the Syrians and winning their autonomy although they were still considered a *"province"* of the Seleucid Kingdom. This ended upon the death of Antiochus in 129 BCE. The Romans and the Hasmoneans had established an *"alliance"* which lasted up until the time of Pompey in 63 BCE.

During this time period, the Maccabees reestablished the Kingdom of Israel. It was to eventually become extremely corrupt. Caught between the fading and fractured Greek Empires and the new Roman overlords, the Jews were profoundly affected by the corrupt ways of these peoples. Whether a *"king"*, a Hellenist, a Priest or Pharisee, many became corrupt.

ROMANS

From approximately 129 BCE until 63 BCE this priestly family ruled an independent state. Thereafter, the Romans enter the pictured in the Jewish peoples long history, for the Romans had already annexed Greece in 146 BCE making Israel and their *"alliance"* an unnecessary burden. In 63 BCE the Roman general Pompey took Jerusalem, thus ending the Hasmonean rule and beginning the Roman rule.

The Hasmonean dynasty did not end with their defeat by the Romans, only their independence. Depending on whether the Jewishness of Antipater (he was an Idumaean convert) father of Herod is counted, the Hasmonean dynasty either ended in 63 BCE or 37 BCE. If the circumcision of Antipater, called *"Antipas"*, Herod's father is to have any real meaning, the Hasmonean dynasty ended with the death of the last Hasmonean male heir and beginning with the *"Idumean Jew"* Antipater, another dynasty began.

To be fair, Herod's people (the Idumaeans) had earlier been forcibly converted by John Hyrcanus. According to Josephus, most if not all of the Idumaeans, many thousands (all that were in the land) were circumcised and took on the Law of Moses and became no different than the other Jews, and were indeed called "*Jews*". This alone may help explain much of the red hair.

A telling incident occurred sometime about 30 years or so after the death of Jesus when a party of 20 thousand defenders, Jews still called *"Idumaeans"* (Idumaean Jews) rushed to Jerusalem in defense of the Temple to help fight the Romans, but were denied entry into the city and rebuffed by those unwilling souls of the Jews inside. Part of a speech by one of their generals named Simon quoted by Josephus, tells of how dedicated they were as *"Jews"* in defense of their GOD and the Temple in spite of their reception.

"But if these men have been more merciful than the public necessarily required , we that are Idumeans will preserve this house of GOD, <u>and will fight for our common country</u>, and will oppose by war as well those that attack them from abroad, as those that betray them from within. Here we abide before the walls in our armor, until either the Romans grow weary in waiting for you, <u>or you becomes friends of liberty, and repent of what you have done against it</u>". (The Jewish War: Book 4, Chapter 4, Paragraph 4:281-282 Flavius Josephus)

The Idumaeans were defending not only the Temple against the Romans, but against the corrupt Jews and Priests within Jerusalem's walls. They were making a powerful statement against Jewish hypocrisy as well. This took place not long before the Romans finally destroyed the Temple of YHWH in 70 CE. By not accepting such help when offered is profoundly enlightening when the dire situation they were all in with the Romans is assessed.

The time of the Hasmoneans especially, and thereafter until the Temple of YHWH was destroyed in 70 CE, was without a doubt the most corrupt, the bloodiest and most disgusting in all of Jewish history while the Jewish people were still on their inherited land.

Aside from the bloodletting and intrigue from their bankrupt souls, neither the Hasmonean "*priests*", were of the correct line (Zadok) of Priests of the linage of Aaron to hold that office, nor were the Maccabees or Idumaean "*kings*" of the SEED of David, the correct pedigree to sit upon his throne. For a King of Israel to be of the SEED of Esau is profoundly perverted. For a while, the *"High Priest"* held the position of *"High Priest"* and of *"king"* together. To anyone who knew the Law of Moses, the holding of these dual positions was sick and was outside the Law of Moses.

There are no words to describe the amount of mayhem and human carnage that existed during the time of these twisted lost souls. Parents murdered children, children murdered parents, brother murdered brother, sisters, brothers, aunts, uncles and cousins all conspired and killed each other for gain, jealousy, wealth, the priesthood and power. Priests, Pharisees, Sadducee, Essene, Samaritans, Sacraii, Zealots, Herodians, Hellenists, Idumaeans, Greeks, Romans and Jewish laymen were all part of the mosaic of an extremely sick society and time in the existence of Israel. It was a *"free for all"* of every despicable evil known to man. For a period of approximately 200 years or more, the land of Israel experienced and underwent some of the saddest days ever in it's long history.

When compared to the first Kingdom of Israel / Judah and their kings (before and after the split), the second Kingdom of Israel was almost unrecognizable during the time of Herod, who was himself little more than a murderous crazy guy who liked to build big stone things. Along with the *"murderous crazy guy"* Herod, were the *"multifaceted corrupt"* Temple Priests, the *"second banana"* Pharisees, the *"kill it if it moves"* Zealots, and finally the *"good cop, bad cop"* Roman occupiers. The *"second"* Kingdom of Israel during the time of Jesus was truly in a sad state of affairs. In many respects, the little kingdom of Israel took on the persona of all that was rotten in Rome.

ROMAN RULE

During the time of Jesus, it was the Romans who were the worlds *"super power"*.

The Romans, other than carrying out the sentence of death for Jesus passed down by the priests at the end of his life, were of little real influence or consequence in the daily existence of Jesus. Jesus understood well that it was because of the sins of his own people that they were subjugated by Rome. The Jews were semi-autonomous, with the Romans leaving them to govern themselves with regard to their own religious laws, but only in so far as it did not overstep existing Roman Law. The Romans seemed to be a bit more politically sensitive to the religious time bomb they were sitting on than were the Greeks who proceeded them, or perhaps they just had more experience.

The different Roman governors from various jurisdictions had their own personal internal rivalry and power struggles which at times spilled over into the world of their subjugated peoples. But by and large, this was usually less by design than by their own corruption and ineptitude.

Other than their own internal disputes, the primary interest of the Romans was in receiving the tax money from the Jews and in maintaining the peace so this could be accomplished. As long as the Jewish inhabitants paid their taxes and did not make any trouble, they were more or less left to their own devices. This is not to say that the Romans were not involved with all kinds of mischief in their conspiracies to control the Jewish population and to increase their own grip on power. They were not adverse to playing one side off of another to increase their own power or in manipulating for gain. They were adept, and often inept, at playing the various factions and sects against one another. But primarily, it was revenue, the tax money that they wanted. And the more they could increase their tax base, the more money, influence and power they would wield. Keeping the peace became a prime objective.

BETHLEHEM / NAZARETH

An example of the topic of taxes, is evident in the story of how Jesus came to be born in Bethlehem in the first place. According to the Gospel of Luke, Joseph had to return to his ancestral home (house of David) to pay his taxes. As the pedigree of Joseph dictated that he return to his ancestral inheritance in Bethlehem to accomplish this Roman law. Mary who was with child, delivered Jesus in Bethlehem instead of Nazareth to which they later returned and where he was raised.

Luke 2:1-7, (1), [1] And it came to pass in those days, that there went out a decree from Caesar Augustus, that all the world should be taxed. (2) (And this taxing was first made when Cyrenius was governor of Syria.) (3) And all went to be taxed, every one into his own city. (4) And Joseph also went up from Galilee, out of the city of Nazareth, into Judaea, unto the city of David, which is called Bethlehem; (because he was of the house and lineage of David:) (5) To be taxed with Mary his espoused wife, being great with child. (6) And so it was, that, while they were there, the days were accomplished that she should be delivered. (7) And she brought forth her firstborn son, and wrapped him in swaddling clothes, and laid him in a manger; because there was no room for them in the inn

A revealing part of this story is the apparent humble background of Jesus, in that his parents could not afford a lamb for a burnt offering as part of the atonement after the purification of the mother (Luke 2:21-24). The Law (Leviticus 12:1-8) allowed in such cases, instead of a lamb for the burnt offering, a pigeon or turtledove as a sin offering for those who could afford it. They were to bring two turtledoves or two pigeons to offer instead, one for the burnt offering, and the other for the sin offering for those who were poor.

This is an example of the Law at work. And along with the circumcision of Jesus, it shows how very much the Law of Moses was a part of every aspect of the life of a Jewish family, beginning from ones birth. This was as true for Jesus as for any Jewish baby born to Israel. And for the first born son such as Jesus was, it was even more so.

Although the story in Luke is somewhat misleading because it leaves out the full atonement requirement which includes a lamb of the first year for a burnt offering, it nevertheless is interesting. Joseph was obviously of humble origins and could not afford a lamb for the atonement of his wife. So, from the very beginning of the story of Jesus is illustrated just how very much the Law of Moses was a part of every aspect of the life of Jesus and of Israel.

'I HALLOWED UNTO ME'

Luke 2:21-24 (21) And when eight days were accomplished for the circumcising of the child, his name was called JESUS, which was so named of the angel before he was conceived in the womb. (22) And when the days of her purification according to the Law of Moses were accomplished, they brought him to Jerusalem, to present him to the Lord; (23) (As it is written in the law of the Lord, Every male that openeth the womb shall be called holy to the Lord;) (24) And to offer a sacrifice according to that which is said in the Law of the Lord, A pair of turtledoves, or two young pigeons.

Additionally, the scripture in Exodus regarding the *"male"* is misquoted in Luke 2:23, for Exodus 13:1 refers to the *"first born male"* which had an entirely different status than the other males born. *"And she brought forth her firstborn son, and wrapped him in swaddling clothes, and laid him in a manger; because there was no room for them in the inn"* (Luke 2:7). As it was mentioned in verse seven that Jesus was her *"first born son"*, verse 23, the writer if not Jewish, may not have known the significance. This may be as well, another example of where the author being unfamiliar with the Law of Moses, either did not know or appreciate the difference between the *"first born male"*, the *"first born"* or a *"male"* born because he was not Jewish.

Exodus 13:1-2, 15, (1) And YHWH spoke unto Moses, saying: (2) 'Sanctify unto Me all the first-born, whatsoever openeth the womb among the sons of Israel, both of man and of beast, it is Mine.' ….but all the first-born of my sons I redeem.

Numbers 3:13, (13) for all the first-born are Mine: on the day that I smote all the first-born in the land of Egypt I hallowed unto Me all the first-born in Israel, both man and beast, Mine they shall be: I am YHWH.'

Exodus 22:28, (28) .... *The first-born of thy sons shalt <u>thou give unto Me</u>.*

The first born male in Israel is a type of *"wave"* offering to GOD which is redeemed. First born males of Israel belong to YHWH and are very special.

FIRST BORN JESUS

According to the Gospels, Jesus was the first born son. First born males of Israel belong to YHWH. According to the Law, they must be *"redeemed"*.

According the Safer Torah (Exodus 4:22), not only is *Israel* YHWH'S first born son but all first born sons of Israel belong to YHWH and are *"HIS"*.

To YHWH GOD, all first born males of Israel are *"hallowed"* unto YHWH and belong to HIM. They are made *"holy"* to GOD. This was true many centuries before Jesus was born, during the time of Jesus and is true up until the present time. The Hebrew root word used in Numbers 3:13 for *"hallowed"* stems from (*Koof-Dalet-Shin*) meaning *"separation"*. The idea of *"apartness"* and *"sacredness"* come from this as well, and finally is the root for *"holy"*. There are several other words derived from this root with similar or related meanings such as in *"consecrated"*, but the idea is one of *"holiness"* whether referring to the *"sanctuary"*, someone or even something *"set aside"* such as the holy portion for priests.

JEWS / PRIESTS / PHARISEES / SADDUCEE / ROMANS

So the historical, cultural, military, political and religious time leading up to and including the life of *"first born male"* Jesus, sets the stage for his own ministry to his people Israel, and the context in which it all took place.

This is part of the world of Jesus. The things which he did, and the things which he said, and the things he said he believed and taught must be understood within this context. Jesus had very little, almost no contact with any people outside of his own people Israel. With the possible exception of the occasional Samaritan and a Canaanite which it is written he had contact with, this is so. Of course, there were the Romans. But his entire world was Israel, the Temple of YHWH and the Jewish people. Anything inconsistent with this understanding distorts the narrative regarding his life.

As Jesus was born, lived and died as a practicing Jew under the Law of Moses in a Jewish kingdom located in the land of Israel, much of the story of Jesus has to do with the Law and the Prophets. His life and the word which he spoke is approached from this perspective as the entire religion of Christianity that is now based on his life, in all reality, hinges on the Law of Moses and the words of Prophets. Although one may be sure that few if any Christians are aware of this. To them the Law is archaic.

For <u>according to the Gospels</u>, the Law of Moses and the Prophets were the basis for his existence and his death for his people Israel. And so therefore, the Law of Moses and the Prophets are the *"base"* from which the source of the Christian Bible springs. That said, even though it would be difficult to find almost anything remotely *"legal"* within Christianity today that would lead the reader to understand this. The Law dominated the life of Jesus.

HEBREW BIBLE – LAW OF MOSES – SAFER TORAH

Because the basis for which the Gospels rests is on the Law of Moses and the Prophets, there is much in this book which explains or discusses in some aspect, the conversations pertaining to Law which occurred between Jesus, the Priests and rabbis of his day. Some of it may be too detailed for many, but it must be understood as discussed before, that the *"Law"* by definition is a *legal code* and therefore is *technical*. It consists of detailed Laws, Statutes Commandments, and Ordinances given to Israel to live by, by YHWH. The entire discussion of the Gospels centers on and around the Law of Moses.

By either breaking the Law or not keeping the Law, it became literally a matter of life or death for Israel. This was true both as a people collectively and for the individual. There are many examples of Israel being punished both collectively because of sin as well as individuals being punished for their sin all throughout the Hebrew Bible. It is the Law of Moses, that is comprised of these detailed Laws, Commandments, Statutes and Ordinances which was the world in which Jesus existed.

Because the basis for the existence of Jesus was the Law of Moses of which he lived, preached and died, addressing the Law itself is imperative.

THE JEWISH WORLD OF JESUS

Only the Law and the Prophets existed during his lifetime. There was no such thing as *"Christianity"*. And the false prophet of the surrounding *"mixed"* peoples had not been born yet or entered into his cave. His own personal perverted hallucinations of blood and gore, establishing his ghoulish nightmare of a religion was still several centuries into the future. Also, the Jews of Jesus's day, even those who professed belief in him, would be shocked and would not recognize today what is called *"Christianity"* or *"Christians"*. For in many respects the followers of Jesus were Jews who still sacrificed in the Temple and went to synagogue with fellow Jews. So in the early days, followers in Jesus and the early followers of the rabbis often met and worshiped together in the same place. These were the beginnings of what would eventually become two separate new religions.

The Christian religion today, could be called a *"virtual religion"* as it is not of <u>this world</u>. For Jesus said himself that his kingdom was not of this world. The non Hellenist Jews, practiced a form of religious observance based on the Law of Moses as taught to them by the Temple Priests the <u>teachers</u> and <u>judges</u> of Israel. As for the hallucinating cave dweller, he would not exist nor his vision of hate would not spawn any followers for several hundred years.

BACKGROUND

Understanding the background and many of the issues which surrounded the ministry of Jesus gives one a better feel for what he was up against as he preached to Israel and a better comprehension of some of the nuances of Law discussed. For it was the Law, including the idea of *"blasphemy"* contained within it, which he was accused of and for which his death was called for by the Priests. As has been stated, it may have been the Romans who crucified Jesus, but it was the Priests and the Law of Moses used to condemned him.

HEROD THE NOT SO GREAT

Herod may have been certifiably insane. At least by many accounts he was *"mad"*. He may not have been a *"Nero"* or a *"Caligula"*, but he would not have felt out of place in their company. The *"great"* part of his name had more to do with his building projects than his rule as client *"king"* of Judea to the Romans. The Herodian life style that he led was considered decadent by most of the Jewish population, and the antipathy towards Herod may have been less a reflection of the fact that he was the son of an Idumean *"convert"* who as *"king"*, showed little true regard for his Jewish religion, than to the sick life style and world in which he belonged. For had his moral compass been more in tune with the Statutes of GOD, the words of his subjects may have been kinder to him. But Herod was decadent.

Some historians say that Herod was an *"observant"* Jew, but *"observant"* is a relative term. The number of people that he reportedly was either directly or indirectly responsible for having murdered, would give new meaning to the term *"observant"*. His pedigree was probably far less an issue than life style.

For along with most of the rest of the Idumeans, his father Antipater and his house was converted *"forcibly"* by John Hyrcanus (134 BCE-104 BCE). Had Herod attempted to live according to the Law of Moses, or even to pretend to, one may suppose that his life and that of the Jews in Judea may have fared much better, and the subsequent events that led up to destruction of the Temple in 70 CE may have had a different outcome. But this was not to be.

The ascension of the Ideumeans as a people within Jewish society, even though they were now as *"Jews"* according to Josepheus, may be another hint as to the deterioration of Israel's relationship with it's GOD. For now it had a king of the House of Esau. Many of today's armchair psychologists say that Herod's building fetish was his way of compensating for his lack of respect by the Jewish population, who did not recognize his *"Jewishness"*. In other words, Herod was trying to win acceptance through his many *Jewish* building projects. His over compensation as a *builder* of Jewish things holy, was his way of winning acceptance. In some way perhaps we should be thankful for this effort. Then, there is the Freudian angle, some will no doubt bring up.

But executing many members of his own family, including one of his ten wives including three of his own sons, a mother-in-law, and a brother-in-law may have had a considerable impact on why he was not so acceptable to the Jewish population. He is known to have executed these six members of his own family and possibly conspired to kill even more. This does not include other real or perceived enemies not related to him. *Not* being related to the *"king"* during his time would have been an advantage one might suppose.

As mentioned, other than his actions as written in the Christian Bible, he has become famous for his building projects. His expansion of the Temple Mount and the rebuilding of the Temple of YHWH are two of his most well known building projects. The Herodium, Masada fortress, Caesarea, the walled inclosure of the Cave of the Patriarchs where Abraham, Isaac and Jacob are buried are other monuments to his insecurity. Although, given the current onslaught of de-legitimization efforts by most of Israel's enemies, these lasting monuments built by Herod for whatever reason are hard to ignore.

As discussed, what is commonly referred to as the *"Wailing Wall"* or *"Western Wall"* (Kotel), at the Temple Mount in the Old City of Jerusalem, is but the western side of the retaining wall built around the Temple, used to expand the size of the ancient Temple Mount itself. This was one of Herod's building projects. Huge blocks of stone were stacked on top of one another and filled with earth to expand the size of the Temple Mount grounds. There are many Jewish people today who believe that this retaining wall was part of the ancient Temple of YHWH itself and are unaware of what it actually is.

To see such reverence given to this retaining wall today by worshipers is truly sad. In many ways it is like praying at, crying on and kissing a fence. The rabbis protect and assign reverence to this retaining wall far in excess of what it actually is. It is sad commentary for the Jewish people.

"*Sad*", because just above this retaining wall is the Jewish people's true place of worship which the leaders of Israel have quite literally given away the keys to, after having won it in the 1967 war. The Temple Mount is currently "*occupied*" by Israel's sworn enemy who have their own unholy outhouse of worship occupying it's site, and who curse the GOD of Israel and his people on a daily basis, and lust after their blood without end.

BABY KILLER

According to the Gospel of Matthew (2:1-23), King Herod upon hearing that the "*messiah*" was born, wanted to kill him but he was not able to find him, so he ordered all of the male infants of Bethlehem and the "*coasts*" to be slain. According to this Gospel, this was all the males, up to two years of age. Some historians are not convinced that this took place because of the scant evidence to support it. But given his known lists of murders and executions, it is not much of a stretch to believe such a thing happened exactly the way that it is written by this "*observant*" Jew called "*Herod*" .

But Joseph the father of Jesus, was aware of the plot, having been warned in a dream. Joseph fled to Egypt taking his wife and new born son and remained there until word came that Herod was dead.

CHAPTER THREE

JESUS THE JEW

Jesus the Jew was *"Jewish"*. Jesus the Jew was *not* a Christian but lived as a Jew by the Law of Moses.

Jesus lived his entire life as a *"Jew"*, according to the Law of Moses and was sentenced to death from this very Law, as a *"Jew"*.

This statement that Jesus was not a Christian may seem obvious to some and come as a shock to others, yet, Jesus the Jew was an observant son of Jacob and was never a "*Christian*"..

Jesus was an *"observant"* Jew. He lived by the Law. Although, this concept is a modern concept unavailable to the Jews of his time. By *"observant"* is meant that Jews were either followers of the Law of Moses and offered sacrifice at the Temple of YHWH, or were Hellenists for the most part. They may have been either very pious and observant Jews or Jews not so observant, but they were Jews nevertheless. There was only one religion of Israel and it was centered on the Temple of YHWH in Jerusalem and was not called "*Judaism*". This "*religion*" did not exist *yet*.

As the "*religion*" of Israel during the time of Jesus was based on the Temple of YHWH and the Law of Moses, it was very simple and easy to live by. Most people would not have had much of a problem remaining observant for in reality, it was the Temple priests and Levites who did all of the "*work*".

And as the concept of "*religion*" is concerned, most observant Jews of his day, no doubt might be considered "*orthodox*" by today's standards but with a completely different meaning. Not by today's "*rabbis*" definition of *their* own religion, but of their observance regarding the Temple of YHWH and the observing the Laws of the Safer Torah, new moons and the holy feast days. There was no "*Talmud*" with it's many perversions of the Law of Moses nor 613 "*mizvot*". Life was much more simple as is the Law of Moses itself.

The world which Jesus would be born into was relatively simple.

HIS WORLD

His small world was one in which as a carpenter, he made a meager living working with his hands, and who no doubt looked forward to Shabbat (the Sabbath) when he could rest. Additionally, as a youth while growing up in Israel, Jesus spent time going to the local synagogue created by the rabbis and listening to the adults discuss the Law. As the Temple of YHWH was still very active in sacrificing each day, and very busy with many Temple servants and priests keeping it running, the synagogue was a meeting place to read and to study. It was not a house of worship nor a religion. It would only become a *"religion"* after the Temple was destroyed. This was an alien concept to the people of ancient Israel. Only the Temple was holy.

For the Christian or others who may be confused about the *synagogue*, it was in no way connected to nor associated with the Temple of YHWH. It was purely a secular creation of relatively recent origins running parallel to, but not part of the Temple. It was led by rabbis who wrote their own books which were different than the written word of GOD taught by the Temple Priests. It more or less ran in parallel to the Temple religion until in 70 CE. during the First Jewish Revolt. The Romans destroyed the religion of Israel by razing the Temple. In 135 after the second Jewish revolt and the dispersal of most of Israel's people, what the rabbis had been doing slowly became a *"religion"* itself by default, for the Jewish people. Fast forward 2,000 years and we have the mess we have today called *"Rabbinic Judaism"*, which in many ways is more of a *cultural dinosaur* based more on *tradition* than the fear of GOD.

The religion of ancient Israel was one of sacrificing to YHWH in HIS Temple. The every day life of the average Israelite would have been one of working and taking care of his family and remaining sanctified before his GOD YHWH. The dietary laws, remaining pure, going to the *mikvah* (ritual bath), circumcision, observing the rhythm of Sabbath, new moons, holy days and festivals would have been ingrained into them and they would not have needed help from any secular, self professed pontifications of the pious.

All of the everyday things associated with life were taught and handed down. The rabbis only became a necessary evil, long after the exile when Israel was cut off from it's Temple, it's Priests and it's land, and the rabbis and their synagogues became a religion of the Jewish people *by default*. And as Spinoza would later find out, once they became the religious authority, they could excommunicate or threaten the people to keep the community in line.

The Pharisees taught some of the true Law of Moses written in the Safer Torah and their own confusing writings not in the Safer Torah. Jesus as written in the Gospels, had gone to these synagogues as a youth, and as an adult. As this was the meeting place of laymen where discussing, learning and teaching was done. It was generally a meeting place for reading and informal discussion of the Law by exiles begun in Babylon. It became a meeting place of minds. Yet the Jewish people were never given the task of teaching GOD'S holy word to Israel. The rabbis attempt at usurping YHWH'S ministers who were given this role as their mission to Israel has perverted HIS Law beyond description. Like giving the *"village idiot"* a volume of Law to interpret, the rabbis made a mockery of YHWH'S Law.

Unlike the synagogue, the Temple was the place one brought their offering to GOD YHWH to be sacrificed and burned on HIS alter. It was the place of the Priests and the Levites who had been teaching GOD'S Law since Aaron. The Temple was the place of worship. The Temple was the place of the meeting of minds, the primary place. The Temple Priests were the ultimate authority on the word of GOD written in the Safer Torah for countless generations. The Priests and Levite ministers taught, but did most all of the hard work in GOD'S holy sanctuary while the rest of Israel lived a fairly simple life. By stepping into this arena and competing with the Priests, the secular Jewish *"rabbis"* went in way over their collective head, and were out of their league.

Compared to the Temple, the synagogue was like a *"hand me down"* intellectual mind meld between like minded gray matter. Whether everyone in the beginning who went to these gatherings believed in the so called *"oral law"* or if it was mandatory to do so is not known although doubtful. But slowly they took on the air of a crazed mad man creating a *"law"* of their own for every possible thought, or conceivable movement, action, inaction or task either known or unknown to Jewish kind. When they got to 613 they stopped and made the number *"holy"*, as now they were righteous in their own eyes.

But it was the responsibility of the Levites to teach Israel the Law, not the self appointed pious Jews from the streets and fields. Levites were ordained and hand picked by GOD for this task as HIS ministers. *Jews were not.*

Malachi 2:7, (7) For the Priest's lips should keep knowledge, and they should <u>seek the Law at his mouth; for he is the messenger of YHWH of hosts.</u>

If GOD'S holy servants of Levi, the Priest's lips are the *"messenger of YHWH"*, what does that say about the secular laymen men of Judah?

The practice of meeting on Shabbat and reading the Torah developed earlier while in exile in Babylon after the Jewish people had been suddenly ripped from their land and their Temple destroyed during the first short exile. But even after the rebuilding of the Temple of YHWH upon the return of the Jewish community from exile, the practice of meeting on Shabbat and reading the Torah, learning and teaching from the Law of Moses continued.

The Jews who became leaders of these *"synagogues"* were called *Pharisees / Rabbis* and were to eventually become enemies of the priesthood, directly challenging their authority. Largely because of the Christian religion, the negative and very *"loaded"* term *"Pharisee"* was eventually dropped and *"Rabbi"*, although still very negative, was kept, adopted and used till today.

These rabbis continued a *"tradition"* of interpreting the Law of Moses and passing it down orally for a while. They called this the *"<u>oral law" which they claimed too, was given to Moses</u>* at Sinai along with written Commandments (Safer Torah). The priests with the Law of Moses (Safer Torah), and the rabbis with their *"oral law"* would eventually become bitter enemies. Within a few hundred years after this period of Jesus, the *"oral law"* of the rabbis would be written down, and called the *"Mishnah"*. The Mishnah is a *"commentary"* on the Safer Torah. Still later a *"commentary"* of the Mishnah would be written down and called the *"Gemara"*. This was essentially a commentary on a commentary. Together, they are what is called today, the *"Talmud"* (Mishnah & Gemara). Jesus would have been exposed to this stuff.

Much of the words of this same Mishnah, before having been written down, would have been the words which Jesus would have heard in the synagogue as a youth. The *"Mishnah"* is a commentary on the Safer Torah, the rabbis say that it came down to them from GOD with Moses from Mount Sinai. Although there was no such thing as a *"rabbi"* on mount Sinai nor an *"oral law"* on said holy hill. According to them it was necessary, as the Safer Torah is too difficult to understand. Then again, it might be argued that the rabbis just lacked the common sense needed to comprehend the words of GOD which HE meant for all of Israel to be able to understand.

The Mishnah was a commentary on the Safer Torah, because it was so silly no one could understand it, another commentary was put together. The Gemara too was later written as a commentary on the commentary (Mishna). Sort of like a *"translation of a translation"*. The Gemara too is part of the *"oral tradition"* of the rabbis. By their own words, none of these books were to have been written down according to GOD, yet they did write them down. Jesus was probably spared much of it's nonsense as it was not written down until even later. Nevertheless, as Jesus was growing up, he heard the silliness of this *"stuff"* as it was discussed in synagogue in Nazareth *"orally"*.

LIFE RHYTHM

Growing up, Jesus would have been a typical Jew of his day, having been circumcised on the eighth day after birth and growing up observing the Law of Moses and festivals with the rest of his family and Israel as the people of GOD. Wheat, balsam, honey, oil and balm were produced and exported. Cattle, sheep, goats, camels, horses and asses were raised and sold, making for a mobile society. Life was simple, revolving around the Sabbaths, new moons and seasonal feasts. The natural rhythm of life seldom changed.

The rhythm of life which Jesus would have been familiar with was one which moved very slowly, and for the most part changed very little from one generation to the next. His world was a world without any major inventions or developments, few changes of existing technology, with no new updates, upgrades or new editions, no downloads to install, nothing to refresh or file, nothing to browse or store, no viruses to scan for, bugs to find and few crashes. The world of Jesus was already an ancient Israelite world.

Other than possibly Uncle Gideon getting a new ass, or cousin Sarah having a new baby, or a new baby brother being circumcised, things changed very little. Life's rhythm was relatively constant. The life that your father knew was the same as your own, and would be the same life that your own son would live. No *"generation gap"* existed. Music, clothes and food from generation to generation changed not. Leisure time, children games and life was the same. Change was something seasons did.

It was a world which revolved around the Temple of YHWH and HIS priests. From one year to the next, it was a year which was governed by the new moons, new year, sacrifice, first fruits and feasts. Shabbat and YHWH'S holy days were observed with a singular regularity not changed. As the _religion_ of Israel was basically an agricultural based religion governed by the changing of the seasons, the harvests and first fruits, it was a slow moving predictable life for the average Israelite. Jesus lived in an agrarian society. Three times a year during *Hag Ha Mazot, Hag Shvuot, and Hag Sukkot*, "all males" were to present themselves before YHWH in Jerusalem. These three *"pilgrimage festivals"* are associated in some form or another with agriculture such as the *rippening of the barley* before Pesach and the wave of the *sheaf offering during Hag HaMazot*, the Feast of Harvest (*first fruits*) during Shuvot, or with the *feast of Ingathering* (Sukkot), a type of last harvest called *booths*.

It was not until after the Temple of YHWH and HIS priesthood was destroyed long after Jesus was gone, did the newly created religion called *"Rabbinic Judaism"* of the rabbis institute radical changes in the way which the Jewish people worshiped and lived their lives. While the Temple of YHWH still stood, life for the average Jew in Israel was one of a constant cyclical observance of the Law and offering before YHWH.

That being said, there was only one religion, and it was **not** Rabbinic Judaism. As long as the Temple of YHWH stood and sacrifice was still offered to YHWH, the religion of Israel was the worship of YHWH through the observance of HIS Laws in the Safer Torah and being taught the Law by HIS priests. The offering of sacrifice at the Temple of YHWH and observing HIS Statutes and Ordinances concerning ritual purity and keeping of HIS Commandments was done without the need for lay people to sit around in large rooms and argue endlessly on what was the Law pertaining to a certain minor issue. Being an observant Jew and life itself was much more simple. And until the Temple's destruction the rhythm of life revolved around births and deaths, feasts, new moons and yearly seasonal changes.

JEWISH WORLD / GENTILE WORLD

To fully appreciate the world in which Jesus lived, it is completely necessary to remove oneself from the present, and to put oneself in the place of an ancient Israelite living under the Law of Moses. And while being under the Law of Moses, one is being buffeted about by false prophets, Hellenism, foreign military powers, diverse philosophies, religious sects, conspiracies, revolutionaries and corrupt priests, all together at the same time.

On top of this, after reading the Gospels, one may get the impression that the land was filled with vexed lunatics, lepers, prostitutes, possessed people full of demons, the deaf, the dumb, the blind, the lame and unnamed incurable diseases, violence, infanticide, bloodshed, religious and terrorist fanatics and death. It is no wonder that Jesus represented hope to so many people. Even if in the end, most did not believe.

RELIGION

As has been stated, if one is to comprehend the world in which Jesus lived, it is imperative that one understand that the ***only*** religion which existed in ancient Israel was the Temple and worship of YHWH. Synagogues may have been places where people met, studied, learned, taught, debated and discussed "*law*", but it was not a "*religion*", just a social club for men.

There existed various sects of religious thought regarding the Law of Moses, for example that of the Pharisees and the Sadducee during the time of Jesus. The Pharisees were not the only Jewish sect, just the loudest. Their main opponents at that time were the Sadducee who for the most part supported the priests. But the Temple of YHWH with it's priests and Levite ministers was the ***only*** "*religion*" of Jesus and of Israel. The Pharisees were by and large opponents of the Priests, and the Sadducee. There were other differences, but this is generally where they stood relative to the Temple of YHWH.

According to the Gospels, Jesus new the Safer Torah and the Prophets. So it must have been very frustrating for him when dealing with the Pharisees. For they "*thought*" they new the "*Law*" of Moses, but in reality they only knew the corrupt interpretation of their own so called "*oral law*" from the rabbis. For whether their "*stuff*" was written down yet or not did not really matter, as it distorted their understanding of the true word of GOD. Jesus had to have been aware of this when he was discussing details of the Law with them.

This is important to digest, as Jesus was not just debating points of the Law with Pharisees, for much of their understanding of what they thought was the *Law,* was not actually *Law*, as they were heavily influenced by the "*oral laws*" (traditions) of other rabbis and were without a clue as to the real Law.

CRAZIES - LUNATICS – DEMONS - RABBIS

As stated earlier, if one reads just the four Gospels, one will see that for whatever reason, the land of Israel during the time of Jesus, appeared to have been chock full of insane, and crazy lunatics full of demons, possessed with evil spirits, and wreaking all manor of havoc on the Jewish people.

Additionally as mentioned, there were the lame, blind, diseased and the mysteriously ill. Aside from a land oozing with possessed and sick people, the political intrigue, bloodletting, conspiracies and religious mayhem was enough to keep the people on edge. To say the least.

Another thing to remember as well, the people were much more dependent on their *"learned"* leaders for teaching them the Law and the finer points of how to live. Most sons would have learned the basic Laws of Moses regarding keeping Shabbat and Laws of sanctification, circumcision and purity as well as others from their Priests passed down to their fathers. The same goes for wives and mothers, receiving teachings passed down from the Priests to Fathers, sons, wives and daughters. Levites were teachers of Law.

Deuteronomy 33:8, 10, (8) _And of Levi_ he said: Thy Thummim and Thy Urim be with Thy holy one, ….(10) _They shall teach Jacob Thine Ordinances, and Israel Thy Law;_

Daughters would have learned from their mothers the Laws which pertained to ritual purity and other related statutes associated with blood purity after child birth, monthly blood flow and related ordinances as well as keeping the home *"clean"* as in *"pure"* regarding sanctification. Whenever a question arose, the Priests would have been consulted if no one knew. It may not be too much of an exaggeration to say that as regarding the Law, they were totally dependent on their religious leaders. This (Malachi 2:7) was generally the responsibility of the Priests and of the Levites. But in the household itself, the responsibility fell on the father as the head of the house to make sure that they were doing things correctly according to the Law. When a question arose, he went to the Levites and Priest. There were far fewer *"Laws"* of Moses then, than there are *"oral laws"* of Rabbinic Judaism religion today.

If Levitical Priests are the *messenger of YHWH of hosts* then secular Jewish laymen called *"Pharisees"* / *"Rabbis"* are the exact opposite. If the Priests taught _Law_ and truth, then the rabbis taught _anti-law_ confusion, stories and lies. Today's plethora of rabbinic doctrinal confusion is living proof of this. The Priests had ONE LAW, the rabbis have many, many conflicting laws.

"Synagogue", Greek for _assembly,_ existed everywhere full of Pharisees who were teaching things **not** written in the Safer Torah, the Law of Moses and Laws which were interpreted differently than the Priest's teachings. This was a relatively new creation by laymen who were not of the Temple Priests nor who had been instructed by GOD to teach the people. The term for *Pharisee* in Hebrew originates from the root meaning to *"separate"*, *"set apart"* (above the people). They basically set themselves up as an *"authority"* on the Law in contrast to, and competed with the Priests, becoming *"pious secular Jews"*.

This presented the people with a very unique problem, *"who and what to believe?"*. Life was difficult enough, but now the people had two competing *"authorities"* on the meaning of the Law. The *"laws"* of the rabbis as they *contradicted* the Law of Moses and HIS Priests, was something Jesus was constantly confronting them about. What made the man made laws of these *"rabbis"* so dangerous, and still does, is that they mix their own invented foolishness in with the Law of Moses. The danger was in a father having a question of Law, but believing the words of a rabbi without bothering to ask a Priest, or just becoming confused by the contradiction between the two. Or today, there are no longer Temple Priests or Levites versed in the Law to ask.

When someone like John the Baptist or Jesus showed up on the scene, it became imperative that the people knew the Law well enough to be able to understand what stood before them. Jesus said this very thing himself. Were they false prophets? How well Jesus knew the Law and the Prophets himself may be debated, but apparently from the Gospels he knew TaNaKh well enough to shut the Pharisees up from time to time and win their wrath. Also, according to the Gospels, there were Pharisees who followed him as well.

KNOWING TORAH

If Jesus knew Torah as well as he seemed to have, his indignation and outrage at the Pharisees, as indicated in the Gospels (Matthew 23), would make sense. This chapter is worth quoting for it not only sums up in many respects the feelings of Jesus towards the Pharisees, but more importantly it illuminates his discussions with the Pharisees regarding the Law throughout the Gospels with their _traditions_. As this is being read recall that as Jesus was growing up, he often sat at the feet of these same people listening to them.

Matthew 23:1-36 (1) THEN spake Jesus to the multitude, and to his disciples, (2) Saying, The scribes and the Pharisees sit in Moses' seat: (3) All therefore whatsoever they bid you observe, that observe and do; but do not ye after their works: <u>for they say, and do not.</u> (4) For they bind heavy burdens and grievous to be borne, and lay them on men's shoulders; but they themselves will not move them with one of their fingers. (5) <u>But all their works they do for to be seen of men</u>: they make broad their phylacteries, and enlarge the borders of their garments, (6) And love the uppermost rooms at feasts, and the chief seats in the synagogues, (7) And greetings in the markets, <u>and to be called of men, Rabbi, Rabbi.</u>(8) But be not ye called Rabbi: for one is your Master, even Christ; and all ye are brethren. (9)And call no man your father upon the earth: for one is your Father, which is in heaven.(10) Neither be ye called masters: for one is your Master, even Christ.
11 But he that is greatest among you shall be your servant. (12) And whosoever shall exalt himself shall be abased; and he that shall humble himself shall be exalted. (13) <u>But woe unto you, Scribes and Pharisees, hypocrites! for ye shut up the kingdom of heaven against men: for ye neither go in yourselves, neither suffer ye them that are entering to go in.</u> (14) Woe unto you, Scribes and Pharisees, hypocrites! for ye devour widows' houses, <u>and for a pretence make long prayer</u>: therefore ye shall receive the greater damnation.(15) Woe unto you, Scribes and Pharisees, hypocrites! for ye compass sea and land to make one proselyte, and when he is made, <u>ye make him twofold more the child of hell than yourselves</u>. (16) Woe unto you, ye blind guides, which say, Whosoever shall swear by the Temple, it is nothing; but whosoever shall swear by the gold of the Temple, he is a debtor! (17) Ye fools and blind: for whether is greater, the gold, or the Temple that sanctifieth the gold? (18) And, Whosoever shall swear by the Altar, it is nothing; but whosoever sweareth by the gift that is upon it, he is guilty. (19)Ye fools and blind: for whether is greater, the gift, or the Altar that sanctifieth the gift? (20) Whoso therefore shall swear by the Altar, sweareth by it, and by all things thereon. (21) And whoso shall swear by the Temple, sweareth by it, and by him that dwelleth therein. (22) And he that shall swear by heaven, sweareth by the throne of God, and by him that sitteth thereon. (23) <u>Woe unto you, scribes and Pharisees, hypocrites! for ye pay tithe of mint and anise and cummin, and have omitted the weightier matters of the law, judgment, mercy, and faith</u>: these ought ye to have done, and not to leave the other undone. (24) Ye blind guides, which strain at a gnat, and swallow a camel. (25) Woe unto you, Scribes and Pharisees, hypocrites! for ye make clean the outside of the cup and of the platter, but within they are full of extortion and excess. (26) Thou blind Pharisee, cleanse first that which is within the cup and platter, that the outside of them may be clean also. (27) Woe unto you, Scribes and Pharisees, hypocrites! for ye are like unto whited sepulchres, which indeed appear beautiful outward, but are within full of dead men's bones, and of all uncleanness. (28) <u>Even so ye also outwardly appear righteous unto men, but within ye are full of

hypocrisy and iniquity. (29) Woe unto you, Scribes and Pharisees, hypocrites! because ye build the tombs of the prophets, and garnish the sepulchres of the righteous, (30)And say, If we had been in the days of our fathers, we would not have been partakers with them in the blood of the prophets. (31) Wherefore ye be witnesses unto yourselves, that ye are the children of them which killed the prophets. (32) Fill ye up then the measure of your fathers. (33) Ye serpents, ye generation of vipers, how can ye escape the damnation of hell? (34) Wherefore, behold, I send unto you prophets, and wise men, and scribes: and some of them ye shall kill and crucify; and some of them shall ye scourge in your synagogues, and persecute them from city to city: (35) That upon you may come all the righteous blood shed upon the earth, from the blood of righteous Abel unto the blood of Zacharias son of Barachias, whom ye slew between the Temple and the Altar. (36) Verily I say unto you, All these things shall come upon this generation. (37) O Jerusalem, Jerusalem, thou that killest the prophets, and stonest them which are sent unto thee, how often would I have gathered thy children together, even as a hen gathereth her chickens under her wings, and ye would not! (38) Behold, your house is left unto you desolate. (39 For I say unto you, Ye shall not see me henceforth, till ye shall say, Blessed is he that cometh in the name of the Lord.

Jesus would have been taught the Safer Torah, and he would have heard the *"stuff"* concocted by the Pharisees as well. It did not take a genius to see the weakness of the words of these rabbis when compared to the written words of the Law. This *stuff, "tradition"* has now all but supplanted the word of GOD in authority to the Orthodox Jews and to most other Jewish people who are unaware. The mixture of the Law of Moses with the nonsense of the rabbis has caused no end of grief to the Jewish people, beginning even before the time of Jesus. This is important because it is this very same *"stuff"* that Jesus was dealing with while he was preaching. Moreover, Jesus apparently was a very astute observer of people. His words just cited against the hypocrisy of the rabbis is telling. He must have been a very good student, watching their every move, and listening to their every word.

THE LAW OF MOSES VS OTHER 'STUFF'

This topic is important as it is the *"Law"* which was discussed throughout the Gospels, and as it was the *"Law"* which the Pharisees and the Priests used to condemn Jesus to death. During the time of Jesus, the teaching of the Priests and Levites to Israel was only that of the Commandments of YHWH, HIS Ordinances and HIS Statutes as written in the Law of Moses, the Safer Torah. The Priests did not **have**, **accept** or **believe** in the so called *"oral law"*.

As the Mishna was still unwritten at that time and was a creation of the rabbis, it was only recited and memorized by them. Contrary to the written Law of Moses, the rabbis were teaching their so called *"oral law"* in their synagogues, many things which contradicted the Law of Moses. At that time, the Priests and the rabbis were the two most influential groups on the peoples religious lives. Jews such as Jesus would have been exposed to the laws and doctrines from both of these influential groups as well as others.

Growing up, Jesus apparently was intelligent enough to be able to absorb both of these conflicting teachings and was wise enough to be able to master the truth between the two. He could tell the difference and knew the truth.

Relative to the Temple of YHWH Priests and the Law of Moses, the Pharisees and their assorted *"rabbis"* and *"sages"* acted in many respects as a *"fifth column"* within the kingdom. Instead of throwing their support behind the Temple Priests, who were having to deal with the Romans and the steadily encroaching Hellenism on the Jewish people, they became the Priests chief adversaries. If this were not bad enough, there were all of the other factions, sects and misguided souls vying for the peoples hearts and minds.

The Temple Priests were corrupt but it was less from their understanding of the Law than from their application of the Law. For the most part, they knew the truth of the Law but it was the affliction of their own corruption which determined how they executed their office. Contrary to the Priests who learned the Law of Moses, the Pharisees and their rabbis only studied the works of each other (the phrase *"blind leading the blind"* comes to mind), and had only a very weak understanding of the actual written Law of Moses.

The Jewish people were caught between these two diametrically opposing forces. Jesus was right in the middle of them. These two groups were enemies of each other and were teaching different things (law) to the people. For those Jews who were seriously trying to keep GOD'S Law, this made it even more difficult. It was this tug-of-war for the hearts and minds of the people that was going on between the Priests of GOD and the rabbis of the Pharisees, at the same time that the Jewish people were listening to the words of John the Baptist and Jesus and trying to make sense of it all.

And this is but just one of the many *"tug-of-wars"* going on at the same time, and the average Jew was caught in the middle, trying to contend with all of it simultaneously while under Roman occupation. These were trying times for GOD'S sons. Jesus grew up himself, having to cut his way through all of these different doctrines to understand the truth about GOD'S word.

And according to the Gospels, Jesus was taken to synagogue from an early age, he would have had an uphill climb from his youth to separate the Law of Moses out from the words of secular Jewish laymen he had heard.

RESEARCH THE LAW AND THE PROPHETS

It is not as if a person could go to the local library and research *"lies of the Pharisees"*, *"which of the rabbis is not crazy"*, *"how to tell a false prophet"*, *"how to know the real messiah"* or do a web search on his computer at home to investigate a particular aspect of a Statute or Ordinance of YHWH'S Law. They would not have had a Safer Torah in their home to read or to research. These documents (animal hide scrolls) were extremely expensive, requiring the hides of many animals, time, money and a scribe to complete the writing over a year or so. It was mainly only the priests and the king, or the wealthy class who could afford to have a copy. Simply put, there were no *"books"* in the house to reference at one's leisure as one might today.

The people were entirely dependent on their religious *"shepherds"* for guidance. The people studied and lived the Law. It was living the Law and passing it down, which was the the most practical way of remembering GOD'S Law. But even still, it was difficult to carry around in one's head, all of the details of Laws of the Safer Torah for total recall whenever necessary. This was especially so in rare situations with false prophets or messiahs.

When situations developed like that during the time of Jesus, when both he and John the Baptist were making a lot of *"news"*, it was a time of much consternation for the Jewish people, as the people had to either know and recall the Law as well as the prophets, or ask those in positions of authority to explain to them all of the many things which they were seeing and hearing from John and from Jesus. Israel was aware of the idea that a son of David would come and save them. This is what they believed. So when a prophet, healer, teacher etc. arose, it was a time of great anxiety and excitement. As Jesus came about during a time of extreme political, social and religious unrest, many of the people of Israel were drawn to the figure of Jesus, putting them in a extremely vulnerable position. Neither priests nor rabbis were of much help. The times were very hard and the hope he offered was enticing.

When it came to the Prophets, many of the scriptures, as the Gospels attest, were known by the people. But for some of the finer points of either the Law or prophesy, they would often need to consult a Priest who would have a copy of the Safer Torah, and the books of the Prophets. As mentioned, it must be remembered as well, that the Hebrew Bible as we know it today was an entire catalog of holy books, not yet canonized into one book. Although the first five books of the Law of Moses as the Safer Torah would have existed already for many hundreds of years as it was a Law from YHWH that even the king was to read. For when GOD told Israel of the responsibilities of their king, it was reading the Law which HE required of him.

Deuteronomy 17:18-20, (18) And it shall be, <u>when he sitteth upon the throne</u> of his kingdom, that he shall write him a copy of this <u>law in a book</u>, out of that which is before the priests the Levites. (19) And it shall be with him, <u>and he shall read therein all the days of his life; that he may learn to fear YHWH his God, to keep all the words of this law and these statutes, to do them;</u> (20) that his heart be not lifted up above his brethren, and that he turn not aside from the commandment, to the right hand, or to the left; to the end that he may prolong his days in his kingdom, he and his children, in the midst of Israel.

A PLACE TO MEET

In the beginning when meeting on the Sabbath first began in Israel, it must have been a pleasant experience. As it was the Sabbath and no one could work, the men of the community could meet, relax, read and discuss the Law. As it was not a religion yet, for the Temple of YHWH still stood, the atmosphere must have been very casual and enjoyable to be in. This was probably what Jesus experienced as he was growing up. Nevertheless, it is very doubtful that he could be considered one of them (Pharisee).

As the example of Jesus later indicated, he was ***not*** a *"Rabbinic Jew"* even though he went to synagogue, listened and learned. But as his words towards the Pharisees were to show, he listened and paid close attention to what they had been teaching while growing up. That Jesus had such strong feelings against the Pharisees is testament to his own awareness of the truth of the Safer Torah. In other words, Jesus was able to distinguish between the truth of the words written in the Law of Moses and their own *"stuff"* the rabbis were creating in the name of GOD. He also showed admiration for their zeal.

As discussed, most adult males would have been well versed in most of the every day living points of the Law. They would have grown up being taught first by their own father, per the commandment to do so by the Law itself. No doubt, Joseph taught his son Jesus as much of the Law as he could while Jesus was still young. It may well be that Joseph himself did not grow up under the feet of these Pharisees during his own generation and really knew *"Torah"* from the written word of GOD. As the sect of the Pharisees grew slowly after the return of the Jews from Babylon where they and their *"sage babel"* conspiracy was first hatched, no doubt there were still men of GOD who were not influenced by the rabbi loonies and actually knew the Law.

Deuteronomy 6:4-7, (4) Hear, O Israel: YHWH is our God, YHWH is one. (5) And thou shalt love YHWH thy God with all thy heart, and with all thy soul, and with all thy might. (6) And these words, which I command thee this day, shall be upon thy heart; (7) and thou shalt teach them diligently unto thy children, and shalt talk of them when thou sittest in thy house, and when thou walkest by the way, and when thou liest down, and when thou risest up. (first part of the Shema)

The father's primary source of the Law was the priests and the Levites who kept the Law of Moses like all of the people but whose task it was to also teach the Law, but also the priests kept those specific laws which pertained to only the priests. They were well versed in the Law and part of their duty as priests was to teach the Law to Israel. Growing up from one generation to the next in service to the Holy Temple, the Levites were in a legal, technical world of the Law of Moses so far removed from the every day Israelite, that for any of Israel outside the walls of the Temple to even pretend to know the Law let alone write their own books and say they came from GOD is preposterous and the very height of gall (*chutzpah*), bordering on blasphemy. Unlike the ignorance of rabbis, the issue with priests was not a lack of knowledge of Law but their own corruption and it's subsequent affect.

Deuteronomy 4:8-10, (8) And what great nation is there, that hath statutes and ordinances so righteous as all this law, which I set before you this day? (9) Only take heed to thyself, and keep thy soul diligently, lest thou forget the things which thine eyes saw, and lest they depart from thy heart all the days of thy life; but make them known unto thy children and thy children's children; (10) the day that thou stoodest before YHWH thy God in Horeb, when YHWH said unto me: 'Assemble Me the people, and I will make them hear My words that they may learn to fear Me all the days that they live upon the earth, and that they may teach their children.'

The obvious problem here is, with the invention and the development of the *"synagogue system"*, and the Rabbinic schools, their parallel teachings were often as not, at variance on many of the key issues with that of the Priests and Levites who taught the Law of Moses using only the written Safer Torah.

TO BELIEVE OR NOT TO BELIEVE

It cannot be emphasized enough the confusion which ensued regarding the Law, because of the competing teachings of the rabbis. Between the Law of Moses taught by the Priests, the so called *"oral law"* of the Pharisees taught by the rabbis, the doctrines of the other Jewish sects such as the Sadducee and Roman Law, the people had much to learn, remember and to choose from. With this in mind, it may be easier to understand the vitriol of Jesus toward the Pharisees in Matthew 23.

The Jewish people were caught between several life threatening or life altering forces. The *"fear of GOD"* was not just an expression. Aside from the teachings of Jesus, the Temple Priests, rabbis and other of the several Jewish groups, there were the Hellenists who were for total assimilation all together. And of course, there were the seemingly all powerful Romans.

The average Jew listening to Jesus had much to give up, and much to accept in following Jesus. At the same time, Jesus represented what appeared to be real hope for many desperate people. It was not so simple. The Jewish people had approximately already 1,500 years of worshiping YHWH since the time of Abraham. This is often over looked, but should never be forgotten. The threat of being cut off from his GOD by following Jesus and also being cut off from his own people, was a very immediate and real concern to anyone of Israel who was contemplating accepting and following Jesus as the *"Christ"*, the *anointed one* of GOD. For the Law of Moses specifically names these two curses to any of Israel who follow another "*god*". They would be *cut off from YHWH*, and they would be *cut off from their own people Israel*.

This was an extremely difficult and potentially traumatic situation which only a Jew was faced with. For within the Law he could / would be cut off. As is repeated often, later Gentile converts to the new "*religion*" being spread by Paul, were not faced with this dilemma and this was a major difference.

It is not like a Gentile today deciding he wants to become a Christian and professes that he "*believes*", is baptized and forfeits nothing to do so. Or to give up one's belief in Zeus. But for a Jew to follow Jesus, his very life and relationship with the GOD of his forefathers for the previous 1,500 years was in the balance. According to the Law of Moses, a Jew could be "*cut off*".

For following a false prophet, believing in any GOD but YHWH, or worshiping and believing in any name but "*YHWH*" was forbidden to the Jew by his Law as given to Moses. For a person not versed in the Law of Moses or born into that Law, these concerns and fears do not exist and the fear would be neither understood nor be appreciated. But they were very real. If one thinks of Israel more as a *family* than as a kingdom or as a modern nation state made up of strangers, the concept of being *cut off forever*, which GOD uses HIMSELF as a threat many times, has much more meaning. "*YHWH*" is the Father of Israel. The fear of being "*cut off*" from both your Father GOD YHWH and your own family of Israel was very real and very immediate.

Many of the things which Jesus said, would have raised questions about the Law, which they did, and caused strong concern for a Jewish follower of that Law. For a Jew to have have accepted Jesus on faith as being something for which he may not have been, jeopardized many, many, generations of faith by that individual and his fathers "*house*" he represented. For he would have been cutting off his own heirs from his own SEED. Unless one was apathetic, belief in "*Jesus*" would have been an incredibly heart wrenching decision. Not so with a Gentile hearing for the first time the message of Jesus. The difference between these two peoples is like day and night. This dilemma still exists for the Jewish person today. Even if he is unaware of this potential danger when contemplating any name other than that of YHWH, the name of his own GOD, although he cannot pronounce it. This is true, even as perverted as Rabbinic Judaism is today, the curse and the threat remain.

JESUS AND THE LAW

Now that the groundwork has been set and what led up to the time of Jesus and the time that he lived, what was the attitude of Jesus to the "*Law of Moses*"? How did his words and actions stack up against the Law which permeated absolutely every aspect of Jewish life? For it was the Law which he was born into, and ultimately the Law which sentenced him to death.

Some of this has been touched on such as his words about keeping the Commandments. Much more will be said regarding this as it is in many ways central to understanding his message.

CHAPTER FOUR

THE LAW

LETTER OF THE LAW / SPIRIT OF THE LAW

Deuteronomy 4:7-8, (7) For what great nation is there, that hath God so nigh unto them, as YHWH our God is whensoever we call upon Him? (8) And what great nation is there, that hath Statutes and Ordinances so righteous as all this Law, which I set before you this day?

Before a discussion of Jesus and his attitude towards the Law, a look at Israel's attitude, relation and history with their Law is important. For the Law was a blessing and a gift from GOD to Israel to live by, for life.

It has often been said and written by Christian theologians that the Jewish people were guilty of adhering to the *"letter of the Law"* without feeling, without the *"spirit of the Law"*. That they implemented the Law without the true *"spirit"* of the Law. This idea by many Christians was especially true regarding the trial and death of Jesus. No doubt, this happened. And perhaps it happened more often than one might like to admit. Yet, it was the *"letter"* of the Law for which Israel was responsible. Stoning a person to death could not always have been easy. Getting into the *"spirit"* of a stoning sounds silly. Yet, a dispassionate law enforcer sometimes may be preferable to an emotional policeman who takes his work a bit too personal.

As mentioned often, the Law by it's very nature is *"technical"*. It is difficult therefore to fault Israel for the times that they were over zealous in it's application for they had good reason not to ignore the *"letter"* of the Law. Therefore whether they agreed in spirit or not was irrelevant. Even when they had become either corrupt or misguided in their understanding, fear of GOD'S Law was part of their history, engrained into their DNA and there are more than a few examples in TaNaKh that may explain why their dogmatic observance to it's Statutes and Ordinances existed, and why Gentiles do not understand.

Two examples from Israel's history of where the *"letter"* trumped *"spirit"* may perhaps shed light on this idea and illustrate the seriousness of the *"letter"* and why it was so important, *"Till heaven and earth pass, one jot or one tittle shall in no wise pass from the law, till all be fulfilled"*. A *"jot"* is understood to be the smallest Hebrew letter *"yod"*. And a *"tittle"* is said to represent the smallest stroke of the pen when writing a Hebrew letter. Jesus was alluding to the *letter* of the Law not it's *spirit*.

'STRANGE FIRE'

Take for example Aaron and his sons. In Leviticus Chapter 10, Nadab and Abihu two of Aaron's sons, took each of them a censer and put on fire and incense and offered it before YHWH. In the text it is referred to as offering *"strange"* fire. Why was it called *"strange"* fire? It was called *"strange"* fire because YHWH had not *"commanded"* it. The Hebrew root for the word for *strange* used in this story is *"Zyin-Resh-Heh"* which is translated as *"cause to fly", "scatter"* and *"winnow"*. All of these words are words which have the same general meaning of to *"disperse"*, as is something put to the wind. Something that has either lost control or which has no control over their lives.

What happened next in the story is profound and almost shocking. *"And Nadab and Abihu, the sons of Aaron, took each of them his censer, and put fire therein, and laid incense thereon, and offered strange fire before YHWH, which He had not commanded them, And there came forth fire from before YHWH, and devoured them, and they died before YHWH" (Leviticus 10:1-2).*

Did the brothers offer incense before YHWH out of maliciousness? No doubt they thought that they were being respectful, even pious before GOD. Yet, GOD roasted the two of them faster than you can yell *"marshmallow"*. There is a reason for the Law which YHWH gave to Israel to live by. Not only is there a reason for the existence of the Law, but there is a reason for all the Commandments, the Statutes and Ordinances which make it up. We may not always understand why certain Commandments exist, but YHWH does. And that is the point. GOD is GOD. YHWH burned them up and hardly allowed Aaron to mourn. The lesson here is that *"to obey is better than sacrifice"*.

The *"strange"* fire offered before YHWH which YHWH had not commanded is referred to by a word meaning to *"scatter"*. Historically, it is by Israel not obeying YHWH'S Statutes that they are *winnowed*, and *scattered* to the wind.

YHWH warns Israel not to *"add"* or to *"diminish"* from HIS Law (Deuteronomy 4:2 ; Deuteronomy 13:1). These warnings are meant to protect Israel. For every time Israel disobeyed YHWH, HE scattered them. Whether it was the northern Kingdom of Israel, or the southern Kingdom of Judah, YHWH exiled and scattered them for not obeying HIS Law. And whether this was adding or subtracting from HIS commandments, the results were always the same. Israel was *"scattered"* as chaff to the wind.

Before Israel crossed the Jordan River to inherit the land, YHWH warned what would happen to them if they disobeyed HIS *"commandments"*. They would be *"scattered"* amongst the nations. And as with the strange fire, Israel would become *"estranged"* from their GOD YHWH.

Deuteronomy 4:26-27, (26) I call heaven and earth to witness against you this day, that ye shall soon utterly perish from off the land whereunto ye go over the Jordan to possess it; ye shall not prolong your days upon it, but shall utterly be destroyed. (27) And YHWH shall scatter you among the peoples, and ye shall be left few in number among the nations, whither YHWH shall lead you away.

Deuteronomy 28:64, (64) And YHWH shall scatter thee among all peoples, from the one end of the earth even unto the other end of the earth;

The Hebrew for *"scatter"* is different here, but the idea is the same. If Nadab ben Aaron and Abihu ben Aaron were guilty of anything, it was *"adding"* to YHWH'S Commandments. By bringing a *"strange"* fire before YHWH that HE did not *"command"*, they were destroyed. Nadab and Abihu brought a *"scattering"* fire before YHWH. A fire not commanded. The type of thing done which results in the *"scattering"* of Israel. And it is this connection to the word *"scatter"* which is made. By disobeying GOD'S Law, Israel is *"scattered"*. A *"strange"* fire is a *"scattering"* fire. Yet even in this, there is compassion, for YHWH said that HE scatter Israel but would gather Israel and return them to their inheritance when they turn to HIM.

Deuteronomy 30:3, (3) that then YHWH thy God will turn thy captivity, and have <u>compassion</u> upon thee, and will <u>return and gather thee</u> from all the peoples, whither YHWH thy God <u>hath scattered thee.</u>

Not obeying YHWH or HIS commandments, whether it is by an *act* of doing a thing not commanded, or by an act of *omission*, it is not tolerated by GOD.

'YHWH HAD BROKEN FORTH'

After David had become King of all Israel, he decided to bring up the Ark of GOD from Baale-judah where it had rested. In doing so a new cart was made and the two sons of Abinadab, Uzzah and Ahio drove the cart. It was the two sons of Abinadab in whose house the Ark of GOD had rested after having been sent back by the Philistines, who steered the cart.

Previously, YHWH had destroyed 50,070 men of Beth-shemesh for even gazing upon the Ark of YHWH when it had arrived (I Samuel 6:19-21). The Philistines had earlier captured and then returned the Ark of GOD. Men had looked upon it and paid with their lives. Word was sent to come and take it.

The country was *"hill"* country which is mentioned twice. As the Ark of GOD was being taken on the cart, the oxen stumbled. Uzzah put forth his hand to the Ark of GOD and *"took hold of it"*. One might do such a thing before even having time to think in order to steady an object as an automatic reflex. Yet, this act displeased YHWH who killed him, as with Nadab and Abihu. *"And when they came to the threshing-floor of Nacon, Uzzah put forth his hand to the ark of God, and took hold of it; for the oxen stumbled. And the anger of YHWH was kindled against Uzzah; and God smote him there for his error; and there he died by the ark of God" (II Samuel 6:6-7).*

One may ask what does all of this have to do with the *"letter of the Law"* and the *"spirit of the Law"*? Was not Uzzah trying to protect a precious object? Was his *"error"* in trying to protect GOD'S holy Ark a sin? If so, the sin of Uzzah aside from actually touching the holy Ark, seemed to be not trusting or believing in GOD enough to know that the Ark was safe without his hand.

The *"letter of the Law"* is very closely associated with the *"fear"* of GOD. If these stories illustrate anything, they illustrates that understanding the concept of the *"letter"* of the Law is something which the Nations would be hard pressed to either appreciate or comprehend. The Christian world which often is too quick to judge Israel and the Jewish people, does not understand the ancient principle of *"fear"* of GOD which was already a 1,500 years old *"emotion"* by the time of Jesus. It was not only part of Israel's DNA but was an integral component of their psyche. Beginning with Abraham the grandfather of Israel (Jacob), the idea of *"fear"* of GOD was ingrained into Abraham's SEED. The idea of approaching GOD'S Law in the *spirit* without the *"letter"* would never have occurred to those who were given the Law to live by. At least not in the sense that most Christians might practice this concept. There was no real separation between Law and *"spirit"* in that sense.

Better the letter of the Law without *"spirit"* than having the *"spirit"* of the Law without any Law. GOD would often challenge and berate Israel telling them that *"to obey"* is better than sacrifice.

Proverbs 21:3, (3) To do righteousness and justice is more acceptable to YHWH than sacrifice.

Was he saying not to obey the Law? God forbid! He was making a statement regarding being righteous and doing justice. As Samuel said to King Saul.....

I Samuel 15:22, (22) And Samuel said: 'Hath YHWH as great delight in burnt-offerings and sacrifices, as in hearkening to the voice of YHWH? <u>Behold, to obey is better than sacrifice, and to hearken than the fat of rams.</u>

Was the Prophet Samuel saying not to offer sacrifice? NO, he was saying that obeying GOD was more important. Obeying GOD is more important.

Hopefully, the story of the death of Aaron's two sons and the death of the son of Abinadab show, being in the spirit and making an offering to YHWH or steadying the holy ark with ones hand is not acceptable. Their *"intentions"* may have been honorable. They may have been *"in the spirit"*. Nevertheless, as with the expression, *"the road to hell is paved with good intentions"*, being in the spirit is not the point. To obey and to fear GOD is the point.

If the story of these deaths seem a bit harsh in today's world, then remove yourself from this world as best you can. Make an attempt to understand that YHWH the GOD of heaven and earth and all beyond had made contact with mankind and blessed him with HIS eternal Law to live by, *And what great nation is there, that hath Statutes and Ordinances so righteous as all this Law, which I set before you this day?* What great nation but Israel!

Remember that GOD is wiser than us and by living as we are told, his blessings of the Law become real. To add or subtract from the holy will and the perfect word of the living GOD invites disaster, even if in the *spirit.*

'THE FEAR OF YHWH IS THE BEGINNING OF WISDOM'

So for those who are quick to judge a people born into the Law of YHWH, these stories just discussed and many others, they may want to take into account. YHWH had blessed Israel, and part of that blessing was teaching them the *"fear of GOD"*. And with the *"fear of GOD"*, comes obeying the *"letter of the Law"*, even if one may not feel the spirit, the Law must be kept.

Hosea 4:6, (6) My people are destroyed for lack of knowledge; because thou hast rejected knowledge, I will also reject thee, that thou shalt be no priest to Me; seeing thou hast forgotten the Law of thy God, I also will forget thy children

Obeying GOD'S Law, is Knowledge. Knowledge, is the fear of GOD. The fear of GOD, is the beginning of wisdom.

Psalms 111:10, (10) <u>The fear of YHWH is the beginning of wisdom;</u> a good understanding have all they that do thereafter; His praise endureth for ever.

By the same token, those who hate knowledge have no fear of their GOD.

Proverbs 1:29, (29) For that <u>they Hated Knowledge,</u> and did <u>not choose the Fear</u> of YHWH;

'HE HATH COMMANDED HIS COVENANT FOREVER'

Is there any doubt but that YHWH'S Covenant is forever? In their haste, did the followers of Jesus not *"throw the baby out with the bath water"?* For the early Jewish believers kept the Law of Moses. Only later after Jewish believers were no more in the majority, and finally were no where to be seen, did the

Gentiles discard the Law and hang their hat entirely on *"grace"*. Christianity then became a mish-mash of pagan and other forms of worshihp.

'MY THOUGHTS ARE NOT YOUR THOUGHTS'

Isaiah 55:8-11, (8) <u>For My thoughts are not your thoughts, neither are your ways My ways, saith YHWH.</u> (9) For as the heavens are higher than the earth, so are <u>My ways higher than your ways,</u> and My thoughts than your thoughts. (10) For as the rain cometh down and the snow from heaven, and returneth not thither, except it water the earth, and make it bring forth and bud, and give SEED to the sower and bread to the eater; (11) So shall My word be that goeth forth out of My mouth: <u>it shall not return unto Me void, except it accomplish that which I please, and make the thing whereto I sent it prosper.</u>

Did Jesus have this in mind when he said that not one *jot* or *tittle* would fail from the Law until all had been accomplished? The word of YHWH is the Law of YHWH, and the Law of YHWH is the word of YHWH.

Many of the stories of Jesus are stories of compassion, especially regarding the seemingly harshness of the Law. And in many ways it is because of his compassion for which he is still remembered. This is brought out beautifully in the story of Jesus and the adulteress story regarding stoning. And many of the things which Jesus said in the continuous confrontations he had with the Pharisees were true, but often they were not what was said in the Law. His teaching on divorce is an example of what may be considered by today's standards, *"enlightened thinking"*. Nevertheless, the question remains, was he teaching the Law as it is written in the Safer Torah, or was he changing the Law as he appeared to be doing. Is his view on adultery good for marriage?

The quote from the Prophet Isaiah was given for a good reason. Why GOD wrote the Law as HE did is not for man to question. The Law of YHWH is on many levels a reflection of GOD'S ways. And as YHWH said, *"so are My ways higher than your ways"*. It is precisely because GOD'S thoughts and GOD'S ways are *"higher"* than those of GOD'S creation, that GOD'S creation has absolutely no business questioning GOD, second guessing GOD, or altering GOD'S holy words as written in HIS holy Law, *"For as the heavens are higher than the earth"*. An adulteress is to be stoned to death.

YHWH gave HIS Law to Israel. This Law is a **blessing** to Israel. The Law is **perfect**. Whether Israel sees it as such is not important. GOD did not have Moses write a Law that was sort of OK, but YHWH gave to Moses Laws which were holy and righteousness from YHWH himself. YHWH did not create a body of work to give to Israel which was anything but the best. For anyone of GOD'S creation to be so arrogant as to think that they can improve on what is holy and righteous from YHWH is the height of perversity. This is true for Jesus and for the rabbis or anyone else who thinks to improve on what GOD has created. Does man think that GOD gave to him just a *"rough draft"* of HIS Law for man to rework and interpret as he saw fit? For this is the short coming of the rabbis. They have rewritten GOD'S Law.

Can man improve on the heavens which GOD created? Or can man improve on the earth which GOD has created? So, why is it then that mankind, who is a creation of GOD himself, think that he has the wisdom to improve on the Law of YHWH who is higher than the earth and beyond the heavens?

JESUS

From the time that Jesus was born, the Law became part of his existence. And as with every male born in Israel, especially every first born male in the family, Jesus was circumcised per the Law of Moses on the eighth day, and sacrifice was offered to YHWH for his being the first born male.

Luke 2:21-24, (21) <u>And when eight days were accomplished for the circumcising of the child</u>, his name was called Jesus which was so named of the angel before he was conceived in the womb. (22) And when the days of her purification <u>according to the law of Moses</u> were accomplished, they brought him to Jerusalem, to present him to the Lord; (23) As it is written in the law of the Lord, Every male that openeth the womb shall be called holy to the Lord;) (24) And to offer a sacrifice according to that which is said in the law of the Lord, a pair of turtledoves, or two young pigeons

The line in verse 23 actually pertains to every *"first born male"* according to the Law, not to every male (Exodus 13:12-16). Likewise, verse 24 pertains only to those too poor to offer a lamb for a burnt offering and a young pigeon or turtle-dove for a sin offering. Regardless, Jesus was the first born male.

JESUS AND THE SAFER TORAH

Jesus was pretty consistent in his words about keeping the Law. Whether one agreed with his interpretation of it or not. There are a few questions regarding his interpretation on several Laws which appear to be radically different than that written in the Safer Torah. He seemed to have paraphrased Isaiah 55:11.

Matthew 5:17-18, [17] Think not that I am come to destroy the Law, or the prophets: I am not come to destroy, but to fulfil. (18) For verily I say unto you, <u>Till heaven and earth pass, one jot or one tittle shall in no wise pass from the law, till all be fulfilled</u>.

His words concerning the Law say much regarding his attitude about keeping the Law and help explain some of his other words which may not be so clear.

THE LAW AND GRACE

Is the Law dead? Has the eternal Law of the Almighty GOD ended because of an assumption made by an ancient few? GOD forbid! The Law is not dead and GOD has stated that it will live written on the hearts of Israel, all of it including priests who will make sacrifice offerings to the Most High. YHWH has said that HE will make it so that Israel will never have to teach HIS Law again, as HE will have put it in the heart of Israel, (Jeremiah 31:31-34). King David had this to say about the beauty of YHWH'S Law.

Psalms 19:8-11, (8) <u>The Law of YHWH is perfect, restoring the soul</u>; the Testimony of YHWH is sure, <u>making wise the simple</u>. (9) The Precepts of YHWH are right, <u>rejoicing the heart</u>; the Commandment of YHWH is pure, <u>enlightening the eyes</u>. (10) The Fear of YHWH is clean, <u>enduring for ever</u>; the Ordinances of YHWH are true, <u>they are righteous altogether</u>; (11) More to be desired are they than gold, yea, than much fine gold; sweeter also than honey and the honeycomb.

"More to be desired are they than gold, yea, than much fine gold; sweeter also than honey and the honeycomb"

The Law of YHWH is a *"blessing"* given to HIS first born son Israel.

'FOR OUT OF ZION SHALL GO FORTH THE LAW'

The *"Law"* will continue to be kept and the Nations will learn HIS ways and walk in HIS paths. The Law of YHWH is *not* dead but is alive now, and according to the Prophets of YHWH, it will continue to live.

Micah 4:1-2, (1) But in the end of days it shall come to pass, that the mountain of YHWH'S house shall be established as the top of the mountains, and it shall be exalted above the hills; and peoples shall flow unto it. (2) And many nations shall go and say: 'Come ye, and let us go up to the mountain of YHWH, and to the house of the God of Jacob; and He will teach us of His ways, and we will walk in His paths'; for out of Zion shall go forth the LAW, and the word of YHWH from Jerusalem.

Because according to most Christian doctrine, the Law is considered void, they pay little attention to it's tenants nor attempt to understand it. But this is a mistake. Jesus said to Israel, that if they were to enter into eternal life, they must keep the Commandments. If this is so for GOD'S chosen SEED, is it not all the more so for the Nations? If many Nations are to be joined with Israel in the worship of YHWH as per the prophets, then there is but one Law for all.

Isaiah 56:6-8, (6) Also the aliens, that join themselves to YHWH, to minister unto Him, and to love the name of YHWH, to be His servants, every one that keepeth the Sabbath from profaning it, and holdeth fast by My Covenant: (7) Even them will I bring to My holy mountain, and make them joyful in My house of prayer; their burnt-offerings and their sacrifices shall be acceptable upon Mine altar; for My house shall be called a House of Prayer for all peoples. (8) Saith the Lord YHWH who gathereth the dispersed of Israel: yet I will gather others to him, beside those of him that are gathered.

GOD speaks of a time when the Gentiles will worship YHWH along with Israel, keeping HIS Sabbaths and keeping HIS Covenant of Law, offering their burnt sacrifices to HIM upon HIS alter. The Law did not end with Jesus.

The Law of Moses is a living breathing blessing from YHWH. It is a gift of such importance and of such great magnitude, there are no words to describe it's relevance. This is true not only for the past, but of today as well. Perhaps it is even more important today. The Law of Moses is a wonder gift. It is the guide for man, being GOD'S map for HIS holy path for Israel. Ultimately all Nations must walk by it. In YHWH the Law binds all Nations as one.

'I GIVE UNTO YOU'

By Jesus saying, *"a new commandment I give unto you"*, was Jesus taking a page out from the Pharisees by apparently *"adding"* or *"subtracting"* from the Safer Torah? Did he actually mean a *"new"* commandment?

One of the most important Laws of GOD written in the **Safer Torah**, is the Law *not* to *add* anything *to* the word of GOD and *not* to *subtract* anything *from* the word of GOD. A person does not need to be either a biblical scholar or a genius to understand what this means. Yet, in volumes the rabbis add, subtract, multiply, divide, calculate, miscalculate and guess the Law of GOD.

Deuteronomy 4:2, (2) Ye shall NOT add unto the word which I Command you, NEITHER shall ye diminish from it, THAT ye may keep the Commandments of YHWH your God which I Command you.

It is paramount that this scripture regarding *not adding or diminishing* be remembered as the words of Jesus are discussed. For at best, Jesus seemed to be skirting this issue very closely. But then again as with all of the controversial scriptures, this really depends allot on the faith one has in the translation which has been handed down to us.

In Deuteronomy, GOD is saying by the hand of Moses, not to do anything, either by adding to HIS Law or by taking from HIS Law in any way. The Commandments of GOD are holy, sacrosanct and not to be altered in any fashion. They are perfect. This not only means *not* to add or to take away from the existing text of the word of GOD itself, but this includes as well the writing of other books by man, and attributing those writings to GOD.

By the rabbis writing their own books, and not physically tampering with the actual word of GOD itself in HIS BOOK, perhaps they thought to fool a few people or even GOD. And no doubt they have fooled a few people. They wrote their own books and then attributed them to GOD as if they were really HIS words. This is all that the Talmud, the supposed *"oral law"* is. They are books written by Jewish guys wearing funny looking clothes. They are read, studied, discussed, debated, and argued over. They have supplanted the very Safer Torah which they purport to explain. It is a perversion on a colossal scale because they have not only defiled GOD'S perfect Law, but because with it they have led Israel astray. But GOD is neither fooled nor mocked.

As for Jesus, it is difficult to be certain what Jesus meant regarding a *"new commandment"*, for as discussed elsewhere, the Greek from which the English translation has come down, is itself vague.

'A NEW COMMANDMENT'

Jesus said to keep the Law which forbids adding anything to it , Yet Jesus speaks as if he is giving a *"new"* commandment himself. Although as mentioned, it is hard to know if this was the case or not, both because of the translation which we are dealing with, and the subject. Was he really?

John 13:34 (34) A new commandment I give unto you, That ye love one another; as I have loved you, that ye also love one another.

The mere idea that anyone would or could give Israel a *"new"* commandment is quite unbelievable. For a people who were bound by the Commandments of the Law of YHWH in HIS Safer Torah, this would be unprecedented. It not only was not done, but it was forbidden within the very Law which Jesus said that Israel must obey to enter into life. But much more than this, adding or taking away from the Law was more than forbidden, it was outrageous and outside the Law of GOD. If Jesus really meant that he was giving a *"new"* commandment, then he was *"adding"* to the Law of Moses, contrary to it's commandment not to do so. It would have been interpreted as a *new doctrine.*

One must picture many thousands of Israel in the desert at the base of Sinai receiving the Law of Moses and Priests sprinkling the blood of the Covenant on them. Then, visualize Jesus telling a group of descendants of Israel that he was giving to them a *"new commandment"*. As if somehow GOD had forgotten one and Jesus was bringing it to Israel 1,500 years later.

The Greek word *"kainos"* is the origin of the word used in translation for the word *"new"*. It is a word which can also mean *"fresh"*, as in *age, unworn* or *unused*. The Greeks, not being under the Law, may not have been as careful as they could have been in translating some words, not fully appreciating the consequences of what they were writing. Other related meanings of *"kainos"* are a *new kind, unprecedented, novel, uncommon* and *unheard of.*

Could it be in a way, that Jesus was being sarcastic here? Is it perhaps at least possible that Jesus was saying that he was ***not*** giving a *"new"* commandment, but refreshing their memory of a commandment which they have not been keeping? Was Jesus berating them in a fashion about not practicing brotherly love? If so, it would explain away the *"new"* with *"fresh"*, thereby Jesus would not be *"adding"* a new commandment, but telling his followers that this idea is old and they need to practice it more.

Could it possibly be that the Greek for *"fresh/unused"* was not saying *"new"*, but was really saying that they were not practicing brotherly love as is already written in their Law? For it is actually written in the Safer Torah already. In other words, was he just stating the obvious, that they had not been practicing the Law which they already possessed?

Leviticus 19:17-18, (17) Thou shalt not hate thy brother in thy heart

Aside from the word *"new"* when translated, whether or not care was fully appreciated regarding the word *"commandment"* too is in question. This would apply to not only the Greek but also the English translation as well. The Greek word used for *"commandment"* is *"entole'"*, which is normally translated meaning an *"injunction"* i.e. an authoritative prescription. Injunction normally has the sense of meaning an *"order"*. Other possible meanings of *"entole'"* besides injunction and order are, *"command"* and *"behest"*. That the translators saw fit to use these two English words, *"new commandment"* is something we must deal with, but may not be accurate.

The Greek *"entole'"* appears to be used in the TaNaKh to always mean either *"command"* or *"commandment"*. It was not found to mean any thing else. This includes the Five Books of Moses, the Prophets and Writings, all of the Hebrew Bible. This holds true for the Christian Bible as well.

Returning to *"kainos"*, it is very consistent as well, being used for *"a new"* or *"new"* throughout the Hebrew Bible and the Christian Bible.

Was Jesus just giving his followers instruction on how to behave themselves towards each other after he was gone? Was he just instructing his disciples on how to conduct themselves and behave? As if to say, *'You already have the Law, so keep it'*. Was this possibly all that was transpiring between him and the people who would represent him? As if to say, *'Behave yourselves, and especially be nice to one another as people are watching you and how you reflect on me and my message when I am gone. Keep the commandments and not hate one another'*. Jesus often seemed to be frustrated with his followers.

Whether or not Jesus was actually giving a new commandment or just commanding his followers how to behave after he was gone is not really clear. The real problem here again is the word *"new"* which can lead one to think that a *"new commandment"* is what he may have said. For had he only said *'I command you to love one another, etc.'* he would not have needed to use the word *"new"* or any variation. As with much of what comes down to us in any language, without having an original Semitic text to study, it is difficult to know exactly what was actually either said or meant by Jesus.

The idea for Israel to love one another is not incompatible with the Law of Moses. For all of the Laws which were given by YHWH, were Laws, which if obeyed and kept by Israel, would be manifested in actual terms in not only Israel loving each other but in their love for GOD.

John 15:10-14, (10) If ye <u>keep my commandments</u>, ye shall abide in my love; even as I have kept <u>my Father's commandments</u>, and abide in his love. (11) These things have I spoken unto you, that my joy might remain in you, and that your joy might be full. (12) <u>This is my commandment, That ye love one another, as I have loved you.</u> (13) Greater love hath no man than this, that a man lay down his life for his friends. (14) Ye are my friends, <u>if ye do whatsoever I command you.</u>

Jesus seems to be making a distinction between "*my commandments*" and "*my Fathers commandments*". As stated, there is a problem with "*my*".

It is difficult to tell if Jesus was actually giving a "*new commandment*", as for Israel to love one another would not seem to be adding to the Law of Moses. There is a problem with the idea of Jesus calling it "*my commandment*", if indeed this is what he said. Although he seems to be making a distinction between himself and "*his*" commandment and that of YHWH, as Jesus refers to "*my Fathers commandments*". As if by doing so, his commandments are different than those of GOD. Yet, at the same time, he states how he and the father are "*one*". His words are unclear.

Deuteronomy 6:4-7, (4) Hear, O Israel: YHWH is our God, YHWH is one. (5) <u>And thou shalt love YHWH thy God with all thy heart, and with all thy soul, and with all thy might.</u> (6) And these words, which I command thee this day, shall be upon thy heart; (7) and thou shalt teach them diligently unto thy children, and shalt talk of them when thou sittest in thy house, and when thou walkest by the way, and when thou liest down, and when thou risest up.

From part of the "*Shema*" we learn what GOD expects of us. If we do as HE has commanded, loving our "*brother*" would *not* be something which would need <u>another</u> "*commandment*". Loving our brother would be the natural outgrowth, outcome, development and benefit from obeying the Commandments of YHWH already given. Therefore in a real sense, aside from the "*new*" commandment of Jesus seemingly "*adding*" to GOD'S words and thereby breaking his Law by doing so, it would have been redundant and unnecessary. Telling his followers to love one another is simply the inverse of not hating their brother, which is written in the Law (Leviticus 19:17-18).

But if he is not really adding to GOD 'S Law, then why is he saying that it is a "*new*" commandment, that it is "*my*" commandment, as distinct from "*my fathers*". On the other hand, if he is not adding to the existing eternal Law of YHWH, then he is really not saying anything but possibly restating an obvious truth from the Law already given. Either way, as with some of the other things that he is reported to have said, it is not really clear. We can only go by what he is reported to have said. So, either he was only restating the obvious already in the Law, or he was really giving a new commandment.

Another possible way to look at this in trying to determine if it really is a new "*commandment*'. One may ask the question, *is* "*That ye love one another, as I have loved you*" a new commandment? It does not appear in the Law of Moses. For Israel to love GOD and to honor ones parents is within HIS Law, but there is no law which states that Israel is to love one another as "*Jesus*" loved them. Brotherly love is a concept not explicitly written in the Safer Torah, but is implied in "*thou shalt not hate thy brother in thy heart*". Nevertheless, if all of Israel were to love YHWH with all of our heart and soul and with all of our might, and hate not our brother in our heart, we will no doubt be loving each other as YHWH loves us. For it is ONE love.

One can argue, that as the words of Jesus are basically the inverse of the Law given in Deuteronomy, *"Thou shalt not hate thy brother in thy heart"*, he therefore cannot be adding anything. If this so, then why did he say it?

John 12:49, (49) For I have not spoken of myself; but the Father which sent me, <u>he gave me a commandment</u>, what I should say, and what I should speak. (50) <u>And I know that HIS Commandment is life everlasting</u>: whatsoever I speak therefore, even <u>as the Father said unto me</u>, so I speak.

Knowing that the Commandments of YHWH are *"Life Everlasting"*, how can Jesus add to this? Is it Life Everlasting, *"plus"*?

Whenever he speaks in this fashion, the words of YHWH come to mind.

Deuteronomy 18:18, (18) I will raise them up a prophet from among their brethren, like unto thee; and <u>I will put My words in his mouth</u>, and he shall speak unto them all that I shall command him.

Jesus seems to say this often as he repeats how his words etc. are those of his *"Father"*. The scripture above is regarding YHWH sending false prophets to try Israel, *"for YHWH your GOD putteth you to proof"* (Deuteronomy 13:4).

Was Jesus sent to *"prove"* Israel? Jesus is saying that the Commandments of YHWH, ie. HIS Law, *"is life everlasting"*. At times Jesus seems to be saying that the *new commandments* are his own. Then he also seems to be saying that they are from the Father. He keeps making this annoying habit of saying *my, mine, his* and *my father* when speaking. It would seem that he would always say *my father* when making these kinds of statements if they are truly *one* and he is speaking for, and in the name of his father.

There are many Laws which deal with Israel and brothers who become poor, in debt, become bondmen or are killed in a quarrel or some other situation which the Law addresses. As stated before, if all of the Commandments of GOD are kept continually by Israel, Israel would not only be blessed, but the need for such a *"new"* Law as *"That ye love one another; as I have loved you, that ye also love one another"* would not be in any way necessary. For it is the existing Law of YHWH itself that needs to be kept. And if keeping the existing Commandments of GOD are to be done as Jesus stated, then it is impossible for Jesus to *"give"* a *"new"* commandment. For doing so would be violating the Law and by definition, be *"adding"* to the Law and thereby breaking the very Law he said to keep.

Think about this. You cannot both *"keep the commandments"* by not adding, and break them by adding a *"new commandment"* at the same time.

John 14:15, (15) If ye love me, keep <u>My commandments</u>.

John 14:21, (21) He that hath <u>My commandments</u>, and keepeth them, he it is that loveth me: and he that loveth me shall be loved of my Father, and I will love him, and will manifest myself to him.

John 14:31, (31) But that the world may know that I love the Father; and as <u>the Father gave M e</u>

commandment, even so I do. Arise, let us go hence.

If "_my commandment_" _is_ an existing Law, then it is **not** a "_new_" Law. So Jesus really was not saying anything new but restating or rather reiterating a biblical imperative. If "_my commandment_" _is_ **not** an existing Law, then it _is_ a new Law. If so, then Jesus was breaking the Law and GOD'S commandments by adding to them a "_new_" commandment to existing Law.

At least two things are clear from the words of Jesus about the Law. First, Jesus said to "_keep the commandments_" of the Law. Second, by due process of elimination, anything that is not commanded in the Law of Moses is not a commandment of GOD and therefore Israel is not obliged to do or to keep.

So whatever Jesus meant by "_new commandment_" is irrelevant and anything else he said not already commanded in the Law of Moses need not be kept.

JESUS & HILLEL

Matthew 7:12, (12) Therefore all things whatsoever ye would that men should do to you, do ye even so to them: for this is the law and the prophets.

Luke 6:31, (31) And as ye would that men should do to you, do ye also to them likewise

Luke 10:25-28 (25) And one day an authority on the law stood up to put Jesus to the test. "Teacher," he asked, "what must I do to receive eternal life?" (26)What is written in the Law?" Jesus replied. "How do you understand it?" (27) He answered, " 'Love the Lord your God with all your heart and with all your soul. Love him with all your strength and with all your mind.' And, 'Love your neighbor as you love yourself.' " (28) "You have answered correctly," Jesus replied. "Do that, and you will live.".

Again, Jesus is saying to Israel to keep GOD'S Commandments.

Leviticus 19:17-18, (17) Thou shalt not hate thy brother in thy heart; thou shalt surely rebuke thy neighbour, and not bear sin because of him. (18) Thou shalt not take vengeance, nor bear any grudge against the children of thy people, but thou shalt love thy neighbour as thyself: I am YHWH.

This man appeared to be paraphrasing Deuteronomy 6:5 and Hillel the Elder (110 BCE -10 CE), and Leviticus 19:18.

Hillel is quoted as saying, "_What is hateful to you, do not do to your fellow: this is the whole Torah; the rest is commentary; go and learn"_ (Shab. 31a). Hillel understood that brotherly love was the fundamental principle of Jewish moral law, and his approach to the Law was based in many respects on this principle. How can Israel say he loves YHWH and not love his brother?

Jesus appeared to be paraphrasing Hillel regarding the "_Golden Rule_". This often referred to "_Golden Rule_" is quoted by Christians on a regular basis as a type of proverb of how to live one's life. One wonders if many are aware that they are actually quoting a famous rabbi and not Jesus.

One could add to this from the book of Leviticus.

Leviticus 19:34, (34) The stranger that sojourneth with you shall be unto you as the home-born among you, <u>and thou shalt love him as thyself</u>; for ye were strangers in the land of Egypt: I am YHWH your God.

YHWH goes to great length to remind Israel and often, that they were once strangers in a strange land, and to therefore treat strangers kindly.

Exodus 22:20-22, (20) <u>And a stranger shalt thou not wrong, neither shalt thou oppress him; for ye were strangers in the land of Egypt</u> (21) Ye shall not afflict any widow, or fatherless child. (22) If thou afflict them in any wise -- for if they cry at all unto Me, I will surely hear their cry --

CONTRADICTIONS

Using this same scripture from Matthew regarding the *"Golden Rule"*, how does this idea jibe with turning the other cheek? This *"rule"* it must be recalled, is not a Law, but a *"philosophy"* of life from the lips of a rabbi. Does turning the other cheek *"keep"* the Law concerning an *"eye for an eye"*? Is there an inherent contradiction in this? Is a man to stand still and receive a blow to the side of his head without giving a blow to his attacker? Or even worse, he is to offer the other side of his face to be struck? *"Therefore all things whatsoever ye would that men should do to you, do ye even so to them: for this is the Law and the prophets"*.

As in the just cited example, was Jesus contradicting his own words as in turning the other cheek, or giving a thief your coat? For Jesus said if struck, give the other cheek, and if your coat is stolen, offer him another garment as well. But is this according to the Law of Moses? Would you not expect a man to strike you back if you hit him? Or would you not expect a man to take back his coat if stolen? Matthew 7:12 is viewed as just this, to expect to be struck if one hits a another man beside the head. And if one takes a man's coat, expect for him to take it back. But then what about Matthew 5:39-40?

Matthew 5:39-40 (39) But I say unto you, That ye resist not evil: but whosoever shall <u>smite thee on thy right cheek, turn to him the other</u> also.(40) And if any man will sue thee at the law, <u>and take away thy coat, let him have thy cloke also.</u>

One must ask, how does this jibe with, *"Therefore all things whatsoever ye would that men should do to you, do ye even so to them: <u>for this is the law</u> and the prophets"*? So is one to smite the cheek of the one who smote your cheek, or is one to turn and give him the other cheek to smite?

Exodus 21:23-24, (23) But if any harm follow, then thou shalt give <u>life for life, (24) eye for eye, tooth for tooth, hand for hand, foot for foot, (25) burning for burning, wound for wound, stripe for stripe.</u>

There are other seeming examples of where Jesus would say something which either clearly contradicted the Law, or was just enough into a *"gray"* area, that there was no way to know for sure what exactly he meant by the words passed down to us. As with the previous example of the word *"new"* in English from the Greek *"kainos"*, did Jesus really mean to be giving Israel a *"new"* commandment, or was this just a poor translation? Was the idea of *"turning the other cheek"* just a figure of speech, or a philosophical view towards violence? Or was Jesus contravening the Law by saying not to respond to violence against ones self, or to a thief who is stealing from you?

According to the Law, if a person strikes you, you strike them back, blow for blow. The words of Jesus seem to contradict this.

Perhaps very few examples of a clear difference in his interpretation of the Law, are the words of Jesus on divorce. Jesus said something profound regarding the Law and *"divorce"*. When asked by the Pharisees regarding whether it was *"lawful"* to put away (divorce) one's wife for *"every cause"*, Jesus answered that but for the act of *"fornication"*, if a man puts away his wife and marries another, he is committing *"adultery"*. Additionally, he is causing the person who marries her, to commit adultery should she remarry.

This quote is extremely important, as it clearly appears to be altering an existing Law in the Safer Torah on divorce. Even a poor translation would be difficult to come up with this particular slant on an existing Law. From most all of the things which Jesus is reputed to have said, this may be the most damaging because it is so hard to miss translate these words without someone either having made them up, or for Jesus to have actually said them.

To fully understand what is being said here, the full quote from Jesus and the Pharisees will be given. As the entire response from Jesus hinges on the actual Law in the question put to him by the Pharisees.

Matthew 19:3-9, (3) The Pharisees also came unto him, <u>tempting him</u>, and saying unto him, <u>Is it</u> lawful <u>for a man to put away his wife for every cause</u>? (4) And he answered and said unto them, Have ye not read, that he which made them at the beginning made them male and female, (5) And said, For this cause shall a man leave father and mother, and shall cleave to his wife: and they twain shall be one flesh? (6) Wherefore they are no more twain, but one flesh. What therefore God hath joined together, let not man put asunder. (7) <u>They say unto him, Why did Moses then command to give a writing of divorcement, and to put her away</u>? (8) He saith unto them, Moses because of the hardness of your hearts suffered you to put away your wives: but from the beginning it was not so. (9) <u>And I say unto you, Whosoever shall put away his wife, except it be for fornication, and shall marry another, committeth adultery: and whoso marrieth her which is put away doth commit adultery</u>.

Jesus acknowledges the Law of Moses, but then appears to *"add?"* something extra which is not part of the Law regarding divorce, saying only in the instance of *"fornication"* is it *"lawful"*, as he responds.

But what does the Law itself actually say regarding divorce?

Deuteronomy 24:1, (1) <u>When a man taketh a wife</u>, and marrieth her, then it cometh to pass, if she find no favour in his eyes, <u>because he hath found some unseemly thing in her, that he writeth her a bill of divorcement</u>, and giveth it in her hand, and sendeth her out of his house

According to the Law of GOD, it is *"lawful"* to divorce one's wife, if in her is found something *"unseemly"* by her husband. The Law is general, and does not state specifically or qualify the reasons for what is *"unseemly"*. The Hebrew word used here is *"ervah"* (*Ayin-Resh-Vav-Heh*) from the root (*Ayin-Resh-Heh*) meaning *"be naked, bare"*. It translates as *"nakedness"*, with the idea of finding something *"shameful"*, implying something *"indecent or improper behavior"*. In Hebrew as when the word *"naked"* in English is used, it normally refers to something shameful being exposed or having occurred.

The rest of the Law pertaining to divorce states that she can remarry, as well as the man. But once she remarries, she cannot return to her husband.

Deuteronomy 24:2-4, (2) and she departeth out of his house, and goeth and becometh another man's wife, (3) and the latter husband hateth her, and writeth her a bill of divorcement, and giveth it in her hand, and sendeth her out of his house; or if the latter husband die, who took her to be his wife; (4) *her former husband, who sent her away, may not take her again to be his wife, after that she is* *defiled; for that is abomination before YHWH; and thou shalt not cause the land to sin, which* *YHWH thy God giveth thee for an inheritance.*

A divorced and remarried woman cannot return to her former husband. This is the only stipulation regarding divorce *after* a bill of divorcement is given. This is the Law on divorce.

Again, the words of Jesus seem to directly contradict the Law of YHWH pertaining to divorce. Jesus is stating three things which are not written in the Law. For Jesus said that a husband can *only* divorce for reason of *"fornication"*, and, the husband will be committing adultery if he remarries, if it was not a divorce for the reason of *"fornication"*. Additionally, the new husband of the divorced wife will be committing adultery as well for marrying the divorced wife under these circumstances. This is not in the Law.

Now in the modern era, one can argue the merits or the fairness of GOD'S Law regarding divorce. Nevertheless, this is the Law as written by the hand of Moses from the words of YHWH GOD, 3,500 yeas ago given at Mount Sinai to Israel. What Jesus appeared to be doing was adding qualifiers to the existing Law saying that only in the case of *"fornication"* may a husband give his wife a bill of divorcement. Then, he appears to go even further as just detailed. But as will be explained, this too is a huge problem.

The Law of Moses concerning divorce continues regarding her remarrying to another man and not *"lawfully"* being able to return to her first husband if her second husband either divorces her or he dies. To return to the first husband under such circumstances, according to the Law, is an *"abomination before YHWH"*. However, nowhere does it qualify the act of divorce as pertaining only for the act of *"fornication"*. Neither does it limit or qualify in any way the first husband's ability to remarry another if he so chooses. Jesus appeared to have *"added"* by determining that the original husband and new husband of the divorced woman will be guilty of *"fornication"* with their respective new spouse. Neither of these concepts are written in the Law of Moses.

There is an even more profound Law which comes into play if a married woman is found *"lying"* with someone other than her husband.

FORNICATION / ADULTERY

Deuteronomy 22:22, (22) If a man be found lying with a woman married to a husband, then they *shall both of them die, the man that lay with the woman, and the woman; so shalt thou put away the* *evil from Israel.*

Here, as stated in the Law itself, if a married woman is *"caught in the act"*, ie. caught *"fornicating"*, both she and her partner in crime would be killed. So, if there is *fornication* involved, it is highly unlikely that a divorce would be forthcoming as they both would be put to death. The husband need not be concerned with a divorce. For if the Law is carried out, his wife and the person she was fornicating with will in all likelihood be stoned to death.

The Law is very clear regarding fornication. For had the husband's wife been found guilty of fornication, which being married constitutes *"adultery"*, there is a very specific sentence for having committed such an offense. She would hardly be in any shape to remarry after having been found guilty of *"fornication"*, for according to the Law, she would have been put to death. Usually death by stoning, was the normal way that punishment for these type offenses were carried out.

Leviticus 20:10 (10) And the man that committeth adultery with another man's wife, even he that committeth adultery with his neighbour's wife, <u>both the adulterer and the adulteress shall surely be put to death.</u>

Assuming she would have wanted to eventually remarry if her husband gave her a divorce to the man she was caught "*lying*" with, both she and her <u>*would be*</u> new "*main squeeze*" would have had a very serious problem doing so. They both would have been killed. There would have been no need for a divorce in the first place. The story of Jesus and the adulteress is all very touching, but not altogether "*kosher*". For the entire issue of "*divorce*" would have been a "*moot point*". The judgment for fornication for a married woman equals death according to the Law, not divorce and a new hubby.

John 8:1-11, (1) Jesus went unto the mount of Olives. (2) And early in the morning he came again into the temple, and all the people came unto him; and he sat down, and taught them. (3) And the <u>scribes and Pharisees brought unto him a woman taken in adultery;</u> and when they had set her in the midst, (4) They say unto him, <u>Master, this woman was taken in adultery, in the very act.</u> (5) Now Moses in the law commanded us, that such should be stoned: but what sayest thou? (6) This they said, tempting him, that they might have to accuse him. But Jesus stooped down, and with his finger wrote on the ground, as though he heard them not. (7) So when they continued asking him, he lifted up himself, <u>and said unto them, HE THAT IS WITHOUT SIN among you, let him first cast a stone at her.</u> (8) And again he stooped down, and wrote on the ground. (9) And they which heard it, being convicted by their own conscience, went out one by one, beginning at the eldest, even unto the last: and Jesus was left alone, and the woman standing in the midst. (10) When Jesus had lifted up himself, and saw none but the woman, he said unto her, <u>Woman, where are those thine accusers? hath no man condemned thee? (11) She said, No man, Lord. And Jesus said unto her, Neither do I condemn thee: go, and sin no more.</u>

The idea here is, that if a married woman had been accused of "*fornication*", and had been found guilty of "*fornication*", she is guilty of "*adultery*". As a married woman either being accused of the act or caught in the act of having sex with someone other than her husband, and having been found guilty, this would have gotten her the death sentence. She would not have had the opportunity to marry anyone else, nor would her own husband need to go through a messy divorce procedure, as she would have been put to death. So, remarrying was not an option for her. Neither would her lover been able to contemplate any personal ideas of future wedded bliss, for he too would have been put to death. The woman was caught "*in the very act*". This is death.

So, herein lies an extremely weak link in the discussion by Jesus regarding divorce. A man would have no need to put away his wife for fornication. She would be put to death if found guilty of this offense. The discussion itself becomes moot and ends there. As she was caught in the act, she would die.

So, the discussion then returns to the question of divorce according to the Law, "*When a man taketh a wife, and marrieth her, then it cometh to pass, if she find no favour in his eyes, because he hath found some unseemly thing in her, that he writeth her a bill of divorcement, and giveth it in her hand, and sendeth her out of his house*". This is the Law on divorce.

The act of *proven fornication* concerning a married woman then becomes **not** just *fornication* or <u>grounds for divorce</u>, but the act of *adultery* according to the Law is grounds for **death.** Divorce would not be necessary as she would have been stoned to death, and as the very recently deceased wife, remarrying would hardly have been an option for her or her lover. For he too, would have no need to be making honeymoon plans. They both would have died.

'WITH SIN'

The story itself is truly ingenious though. And the *"guilt trip"* he put on the Pharisees was quite extraordinary. Although, had they known the Law, his words could easily have been refuted. But there is an even more interesting side line here regarding Jesus himself. Was Jesus *"with sin"* so that he was not compelled to obey the Law of Moses himself? Did Jesus exclude himself from stoning her because he was *"with sin"*, or was he just acting above it all? But Jesus said one must keep the Commandments. The Commandments stipulate that the *"adulterer"* should die according to the Law which he said Israel must keep. So what is it to be? Keep the Commandments or not to keep the Commandments? Was this what Jesus meant when he said, *"And he said unto him, <u>Why callest thou me good</u>? there is none good but one, that is, God: but if thou wilt enter into life, <u>keep the Commandments</u>."* (Matthew 19:17). Was Jesus referring to <u>his own sin</u>? Was Jesus a man *"with sin"?*

Was Jesus saying here that he too was with sin and could not cast a stone? He appears to be addressing only them, excluding himself. It is very clever what he said. But he does not seem to be keeping the Law of Moses himself.

So was Jesus playing loose with the Law? This is a great story, a great object lesson on the meaning of compassion. But would it hold up in the court of the Law before Moses or Aaron? It is doubtful that it would. The Law makes allowances for all kinds of situations, but this story calls for stoning to death.

The Laws discuss (Deuteronomy 22:23-29) regarding a betrothed damsel who is *"deflowered"* by someone other than her betrothed is a good example. Was she in the city where her cry would be heard or in a field where her cries would not be heard? There is much room for *"compassion"* in the Laws of GOD. When one studies all of HIS Laws, a clear picture of a merciful and compassionate GOD emerges. But for a married woman caught in the act of committing adultery however, there does not seem to be much *"wiggle room"*. She would be stoned to death. For she has not just sinned against her husband by violating his honor and his sanctification before his GOD by her act of fornication / adultery, she sinned against the living GOD by her act.

ADULTERY REVISITED

As with his words regarding the adulteress (John 8:1-11), they may not be compelling to someone outside the Law, but she should have been put to death according to the Law. Jesus did not say to stone her according to the Law, but played on the conscience of the accusers, knowing full well that all men sin. He changed the subject and redirected the focus of the discussion. His compassion for her was profound and powerful. But at the same time, Jesus said to *keep* the Commandments, but in her case he did not.

Leviticus 20:10, (10) And the man that committeth adultery with another man's wife, even he that committeth adultery with his neighbour's wife, <u>both the adulterer and the adulteress shall surely be put to death.</u>

There is a clear conflict going on here. Do we keep the Law or ignore the Law? So how are we to understand his words and actions in this example, when both seem to be at such variance with the Law of YHWH itself? This goes back to the idea of *"do as I say, not as I do"* type of preaching which Jesus seemed to often be saying.

Looking again at the story of the adulteress, one may ask why such a harsh penalty? The people of

Israel lived in small communities. They were a very closely knit community composed of the immediate family, extended family and *"house"*, the clan, tribe and people. Israel is a people related by blood ties. In today's world the intellectuals may argue if the Jews are a race or not, but they did begin as a family related by blood ties and DNA passed down from Abraham in his SEED to his circumcised sons. It was this same SEED which was **blessed**. They were a large extended family of Abraham's SEED. Today's Y-DNA studies indicate that the SEED of Abraham is still closely related by blood, much more so than many would think.

In this setting, the adulteress would have brought shame on her husband and the entire family. If they had children, those children would eventually become aware of the adultery of their mother and have to bear the stigma of it for the rest of their life. Her act would in turn become a part of the family history, extended family, house, clan, tribe and to all of Israel. She would not have been some anonymous woman on the six o'clock news caught by an angry husband, beaten in public and soon forgotten. She would have been "X" daughter of "Y" of the "Z" clan who shamed her entire family and of whom now everyone is talking about. The knowledge of this shame would have been remembered for many generations, as oral history was a large part of Middle Eastern culture. One may assume that death by stoning did deter.

A person's reputation and pedigree was extremely important and was often all that existed regarding ones status in society, ie. *"one's good name"*. If any part of your family was caught up in a scandal, the family might suffer for many years if not generations. The entire family suffered. For example when it came time for the son or daughter of a disgraced family to marry, the past family scandal is something which would have been considered and could influence and limit the availability of a potential marriage partner. So adultery was very serious, and the Law pertaining to it was very serious.

The idea of *shame* and dishonor 2,000 years ago was much different than it is today. It was extremely powerful emotion. How much of a deterrent the death penalty for adultery was 2,000 years ago was, can only be surmised. But one can feel fairly certain that it was a much more powerful deterrent than today's justice system. And as for the children of such a situation where the mother was stoned to death for adultery or a father was stoned to death for his part, *adultery* was probably far less common than it is today. One may suspect the shame brought to a family was more of a deterrent than death by stoning.

By way of example, *"honor killings"* are still common in the Middle East amongst the Arabs today, because of the powerful sense of *"shame"* and *"dishonor"* such a thing as fornication by a woman or adultery (proven or not) can bring to the family. Whether one agrees or disagrees, it is a reality.

The shame and dishonor she would have brought to not only herself, but to her husband, her children and her family cannot be ignored. There was a reason why these *"Laws"* existed. Much of it had to do with the people of Canaan who preceded Israel on the *"holy land"* whom GOD abhorred.

So in retrospect, were the words of Jesus with the adulteress actually a benefit to either her, her husband and family, or to Israel, or was it a type of appeasement which not only contradicted the Law which Jesus said to keep, but also only helped to confuse the issue and weaken GOD'S Law? Telling the adulteress to *"go, and sin no more"* does not take into the consideration the above several paragraphs, and only exacerbates the situation.

'ADDING AND DIMINISHING'

There are a number of questions regarding the words and teachings of Jesus with regard to the Law of Moses. Some of his sayings appear to be either in direct *opposition* to the Law, *contradict* the Law, or *add / subtract* something *to / from* the Law. Or in the case of adultery, he seems to have rewritten it.

However, Jesus was right on, with regard to many of the understandings of the Law when confronted by the priests and rabbis. And in many instances he not only out shown them with his understanding of the Law, but he did so in a fashion which revealed how really bankrupt these people (Priests, Pharisee, Sadducee, Scribes) were intellectually. Jesus appeared to have had a very low opinion of them. The many instances when they were unable to respond for lack of knowledge of Law are truly remarkable such as with the adulteress.

Jesus said some profound things regarding the Law in the words which are attributed to him which leaves many questions. Some of the words attributed to Jesus appear to directly contradict his own words as well as the Law of Moses such as the *"turn the other cheek"* demonstrates.

To the uninitiated believer in Jesus, these minute details of Law may seem somewhat frivolous. This would especially be true to the majority of Christians who relate to the Law as little more than an ancient relic of the past. But this could not be farther from the truth. As Jesus said to keep the Commandments, and then said to turn the other cheek which is opposite from the Commandment, a contradiction appears. They are exact opposites. Herein lies the problem for an Israelite under the Law. Jesus seemed to be saying two different things. To keep the Law as in an "eye for an eye", *"But if any harm follow, then thou shalt give life for life, eye for eye, tooth for tooth, hand for hand, foot for foot, burning for burning, wound for wound, stripe for stripe"*, or as Jesus said to *"turn the other cheek"*. There's a clear problem here. It cannot be both *"wound for wound"* and *"turn the other cheek"*.

SWEAR

Another example regarding *"swearing"* shows how Jesus differed from the Law of Moses and seemed to contradict himself as well. Jesus is quoted as saying not to swear at all.

Matthew 5:34, (34) But I say unto you, <u>Swear not at all</u>; neither by heaven; for it is God's throne"

Yet when berating the Scribes and Pharisees (Matthew 23:16-22) for their hypocrisy regarding swearing, he explains that it is swearing by that which has either been sanctified holy or is holy (Alter, Throne, Temple) when making their oath, is that which makes it acceptable to GOD.

But what does the Law of Moses say regarding *"swearing"*? It said to swear by *"YHWH"*.

Once again to the uninitiated these minute details of Law may seem frivolous and beside the point to most Christians. But this is far from the truth. As Jesus said for Israel to keep the Commandments, to say *"swear not at all"* is the exact opposite. Herein lies the problem for an Israelite under the Law.

'AND BY HIS NAME SHALT THOU SWEAR'

Deuteronomy 6:13, (13) Thou shalt fear YHWH thy God; and Him shalt thou serve, <u>and by His Name shalt thou Swear.</u>

Leviticus 19:12, (12) And ye shall <u>not Swear by My Name falsely</u>, so that thou profane the Name of thy God: I am YHWH.

The Law is clear regarding swearing. Israel is to swear by the name of "**YHWH**", but Israel is not to swear *falsely* in the name of YHWH, for by doing so they will be profaning HIS holy name.

At the time of Jesus when the name of "*YHWH*" was still known and pronounced, swearing was something which people still did and it was done in the name of "*YHWH*". During the time of Jesus, it was still common to swear as Jesus spoke of *"swearing"*. And it was not too long after the time of Jesus after the Temple had been destroyed that the rabbis banned the use of GOD'S holy name, *"YHWH"*. Even though, it was by the name *"YHWH"* by which people were commanded to swear according to the Law. So *swearing* and *uttering* the name of *"YHWH"*, GOD'S holy name, were still done during this time period. Else, the rabbis would hardly have felt the need to issue such a ban on the utterance of the name of "*YHWH*" and forbid it's use.

History tells us that the reason used by the rabbis to forbid the use of YHWH'S name, is Leviticus 19:12. By misapplying this Commandment to not swear at all, they are *"diminishing"* from GOD'S Law of Deuteronomy 6:13 telling us how to swear. Jesus and the rabbis seem to be in agreement.

Going back as far as Abraham, swearing (swearing an oath or covenant, or making a vow) was taken very seriously. The example of Abraham making his servant swear to him (Genesis 24:1-4), was a type of formal swearing far in excess of today's swearing on a bible. The servant swore by "*YHWH*".

The example of Abraham sending off his servant on a mission to procure a wife for his son Isaac, is very similar in some respects to Jacob and Joseph later when Jacob makes Joseph promise him that he would (Genesis 47:29) not bury him in Egypt but carry him back to be buried with *"my fathers"*. It has the air of a very formal legal procedure or rite, which when once made, was binding between the parties before the living GOD. The two examples of swearing, one by Abraham and the other by Jacob are here given.

Genesis 24:2-3, (2) And Abraham said unto his servant, the elder of his house, that ruled over all that he had: '<u>Put, I pray thee, thy hand under my thigh. (3) And I will make thee SWEAR BY YHWH</u>, the God of heaven and the God of the earth, that thou shalt not take a wife for my son of the daughters of the Canaanites, among whom I dwell.

Genesis 47:29, (29) And the time drew near that Israel must die; and he called his son Joseph, and said unto him: 'If now I have found favour in thy sight, put, <u>I pray thee, thy hand under my thigh</u>, and deal kindly and truly with me; bury me not, I pray thee, in Egypt.

There is significant reason for this symbolic act which has to do with the Hebrew word for "*thigh*". The word for thigh is also the word for "*loin*", as the "*seat of procreative power*". It has the sense of ones "*being*", and ones strength. It is the essence of a mans source of power. Just as the "*right hand*" is the sign of strength, or a mans SEED is no different than his being, So too, by Abraham's servant putting his hand near the seat of procreative power and swearing by the name of "*YHWH*", he was by his oath of swearing, also making a connection between Abraham's SEED and the SEED of Isaac which the servant was safeguarding by his mission to Abraham's family. Especially in the case of Abraham, it was also the future procreative power of his son Isaac which concerned him, because of the blessing of YHWH regarding Abraham's SEED. The blessing was on <u>*his*</u> *"SEED".*

'I SWEAR'

Abraham makes his servant *"swear"*. Swearing oaths 3,500 years ago was a very serious act if with another individual or for sure with GOD when HIS name was invoked. It had an air of holiness attached to it as it was before GOD Almighty YHWH, and as in the case of Abraham his servant was commanded to swear by **"YHWH"**.

The Hebrew word used for *"swear"* can also mean *"[to take an] oath"*. It's root comes from the Hebrew word for *"seven"* (*Shin-Bet-Ayin*), to *"seven oneself"* or *"bind oneself by seven things"*. The best example of this is when Abraham bought the well from Abimelech.

Genesis 21:28-31, (28) <u>And Abraham set seven</u> ewe-lambs of the flock by themselves. (29) And Abimelech said unto Abraham: '<u>What mean these seven</u> ewe-lambs which thou hast set by themselves?' (30) And he said: '<u>Verily, these seven ewe-lambs shalt thou take of my hand, that it may be a witness</u> unto me, that I have digged this well.' (31) Wherefore that place was called <u>Beer-sheba</u>; because there they swore both of them.

In the story of Abraham buying the well, Abraham had already given sheep and oxen to Abimelech. The seven ewe-lambs he set aside were *"witness"* to their *Covenant* event. The well *BeerSheva*, by which today the city is called, is understood as *"well of <u>seven</u>"*, *"<u>swearing</u> by <u>seven</u>"* or *"well of <u>oath</u>"*.

These examples are to illustrate the importance of swearing an oath. The vow made to YHWH by the mother of Samuel (I Samuel 1:11) is but another example of calling on the name of *"YHWH"* when either oath taking or vow making is performed by an individual of Israel.

"Swearing" in the name of *"YHWH"* for what ever reason, was done, and it was taken seriously by the people of Israel. Therefore, it is in this vein that what Jesus had to say regarding this Commandment of GOD about swearing, is problematic. YHWH said to swear in HIS name. Jesus said not to swear at all. Which is it? Is this a case of Jesus being influenced by rabbis?

'BY HIS NAME '

YHWH is very specific regarding *"vows"* and swearing of *"oaths"*. It is by the name of *"YHWH"* that *we are to swear*. Swearing is not something to be taken lightly as the person doing the swearing will surely be held accountable. But swearing was not only permitted, but the guidelines for swearing were explained to Israel on how it was to be done according to the Law which GOD gave to them by the hand of Moses (Deuteronomy 6:13).

Deuteronomy 10:20, (20) Thou shalt fear YHWH thy God; Him shalt thou serve; and to Him shalt thou cleave, <u>and by His Name shalt thou Swear</u>.

Numbers 30:3, (3) When a man <u>voweth</u> a <u>vow</u> unto YHWH, or <u>sweareth</u> an <u>oath</u> to bind his soul with a bond, <u>he shall not break his word</u>; he shall do according to all that proceedeth out of his mouth.

We are commanded quite clearly to <u>*swear by the name of YHWH*</u>, <u>*to not break our word*</u>, we will be <u>*held accountable for all that we swear*</u>, and we are <u>*not to swear falsely,*</u> as did the false prophets (Leviticus 19:12).

So by Jesus saying *"<u>Swear not at all</u>; neither by heaven; for it is God's throne"*, we have what appears to be either the *<u>addition</u>* of a new *"commandment"*, a *<u>contradiction</u>* of the existing Law, or a *<u>diminishing</u>* of the existing Law. Possibly, it is all three. Or was Jesus just giving his own advice and saying to be *"honest"* with ones words and not take swearing lightly.

The complete scripture in Matthew attributed to Jesus, is the following.

Matthew 5:33-37, (33) Again, ye have heard that it hath been said by them of old time, Thou shalt not forswear thyself, but shalt perform unto the Lord thine oaths: (34) But I say unto you, <u>Swear not at all</u>; neither by <u>heaven</u>; for it is God's <u>throne</u>: (35) Nor by the <u>earth</u>; for it is his footstool: neither by <u>Jerusalem</u>; for it is the city of the great King. (36) <u>Neither shalt thou swear</u> by <u>thy head</u>, because thou canst not make one hair white or black. (37) But let your communication be, Yea, yea; Nay, nay: for whatsoever is more than these cometh of evil.

In attempting to give this scripture the benefit of the doubt, a literal translation from the Greek was studied. The idea was that perhaps Jesus was only speaking of people who were "*swearing*" by things *other* than the name of "*YHWH*" such as by "*heaven*", the "*throne*" of GOD, by the *earth*, by *Jerusalem*, or by one's own *head*. But the "*at all*" is difficult to get around. It reads as if Jesus is saying that a person under the Law of Moses, who is commanded to swear in the name of YHWH, is being told by Jesus to no longer swear at all or for any reason whatsoever.

Remember, as a people who lived by the Law of GOD, every word of Jesus was weighed and scrutinized against the Law of YHWH and the words of HIS Prophets by the people of Israel.

It did not take either a majority of his words contradicting the Law of Moses or a minority of his words. The words attributed to Jesus cited above alone, were themselves enough for some who knew the Law, to not believe in him.

In forbearing the act of swearing when GOD said in HIS Law to swear, Jesus seems to taking his cue from the rabbis who themselves later forbid the utterance of the name of YHWH when YHWH said to swear by HIS name.

THINGS THAT DEFILE

In Chapter 15 of Matthew, Jesus speaks of those things which defile. On a purely philosophical level, it is difficult to argue with what he had to say. But although his words in many respects could be considered true, the Law of YHWH is about Commandments, Statutes and Ordinances. But these are two different issues. What a person utters is important, but the discussion is *food*.

In the Law, what is allowed for Israel to eat which is "*clean*", and that which is considered "*unclean*" are given (Leviticus 11:1-47). They are specific and cover mammals, fish, fowl and other assorted creatures clean and unclean.

A question arose regarding the washing of hands before eating. The Pharisees accused the disciples of Jesus of eating without first washing. One may have thought that not praying before eating would have been the more obvious "*offense*". But it was that of not washing first before eating that offended the Pharisees. Jesus changed the subject abruptly and accused them of their own hypocrisy with their own "*traditions*". They have a prayer for hand washing.

Matthew 15:1-3 (1) THEN came to Jesus scribes and Pharisees, which were of Jerusalem, saying,(2) Why do thy disciples <u>transgress the tradition of the elders? for they wash not their hands</u> when they eat bread.(3) But he answered and said unto them, <u>Why do ye also transgress the Commandment of God by your tradition?</u>

Because this prayer regarding "*washing*" is said as one of the very first "*blessings*" recited after an Orthodox Jew rises from bed in the morning, he begins the day by attributing a lie to YHWH his GOD at the beginning of the day, and continues it each time he washes his hand until he returns to bed. The prayer is, "*Blessed art thou, O Lord our God, King of the Universe, who hast sanctified us with thy commandments, and commanded us concerning the washing of the hands".* This prayer is recited numerous times daily.

GOD YHWH **never** commanded Israel *"concerning the washing of the hands".* This was a concoction made up by some of the *"carbon based bi-peds"* which HE had created called *"rabbis",* not HIS own Commandment.

So, an Orthodox Jew practically begins and ends his day, telling a lie and attributing that lie to GOD. For each time that he recites this prayer or any other prayer that attributes a Commandment to YHWH, when none is written in the Safer Torah, he is putting words into the mouth of GOD, no different than a false prophet who did this and lied to Israel, was condemned by GOD to death. There is no difference. For the rabbis, who have so many of Israel's people focused on their own *"commandments"* and *"traditions"* from their own supposed *"oral law",* have made themselves as *"prophets"* to Israel. They have by their *"traditions"* taken Israel's attention away from GOD'S word and GOD'S holy commandments. For by keeping these many *"laws"* created by man, they *"made the commandments of GOD of none effect".* And for this they are guilty of an offense so serious, it's sentence is death.

Deuteronomy 18:20, (20) But the prophet, that shall speak a word presumptuously in My Name, which I have not commanded him to speak, or that shall speak in the name of other gods, that same prophet shall die.

Jesus was correct in his condemnation of the Pharisees in what they did, and by extension, what their rabbinic descendants are still doing today, *"Why do ye also transgress the Commandment of God by your tradition?".*

Matthew 15:17-20, (17) Do not ye yet understand, that whatsoever entereth in at the mouth goeth into the belly, and is cast out into the draught? (18) But those things which proceed out of the mouth come forth from the heart; and they defile the man. (19) For out of the heart proceed evil thoughts, murders, adulteries, fornications, thefts, false witness, blasphemies: (20) These are the things which defile a man: but to eat with unwashen hands defileth not a man.

Jesus was **not** saying *not* to keep GOD'S Law regarding clean and unclean food. He was commenting on the *"traditions"* (oral law) of the rabbis, and he was also making a point about their hypocrisy. There is no Law about washing of hands, either before eating or after eating nor does it defile a man. Just like there is no Law regarding any kind of *"drink"* on Passover (Pesach). The washing of hands is a *"tradition"* developed by man and has become in *their* religion (Rabbinic Judaism), as if it was etched on a stone sent by GOD from HIS heavenly abode and handed to the local rabbi. Only it is not. It is silly nonsense spoken by GOD'S creation of carbon based bipeds, and written down into their books to give it legitimacy. Some Christians see this is proof that *"keeping kosher"* is no longer necessary for anyone, Jew or Gentile.

Jesus was not saying to his fellow Jews that it did not matter what they put into their mouth, that only that which came out of it defiled them. He was making the point that the Pharisees were hypocrites with their man made *"traditions"* and that all of the things he listed were evil and came from mans heart and should not be done. This is true. But at **no** time did he state that it was then, OK to not keep GOD'S Law pertaining to clean and unclean food.

Concerning what comes out of a mans mouth Jesus was making a valid point, that what comes from mans mouth is a reflection of the state of mans heart. He was not declaring in any way not to obey

GOD'S Law, to eat blood or unclean animals. This is an assumption by *believers,* not the words of Jesus.

What did Jesus say to Israel concerning entering eternal life? He said to *keep* the Commandments. What do the Commandments say about *"clean"* and **"unclean"** animals? **Read the Law. The Law is specific. Keep the Law!**

'I CAME NOT TO SEND PEACE, BUT A SWORD'

Jesus said that he came to bring '*division*' on earth.

Matthew 10:34-36, (34) <u>*Think not that I am come to send peace on earth: I came not to send peace, but a sword. (35) For I am come to set a man at variance against his father, and the daughter against her mother, and the daughter in law against her mother in law. (36) And a man's foes shall be they of his own household.*</u>

Luke 12:49, 51, (49) <u>*I am come to send fire on the earth; ... (51) Suppose ye that I am come to give peace on earth? I tell you, Nay; but rather division:*</u>

How do these words stack up against the Law of YHWH? One of the commandments given to Moses was to honor one's father and mother.

Exodus 20:12, (12) <u>*Honour thy father and thy mother,*</u> *that thy days may be long upon the land which YHWH thy God giveth thee.*

Deuteronomy 5:16, (16) <u>*Honour thy father and thy mother, as YHWH thy God commanded thee;*</u> *that thy days may be long, and that it may go well with thee, upon the land which YHWH thy God giveth thee.*

The Law is explicit concerning honoring one's father and mother. Jesus did not say *"not"* to honor them but his words are unclear as to what he meant.

What did Jesus mean by, *"Suppose ye that I am come to give peace on earth? I tell you, Nay; but rather division"*?

If the *"messiah"* is not coming to bring *"peace"*, what did they, or do we now need of him? Division, we have plenty. There is no shortage, our storehouse is full and overflowing. There are ships with *"division"* yet to be unloaded.

This is a statement in general. The entire idea of the coming of the *"messiah"* to Israel is to save Israel. As for the world, it is to bring everlasting peace to the earth. The nations will be judged, and justice will prevail. Nations will worship YHWH and will know HIS holy name. So, if a *"messiah"* comes, any *"messiah"* preaching and bringing anything but *"peace"*, what is the point? The earth already has enough *"division"*, *"fire"* and *"sword"*.

Luke 14:26, (26) <u>*If any man come to me, and hate not*</u> *his father, and mother, and wife, and children, and brethren, and sisters, yea, and his own life also,* <u>*he cannot be my disciple.*</u>

Yet, he also said to honor ones father and mother......................?

Mathew 19:19, (19) <u>*Honour thy father and thy mother:*</u> *..*

In the Book of Deuteronomy a curse is uttered for anyone who dishonors his father or mother. This is a good indication of the seriousness of the Law given in the Law of Moses. What is Israel to make of *"and hate not".*

Deuteronomy 27:16 (16) <u>Cursed be he that dishonoureth his father or his mother</u>. And all the people shall say: Amen.

The words of the prophets are echoed once again in Proverbs where King Solomon speaks of hearkening to the father and mother who bore thee.

Proverbs 23:22, (22) <u>Hearken unto thy father that begot thee, and despise not thy mother when she is old.</u>

These words resonate with warning regarding one's father and mother. GOD does not take lightly when one dishonors those who begot them. This is Law.

Jesus seemed to be paraphrasing the Prophet Micah regarding the division between family members. But Jesus is on the negative side of the words of Micah in that Micah was bemoaning the division which Jesus said he was bringing. Micah was stating that as for him, he will look unto YHWH.

With this scripture of the Prophet Micah in mind, when the words of Jesus are read, it appears more like he was bringing trouble and dissension rather than peace and prosperity to Israel, *"I am come to send fire on the earth".* During his day and after, Israel was divided regarding him. Did Jesus bring healing to Israel? Where was peace and prosperity? What did he accomplish?

The Prophet Micah was speaking of a time when the *"godly"* man had perished out of the land, and *"upright"* men were no more (Micah 7:2). He speaks of an ungodly time, of a period of godlessness, *"The godly man is perished out of the earth, and the upright among men is no more; they all lie in wait for blood; they hunt every man his brother with a net".* Is this not the very thing that Jesus said that he was bringing, hate, division, fire and sword?

Micah 7:6-7, (6) For the son <u>dishonoureth</u> the father, the daughter riseth up <u>against</u> her mother, the daughter-in-law <u>against</u> her mother-in-law; a man's <u>enemies</u> are the men of his own house. (7) '<u>But as for me, I will look unto YHWH; I will wait for the God of my Salvation; my God will hear me.</u>

'BUT AS FOR ME, I WILL LOOK UNTO YHWH'

The Prophet Micah, after viewing the situation of the state of godlessness that surrounded him, states in his determination that YHWH alone is GOD, and he will wait for YHWH'S *"salvation"*. And that YHWH his GOD will *"hear"* him (when he calls **HIS** name). As if to say that by example, the words which Jesus spoke were words whereby one is not *"looking unto YHWH"* or waiting for the *"GOD of my salvation"*. In contra distinction to the scripture of the Prophet Micah, the Gospels appear to show the words of Jesus in a negative light. In that what he was preaching appears to be at direct variance with what is good and what is right in *"looking to YHWH"* and waiting for the *"GOD of my salvation"*. Much and often the TaNaKh speaks of YHWH.

Psalms 83:19, (19) That they may know that it is <u>Thou alone whose name is YHWH,</u> the Most High over all the earth.

Psalms 4:9, (9) In peace will I both lay me down and sleep; <u>for Thou, YHWH,</u> makest me dwell alone in safety.

Psalms 18:32-36, (32) For who is God, save YHWH? And who is a Rock, except our God? (33) The God that girdeth me with strength, and maketh my way straight; (34) Who maketh my feet like hinds', and setteth me upon my high places; (35) Who traineth my hands for war, so that mine arms do bend a bow of brass. (36) Thou hast also given me Thy shield of salvation, and Thy right hand hath holden me up; and Thy condescension hath made me great.

ELIJAH

What does GOD'S Prophet Malachi have to say by GOD'S word in an apparent allusion to dishonoring one's father and one's mother?

The Jewish people have long believed that the Prophet Elijah would come before the Messiah, leading the way and preparing the people for his arrival. A *"tradition"* developed from the rabbis during Israel's longest exile to pour a cup of wine for Elijah and open the door for Elijah to enter during Passover in anticipation of his arrival as Prophet before the messiah *"mesiach"*.

Isaiah 40:3, (3) Hark! one calleth: 'Clear ye in the wilderness the way of YHWH, make plain in the desert a highway for our God.

Like most *"traditions"* within Rabbinic Judaism, this *"tradition"* of opening up the door for the prophet Elijah and pouring him a cup of wine, as with most of it's other traditions has no basis in scripture but usually comes from a kernel of an idea roughly based on something found in TaNaKh. But usually, it just comes from a kernel of an idea from the very fertile mind of man and has absolutely no connection to the Safer Torah or the word of GOD at all. Much of Jewish culture today, specially *"religious culture"* is based on just such nonsense. Inventions by the rabbis permeate Jewish culture.

There is neither any connection of Passover to the Prophet Elijah, the drinking of fermented grapes, which is forbidden, nor the opening of doors.

Much of the thinking behind this tradition, given the fact that Elijah did not die but was taken up to heaven on a flaming chariot, and scriptures like this one from the Prophet Malachi, have given hope to the Jewish people through much suffering and lends itself to ever more *"new"* traditions.

Malachi 3:22-24, (22) Remember ye the law of Moses My servant, which I commanded unto him in Horeb for all Israel, even statutes and ordinances. (23) Behold, I will send you Elijah the prophet before the coming of the great and terrible day of YHWH. (24) And he shall turn the heart of the fathers to the children, and the heart of the children to their fathers; lest I come and smite the land with utter destruction.

According to the Prophet Malachi, the Prophet Elijah *will* come. Elijah will come before the *"great and terrible day of YHWH"*. He will come not before the day of Jesus or the day of Simeon bar Kochba or Shabbetai Zvi but *before the coming of the great and terrible day of YHWH*. YHWH is *Savior*.

Hosea 13:4, (4) Yet I am YHWH thy God from the land of Egypt; and thou knowest no God but Me, and BESIDE ME THERE IS NO SAVIOUR.

In this scripture of Malachi 3:24, it is interesting that of all of the things which could have been mentioned regarding Israel's behavior, before the great and terrible day of YHWH, it is the relationship of the children to their fathers and fathers to the children that GOD had his Prophet Malachi utter.

It is significant for several reasons, not the least of which is that it is just the opposite of the words of Jesus bringing *division, fire* and a *sword*.

But of the Prophet Malachi, his words are understandable. For the relation of parent and child, in this case the father and his children, is the basic family unit. If it is not honored according to GOD'S Law, nothing beyond it whether one's "*house*", clan, tribe or people has a base from which to thrive. For all starts with the individual and his GOD and his heart honoring his father.

It is said by economists that the family is the "*basic economic unit*". Likewise, the family is the "*basic civil unit*". For just like an economy cannot function if all of the "*families*" of a civilization are corrupt and out of sync, so is a society dis-functional (read: chaos) when the basic family unit of it's population is broken and does not work. As if to say, the love, honor and respect of children for their father in a family, like that of Israel for YHWH their Father, is what makes everything work. The Prophet Elijah will address this issue before the day of YHWH.

For the family is the foundation from which all else is built on. Without this basic family unit functioning according to how it was designed, the rest does not work. The basic family unit is the bedrock of society. Sociologists understand this on another level. But with GOD, it has much more relevance for Israel on a spiritual level. For Israel, to honor one's father and mother is a commandment from GOD HIMSELF. Israel is the son of GOD and YHWH is the Father of Israel. Israel must understand that they are GOD'S sons and must act accordingly, "*ye shall therefore be holy, for I am holy* ".

John 8:41, (41) Ye do the deeds of your father. Then said they to him, we be not born of fornication; we have one Father, even GOD

Jesus was using this conversation (John 8:31-47) to tell the listeners how evil they were and that **had** they truly been of GOD, they would have heard his words. He was **not** saying that Israel was not GOD'S sons, but that *this generation* was an evil rebellious generation. Because they do not believe his words, he is implying that they are not the sons of GOD. In some way this is reminiscent of the evil generation YHWH did not allow to enter into Canaan.

John 10:34, (34) Jesus answered them, Is it not written in your law, I said, <u>Ye are gods</u>?

Psalm 82:6, (6) I have said, <u>Ye are gods</u>; and all of you are <u>children of the most High</u>.

Hosea 11:1, (1) When Israel was a child, then I loved him, <u>and out of Egypt I called My son</u>.

Israel's entire existence is based on "*family*", with YHWH as Father of Israel. It begins from the bottom up with the immediate family unit of father and mother continuing through "*house*", "*clan*", "*tribe*" and "*people*" of Israel whose Father is YHWH GOD. If children are not honoring their father *here*, then they are not honoring YHWH GOD their Father *there*, for they are the same family unit. Israel is YHWH'S first born son. YHWH is Israel's Father.

Exodus 4:22, (22) And thou shalt say unto Pharaoh: <u>Thus saith YHWH: Israel is My son, My first-born</u>.

Thus YHWH has his Prophet Malachi tell Israel that HE will have HIS Prophet Elijah turn the hearts of the fathers to the children and will turn the hearts of the children to the father, "*lest I come and smite the land with utter destruction*". The relationship of father and son is an unbroken chain.

Neither John the Baptist, of whom Jesus said was the Prophet Elijah, nor Jesus himself brought the heart of the fathers to the children or the hearts of the children to the fathers from the story in the Gospels. To the contrary, the very words of Jesus earlier quoted, state just the opposite. Jesus brought "*division*". And John the Baptist barely makes a presence in the Gospels.

Matthew 11:11-14, (11) Verily I say unto you, Among them that are born of women there hath not risen a greater than <u>John the Baptist</u>: notwithstanding he that is least in the kingdom of heaven is *greater than he. (12) And from the days of <u>John the Baptist</u> until now the kingdom of heaven <u>suffereth violence, and the <u>violent</u> take it by force</u>. (13) For all the prophets and the law prophesied until John. (14) <u>And if ye will receive it, this is Elijah, which was for to come</u>.*

John the Baptist spent his adult life baptizing Israel for the remission of sins and who lived in the wilderness. But neither he nor Jesus could be accused of bringing hearts together or making peace between the Jews of Israel. For at a time in Israel's history when Israel was at one of it's lowest places, the *"division"* which Jesus brought was not helpful, and could arguably be said to have made a bad situation even worse than it already was. And yet having said this, rightly or wrongly to many who believed in him, he also gave hope of a future time of peace. But to those who did not believe in him, he was the cause of trouble and schism. The messiah was to have brought eternal peace.

It is for this reason, the divisiveness of the words of Jesus that his words seem to be at variance with the Law of GOD, and appear to be in contradiction to it. Additionally, as the Prophet Elijah is to prepare the way for YHWH Israel's messiah, the division, schism and issues which Jesus brought with him seem to be a very long way from peace and prosperity, and youthful visions of joy, that many of GOD'S Prophets prophesied about.

'COMMANDMENTS'

This is mentioned often, but for a reason which in many ways is the basis of everything that Jesus said, *"keep the commandments"*, was directed at Israel.

Matthew 19:17, (17) And he said unto him, Why callest thou me good? <u>there is none good but one, that is, God: ......but if thou wilt enter into life, keep the Commandments</u>.

Jesus is saying very plainly that for those of Israel who wish to enter into eternal life, he must keep all of GOD'S Commandments. It is not an option. At times, Jesus often seemed to be toying with the Pharisees and others knowing that they did not know their Law as they should have. The earlier example of the adulteress is a prime example. A people versed in the Law and who were living it, no doubt would have already put the woman and her lover to death. End of story. Yet, with this generation we get the sense that Jesus is discussing the situation with them as if bargaining the cost of grapes.

The Law of Moses was *not* a Covenant between YHWH GOD and Israel in which Israel was given the <u>option</u> in their Covenant to pick and choose only those Laws which they wanted. Or, as the Christians have done, to throw out the Law of Moses completely. For once Israel agreed to GOD'S offer of Covenant, they were bound by all of it's tenants and held to all of it's precepts as given by GOD. They had agreed to all of the words spoken to them by the Prophet Moses, *"And all the people answered together, and said: '<u>All</u> that YHWH hath spoken we will do.' And Moses reported the words of the people unto YHWH"*. It must be understood that at no time did Jesus ever say *"not"* to keep GOD'S Law. To the contrary, he said on many occasions to *"keep"* GOD'S Law, and that none of the Law would fail. It was only to Israel who <u>already had</u> the Law to *"keep"*, not the Nations, to whom Jesus addressed.

Whether Jesus himself kept the Law or not is not the point here. That is for GOD to decide. The words attributed to Jesus state clearly that Israel must keep GOD'S Commandments. This is extremely important for Israel to know. For it was they who had the Law in the first place, not the Gentiles. For you must either already have something, or acquire that something before you can *"keep"* that something. Israel possessed the Law and all it's Commandments. Jesus told them to *"keep"*, as in *obey*, the Law which they already possessed.

Jesus was saying GOD'S statutes in HIS Law with Israel are eternal and to keep them if Israel wants to *"enter into life"*. It is they who have the Law. It is theirs to keep. What else did Jesus say concerning the Law of GOD and HIS commandments? He said that nothing from the Law would *"fail"*. That is, the Commandments of GOD, all of the Statutes, the blessings and the curses associated with either keeping GOD'S Law or not keeping GOD'S Law would not *"fail"* and would be *"fulfilled"*. Israel must keep the Law.

Matthew 5:17-22, (17), Think not that I am come to destroy the law, or the prophets: I am not come to destroy, but to fulfil. (18) For verily I say unto you, Till heaven and earth pass, one jot or one tittle shall in no wise pass from the law, till all be fulfilled. (19) Whosoever therefore shall break one of these least commandments, and shall teach men so, he shall be called the least in the kingdom of heaven: but whosoever shall do and teach them, the same shall be called great in the kingdom of heaven.(20) For I say unto you, That except your righteousness shall exceed the righteousness of the Scribes and Pharisees, ye shall in no case enter into the kingdom of heaven.

When one considers the many different doctrines of the modern day Christian churches around the globe, and when many of their doctrines are compared next to the words of Jesus and against what he said about the Law, a very clear picture, albeit a distorted picture, comes into focus.

For aside from the words of Paul, who was not Jesus, the words of Jesus spoken to his people Israel, are that his people Israel must obey and keep the Commandments of the Law of YHWH their GOD. Even if one accepts that Jesus said to *keep my commandments*, (John 14:15), *"If ye love me, keep my commandments"*, he also said to keep **the** Commandments. If Jesus said to keep his commandments *and* to keep GOD'S Commandments, then by definition, the *keeper* of GOD'S Commandments would be on safe ground for anything outside GOD'S Law would be forbidden. In simple terms, *keeping GOD'S Law would cancel out anything that was unlawful.*

Once again, the words of Jesus absolutely must be kept in perspective. For his audience according to the Gospels, was Israel, not Botswana, Uruguay or Tahiti. By his own admission, he came preaching to his own people Israel, and not to anyone else, admonishing his followers to do the same.

What was the context in which these words were spoken. Who was Jesus the Jew speaking to? Who was his focus on? Who was the target audience of his words? It was the Jewish people and the remnant of Israel it's lost sheep who were scattered, who had been given the Law of Moses by their GOD YHWH and accepted by them at Sinai. The target audience of Jesus his entire life was to his own people Israel wherever they were scattered. One must ask then, how does this square with some of the other words attributed Jesus regarding sending out his disciples to the nations? Israel was scattered in the nations.

'THAN ONE TITTLE OF THE LAW TO FAIL'

When Jesus said that nothing of the Law would fail, Jesus was saying that not one *"iota"* of the Law of GOD will not be accomplished, not one *"yood"*. Everything written in the Law of GOD will be done, both the good, ie. the blessing and the bad, ie. the curse. But as well, this includes GOD'S *mercy-compassion*, which is often overlooked. For YHWH is GOD, not man. Every word of GOD will bear the fruit of YHWH'S will, including YHWH'S mercy.

Hosea 11:8-9, (8) How shall I give thee up, Ephraim? How shall I surrender thee, Israel? How shall I make thee as Admah? How shall I set thee as Zeboim? My heart is turned within Me, My compassions are kindled together. (9) I will not execute the fierceness of Mine anger, I will not return to destroy Ephraim; for I am God, and not man, the Holy One in the midst of thee; and I will not come in fury

Psalms 25:6, (6) Remember, O YHWH, <u>Thy compassions and Thy mercies</u>; for they have been from of old.

The *"GOD of Mercy"* is a key component even within GOD'S Law to HIS people. For without GOD'S mercy, the Law and the Prophets would have had far, far fewer words to write or to speak. In Deuteronomy in the Law of Moses, GOD speaks of HIS mercy towards HIS people Israel.

Exodus 34:5-7 (5) And YHWH descended in the cloud, and stood with him there, and proclaimed the Name of YHWH. (6) And YHWH passed by before him, and proclaimed: 'YHWH, YHWH, <u>God, Merciful and Gracious</u>, long-suffering, and abundant in goodness and truth; (7) <u>keeping Mercy unto the thousandth generation, forgiving iniquity and transgression and sin</u>; and that will by no means clear the guilty; visiting the iniquity of the fathers upon the children, and upon the children's children, unto the third and unto the fourth generation.'

GOD punishes for sin, but HE forgives sin as well. And for those who keep HIS Commandments, HE is faithful for a thousand generations, forgiving the sin of HIS people. But for those who hate HIM, HE will repay that sin upon their head. HE is merciful towards HIS people Israel, but HE will also punish them for their sins against HIM and HIS Law. This can still be observed.

'WHO KEEPETH COVENANT AND MERCY'

Deuteronomy 7:9-13, (9) Know therefore that YHWH thy God, He is God; the faithful God, <u>who keepeth Covenant and Mercy with them that love Him and Keep His Commandments</u> to a thousand generations; (10) and repayeth them that hate Him to their face, to destroy them; He will not be slack to him that hateth Him, He will repay him to his face. (11) Thou shalt therefore keep the Commandment, and the Statutes, and the Ordinances, which I Command thee this day, to do them. (12) And it shall come to pass, <u>because ye hearken to these Ordinances, and keep, and do them, that YHWH thy God shall keep with thee the Covenant and the Mercy which He Swore unto thy fathers,</u>(13) and He will love thee, and bless thee, and multiply thee; ....

This sums up Israel's relationship with their GOD that YHWH swore to Israel's forefathers. HE will keep HIS oath. But HE will hold Abraham's SEED to the Statutes and Ordinances of HIS Covenant, to do them. Part of the *Covenant* is GOD'S *"mercy"* with HIS people, *"which HE swore"*. When GOD swears, HE cannot swear by a higher authority, for there is no higher authority than HE, so HE swears by HIMSELF.

Isaiah 45:23, (23) <u>By Myself have I sworn</u>, the word is gone forth from My mouth in righteousness, and shall not come back, that unto Me every knee shall bow, every tongue shall swear

GOD loves HIS people Israel and knows that Israel is but flesh and bone. GOD seems to constantly remind HIMSELF of this fact which is very closely connected with HIS mercy towards HIS people. GOD'S mercy and compassion existed along with HIS salvation long before Jesus. By telling Israel to keep GOD'S Commandments, Jesus was possibly reminding them of the connection between YHWH'S *"Covenant and Mercy"* which HE has had with Israel already for many generations. Mercy began not with Jesus.

'SO HE REMEMBERED THAT THEY WERE BUT FLESH'

Psalms 78:38-39, (38) But He, being <u>full of compassion, forgiveth iniquity,</u> and destroyeth not; yea, many a time doth He turn His anger away, and doth not stir up all His wrath. (39) <u>So He remembered that they were but flesh,</u> a wind that passeth away, and cometh not again.

GOD will not forget HIS Covenant with Abraham, Isaac and Jacob. HE will become *angry*, HE will *punish* and HE will *exile*, but HE will also *return* Jacob to his home and have *compassion*, HE will *forgive* and HE will have *mercy*, for YHWH is a *"merciful GOD"*. Praise HIS holy name.

Many of the Christians believe that Jesus represents GOD'S mercy to Israel. But it is YHWH who is the mercy of Israel. For YHWH is the GOD of Mercy. And the GOD of Mercy is the GOD of Israel. YHWH is HIS name.

Deuteronomy 4:31, (31) <u>for YHWH thy God is a merciful God</u>; He will not fail thee, neither destroy thee, nor forget the covenant of thy fathers which He swore unto them.

Micah 7:18-20, (18) Who is a God like unto Thee, that <u>pardoneth the iniquity,</u> and passeth by the transgression of the remnant of His heritage? He retaineth not His anger for ever, because He <u>delighteth in Mercy.</u> (19) He will again have <u>Compassion</u> upon us; He will subdue our iniquities; and <u>Thou wilt cast all their sins into the depths of the sea.</u> (20) Thou wilt show faithfulness to Jacob, mercy to Abraham, as Thou hast sworn unto our fathers from the days of old.

Returning to the words of Jesus and the Law of Moses, it must be said that you cannot have it both ways. Either the entire Law of YHWH must be kept, or the entire Law of YHWH does not need to be kept. Picking and choosing is <u>not</u> an option for Israel. For this idea of picking and choosing which of GOD'S Law one needs to keep is what is done within Rabbinic Judaism.

Within Rabbinic Judaism today, this distortion of Torah observance can be witnessed within the various denominations from the Ultra Orthodox on down to something called *"Flexodox"* and all that is in between (Ultra-Orthodox, Orthodox, Conservative, Reform, Reconstructionist, Humanistic and Flexodox). Within Orthodox alone, there are many extreme divisions and doctrines of man. On a graduated scale of a continual and ever decreasing level of observance of GOD'S holy Commandments, each of these different absurd bankrupt perversions within it's own religious doctrine, beginning with it's base in the Talmud, exhibit an extremely skewed view of what YHWH expects of them. Their traditions Jesus may have had in mind when he told them, *"Ye blind guides, which strain at a gnat, and swallow a camel"*. rabbis create *"law"* for every conceivable state of existence and task and in doing so, they miss the the big picture completely, the Law of YHWH itself.

As there is no Temple of YHWH today because of Israel's sins, some of the observances cannot be performed, as in offerings of sacrifice upon the alter. However, <u>all</u> Commandments which <u>can</u> be kept, <u>must</u> be kept <u>by</u> Israel. This refers to the Laws in the Safer Torah *only*, not the so called *"oral law"*.

If the statements by Jesus about keeping the Law are to be taken at face value, then anything else that is written in the Gospels which appears to contradict his words related to the idea of keeping GOD'S Law, is not accurate. You cannot both keep the Law of Moses in it's entirety and not keep the Law of Moses in it's entirety. It must be recalled when Jesus preached, the Temple and the daily sacrifice still existed. Offerings were being made.

As there is no such thing as being *"a little bit pregnant"*. Time and again, the words attributed to Jesus for Israel, is that he was saying the Commandments of the Law must be kept. Not only was he saying that the Law and it's Commandments must be kept, but <u>all of the Law</u> must be kept and that none of it would be overlooked by GOD. Obeying GOD'S Law for Israel was not an option, but was the verbal contract they had agreed to at Sinai with YHWH, every <u>jot and tittle</u>. In this, Jesus was not saying anything new. The *"Blood of the Covenant"* was sprinkled on Israel. Israel is under Covenant.

Exodus 24:8, (8) And Moses took the blood, and sprinkled it on the people, and said: 'Behold the Blood of the Covenant, which YHWH hath made with you in agreement with all these words.'

Jesus said that none of the words of the Law which Israel accepted at Sinai or the words of the prophets given to GOD'S servants would fail "*And it is easier for heaven and earth to pass, than one tittle of the law to fail*". Does this jibe with the words written in the Safer Torah, the Law of GOD itself?

Isaiah 55:11, (11) So shall My word be that goeth forth out of My mouth: it shall not return unto Me void, except it accomplish that which I please, and make the thing whereto I sent it prosper.

Leviticus 26:25, (25) And I will bring a sword upon you, that shall execute the vengeance of the Covenant;

Deuteronomy 4:27, (27) And YHWH shall scatter you among the peoples, and ye shall be left few in number among the nations, whither YHWH shall lead you away.

Deuteronomy 29:20, (20) and YHWH shall separate him unto evil out of all the tribes of Israel, according to all the curses of the Covenant that is written in this Book of the Law.

Ezekiel 6:10, (10) And they shall know that I am YHWH; I have not said in vain that I would do this evil unto them.

For the Covenant says plainly that Israel would be held accountable to all of the words in the Law, *which they agreed to.* Else, they would be severely punished. It was the curse of breaking the Law, Gentiles did not have to face.

Exodus 19:8 (8) And all the people answered together, and said: 'All that YHWH hath spoken we will do.' And Moses reported the words of the people unto YHWH.

GOD heard Israel, and Moses was HIS witness. And it may be for this reason, that in anticipation of these stiff necked people possibly changing or attempting to change HIS Law, as if they could fool GOD by such tactics, that YHWH had HIS prophets write more than once about not changing, either by *adding to* or *subtracting from* the word of GOD. GOD'S curse on Israel alone is proof enough of the power of the Law when it is not kept.

HIS word and HIS Law is eternal truth. GOD said what would happen with Israel concerning HIS Covenant, good and bad. YHWH'S Covenant with Israel is a living breathing reality not a *religion*. It is GOD'S eternal promise for HIS people who grasp HIS offer and take HIM to heart. HIS mercy is an eternal burning sun and GOD'S compassion, which is reborn each day.

Isaiah 54:7-8, (7) For a small moment have I forsaken thee; but with great Compassion will I gather thee. (8) In a little wrath I hid My face from thee for a moment; but with Everlasting Kindness will I have Compassion on thee, saith YHWH thy Redeemer.

'THAT YE MAY KEEP THE COMMANDMENTS OF YHWH'

In regard to not adding to or diminishing from the word of GOD, what harm can it do? To answer this, a look at the Law itself and what it says concerning either "*adding*" or "*subtracting*" anything from the word of GOD is necessary. Knowing the repercussions of adding and diminishing to the Safer Torah, are important as they relate directly to the words of Jesus for some of his words appear to change the Law as written in the Safer Torah. As the words attributed to Jesus regarding "*divorce*" seem to indicate, his verbal adding to GOD'S holy word, appears to have been done. The books written by the rabbis and added to the Safer Torah are a more serious case in point.

In telling Israel to *"keep the commandments"*, was Jesus telling Israel to *"do as I say not as I do"?* In some respects it appears that on occasion Jesus did deliberately mislead Israel and then reminded them to keep the Law to see if they would catch him. Even going so far as chiding them that they did not know the Law of Moses, for had they known it, they would have known if his *"doctrine"* was from GOD or was his own. For he seemed to have known the Law well enough to debate with the rabbis but the rabbis were so full of their own man made *"laws"*, they could not tell if what he said was from the Law of Moses or not. They were blinded by their own *"traditions"*. It was as if Jesus was saying to them to *"catch me"*. Obey GOD'S Law and HIS Law will act as a *"sieve"*, and filter out all doctrine that is not truly HIS doctrine.

'WHAT NEW DOCTRINE IS THIS?'

Mark 1:27 (27) And they were all amazed, insomuch that they questioned among themselves, saying, What thing is this? what new doctrine is this?

The *"doctrine"* that Jesus preached apparently sounded strange to the Pharisaic listeners. Even if he had read straight from the Safer Torah, much of what they heard would have sounded *"strange"* to them. Much of it would have sounded *"strange"* to the Pharisees as the rabbis of his time would not have been very well versed in the Safer Torah because of all of their own nonsense (traditions) which they were memorizing. For even had they recognized the words from the Safer Torah, their understanding would have been so skewed by the nonsense of their own so called *"oral law"*, that they had been brainwashing themselves with, that it would have barely registered. Additionally, much of the *"doctrine"* Jesus preached would have sounded odd anyway as he was difficult to understand and it often did seem to be at variance with the Law which may have been the point all along.

Had the people been keeping the Law as it was given to them by Moses, then they would have known if the words of Jesus were from the Safer Torah or not. *"If any man will do his will, he shall know of the doctrine, whether it be of God, or whether I speak of myself"*.

If the average Jew was confused by other self styled know-it-all Jews (false prophets, religious teachers, the Pharisees, Scribe, Sadduce, Essene and the Priest), about the Law of GOD, how were they going to know if Jesus was a false prophet or a false messiah. Jesus said as much himself.

John 7:14-24, (14) Now about the midst of the feast Jesus went up into the temple, and taught. (15) And the Jews marvelled, saying, How knoweth this man letters, having never learned? (16) Jesus answered them, and said, My doctrine is not mine, but his that sent me. (17) If any man will do his will, he shall know of the doctrine, whether it be of God, or whether I speak of myself. (18) He that speaketh of himself seeketh his own glory: but he that seeketh his glory that sent him, the same is true, and no unrighteousness is in him. (19) Did not Moses give you the Law, and yet none of you keepeth the Law? Why go ye about to kill me? (20) The people answered and said, Thou hast a devil: who goeth about to kill thee? (21) Jesus answered and said unto them, I have done one work, and ye all marvel. (22) Moses therefore gave unto you circumcision; (not because it is of Moses, but of the fathers;) and ye on the Sabbath day circumcise a man. (23) If a man on the Sabbath day receive circumcision, that the law of Moses should not be broken; are ye angry at me, because I have made a man every whit whole on the Sabbath day? (24) Judge not according to the appearance, but judge righteous judgment.

And just in case they did not fully understand his words, he stated plainly that they do not keep the Law of Moses. As if to say, you cannot possibly know if my words are my own or not, because you do not know the Law of Moses yourself. If you kept the Law of Moses, you would be able to recognize the Law of Moses. In essence saying, *"it takes one to know one"*. One may recall how easily they could have brushed aside his words regarding the example of the *"adulteress"* from before, had they known the Law.

There were several things going on here at once (Aside from the writer reminding us that during the feast, Jews went up into the Temple. Who else would it be?), but the line referring to if Israel was doing *"HIS will"* (the Law of the Father), they would *"know"* if what Jesus said (doctrine) was from GOD or from Jesus. In many respects, this seems to sum up his ministry. As he had told them that <u>nothing</u> from the Law would <u>fail</u> and that he had come to <u>fulfill the Law</u>, and for Israel to <u>keep</u> the Law if they wanted to enter life. And as the quote above showed, he admonished them for not knowing and keeping their own Law. The more this is understood, it seems Jesus was almost *"toying"* with them in their ignorance of the Law, leaving clues for them to follow like bread crumbs. Until in the end, the Priests had finally had enough. Did Jesus purposely tempt or try (proof) the Priests who actually knew the Law, until they had no recourse but to put a stop to it and condemn him to death for blasphemy? A fate he knew was his from the beginning?

Which leads back to the writings of the rabbis today. If by accusing the Jews of not knowing the Laws of the Safer Torah 2,000 years ago was any indication of the poor state of affairs back then, just fast forward to today's situation after those 2,000 years of added confusion with the written words of the rabbis now taught as if they were the holy words of YHWH HIMSELF. Rabbinic seminaries (yeshivot) exist all over the world spreading their own writings much as some wild beasts enjoy a good roll in the scent of the carcass of a recent kill spreading the smell of death on themselves. For what had only previously been remembered, was later written down and added to and added to. What are today's Jewish people to make of the words of Jesus from 2,000 years ago, when all they have to compare his words against are the ramblings and the mad grunts and groans of man made *"laws"* created by the rabbis? The rabbis do not keep the Law of Moses today either, even less so than when Jesus berated them.

KEEPERS OF THE LAW

The earliest followers of Jesus were keepers of the Law according to the words written in the Christian Bible. This changed drastically as later Paul spread this now, *"new religion"* to the Gentile world. It was Paul who began throwing out the Law, but it was the later Gentiles who not only jettisoned the Law of Moses completely, but they somehow even managed to change the Sabbath of GOD, HIS day of rest, the one which HE said was **<u>holy</u>** to HIM and was holy to Jesus, to the first day of the week (from Saturday to Sunday). And not only this, but somehow, rabbits started laying eggs, in what they called "Easter"! If the Hebrew Bible is accepted as the foundation of / for Christianity as is proclaimed by it's believers, then without the Patriarchs, the Law of Moses and the Prophets there would be no religion called Christianity. What was the meaning of forsaking GOD'S most holy Sabbath? Did Jesus say anything concerning <u>*Sunday*</u>?

What justified this change? It is known why they did it (Jesus was raised on Sunday), but how did they justify making it GOD'S holy day when it was never GOD'S holy day to GOD, Israel, the Jewish people or to Jesus? What does the Law of Moses say about keeping *"Shabbat"*?

Exodus 20:8, (8) Remember the Sabbath day, to keep it holy.

Did not Jesus himself say to keep the Commandments? Keeping YHWH'S Sabbath is written in the *"Law"*. But the Christian will say the *"Law"* is dead. The Law is not dead. Followers of Jesus must keep GOD'S Sabbath.

Long before the Law of Moses was given at Sinai, the seventh day was a holy day to GOD having been established at the time of creation when YHWH finished HIS work. It was *"HIS"* holy day, the day which HE *"hallowed"*. Only much later, did the Law of Moses, when given at Mount Sinai, establish keeping GOD'S Sabbath as written law commanding all of Israel to keep. For just as circumcision of Abraham's sons existed long before the Law of Moses was written down establishing it as *"Law"*, so did GOD'S holy Sabbath on the *"seventh"* day exist. Therefore, the holiness of the Sabbath day existed long before it was written into Law to keep. From the start it was *"holy"*.

If YHWH *"blessed"* the Sabbath day (seventh) and *"hallowed it"*, what does that say about the other days of the week? Additionally, if Jesus said to keep *all* of the Commandments, why is the Commandment to keep the Sabbath day of YHWH not only ignored, but changed altogether?

Whatever else Jesus was, he was a Jew who observed the Sabbath of YHWH GOD. Whether he violated the Sabbath or not is a judgment for GOD. But keeping the Commandments he said to do, and that included keeping GOD'S Sabbath which is the seventh day of the week, not the first day of the week. What the Christians make of this is beyond ones thinking. It is understood why they made *"Sunday"* their *"Sabbath"* day of rest according to their tradition, but there is nothing in the words of Jesus that would even hint of such a perversion. It certainly did not come from either Jesus or the Jewish believers. By ignoring YHWH'S holy Sabbath and HIS Law, the new religion codified by the Gentiles, *"threw the baby out with the bath water"*.

The rabbis write their own books and make up their own doctrine to fit their own religion. Thus, do the Christians write their own books and make up their own doctrine to fit there own religion. In the entire Talmud, not once does the written formula found all throughout GOD'S holy word in the Hebrew Bible say, *"Thus saith YHWH"*. Neither in all of the Gospels in the words attributed to Jesus does the formula exist stating, *"Thus saith YHWH"*.

BLOOD AND FLESH

The eating of blood was forbidden by YHWH, even as far back as the time of Noah long before the Law was given, it was commanded to Noah by GOD that it was not to be eaten. For life is in the blood.

Genesis 9:3-4, (3) Every moving thing that liveth shall be for food for you; as the green herb have I given you all. (4) Only flesh with the life thereof, which is the blood thereof, shall ye not eat.

One of the more troubling aspects that a Jew who is living by the Law of Moses might find, is the idea even symbolically of *drinking blood*. Eating the blood of an animal is so far removed from the Law where it is forbidden to do so, that it is one of the more bazaar aspects of the teachings of Jesus. Even more bazaar is the concept of symbolically *drinking the blood of a human* being. Add to this the symbolic *eating of the flesh* of Jesus, and you have a truly disturbing act. Metaphor or not, this choice of symbolism of all that may have been chosen but was not, was very troubling to Israel then and should be now. For these things are extremely taboo for Israel.

This metaphor of his blood and his flesh, like many of the symbolic acts of Jesus were meant to inspire and bring a feeling of pathos to his story. At least to give a feeling of connection for the participant. And yet, even as a symbolic act, they are troubling to an observant Jew. Drinking the blood of a human being and eating his flesh, are against the Law of Moses and would have been repulsive to all observant Jews hearing it, and one may suspect the non-observant as well.

BLOOD FLESH AND PASSOVER

The scripture regarding *"blood"* and *"flesh"* of Jesus in the Book of Matthew speaks of a symbolic act, but are we witnessing Jesus drinking *wine*?

*Matthew 26:26-29, And as they were eating, Jesus took **bread**, and blessed it, and brake it, and gave it to the disciples, and said, Take, eat; <u>this is my body.</u> (27) And he took the <u>cup</u>, and gave thanks, and gave it to them, saying, <u>Drink</u> ye all of it; (28) For <u>this is my blood</u> of the new testament, which is shed for many for the remission of sins. (29) But I say unto you, I will not drink henceforth of <u>this fruit of the vine</u>, until that day when I drink it new with you in my Father's kingdom.*

This story is repeated again with varying degrees of difference in each of the books of Mark and Luke. But interestingly enough, *<u>not one of them states that it was actually wine in the cup</u>*, or that he himself actually drank wine. Why is this important. Fermented / leavened food is forbidden on Passover!

A look at the literal Greek translation indicates the same regarding the story. It could have been water for all that is actually known or grape juice. The assumption is, that because immediately after his telling his disciples to eat his flesh and to drink his blood, he declared that he would not drink *"this fruit of the vine"* until etc., etc. It is inferred from this, and also because rabbis drink fermented grapes during Passover. It is assumed that wine was what was in the cup. But as was stated, it may have been grape juice in stead.

A review of the Greek translation of *"this"* (hoo'-tos) indicates that *"this"* is correct, however, it is still unknown whether *"this"* was added by the translator or if it actually existed in the original. Depending on several other criteria, it can have the sense also of *"he, she, it"*. However, it would not change the issue of *"fruit of the vine"* regardless of which word was used.

The main point is however, that without *"this, he, she* or *it"*, the possible understanding can have a radically different meaning. Just for starters, it would indicate the difference as to whether they were possibly drinking wine or not. This is important because the eating of *fermented* or **leavened** food (theses two words are often used interchangeably and mean the same thing), whether solid or liquid, was forbidden on Passover according to the Law.

The drinking of wine or any liquid for that matter was <u>*never*</u> a part of Passover in the story of the Passover in Exodus, the Safer Torah, the Law of Moses or the Hebrew Bible. It is not written and cannot be found anywhere in the Law of GOD pertaining to the Passover Seder. It is for this reason that today, Karaite Jews do not drink wine or any fermented beverage during Passover. The drinking of wine during Passover was added to the Passover Seder by Rabbinic Jews, but is not part of GOD'S instruction for Passover, nor is it to be found anywhere in the Safer Torah regarding Pesach. It is for this reason, that the Passover Seder story in the Gospels is of particular interest. Did Jesus drink wine during the Passover Seder?

PASSOVER AND WINE

During Passover, the drinking or eating of any *"fermented"* or *"leavened"* food is forbidden to **all** of Israel.

Jesus did not appear to have drunk the *"wine"* at the Passover Seder in the stories of Matthew 26:17-30 and Luke 22:7-23. However, he appeared to have encouraged his fellow Jews to do so. In Mark 14:12-25, however there is a possibility in verse 23 with *"and they all drank"*. But this quote comes *after* he blessed the wine and gave *"it to them"*. Was he of *"them"*? And was he encouraging them to drink wine, if it was wine, to desecrate the Passover?

The real issue as to whether or not he drank wine, or whether he was a Nazirite (as some believe) or not has to do with *"no more"* in verse 25. The literal translation from the Greek also has *"no more"* which could easily mean that at some time, he drank the *"produce of the vine"*, which would have ended his Nazirite vow had he been one. But even more important, he was cursed if he drank wine during Passover for wine is liquid fermented / leavened food and is absolutely forbidden. It is a very serious question.

Mark 14:23-25 (23) And <u>he took the cup</u>, and when he had given thanks, <u>he gave it to them</u>: and <u>they all drank</u> of it. (24) And he said unto them, This is my blood of the new testament, which is shed for many. (25) Verily I say unto you, I will drink <u>no more</u> of the <u>fruit of the vine</u>, until that day that I drink it new in the kingdom of God (King James Version).

A quick look at a *literal* translation of the Greek Christian Bible seems to confirm that of Mark.

Mark 14:23-25, 23 and having <u>taken the cup</u>, having given thanks, he gave to them, and <u>they drank</u> of it – all; (24) and he said to them, 'This is my blood of the new covenant, which for many is being poured out; (25) verily I say to you, that <u>no more</u> may I drink of the <u>produce of the vine</u> till that day when I may drink it new in the reign of GOD.' (Young's Literal Translation).

Assuming Jesus knew the Law of Moses, he would have known that he not only was not required to drink wine during Passover, but he was not required to drink anything. There is nothing in the Safer Torah regarding Passover about drinking wine or anything else. If Jesus was unaware that he was not required to drink wine during Passover it would say allot about his knowledge of the Law, as wine is forbidden. If Jesus was a Nazirite (which is doubtful), he would have known GOD'S statutes (Numbers 6:1-21) of a Nazirite vow. Although this writer does not believe that he was a Nazirite.

As drinking wine or any liquid for that matter is not part of the original instructions from GOD concerning the Passover Seder, it becomes a moot point other than the fact that he may have at some point had *"produce of the vine"*, but *"no more"*. As with many *"traditions"* invented by Rabbinic Judaism over many generations, the drinking of wine during Passover is not written in the Hebrew Bible, nor is it required nor does it have anything to do with the Passover Seder whatsoever. Drinking of any liquid is not mentioned. It is interesting that even if he did not drink wine, if it existed at all during their Passover Seder, it would show a reflection of the influence of the rabbis.

The example of the wine, and many, many other created customs, have nothing to do at all with what is actually written in the Hebrew Bible but are *traditions added by the rabbis*. This is really a prime example of why not "*adding*" anything to the Safer Torah as commanded by GOD, is so wrong. There is a "*curse*" by GOD for consuming "*leaven*" during Pesach.

Exodus 12:8, 14, (8) And they shall eat the <u>*flesh*</u> *in that night, roast with fire, and* <u>*unleavened bread*</u>*; with* <u>*bitter herbs*</u> *they shall eat it.................(14) And this day shall be unto you for a memorial, and ye shall keep it a feast to YHWH; throughout your generations ye shall keep it a feast by an ordinance* <u>*for ever*</u>*.*

'WINE'?

"*Flesh*", "*bitter herbs*" and "*unleavened bread*" are required for Passover. No mention of any kind is made of wine, water, milk, beer or any liquid. No mention is made of drink at all, only solid food. One may even ask, was it GOD'S intention that no liquid at all be consumed during Pesach?

For more details all of Exodus Chapter 12 should be read. It is a long chapter, but no where within the Commandment to keep the Passover as described, does it mention any kind of drink, neither in Deuteronomy or in Numbers.

Wine is the natural fermentation (leavening) process brought about from naturally occurring yeast of grapes which produces the wine. It is very similar to the naturally occurring yeast in dough which produces bread as well as the yeast used to make beer. It is for this very reason that bread has often been called "*liquid beer*". The process for making wine, beer or bread necessitates the use of either naturally occurring yeast, or added yeast. The end results is the same. They all undergo a leavening or fermenting process As stated, this is why Karaite Jews do not drink wine (or any other alcoholic beverage) during Pesach (Passover). It is "*not written*" to do so in the **SAFER TORAH**, plus, the fermentation of grapes are forbidden just as leavened bread would be. They are both forbidden during Passover (Pesach).

The JPS 1917 translation of the text in Exodus reads as follows. The King James translation is almost identical.

Exodus 12:15, 19-20, (15) Seven days shall ye eat <u>*unleavened*</u> *bread; howbeit the first day ye shall put away* <u>*leaven*</u> *out of your houses; for whosoever eateth* <u>*leavened*</u> *bread from the first day until the seventh day, that soul shall be cut off from Israel.....(19) Seven days shall there be no* <u>*leaven*</u> *found in your houses; for whosoever eateth that which is* <u>*leavened*</u>*, that soul shall be cut off from the congregation of Israel, whether he be a sojourner, or one that is born in the land. (20) Ye shall eat nothing* <u>*leavened*</u>*; in all your habitations shall ye eat* <u>*unleavened*</u> *bread.'*

A literal translation of the Greek actually uses the words *fermented* 12:15, 19-20 in Exodus. As stated previously, often the words *fermented* and "*leavened*" are used interchangeably as they mean the same thing.

Exodus 12:20, (20) anything <u>*fermented*</u> *ye do not eat, in all your dwellings ye do not eat* <u>*unleavened things*</u> (Young's Literal Translation)

The use of *leaven* and *fermented* are used interchangeably in these scriptures.

The use of "*leaven*" and "*fermented*" are continued in 13:3, 7.

Exodus 13:3....and any thing __fermented__ is not eaten (Young's Literal Translation).

The idea here is that the *"rabbis"* **added** to the Safer Torah instructions of the Passover meal, by including a *"drink"* to go with the unleavened / non fermented bread. And not just any drink, but one which was fermented from grapes to become an alcoholic drink called *"wine"*. This is **FORBIDDEN** during Pesach (Passover). A argument can be made that it only refers to *"bread"* or solid food. But even 2,400 years ago, as the *"Passover Letter"* will show, liquid drink was understood and known to be *"leaven"* as well and forbidden by Jews at Passover, primarily because of the process to make it.

THE PASSOVER LETTER

In 1907 during an excavation, a papyrus letter was discovered on Elephantine Island (Egypt), reminding the Jewish occupants of the island how to keep Passover. The date of this letter was approximately 419 BCE, being sent to the Jewish mercenary garrison on this Egyptian island as Jews had fled to all corners of the Middle East because of the earlier exile to Babylon of Judah.

After conquering the Babylonians, King Darius of Persia was very good to the Jewish people and had allowed them to rebuild the Temple in Jerusalem. It was during this same time frame that this letter was sent to the Jewish garrison on Elephantine Island in the middle of the Nile River, also known as *"Yeb"* . Historians refer to this letter as *"A Passover Letter"*. It was written in Aramaic and is currently in *"Staatliche Museen"*, Berlin, Germany. The letter instructs the Jewish garrison so far removed from the rest of the Jewish world, how and when to conduct *Passover* and *Feast of Unleavened Bread*.

'A PASSOVER LETTER'

"(1) To my brothers, (2) Yedaniah and his colleagues of the Judahite garrison, (from) your brother Hananiah, May the gods seek the welfare of my brothers. (3) Now this year, the 5th of King Darius, word was sent from the king to Arsames, saying: (4) In the month of Nisan, let there be a Passover for the Judahite garrison. Now accordingly count fourteen (5) days of the month Nisan and keep the Passover, and from the 15th day to the 21st day of Nisan (6) are seven days of Unleavened Bread. Be clean and take heed. Do not work (7) on the 15th day and on the 21st day. Also, drink no intoxicants; and anything in which there is leaven, (8) do not eat, from the 15th day from sunset until the 21st day of Nisan, seven (9) days, let it not be seen among you; do not bring it into your houses, but seal it up during those days. (10) Let this be done as King Darius commanded. To my brethren, Yedaniah and his colleagues of the Judahite garrison, (from) your brother Hananiah."

This is truly an incredible letter, absolutely astounding. The author is reminding the Jewish garrison not to drink anything which is *fermented* during Passover. In this letter, the writer Hananiah is reminding his brothers so far away, not to drink intoxicants during Passover, *"Also, drink no intoxicants; and anything in which there is leaven"*. The people of ancient Israel were not a bunch of back woods yahoos who were not aware that *"intoxicants"* were *fermented* beverages that were made by a process no different than the making of *leavened* bread. Whether it is *solid* bread or *liquid* wine, *leavening* and *fermentation* are the basic same process, and both are forbidden to Israel during Passover. There is no difference.

WHAT WAS IN THE CUP

A very careful reading of the scripture does not indicate what was either in the cup, or that Jesus actually drank from it himself. This is critical because it is Pesach (Passover) and drinking wine, as stated, is not part of this ritual. As covered, there is nothing in all of the entire Hebrew Bible, especially in the Safer Torah that even hints at drinking **anything**, let alone drinking wine. Exodus 12:1-11 gives the entire account of Passover and what is to be performed. There are only three items of food mentioned. The **meat** (lamb or goat), the **bread** (unleavened), and bitter **herbs** (vegetables). No mention is made of drink. None at all. Note that Passover also marks the *"first month of the year"* for Israel. What rabbis call "Rosh HaShana" is the seventh month.

Exodus 12:1-11, (1) And YHWH spoke unto Moses and Aaron in the land of Egypt, saying: (2) <u>'This Month shall be unto you the Beginning of Months; it shall be the First Month of the Year to you</u>. (3) Speak ye unto all the congregation of Israel, saying: In the tenth day of this month they shall take to them every man a <u>lamb</u>, according to their fathers' houses, a <u>lamb</u> for a household; (4) and if the household be too little for a <u>lamb</u>, then shall he and his neighbour next unto his house take one according to the number of the souls; according to every man's eating ye shall make your count for the <u>lamb</u>. (5) Your <u>lamb</u> shall be without blemish, a male of the first year; ye shall take it from the <u>sheep</u>, or from the <u>goats</u>; (6) and ye shall keep it unto the fourteenth day of the same month; and the whole assembly of the congregation of Israel shall kill it at dusk. (7) And they shall take of the blood, and put it on the two side-posts and on the lintel, upon the houses wherein they shall eat it. (8) And they shall <u>eat the flesh</u> in that night, roast with fire, and <u>unleavened bread</u>; with <u>bitter herbs</u> they shall eat it. (9) Eat not of it raw, nor sodden at all with water, but roast with fire; its head with its legs and with the inwards thereof. (10) And ye shall let nothing of it remain until the morning; but that which remaineth of it until the morning ye shall burn with fire. (11) And thus shall ye eat it: with your loins girded, your shoes on your feet, and your staff in your hand; <u>and ye shall eat it in haste -- it is YHWH'S passover.</u>

Notice that there is *<u>no mention of any type of liquid</u>* to be drunk.

Perhaps it is because Jesus said in almost the same breath, that he would not drink of the <u>fruit of the vine</u> until he drinks it *"new"* in my *"Father's kingdom"*, that it is *"assumed"* that there was wine in the cup. If added to this the invented Rabbinic practice of drinking wine during Passover, and the confusion comes full circle. For as has been shown, wine was never part of Passover according to the Safer Torah which established the Law of Pesach (Passover). Drinking wine at Passover was an invention from the very fertile minds of the rabbis themselves as part of their own *"tradition"* and according to the *"Passover Letter"*, was still not practiced 400 years previous to the existence of the rabbis. This rabbinic *"tradition"* of drinking wine during Passover may still have been in it's infancy during the time of Jesus, but it clearly was non existent during or right after the Babylonian Exile as there was no such thing as a *"pharisee / rabbi"*. They had not been invented yet.

'THAT SOUL SHALL BE CUT OFF FROM ISRAEL'

The question then arises, had the *"tradition"* of drinking wine during Passover already become established as part of the *"Passover Seder"* during the time of Jesus? It appears to be the case according to the story, but not fully developed. If so, did Jesus drink wine during Passover? *If* he did, then he would have been doing little different than eating leavened bread and would be cursed. He and his followers would have been risking being cursed by GOD YHWH.

Had Jesus or any of the people at the Passover Seder drank wine, they would have been drinking leavened / fermented food and breaking the Law of Passover and thus being in serious danger of the curse from GOD.

Exodus 12:15, (15) Seven days shall ye eat Unleavened Bread; howbeit the first day ye shall put away Leaven out of your houses; for whosoever eateth Leavened Bread from the first day until the seventh day, that soul shall be cut off from Israel.

Exodus 12:19-20, (19) Seven days shall there be No Leaven found in your houses; for whosoever eateth that which is Leavened, that soul shall be cut off from the congregation of Israel, whether he be a sojourner, or one that is born in the land. (20) Ye shall eat nothing Leavened; in all your habitations shall ye eat Unleavened Bread.'

BACK TO FLESH AND BLOOD

Returning to the idea of eating flesh and drinking blood, it is very far outside the Law of GOD to even symbolically do these things. In the Book of John, the story of the *"last supper"* (Passover) is not retold here, however, a more detailed example in another scripture of the metaphor of drinking his blood and eating his flesh is given and is worth quoting.

John 6:47-58, (47) Verily, verily, I say unto you, He that believeth on me hath everlasting life. (48) I am that bread of life. (49) Your fathers did eat manna in the wilderness, and are dead. (50) This is the bread which cometh down from heaven, that a man may eat thereof, and not die. (51) I am the living bread which came down from heaven: if any man eat of this bread, he shall live for ever: and the bread that I will give is my Flesh, which I will give for the life of the world. (52) The Jews therefore strove among themselves, saying, How can this man give us his Flesh to eat? (53) Then Jesus said unto them, Verily, verily, I say unto you, Except ye eat the Flesh of the Son of man, and drink his Blood, ye have no life in you. (54) Whoso eateth my Flesh, and drinketh my Blood, hath eternal life; and I will raise him up at the last day. (55) For my Flesh is meat indeed, and my Blood is drink indeed. (56) He that eateth my Flesh, and drinketh my Blood, dwelleth in me, and I in him. (57) As the living Father hath sent me, and I live by the Father: so he that eateth me, even he shall live by me. (58) This is that bread which came down from heaven: not as your fathers did eat manna, and are dead: he that eateth of this bread shall live for ever.

This is of course all symbolic, however it is still troubling nevertheless, and far outside the Law of Moses which Israel was given to live by.

For as already mentioned (Genesis 9:4), as far back as Noah, before the Law was given, the eating of blood was forbidden. Later at Sinai with the giving of the Law, this was written into Law. So the idea of blood being something not eaten had been around for a long time and known by his followers.

This idea of drinking his blood and eating his flesh seems almost like *"over kill"*. For it seems that the same idea of belief in Jesus and that he was the good shepherd who gave his life for his sheep still works without this. The drinking of blood and eating of flesh idea almost seems gory in comparison. In other words, it did not seem necessary at all, even if only as a metaphor. What did David have to say regarding this topic?

Psalms 16:1-5, (1) Michtam of David. Keep me, O God; for I have taken refuge in Thee. (2) I have said unto YHWH: 'Thou art my Lord; I have no good but in Thee'; (3) As for the holy that are in the earth, they are the excellent in whom is all my delight. (4) <u>Let the idols of them be multiplied that</u> <u>make suit unto another; their drink-offerings of blood will I not offer, nor take their names upon my</u> <u>lips.</u> (5) O YHWH, the portion of mine inheritance and of my cup, Thou maintainest my lot.

'THE LAW AND THAT PROPHET'

YHWH stated on several occasions that he will "*try*" Israel to see if they are keeping HIS Law, and if they really fear their GOD. For the Law *is* Israel's protection, even against false prophets. For in **keeping** GOD'S Law, they are living GOD'S Law. By living GOD'S Law, Israel will not be fooled by a false Prophet, no matter how convincing he is. This was the challenge of Jesus.

The Book of Deuteronomy Chapter 13 quoted before can be summed up with, "*for YHWH your God putteth you to proof, to know whether ye do love YHWH your God with all your heart and with all your soul. After YHWH your God shall ye <u>walk,</u> and Him shall ye <u>fear,</u> and His Commandments shall ye <u>keep,</u> and unto His voice shall ye <u>hearken,</u> and Him shall ye <u>serve,</u> and unto Him shall ye <u>cleave</u>*". Any deviation from HIS Law is known by GOD.

Israel needed to be very careful because there were so many *"prophets", "false prophets", "seers", "dreamers",* those possessed by demons and just plain lunatics about. As has been said, a Jew could not just go home and enter his reference library, or pick out the family bible and see if Jesus met the criteria for a *"regular prophet"* or was a *"false prophet",* or just one of the many crazy *"lunes"* walking about according to what was written on their Safer Torah scroll. They had to either recall all of their learning, or rely on their religious leaders to help them understand. But they had to believe from their *teachers* that what they were hearing was the truth, without an *agenda.*

But with so many conflicting opinions, this became increasingly difficult to do as the Priests were no longer the only source of information and the Pharisees grew stronger and were much more accessible to the average person. The Law was something the people relied on but it was often illusive.

Herein is the problem with the *"rabbis"* (Pharisees), who were little more than secular Jews who thought of themselves as being more *"righteous"* than the ordinary Jew on the street. They looked on themselves as being more pious than the rest of Israel, even challenging the Temple Priests many of who were corrupt. One example of just how sick the Temple Priests were, during the trial of Jesus when he was before Pilate (John 19:15) they yelled *"We have no king but Caesar".* For a Priest of GOD YHWH to utter such a thing is incomprehensible. Regardless, the Pharisees were still but novices.

'WHICH HE SHALL SPEAK IN MY NAME'

There is yet one other scripture which deals with adding or taking away from the Safer Torah. The scripture speaks of GOD sending a Prophet to Israel who will speak *"in the name of YHWH".*

Deuteronomy 18:15-22, (15) <u>*A prophet will YHWH thy God raise up unto thee, from the midst of*</u> <u>*thee, of thy brethren, like unto me; unto him ye shall hearken;*</u> *(16) according to all that thou didst desire of YHWH thy God in Horeb in the day of the assembly, saying: 'Let me not hear again the voice of YHWH my God, neither let me see this great fire any more, that I die not.' (17) And YHWH said unto me: 'They have well said that which they have spoken. (18) I* <u>*will raise them up a prophet*</u> <u>*from among their brethren,*</u> *like unto thee; and I will put* <u>*MY WORDS*</u> *in his mouth, and he shall speak unto them all that I shall command him. (19)* <u>*And it shall come to pass, that whosoever will*</u> <u>*not hearken unto My words which he shall speak in MY NAME, I will require it of him.*</u> *(20) But the prophet, that shall speak a word presumptuously in* <u>*MY NAME,*</u> *which I have not commanded him to speak, or that shall speak* <u>*IN THE NAME OF OTHER, gods, that same prophet shall die.*</u> *' (21) And if thou say in thy heart: 'How shall we know the word which YHWH hath not spoken?' (22)* <u>*When a prophet speaketh IN THE NAME OF YHWH,*</u> *if the thing follow not, nor come to pass, that is the thing which YHWH hath not spoken; the prophet hath spoken it presumptuously, thou shalt not be afraid of him.*

Jesus seemed to always speak in his own name, but also saying at the same time that he and his words were the same as the *"Father"* and he was *"one"*, as with the *"Father"*. This idea is discussed more in detail elsewhere, but the question here is, did Jesus speak *"in the name of YHWH"* by actually uttering YHWH'S name? This issue cannot be emphasized enough. For it goes to the very heart of the entire ministry of Jesus, the name of **"YHWH"**.

Connected with this is the idea that GOD said that a false prophet would die. Jesus died, but it is written that he prophesied his own death. Again, this is yet another example of one of those gray areas. Was he a false prophet who GOD made sure was killed? If a false prophet, it was very convenient for him to die. Or was he a real prophet who went too far and became *"false"?*

Jesus was accused of blasphemy because he said that he was the son of GOD. As discussed, Jesus *was* the son of GOD as are all of the circumcised male SEED descendants of Abraham through Jacob. For it is written in TaNaKh, *"I said: Ye are godlike beings, and all of you sons of the Most High" (Psalm 82:6).* Again, had the rabbis known the Law of Moses, they would never have accuse Jesus of this, but something else they could defend.

Jesus was a son of Israel. As a son of Israel, Jesus, as was all of Israel's circumcised sons, a son of GOD. For Israel is YHWH'S *"first born son"*.

The Christian Bible is often wanting when it comes to details regarding the Laws which were in dispute between the rabbis and Jesus. Jesus appeared to be more often correct than were the rabbis. This *"son of GOD"* discussion was an easy *"win"* for Jesus in his continual *"one-on-one"* with the rabbis. Where the narrative becomes a bit more tricky is when Jesus starts talking about he and the *"Father"* being *"one"*, *"my"* commandments, the *"Fathers"* commandments, *seeing* Jesus is the same as *seeing* the Father etc. Jesus told the Samaritan woman that he was the *"messiah"*. There's no written evidence that Jesus ever corrected his followers when they called him *Lord* and *God.* It may have been all of these references together that the rabbis had in mind.

Much more serious however, was the idea of <u>*in whose name*</u> was Jesus preaching? YHWH had said that he would send Israel a prophet from amongst their own brethren who would speak to them <u>*in HIS*</u> <u>*name*</u>. In Chapter Seven this idea is gone more into depth. But a short discussion is, that Jesus did not appear to be preaching in the name of *"YHWH"*. He seems to be careful to mention the *"Father"* often and saying that he is speaking <u>*for*</u> the Father. He speaks of how they are the same, *"one"* etc., but from the Gospels, Jesus does not appear to have uttered the actual name of GOD his Father, not even once. Was Jesus breaking the Law in this?

Having said this and after researching the Greek Gospels, the Greek translation may have translated "*YHWH*" if it existed in the Hebrew or Aramaic, as "*Lord*" which may not be all of that surprising as they did just this very thing in their translation of the "*Shema*". They did translate "*YHWH*" as "*Lord*". Although in another sense, one might think that a more literal translation of GOD'S holy name would have been more forthcoming, even by these Greek translators. There does not seem to be any evidence that this was the case. If YHWH was ever uttered by Jesus it may remain a secret.

Another point worth mentioning, is that during the life time of Jesus, and for the next generation, the Temple still stood, the name of YHWH would still have been common knowledge and at least by the priests, would have still been uttered. At least until 70 C.E. If the original Semitic language that the Gospels were written in (assuming this was the case) used the name of GOD "*YHWH*", it is almost inconceivable that "*Lord*" or "*my Lord*" would have been substituted at that time by Jewish believers or even by the Greeks.

If however, the Gospels were originally written in Greek, which is at least a possibility, and the name of YHWH was not used, then this may be an even stronger indication that Jesus did not utter the name "*YHWH*" when he was teaching. This would be so, at least if the scribes of the Greek Gospels were not translating "*YHWH*" as "*my Lord*" even at that early period. However having said this, most scholars seem to agree that the Gospels were originally written not in Greek but most likely in Aramaic or possibly the two. If Jesus did utter YHWH'S holy name, there is no written record of it anywhere.

As the ban by the rabbis forbidding the pronunciation of GOD'S name did not occur until approximately sometime in the second century C.E., The Gospels may well have had the name of GOD <u>YHWH</u> written in an original text which was not translated into the Greek, if Greek as has been discussed was not it's original language. The Greeks would not have been sensitive to the "*name*".

The rabbis were still playing only "*second banana*" to the priests as the religious authority, and the rabbinic edict to ban the name of YHWH would hardly have existed this early while the Temple still stood and it's priests existed. Thus, it seems correct if Jesus was preaching or prophesying in the name of YHWH, it would in all likelihood have been written down as such.

According to most historians, the Gospels were all written within the first century C.E. This being said, even though the Gospels were not written until long after the events of Jesus, it would seem that had Jesus called on or spoke in the name of "*YHWH*" it would have been recorded somewhere as such.

So the bottom line is the question, was the teaching and preaching of Jesus and was his prophesying done in the "*name*" of YHWH? There is mention of the "*name*" of GOD, but nowhere does it seem to have actually been uttered, emphasized, written, spoken or said.

Mark 11:9, (9) And they that went before, and they that followed, cried, saying, Hosanna; Blessed is he that cometh <u>in the name of the Lord</u>:

What were these people actually saying? Was <u>*Lord*</u> really <u>*YHWH.*</u> The Greek translation renders <u>*Lord.*</u> But this may or may not be what they really uttered.

Now, for today's Christian, this may seem a trivial point. But it goes to the very heart of the ministry of

Jesus. If Jesus was preaching, teaching and prophesying in the name of YHWH by the Law, even if a false prophet, this is one thing. When *"in the name of YHWH"*, means literally, as saying *"thus saith YHWH"* or even a variation of it. But if he was doing all of these things *only* in his own name, it is an altogether different matter. Some may say that this is a distinction without a difference. But not according to the Law.

SABBATH

Matthew 12:1-14, [1] At that time Jesus went on <u>the Sabbath day</u> through the corn; and his disciples were an hungred, and began to <u>pluck the ears of corn, and to eat</u>. (2) But when the Pharisees saw it, they said unto him, Behold, thy disciples do that which is not lawful to do upon the Sabbath day. (3) But he said unto them, <u>Have ye not read what David did, when he was an hungred, and they that were with him; (4) How he entered into the House of God, and did eat the shewbread, which was not lawful for him to eat, neither for them which were with him, but only for the priests?</u> (5) Or have ye not read in the Law, how that on the Sabbath days the priests in the Temple profane the Sabbath, and are blameless? (6) But I say unto you, That in this place is one greater than the Temple. (7) But if ye had known what this meaneth, I will have mercy, and not sacrifice, ye would not have condemned the guiltless. (8) <u>For the Son of man is Lord even of the sabbath day</u>. (9)And when he was departed thence, he went into their synagogue: (10) And, behold, there was a man which had his hand withered. And they asked him, saying, <u>Is it lawful to heal on the Sabbath days</u>? that they might accuse him. (11) And he said unto them, <u>What man shall there be among you, that shall have one sheep, and if it fall into a pit on the Sabbath day, will he not lay hold on it, and lift it out?</u> (12) How much then is a man better than a sheep? <u>Wherefore it is lawful to do well on the Sabbath days</u>. (13) Then saith he to the man, Stretch forth thine hand. And he stretched it forth; and it was restored whole, like as the other. (14) <u>Then the Pharisees went out, and held a council against him, how they might destroy him.</u>

Along with just about every other statute regarding the Law it seems, Jesus was accused of desecrating the ordinances concerning the Sabbath.

Jesus appears to be equating *circumcision* with *healing* on *Shabbat*. They are both holy. Also, Jesus seems to be saying that just as a male child on the eighth day is to be circumcised so the Law of Moses is not *broken,* so is it within the Law to heal that which is *broken* on the Sabbath. It is interesting on another level too as he appears to be saying that an uncircumcised male child is in a sense not *"whole"* until circumcised. If so, this is an interesting concept. But on a purely legalistic level, Jesus changed the subject, taking their attention away from what his men were doing which was *"plucking"* barley corn.

What does the Law say concerning the *"Sabbath"?*

First off, we know that *"Shabbat"* is a *"holy"* day, YHWH *"hallowed it"*.

Genesis 2:1-3, (1) And the heaven and the earth were finished, and all the host of them. (2) And on the seventh day God finished His work which He had made; and <u>He rested on the seventh day</u> from all His work which He had made. (3) <u>And God blessed the seventh day, and hallowed it</u>; because that in it <u>He rested from all His work</u> which God in creating had made.

MEAT AND BREAD

According to the Safer Torah, on the fifteenth day of the second month after leaving Egypt, the sons of Israel "*murmured*" against YHWH, as they did not like the feeding arrangements. So YHWH told Moses and Aaron to prepare the people for what HE was going to do. YHWH was going to begin feeding them meat *(quail)* every evening and bread *(manna)* every morning. From the beginning of this *"feeding"*, they were to count the days. And by this counting of the days, the *six week days* were established, and by extension, the seventh day of rest became "*official*" for Israel, as their Sabbath called "*Shabbat*" putting it in sync with YHWH'S hallowed day. They were told not to gather the manna or quail on the "*seventh*" day, but gather twice as much on the sixth day. The "*seventh*" day was the day of rest. And the "*seventh*" day of rest has continued thereafter for the next 3,500 years until today.

Exodus 16:4-5, (4) Then said YHWH unto Moses: 'Behold, I will cause to rain bread from heaven for you; and the people shall go out and gather a day's portion every day, that I may prove them, whether they will walk in My law, or not. (5) And it shall come to pass on the sixth day that they shall prepare that which they bring in, and it shall be twice as much as they gather daily.'

YHWH fed Israel "*quail*" in the evening and "*'manna*" in the morning for six days. They were told to gather twice as much on the sixth day, as the next day was the "*Sabbath*", there would be no quail or bread and no "*gathering*".

Exodus 16:22-23, (22) (22) And it came to pass that on the sixth day they gathered twice as much bread, two omers for each one; and all the rulers of the congregation came and told Moses (23) And he said unto them: 'This is that which YHWH hath spoken: To-morrow is a solemn rest, a Holy Sabbath unto YHWH........'

This marked the beginning of the counting of the Hebrew "*Shabbat*", until this very day. For just as the *"first month"*, of the Hebrew year had it's start (Exodus 12:1-2) with Pesach, so did the official counting of the six days of the week leading up to Shabbat have a beginning for Israel. The quail and the heavenly bread continued for the next forty years of wandering in the desert.

A person once asked how do we know that *"Shabbat"* is *"Shabbat"?* We know because it has been observed by Israel and by the Jewish people since it was first instituted by YHWH during the desert wandering of Israel, approximately 3,500 years ago. During the worst of times while scattered to the four corners of the earth in exile, and during the best of times, it has continued unabated since GOD sent heavenly food in the desert to feed Israel, many, many generations ago. In addition, the rest of the world adopted the seven day week as well. Although almost no Gentiles and very few Jews could tell how, where or when the seven day week was first observed or why it began or for that matter, when the first month on the Hebrew year is.

The *quail* and *manna* continued forty years until that entire generation had died out, but for Joshua and Caleb, until Israel had crossed into the promised land, were circumcised and celebrated their first Passover *in the land*.

Joshua 4:19, (19) And the people came up out of the Jordan on the tenth day of the first month, and encamped in Gilgal, on the east border of Jericho.

Joshua 5:2, (2) At that time YHWH said unto Joshua: 'Make thee knives of flint, and circumcise again the sons of Israel the second time.'

It is interesting to note, that Israel crossed the Jordan into Canaan on the tenth day of the first month of the year, the day when the pascal lamb is separated out in preparation for Pesach (Exodus 12:1-6), then after the crossing, all of Israel was circumcised. Then on the fourteenth day of the month, the first Pesach was celebrated in the promised land. Israel began eating the produce of the land and immediately the quail and the bread ceased from GOD.

Joshua 5:10-12, (10) And the sons of Israel encamped in Gilgal; <u>and they kept the passover on the</u> *<u>fourteenth day of the month</u> at even in the plains of Jericho. (11) <u>And they did eat of the produce of</u>* *<u>the land on the morrow after the passover,</u> unleavened cakes and parched corn, in the selfsame day.* *(12) <u>And the manna ceased on the morrow,</u> after they had eaten of the produce of the land; neither* *had the sons of Israel manna any more; but they did eat of the fruit of the land of Canaan that year.*

So far, we know that Shabbat is a holy day, and that the gathering food on this day is forbidden. Does this mean that if one picks an ear of corn to put to his mouth to eat, that he is *"gathering"*, if it is on Shabbat?

If he is eating it straight away, does it matter if he picked it up off of his table, or from the corn stalk itself? Once again, as with other stories in the Gospels, this one seems to cut close to the edge. Were the followers of Jesus desecrating the Sabbath by picking ears of *"corn"* in the field to eat? Or were they doing something altogether different and were *"gathering"* it.

A quick analysis of Matthew12:1 might help one arrive at an answer.

Matthew 12:1-2, (1) At that time Jesus went on <u>the Sabbath day</u> through the corn; and his disciples *were an hungred, and began to <u>pluck the ears of corn, and to eat.</u> (2) But when the Pharisees saw it,* *they said unto him, Behold, thy disciples do that which is not lawful to do upon the Sabbath day*

The disciples of Jesus were not picking a couple of ears of *"corn"* to eat, as in *"corn on the cob"*. In other words, they were not eating *"maze"*. For *"corn"* or *"maze"* was a *"new world"* crop which did not exist in Israel 2,000 years ago. During the time of Jesus, *"corn"* only existed in the Americas. The followers of Jesus were picking *"barley corn"* which did exist in Israel. Barley corn grows in the field on a stalk similar to wheat and is very small.

In order to get enough barley *"corn"* to satisfy one's appetite, a large amount of barley corn would have been necessary as the *"ears"* were about the size of the end of a sharpened pencil. Thus, it would have been necessary for the disciples to pick a quantity of barley corn from the stalks. So, unlike picking an ear or two of *"maze"* corn to eat, his followers were picking *allot* of barley corn. Feeding on barley corn would have been very *"labor intensive"*.

The question arises, as there are so few details, were his men walking through the field and just raking their hands across the stalks as they crossed the field, and eating as they went? Or were they stopped in one area of the field *"pigging out"*? Does it really make a difference?

It did seem to matter to the rabbis. So in this respect, the disciples of Jesus did appear to be desecrating the Sabbath by *"gathering"*, especially in the eyes of the Pharisees. Jesus changed the subject to David eating the *"show bread"* while on the run from King Saul. But the question still remains unanswered and is important. By all accounts, his followers did appear to have violated the Law of the Sabbath. And as far as David and the *"show bread"* goes, this was an entirely different situation, completely different than the followers of Jesus *"plucking"* barley corn from a field on Shabbat.

Exodus 16:25-29, (25) And Moses said: 'Eat that to-day; for to-day is a <u>Sabbath</u> unto YHWH; to-day *ye shall not find it in the field. (26) <u>Six days ye shall gather it</u>; but on the <u>seventh</u> day is the <u>Sabbath</u>,* *in it there shall be none.' (27) And it came to pass on the <u>seventh</u> day, that there went out some of* *the people to <u>gather</u>, and they found none. (28) And YHWH said unto Moses: 'How long refuse ye to* *keep My Commandments and My Laws? (29) <u>See that YHWH hath given you the Sabbath; therefore</u>* *<u>He giveth you on the sixth day the bread of two days; abide ye every man in his place, let no man go</u>*

out of his place on the seventh day.'

What is the Law of Shabbat?

Exodus 20:8-11, (8) Remember the Sabbath day, to keep it holy. (9) Six days shalt thou labour, and do all thy work; (10) but the seventh day is a Sabbath unto YHWH thy God, in it thou shalt not do any manner of work, thou, nor thy son, nor thy daughter, nor thy man-servant, nor thy maid-servant, nor thy cattle, nor thy stranger that is within thy gates; (11) for in six days YHWH made heaven and earth, the sea, and all that in them is, and rested on the seventh day; wherefore YHWH blessed the Sabbath day, and hallowed it.

Work is forbidden on Shabbat. Here, the rabbis appear to have been right.

Whether the followers of Jesus were *"working"* when they picked the barley corn, is a matter of interpretation, but it certainly appears that they were.

We also know that *"profaning"* the Sabbath was punishable by *"death",* and being *"cut off"* from Israel. So it would have been an extremely serious offense for Jesus and his men to be charged with profaning the Sabbath.

Exodus 31:14-17, (14) Ye shall keep the Sabbath therefore, for it is holy unto you; every one that profaneth it shall surely be put to death; for whosoever doeth any work therein, that soul shall be cut off from among his people. (15) Six days shall work be done; but on the seventh day is a Sabbath of solemn rest, holy to YHWH; whosoever doeth any work in the Sabbath day, he shall surely be put to death. (16) Wherefore the sons of Israel shall keep the Sabbath, to observe the Sabbath throughout their generations, for a Perpetual Covenant. (17) It is a Sign between Me and the sons of Israel For Ever; for in six days YHWH made heaven and earth, and on the seventh day He ceased from work and rested.'

So we find out a few more things about Shabbat. Aside from a person of Israel being *"put to death"* and being *"cut off"* from Israel if it is *"profaned"* by them, Shabbat is an *eternal "sign",* a *"perpetual Covenant"* between YHWH and Israel. It is *"for ever".* It is *"everlasting."* It is *"eternal".* The Greek copy of the Hebrew Bible had been around already for 300 years by the time of Jesus, so claiming ignorance of this fact by any of his Jewish followers or the Greeks is a weak argument. One might think that Christians would be interested in this piece of news regarding YHWH'S Holy Sabbath.

There is even more about Shabbat, as YHWH speaks to Moses and explains to him how *by keeping the "sign" of the Sabbath, Israel will know that it is YHWH who "sanctifies" Israel.* In other words, by Israel keeping the Sabbath of GOD, Israel will understand that it is YHWH who makes them *"holy",* for Israel is a holy people to YHWH. For as YHWH is holy, HIS people must be holy. Israel is sanctified, set aside, made holy, as the holy portion of GOD, HIS inheritance. It is YHWH who *sanctifies* Israel. Israel must keep Shabbat.

YHWH separated out the nations and set their boundaries, but Israel HE kept for HIMSELF. Israel is YHWH'S people, HIS inheritance, HIS holy portion.

Deuteronomy 32:7-9, (7) Remember the days of old, consider the years of many generations; ask thy father, and he will declare unto thee, thine elders, and they will tell thee. (8) When the Most High gave to the nations their inheritance, when He separated the children of men, He set the borders of the peoples according to the number of the sons of Israel. (9) For the portion of YHWH is His people, Jacob the lot of His inheritance.

To paraphrase an old Jewish saying, *'More than the Jews keep Shabbat, Shabbat has kept the Jews'.*

WHAT IS WORK?

What does the Law say? Were the followers of Jesus *"working"* on GOD'S Sabbath when they *"plucked"* the barley corn from the sheaves on the stalk?

Exodus 35:2-3, (2) Six days shall work be done, but on the seventh day there shall be to you a holy day, a Sabbath of solemn rest to YHWH; whosoever doeth any work therein shall be put to death. (3) Ye shall kindle no fire throughout your habitations upon the Sabbath day.'

We learn that a person of Israel is forbidden to *"kindle"* a fire on Shabbat.

There is not allot of detail regarding Sabbath and what constitutes *"work"*. But there are a few examples of where people were caught on Shabbat doing something which constituted *"work"*. Is *"gathering"* considered *"work"*.

Numbers 15:32-36, (32) And while the sons of Israel were in the wilderness, they found a man gathering sticks upon the Sabbath day. (33) And they that found him gathering sticks brought him unto Moses and Aaron, and unto all the congregation. (34) And they put him in ward, because it had not been declared what should be done to him. (35) And YHWH said unto Moses: 'The man shall surely be put to death; all the congregation shall stone him with stones without the camp.' (36) And all the congregation brought him without the camp, and stoned him with stones, and he died, as YHWH commanded Moses.

We learn that along with the *"kindling"* of a fire mentioned in the other example, the *"gathering"* of sticks too is a form of *"work"* forbidden on Shabbat. This idea of *"gathering"*, was what the followers of Jesus were charged. Even though the story of gathering sticks for a fire is different, it is the act of *"gathering"* itself that violates the Sabbath.

One needs to have a bit of an imagination to understand just how labor intensive building a fire would have been in a desert, amongst hundreds of thousands of other people, 3,500 years ago. Without matches, liquid fuel or other modern conveniences, it took allot of *"work"* to build a fire not even including finding the material to burn. One such *"work"* would have been finding enough of dry *"anything"* to burn amongst several hundreds of thousands of other people doing the same. And in the desert. Therefore, the *"gathering"* alone was not such a simple thing. It took considerable effort.

As they were in the desert where aside from the competition to find material which would have been steep, there just was not that much burnable material to begin with. Their search would take them increasingly farther from camp.

This idea of *"gathering"* needs to be recalled when the conversation between Jesus and the people was taking place regarding the *"corn"* gathering incident. The real problem with this incident as mentioned, was were they really *"gathering"* to take with them as in *"harvesting"*, or were they just eating. If they were just eating, then it becomes a question of, what is the difference in eating barley corn from the sheaves of a stalk and eating from a plate, if eating, not *"gathering / harvesting"* is what your *"intention"* is. Does intent matter? It is not so clear. All we have to go by is the story in the Gospels which creates as many questions as it leaves answers. Either way, his followers would have needed to *"pluck"* from allot of stalks, and glean the barley corn from many sheaves to make a meal. And herein lies the *"work"*.

Returning to the idea of gathering sticks for a fire, the *"gathering"* of sticks is but one part of what is necessary to *"kindle a fire"*. It does not even include what it must have taken to actually *"kindle"* a fire using sticks, flint rock, twine and balls of easily burnable *"starter"* to get it going. So it does not take much imagination to see just how much *"work"* was involved in having a fire. One could hardly have spent allot of time *"resting"* on Shabbat, while trying to either maintain an existing fire or while doing all of the different tasks necessary to building one from scratch.

GATHER - GLEAN - PICK - PLUCK

With the instructions given at the time of the quail and bread *"gathering"* was a Hebrew word which meant literally to *"gather"*, to *"glean"* to *"pick"* or *"pluck"* as in a field of harvest as with grapes or even stones. It has more of a commercial type connotation. The word used referring to the man who was caught *"gathering"* sticks on Shabbat, was a Hebrew word which specifically means *"gathering stubble"*. They are different words, but create the same kind of outcome. They are both considered *"profaning"* the Sabbath if done on Shabbat, and require the death penalty. Were Jesus and his followers *"profaning"*the Sabbath by picking raw barley corn off of the stalks to eat? It is hard to know exactly, but the evidence seems against them.

One other thing, had Jesus taught his disciples that it was OK to *pluck* the barley corn on Shabbat? Was Jesus only responding to the Pharisees, or had he also been teaching that their *plucking* was not in violation of YHWH'S Sabbath in responding to his followers questions? Did Jesus at any time *rebuke* his followers for *plucking* barley corn on Sabbath? It is one thing to violate the Sabbath yourself and desecrate GOD'S holy day, but an even more serious offense would have occurred if he was teaching his followers to do so as well. Surely the question arose. But there is neither record of his teaching or their asking this nor of his having rebuked them for doing so.

Jesus seemed to have addressed this very idea regarding keeping or breaking commandments and teaching others to do so.

Matthew 5:19 (19) Whosoever therefore shall break one of these least Commandments, <u>and shall teach men so</u>, he shall be called the least in the kingdom of heaven: but whosoever shall <u>do and teach</u> them, the same shall be called great in the kingdom of heaven.

'MY COVENANT SHALL BE IN YOUR FLESH'

One other thing is the Law regarding circumcision, as was mentioned by Jesus to defend himself when approached regarding keeping the Sabbath. Part of the discussion was concerning circumcision on Shabbat. The Law is very clear what Israel is to do on the eighth day of a male born to Israel.

CIRCUMCISION

Genesis 17:9-12, (9) And God said unto Abraham: 'And as for thee, thou shalt keep My Covenant, thou, and thy SEED after thee throughout their generations. (10) This is My Covenant, which ye shall keep, between Me and you and thy SEED after thee: every male among you shall be Circumcised. (11) And ye shall be Circumcised in the flesh of your foreskin; <u>and it shall be a token of a Covenant betwixt Me and you.</u> (12) <u>And he that is eight days old shall be Circumcised among you, every male throughout your generations,</u> he that is born in the house, or bought with money of any foreigner, that is not of thy SEED.

But there is a warning to Israel about the SEED Covenant of circumcision. It continues.

Genesis 17:13-14, (13) He that is born in thy house, and he that is bought with thy money, must needs be circumcised; and My Covenant shall be in your flesh for an everlasting Covenant. (14) <u>And the uncircumcised male who is not circumcised in the flesh of his foreskin, that soul shall be cut off from his people; he hath broken My covenant.</u>'

Leviticus 12:1-4, (1) And YHWH spoke unto Moses, saying: (2) Speak unto the sons of Israel, saying: If a woman be delivered, and bear a <u>man-child</u>, then she shall be unclean seven days; as in the days of the impurity of her sickness shall she be unclean. (3) <u>And in the eighth day the flesh of his foreskin shall be Circumcised.</u> (4) And she shall continue in the blood of purification three and thirty days; she shall touch no hallowed thing, nor come into the sanctuary, until the days of her purification be fulfilled.

If Jesus had being challenged on whether or not to circumcise on Shabbat, according to the Law there are no allowances for whether or not to circumcise on the eighth day if it falls on Shabbat. On the eighth day after birth, a male child is to be circumcised. Surely GOD knew before HE made the Law that sons born to Israel would need to be circumcised on Shabbat, as the eighth day after birth for many would surely fall on this holy day.

Likewise, YHWH would have known that man would be in situations where an act, or acts of *"healing"* would have to be performed on Shabbat. If a child falls down and hurts his head so that he is bleeding, and it is Shabbat, a parent would not hesitate to clean and to bandage the wound. This seemed to be what Jesus was alluding to. Today, even the rabbis themselves agree that it is permissible to save a life on Shabbat. In Matthew Chapter 12, Jesus seemed to be equating circumcision on Shabbat to healing. Both of these events, according to what he seemed to be saying, makes a person *"whole"*.

Mark 3:4 (4) And he saith unto them, <u>Is it lawful to do good on the Sabbath days, or to do evil? to save life, or to kill?</u> But they held their peace.

Luke 6:9, (9) Then said Jesus unto them, I will ask you one thing; <u>Is it lawful on the Sabbath days to do good, or to do evil? to save life, or to destroy it?</u>

'THEN CAME DAVID TO NOB'

As Jesus often seemed to do, he would have the rabbis comparing apples and oranges by changing the subject. When the Pharisees approached Jesus and his followers about *"plucking"* on the Sabbath, he very adeptly changed the subject to King David eating the *"show bread"*. These two situations were entirely different. The story regarding David and his men eating the *"show bread"* is not exactly accurate in the Gospels according to the story in First Samuel itself. So, what exactly did happen with David in this story?

Matthew 12:3-4, (3) But he said unto them, Have ye not read what David did, when he was ahungered, and they that were with him; (4) How he entered into the <u>House of God</u>, and did eat the shewbread, which was not lawful for him to eat, neither for them which were with him, but only for the priests?

I Samuel 21:1-7. (1) And he arose and departed; and Jonathan went into the city. (2) <u>Then came David to Nob to Ahimelech the priest;</u> and Ahimelech came to meet David trembling, and said unto him: 'Why art thou alone, and no man with thee?' (3) And David said unto Ahimelech the priest: 'The king hath commanded me a business, and hath said unto me: Let no man know any thing of *the business whereabout I send thee, and what I have commanded thee; and the young men have I appointed to such and such a place. (4) Now therefore what is under thy hand? five loaves of bread? give them in my hand, or whatsoever there is present.' (5) And the priest answered David, and said: 'There is no common bread under my hand, but there is holy bread; if only the young men have kept themselves from women.' (6) And David answered the priest, and said unto him: 'Of a truth women have been kept from us about these three days; when I came out, the vessels of the young men were holy, though it was but a common journey; how much more then to-day, when there shall be holy bread in their vessels?' (7) So the priest gave him holy bread; for there was no bread there but the showbread, that was taken from before YHWH, to put hot bread in the day when it was taken away.*

In Matthew Chapter 12, Jesus is quoted as saying that David went into the House of GOD and ate the *"showbread"*. David was not in the House of GOD, but in a priestly city called *"Nob"*. It appears to have been one of the Priestly cities assigned to them located somewhere north of Jerusalem in the tribal territory of Benjamin. The bread in question was *"holy bread"* taken from the Temple of YHWH after having been replaced with fresh bread. This was done on a regular basis every Sabbath. The *"show bread"* which was removed, the Priests of YHWH were then allowed to eat, *"in a holy place"*.

The *"showbread"* was the responsibility of the *"sons of Kohath"*, who were descendants of the second son of Levi, to have the bread continually remain on the *"Table of Showbread"* before YHWH in his Temple.

Leviticus 24:5-9, (5) And thou shalt take fine flour, and bake twelve cakes thereof: two tenth parts of an ephah shall be in one cake. (6) And thou shalt set them in two rows, six in a row, upon the pure table before YHWH. (7) And thou shalt put pure frankincense with each row, that it may be to the bread for a memorial-part, even an offering made by fire unto YHWH. (8) Every Sabbath day he shall set it in order before YHWH continually; it is from the Sons of Israel, an Everlasting Ccovenant. (9) And it shall be for Aaron and his Sons; and they shall eat it in a holy place; for it is most holy unto him of the offerings of YHWH made by fire, a perpetual due.'

The change of subject by Jesus from his *"corn pluckers"*, to David eating the *"showbread"* seems to be more of Jesus redirecting (or misdirecting) the Pharisees attention away from his followers and what they were doing, than any connection to David. Does Nob being a priestly city mean that it is a *"holy place"*? Does it qualify as a *"holy place"* to eat the *"holy bread"*? In other words, what was the holy bread doing their in the first place, unless the priestly cities took on an amount of "*holiness*" which allowed them to eat *"holy bread"* away from the Temple of YHWH in Jerusalem where it had been placed before YHWH? But *"holy place"* was not a designation assigned to the priestly cities. "*And it shall be for Aaron and his Sons; and they shall eat it in a Holy Place; for it is most holy unto him of the offerings of YHWH made by fire, a perpetual due".*

'AND THEY SHALL EAT IT IN A HOLY PLACE'

The question then arises, were the priests suppose to have eaten the holy bread within the Temple of YHWH sanctuary in Jerusalem? Or could they eat it in a priestly city *"And Nob, the city of the priests"*? If so and the bread was taken to Nob, does it lose it's holiness not being in GOD'S sanctuary? And therefore, for David and his men, who according to the story were "*sanctified*", therefore eating the bread was not a problem for YHWH? The Safer Torah does not state Levite cities were **holy**, only they were given the cities as their possession. Even the *six cities of refuge* were not called **holy**.

Was Nob considered a holy place for priests to eat *"holy bread"*? Was Jesus purposely misquoting scripture to see if they would catch him? David did not enter the Temple of YHWH. David was not even in Jerusalem when this incident occurred. And there is no indication that *"Nob"* was *"holy"*. In addition, the city of *"Nob"* is not listed as one of the 48 cities set aside for the Levites or as one of the six Cities of Refuge, but is only listed in the story of David and the holy bread, and as one of the cities of Benjamin. It could be that one of the Levite cities was also called by another name (Almon?), or possibly one of the original Levite cities no longer existed (Almon?) and Nob became a replacement. The Levite city of Almon is mentioned but once in all of TaNaKh. Most texts clearly show Nob as a city associated with the tribe of Benjamin and the cities of Gibeon, Ramah, Geba, Anathoth and *Almon*.

For sure, the priest Ahimelech was intimidated by seeing David and his men appear suddenly from out of no where. He may only have offered the holy bread for this reason, knowing that it was bread which was off limits to the general population of Israel to eat. Nevertheless, for the son-in-law of King Saul and one of the chief captains of the host of Israel, the bread was offered by the Priest after being convinced that the men had not been with women and were sanctified. But even still, was this act *"kosher"*?

BLASPHEMY

When looking at the discussion between Jesus, the Priests and the Pharisees, it becomes clear soon enough that the these two opposing groups had at least one thing in common although their many differences remained. The Pharisees who were constantly confronting Jesus throughout most of his ministry seemed mainly interested in the minutia of the Law. Their constant conflict with Jesus was much more over the interpretation of the Ordinances, Statutes and Commandments of the Law. Whereas the Priests appeared only interested in who Jesus was. Was he a *"blasphemer"*? Who was Jesus as he relates to the idea of *"blasphemy"*? Did he desecrate the name of GOD?

Hosea 11:1, (1) When Israel was a child, then I loved him, <u>and out of Egypt I called My son.</u>

If Israel is called *"My son"*, how is Jesus, a son of Israel, the son of GOD, a blasphemer? For YHWH is the Father of Israel, the Rock from which Israel is hewn. If Jesus was condemned because he said he was a son of GOD, then he was innocent, as Israel is the son of GOD, *"My first born"*. If Jesus was condemned because he said he was the *"messiah"*, then that was a different issue. Additionally, if the Priests condemned Jesus to death because he said there was no difference between himself and GOD, then they would no doubt have had grounds to pass the death sentence as it existed. And the words attributed to Jesus seem to indicate that this is what he was saying.

John 14:9-11, (9).......<u>he that hath seen me hath seen the father</u>, and how sayest thou, then Show us the Father? (10) Believest thou not that I am in the Father, and the Father in me? The words I speak unto you I speak not of myself: but the Father that dwelleth in me, he doeth the works (11) Believe me that I am in the Father, and the Father in me; <u>or else believe me for the very works sake</u>

Deuteronomy 32:6, 9, 18, (6) Do ye thus requite YHWH, O foolish people and unwise? <u>is not He thy Father that hath gotten thee?</u> hath He not made thee, and established thee?..... (9) For the portion of YHWH is <u>His people,</u> Jacob the lot of His inheritance.....(18) <u>Of the Rock that begot</u> thee thou wast unmindful, and didst forget God that bore thee.

The idea of whether Jesus was a false messiah or not seemed to be only part of the larger issue of blasphemy itself. This may be in part why the Temple Priests did not really enter into the picture until near the end of the life of Jesus. Before he became so popular, only the Pharisees noticed his doctrine and questioned him as they were mostly posturing. For sure the Priests would have been aware of

Jesus, but until issues of *"blasphemy"* became more prevalent, their interest seemed minimal. Only after Jesus became a huge issue did the Priests interest in Jesus pick up. They would have entered eventually regardless, because of their own status as religious authority.

However, not until Jesus appeared to be either a threat to their own authority, or possibly cause problems with the Romans, did the interest of the Priests rise and did they get involved. But most of their interest revolved around the question of *"blasphemy"*. For the words of Jesus about being *"one"* with the Father, *seeing* Jesus was *seeing* the Father, would have gotten much attention from the Priests, for they saw Jesus making himself the *same* as GOD.

John 10:33, (33) The Jews answered him, saying, For a good work we stone thee not; but for blasphemy; and because that thou, being a man, makest thyself God.

What the Priests and the Pharisees seemed to share in common was for the immediate demise of one said Jew named Jesus. As with *Pilate* and *Herod,* their mutual antipathy for Jesus seemed to give them common ground.

Luke 23:12, (12) And the same day Pilate and Herod were made friends together: for before they were at enmity between themselves.

As were Pilate and Herod Antipas who were brought together over the situation of one of their subjugated peoples in Jesus, so too, were the priests and the Pharisees in apparent agreement regarding their fellow Jew Jesus. They wanted him dead.

Mark 14:61-65 (61) But he held his peace, and answered nothing. Again the high priest asked him, and said unto him, Art thou the Christ, the Son of the Blessed? (62) And Jesus said, I am: and ye shall see the Son of man sitting on the right hand of power, and coming in the clouds of heaven. (63) Then the high priest rent his clothes, and saith, What need we any further witnesses? (64) Ye have heard the blasphemy: what think ye? And they all condemned him to be guilty of death. (65) And some began to spit on him, and to cover his face, and to buffet him, and to say unto him, Prophesy: and the servants did strike him with the palms of their hands.

In the Law of Moses, the act of blasphemy was punishable by death by stoning (Deuteronomy Chapter 13:1-12). Part of this scripture reads, *"And thou shalt stone him with stones, that he die; because he hath sought to draw thee away from YHWH thy God".*

Whether or not Jesus qualified to be stoned to death or not, the Priests believed that he had blasphemed GOD YHWH. And it is for this reason that they called for the Romans and insisted they administer the death sentence. It is not clear whether Israel was allowed to execute. Capitol punishment was administered by Rome. Jesus was crucified according to Roman Law. It does not appear that the Sanhedrin had the authority to administer the death sentence at this time although it appears that Pilate could have returned Jesus to the Priests for some type of punishment short of death. The Sanhedrin had found Jesus guilty of blasphemy which called for his death according to the Law of Moses. But Jesus was crucified according to Roman Law as *"King of the Jews".*

John 19:6 (6) When the chief priests therefore and officers saw him, they cried out, saying, Crucify him, crucify him. Pilate saith unto them, Take ye him, and crucify him: for I find no fault in him.

Jesus had been accused, amongst other things, of saying that he would or could destroy the Temple of

YHWH and rebuild it in three days (Mark 14:58). This alone was enough to get all of the attention of the Priests. Although Jesus was speaking of his own body, it was enough to freak out the Temple Priests. Jesus had to die. The priests main concern was the Temple of YHWH. The Priests were guardians of GOD'S holy Temple. For anyone to even hint at it's destruction would invite the full weight of their wrath.

Matthew 26:62-68 (62) And the high priest arose, and said unto him, Answerest thou nothing? what is it which these witness against thee? (63) But Jesus held his peace. And the high priest answered and said unto him, I adjure thee by the living God, that thou tell us whether thou be the Christ, the Son of God. (64) Jesus saith unto him, Thou hast said: nevertheless I say unto you, Hereafter shall ye see the Son of man sitting on the right hand of power, and coming in the clouds of heaven. (65) Then the high priest rent his clothes, saying, He hath spoken blasphemy; what further need have we of witnesses? behold, now ye have heard his blasphemy.(66) What think ye? They answered and said, He is guilty of death. (67) Then did they spit in his face, and buffeted him; and others smote him with the palms of their hands, (68) Saying, Prophesy unto us, thou Christ, Who is he that smote thee?

Many times throughout the history of Israel, the Levites fought to the death to protect the most holy site of YHWH GOD and the people of Israel. Long after the death of Jesus, it would be the Romans themselves whom the Levites would fight to the death on their Holy Temple Mount. Like killer bees in a hive fighting to protect the queen, the Priests and the Levitical ministers of the Temple of YHWH were extremely protective of all which was their GOD'S Temple and their own livelihood. Jesus was a threat to the priests. He was a threat on many different levels, not the least of which was their own authority over Israel as the guardians of the Holy of Holies.

Matthew 26:65 (65) Then the high priest rent his clothes, saying, He hath spoken blasphemy; what further need have we of witnesses? behold, now ye have heard his blasphemy.

The idea of blasphemy was of concern to the Pharisees as well, but for the Pharisees who saw themselves to be *"legal"* experts, professing to be guardians of the Law of Moses, it was more on a level of *"doctrine"* than blasphemy against GOD. They were lay people with no authority. Although they themselves had no idea what was written in the Safer Torah, their feelings were hurt by Jesus who was continually *"showing them up"* regarding the Law in their confrontations with him. They wanted revenge.

The Pharisees wanted him dead, but their reasons seemed to be less one of blasphemy against GOD and more regarding their own fragile *"egos"*. For Jesus put them to shame on more than one occasion. He had embarrassed them. Whether Jesus was always right or not is not the point. He usually left them speechless and unable to respond to him. The Pharisees were strictly amateurs regarding the Law of Moses. Jesus took advantage of this.

The *"heavy weights"* were the Temple Priests who were responsible by Law to teach the people of Israel GOD'S Commandments. This they had been doing for many hundreds of years and for countless generations. The secular Jews called *"rabbis"* were new at this as they were pious Jews who had only recently, when compared to the Temple Priests, taken it upon themselves to know the *"Law"*. They had been teaching their own *"stuff"* regarding the interpretation of the Law and making it up as they went. So their own ineptitude and ignorance of the Law of Moses was probably easy for a knowledgeable Jew in the Law to make look silly. This Jesus did in several well documented instances. These *"instances"* were surely enough to raise the ire of the Pharisees enough to want him *"silenced"*.

But for the Temple Priests, their view of Jesus seemed to be more directed at whether or not Jesus was committing *"blasphemy"*. According to the Law, blasphemy was punishable by death. The finer points of the Law which appeared to consume the Pharisees, did not seem to be of much interest to the Priests. The interest of the Priests in Jesus was concerned much more with what he had to say about YHWH. Was Jesus guilty of blasphemy and therefore worthy of death?

There is further evidence that the Priests and the Pharisees may have helped *"stack the deck"* against Jesus when he was before Pilate and an offer to free Jesus was put before the crowd. Whether or not the crowd really screamed for death is true or not is a bit circumspect. At least not unless the story of the conspiracy was accurate. The outcome of this scene of Pilate washing his hands and absolving himself of any responsibility of the death of Jesus has become synonymous with the guilt of the Jews for causing his death.

Some historians have a more sinister view to his trial with an understanding between the Priests, the Sanhedrin and the Romans. To maintain order and remain in authority the theory goes, some see a much larger *"conspiracy"*, almost like a *"gentleman's agreement"* in their attitude and handling of the whole affair between the Jewish authorities and the Romans. According to this view, they all wanted the Jesus problem to go away and saw that it did.

TRIAL OF HIS LIFE

The question here is not whether he was put to death for blasphemy or not. But, was the accusation of blasphemy justified and did he get a fair trial? In other words, was the entire situation of Jesus when he was brought before the Priests in accordance with the Law of Moses? Was Jesus guilty of blasphemy because he, *"makest thyself GOD"*, or because he said that he was the *"messiah"*? Was the charge of *"blasphemy"* according to the Law? Were there witnesses according to the Law? Was his sentence carried out according to the Law? The entire story of the life and death of Jesus boils down to these questions. For according to the Law, *"blasphemy"* is punishable by *"stoning"*. The following story of the *"Israelitish"* woman's son who blasphemed YHWH is the text book case of this act and it's repercussions. Leviticus 24:10-23 contains both the Law regarding blasphemy and an example of blasphemy by the son of the Israelite woman who had married and Egyptian man and had a son who cursed YHWH.

Leviticus 24:14-16, (14) 'Bring forth him that hath cursed <u>without the camp</u>; and let all that heard him lay their hands upon his head, <u>and let all the congregation stone him</u>. (15) And thou shalt speak unto the sons of Israel, saying: <u>Whosoever curseth his God shall bear his sin</u>. (16) And <u>he that blasphemeth the name of YHWH</u>, he shall surely be put to death; all the congregation shall certainly <u>stone him</u>; as well the stranger, as the home-born, when he blasphemeth the Name, <u>shall be put to death</u>.

As with many other things about the life and death of Jesus, even his death sentence leaves questions as to whether the proper sentence was carried out according to the Law for blasphemy. The priests spit on and slapped Jesus. According to the Law, it was not carried out strictly by the Law. For according to the law, Jesus should have been taken outside the *"camp"*, of the congregation place of the people, and stoned to death by Israel. He was neither taken outside the city nor stoned by Israel. For Rome was in charge, and Israel did not have complete autonomy. Was this *"kosher"*.

HOLY GHOST

Mark 3:28-30, (28) Verily I say unto you, <u>All sins shall be forgiven</u> unto the sons of men, <u>and</u>
<u>blasphemies</u> wherewith soever <u>they shall blaspheme</u>: (29) <u>But he that shall blaspheme against the</u>
<u>Holy Ghost hath never forgiveness</u>, but is in danger of eternal damnation: (30) Because they said,
He hath an unclean spirit.

These words of Jesus stand in sharp contrast to the Law given in Leviticus 24:16 regarding a person
who blasphemes the name of YHWH.

The words of Jesus appear to be saying that a person can or will be forgiven blaspheming the holy
name of *"YHWH"*. But the *"holy ghost"* (holy spirit) which is seldom mentioned in the Hebrew Bible,
seems to have taken on a status and an anthropomorphic persona for which now, it has become possible
to blaspheme. This is something new. No such thing like it exists in the Hebrew Bible where the term
"holy spirit" (ruach ha-kodesh) is written only three times. Twice it is written in Isaiah 63 where GOD
has HIS Prophet Isaiah speak of how Israel grieved GOD, and once it is written in Psalm 51where
David asks GOD for mercy after his sin with BathSheba.

Isaiah 63:10-11, (10) But they rebelled, and grieved <u>His holy spirit</u>; therefore He was turned to be
their enemy, Himself fought against them. (11) Then His people remembered the days of old, the
days of Moses: 'Where is He that brought them up out of the sea with the shepherds of His flock?
Where is He that put <u>His holy spirit</u> in the midst of them?

Psalm 51:13, (13) Cast me not away from Thy presence; and take not <u>Thy holy spirit</u> from me.

But there is nothing in the Law of Moses regarding blasphemy against the *"holy spirit"*. How
misleading this would be if what is meant is that GOD will forgive a person for blasphemy against HIS
holy name, but a person would not be forgiven if they blasphemed the *"holy ghost"*. There is no Law.

The example of blasphemy in the Safer Torah is the story of the Israelitish woman whose Egyptian son
by her Egyptian husband, blasphemed the name of YHWH (Leviticus 24:10-23) according to but one
(?) witness, and stoned. with the statement by Jesus that a person who blasphemes the *"holy ghost"*has
*"never"*forgiveness and is in danger of eternal damnation.

Is this a new Law, a new commandment or a new interpretation of the Law being put forth by Jesus. Is
this another case where he appears to be adding or taking away from the Law of Moses? There is no
such Law in Safer Torah.

IN THE BOSOM OF ABRAHAM

There is an interesting story in the Book of Luke about a rich man and a poor man (Luke 16:19-31).
The rich man before he died did not give to the poor. When the poor man died he went to be with
Abraham and the rich man went to hell. The rich man cried out and asked Abraham to warn his five
brothers. Abraham tells them they already have Moses and the Prophets, *"let them hear them"*. The
rich man asks Abraham to send someone risen from the dead, as only then would they repent. Abraham
responds. *"And he said unto him, If they hear not Moses and the prophets, neither will they be*
persuaded, though one rose from the dead.".

Jesus is making a statement about keeping GOD'S Law and seems to be making a comment on his own ministry in some respects. Often he told Israel in one manner or another to keep the Law, even chastising them for not knowing it. His attitude from the beginning was very positive towards the Law of Moses. His own life is a separate issue than his message regarding Israel keeping the Law of Moses. As has been mentioned, his life seemed to be one of, *"do as I say and keep the Law of Moses and HIS Commandments, not do as I do"*.

If Israel will not hear Moses and the Prophets, then warning them with one raised from the dead or working miracles will not convince them. How true.

HOLY OIL – PERFUME – STONING - CRUCIFIXION

Unless Jesus really was the son of David, and David's anointing by the Prophet Samuel with *"Holy Oil"* mattered in the life story of Jesus, Jesus was never *"anointed"* as the *"messiah"* of Israel. Does it matter?

As is with so many of the events in his life, does the anointing of Jesus with perfume in the house of Simeon the leper count as an *"anointing"*? Or was the assumption that Jesus was the SEED of David enough to qualify him as being the *"anointed"*, yet he was born of a virgin? If Jesus really was the anointed messiah of GOD, what was a leper doing with a house full of people, and what was Jesus doing there, when according to the Law, the leper should have been *"outside"* and separated from Israel as not to defile them? Then again, as several stories have shown, a person can be called *"anointed"* as in *"chosen"* for a task, without having been anointed with *"anointing oil"*.

Numbers 5:1-4,(1) And YHWH spoke unto Moses, saying: (2) 'Command the sons of Israel, that they put out of the camp every leper, and every one that hath an issue, and whosoever is unclean by the dead; (3) both male and female shall ye put out, without the camp shall ye put them; that they defile not their camp, in the midst whereof I dwell.' (4) And the sons of Israel did so, and put them out without the camp; as YHWH spoke unto Moses, so did the sons of Israel.

If Jesus was guilty of *"blasphemy"* he should have been taken outside the town and stoned to death. Yet, as we know he was crucified by Romans not stoned by Israel. Does this count? Did Jesus actually *"blaspheme"* the name of YHWH according to the Law? Even this is not clear as *"the Name"* does not appear to have been uttered in the translated text of the Gospels. If Jesus never uttered the name of GOD *"YHWH"*, was it still possible to blaspheme the name?

According to the strict definition of the Law, Jesus does not appear to have *blasphemed* the name of YHWH according to the information available in the Gospels as it is unknown whether Jesus actually uttered the name of YHWH.

Returning to *"anointing"*, there is no *"Law"* pertaining to *"anointing"* of a messiah, so the issue comes down to whether or not Jesus was a *"messiah"*, a prophet of YHWH, or a false prophet to test Israel becomes the question.

JESUS AND THE LAW

The attitude of Jesus towards the Law of Moses was for Israel to *keep the Commandments*, that nothing of the Law would *"fail"*. Was the death of Jesus himself, *"proof"* that the Law would not *fail*? That somehow he had *not* kept the Law and the Law sentenced him to death? The Law says that all men will die for their own sin. Was the death of Jesus not *"proof"* of the unfailing power of the Law? For he said he came to fulfill the Law. Is this scripture what he meant?

Matthew 5:17, (17) Think not that I am come to destroy the Law, or the prophets: I am not come to destroy, but to fulfil.

Was his death not *evidence* of the truth of the Commandments of the Law?

Whether he did or did not himself keep the Law, this was what he taught to his followers, to keep the Commandments.

Additionally, he taught his followers to go out to the Nations and to teach the lost sheep of the House of Israel, to **keep** the Law to *"enter life"*. For it was Israel who *"possessed"* the Law which allowed them to *"keep"* the Law. The Law encompasses all aspects of life. If his listeners obey him and *"keep"* the Commandments of the Law, their actions would keep them from violating that very Law itself. For whether he did or did not himself keep the Law, to keep the Commandments of the Law was what he taught to his followers.

Did Jesus blaspheme YHWH according to the Law of Moses. It is not clear, even though his own followers called him Lord before he died and called him *"God"* after he died. Did Jesus blaspheme the *"name"* of YHWH according to the Law? There is no definitive answer according to the text of the Gospels. For it is unknown if Jesus even uttered HIS name, *"YHWH"*.

As for his other sayings about his words and himself being *"one"with* the Father, this too appears to be a gray area as regards the Law of blasphemy itself. Although according to the words of the Priests, it was because Jesus made himself equal to GOD, was why they condemned him. This in itself seemed to be their justification for accusing him of *"blasphemy"*.

John 10:33 (33) The Jews answered him, saying, For a good work we stone thee not; but for blasphemy; and because that thou, being a man, makest thyself God.

As with many of his words and actions, they appear to cut very close to the edge without definitively going over. Whether he ever spoke the name of YHWH and actually blasphemed it is unknown especially because of the Greek translation. Only GOD YHWH knows the truth.

CONCLUSION

As regards the Law itself, the attitude of Jesus towards the Law was for Israel to obey and keep GOD'S Commandments as he stated when responding about entering life. His attitude seemed to reflect a reverence for the Law. In other words, Jesus was very positive towards the Law exhorting Israel to *"keep the Commandments"* of GOD. Regardless of his other words, this idea he repeated often.

Matthew 19:16-17, (16) And, behold, one came and said unto him, Good Master, what good thing shall I do, that I may have eternal life? (17) And he said unto him, Why callest thou me good? there is none good but one, that is, God: but if thou wilt enter into life, keep the Commandments.

During his ministry it was GOD'S Law which he said he came to *teach* to the Lost Sheep of the House of Israel to *keep* HIS Commandments. It was only Israel who had (possessed) the Commandments, so it was Israel to whom he was speaking. The Nations neither were given the Law to keep, nor had the Law to keep, for indeed Christians rejected the Law. All of Israel was under Covenant Law with GOD YHWH to keep HIS Law. Jesus was telling Israel to keep the Commandments of GOD which HE had given them to live by.

Isaiah 55:11, (11) So shall My word be that goeth forth out of My mouth: it shall not return unto Me void, <u>except it accomplish that which I please, and make the thing whereto I sent it prosper.</u>

The *"vengeance of the Law"*. He understood that none of it would fail, every *"jot"* and every *"tittle"* of the Law of YHWH would be accomplished.

Matthew 5:17-20, (17) <u>Think not that I am come to destroy the LAW, or the Prophets:</u> I am not come to destroy, but to fulfil. (18) For verily I say unto you, Till heaven and earth pass, one jot or one tittle shall in no wise pass from the LAW, till all be fulfilled. (19) Whosoever therefore shall break one of these least Commandments, and shall teach men so, he shall be called the least in the kingdom of heaven: <u>but whosoever shall DO and TEACH them,</u> the same shall be called great in the kingdom of heaven. (20) For I say unto you, That except your righteousness shall exceed the righteousness of the scribes and Pharisees, ye shall in no case enter into the kingdom of heaven.

Jesus said to *do* and *keep* the Commandments and to *teach* the Commandments and to *live* by every word of GOD. These words are difficult to get around, as is the Law of Moses and as are the words of the Prophets of YHWH, the living GOD. Put plainly, Jesus said to keep the Law of Moses to live.

During his ministry it was GOD'S Law which he said he came to tell the Lost Sheep of the House of Israel to keep. Quoting from Deuteronomy 8:3, Jesus reminds his listeners that man does not live only by bread, but by every word which comes from GOD. The Law of YHWH is the word of GOD.

Luke 4:4, (4) And Jesus answered him, saying, <u>It is written, That man shall not live by bread alone, but by Every Word of God.</u>

For Israel, every word of GOD is HIS Law, HIS Commandments HIS Statutes and HIS Ordinances to keep and to do them. And to teach them to their children. Jesus had said to *"keep"* the Commandments and to *"teach"* the Commandments.

Deuteronomy 6:4-7, (4) Hear, O Israel: YHWH is our God, YHWH is one. (5) And thou shalt love YHWH thy God with all thy heart, and with all thy soul, and with all thy might. (6) And these words, which I command thee this day, shall be upon thy heart; (7) <u>and thou shalt teach them diligently unto thy children,</u> and shalt talk of them when thou sittest in thy house, and when thou walkest by the way, and when thou liest down, and when thou risest up.

Anything that he said or did himself which appears to be outside the Law would be between him and YHWH Father of Israel. But his message after the chaff has been separated from the SEED, was to *live by the Law, <u>obey</u> the Law, <u>keep</u> the Law* and to *<u>teach</u> the Commandments of the Law* of GOD given to Israel. And that all of the Law would be accounted for, *"every jot and every tittle"*. Keeping the Law is life, not keeping the Law is death.

If understood in this light, this appeared to have been fulfilled by his own death. *"I am not come to destroy, but to fulfill",* if he answered for his own sins, and if he blasphemed GOD and Jesus was guilty of these things, then the *"vengeance of the Law"* did not fail.

Luke 16:17, (17) And it is easier for heaven and earth to pass, than one tittle of the Law to fail.

CHAPTER FIVE

JESUS AND THE PROPHETS

In the Gospels are countless references to either the Prophets and a prophesy which is being "*fulfilled*" in Jesus or the Law which is being kept by some action in the story. Sometimes it is just quoting a Prophet or a Psalm without something apparently being "*fulfilled*", but nevertheless making a connection to an event. More often than not it is an attempt to connect to Jesus somehow.

Amos 3:7, (7) For the Lord YHWH will do nothing, but He revealeth His counsel unto His servants the prophets.

The Jewish people during the time of Jesus were faced with many questions about him and his words and his actions. Did the Prophets speak of Jesus before his arrival? Several of these "*fulfilled*" statements here are looked at.

'THAT IT MIGHT BE FULFILLED'

Matthew 1:22-23 (22) Now all of this was done, <u>that it might be fulfilled</u> which was spoken of the Lord by the prophet saying, (23) Behold a <u>virgin</u> shall be with child, and shall bring forth a son, and they shall call his name Immanuel …..which being interpreted is GOD with us

'VIRGIN / YOUNG WOMAN'

In the Christian Bible, a *"virgin"* birth is foretold concerning Jesus (Matthew 1:23). Indeed, today an entire religion is based on the premiss that the mother of Jesus was a virgin when he was conceived and she herself is worshiped as *"Mary mother of GOD"*. But is this what the scripture really said?

Jewish scholars have long disputed the Hebrew translation of the Prophet Isaiah used for the *"virgin birth"*. In the Christian Bible, the scripture from Isaiah which is used is Isaiah 7:14, but Matthew 1:23 reads as the following. *"Therefore the Lord himself will give you a sign; 'Behold, a <u>virgin</u> shall* *conceive and bear a son, and shall call his name Immanuel'."*

In the original Hebrew of Isaiah 7:14, the two words used in Isaiah which have been translated as *"virgin"* in the Christian Bible were *(Ain-Lamed-Mem-Heh)*, pronounced *"all-mah"* and *(Heh-Resh-Heh)*, pronounced *"Ha-rah"*. The word *"all-mah"* has the definite article before it so all together it reads as *"Ha-all-mah ha-rah"* phonetically.

The actual meaning of these two words is a bit more complex than the simple rendering in the English translation. The young woman (who is sexually ripe) *"all-mah"* will become pregnant (conceive) *"ha-rah"*.

"All-mah" in Hebrew means *"young woman"*, a young woman who is *"sexual ripe"*, a *"maid"* or *"newly married"*. The Hebrew root of this word is *(Ain-Lamed-Mem)*, meaning *"mature sexually"*. This word is a noun in the Hebrew.

"Ha-rah" in Hebrew means *"pregnant"*. The Hebrew root of this word is *(Heh-Resh-Heh)* meaning *"conceive, become pregnant"*. This word is a feminine adjective in agreement with the noun, *'A sexually mature maiden will become pregnant'*. The original Hebrew Isaiah reads as follows.

Isaiah 7:14, (14) Therefore the My Lord Himself shall give you a sign: behold, the <u>young woman</u> shall conceive, and bear a son, and shall call his name Immanuel.

Neither of these Hebrew words means *"virgin"*. The truth of the matter is, had this bad translation not occurred, it would have made the entire story of Jesus more believable to the skeptics and unbelievers. Being a virgin and giving birth does not in any way make the story more acceptable to the Jewish population. As with another discussion in this book regarding the genealogy of Jesus being quite literally all over the place and not reliable, neither of these two stories (virgin birth & Davidic pedigree) helps the *"case"* for Jesus but in fact detracts from the believability quotient.

For aside from none of the listed genealogies in the Gospels matching that of King David, if Jesus was conceived by the *"Holy Ghost"* as well (Matthew 1:20), it makes the entire pedigree a moot point as well and much more difficult to believe. In deed, to make sure that the story of his miraculous birth is fully appreciated by the skeptics, verse 25 states that Joseph did not *"know"* his wife until <u>*after*</u> his first born son Jesus was born. Thereby making any probability of Jesus being of Joseph's SEED, and therefore of David's SEED or not, all but impossible. It therefore makes the idea that Jesus is the *"son"* of David a moot point. Was Jesus missing his male "Y" Chromosome, as this can only come from his flesh and blood biological father?

Having said this, it is well understood and accepted that to GOD all things are possible, even virgin birth, if HE so chooses. Nevertheless, aside from the father of Jesus who raised him being of the SEED of David himself, there is no biological connection to David and thus, also makes the idea Jesus having been *"anointed"* (through David as his SEED), a moot point if of virgin birth.

Assuming that Joseph did not impregnate Mary as the story said, then the only actual biological *"pedigree"* that Jesus can lay claim to is through his mother. According to the Gospels, Mary the mother of Jesus and Elizabeth the mother of John the Baptist were cousins (Luke 1:36). Additionally, according to Luke 1:5, Elizabeth was of the *"daughters of Aaron"*. This would mean then that the mother of Jesus too, was likely but not definitely of the *"daughters of Aaron"*. This does not mean that Mary nor Elizabeth was of the SEED of Aaron, as neither would have his Y Chromosome, thereby not possessing his Y-DNA. Therefore, if Jesus had no biological father, and if his mother was of the *"daughters"* of priests descended from Aaron, then Jesus had one "X" Chromosome and no "Y" Chromosome, biologically speaking that is.

Hebrew Bible linage of Israel is always *"parilineal"*, and the pedigree of the priest (sons of Aaron) is always determined from father to son, patrilineally.

The Gospels state through his father, Jesus was a descendant of David and his cousin John descendant of Aaron (Luke 1:5) as his father was a Priest. John would have been a second cousin to Jesus.

VIRGIN DAMSEL IN DISTRESS

Returning to the issue of *"virgin"*, an example in the Hebrew where the word which actually does mean *"virgin"* shows the difference between a *"young woman"* as in Isaiah 7:14, and that of Deuteronomy 22:23-29 is important.

The example of the use of this word in Hebrew is with the Law pertaining to a *"damsel"* who was found by a man and who did *"lie"* with her. There are several different scenarios which have different penalties associated with them depending on each individual circumstance. But the word used for *"virgin"* is important for the above stated reasons. As these Laws deal with technical issues and are life and death matters, which words were used in describing these individuals was critical.

Deuteronomy 22:23-29, (23) If there be a <u>damsel</u> *that is a <u>virgin betrothed</u> unto a man, and a man find her in the city, and lie with her; (24) then ye shall bring them both out unto the gate of that city, and ye shall <u>stone them with stones</u> that they die: the* <u>damsel</u>*, because she cried not, being in the city; and the man, <u>because he hath humbled his neighbour's wife</u>; so thou shalt put away the evil from the midst of thee. (25) But if the man find the* <u>damsel</u> *that is <u>betrothed</u> in the field, and the man take hold of her, and lie with her; then the man only that lay with her shall die. (26) But unto the* <u>damsel</u> *thou shalt do nothing; there is in the* <u>damsel</u> *no sin worthy of death; for as when a man riseth against his neighbour, and slayeth him, even so is this matter. (27) For he found her in the field; the <u>betrothed</u>* <u>damsel</u> *cried, and there was none to save her. (28) If a man find a* <u>damsel</u> *that is <u>a virgin, that is not betrothed</u>, and lay hold on her, and lie with her, and they be found; (29) then the man that lay with her shall give unto the* <u>damsel's</u> *father fifty shekels of silver, and she shall be his wife, because he hath humbled her; he may not put her away all his days.*

Breaking down these scriptures will help understand better what is meant by *"damsel"*, *"virgin"* and *"betrothed"* so Isaiah 7:14 will make more sense.

<u>Damsel</u> is used eight times. It translates as *"girl"*, *"damsel"* from (*Nun-Ayin-Resh*). When paired in conjunction with other words, *"little girl", young daughters", "young woman"* (marriageable), *"betrothed girl"* or *"maids"*.

Interestingly enough, the feminine form of the word which has the feminine *"Heh"* ending is not used, but a masculine form is written instead. At first it was thought that it might have been a scribal error (from Ancient Hebrew [also called Paleo-Hebrew] pre-exile to Babylon, to post Babylonian Modern Hebrew), but after checking against the ancient Samaritan Pentateuch (Safer Torah) to see what was written, it is the same spelling but it has different accent marks in the modern Hebrew script which renders it feminine.

The Hebrew word for *"virgin"* is used twice, and *"betroth"* is used four times. It is the same word the Prophet Hosea uses in 2:21-22 figuratively when referring to Israel being *"betrothed"* to YHWH.

Hosea 2:21-22, (21) And I will __betroth__ thee unto Me for ever; yea, I will __betroth__ thee unto Me in righteousness, and in justice, and in lovingkindness, and in compassion. (22) And I will __betroth__ thee unto Me in faithfulness; and thou shalt know YHWH.

The Hebrew word used for *"virgin"* is pronounced *"b-toolah"* (*Bet-Tav-Vav-Lamed-Heh*). It is used __specifically__ in the Law quoted in Deuteronomy regarding a *"virgin"* who a man found and did *"lie"* with.

Neither *"b-toolah"*, or any of the other words, either alone or in conjunction with another is used in Isaiah 7:14 to mean *"virgin"*. In other words, the English rendering of the Hebrew word for *"virgin"* is dubious at best and is a bad translation. The Hebrew in Isaiah 7:14 clearly means *"young woman"*.

The best example of the word *"virgin"* in Hebrew, is with the High Priest.

Leviticus 21:13-14, (13) And he shall take a wife in her __virginity__. (14) A widow, or one divorced, or a profaned woman, or a harlot, these shall he not take; but a __virgin__ of his own people shall he take to wife.

The Law pertaining to the priesthood was very strict. There are other ordinances pertaining the the High Priest and his wife (Ezekiel 44:22). For instance, the *"virgin"* could only be of *"Israel"*, and he *was* allowed to marry a widow, but *only* if she were the widow of a *"Priest"*. There were many built in advantages for a priest to marry the widow of another priest, for she would come with an encyclopedic wealth of experience and knowledge pertaining to the Laws of purity and keeping the home of the Priest in a *"sanctified"* state of cleanliness. Additionally, it would keep her from becoming either a burden as a widow on other parts of her family or of becoming destitute after her husband died.

Returning to *"virgin"*, the word in Hebrew is *"b-toolah"* regarding the wife to be for the Priest. The priest could marry only a *"virgin" (b-toolah)*. And this is not the word used in Isaiah 7:14. The following JPS 1917 Hebrew / English translation is the correct translation of this (Isaiah 7:14) scripture, not that of the King James Isaiah 7:14.

Isaiah 7:14, (14) Therefore My Lord Himself shall give you a sign: behold, the __young woman__ shall conceive, and bear a son, and shall call his name Immanuel.

According to this scripture then, not only was Jesus not of a miraculous virgin birth, although it is possible she was a virgin at the time she married, Jesus was not named *"Immanuel"*, but was called *"Yeshua"*, *"Jesus"* in Greek, meaning *"salvation"* not *"God is with us"*.

IMMANUEL / YESHUA

When that entire seventh chapter in Isaiah is read, the story and prophesy regarding the ultimate demise of the northern Kingdom of Israel is foretold. Israel is often referred to as *"Samaria"* or poetically referred to at times as *"Ephraim"*. As later with sieges in the kingdom of Judah against Jerusalem with various armies, the prophets of GOD often used births and deaths, the cost and availability of staple goods etc., to signify time and coming future events. With the idolatrous northern Kingdom of Israel, the birth of a child named *"Immanuel"*, is foretold. YHWH has the Prophet Isaiah tell King Ahaz of Judah of the coming destruction of both Israel and Assyria.

The name of Jesus in Hebrew is *"Yeshua"* and means *"salvation"*. The name given in Isaiah is *"Immanuel"* and means *"GOD is with us"*. A Jew reading the prophets during his life time would have made no connection between a young woman becoming pregnant and having a baby called Immanuel, and Jesus being born of the *"Holy Ghost"*. There is no *"Holy Ghost"* in the Isaiah scripture. They would have seen no relation to Isaiah 7:14 and Jesus.

'FOR THUS IT IS WRITTEN BY THE PROPHET'

Matthew 2:5-6 And they said unto him, In Bethlehem of Judea: <u>for thus is it written by the prophet,</u> (6) And thou Bethlehem in the land of Judah art not the least amongst the princes of Judah: for out of thee shall come a Governor that shall rule my people Israel

This is a paraphrase of several scriptures referring to King David. Per the prophets, there is no doubt that David or his SEED will be king again.

'THEN WAS FULFILLED'

Matthew 2:17-18 (17) <u>Then was fulfilled</u> that which was spoken by Jeremiah the Prophet, saying, (18) In Ramah was there a voice heard, lamentation, and weeping, and great mourning. Rachel weeping for her children, and would not be comforted, because they are not

Herod slew many infants in his quest to kill what was rumored to be the birth of the *"messiah"* or a *"king"* in Beth-lehem *"and in all the coast"*. Herod was not a man who enjoyed competition. Joseph was warned to flee to Egypt. Allusions are made to Israel's former status there in Chapter 2 of Matthew.

The quote from Jeremiah 31:15 is from a long chapter about GOD'S love for Ephraim (Israel) and how they will return and live according to GOD'S Law written on their heart as a *"new Covenant"* where they will no longer be taught the Law of YHWH but each will know it *"by heart"*.

It is about a time in the future when Israel returns and will never *"be thrown down any more forever"*. Regarding Rachel weeping, a careful reading of the scripture will show that she was weeping because *"they were not"*. Israel was *"missing"*, away in captivity, exiled. The Prophet Jeremiah lived during the last days of the Kingdom of Judah. The ten northern tribes of Israel had long been in exile. The Prophet Jeremiah said *"refrain thy voice from weeping"*. For YHWH will return Israel from the land of their enemy from being *"chastised"*. Except for this one verse about Rachel weeping, the other thirty nine verses are up beat. The entire chapter is very positive and speaks of GOD'S love and the reestablishment of Israel and Judah by YHWH to *"build"* and to *"plant"*. Overall it is a very up lifting and positive chapter. Any connection to Herod killing babies is a stretch. The Prophet Jeremiah said not to weep, YHWH will restore Israel from their exile where scattered.

Additionally. This one verse in Jeremiah speaks of *"Rama"*. The Hebrew means simply either *"the Height"*, and thus *"Rama"*, or is often a common attachment to a name as for example, *"the height of Sharon"* (Ramat Ha-Sharon). There are many such place names in Israel.

In ancient Israel, there existed such a town called *"Ramah"* in the tribal territory of Benjamin to the north of Jerusalem (Bethlehem is to the south of Jerusalem) which was one of the cities which was part of the Prophet Samuel's circuit. Bethlehem is always referred to as Bethlehem or sometimes Bethlehem-Ephrath because of it's close proximity to Ephrath. Any association of *"Ramah"* with Bethlehem is dubious with no biblical source.

The allusion they were attempting to make may have been from the Prophet Micah, however they misquoted him and the geography, if this was the case.

Micah 5:1, (1) But thou, <u>Beth-lehem Ephrathah,</u> which art little to be among the thousands of Judah, <u>out of thee shall one come forth unto Me that is to be ruler in Israel;</u> whose goings forth are from of old, from ancient days.

This scripture refers to David as he was from *Bethlehem*. However, there is no connection to *David, Beth-lehem or Beth-lehem Ephratha* with *"Ramah"*.

'THAT IT MIGHT BE FULFILLED'

Matthew 2:23, And he came and dwelt in the city called Nazareth <u>that it might be fulfilled</u> which was spoken by the prophets, <u>He shall be called a Nazarene</u>

The question is, *"he who?"* would be called a Nazarene?

If this scripture is only saying that Jesus would be called a Nazarene because he was from Nazareth, there is no issue, though there is no Hebrew prophesy. For people were often referred to by their village or town or some other identifying *handle* as many Israelites had the same name. People were often called by their town or trade. However, the reference source for this scripture is given as Judges 13:5 (King James Version, New Encyclopedic Reference Edition, Zondervan Publishing House) which refers to the Prophet Sampson.

Sampson was a *"Nazarite"* from birth. He was a *"Nazarite"*, a man who was consecrated to GOD. Sampson was not from *"Nazareth"*, the town. Therefore, he was not a *"Nazarene"*. The words of the Prophet regarding Sampson are about his being a servant of GOD as a *"Nazarite"*, not about what village he was from. A *"Nazarene"* is someone from *"Nazareth"*. Sampson was from *"Zorah"* of the tribe of Dan, a Danite not a Jew of Judah.

There is no indication in the Hebrew Bible or the Christian Bible that Jesus was a *"Nazarite"*, according to the Law pertaining to a Nazarite (Numbers 6:1-21). For Sampson was a Nazarite from his birth. And the scripture given as being *"fulfilled"* is regarding Sampson, and in using it to refer to Jesus is incorrect on several levels just discussed. And given the details of his ministry, it is highly unlikely that Jesus was a *"Nazarite"* as his association with leprous people and the diseased and with the dead would have ended this vow quickly. Jesus would have had an extremely difficult time not breaking his Nazarite vow if in deed he had made the vow of a *Nazarite*.

Additionally, there is no scripture which indicates that either *"a"* or *"the"* messiah would come from *"Nazareth"* in the Hebrew Bible or would be a *"Nazarene"*. The scripture in Matthew 2:23 does not make any sense as it does not say *where* or *who's* words were fulfilled. The question could then be asked, *"what was fulfilled"?* There is no prophesy about a *"Nazarene"*.

This is relevant for several reasons. The house of David came from Bethlehem in Judah, not from Nazareth in the north of the country, although the Gospels indicate that Joseph and Mary were in Bethlehem just long enough for Jesus to be born there. The *"Messiah"* of Israel is not associated with either being a *Nazarite* or being from *Nazareth*. There is no connection.

Why the Gospels associate Jesus with the city of Nazareth does not make much sense, if it in any way is to lend credence to his being the messiah. For his being raised in Nazareth means nothing either in prophesy or in his story.

If the translator was attempting to make a connection not knowing the Law of a Nazarite or even what one was, this would make sense. A Greek may not have known the difference between a *"Nazarene"* and a *Nazarite"* and was attempting to draw a connection between Jesus being born in Bethlehem but raised in Nazareth. Like the example of Isaiah 42:1-4 which is discussed, the early Christian translators or redactors were not above altering the Hebrew scripture to fit their doctrine, or referencing Hebrew scripture erroneously.

In a very similar vein to the genealogy of Jesus which does not add up, the *Nazarene* issue detracts but adds nothing to his being the *messiah*. The same thing can be said regarding the *virgin* birth discussed. It only distracts from the story and adds nothing to it, using scripture unrelated and out of context.

It was common to associate people with a town or other distinguishing features such as occupation or physique, as often people had the same common name so towns or other words were used to distinguish them. But this is not the case here as Judges 13:5 clearly refers to a *"Nazarite"*.

Nevertheless, Matthew 2:23 is irrelevant other than Jesus just being called after his town. There is nothing in the scriptures of the Hebrew Bible that indicate something was *"fulfilled"* by Jesus having been born in Nazareth. Neither is there any indication in the gospels that he was ever a *"Nazarite"*.

'OF WHOM MOSES IN THE LAW, AND THE PROPHETS'

John 1:45, (45) Philip findeth Nathanael, and saith unto him, We have found him, of whom Moses in the law, and the prophets, did write, Jesus of Nazareth, the son of Joseph.

There is no reference to *"Jesus of Nazareth", "Jesus son of Joseph"* or *"Jesus"* in the Law of Moses or the Prophets, nor as just discussed, of a *"prophet"* or *"messiah"* from the city of Nazareth. If one studies the prophets or evaluates each of the examples either given in the Gospels or used as the source reference by the Christian Bible, no evidence of such a prophet or messiah exists from Nazareth. There are many gaps between the life of Jesus and any clear biblical evidence in the Hebrew scriptures regarding his life. In addition, there is no connection in the Hebrew Bible to Nazareth at all. **The city of Nazareth is not mentioned once in all of the Hebrew Bible.** If it existed at all, it was not mentioned in any scripture, text or book. Not by this name. There was neither a Nazarene, a Nazareth nor a Nazarite from a Nazareth in all of the Hebrew books which make up the entire Hebrew Bible.

The scriptures of Matthew 2:23 or John 1:45 do not appear to be saying that Jesus was to have been a *"Nazarite"*, only that it was prophesied that apparently he (the prophet / messiah?) would be from there, from Nazareth the city. However, it is saying that Moses in the Law and the prophets spoke of (Jesus? / prophet / messiah?) being from *"Nazareth"*. It, like many things regarding his life and his words, are not clear. The Gospels do not give the source for this pronouncement, but many Christian Bibles will give the following biblical scriptures as supporting the line about Moses and the Prophets

(Gen. 3:15, Deut.18:18, Is. 4:2, Mic. 5:2, Zech. 6:12, [John 5:39, 45-47]. It also referenced Judges 13:5 regarding Samson. Once again, these scriptures speak of events, such as Sampson being a Nazarite, but there is no connection at all to Jesus or a town called *"Nazareth"*. There is no evidence that Jesus was ever a Nazarite. Given his ministry it is difficult to see how he could have kept from violating the Laws pertaining to a Nazarite vow if one.

This reference to Sampson appears much more like an editor who is totally unfamiliar with the Law or Hebrew scripture, who was attempting to make a connection to *"Nazareth"* the city and Jesus with the Hebrew Bible text, not knowing apparently that the Hebrew Bible text was speaking of a person who was a *"Nazarite"* (Sampson), and having absolutely no connection with and having nothing whatsoever to do with the city of Nazareth, Jesus or another.

'THAT IT IS WRITTEN'

Luke 24:44-48, (44) And he said unto them, These are the words which I spake unto you, while I was yet with you, that all things must be fulfilled, <u>which were written in the law of Moses, and in the prophets, and in the psalms, concerning me.</u> (45) Then opened he their understanding, that they might understand the scriptures, (46) And said unto them, <u>Thus it is written</u>, and thus it behoved Christ to suffer, and to rise from the dead the third day: (47) And that repentance and remission of sins should be preached <u>in his name</u> among all nations, beginning at Jerusalem. (48) And ye are witnesses of these things.

As for Moses and the Law having spoken of Jesus, there is no evidence of this either, especially in the references given. If Moses ever spoke *of* Jesus, referred *to* Jesus or prophesied *about* Jesus, it was not recorded. There are many scriptures in the TaNaKh which are so generic, anyone could apply their words to another situation. Whether or not there is any real connection or not however, is an entirely different question. If Moses wrote of Jesus he lost the cow hide it was on. Does the Hebrew Bible speak of the *"messiah"* of Israel who would *"suffer"* and *"rise from the dead on the third day"*?

Was he referring to the Prophet Hosea who spoke of Israel, but not the messiah, and not GOD, who was being raised up.

Hosea 6:1-2, (1) 'Come, and let us return unto YHWH; for He hath torn, and He will heal us, He hath smitten, and He will bind us up. (2) <u>After two days will He revive us, on the third day He will raise us up, that we may live in His presence.</u>

The Prophet Hosea speaks of YHWH healing HIS people (Ephraim and Judah) but the prophesy is not regarding a *"messiah"*. If so, YHWH is HE.

Many Christians interpret in Isaiah 53, as being the *"suffering servant"* and apply it to Jesus. This entire chapter could be applied to King David or to some of the many prophets of GOD killed by HIS people Israel. For a careful search of the Psalms shows how much of a *"suffering servant"* David truly was. David did not suffer from the enemies outside of Israel, but from those from within Israel. Additionally, any ancient Prophet of YHWH in Israel suffered greatly at the hands of the people. Israel was castigated often by YHWH for killing HIS Prophets that HE sent to them. The suffering Prophet Jeremiah is a good example of this.

Jeremiah 15:15-18, (15) Thou, O YHWH, knowest; remember me, and think of me, <u>and avenge me of my persecutors</u>; take me not away because of Thy long-suffering; <u>know that for Thy sake I have</u>

suffered taunts. (16) Thy words were found, and I did eat them; and Thy words were unto me a joy and the rejoicing of my heart; because Thy Name was called on me, O YHWH God of hosts. (17) I sat not in the assembly of them that make merry, nor rejoiced; I sat alone because of Thy hand; for Thou hast filled me with indignation. (18) Why is my pain perpetual, and my wound incurable, so that it refuseth to be healed? Wilt Thou indeed be unto me as a deceitful brook, as waters that fail?

It was not for the faint of heart to be chosen by GOD to be GOD'S messenger to Israel HIS people. Israel seldom wanted to hear the truth, prophets beware.

The thing regarding both of the two examples given above, is that in neither one of them do they say that this person is the "*messiah*". YHWH told Israel very clearly that HE would send HIS Prophet to tell Israel of what HIS intentions would be. At no place does YHWH ever say that HE would send a "*messiah*" who would suffer, be killed and then be raised on the third day. Isaiah 53 is interesting, but one must make the mental leap himself, to make the connection to Jesus on their own, as the scripture does not do it itself, "*For the Lord YHWH will do nothing, but He revealeth His counsel unto His servants the prophets*". There is no evidence that YHWH "*revealed*" Jesus to Israel's prophets.

'IT IS WRITTEN'

Matthew 4:3-4, And when the tempter came unto him, he said, If thou be the son of GOD, command that these stones be made bread. (4) But he answered and said, it is written, Man shall not live by bread alone, but by every word that proceedeth out of the mouth of GOD.

This is a quote from Deuteronomy and is part of a long instruction from Moses to Israel about their relationship with GOD and HIS Law and to observe all of YHWH'S Commandments as they were preparing to take possession of the promised land.

Deuteronomy 8:1-3, (1) All the commandment which I command thee this day shall ye observe to do, that ye may live, and multiply, and go in and possess the land which YHWH swore unto your fathers. (2) And thou shalt remember all the way which YHWH thy God hath led thee these forty years in the wilderness, that He might afflict thee, to prove thee, to know what was in thy heart, whether thou wouldest keep His commandments, or no. (3) And He afflicted thee, and suffered thee to hunger, and fed thee with manna, which thou knewest not, neither did thy fathers know; that He might make thee know that man doth not live by bread only, but by every thing that proceedeth out of the mouth of YHWH doth man live.

What if anything, this has to do with Jesus being tempted by the "*devil*" to turn stones into bread is anyone's guess. The symbolism is appreciated, for what was quoted is true. Man will and must live by every word from GOD. But again, as with most of the quotes from the Hebrew Bible, the quote is true. But it is making any kind of a connection to what is happening in the narrative that is the problem. Jesus could have responded with any number of similar quotes from the writings of the Safer Torah, and they would have been equally as profound, and true but with no connection to his story.

The same thing can be said about the next quote when Jesus was "*tempted*", and yet again with the last or the third temptation.

'FOR IT IS WRITTEN'

Matthew 4:6 (6) And saith unto him, If thou be the son of God, cast thyself down: <u>for it is written,</u> <u>He shall give his angels charge concerning thee</u>: and in their hands they shall bear thee up, lest at any time thou dash thy foot against a stone

Mathew 4:10 (10) Then saith Jesus unto him, get thee hence Satan: <u>for it is written,</u> Thou shalt worship the Lord thy God, <u>and him alone shalt thy serve.</u>

These two scriptures from Matthew appear to have been taken from those Hebrew Scriptures below. It is difficult to argue with these words, just the connection to the story which prompted the response.

Psalms 91:9-11, (9) For thou hast made YHWH who is my refuge, even the Most High, thy habitation. (10) There shall no evil befall thee, neither shall any plague come nigh thy tent. (11) <u>For</u> <u>He will give His angels charge over thee, to keep thee in all thy ways.</u>

Deuteronomy 6:13, (13) Thou shalt fear YHWH thy God; <u>and Him shalt thou serve</u>, and by His name shalt thou swear

The thing which must be kept in mind is that most, if not all of the scriptures referenced in the Gospels regarding Jesus, exist or were put there for a reason. The reason in most all cases is to either show that Jesus was the long awaited *"messiah"* and / or he completed some prophesy about the messiah, and thus evidence of him and his ministry were somehow foretold. The main issue with most, if not all of the scripture references referenced in the Hebrew Bible given in the Gospels is that they neither speak of Jesus, are misquoted, misapplied or are totally disconnected and irrelevant to either his life or the situation in the story when the reference was made. In many cases it is merely restating an obvious truth.

The feeling one gets is that a redactor or editor came in and having sought throughout the Hebrew scriptures, looked for, found and inserted random scriptures which they believed would help the Gospel account of Jesus being the messiah. The use of these scriptures to show how something was *fulfilled*, such as the example of Samson the Nazarite and Jesus being from Nazareth show this clearly. For as with this example, often the editor had no clue or knowledge of Jewish Law and his own agenda through his editing is exposed.

'THAT IT MIGHT BE FULFILLED'

Matthew 4:13, (13) And leaving Nazareth, he came and dwelt in Capernaum, which is upon the sea coast, in the borders of Zabulon and Nephthalim: (14) <u>That it might be fulfilled</u> which was spoken by Esaias the prophet, saying, …..

'LIGHT IS SPRUNG UP'

When Jesus started preaching, one of the first scriptures which alludes to his being the *"messiah"*, is a scripture referencing the Prophet Isaiah.

The prophesy the Prophet Isaiah mentions indicates a person who will sit upon the throne of David *"<u>whose name is called</u>"* **"Pele-joez-el-gibbor-Abi-ad-sar-shalom"**, meaning *"That the government may* be increased, *And of peace there be no end"*. Matthew 4 continues with verses 15-16.

Matthew 4:15-16, (15) The land of Zabulon, and the land of Nephthalim, by the way of the sea, beyond Jordan, Galilee of the Gentiles; (16) The people which sat in darkness saw great light; and to them which sat in the region and shadow of death light is sprung up.

Matthew 4:15-16 is quoting from the last half of Isaiah 8:23 through Isaiah 9:1 (JPS 1917). It is later in verse 5 it speaks of a child being born who is called *"Pele-joez-el-gibbor-Abi-ad-sar-shalom"*.

Jesus brought much strife during his life time not peace, and from his own words he came to bring *"division"*. The reference in Isaiah is of someone whose name is *"Pele-joez-el-gibbor-Abi-ad-sar-shalom"*. The *"peace"* of the child which Isaiah speaks of, has not come. Having said this, it is realized that Christianity for the most part, is more of an *"ethereal"* type of religion than is the ancient Temple religion of Israel and that most Christians relate to their religion in more of a *"spiritual"* way than that on earth. It was to Israel Jesus came. And by all available evidence including his own words, he did not bring *"peace"* but *"division"*. The scripture in Isaiah refers to someone bringing *"peace, justice and righteousness"*, not *"fire, sword and division"*.

Below are the scriptures of the Prophet Isaiah mentioned in Matthew 4:15-16.

Isaiah 8:23, (23) For is there no gloom to her that was stedfast? Now the former hath lightly afflicted the land of Zebulun and the land of Naphtali, but the latter hath dealt a more grievous blow by the way of the sea, beyond the Jordan, in the district of the nations.

Isaiah 9:1-5, (1) The people that walked in darkness have seen a great light; they that dwelt in the land of the shadow of death, upon them hath the light shined. (2) Thou hast multiplied the nation, Thou hast increased their joy; they joy before Thee according to the joy in harvest, as men rejoice when they divide the spoil. (3) For the yoke of his burden, and the staff of his shoulder, the rod of his oppressor, Thou hast broken as in the day of Midian. (4) For every boot stamped with fierceness, and every cloak rolled in blood, shall even be for burning, for fuel of fire. (5) For a child is born unto us, a son is given unto us; and the government is upon his shoulder; and his name is called Pele-joez-el-gibbor-Abi-ad-sar-shalom; (6) That the government may be increased, and of PEACE there be NO END, upon the throne of David, and upon his kingdom, to establish it, and to uphold it through JUSTICE and through RIGHTEOUSNESS from henceforth even FOR EVER. The zeal of YHWH of hosts doth perform this.

The feeling one gets after a while from many of the scriptures given in the Gospels by Jesus or others, was that he was constantly testing Israel to see if they knew their Law and their Prophets. For many of the scriptures, as was just cited, do not appear to have any connection to Jesus at all. Jesus does not seem to have been challenged by anyone on this matter.

Jesus, said,*"Think not that I am come to send peace on earth: I came **not** to send peace, but a sword. (Matthew 10:34); "Suppose ye that I am come to give peace on earth? I tell you, Nay; but rather division"* (Luke 12:51).

How do the words attributed to Jesus square with the words of the Prophet Isaiah regarding *"for a child is born"*? The Prophet Isaiah speaks of someone who will govern and bring peace and Jesus speaks of himself as bringing *strife* and a *sword* of *division* between father and son, mother and daughter etc. As if Jesus is saying, *'You think that I come to bring peace to you? No, I bring division. I bring a **sword**. I bring you the opposite of peace.'*

What does Jesus say himself about the *sword*. Matthew 26:52 *"Then said Jesus unto him, Put up again thy **sword** into his place: for all they that take the **sword** shall perish with the **sword"**. Did Jesus perish for bringing a *sword, fire and division*? Jesus brought the opposite of peace.

If all of the scriptures are read (Matthew 10:34-39 and Luke 12:49-53), it is difficult to understand his words in any other way. So much of what Jesus said not only appears to contradict his own words spoken in other places, but they appear as well to contradict the words of the Law and the Prophets. In this case, it is the Prophet Isaiah of whom the words of Jesus appear to be at variance with. In the Gospels, it is often a scripture from the Hebrew Bible which contradicts his words or an event that is given as evidence or proof.

On the Sermon on the Mount, Jesus said, *"Blessed be the peacemakers, for they shall be called the children of God"* (Matthew 5:9). How does this compare to bringing a *sword* and *division* upon the earth by himself?

Then again, Jesus speaks much about *"love"*, that his followers were to love one another as *"his Father"* loved him and as he loved them etc. (John 13:31-35, 15:12-17). These examples of Jesus extolling the virtues of *"love"* are in stark contrast to his words of *"division"*, *"fire"* and a *"sword"*.

Did Jesus fulfill the prophesy of Isaiah regarding *"of peace there be no end"*? Was Jesus a *"peacemaker"*? If so, where is his peace with *"no end"*?

'THAT IT MIGHT BE FULFILLED'

Matthew 12:17-21 (17) That it might be fulfilled which was spoken by Esaias the prophet, saying,(18) Behold my servant, whom I have chosen; my beloved, in whom my soul is well pleased: I will put my spirit upon him, and he shall shew judgment to the Gentiles. (19) He shall not strive, nor cry; neither shall any man hear his voice in the streets.(20) A bruised reed shall he not break, and smoking flax shall he not quench, till he send forth judgment unto victory. (21) And in his name shall the Gentiles trust.

'IN HIS NAME SHALL THE GENTILES TRUST' ???

The just quoted verse from Matthew12:17-21 is supposedly quoting from Isaiah 42:1-4. However there is a very serious problem on several levels.

As was mentioned in the Preface, this may be good example of a scribe either taking liberties or one who has an agenda or both. It is doubtful that too many people are aware of this *"creative error"*. It is startling for several reasons.

The scripture given in Matthew 12:17-21 are quoted as being words of the Prophet Isaiah are incorrect and in no way support the assertion previously given in the Gospel, that Isaiah 42:1-4, purportedly is speaking of Jesus.

The Hebrew scripture of the Prophet Isaiah given as a prophesy *"fulfilled"*, by Jesus, does not support the English translation given in the *same* King James Bible. The King James scripture of Isaiah reads as the following.*'And the isles shall wait for his teaching* (Law)'. Literally it reads *"Torah"* (42:4).

Isaiah 42:1-4, (1) Behold My servant, whom I uphold; Mine elect, in whom My soul delighteth; I have put My spirit upon him, he shall make the right to go forth to the nations. (2) He shall not cry, nor lift up, nor cause his voice to be heard in the street. (3) A bruised reed shall he not break, and the dimly burning wick shall he not quench; he shall make the right to go forth according to the truth. (4) He *shall not fail nor be crushed, till he have set the right in the earth; **and the isles shall wait for his teaching.***

The translation of Isaiah given in the same King James Bible as well as in the 1917 JPS, when compared to a literal translation of the Greek Gospel of Matthew reads considerably different, especially the last line in the Gospel which reads, *"And in his name shall the Gentiles trust"*. This last line is an example of a scribe being very creative when compared to the actual Hebrew.

Some translations of Isaiah have, *"and the isles shall wait for his **Law**"*, as *"torah"* not only means *"instruction" (teaching)* but means *"Law"*. This may point in part to the reason it was changed, as the original Hebrew itself is a problem with regard to Christian doctrine as *"the Law"* was not part of the Christian equation, for the *"Law"* was to have been replaced by *"grace"*. And this may be why the *"scribe"* in his translation went from the *"isles"* waiting *"for HIS Law"* to *"in his name shall the Gentiles trust"* in the first place.

" HIS Law" can refer to none other than **YHWH**, the GOD of Israel who gave the **Law** of Moses to Israel at Mount Sinai. So here we have at least two doctrinal issues which the author of the Greek was not able to overcome. That of *"YHWH"* and that of *"Law"*. So he changed them to refer to *"Jesus"* and the *"Gentile"* instead of *"Law"*.

The Greek translation of Isaiah 42 renders, *"And upon his name nations shall hope"*, which is almost identical to the King James version *"And in his name nations shall hope"*. So seemingly the bad translation of Isaiah 42 given in Matthew 12 in the King James Version comes from the Greek translation of the Isaiah text. In other words, it appears to have originated from the Greeks.

By no stretch of the imagination from the original Hebrew of the Prophet Isaiah cited, can any connection be made from *"and the isles shall wait for his teaching/Law"* to *"And in his name shall the Gentiles trust"*. This would not even pass as a bad translation, but a 100% corruption of the scripture to fit the mind set of the person who wrote it. It was made up by the writer to fit his own agenda and to *"fulfill"* his own doctrine, not a prophesy about Jesus.

As touched on, within the same King James Bible itself, the actual translation of Isaiah 42:1-4 is translated as it actually exists in Hebrew, similar to the JPS Hebrew translation, *"and the isles shall wait for his law"*. It is different than the *same* scripture quoted in Matthew Chapter 12:21 in the *same* bible incorrectly *"And in his name shall the Gentiles trust"*. So in the *same* Christian Bible (King James), there are two different *"translations"* of Isaiah Chapter 42:4 of the *same* scripture.

This in and of itself is a problem, yet it can be dealt with. But what it does, is that it raises serious questions about the integrity of ***all*** of what is written in the Christian Bible. For if something this blatant exists, what other less obvious secrets exists within the text? How many other liberties were taken?

'FOR A LIGHT OF THE NATIONS'

Another interesting aspect of this scripture, is that it is a lead up to a scripture which is often quoted. If one reads the entire forty second chapter of Isaiah. They will see that YHWH is extremely jealous for HIS holy name.

*Isaiah 42:8, (8) I am YHWH, that is My name; and **My glory will I not give to another**, neither My praise to graven images.*

It is the collective people of Israel who are *for a light of the nations.*

Isaiah 49:6, (6) Yea, He saith: 'It is too light a thing that thou shouldest be My servant to raise up the tribes of Jacob, and to restore the offspring of Israel; I will also give thee <u>for a light of the nations</u>, that <u>My salvation</u> may be unto the end of the earth.'

YHWH repeatedly refers to HIS own name and how it is HE who is Savior of Israel, and it is HE who is "*salvation*" of the nations.

Yet, Jesus tells his Jewish followers that they will die in their sins if they do not believe in *<u>him</u>*, presumably as their salvation. When it is YHWH GOD.

John 8:21-24, (21) Then said Jesus again unto them, I go my way, and ye shall seek me, <u>and shall die in your sins</u>: whither I go, ye cannot come. (22) Then said the Jews, Will he kill himself? because he saith, Whither I go, ye cannot come. (23) And he said unto them, Ye are from beneath; I am from above: ye are of this world; I am not of this world. (24) <u>I said therefore unto you, that ye shall die in your sins: for if ye believe not that I am he, ye shall die in your sins.</u>

" He who"? But then GOD said that we all sin and all die for our own sin.

'LIFE THROUGH HIS NAME'

Several times in the Gospels the name of Jesus is equated with that of YHWH, or this is inferred from the text. In John 20:31 we have a clear example of Jesus adding his own name to that of YHWH as Israel's savior and giver of life. Jesus is saying everlasting life is through his own name.

John 20:31 (31) But these are written, that ye might believe that Jesus is the Christ, the Son of God; <u>and that believing ye might have life through his name.</u>"

" Life through his name"? But what does YHWH have to say?

Isaiah 43:3, (3) For <u>I am YHWH</u> thy God, The Holy One of Israel, <u>thy Saviour;</u>

Isaiah 44:6 (6) Thus saith YHWH, the King of Israel, and his Redeemer YHWH of hosts: I am the first, and I am the last, and <u>beside Me there is no God</u>.

Isaiah 43:25, (25) I<u>, even I, am He that blotteth out thy transgressions for Mine own sake; and thy sins I will not remember.</u>

Isaiah 45:5, (5) <u>I am YHWH</u>, and there is none else, <u>beside Me there is no God</u>

Isaiah 43:11, (11) I, even I, am YHWH; and <u>beside Me there is no Saviour.</u>

Hosea 13:4, (4) Yet I am YHWH thy God from the land of Egypt; and thou knowest no God but Me, and <u>beside Me there is no Saviour.</u>

Joel 3:5, (5) And it shall come to pass, that <u>whosoever shall call on the name of YHWH shall be delivered...</u>

There are many scriptures which state that it is YHWH alone "*who*" is **GOD** and that it is YHWH alone "*who*" is **Savior** to Israel and who is "*salvation*".

Psalms 3:9, (9) <u>Salvation belongeth unto YHWH</u>; Thy blessing be upon Thy people. Selah

How knowing all of this from GOD'S own words, can the words of Jesus be explained, integrated, absorbed or otherwise added to the words of YHWH without contradiction or causing problems for an observant Jew.

Is not YHWH GOD and Savior. Yes HE is. Then how can the utterance or the call to _another name_ when in distress be made by ones lips?

One can see from just the Prophet Isaiah alone how much that YHWH GOD thinks of HIMSELF and of HIS name. And it is the NAME itself which is the key here to understanding the issue of the name of "*Jesus*". The gray area of saying that we are "*one*", "*I and my Father are one*" makes the entire understanding a little murky. By this is meant that so much of what Jesus said, depends on whether or not one believes that he was no different than GOD. ie., **GOD in the flesh**. It was this very issue for which the Priests of YHWH condemned Jesus. This was essentially what Jesus was claiming. It is this same issue which has always been so troubling to many Jewish people.

In all of the Five Books of the Law, fifteen Books of the Prophets and the thirteen Books of Writings comprising 2,264 pages in book form, there is no one who comes even close to either having been or claimed to have been such as Jesus. Neither Abraham, Moses, Elijah, David, or Samuel either individually or all together came close to proclaiming or exclaiming some of the things that Jesus is reputed to have said in referring to himself.

Many of the words in the Gospels to a Jewish person are truly astounding because of the Law and the warnings from YHWH. But also, because of the many words of praise, hope and obedience of HIS flock who wait for HIM.

Psalms 50:14-15, (14) Offer unto God the sacrifice of thanksgiving; and pay thy vows unto the Most High; (15) And call upon Me in the day of trouble; I will deliver thee, and thou shalt honour Me.'

Psalms 33:12, (12) Happy is the nation whose God is YHWH; the people whom He hath chosen for His own inheritance

Psalm 33:21, (21) For in Him doth our heart rejoice, because we have trusted in His holy name.

According to the Hebrew Bible, all men sin. This would have to include Jesus, born in the blood of woman. As did many of ancient Israel, Jesus could perform miracles, speak words of wisdom and teach, but still be a man who is with sin. The Gospels never said Jesus was sinless, only that he came to save.

According to the Hebrew Bible, all men sin, all men die for their own sins, and that another cannot give to GOD a ransom for him (I Kings 8:46); (Deuteronomy 24:16); (Psalms 49:8-9). The question then becomes, did Jesus die for his own sins?

In Matthew 1:21, it does not say that Jesus came "*to die for*" the sins of Israel, but that he came "*to save his people from their sins*". Did not Jesus tell Israel to obey and to _keep the Commandments_ if they wanted to "*enter life*" ? Was he not warning Israel to obey GOD'S Commandments to keep from continually sinning before HIM? In this, he was surely acting in the capacity of a prophet, even if he was not the messiah. For even if he was a false prophet sent to try Israel, if they listened carefully to his words and kept the Commandments, nothing else he said would matter. Keeping GOD'S Commandments could surely be interpreted as saving Israel from their sins.

'IN THEM IS FULFILLED THE PROPHESY'

Matthew 13:14-14, (14) And in them is fulfilled the prophecy of Esaias, which saith, By hearing ye shall hear, and shall not understand; and seeing ye shall see, and shall not perceive: (14) For this people's heart is waxed gross, and their ears are dull of hearing, and their eyes they have closed; lest at any time they should see with their eyes, and hear with their ears, and should understand with their heart, and should be converted, and I should heal them.

It is not clear if this was to have been a direct quote or a paraphrasing of scripture. These words were often used in referring to Israel in TaNaKh by the Prophets when Israel was not behaving and was a *"rebellious"* house, and usually when they went astray worshiping idols. They became as their idols.

Jeremiah 5:21, (21) Hear now this, O foolish people, and without understanding, that have <u>eyes</u>, and <u>see not</u>, that have <u>ears</u>, and <u>hear not</u>:

Ezekiel 12:1-2, (1) The word of YHWH also came unto me, saying: (2) 'Son of man, thou dwellest in the midst of the rebellious house, that have <u>eyes</u> to see, and <u>see not</u>, that have <u>ears</u> to hear, and <u>hear not</u>; for they are a rebellious house.

Isaiah 40:18-21,(18) <u>To whom then will ye liken God?</u> Or what likeness will ye compare unto Him? (19) The image perchance, which the craftsman hath melted, and the goldsmith spread over with gold, the silversmith casting silver chains? (20) A holm-oak is set apart, he chooseth a tree that will not rot; he seeketh unto him a cunning craftsman to set up an image, that shall not be moved. (21) <u>Know ye not? hear ye not?</u> Hath it not been told you from the beginning? Have ye not understood the foundations of the earth?

These three Prophets employed these lines to castigate and shame GOD'S inheritance for their behavior. Psalm 115:3-8 also berates Israel for their sin.

It simultaneously refers to both the pagan idols themselves made by hand and worshiped, and to Israel at times when they are behaving just like the idols they worshiped, which could neither hear nor see. It was an analogy the Prophets of YHWH went to allot. Isaiah Chapter 44 is a sarcastic, almost cynical observation of the state of man and the idols he worshiped.

Today, these very words could be applied to man who has now replaced his hand crafted miniature GOD with his hand crafted technology, as *"science"* has largely replaced GOD as man's new *"idol"* to worship. Mainly for the non religious, one has only to listen to the excitement of people referring to their new upgraded gadget to understand their reverence for the *"god"* of technology. Truly GOD fearing people too become excited, but from a different angle. They understand the truth behind the science. To the non GOD fearing, science has become their truth. Only an *"alter"* is lacking.

YHWH declares HIS omniscience as the GOD of Israel and juxtaposed the worthlessness of man made objects that GOD'S creation makes and bows down to, all the while as man is expecting from that object things for which it cannot provide. GOD returns back to HIS earlier theme regarding HIMSELF and Israel. Isaiah 44:1-28 should be read in it's entirety.

According to the Gospel of Matthew (13:11), the purpose of Jesus speaking in parables was because his words were only meant for his disciples to understand. Yet, as the scriptures often indicate they seldom understood what he was talking about unless they asked him to explain his words. Moreover, if his message was so important to Israel to save his people, it would seem that speaking plainly so all could understand his words would make much more sense and be considerably more efficient than speaking in riddles.

His reference to Isaiah is comparing the people other than his followers to those idol worshipers and / or idols themselves which cannot hear nor see.

The fact that the Jews of Israel did not believe in him did not necessarily mean a scripture was fulfilled, but it did mean that they were not convinced that Jesus was the long awaited messiah, or that he was a prophet, or was *"one"* with GOD, or that his words came from GOD the Father. Many no doubt were confused by his words. His words often appeared to sound strange. *"And it came to pass, when Jesus had ended these sayings, the people were astonished at his doctrine"* (Matthew 7:28).

It was not just what he said, but how he said it which also got their attention. This idea can largely be summed up with the scripture which was asked concerning his *"doctrine"* as perceived by his listeners.

Mark 1:27, (27) And they were all amazed, insomuch that they questioned among themselves, saying, _What thing is this? what new doctrine is this?_ for with authority commandeth he even the unclean spirits, and they do obey him.

Closely connected with the quote of Isaiah is another reference to the *"fulfillment"* of something in Matthew 13:35.

'THAT IT MIGHT BE FULFILLED'

Matthew 13:34-35, (34) All these things spake Jesus unto the multitude in parables; and without a parable spake he not unto them: (35) _That it might be fulfilled_ which was spoken by _the prophet_, saying, I will open my mouth in parables; I will utter things which have been kept secret from the foundation of the world.

One might ask, if secret things were to be uttered, then what was the purpose of speaking in parables, but for them to remain secret?

The closest scripture in the Hebrew Bible to the scripture of Matthew 13:35 ("the prophet") is credited to Asaph, one of the Temple Priests. Asaph's following Psalm tells a brief history of the wonders and the might of YHWH GOD of Israel as had been told and passed down from fathers to sons. According to the Christian Bible (Zondervan KJV) and a search of the Hebrew scriptures, indicates that it is the only scripture in the Hebrew Bible that Matthew 13:34-35 appears to be referencing. The Psalm of Asaph does not speak of *"secrets"*, but of greatness, mercy and salvation of YHWH the GOD of Israel. Israel is reminded of GOD'S Law, to keep Commandments.

Just how this connects with the story in the Gospel and the use of parables by Jesus is neither clear nor does it seem to be relevant. Jesus was apparently speaking of something akin to a *"mystery"* which is not explained in the Gospels other than to what he said earlier that he was speaking to his followers understanding, not to the others. One may simply ask, then why waste so much time teaching and preaching in parables, if by doing so, he knew most would not be able to comprehend his words? Even his followers could not comprehend his words most of the time. The complete Psalm of Asaph (Psalm 78:1-70) does not refer to secrets or mysteries but of GOD'S Law passed down and told from generation to generation.

Jesus speaks of uttering things that have been kept *"secret"* since the foundation of the world. What would that be? If something was *"fulfilled"* what was it? The closest thing said by Asaph or any other which closely approximates the words of Jesus, only speak of the incredible omnipotence and *"wondrousworks"* of YHWH GOD of Israel. We know YHWH is great.

Psalms 78:1-7, (1) Maschil of Asaph. Give ear, O my people, to my teaching; incline your ears to the words of my mouth. (2) I will open my mouth with a parable; I will utter dark sayings concerning days of old; (3) That which we have heard and known, and our fathers have told us, (4) We will not hide from their children, telling to the generation to come the praises of YHWH, and His strength, and His wondrous works that He hath done. (5) For He established a Testimony in Jacob, and appointed a Law in Israel, which He Commanded our fathers, that they should make them known to their children; (6) That the generation to come might know them, even the children that should be born; who should arise and tell them to their children, (7) That they might put their confidence in God, and not forget the works of God, but Keep His Commandments;

In a cynical world, talk of splitting of seas, prophets calling fire from the sky and bringing to life dead children may seem preposterous. Perhaps this is what the Priest Asaph had in mind regarding the telling of the *"days of old"*. These and other *"wonderous works"* remind Israel to *"put their confidence in God, and not forget the works of God, but Keep His Commandments* .

So what, may one ask, was *"fulfilled"* in Matthew 13:34-35?

CLOAK

As just mentioned, if the *"message"* of Jesus was such an *"important"* message, a matter of life and death it would seem as regarding *saving his people from sin, "salvation"* of Israel, why would anything which was so important, be said in any way other than in plain simple language so all could understand? Why would anything so important be made so difficult to know?

Why would something as important as *"salvation"* be cloaked under so much secrecy, mystery and subterfuge? Why the deception? Why was so much of his words covered in a thick layer of parables and riddles making them so difficult for Israel to comprehend? What was the reason? What purpose did it serve? If there is a fire in a theater, the messenger does not yell out a riddle. He would scream out in a very loud and clear voice the warning. Would not salvation be such a warning? Was not saving Israel from sin the message?

Psalms 34:23, (23) YHWH redeemeth the soul of His servants; and none of them that take refuge in Him shall be desolate.

'WELL DID ESAIAS PROPHESY OF YOU'

Matthew 15:1-3 (1) Then came to Jesus Scribes and Pharisees, which were of Jerusalem, saying,(2) Why do thy disciples transgress the TRADITION of the ELDERS? for they wash not their hands when they eat bread.(3) But he answered and said unto them, Why do ye also transgress the Commandment of God by YOUR TRADITION?

There is little doubt, that this response by Jesus was directed at the *"oral"*traditions, ie., the supposed *"oral law"*which the Pharisaic Rabbinate Jews had been practicing and developing. These *"traditions"* were discussed earlier. For even back then as this episode shows, evidence existed that the Law of Moses was slowly being evaporated and eroded by the invented nonsense created by the rabbis. Having listened to them growing up, Jesus was aware of this. The sanctity of GOD'S holy word as written in the Safer Torah was slowly being supplanted by the unholy words invented and created by man and put into GOD'S mouth *as if HIS own*.

The term "*tradition*" is little more than a "*catch phrase*" for the man made observances, "*oral law*" *(Talmud)* created by observant Jews in addition to the Laws of GOD "*Laws of Moses*" (Safer Torah). The issue as Jesus so artfully observed, is that these "*traditions*" more times than not <u>*replace*</u> the Laws of Moses. Jesus was accusing these rabbis with their "*oral law*" of not keeping YHWH'S Law and "*transgressing*" HIS Law, even 2,000 years ago with their own self made "*traditions, "Why do ye also transgress the Commandment of God by your tradition"?* This is amazing.

There are at least a few things happening here as per the words of the Rabbis. They appear to be more concerned with whether the children of GOD wash their hands before eating, (and presumably recite their man made prayer), than themselves obeying YHWH'S written word in the Safer Torah. In truth, this probably had more to do with the followers of Jesus not regurgitating their (Rabbinic) man made prayers (bracha), than whether the Jews washed their hands before eating. For the writers of the Christian Bible, it may be that because they did not appreciate the exchange between Jesus and Pharisees and hand washing, they possibly focused on what was to them the more obvious issue of *cleanliness*. But this exchange had nothing to do with cleanliness. The words of Jesus were not about "*purity*" or "*cleanliness*", but about keeping the Law of Moses and a comment about the rabbi's *traditions*. His damning indictment against the rabbis for ignoring the Law of GOD and replacing it with their own invented "*oral law*" and <u>*traditions*</u> associated with it 2,000 years ago, is important for Jewish people reading this today to know.

Mark 7:8-9, (8) <u>For laying aside the Commandment of God, ye hold the tradition of men</u>, as the washing of pots and cups: and many other such like things ye do. () And he said unto them, Full well <u>ye reject the Commandment of God, that ye may keep your own tradition</u>.

As was mentioned, within this account in Matthew 15, is an even more important undercurrent regarding the *Law of Moses* <u>verses</u> the *traditions* of the rabbis, which in reality has nothing at all to do with either cleanliness or hand washing. For without a doubt, the rabbis had been listening to every word, and watching every action in order to catch either Jesus or his disciples. When the followers of Jesus were about to eat and did not say "*their*" Rabbinic prayer (for there is no Law concerning either washing or prayer before eating), what they either did or did not do was witnessed by the Pharisees and thus the verbal exchange with Jesus. But these rabbis were judging from their own "*oral law*", not that of the Law in the Safer Torah, and this was the point of the response of Jesus and the real issue at hand.

For normally, a "*bracha*" (blessing) by the rabbis is said while washing the hands before eating. The Pharisees would have noticed it's absence by the followers of Jesus and therefore the self righteous condemnation. Whatever it was exactly which prompted the rabbis to get themselves all worked up, it was not anything of the Law of Moses which was not being kept by the followers of Jesus. And this is the point. The rabbis did not know the Law.

'TEACHING FOR DOCTRINES THE COMMANDMENTS OF MEN'

This scene in Matthew 15:9, in and of itself might be a microcosm of the entire mindset of the Pharisees and the attitude of Jesus to them. The steady corrosion of the so called *oral law* upon the Law of Moses was already garnering the attention of the Jewish people. For surely Jesus was not the first or only person under the Law who noticed what was going on by these *traditions* created by other self righteous Jews. Rabbis were Jews who tried to hold their pious heads a little bit higher than the average Jew and thought of themselves as guardians of GOD'S Law, even at times above the priests.

According to the Christian St. Jerome (347 CE – 420 CE) living in Israel 350 years later, he expressed how the Jews of the land made fun of these *"rabbis"* and called them the *"increasers"*. Those who *"added"* to the Law. St Jerome had studied with the "Jewish Christians" and is said to have been the original author of the *"Gospel of the Hebrews"* which emphasizes obeying the Commandments of the Law, reputed to have been the original source for the Gospel of Matthew. So even after this much time had elapsed after the destruction of the Holy Temple of YHWH, the Jewish people still were not bowled over by, nor accepted either the piety of these rabbis or their *"second torah"* which they were creating, inventing, writing and espousing. St. Jerome lived in the Land of Israel, is credited with writing the Latin Vulgate.

'MADE THE COMMANDMENTS OF GOD OF NONE EFFECT'

Essentially what the rabbis had done with their creativity was to cancel out GOD'S *written* Law and replace it with their own *oral* law but giving it more or less the same name and mixing them together and confusing the people.

Matthew 15:6-9 (6).......... Thus have ye made the Commandment of God of none effect by YOUR TRADITION. (7) Ye hypocrites, well did Esaias prophesy of you, saying,(8) This people draweth nigh unto me with their mouth, and honoureth me with their lips; but their heart is far from me.(9)But in vain they do worship me, teaching for doctrines the commandments of men.

This scripture appears to be paraphrasing Isaiah 29:13.

Isaiah 29:13, (13) And the Lord said: Forasmuch as this people draw near, and with their mouth and with their lips do honour Me, but have removed their heart far from Me, and their fear of Me is a commandment of men learned by rote;

Here, the Prophet Isaiah speaks of vain repetitious prayers learned and recited from memory with no heart. For their heart is not concerned with the Law of GOD, but concerned only with the *"doctrines the commandments of men"*. These are man's commandments that they have learned by *"rote"* without heart, without soul, and with little or *no real or actual fear of GOD YHWH* and his word. Their oral law is dangerous because they mix in with it the Law of Moses. Like taking the very best wine known to exist and mixing in with it the very worst wine available. It is still *"wine"*, but it is no more perfect wine. Mixing *truth* and *lie* together is what the Talmud is. It is very corrupt.

This accusation by Jesus could probably be made against any religion today, Jewish, Christian or other. It is especially true of the *"descendants of tradition"* of whom Jesus was speaking. *"Tradition"* is the rabbi's middle name and reciting mind numbing prayers and blessings learned from memory is exactly what Jesus was speaking about even 2,000 years ago. He was right.

'IT IS WRITTEN'

Matthew 21:12-13, (12) And Jesus went into the Temple of God, and cast out all them that sold and bought in the Temple, and overthrew the tables of the moneychangers, and the seats of them that sold doves,(13) said unto them, It is written, My house shall be called the House of Prayer; but ye have made it a den of thieves.

Jesus was paraphrasing from Isaiah here, of whom Jesus seemed to be in sync with for Isaiah is often quoted by him. The Prophets speak of a time coming when all of the nations (those who still exist after judgment) will worship YHWH for HIS Holy Temple is a house of prayer, *"for all peoples"*.

Isaiah 56:6-8, (6) <u>Also the aliens</u>, that join themselves to YHWH, to minister unto Him, and to <u>love the name of YHWH</u>, to be His servants, every one that <u>keepeth the Sabbath</u> from profaning it, and <u>holdeth fast by My Covenant</u>: (7) Even them will I bring to My holy mountain, and make them joyful in My house of prayer; their burnt-offerings and their sacrifices shall be acceptable upon Mine altar; <u>for My house shall be called a House of Prayer for all peoples</u>. (8) Saith the Lord YHWH who gathereth the dispersed of Israel: yet I will gather <u>others</u> to him, <u>beside those</u> of him that are gathered.

This idea of other nations being joined to Israel and worshiping YHWH is echoed throughout the books of the Prophets. However, most of the Prophets seem to indicate that this will not take place until sometime in future after *judgment*. They speak of sacrifice and burnt offerings made to YHWH, keeping HIS Sabbaths and the Law of the Covenant. The Prophet Micah had this to say about the future when the nations would come to know YHWH.

Micah 7:16-20, (16) <u>The nations shall see and be put to shame</u> for all their might; <u>they shall</u> lay their hand upon their mouth, their ears shall be deaf. (17) <u>They shall</u> lick the dust like a serpent; like crawling things of the earth they shall come trembling out of their close places; <u>they shall come with fear unto YHWH our God, and shall be afraid because of Thee</u>. (18) Who is a God like unto Thee, that pardoneth the iniquity, and passeth by the transgression of the remnant of His heritage? He retaineth not His anger for ever, because He delighteth in mercy. (19) He will again have compassion upon us; He will subdue our iniquities; and Thou wilt cast all their sins into the depths of the sea. (20) Thou wilt show faithfulness to Jacob, mercy to Abraham, as Thou hast sworn unto our fathers from the days of old.

There are many prophesies regarding YHWH'S mercy and compassion to HIS *"heritage"* Israel, but also to the nations who will come to know and fear the name of YHWH. Still, sacrifice and burnt offerings are to be made.

Psalms 34:12, (12) Come, ye children, hearken unto me; <u>I will teach you the Fear of YHWH</u>.

The exact situation with Jesus overturning the money changers (for money was exchanged for animals, money was put into the Temple treasury, vows were met and could include funds toward the Temple etc.) is not clear, unless as with many other priestly functions, they had become corrupt and the situation was so perverse that his actions would make sense at such a time. The priests had many tasks to perform and functions to carry out in the running of the Holy Temple. For it was a huge undertaking every day to keep it running. It may have been that their function as guardians had slowly over time taken on more of a market or bazaar quality to it than just adhering to their duties and tasks as Priests and Levites. This appears to be the case.

Dealing with Temple money was a normal part of the daily running of the Temple of YHWH. There are examples of this throughout TaNaKh. Money was brought to the Temple and deposited into the Temple treasury for many different reasons including it's building and upkeep (Ezra 2:68-69; II Kings 12:5-17). The part regarding the selling of *"doves"* too would be legitimate, as they were sacrificed on a regular basis, such as with the mother of Jesus (Luke 2:21-24). Instead of all of Israel bringing animals to be sacrificed, often they were *"sold"* for the offering.

'FOR IT IS WRITTEN'

Matthew 26:31, (31) Then saith Jesus unto them, All ye shall be offended because of me this night: for it is written, I will smite the shepherd, and the sheep of the flock shall be scattered abroad.

In this scripture, Jesus again is alluding to a future event. In this case it is his followers scattering upon his own arrest and eventual death. In the scripture in Matthew, Jesus seems to be quoting from the Prophet Zechariah 13:7.

Zechariah 13:7, (7) Awake, O sword, against My shepherd, and against the man that is near unto Me, saith YHWH of hosts; smite the shepherd, and the sheep shall be scattered; and I will turn My hand upon the little ones.

The Prophet Zachariah is speaking about a time of the end when Israel has been tried, turns and calls on the name of GOD, and GOD forgives them.

Jesus may be making an analogy between his situation and that of a future event as told by the Prophet Zachariah with himself as the *shepherd*. But aside from David being the shepherd of Israel, YHWH HIMSELF often is portrayed as the Shepherd of Israel and Israel as HIS flock. As well, Israel's evil leaders are often portrayed as bad shepherds. But YHWH is *"Shepherd"*.

Psalms 95:6-7, (6) O come, let us bow down and bend the knee; let us kneel before YHWH our Maker; (7) For He is our God, and we are the people of His pasture, and the flock of His hand. ....

'THEN IT WAS FULFILLED'

After Judas hung himself, Jesus quotes again about a prophesy being fulfilled regarding the money which had been paid to Judas by the Temple Priests for his betrayal. Unfortunately, who ever put these words to ink got it wrong and the quote is actually from the Prophet Zechariah (11:11-13) not Jeremiah as written in Matthew 27:9-10.

Matthew 27:9-10, (9) Then was fulfilled which was spoken by Jeremy the prophet, saying, And they took the thirty pieces of silver, the price of him that was valued,(10) And gave them for the potter's field, as the Lord appointed me.

Once again the writer makes another mistake, but this time he quotes the wrong Prophet entirely instead of making up a scripture. The writer (or editor) of Matthew gives the source of the *"fulfilled"* item as *"Jeremy"* (other sources as "Jeremiah"). But the actual Prophet is Zechariah. In the story in Matthew, the Priests refused to keep the *"betrayal"* money after Judas had tried to return it to them. They did not want to put it into the Temple treasury. For they considered it *"blood money"* both because it was for the betrayal of Jesus, whom they were sentencing to death, and perhaps because of the suicide of Judas. And no doubt, their own guilt played a part. So they took the money and bought a field for the burial of strangers.

But in the Book of Zachariah, the *"prophesy"* is a bit different. The money *is* put into the treasury. The outcome is basically the opposite in nature.

Zechariah 11:11-13, (11) And it was broken in that day; and the poor of the flock that gave heed unto me knew of a truth that it was the word of YHWH. (12) And I said unto them: 'If ye think good, give me my hire; and if not, forbear.' <u>So they weighed for my hire thirty pieces of silver.</u> (13) And YHWH said unto me: '<u>Cast it into the treasury, the goodly price that I was prized at of them.' And I took the thirty pieces of silver, and cast them into the treasury, in the house of YHWH</u>

The entire chapter deals with Israel and Judah and how YHWH will allow them to be smitten and will not deliver them. He would break the brotherhood between them. YHWH was very angry in HIS words.

As with another scripture where the last line quoted in the Gospel, is completely different than the actual scripture in the Hebrew Bible, so is Matthew 27:9-10 opposite of Zachariah 11:12-13. Compare Matthew 12:17-21 and Isaiah 42:1-4. Verse 12:21 in Matthew has been rewritten. When compared, Matthew 27:9-10 and Zachariah 11:12-13 are different. In Zachariah, the money *is* put into the treasury in verse thirteen.

This last line of Matthew 27:10 is the opposite as Zachariah 11:13 which like Matthew 12:21 is non existent in Isaiah 42:4, it refers to and gives question to the integrity of persons writing some of these books or at least their editors.

So what does this mean? The scriptures cited are not only misquoted, but have the exact opposite out come. But as stated, what is even more important from this authors view, is the motive(s) of the person or persons writing these books. The reference to the Prophet Zechariah has no connection to the story.

'THAT IT MIGHT BE FULFILLED'

Upon the crucifixion of Jesus, according to the story, *"lots"* were cast for his garments.

Matthew 27:35, (35) And they crucified him, and parted his garments, casting lots: <u>that it might be fulfilled</u>which was spoken by the prophet, <u>They parted my garments among them, and upon my vesture did they cast lots.</u>

In this *"fulfilled"* prophesy, the Gospel is referring to a Psalm where David is bemoaning how he is constantly beset by his enemies. Contrary to what many might think regarding most if not all of these types of Psalms from David, he was not talking about the Philistines, the Moabites or the Assyrians. David was continually beset by internal strife, *"court intrigue"*. It was those closest to him that was his biggest heartache. He wrote constantly about such themes. David never bemoaned the enemies outside of Israel, it was always those who were closest to this former shepherd boy whom he wrote about. The Prophet Nathan told David that the sword would never depart from his house because of the taking of BathSheba and the slaying of Uriah the Hittite (I Samuel 12:7-12), *"But the thing that David had done displeased YHWH"*.

So, David was beset the remainder of his life with problems within his kingdom with family and friends. David could trust in no one but YHWH.

Psalms 55:13-16, (13) For it was not an enemy that taunted me, then I could have borne it; neither was it mine adversary that did magnify himself against me, then I would have hid myself from him. (14) But it was thou, a man mine equal, my companion, and my familiar friend; (15) We took sweet counsel together, in the house of God we walked with the throng. (16) May He incite death against them, let them go down alive into the nether-world; for evil is in their dwelling, and within them.

David understood well the meaning of GOD'S mercy, HIS compassion and HIS deliverance. For if David's Psalms say anything about David, it is that David was truly a man of faith and understood well his place before YHWH.

Psalm 22:19 is a powerful metaphor regarding the hornets nest David lived in. Verse 19 is not the only quote used by Jesus. For when he was on the cross, he is reputed to have quoted from Psalm 22:2, " *My God, my God, why hast Thou forsaken me*". For a better feel for what David was saying, more of the Psalm is given. David eventually ended this long Psalm of 32 verses on a positive note of hope, but from the middle of his Psalm is the following.

Psalm 22:12-20, (12) Be not far from me; for trouble is near; for there is none to help. (13) Many bulls have encompassed me; strong bulls of Bashan have beset me round. (14) They open wide their mouth against me, as a ravening and a roaring lion. (15) I am poured out like water, and all my bones are out of joint; my heart is become like wax; it is melted in mine inmost parts. (16) My strength is dried up like a potsherd; and my tongue cleaveth to my throat; and Thou layest me in the dust of death. (17) For dogs have encompassed me; a company of evil-doers have inclosed me; like a lion, they are at my hands and my feet. (18) I may count all my bones; they look and gloat over me. (19) They part my garments among them, and for my vesture do they cast lots. (20) But Thou, O YHWH, be not far off; O Thou my strength, hasten to help me.

No doubt the words of David were used often by Israel for their beauty and their simplicity of expression. Quoting David does not fulfill a prophesy.

As famous as Jesus was throughout the Kingdom of Israel, he must have been popular as well with the Romans. For his story would surely have made it's way back to Rome and to other provinces. Anything he possessed would have had some *"token"* value, either sentimental or monetary. Then again, it may have been some kind of a cultural perversion to own a piece of history. The Romans were not above barbarity. This part of mankind has not changed.

'AS IT IS WRITTEN IN THE PROPHETS'

Mark 1:1-3, (1) THE beginning of the gospel of Jesus Christ, the Son of God; (2) As it is written in the prophets, Behold, I send my messenger before thy face, which shall prepare thy way before thee. (3) The voice of one crying in the wilderness, Prepare ye the way of the Lord, make his paths straight.

Not allot is known of John the Baptist other than as with Jesus, John the Baptist managed to make a few too many powerful enemies. According to scripture he was the second cousin of Jesus through their respective mothers. John's father was a priest and his mother the daughter of a priest. The scripture alluding to Elijah the Prophet, who John the Baptist said he was not (John 1:19-21), although the prophesy of his birth was that he would have the *"spirit of Elijah"* Luke 1:17), and Jesus said that John was Elijah (Matthew 11:13-14), was to demonstrate how a prophet was preparing the way for the *"messiah"*. Although they did not agree as to who John was. Additionally, it is not clear just how much *"preparing"* the way John did for Jesus as he gets very little print in the Gospels.

Isaiah 40:1-3, (1) Comfort ye, comfort ye My people, saith your God. (2) Bid Jerusalem take heart, and proclaim unto her, that her time of service is accomplished, that her guilt is paid off; that she hath received of YHWH'S hand double for all her sins. (3) <u>Hark! one calleth: 'Clear ye in the wilderness the way of YHWH, make plain in the desert a highway for our God. (4) Every valley shall be lifted up, and every mountain and hill shall be made low; and the rugged shall be made level, and the rough places a plain;</u>

Malachi 3:22-24, (22) Remember ye the law of Moses My servant, which I commanded unto him in Horeb for all Israel, even statutes and ordinances. (23) <u>Behold, I will send you Elijah the prophet before the coming of the great and terrible day of YHWH.</u> (24) And he shall turn the heart of the fathers to the children, and the heart of the children to their fathers; lest I come and smite the land with utter destruction.

John the Baptist declares that he his not the messiah, but was sent before him. Additionally, he declares that Jesus is the *"Lamb of God"* who would take away the *"<u>sin of the world"</u>* (John 1:29). this is a considerably different message than that of to *"save his people from their sins"*.

John 1:29, (29) The next day John seeth Jesus coming unto him, and saith, Behold the Lamb of God, <u>which taketh away the sin of the world.</u>

John 3:28, (28) Ye yourselves bear me witness, that I said, I am not the Christ, <u>but that I am sent before him.</u>

In the Book of Luke there is an extended version of this *"prophesy"*.

Luke 3:4-6, (4) As it is written in the book of the words of Esaias the prophet, saying, <u>The voice of one crying in the wilderness, Prepare ye the way of the Lord, make his paths straight.</u> (5) Every valley shall be filled, and every mountain and hill shall be brought low; and the crooked shall be made straight, and the rough ways shall be made smooth; (6) And all flesh shall see the salvation of God.

However, as stated regarding Psalms, quoting famous Kings or prophets does not mean a thing either is true or fulfilled a prophesy. Today, people often quote scripture under certain circumstances as there is much wisdom there.

The quote of John and that regarding Jesus in Matthew appear to be in conflict. For Matthew 1:21 states according to the angle that Jesus was born to *"save <u>his people</u> from their sins."*. *"His people"* is **Israel**. But that does not seem to be the idea in John 1:29,*"which taketh away the sin of <u>the world"</u>*. *"His people"* and *"the world"*are two very different concepts. For *"his people"* represent Israel, GOD'S elect. *"The world"* represents what apparently the editors wrote after Jesus.

Within the Gospels there are two very distinct and competing messages. One is of Jesus and Israel and the other is of Jesus and the Gentiles/Nations/world. They often contradict each other and appear to be saying two different things which are not compatible one to the other. The overall feeling is one of Jesus bringing a message to his people Israel, and later editors adapting it to fit a much larger audience. Traces of this can be seen all throughout the Gospels, especially with regard to telling his followers he came only for Israel and for them to avoid the Gentiles. And later scriptures which contradict these words.

Returning back again to the topic of *"name"*, the Prophet Isaiah spoke of a Prophet who would prepare the way for *"YHWH"* not *"Jesus"*. And according to the Gospels, John the Baptist *"baptized"* Jesus for the remission of sins. If Jesus was *"one"* with GOD the Father, how is this possible? How can a man with sin forgive sin? And if he was one with GOD who is without sin, how and why is he baptized for the remission of sin?

YHWH is YHWH. Jesus is Jesus. David is David. Unless YHWH was both GOD and man, Father and son, creator and created, David and prophet, the heavenly limitless eternal and the earthly limited mortal, sinner and sinless etc., it is very difficult to accept John as a prophet, or the *"prophesy"* (Isaiah 40:3) which clearly speaks of *"YHWH"* the personal name of GOD in the Hebrew, not *"Lord"*, not *"Jesus"*, not anyone else. Also, Malachi 3:24 speaks of *"YHWH"* not any other. YHWH and Jesus are two different names.

Also, why would Jesus need to be baptized for the remission of sin? And how can Jesus bring salvation to a people, *"his people"*, who already had salvation in YHWH their GOD? Israel is his people. If Jesus was equal to GOD, how was he with sin and in need of forgiveness in being baptized by John for their remission? *"He that is without sin among you, let him first cast a stone at her"* (John 8:7). Why did Jesus not cast the first stone?

Isaiah 45:17, (17) O Israel, that art saved by YHWH with an Everlasting Salvation; ye shall not be ashamed nor confounded world without end.

Psalms 96:1-3, (1) O sing unto YHWH a new song; sing unto YHWH, all the earth. (2) Sing unto YHWH, bless His name; proclaim His Salvation from day to day. (3) Declare His glory among the nations, His marvellous works among all the peoples.

Salvation in YHWH for Israel, was neither unknown nor a new concept.

As for John the Baptist, the idea of a *"prophet"* who it was prophesied at birth would lead the way for the one bringing salvation (Luke 1:67-80), but who denied he was Elijah, and as a *"prophet"* had to send his own followers to inquire of Jesus to determine who Jesus was (Luke 7:19-23), does not seem much like a prophet when compared to the ancient prophets of GOD.

Mark 1:1-3 translates *"YHWH"* as *"Lord"* and appears to be paraphrasing Isaiah 40:3. This is another clear example of the *"name"* of GOD, being changed into a *"title"* for GOD. The Prophet Isaiah was clearly speaking of *"YHWH"* GOD of all creation, Lord of the Universe, maker of heaven and earth, the *"Savior"* of Israel. But this writer is attempting to apply it to Jesus.

'AND HAVE YE NOT READ IN THE SCRIPTURE'

Jesus tells a parable of the owner of a vineyard who rented / leased is vineyard out to a bad husbandman. The husbandman beat and killed the servants of the owner when they were sent to collect. The owner finally sent his son, thinking that surely the son of the owner will be respected. But instead he was killed by the bad husbandman. Then Jesus asks the question.

Mark 12:9-10, (9) What shall therefore the lord of the vineyard do? he will come and destroy the husbandmen, and will give the vineyard unto others.(10) And have ye not read this scripture; The stone which the builders rejected is become the head of the corner:

It is a good story, but what has it to do with Jesus? It appears to be a quote from Psalm 118:22 about David, GOD'S salvation, and HIS mercy being forever. Jesus seems to be saying that it is he who is the son of the owner who was rejected (the rejected builders stone), but will become the *"head of the corner"*. If by *"others"* these lines are referring to anyone but the SEED of Abraham, Isaac and Jacob, then his words contradict every Covenant and oath written in the Safer Torah, Prophets and Writings, the entire Hebrew Bible. Additionally, according to his own words while on the cross when he was quoting King David, it appeared that as a *builders stone,* he was rejected by GOD and forsaken, and *not* made the *"head"* of the corner.

This scripture may be where some believers get the idea that *"Israel"* is the bad husbandman and has been *"replaced"* by the Gentile *"church"*. But the Psalm itself, is of David referring to himself and YHWH'S mercy/salvation.

'THIS DAY IS THIS SCRIPTURE FILLED'

In an apparent reference to himself, Jesus preaches in a synagogue and recites the words of the Prophet who seemingly is his favorite, the Prophet Isaiah.

Luke 4:16-19, (16) And he came to Nazareth, where he had been brought up: and, as his custom was, he went into the synagogue on the Sabbath day, and stood up for to read. (17) And there was delivered unto him the book of the Prophet Esaias. And when he had opened the book, he found the place where it was written, (18) The Spirit of the Lord is upon me, because he hath anointed me to preach the gospel to the poor; he hath sent me to heal the brokenhearted, to preach deliverance to the captives, and recovering of sight to the blind, to set at liberty them that are bruised, (19) To preach the acceptable year of the Lord.

As with several *"quotes"* used from the Prophets, it gets a little messy towards the end with the original words from the Prophet Isaiah being different than those given in Luke.

Isaiah 61:1-2, (1) The spirit of the Lord YHWH is upon me; because YHWH hath anointed me to bring good tidings unto the humble; He hath sent me to bind up the broken-hearted, to proclaim liberty to the captives, and the opening of the eyes to them that are bound; (2) To proclaim the year of YHWH'S good pleasure, and the day of vengeance of our God; to comfort all that mourn;

The entire chapter speaks of YHWH through his prophet Isaiah bringing hope to the humble of Israel. Binding the broken hearted, freeing the captive and restoring sight. But it ends with the words of GOD'S *vengeance* to comfort the mourners. Isaiah continues speaking of Israel rebuilding the waste places, aliens working their fields and Israel being named the *"priests of YHWH"*, being called *"ministers of our GOD"*. Israel will *"eat"* the wealth of the nations, receiving *"double"* for the shame which they endured. YHWH will make an Everlasting Covenant with them, their SEED will be known among the nations, *"that they are the SEED which YHWH hath blessed"* (Isaiah 61:9; 65:23). Israel will rejoice in YHWH'S salvation. GOD YHWH will cause victory and glory to spring forth before all the nations. *"For they are the SEED blessed of YHWH, and their offspring with them"*

The *"glory"* which will *"spring forth"* is YHWH'S glory through Israel HIS people, before the

Gentiles. Israel is the *"SEED which YHWH hath blessed"*.

Isaiah 46:13, (13) I bring near My righteousness, it shall not be far off, and My Salvation shall not tarry; and I will place Salvation in Zion <u>for Israel My glory</u>.

It is Israel who has endured the shame of their sin and who will *"spring forth before all the nations"*. For Israel is a nation of priests, the holy SEED.

At this point Jesus was apparently doing fine before the Pharisees, as it is hard to get booed when reading from the Prophet of the living GOD. They apparently were OK with his reading from the text. Then Jesus stated, *"This day is this scripture fulfilled in your ears"*. They seemed to be taken by how *gracious* his words were. Jesus continued speaking until they were filled with rage and threw him out of the city and attempted to throw him off a cliff.

Luke 4:23-30, (23) <u>And he said unto them</u>, Ye will surely say unto me this proverb, <u>Physician, heal thyself</u>: whatsoever we have heard done in Capernaum, do also here in thy country. (24) And he said, <u>Verily I say unto you</u>, No prophet is accepted in his own country. (25) <u>But I tell you of a truth</u>, many widows were in Israel in the days of Elias, when the heaven was shut up three years and six months, when great famine was throughout all the land; (26) But unto none of them was Elias sent, save unto Sarepta, a city of Sidon, unto a woman that was a widow. (27) And many lepers were in Israel in the time of Eliseus the prophet; and none of them was cleansed, saving Naaman the Syrian. (28) And all they in the synagogue, <u>when they heard these things, were filled with wrath</u>, (29) And rose up, and thrust him out of the city, and led him unto the brow of the hill whereon their city was built, that they might cast him down headlong. (30) But he passing through the midst of them went his way,

At least in part, Jesus seemed to be alluding to his own time near the end of his life when on the cross, they told him that as he was able to save others, to now save himself (Matthew 27:38-44).

Matthew 27:42, (42) <u>He saved others; himself he cannot save</u>. If he be the King of Israel, let him now come down from the cross, and we will believe him.

In the end, what scripture was *"fulfilled"* is not clear as the words of the Prophet Isaiah speak of future events not yet having taking place, and do not seem to have much in common with Jesus or his own words.

One thing needs to be stated if it is not already understood about GOD'S prophets. GOD'S prophets were sent to Israel. Whether they were sent to the north to the tribes in Samaria or later to Judah in the south or during the exile. Their words resonate with affection towards HIS people. The prophesies by GOD'S prophets unless clearly stated otherwise such as with the Prophet Jonah, are not about the nations but are only concerning HIS people Israel. Any attempt to stretch the words of GOD'S prophets beyond their given parameters of HIS people Israel, is not only inaccurate, but is dishonest, disingenuous and wrong. The prophets and prophesy are generally very specific and not given so they can be made to apply to whoever wants to use them for their own given purpose.

'AS IT IS WRITTEN'

John 12:14-15, (14) And Jesus, when he had found a young ass, sat thereon; as it is written, (15)

Fear not, daughter of Sion: behold, thy King cometh, sitting on an ass's colt.(also Matthew 21:5).

This is a partial quote from the Prophet Zechariah 9:9 which speaks of YHWH as Savior of Israel. In the Gospel story of the *"triumphant"* entry into Jerusalem, it was during one of the *"feasts"*. None of the Gospels identify exactly which one it is, but from the story, it appears to be *"Sukkot"*, or as it is called by Christians, *"Feast of Tabernacles"*. Nevertheless, as it is often written, it was a *"feast of the Jews"* just in case the reader did not know who these people living in Israel were.

As the Kings of Israel seemed to prefer an ass (or mule) to other modes of transportation, and that Jesus or any other rode on an ass as opposed to an other type of animal such as a horse is not unusual. An ass was much smaller, sure footed in an uneven rock strewn land, easier to keep and cheaper to feed than a horse or camel, and was the *"people wagon"* of the masses. Some of the kings used chariots, but David preferred an ass. The _ass_ of the king was symbolic of his throne. So much so, it was used to install a king.

So Israel would get the message of King David's choice of successor, he had Solomon ride on the king's *"mule"* (I Kings 1:33-34) in front of all Israel for them to see, as Solomon rode to Gihon to be anointed King by the Priest Zadok. Asses were as common as sandals, but the kings ass was special.

Zacheriah 9:9, (9) Rejoice greatly, O daughter of Zion; shout, O daughter of Jerusalem: behold, thy King cometh unto thee: he is just, and having Salvation; lowly, and riding upon an ass, and upon a colt the foal of an ass.

The entire chapter is about YHWH as Savior to Israel. In verse 10-11 we are reminded of the *"Covenant of Blood"* and salvation Israel has in YHWH.

(10) And I will cut off the chariot from Ephraim, and the horse from Jerusalem, and the battle bow shall be cut off, and he shall speak peace unto the nations; and his dominion shall be from sea to sea, and from the River to the ends of the earth. (11) As for thee also, because of the Blood of thy Covenant I send forth thy prisoners out of the pit wherein is no water.

No doubt most of the people had and / or rode asses as they were both the common mode of transportation and were work animals. They still fill the Middle East today, including Israel, as beasts of burden and as transportation. That Jesus entered Jerusalem on this creature other than by walking, would have been expected. Bedouin are seen every day entering Jerusalem on an ass. So the point of the story was that Jesus fulfilled *"prophesy"* as *"king"* because he rode on, and entered into Jerusalem on an ass?

'MIGHT BE FULFILLED'

John 12:37-41, (37) But though he had done so many miracles before them, yet they believed not on him: (38) That the saying of Esaias the prophet might be fulfilled, which he spake, Lord, who hath believed our report? and to whom hath the arm of the Lord been revealed? (39) Therefore they could not believe, because that Esaias said again,(40) He hath blinded their eyes, and hardened their heart; that they should not see with their eyes, nor understand with their heart, and be converted, and I should heal them. (41) These things said Esaias, when he saw his glory, and spake of him.

One of things noticeable here is as in other places in the Gospels, an emphasis is placed on *"miracles"*. When it is these very things which Israel needed to be careful of. For they could be a way of deceiving the people. For **ONLY** the Commandments of the Law mattered. The eternal Statutes and Ordinances of YHWH trumped any *"works"* by a prophet. It was the words of Jesus as they stacked up against the Law of Moses which was the big issue, not *"miracles"*. Except for when Jesus healed on Shabbat, his miracles were never at issue. It was his *"doctrine"* and words which were the issue.

This is basically the same prophesy discussed already regarding the people not hearing or seeing for their blindness. Jesus is saying that he is the truth, but the people cannot see his truth for their own spiritual blindness.

The thing with this scripture of Isaiah and with the many others like it, is that it could be applied to just about any one of the many generations of Israel throughout their very long history. It is a true statement if Jesus said it or not.
Because someone does not believe a thing, does not mean that thing is true. It may be that Israel had good reason not to believe his *"doctrine"* if different than the Law of Moses and whose commandments he said ot keep.

'THAT THE SCRIPTURE MIGHT BE FULFILLED'

*John 13:18, (18) I speak not of you all: I know whom I have chosen: <u>but that the scripture may be</u>
<u>fulfilled,</u> He that eateth bread with me hath lifted up his heel against me.*

Jesus is quoting from King David.

As already discussed, King David lamented often of the conspiracies and intrigue which surrounded him. When he was not praising YHWH, more often than not as mentioned, it was *"court intrigue"* which he was speaking about. The *"enemies"* which he often mentions were not the Assyrians, Arameans or the Edomites, but those of his own people, in his own court.

He was not concerned with the many enemies of Israel, for they were much easier for him to deal with. As the leader of the army of Israel, David was without peer as a military commander. Not because of his military prowess, but because of his faith in his GOD. But it was those who were closest to him who gave him the most trouble and who provided him with the most pain.

*Psalms 41:10, (10) <u>Yea, mine own familiar friend, in whom I trusted, which did eat of my bread,</u>
<u>hath lifted up his heel against me.</u>*

Also, this author has long suspected that many of these words which are often quoted are idiomatic expression common to their day, *"hath lifted up his heel against me"* could easily be such an expression. As for David, with his immediate family this was so, as GOD told him because of his sin, what would happen. YHWH had the Prophet Nathan tell David what he could expect because of his sin regarding Uriah the Hittite.

*II Samuel 12:10, (10) Now therefore <u>the sword shall never depart from thine house;</u> because thou
hast despised me, and hast taken the wife of Uriah the Hittite to be thy wife.*

The Prophet Nathan had several other things to say, and as the life of David even as King of Israel shows, David's woes were not limited to just of his family. Nevertheless, YHWH told David, "*And David said unto Nathan, I have sinned against YHWH. And Nathan said unto David, YHWH also hath put away thy sin; thou shalt not die.*" (By this it is understood to mean *eternal death*, not that of dying a natural death which all are afflicted with).

There were few if any, in all of TaNaKh, who were loved as much or were loved more than was David by his GOD YHWH.

By using this scripture, Jesus seemed to be equating himself as being like David surrounded by those of Israel who *"eateth bread with me"* and who conspired and plotted against him. Or to be even more specific, Judas who ate bread with him and who ultimately betrayed him. Although according to the story, it was *preordained* that Judas would betray him as part of the plan.

As with any of the scripture references, the many parables and stories within the Hebrew Bible could be applied to many people and to many situations. That Jesus was betrayed, as are many in life, does not mean that the application of David's words are any more meaningful to him than they are to the reader or to another. Everyone is betrayed by someone close to them at some point in their life. David's words are well appreciated by many.

One of the issues with supposedly Moses, the Prophets and Psalms attesting to the identity of Jesus, is that it becomes a very wide playing field of scripture which one can then pick and choose from. As many of the scriptures cited both in the Christian Bible and in the Hebrew Bible are parables of one sort or another, it then becomes even more difficult to either apply them to Jesus or even to argue in an intelligent manner of their disconnection from him or his life. The point is, these scripture references in general do not actually prove or show anything. Besides, according to the story, Judas was appointed for his task. If Judas was part of the plan, how did he *life his heel*?

THE LEGAL CONTEXT

It is within the context of the **"*Law*"** that each and every issue regarding Jesus and his life must be viewed if one is to appreciate the circumstances which surrounded him during his life time. This will be repeated often to remind the reader that as stated, Jesus did not live in a vacuum. Everything that he said and everything that he did, was seen and interpreted through the eyes of a people who lived according to the Law of Moses and the Prophets.

The average Jew, the priest, Pharisee, Sadducee, Essene, Zealot, Sicarri, Herodian, Scribe, publican etc., viewed all of his words and his actions within not only the Jewish narrative, but within their own narrow view of the Law and the Prophets. For *"miracles"* aside, Jesus was viewed largely by his words and actions by the majority of Israel, not on *"miracles"* performed.

Jesus was a Jew and his people were Jews, the world which they knew, and the culture in which they lived was Jewish. They worshiped and sacrificed to the GOD of Israel, *"YHWH"* in HIS Temple. The life and death of Jesus must be seen completely and totally within this context, else a full comprehension of the words written and actions in the Gospels will be distorted by historical, cultural and religious bias. It is for this reason, that most church doctrine today is at variance in most respects with the words of Jesus 2,000 years ago.

One must disassociate the words of Jesus from the rest of the words of those who came after him and whose writings fill up many pages within the Christian Bible after the Gospels. As has already been pointed out, Jesus spoke to a Jewish audience and said on several occasions that he came only for the Lost Sheep of the House of Israel. He instructed his disciples to avoid and not to go to the nations but to the Lost Sheep of the House of Israel. This is necessary to repeat because all of this changed after he was gone. For beginning with Paul, it later accelerated exponentially within the Gentile world view, as they reworked and messaged his words into their very own world specific view and doctrine of salvation for the nations.

Psalms 98:1-3, (1) A Psalm. O sing unto YHWH a new song; for He hath done marvellous things; His right hand, and His holy arm, hath <u>wrought salvation</u> for Him. (2) <u>YHWH hath made known His salvation</u>; His righteousness hath He revealed in the sight of the nations. (3) He hath remembered <u>His mercy</u> and His faithfulness toward the house of Israel; <u>all the ends of the earth have seen the Salvation of our God</u>.

Many early and important church writings which differed from the four Gospels which have comes down to us have been lost or ignored. There is significant evidence of texts such as the "Hebrew Gospel" which showed the atachment of the Jewish believers (Ebionites) to the Law of Moses. This attachment to the Commandments by the Jewish believers was later watered down by Paul and then completely jetisoned by the Gentile Nations.

GENEALOGY

The Gospels either refer to the Prophets or quote them often in regard to Jesus, both to what he was saying and to his actions.

Beginning with his pedigree, there is a discrepancy, as the genealogy lists are vastly different, both from each other and from that of King David given in the Hebrew Bible. Matthew lists the pedigree from Abraham to Jesus. Luke lists the pedigree from Jesus to Adam. Only two Gospel lists are given here although when compared to that of David, none of the three pedigrees match.

<u>28 generations between David and Jesus</u>

<u>Matthew 1:1-17</u>, THE book of the generation of Jesus Christ, the son of David, the son of Abraham.
2 Abraham begat Isaac; and Isaac begat Jacob; and Jacob begat Judas and his brethren;
3 And Judas begat Phares and Zara of Thamar; and Phares begat Esrom; and Esrom begat Aram;
4 And Aram begat Aminadab; and Aminadab begat Naasson; and Naasson begat Salmon;
5 And Salmon begat Booz of Rachab; and Booz begat Obed of Ruth; and Obed begat Jesse;
6 And Jesse begat <u>DAVID the king</u>; and David the king begat <u>SOLOMON</u> of her that had been the wife of Urias;
7 And Solomon begat <u>Roboam</u>; and Roboam begat <u>Abia</u>; and Abia begat <u>Asa</u>;
8 And Asa begat <u>Josaphat</u>; and Josaphat begat <u>Joram</u>; and Joram begat <u>Ozias</u>;
9 And Ozias begat <u>Joatham</u>; and Joatham begat <u>Achaz</u>; and Achaz begat <u>Ezekias</u>;
10 And Ezekias begat <u>Manasses</u>; and Manasses begat <u>Amon</u>; and Amon begat <u>Josias</u>;
11 And Josias begat <u>Jechonias</u> and his brethren, about the time they were carried away to Babylon:
12 And after they were brought to Babylon, Jechonias begat <u>Salathiel</u>; and Salathiel begat <u>Zorobabel</u>;
13 And Zorobabel begat <u>Abiud</u>; and Abiud begat <u>Eliakim</u>; and Eliakim begat <u>Azor</u>;
14 And Azor begat <u>Sadoc</u>; and Sadoc begat <u>Achim</u>; and Achim begat <u>Eliud</u>;
15 And Eliud begat <u>Eleazar</u>; and Eleazar begat <u>Matthan</u>; and Matthan begat <u>Jacob</u>;

16 And Jacob begat <u>Joseph</u> the husband of Mary, of whom was born <u>Jesus</u>, who is called Christ.
17 So all the generations from Abraham to David are fourteen generations; and from David until the carrying away into Babylon are fourteen generations; and from the carrying away into Babylon unto Christ are fourteen generations.

<u>42 generations between Jesus and David</u>

<u>*Luke 3:23-38*</u>*, 23 And <u>Jesus</u> himself began to be about thirty years of age, being (as was supposed) the son of <u>Joseph</u>, which was the son of <u>Heli</u>,*
24 Which was the son of <u>Matthat</u>, which was the son of <u>Levi</u>, which was the son of <u>Melchi</u>, which was the son of <u>Janna</u>, which was the son of <u>Joseph</u>,
25 Which was the son of <u>Mattathias</u>, which was the son of <u>Amos</u>, which was the son of <u>Naum</u>, which was the son of <u>Esli</u>, which was the son of <u>Nagge</u>,
26 Which was the son of <u>Maath</u>, which was the son of <u>Mattathias</u>, which was the son of <u>Semei</u>, which was the son of <u>Joseph</u>, which was the son of <u>Juda</u>,
27 Which was the son of <u>Joanna</u>, which was the son of <u>Rhesa</u>, which was the son of <u>Zorobabel</u>, which was the son of <u>Salathiel</u>, which was the son of <u>Neri</u>,
28 Which was the son of <u>Melchi</u>, which was the son of <u>Addi</u>, which was the son of <u>Cosam</u>, which was the son of <u>Elmodam</u>, which was the son of <u>Er</u>,
29 Which was the son of <u>Jose</u>, which was the son of <u>Eliezer</u>, which was the son of <u>Jorim</u>, which was the son of <u>Matthat</u>, which was the son of <u>Levi</u>,
30 Which was the son of <u>Simeon</u>, which was the son of <u>Juda</u>, which was the son of <u>Joseph</u>, which was the son of <u>Jonan</u>, which was the son of <u>Eliakim</u>,
31 Which was the son of <u>Melea</u>, which was the son of <u>Menan</u>, which was the son of <u>Mattatha</u>, which was the son of <u>NATHAN</u>, <u>which was the son of DAVID</u>,
32 Which was the son of Jesse, which was the son of Obed, which was the son of Booz, which was the son of Salmon, which was the son of Naasson,
33 Which was the son of Aminadab, which was the son of Aram, which was the son of Esrom, which was the son of Phares, which was the son of Juda,
34 Which was the son of Jacob, which was the son of Isaac, which was the son of Abraham, which was the son of Thara, which was the son of Nachor,
35 Which was the son of Saruch, which was the son of Ragau, which was the son of Phalec, which was the son of Heber, which was the son of Sala,
36 Which was the son of Cainan, which was the son of Arphaxad, which was the son of Sem, which was the son of Noe, which was the son of Lamech,
37 Which was the son of Mathusala, which was the son of Enoch, which was the son of Jared, which was the son of Maleleel, which was the son of Cainan,
38 Which was the son of Enos, which was the son of Seth, which was the son of Adam, which was the son of God.

They all three (Matthew, Luke, Hebrew Bible [I Chronicles 3:1-24, 14:3-7, II Samuel 5:13-16, I & II Kings]) differ one from the other. Nevertheless, Jesus could still have been from the linage of King David, as David had a huge number of sons, even though most of them are not listed.

Much energy and time has been spent researching David's offspring in TaNaKh, and there are without a doubt, many thousands of his sons both in TaNaKh and with us today. If an accurate count were possible, it would probably render several hundred thousand descendants of David's SEED. The descendants of Aaron alone are estimated at 350,000 Cohanim by scientists.

With few exceptions, most of the genealogy lists of King David only give the sons of those who were heir to the throne. In a few rare instances, the names of other of the *"royal SEED"* are given. David had many sons and Solomon no doubt had many sons. Most of the kings of Israel had several, if not many wives, producing many offspring. Of King Solomon alone, we only know of one of his sons by name, although King Solomon had seven hundred wives and three hundred concubines. For twenty generations after King David, his sons had many sons who continued to have many sons. If one extrapolates just from the time of King David those sons which are listed until Jesus, the numbers are staggering. Even if one limits these progeny to only one wife and one or two sons, his offspring would be very numerous today. These numbers would be high in spite of all of the catastrophes which have befallen the Jewish people since the time of the Second Temple.

KINGS - I CHRONICLES / MATTHEW - LUKE

Biblical genealogy is always masculine, father to son. It determined if one was an Israelite, Jewish (tribal affiliation, Judah, Levite, Benjaminite, Ephraimite, Danite, Asherite, Gadite etc.). It determined inheritance, the priesthood and who would sit on the throne as king. There are at least two big problems which jump out with that of Jesus. The first is that the genealogy given in Matthew is through David's son <u>Solomon</u>. In the Gospel of Luke, his genealogy is given through David's son <u>Nathan</u>. Both of them cannot be the correct genealogy of Joseph his father.

Of Luke, only David and his son Nathan match, until Jesus and his father Joseph. None of those in the middle match but a questionable one or two come close. The Gospel of Matthew, which is closer to the Hebrew list given in the Hebrew Bible still comes up short. But Jesus need not have been either of these to be a direct descendant of David. It is the fact that the two accounts given in Matthew and Luke do not come close to matching each other becomes the issue. Additionally, had they both stemmed from the same son of David, either Solomon or Nathan, and had differed, it would be easier to deal with. As biblical linage in ancient Israel is always patrilineal, only one of these pedigrees has a chance of being correct. But neither do they match each other, nor match that of David's genealogy given in the Hebrew Bible.

Something else about Matthew was that in Matthew 1:17 the author felt compelled for whatever reason, to proclaim that between Abraham and David, and David and exile to Babylon, and Babylon to Jesus was fourteen generations each (42 generations). Why this was significant is not explained, but the difference between Matthew and Luke in the number of generations becomes all the more glaring because of this pronouncement.

The issue that neither of these two pedigrees match each other aside, and neither of them matches that which is given in the Hebrew Bible of David is interesting. When comparing the list given in the Gospel of Matthew and Luke, and that of David from I Chronicles and I & II Kings is that of the number of generations given in Luke surpasses that of both Matthew and I Chronicles and I & II Kings by as much as fifteen generations. The Hebrew and Matthew lists twenty eight descendants including David to Jesus. The Gospel of Luke lists forty three generations from David to Jesus. The point is, that neither of these genealogy lists add any credibility to the supposed pedigree of Jesus going back to David. They actually do more to destroy any connection to King David due to the wide disparity between them. They weren't really necessary. Having said this it will be repeated, the chance that Jesus was actually a SEED of David (excluding virgin birth) remains high due to the sheer number of offspring that he produced, regardless of these questionable pedigrees. This is being said knowing that he was said to have been of *"virgin"* birth. If Jesus had no earthly father then he could not be a SEED descendant of David regardless.

One final note. Had any of the authors of the Gospels been familiar with the original Hebrew text, it would have been easy for them to compare and synchronize their efforts with the original pedigree of King David. This idea along with their unrelenting use of the term *"the Jews"* gives added weight to the idea that whoever wrote the Gospels, or at least put their draft down in their final form, were completely unfamiliar with Jewish culture, Jewish Law, the Hebrew language or the religion of Israel and it's GOD YHWH.

'AND THY MOTHER THAT BORE THEE'

One other apparent problem, is that in the list of Matthew, Jechoniah (Coniah) the father of Shealtiel father of Zerubbable is listed in the genealogy of Jesus (Matthew 1:12). Not only does it not match that of the Hebrew Bible and given they are several generations off, there is a slight problem here as well, as King Jechoniah _and_ the SEED of King Jechoniah, _both_ were cursed by GOD through his Prophet Jeremiah that his SEED would not sit upon the throne of his father David. It is an exceptionally long and angry curse. The tone of GOD'S words from the Prophet Jeremiah are harsh.

Jeremiah 22:24, 26, 30, (24) As I live, saith YHWH, though Coniah the son of Jehoiakim king of Judah were the signet upon My right hand, yet would I pluck thee thence; …. (26) And I will cast thee out, and thy mother that bore thee, …..(30) Thus saith YHWH: Write ye this man childless, a man that shall not prosper in his days; for no man of his SEED shall prosper, sitting upon the throne of David, and ruling any more in Judah.

When a man is cursed by GOD in TaNaKh, it is usually always his SEED which is mentioned. Once again, Jesus could very easily have been a direct descendant of King David without the use of his genealogy. The problem again is that it was not necessary in as far as his message etc., was concerned. According to the text, along with most of the last several kings of Judah, Jechoniah was an evil king. According to the words of the Prophet Jeremiah, Jechoniah really got on the *"wrong side"* of GOD. This is an especially strong curse not only because he was a son of David of whom GOD truly loved, but because of the tone of the curse and the length of the curse. GOD is very angry here, not just a little bit angry. This is a curse directed at a man and his SEED. To make sure the message gets across, that the SEED of this man will not sit upon the throne of David, *"and thy mother that bore thee"*, the woman who begot him is thrown in *"just for good measure"*.

That Jeconiah and his SEED is cursed by GOD and is listed as part of the genealogy of David from which Jesus was to have descended, *disqualifies* it completely. In the list of sons in I Chronicles 3:1-24, the pedigree which lists the sons of Jeconiah also appears to give the names of Shealtiel *"Zerubbable son of Shealtiel"* given in other scriptures and may be a reflection of one's "House" rather than a direct "father / son" relationship. "*Assir*" appears to have been the son of Jeconiah, but beginning with "Shealtiel", the genealogy appears to pick up that of Zedekiah's sons and continue.

King Jeconiah was carried away captive to Babylon at a relatively young age. Whether or not he even fathered any sons is not known for sure other than possibly "*Assir*" listed above and is actually irrelevant. Given the curse of GOD, none of his descendants were likely to have been in the pedigree of Jesus, or wanted. The pedigree listed in I Chronicles is part of the surviving *"Book of Genealogy"* kept for centuries which eventually ceased. As has been stated, as King David had a huge number of offspring over many centuries, there is no end to the number of possibilities which exist as to his SEED sitting upon his throne without the need of the pedigree of Jeconiah.

Evidence exists that one of the many phantom *redactors* who took part in writing the Gospels may have had a hand in Jeconiah's *pedigree* because he was not familiar enough with the Hebrew scriptures to know that Jeconiah and his SEED had been cursed by GOD and so not noticing, added his name.

'DAVID SHALL BE KING OVER THEM'

Psalms 89:35-40, (35) <u>My Covenant will I not profane, nor alter that which is gone out of My Lips.</u> (36) <u>Once have I sworn by My Holiness: Surely I will not be false unto David; (37) His SEED shall endure for ever, and his throne as the sun before Me.</u> (38) It shall be established for ever as the moon; and be stedfast as the witness in sky.' Selah

In the Book of Ezekiel, the Prophet speaks of David being the *"prince"* over Israel forever. It is a prophecy which alludes to not only the *"SEED"* of David, as so many other prophesies speak of, but of a *"spiritual"* resurrection of David himself to be king over Israel forever. Other prophets speak of this.

It is here where the physical world of the Law of Moses, the Prophets and Writings of GOD YHWH of Israel and the ethereal world of the Christian religion part ways. For according to the Prophets of GOD, the SEED of David nd the spirit of David will reign, bringing *righteousness, justice* and *peace* to HIS people Israel. However, according to the Christian religion, the kingdom of Jesus is a kingdom in heaven etc. Unless Jesus left behind SEED, it is unlikely that he is going to reign. Not according to GOD'S prophets.

'DO THEM'

Ezekiel 37:24-25, (24) <u>And My servant David shall be King over them</u>, and they all shall have one shepherd; they shall also <u>walk</u> in Mine <u>Ordinances</u>, and <u>observe</u> My <u>Statutes</u>, and <u>do them</u>. (25) And they shall dwell in the land that I have given unto Jacob My servant, wherein your fathers dwelt; and they shall dwell therein, they, and their children, and their children's children, for ever; <u>and David My servant shall be their Prince for ever.</u>

Not only will David be king over Israel, but with King David as Israel's shepherd, they will " *walk in <u>Mine Ordinances, and observe My Statutes, and do them</u>*". **Woa-nellie...........!!!** What do we have here but a prophesy of the future king of Israel observing the Statutes and Ordinances of GOD'S *Law.* This does not fit in at all with Christian doctrine of the Law being *"dead".* If GOD'S *""* has replaced GOD'S Law, as most Church doctrine teaches, then why would the future king of Israel of the SEED of David be keeping GOD'S Commandments? Likewise do other prophesies such as Ezekiel regarding GOD YHWH'S Temple 41:1 thru 44:31 where the Prophet speaks of how the Priests the Levites, the sons of Zadok will *"slay",* the *"burnt"* offering, *"sin"* offering and *"guilt"* offering for atonement for Israel's <u>sins</u> and how GOD'S Laws, HIS Ordinances, HIS Statutes and HIS Sabbaths are kept will be observed. So what gives?

We have here within this prophesy, another example of the " *Law"* not being dead, but a Law which is very much alive in the future. David has not returned to his throne as yet, and *"for ever"* has not occurred that we are aware of regarding his reign of *righteousness, justice* and *peace.* The <u>*Ordinances*</u>

and the *Satutes* of YHWH, Israel and his king will *walk* in, Israel and his king will *observe,* and Israel and his king will *do.*

Why is this important? It is important because within the belief system of most Christian doctrines, it is taught that the *"Law"* is dead. Or put another way, the need to offer sacrifice for sin is dead because Jesus supposedly died *"once"* for all of mankind, *"Behold the Lamb of God, which taketh away the sin of the world"*. This John the Baptist said of Jesus which is in line with John 3:16, that GOD sacrificed HIS only son to save the world. Yet, it was said of Jesus, *"for he shall save **his people** from their sins"* *(Matthew 1:21).*

Matthew 10:5 (5) These twelve Jesus sent forth, and commanded them, saying, <u>Go NOT into the way of the Gentiles,</u> and into any city of the Samaritans enter ye not: (6) <u>But go rather to the Lost Sheep of the House of Israel.</u>

Of the overwhelming majority of all of the Gospel scripture which deal with this topic of *"sin"* and *"Israel"*, the scriptures mimic that cited above regarding Israel. The few times it does not agree but appears to contradict cannot be explained in any way other than the many hands which filtered the information after it was originally written down, and altered the focus on Israel to include the entire earth. Also, it is a matter of interpretation. As written elsewhere, going to the nations to preach to scattered Israel, is not the same as going to preach to the nations themselves. Jesus came for Israel.

The *"Law"* is regarded as an archaic aspect of a long completed part of GOD'S plan for mankind according to most Church doctrine. The assumption seems to be by most Christian theologians, that the *"Law"* was the necessary prerequisite for *"Grace",* but with the sacrifice of Jesus, the *"Law"* was no longer needed or relevant. And this especially would include the need for sacrificial offering for *"sin"*. This is the simple understanding of the *"Law"* and of *"Grace"* contrasted in Christianity. But as this book has shown, there are numerous prophesies which clearly indicate that all of the Law will be observed including sacrificial offerings made to YHWH for *"sin"*. So then what did the death of Jesus accomplish? The prophets clearly show offering for *sin* will continue in YHWH'S Temple in the future. Yet, Church doctrine dictates that there is no longer a need for offering of blood to GOD. As Christians accept the Hebrew Bible as part of their Bible, then the words of the Prophets of YHWH are a contradiction of their doctrine regarding sacrifice. The question arises then, *"how do you square that circle"?*

According to the idea of *"grace"*, the Law is not only dead according to much of this idea of it being the *"Old Testament"*, hence it's name, but it is now irrelevant because Jesus died (was sacrificed) *"once"* for all of mankind, hence the *"New Testament"*. *Jesus was to have shed his blood once for all*. Therefore, Temple and *"sacrifice"* is no longer needed or relevant. The word *"Testament"* here meaning the same thing as *"Covenant"*. According to Christian doctrine, the original Covenant of Law at Sinai YHWH made with Israel has ended, and has been replaced with a new *"Covenant"* of . Although as shown, scrifice for sin has not ended, but will continue.

Although the TaNaKh speaks of a New Covenant, what it has to say about this " *new"* Covenant is much different than what the Christians have developed in their own Covenant religion.

Ezekiel 16:59-60, (59) For thus saith the Lord YHWH: I will even deal with thee as thou hast done, who hast despised the oath in breaking the Covenant. (60) <u>Nevertheless I will remember My Covenant with thee</u> in the days of thy youth, and <u>I will establish unto thee an Everlasting Covenant.</u>

The prophets speak of nations bringing their sacrificial offerings to YHWH. In Jeremiah he speaks of HIS priests always being before YHWH to offer sacrifice and that HE will write HIS Law on the hearts of Israel. Additionally, HE speaks of HIS New Covenant (Jeremiah 31:31-34). A Covenant of His Law which will be written on the heart of Israel and Judah, *"But this is the Covenant that I will make with* *the house of Israel after those days, saith YHWH, I will put **My Law** in their inward parts, and in their Heart will I write it; and I will be their God, and they shall be My people".*

Israel has broken their part of the agreement made with YHWH, but YHWH will not forget HIS part of the agreement but will perform it. HE will punish Israel, reminding them of their shame. Nevertheless, HE will heal and HE will write HIS Law upon the hearts of Israel so they will never forget it again.

So, was Jesus trying to say that the messiah and the SEED of David were not necessarily one and the same? It appears that this was what he was alluding to by quoting from this Psalm 110. The prophets speak of the SEED of David restoring his throne, and walking in GOD'S Ordinances and Statutes. And the Prophet Ezekiel speaks of David himself reigning as already mentioned.

Israel, and the Jewish people have always *"assumed"* that because the SEED of David would one day be restored to his throne and would reign, that it was David who must be the *"messiah"* as well. But the possibility exists that YHWH will *"save"*, and David will *"reign"*. They are not mutually exclusive.

Judges 3:9, (9) And when the sons of Israel cried unto YHWH, YHWH raised up a saviour to the sons of Israel,......

The difference between YHWH raising up *"a"* savior, and YHWH being *"the"* savior of Israel, need not be explained other than to say that they are not the same thing. YHWH has always been Israel's *one* and *only "Savior"*.

Nehemiah 9:27, (27) Therefore Thou didst deliver them into the hand of their adversaries, who distressed them; and in the time of their trouble, when they cried unto Thee, Thou heardest from heaven; and according to Thy manifold mercies Thou gavest them Saviours who might save them out of the hand of their adversaries.

'THY SAVIOR'

Isaiah 60:16, (16) Thou shalt also suck the milk of the nations, and shalt suck the breast of kings; and thou shalt know that I YHWH am thy Saviour, and I, the Mighty One of Jacob, thy Redeemer.

Because David was GOD'S anointed, this added weight to the idea that it was David or the SEED of David who was to be the *"messiah"*. Other than the *"saviors"* during the time of Judges just mentioned, when GOD sent his judges and prophets to save his people before there was a king in Israel, it is only YHWH who is Israel's true *"Savior"*. According to the TaNaKh, the only *"Savior"* of Israel ever mentioned in all of the Hebrew Bible as the eternal shield, and sword or help of Israel who would *"save"* them, is *"YHWH"* HIMSELF.

It is by the hand of YHWH that Israel received *a "savior"* such as Gideon or Sampson, but it is *"YHWH"* who ultimately is *the* Savior of Israel. David may be *"anointed"*, but YHWH is his *"right arm"*. David may *reign* as *"King"*, but YHWH will *save* as *"Savior"*. Even the Prophet Malachi speaks of the Prophet Elijah coming before **YHWH**.

Malachi 3:22-23, (22) Remember ye the Law of Moses My servant, which I commanded unto him in Horeb for all Israel, even Statutes and Ordinances. (23) Behold, I will send you Elijah the prophet before the coming of the great and terrible day of YHWH.

As great a king of Israel as King David was, during his life time, King David was not referred to as Israel's *"Savior"*. There no doubt were times when the people may have thought of him in such glowing terms, for David delivered Israel from their enemies even before he was king. But David knew who was the only *true savior* of Israel, and praised him, honoring him all of his life.

Psalms 106:21, (21) They forgot God their Saviour, who had done great things in Egypt;

One has only to read David's Psalms to understand this. YHWH set David upon his throne and blessed him and his SEED for ever. David and his SEED reigned for many generations as King but YHWH was always Israel's Savior.

Isaiah 43:3, 11, (3) <u>For I am YHWH thy God</u>, The Holy One of Israel, <u>thy Saviour;</u>..... (11) I, even I, am YHWH; <u>and beside Me there is no Saviour.</u>

Isaiah 45:21, (21) Declare ye, and bring them near, yea, let them take counsel together: Who hath announced this from ancient time, and declared it of old? <u>Have not I YHWH? And there is no God else beside Me, a just God and a Saviour; there is none beside Me.</u>

Isaiah 49:26, (26) And I will feed them that oppress thee with their own flesh; and they shall be drunken with their own blood, as with sweet wine; <u>and all flesh shall know that I YHWH am thy Saviour, and thy Redeemer, the Mighty One of Jacob.</u>

Who is it that saved Israel time and time again? Who has been Israel's *Savior* always? What name did Israel cry when crying to GOD *to save* them always?

Deuteronomy 33:29, (29) Happy art thou, O Israel, who is like unto thee? <u>a people Saved by YHWH</u>, the shield of thy help, and that is the sword of thy excellency! ...

To whom, and in *"what name"* did David *"call"* to *"save"* him? In what *"name"* did David *"trust"* and *"wait"* for? Who did David himself cry to?

Psalm 54:3, (3) O God, S<u>ave</u> me by <u>Thy Name</u>, and right me by <u>Thy Might</u>.

Psalm 33:20-22, (20) Our soul hath <u>waited for YHWH</u>; He is our help and our shield. (21) <u>For in Him</u> doth our heart rejoice, because we have <u>trusted</u> in <u>His Holy Name</u>. (22) Let <u>Thy mercy</u>, O YHWH, be upon us, according as we have <u>waited</u> for <u>Thee</u>.

There is little doubt that as YHWH'S Prophets have prophesied, that David's SEED will sit upon his throne and reign again and bring peace and prosperity to Israel. But it will be YHWH who will make this all possible as *"Savior"*. David may well be GOD'S instrument for his purpose. We must wait and see.

ANOINTED

Psalms 133:1-3, (1) A Song of Ascents; of David. Behold, how good and how pleasant it is for brethren to dwell together in unity! (2) <u>It is like the precious oil upon the head, coming down upon the beard; even Aaron's beard, that cometh down upon the collar of his garments;</u> (3) Like the dew of Hermon, that cometh down upon the mountains of Zion; for there YHWH commanded the blessing, <u>even life for ever.</u>

It is worth noting the original source for *"messiah"* (christ) as is commonly used in Christianity as in *"Jesus Christ"*. It has been noticed how often the word *"christ"* is used as a surname to Jesus as in *"John Smith"*. Often the name Jesus is dropped and just the word *"christ"* is used alone. When Jesus is referred to as just *"Christ"*, it sounds odd, knowing the original meaning.

The origin of the English word *"Christ"* comes from the Greek *"Khristos"*, which translated the Hebrew word for *"anoint"* (*Mem-Shin-Chet*). The Hebrew generally has the meaning of *"anoint"* but can also mean to "*smear*". But it is almost always used in the sense of to anoint some one, or some thing, to be "*holy*". It is used when the holy anointing oil is poured on to something or somebody to "*consecrate*". It can be sacred vessels, priest or king. The word "*anoint*" is often used as a metaphor, with the idea that either an object or a person has been especially dedicated in the service of something, or someone, usually YHWH GOD. In Christianity, the word "*messiah*" is often interchanged with *Christ, "meshiach"* in Hebrew.

YHWH had Moses create from GOD'S recipe, what was to be the *"holy anointing oil"*. It is the anointing oil which the priest was anointed with. But anointing oil was used to anoint other things as well as the following scripture shows. Still later it would be used to anoint Israel's kings. It was poured on the head of the recipient whether priest or king (Exodus 30:22-33).
"*And thou shalt make it a holy anointing oil, a perfume compounded after the art of the perfumer; it shall be a holy anointing oil.*" (Exodus 30:25).

I Samuel 16:13, (13) Then Samuel took the horn of oil, and anointed him in the midst of his brethren; and the spirit of YHWH came mightily upon David from that day forward. So Samuel rose up, and went to Ramah.

There is no evidence that Jesus was ever "*anointed*" with anointing oil by a prophet. But it may not matter as is it is not a prerequisite for being appointed by GOD to do HIS will, perform a task or to be a "*messiah*".

'AS MOSES LIFTED UP THE SERPENT'

John 3:14-15, (14) And as Moses lifted up the serpent in the wilderness, even so must the Son of man be lifted up: (15) That whosoever believeth in him should not perish, but have eternal life.

Genesis 3:15 speaks of the curse by GOD on the serpent because he *"beguiled"* the woman given to Adam. It is an odd scripture in that it speaks of personal hostility between the *SEED* of the serpent and the "*SEED*" of woman. It is unclear how this relates to Jesus but for the scripture which appears to be associating Jesus with the serpent crafted by Moses.

Numbers 21:5-9, (5) And the people spoke against God, and against Moses: 'Wherefore have ye brought us up out of Egypt to die in the wilderness? for there is no bread, and there is no water; and our soul loatheth this light bread.' (6) And YHWH sent fiery Serpents among the people, and they bit the people; and much people of Israel died. (7) And the people came to Moses, and said: 'We have sinned, because we have spoken against YHWH, and against thee; pray unto YHWH, that He take away the Serpents from us.' And Moses prayed for the people. (8) And YHWH said unto Moses: 'Make thee a fiery Serpent, and set it upon a pole; and it shall come to pass, that every one that is bitten, when he seeth it, shall live.' (9) And Moses made a serpent of brass, and set it upon the pole; and it came to pass, that if a Serpent had bitten any man, when he looked unto the Serpent of brass, he lived

As with the story of Moses, whereby anyone who looked upon the serpent after having being bitten will be live, so too, those who believe in Jesus and "*look on him*", also would live. The analogy, besides the serpent itself, is that as did Israel sin against YHWH *"because we have spoken against YHWH"*, so are Israel as sinners against YHWH. So belief in Jesus will *"save"* them.

Even for the Hebrew Bible the story which surrounds this passage is strange concerning Moses and his serpent on a stick. Why Jesus saw fit to quote it too is odd. Jesus appeared to have compared himself to the incident of Moses with the serpent as being a type healing *"serpent"* himself.

The analogy between Jesus and serpent is understood. It is the choice of this particular story which seems odd. The followers of Jesus must believe, as did Israel when they looked on the serpent of brass made by Moses. Faith?

So now amongst other things, there is eating symbolic flesh of man, drinking symbolic blood of man and believing in a man as (if?) a healing snake. One may begin to understand why so many of Israel had issues with his *doctrine*.

'THESE ARE THE WORDS'

Luke 24:44, (44) And he said unto them, <u>These are the words</u> which I spake unto you, while I was yet with you, that all things must be fulfilled, <u>which were written in the Law of Moses, and in the Prophets, and in the Psalms, concerning me.</u>

After Jesus rose from the dead and appeared to his followers, he made the statement in Luke 24:44. What are the words he is speaking of? The prophesies of the Hebrew Bible, unless otherwise very specific for example that cited regarding the birth of Sampson, can be so general, abstract or, celestial in nature that they can be applied to almost anyone in any situation. And here Jesus includes the Law of Moses, the Prophets and the Psalms saying how they spoke of him. Yet, there is no evidence of this.

Generally it is Isaiah 53 which is used as the *"prophesy"* regarding Jesus, the *"suffering servant"*. For Isaiah, these words seemingly just show up from GOD and are written down. There is little doubt but that these words can very easily be used to define his life and death, if one is a believer. For other than the unwritten personal lives of GOD'S prophets who suffered and were killed, there are few other Jewish figures in the history of the Jewish people who are better defined by these words of Isaiah. But then, none of GOD'S Prophets had their life detailed in writing as was Jesus either. They speak *not* of a *"messiah"* who will *"save"* Israel, and bring *division*, who will die and be resurrected after three days.

According to the Gospels, when Jesus made this statement, it was when he had arisen and showed himself to his followers. He continued speaking telling them how it was written by Moses and the prophets of him that the *"messiah"*was to suffer and to rise on the third day. If there is such a prophesy, it is not with words which clearly speak of Jesus or someone like Jesus, but a parable of an ethereal nature which could be understood and applied to almost anyone. In other words, if YHWH had wanted to hide the coming of Jesus within the words of HIS prophets, then He did a very good job. Then continuing, it is written that *"repentance"* and *"remission of sins"* was to be preached *"among all nations, beginning at Jerusalem"*. If one understands these last words to mean they were to go to all of the nations and preach to the *"lost sheep of the House of Israel"* where they are scattered as he had earlier stated, these words do not conflict with his earlier words and are consistent with his message.

'PRESUMPTUOUSLY'

Deuteronomy 18:15-22 speaks of when Israel enters into the land YHWH had promised to them, that he would raise up to them a prophet from their own people who would speak "*in MY name*". The Hebrew translation does not indicate that GOD would raise up to Israel only one prophet, but by inference, *when needed*, a prophet would be raised up to Israel from their own people. HE said that the Prophet who speaks "*presumptuously in MY name*" or speaks in the name of other "*gods*" "**shall die**". HE continues with how Israel is to know if the Prophet was a "*false prophet*", when a prophet speaks in the "*name of YHWH*" that if the thing "*follow not*" then that prophet hath spoken "*presumptuously*". Israel need not fear him. This is why the continued emphasis by this author on the "*name*" of "**YHWH**".

Psalms 34:10, (10) O fear YHWH, ye His holy ones; for there is no want to them that fear Him.

'HIS NAME'

Given the tenor of GOD YHWH'S words regarding "*HIS name*", when juxtaposed with that of Jesus about *his* own name, it begs the question as to **in whose name** was Jesus preaching. For even with a poor translation where the name of GOD, "*YHWH*" has been translated as "*Lord*" (as was done), the Hebrew phrase which precedes YHWH'S pronouncement would be observed, "*thus saith YHWH*". This is especially true when prophesy is being given. Even the Greek translation would have this proforma introduction before quoting the words of GOD. Yet, no where in the Gospels is there even a hint of such an introduction of a quote from YHWH or that Jesus actually uttered HIS name as did the ancient prophets of GOD YHWH.

But once again, because there is no original Semitic Gospel to study, it is unknown if the name of "*YHWH*" was even mentioned. Referring to "*father*" or to "*God*" is not the same as prophesying *in the name* of "*YHWH*" or quoting YHWH using the standard proforma verbiage "*thus saith YHWH*" preceding GOD'S words .The Greek translation of the Gospels does not indicate that the holy name of "*YHWH*" was ever uttered by Jesus. If this is so, then all of the references that Jesus made about himself and his own name become even more troubling and problematic, especially when chapter 18 of Deuteronomy is read. For whoever the prophet is sent by YHWH, will be sent to prophesy "*in the name of YHWH*", "*in MY name*".

If Jesus was a prophet, in whose *name* was he prophesying?

Ezekiel 14:9, (9) And when the prophet is enticed and speaketh a word, I YHWH have enticed that prophet, and I will stretch out My hand upon him, and will destroy him from the midst of My people Israel.

What does the Law say about false Prophets?

'FOR YHWH YOUR GOD PUTTETH YOU TO PROOF'

Deuteronomy 13:1-6, (1) All this word which I command you, that shall ye observe to do; thou shalt not add thereto, nor diminish from it. (2) If there arise in the midst of thee a prophet, or a dreamer of dreams -- and he give thee a sign or a wonder, (3) and the sign or the wonder come to pass, whereof he spoke unto thee -- saying: 'Let us go after other gods, which thou hast not known, and let *us serve them'; (4) thou shalt not hearken unto the words of that prophet, or unto that dreamer of* *dreams; FOR YHWH YOUR GOD PUTTETH YOU TO PROOF, to know whether ye do love* *YHWH your God with all your heart and with all your soul. (5) After YHWH your God shall ye* *walk, and Him shall ye fear, and His commandments shall ye keep, and unto His voice shall ye* *hearken, and Him shall ye serve, and unto Him shall ye cleave. (6) And that prophet, or that* *dreamer of dreams, shall be put to death; because he hath spoken perversion against YHWH your* *God, who brought you out of the land of Egypt, and redeemed thee out of the house of bondage, to* *draw thee aside out of the way which YHWH thy God Commanded thee to walk in. So shalt thou put* *away the evil from the midst of thee*

Whether YHWH is sending such a prophet HIMSELF or not is not so important as what HE has to say regarding *"for YHWH your GOD putteth you to the proof"*. These prophets which may or may not *"arise"* will be used to test Israel. So, according to the Law in Deuteronomy, even if the given signs and wonders of the prophet *"the sign or the wonder come to pass"*, it is not to be believed as being from YHWH, if Israel is being enticed to go after other *"gods"*. Was Jesus asking Israel to go after *him*, to follow and *"believe"* in *his* *"name"*? According to both chapter 13 and 18 in Deuteronomy regarding false prophets, false prophets are to die. Was Jesus as a *"wolf in sheep's clothing"* enticing Israel to believe in *his name* to *follow him*? Was Jesus as one of these false prophets? Was Jesus performing miracles in his own name? Was his prophesy of his own death conviently added later by an editor to show how what he said would come true?

Deuteronomy 18:18-22, (18) I will raise them up a prophet from among their brethren, like unto *thee; and I will put My words in his mouth, and he shall speak unto them all that I shall command* *him. (19) And it shall come to pass, that whosoever will not hearken unto My words which he shall* *speak in My name, I will require it of him. (20) But the prophet, that shall speak a word* *presumptuously in My Name, which I have not commanded him to speak, or that shall speak in the* *name of other gods, that same prophet shall die.' (21) And if thou say in thy heart: 'How shall we* *know the word which YHWH hath not spoken?' (22) When a prophet speaketh in the name of* *YHWH, if the thing follow not, nor come to pass, that is the thing which YHWH hath not spoken;* *the prophet hath spoken it presumptuously, thou shalt not be afraid of him.*

What does Jesus have to say about false prophets?

Matthew 24:24, (24) For there shall arise false Christs, and false prophets, and shall shew great *signs and wonders; insomuch that, if it were possible, they shall deceive the very elect.*

For he speaks of them warning the people of what they might expect. Jesus seems to be paraphrasing GOD when GOD was warning Israel of false prophets. Was Jesus warning Israel against himself? For he even stated once himself, if they could not believe his words, then believe because of his *"works"* (signs, miracles). At the same time, he could just as easily have been speaking of himself and describing his own words, as he tried to prepare the people to believe in his name and to follow him. Who is *"the very elect"*? The very *"elect"* is GOD'S chosen, who is *"Israel"*.

Isaiah 45:4, (4) For the sake of Jacob My servant, and Israel Mine elect ,..........

Throughout TaNaKh, the *elect* always refers to *Israel*. Always. Beware of miracles. Know the Law.

Deuteronomy 7:6, (6) For thou art **a holy people** *unto YHWH thy God: YHWH thy* <u>*God hath chosen thee to be* **His own treasure**, *out of* **all** *peoples that are upon the face of the earth.*</u>

Psalm 33:12, (12) <u>*Happy is the nation whose God is YHWH*</u>; *the people whom He hath chosen for His own inheritance.*

Isaiah 45:4, (4) For the sake of Jacob My servant, and <u>*Israel Mine elect*</u> *,..........*

YHWH has said time and again, that it is Israel who is HIS *"elect"*. It is *"Israel"* that HE has redeemed, and that Israel is HIS *"chosen"*.

Matthew 7:15-21, (15) <u>*Beware of false prophets, which come to you in sheep's clothing, but inwardly they are ravening wolves.*</u> *(16) Ye shall know them by their fruits. Do men gather grapes of thorns, or figs of thistles? (17) Even so every good tree bringeth forth good fruit; but a corrupt tree bringeth forth evil fruit. (18) A good tree cannot bring forth evil fruit, neither can a corrupt tree bring forth good fruit. (19) Every tree that bringeth not forth good fruit is hewn down, and cast into the fire. (20) Wherefore by their fruits ye shall know them. (21) Not every one that saith unto me, Lord, Lord, shall enter into the kingdom of heaven;* <u>*but he that doeth the will of my Father which is in heaven*</u>.

This last verse states again what Jesus said before about the Law, to "<u>keep the Commandments</u>". What is *"the will of the Father which is in heaven"* but to **obey** and **keep** HIS *Statutes*, HIS *Ordinances* of HIS *Law*. For Israel is YHWH'S *"elect"* (chosen) who are to keep the Commandments of HIS Law. Jesus is saying that only those who keep GOD'S Law will enter the kingdom of heaven. Jesus is consistent regarding obeying the *"Father"* and HIS Law even when some of his other words are not so clear.

Did YHWH say that HE would keep hidden from Israel what HIS plans were from them? For HE has always told Israel of both the good and the bad.

Hosea 5:9, (9) Ephraim shall be desolate in the day of rebuke; <u>*among the tribes of Israel do I make known that which shall surely be.*</u>

Jesus states that you can know a false prophet by their *fruit*. What was the *fruit* of Jesus to Israel? Looking at his life time, he did not seem to do much but bring division and strife to Israel, exactly what he had said he would do. For even after he was gone his followers were still arguing over his words, the Law, Gentiles and circumcision as they tried to relate to his teachings.

Yet, to be fair, today's 2.2 billion Christians seem to be a testimony to his words and the fruit of his labor, assuming this was his intention. For the Jews, he brought division, but for the Gentles he brought hope. As a Jew, this is extremely obvious. However, it is more difficult to understand just what it all means in the total scheme of things. For the majority of Jews rejected him as the Messiah during his lifetime, although he claimed that Israel's messiah, was who he was (John 4:25-26; Mark 14:61-62; Matthew 26:63-64; Luke 22:67-70). In this regard, his *"fruits"* to/for Israel seem few and far between.

The Jews sought to kill Jesus for he had in their eyes violated the Sabbath and made himself equal to GOD and said that he was the *"messiah"*, *"therefore the Jews sought the more to kill him, because he not only had broken the Sabbath, but said also that God was his Father, making himself equal with God"* (John 5:18).

Add to this the charge of *"blasphemy"* from the Priests, and things were not looking too good for Jesus. After the Temple Priests finished with him, his future was bleak, *"....I adjure thee by the living God, that thou tell us whether thou be the Christ, the son of God. Jesus saith unto them,* <u>*Thou hast said:*</u>

nevertheless I say unto you, Hereafter shall ye see the Son of man sitting on the right hand of power, and coming in the clouds of heaven. Then the High Priest rent his clothes, saying, He hath spoken blasphemy; what further need have we of witnesses? Behold, now ye have heard his blasphemy. What think ye? They answered and said, He is guilty of death" (Matthew 26:63-66).

'I HAVE MANIFESTED THY NAME UNTO MEN'

In the Book of John (John 17:6), Jesus speaks of glorifying the name of GOD, *"I have manifested thy **name** unto men"*. Yet there is no real evidence of this. It must be recalled that the ***actual*** name *"YHWH"*, is so important within the narrative of ancient Israel, that it is not possible to over state how very fundamentally crucial it is. Did Jesus utter GOD'S name **YHWH** ever?

It must be asked at this point, when Jesus said that, *"I have manifested thy **name** unto men"*, where in all of the four Gospels is the name of *"**YHWH**"* ever mentioned, given, honored or praised? Where does Jesus ever once utter the most holy name there is in all existence? There is no evidence that he ever did. Does this mean that Jesus was a false prophet and died because of it according to the scripture in Deuteronomy 18:18-22, *"which he shall speak in My name"* ,...... *" But the prophet, that shall speak a word presumptuously in My name, which I have not commanded him to speak, or that shall speak in the name of other gods, that same prophet shall die"*.

Did Jesus utter YHWH'S holy name and then speak *"presumptuously"*? Perhaps one of the more troubling aspects, if not *the* most troubling aspect of the ministry of Jesus is this one issue of *"name"*. There is no evidence that Jesus ever said the name of *"YHWH"*, prayed to *"YHWH"* or prophesied in the name of *"YHWH"*. We are speaking of a GOD whose name is written nearly 7,000 times in TaNaKh. This is not insignificant.

The Book of the Prophet Haggai is small. It consists of only two chapters. Yet within these two chapters the proforma introduction or a variation thereof, is written approximately twenty times before the introduction of the words of the most high GOD *"YHWH"* are given by the Prophet, *"thus saith YHWH of hosts"*. This is said to make the point that even if given the Greek translation of GOD'S holy name *"YHWH"* in the Gospels was changed into *"the Lord"*, the words of Jesus (if a prophet) introducing prophesy in the words of YHWH should still exist in some form. All of TaNaKh is consistent regarding this. But within the narrative of the Gospels, it is absent. Jesus appears to always be speaking in his own name.

'WE ARE ONE'

*John 10:30, (30) **I and my Father are one.***

*John 17:22, (22) And the glory which thou gavest me I have given them; that they may be one, **even as we are one:***

*John 17:26, (26) **And I have declared unto them thy name**, and will declare it: that the love wherewith thou hast loved me may be in them, and I in them.*

Jesus seems to be alluding to the Shema here, where he says that *"I and the Father are one"* and *"we are one"*. As in, his words and his commandments are those from the Father. The Shema reads, *"Hear*

(O) Israel, YHWH our GOD, YHWH (is) ONE". Jesus is clearly stating that there is no difference between himself and his words, and those of GOD the Father.

However, one of the more troubling aspects of the words attributed to him is that he says that he *"declared"* GOD'S name to Israel, yet as already indicated, it is nonexistent in all of the Gospels. But we can already see from the Greek translation of *"YHWH"* as *"Lord"* in the Shema, that had it existed at all, it may have been lost in the translation. *"YHWH"* is the personal name of GOD, not a title. Nevertheless, not once in all four of the Gospels does the *"Tetragrammaton"* of the name of GOD appear. The Greeks when translating the Shema, had to have been aware of the name itself. Were the Greek translators influenced by the *"rabbis"* who forbid the utterance of the holy name and just followed suit by writing *"Lord"* as the rabbis did instead of a phonetic rendering of YHWH?

As the name of *"YHWH"* is written nearly 7,000 times and mentioned, referenced, alluded to, praised, blessed, extolled, held up, prayed to, made vows to and sworn by in the Hebrew Bible many thousands of times, it must be understood that without the name of GOD being mentioned by Jesus, especially regarding the message given by Jesus himself, there is a very serious conflict of interest. For although Jesus mentions often and seems to spare no effort in connecting himself to *"the father"*, or he and the father being *"one"*, and he was sent by *"the father"* or mentions *"his father"*, and will return to *"the father"*, his words were given to him by *"the father"* etc., the silence by Jesus with regard to the actual name of *"YHWH"* as *"Father"* itself is deafening, especially with his emphasis on his own name.

Matthew 23:39 (39) For I say unto you, Ye shall not see me henceforth, till ye shall say, Blessed is he that cometh in the <u>name of the Lord.</u>

Who is Jesus referring to here?

Mark 11:9-10 (9) And they that went before, and they that followed, cried, saying, Hosanna; Blessed is he that cometh in the <u>name of the Lord</u>: (10) Blessed be the kingdom of our father David, that cometh in the <u>name of the Lord</u>: Hosanna in the highest.

One must ask, did these people hear Jesus speak in the *"name of YHWH"*? Did Jesus refer to himself as "LORD"?

John 13:13, (13) Ye call me Master and Lord: and ye say well; <u>for so I am.</u>

John 20:28, (28) And Thomas answered and said unto him, <u>My Lord and my God.</u>

After Thomas, one of the disciples of Jesus is finally convinced of who Jesus is, he makes this astonishing proclamation of the deity of Jesus, as "GOD".

Aside from Jesus being referred to as the *"Lord"*, prayers to the *"Lord"* (GOD), quotes from the prophets referring to the *"Lord"*, there is no *"word"* given by GOD quoted by Jesus as if being given by YHWH. Many times reference is made to the *"Lord"*, about the *"Lord"*. Mention is made of the commandments of the *"Lord"*, angels of the *"Lord"* and the day of the *"Lord"* and others. Yet, *"thus saith YHWH"* does not exist. Not even *"Thus saith the Lord"* from Jesus before quoting prophetic words from YHWH who is GOD.

Jesus said that he was *"Lord"*. Was he saying that he was "YHWH GOD"? Thomas seems to believe so. There is no correction by Jesus rebuking Thomas for calling him "GOD". This alone is extremely troubling.

The term "*Lord*" and "*lord*" are used countless times in the four Gospels. There is a distinct difference in the use and meaning. The first "*Lord*" is usually translated from the Greek as either "*YHWH*", as in the example given of the "*Shema*" (Mark 12:29), or possibly "*GOD*". The "*lord*", is usually referring to "*master*" or similar to "*sir*", is used as a sign of respect.

In many places he constantly is connecting himself with GOD the father, but from the Greek Gospels, let alone the English translation, Jesus does not appear to have mentioned or said the name of GOD once. The name of GOD as GOD says HIMSELF is "*YHWH*". One must ask, *what name* did Jesus "*manifest*" unto men?

'TRULY IN YHWH OUR GOD IS THE SALVATION OF ISRAEL'

The Prophet Jeremiah in Chapter 3, when referring to Judah and Israel, YHWH declares HIS love for HIS people and what would one day be as they are brought to Zion. How "*nations*" would be gathered to it. YHWH is unabashed in HIS affection for HIS people Israel. He says that "*all of the nations*" will be gathered to Jerusalem "*to the name of YHWH*". But HE said something else very profound, "*Truly vain have proved the hills, the uproar on the mountains; truly in **YHWH** our God is the **salvation of** Israel*".

It is scriptures like this which grips the Jewish soul and makes accepting any other "*name*" associated with salvation regarding Israel difficult to digest.

'SALVATION IS OF THE JEWS'

In the encounter Jesus had with the Samaritan woman, he tells her that "*salvation is of the Jews*". On one level he is correct. Yet, what did he really mean when he uttered these words? Was he just stating that regarding the Samaritans, salvation will come through and by the Jews, or was he saying something else? He appeared to be saying this as well as alluding to the prayer of King Solomon above when he dedicated the Temple of YHWH I Kings 8:1-66. Yet, "*truly in YHWH our God is the salvation of Israel*".

John 4:21-26, (21) Jesus saith unto her, Woman, believe me, the hour cometh, when ye shall neither in this mountain, nor yet at Jerusalem, worship the Father. (22) Ye worship ye know not what: we know what we worship: for salvation is of the Jews. (23) But the hour cometh, and now is, when the true worshippers shall worship the Father in spirit and in truth: for the Father seeketh such to worship him. (24) God is a Spirit: and they that worship him must worship him in spirit and in truth. (25) The woman saith unto him, I know that Messias cometh, which is called Christ: when he is come, he will tell us all things. (26) Jesus saith unto her, I that speak unto thee am he.

One must ask the question, who did Israel cry to in time of need, when they needed their "*savior*". It was to "***YHWH***" their GOD and to none other. With utmost respect to David and to his SEED, it will be to YHWH whom Israel will cry to save them, although David may be used as GOD'S sword. As for Jesus, it was not he in Egypt or Canaan saving Israel, but YHWH.

Judges 3:9, 15, (9) And when the children Israel cried unto YHWH, YHWH raised up A Saviour to the Sons of Israel, who saved them, even Othniel the son of Kenaz, Caleb's younger brother.....(15) But when the Sons of Israel cried unto YHWH, YHWH raised them up A Saviour, Ehud the son of

Gera, the Benjamite, a man left-handed; and the Sons of Israel sent a present by him unto Eglon the king of Moab.

Like any son, when afraid or feeling in danger, he will call to his father for help. Likewise, Israel cried to their Father whenever they got into trouble. Only the difference was that their Father was YHWH, who is GOD.

It is *always* the name of *"YHWH"* that Israel cried to. And it was always YHWH who sent a *"savior"*. The entire book of Judges is one continuous motif of Israel being good, sinning, being punished by their GOD YHWH by using their neighbors, Israel crying to YHWH and YHWH sending Israel a *"savior"* to save them. The Book of Judges encapsulates Israel's relationship with their GOD YHWH. It is a cyclical relationship of sin and salvation.

When Moses came to Pharaoh, he did so speaking in the name of *"YHWH"*.

Exodus 5:1-2, (1) And afterward Moses and Aaron came, and said unto Pharaoh: 'Thus saith YHWH, the God of Israel: Let My people go, that they may hold a feast unto Me in the wilderness.' (2) And Pharaoh said: 'Who is YHWH, that I should hearken unto His voice to let Israel go? I know not YHWH, and moreover I will not let Israel go.'

Of course, Pharaoh came to know the name of *"YHWH"* and who he was, and also became aware that he was not good at predicting the future, as he did *"let Israel go"*. Moses reminded YHWH in verse 23 how he had spoken in HIS name, *"YHWH"*, but Pharaoh was inflicting Israel even more and was making matters worse *"For since I came to Pharaoh to speak in Thy name, he hath dealt ill with this people; neither hast Thou delivered Thy people at all"*.

The idea here, is that even the greatest prophet of Israel was always careful to speak only in the name of *"YHWH"*, not in his own name. And Moses was *"no slouch"* when it came to being a Prophet. Without a doubt, Moses was a major player in the historical narrative of Israel, and their greatest Prophet. Fast forward to Jesus and there is no sense from the Gospels of Jesus being a spokesman for GOD *"YHWH"*, so much as for himself, in *his own name*. And THIS, is the main problem with the name issue. One reads the Gospels not with GOD'S name.

At the risk of offending, which is not the intent, the feeling one gets from reading the Gospels, is *"me, me, me"* and *"I, I, I"* and *"Jesus, Jesus, Jesus"* with only lip service being given to an unnamed GOD the father. The *"NAME"* itself is of prime importance. The name of *"YHWH"* it seems, was not mentioned by Jesus. At least not in so far as the text itself reflects. After reading the Gospels, one does not walk away from it feeling that the name of GOD has been either magnified, glorified or honored, based on the written scriptures. There is no feeling at all of *"YHWH, YHWH, YHWH"*.

The reader must study the Gospels in context. The *"context"* of the Gospels is the Hebrew Bible. In the Hebrew Bible, the name of GOD, *"Y-H-W-H"*, is *so* important, that for it to have not even been mentioned by name even once by Jesus, as the author of what Jesus was teaching, if that was the case, becomes a stumbling block of such immense proportions, that nothing else he said or did to many of Israel, would have been of any interest. The oldest Greek texts of the Gospels do not have YHWH written within it's pages.

The accusers of Jesus. Accusing him for saying that he was the *"son of GOD"* were amiss. If Jesus was not speaking *"in the name of YHWH"* as was Moses, who himself was very specific when speaking to both Israel and Pharaoh in that he was not speaking *in his own name*, then the Priests and the Pharisees and others were not paying close enough attention. Jesus was a *"son"* of the *"Father"*. Jesus was a son of GOD, as are *all* of the circumcised sons of Jacob, but the question should be asked, *'was Jesus honoring YHWH and HIS name as he should have been'?*

'BECAUSE HE HATH KNOWN MY NAME'

But what does the Hebrew Bible say about the *name* of GOD? How do we know that this is HIS *name?* Is *salvation* associated with HIS holy *name?*

Psalms 91:14-16, (14) 'Because he hath set his love upon Me, therefore will I deliver him; I will set him on high, because he hath known My Name. (15) He shall call upon Me, and I will answer him; I will be with him in trouble; I will rescue him, and bring him to honour. (16) With long life will I satisfy him, and make Him to behold My Salvation.'

Well, HE said what HIS name is many, many times. There is no mistaken what he calls HIMSELF and that *"YHWH"* is HIS name and the name that HE will be remembered by and that HE is jealous of, just as HE told Moses. This is the name of the GOD of Jesus. The question then continues, did Jesus ever give *"place"* to the name of GOD *YHWH*, and honor HIM? Did he exalt YHWH'S holy name? Did Jesus glorify the name of YHWH?

Exodus 3:13-15, (13) And Moses said unto God: 'Behold, when I come unto the sons of Israel, and shall say unto them: The God of your fathers hath sent me unto you; and they shall say to me: What is His name? what shall I say unto them?' (14) And God said unto Moses: 'I AM THAT I AM'; and He said: 'Thus shalt thou say unto the sons of Israel: I AM hath sent me unto you.' (15) And God said moreover unto Moses: 'Thus shalt thou say unto the sons of Israel: YHWH, the God of your fathers, the God of Abraham, the God of Isaac, and the God of Jacob, hath sent me unto you; this is My name for ever, and this is My memorial unto all generations

Isaiah 42:8, (8) I am YHWH, that is My name; and My glory will I not give to another, neither My praise to graven images.

Amos 5:8...... YHWH is His name

Hosea 12:6, (6) But YHWH, the God of hosts, YHWH is His name.

Ezekiel 39:25, (25) Therefore thus saith the Lord YHWH: Now will I bring back the captivity of Jacob, and have compassion upon the whole house of Israel; and I will be jealous for My holy name.

There are far too many examples in the Hebrew Bible regarding YHWH and HIS holy name to write even a fraction of them all. The point is, that if one reads just the Prophets in the Hebrew Bible, they will see that it is *in the name of "YHWH"* that these prophets speak. Amos does not speak in the name of Amos etc. And Amos was the son of GOD as was Ezekiel, Hosea and Isaiah and all of the prophets. In *YHWH: The Name of GOD*, an attempt was made to explain the unfathomable essence of the name of *YHWH* itself.

FATHERS AND SONS

Jeremiah 3:19, (19) But I said: 'How would I put thee among the sons, and give thee a pleasant land, the goodliest heritage of the nations!' And I said: '<u>Thou shalt call Me, My father</u>; and shalt not turn away from following Me.'

Jesus called his GOD "*Father*", but then most of Israel referred to GOD as their "*Father*", for HE was. Nevertheless, being accused of blasphemy for saying that he was the son of GOD was a serious accusation. Regardless of it's merits, it was very serious to be accused of such a thing in ancient Israel, and could very easily have escalated into his being stoned to death. Yet, he *was* the son of GOD, as are all of the circumcised sons of Jacob. By the leaders of Israel denying Jesus was the son of YHWH, they were in a sense denying their own birthright as GOD'S "*first born son*" as well. So in the Hebrew Bible, who is the "*Father*" and who are the "*sons*" of the "*Father*"?

Isaiah 45:11, (11) <u>Thus saith YHWH</u>, the Holy One of Israel, and his Maker: Ask Me of the things that are to come; <u>concerning My Sons</u>, and concerning the work of My hands, command ye Me.

As YHWH had Moses tell Pharaoh, *"Thus saith YHWH: <u>Israel is My son, My first-born</u>",* HE makes no secret as to *"who"* Israel is to HIM as HE has the Prophet Jeremiah (3:19) state concerning Israel.

Exodus 4:22-23, (22) And thou shalt say unto Pharaoh: <u>Thus saith YHWH: Israel is My son, My first-born</u>. (23) And I have said unto thee: <u>Let My son go</u>, that he may serve Me; and thou hast refused to let him go. Behold, I will slay thy son, thy first-born.' --

The Hebrew word translated as *"first born"* is "*bikor*" *(Bet-Kaf-Resh)* meaning also, *"first fruit"*. The Hebrew is literally *"MY first fruit"* or *"MY first born"*. It can also mean anything that is done "*early*", as in *"new fruit",* as in a rising sun or a woman having her first child, It can also mean "*virgin*". The idea of *"first fruits"* in ancient Israel was huge, and was in many respects central to much of the "*religion*" centered around the Temple of YHWH. The Hebrew word for "*morning*" is "*boker*" from the same Hebrew root, as in the sun *"rising"*. It has the feeling of *fresh* or new *"day"*.

The first born son represented the strength and the might of the father in ancient Israel. Jesus was the first born son of Joseph. The inheritance of the first born son was to be a double portion of that of the other brothers. This is one of the reasons that the stories of the Patriarchs and the rivalry between Ishmael and Isaac, between Jacob and Esau and including Joseph replacing Reuben as first born, whereby Joseph received the double portion as first born through his two sons Ephraim and Manasseh were so dramatic.

Jeremiah 31:9, (9) They shall come with weeping, and with supplications will I lead them; I will cause them to walk by rivers of waters, in a straight way wherein they shall not stumble; <u>for I am become a Father to Israel, and Ephraim is My first-born</u>.

The main problem or issue with the name of "*Jesus*", is that the name of "*Yeshua*" is mentioned often and without hesitancy by Jesus himself, but the name of GOD, **"YHWH"** does not appear to have been part of the narrative.

FOOL

Matthew 5:22, (22) But I say unto you, That whosoever is angry with his brother without a cause shall be in danger of the judgment: and whosoever shall say to his brother, Raca, shall be in danger *of the council: __but whosoever shall say, Thou fool, shall be in danger of hell fire.__*

The number of times that Jesus called another or others *"fool"* or *"fools"* is striking considering what he had to say about calling a person this word. Quite often it was his own followers who were on the receiving end of this word from himself. Yet, how are we to understand it's meaning, when Jesus appeared to be so cavalier with it's use? Jesus spoke in riddles, yet called his followers *"fools"* when they failed to understand.

Another issue is that it seems to fly in the face of the way that Jesus is generally portrayed as a man of love and compassion who would die for others etc. With the exception of the cleansing of the Temple, which is in another league all unto itself, this type of behavior on his part seems almost petty and out of character in comparison.

Matthew 23:17, 19, (7) __Ye fools__ and blind: for whether is greater, the gold, or the temple that sanctifieth the gold?......(19) __Ye fools__ and blind: for whether is greater, the gift, or the altar that sanctifieth the gift?

In Luke, Jesus even has GOD calling a man *"fool"*.

Luke 12:20, (20) But God said unto him, __Thou fool__, this night thy soul shall be required of thee: then whose shall those things be, which thou hast provided?

The story in Luke (Luke 24:13-35) too is strange in that after Jesus was *"resurrected"*, he met two of his followers walking on a road. They were not aware of who he was as the story unfolds, and they were not to recognize him until he made himself known to them. The two men explained why they were sad. That a *"prophet"* had been crucified. And then they say something which is contrary to the words of the Safer Torah and in all of TaNaKh.

Luke 24:21-27, (21) __But we trusted that it had been he which should have redeemed Israel:__ and beside all this, to day is the third day since these things were done. (22) Yea, and certain women also of our company made us astonished, which were early at the sepulchre; (23) And when they found not his body, they came, saying, that they had also seen a vision of angels, which said that he was alive.(24) And certain of them which were with us went to the sepulchre, and found it even so as the women had said: but him they saw not. (25) __Then he said unto them, O fools, and slow of heart to believe all that the prophets have spoken:__ (26) Ought not Christ to have suffered these things, and to enter into his glory? (27) And beginning at Moses and all the prophets, he expounded unto them in all the scriptures the things concerning himself.

Why did Jesus call these two bereaved souls *"fools"* for being sad over his own torture and humiliating crucifixion? What are we to make of, *"but whosoever shall say, Thou fool, shall be in danger of hell fire."*? This scripture seems to be in sync with that of Luke 24:44-46 later where he again mentions Moses and the prophets and showing them how they spoke of him. It would have been nice if more detail had been given so we too could know what Moses and the prophets purportedly said about him.

'REDEEMED'

Jesus, instead of sounding like a son of GOD who had just undergone death and resurrection, hides his true identity and calls his followers *"fools"* because they are sad at what had befallen him! Something is wrong with this scene. Additionally, the two followers had explained to Jesus that they had trusted that it was in Jesus, that Israel would be "*redeemed*". There are so many things wrong with this last statement by these two followers on so many levels.

Israel "*IS*" redeemed by YHWH as a people, **ALREADY**.

The idea of "*redemption*" is very strongly tied in with YHWH freeing Israel from bondage in Egypt and the first born of Israel being "*redeemed*". As this is a topic of discussion all in itself, only a few words will be written here.

Exodus 13:14-15, (14) And it shall be when thy son asketh thee in time to come, saying: What is this? that thou shalt say unto him: By strength of hand YHWH brought us out from Egypt, from the house of bondage; (15) and it came to pass, when Pharaoh would hardly let us go that YHWH slew all the firstborn in the land of Egypt, both the first-born of man, and the first-born of beast; <u>therefore I sacrifice to YHWH all that openeth the womb, being males; but all the first-born of my sons I redeem.</u>

Israel as a holy people to YHWH have been "*redeemed*". Israel's first born males are "*redeemed*" through YHWH taking the tribe of Levi as HIS servants. Since Egypt, Israel was redeemed and remains "*redeemed*" as GOD YHWH'S first born son. He said this himself on so many occasions, it defies normal understanding why it is not better comprehended by HIS own people. The statements in Hebrew about Israel being redeemed are in the past tense. YHWH often reminds Israel of this fact. Israel is a redeemed people.

Exodus 15:13, (13) Thou in Thy love hast led the people that <u>Thou hast redeemed</u>; Thou hast guided them in Thy strength to Thy holy habitation.

The Hebrew for "*redeemed*" here is "*Gimel-Alef-Lamed*" and is past tense. This word has a very strong connection to "*kinsman*" as in an act of redemption on the part of the next of kin, or the taking of a kinsman's widow. One of "*kindred*", often having a duty or right by association to fulfill an obligation (Jeremiah 32:6-8) as in "*right of redemption*".

But there is also another Hebrew word used which is also often translated as "*redeem*", but has a stronger connection to the idea of "*ransom*" which it also is translated as. "*Geh-Dalet-Heh*" means "*ransom*", as in the payment or purchase of something. A price paid. It can also have the meaning as in "*distinguishing*" between two things (Exodus 8:19) as when YHWH put a "*division*" between the land of Goshen where Israel was, and the rest of Egypt when HE cursed Egypt with the plague of flies.

Deuteronomy 7:6-8, (6) <u>For thou art a holy people unto YHWH thy God</u>: YHWH thy God hath <u>chosen</u> thee to be His own <u>treasure</u>, out of <u>all peoples</u> that are upon the face of the earth. (7) YHWH did not set His love upon you, nor choose you, because ye were more in number than any people -- for ye were the fewest of all peoples -- (8) but because YHWH loved you, <u>and because He would keep the oath which He swore unto Your FATHERS</u>, hath YHWH brought you out with a mighty hand, <u>and redeemed you</u> out of the house of bondage, from the hand of Pharaoh king of Egypt.

More than anything else, YHWH would keep HIS oath which HE swore unto Abraham, Isaac and Jacob. YHWH gave HIS WORD!

The idea of both *kinship*, *redemption* and *ransom* are brought out by YHWH in Deuteronomy 7:8 as

HE mentions HIS reason for HIS ransom in HIS love for Israel and, *"because He would keep the oath which He swore unto your fathers"*. What part of *'I have redeemed thee'* in the past tense was not comprehended by these two men or by any others? *Israel is redeemed*!

There are many, many scriptures where YHWH reminds Israel of their being a *"redeemed"* people, and that they are HIS possession.

Isaiah 43:1, (1) But now thus saith YHWH that created thee, O Jacob, and He that formed thee, O Israel: Fear not, for I have Redeemed thee, I have called thee by thy name, thou art Mine.

Isaiah 45:17, (17) O Israel, that art saved by YHWH with an Everlasting Salvation; ye shall not be ashamed nor confounded world without end.

Joel 3:5, (5) And it shall come to pass, that whosoever shall call on the Name of YHWH shall be delivered;

So, what were these two followers of Jesus missing? Did they believe that they were without redemption, without Jesus? Were they only referring to Jesus being their *"messiah"*, and they were disappointed in what had befallen him and he had not arisen yet? Were they not aware that they have been redeemed by GOD and that their salvation is in the name of YHWH and still existed? Did they not know the promise of GOD and their own redemption? Finally, were they not offended by their *"messiah"* calling them *"fools"* because they were sad at his passing?

'THE SIGN OF JONAH'

In the Book of Matthew, Jesus was asked for a *"sign"* from the Pharisees. His response was that they were evil for even asking for a sign. The only *"sign"* that would be given would be that of the Prophet Jonah who was in the belly of the whale for three days and nights. But this was Jonah's fate for fleeing from the face of GOD, not dying.

Jesus was making an analogy between his upcoming three day death and stay in the burial cave (heart of the earth) and Jonah (belly of the whale). As if to say that his own death and resurrection after three days in the burial cave would be the only sign that would be given. He would have had to have been crucified on the fifth day of the week to spend three days in the sepulcher and be raised on the first day of the week. The only thing they really have in common is the number three.

Matthew 12:38-41, (38) Then certain of the scribes and of the Pharisees answered, saying, Master, we would see a sign from thee. (39) But he answered and said unto them, An evil and adulterous generation seeketh after a sign; and there shall no sign be given to it, but the sign of the prophet Jonas: (40) For as Jonas was three days and three nights in the whale's belly; so shall the Son of man be three days and three nights in the heart of the earth. (41) The men of Nineveh shall rise in judgment with this generation, and shall condemn it: because they repented at the preaching of Jonas; and, behold, a greater than Jonas is here.

It is understood what he was saying, given the analogy with the Prophet Jonah. However, in as far as it being a *"sign"*, this is another matter.

'ONE SHOULD DIE'

Jesus spoke often or prophesied regarding his own death. He spoke in terms of returning to the "*father*", that he came to die, he came for the lost "*sheep*". His entire life according to the Gospels was centered around this idea of "*sacrifice*" for his people. Yet, Israel had sacrificial offerings already.

Jesus spoke mostly in riddles, seldom saying plainly to his followers what he was talking about. In many ways his answers seem evasive when asked a simple direct question. His parables are very powerful and often shut the mouths of those attempting to catch him in some grievous offense.

'I AM HE'

Regarding his own identity when asked if he was "*that*" prophet, or the "*messiah*", Jesus would often avoid a direct answer and give another type of answer instead. Or as the practice of the Jewish people has been for centuries, he would answer a question, with a question. Aside from the addition of "*Christ*" as an apparent type of *surname*, or used as a *title* in the Gospels, the idea of his actually being the *messiah* or *christ* is not directly stated but is alluded to. The best example being the Samaritan woman at the well. It is about as close as Jesus ever came to saying plainly that he was the *messiah*. Even before the Temple Priests Jesus seemed to skirt the issue without plainly saying anything although according to the account in Mark (14:62), he said "*I am*" when asked if he was the messiah. The other Gospels differ.

John 4:25-26, (25) The woman saith unto him, *I know that Messias cometh, which is called Christ*:

This exchange with the Samaritan woman seems odd on at least two levels. Her response is redundant in that "*messiah*" and "*christ*" mean the same thing. Unless she was speaking Hebrew and Greek symultaneously, she was actually saying that "*I know that Messiah cometh, which is called Messiah*". Or put another way, *I know that Christ cometh, which is called Christ.* This has all of the earmarks of an editor associating the messiah with Jesus as if "*Christ*" was his name! It would be like saying, "*I know that Bob is coming, which is called Bob*". Was the redactor confused between the Hebrew and Greek not understanding that "*christ*" is not a name, or that *christ* and *messiah* meant the same thing?

Another aspect of this exchange, is that the Samaritans only accept the first five books of the Hebrew Bible, the Safer Torah, which is called the Pentateuch. Prophesies regarding a coming "*messiah*" only exist in the books of the Prophets or other later texts, which are not a part of their holy books and which they do not accept. This woman, presumably along with other Samaritans, either accepted the idea of a "*messiah*" coming as per the ancient Books of the Prophets of their Jewish neighbors which they did not have, or they had their own "*traditions*" regarding YHWH sending a messiah.

CONCLUSION

FULFILLED / UNFULFILLED

So in the final analysis, one has to ask from the standpoint of Moses and the Prophets, just how much of anything was "*fulfilled*". Whether *fulfilled, unfulfilled* or *spilled*, most all of the scriptures which purport to show how an event or prophesy was forecast are bogus. "*Fulfilled*" meaning as in prophetic events of his life which were either foretold regarding himself and Israel his people, either as the "*messiah*" or some other related event. Did Moses really speak of Jesus? Were the words of the Prophets mentioned in the Gospels in any way relevant to Jesus? Were the scriptures given in the

Gospels really speaking of Jesus? Were there too many editors, redactors and scribes with agendas for many of these words to be taken at face value? Additionally, as regards the Law, how did his words and actions jibe relative to the Commandments, Statutes and Ordinances of GOD'S Law?

Neither Moses nor the Prophets spoke of Jesus, or a messiah who was to live and die as Jesus did. There is scant evidence of any kind to the claim of Jesus or a person like him was prophesied.

One must ask, how much of what Jesus said or did was often the opposite of what he either said or what was expected, as with Jesus bringing *fire, sword* and *division*, as opposed to *righteousness, justice* and *peace* regarding David? And what of Jesus bringing "*hate*" between family members?

As for "*sacrifice for sin*" and "*salvation*", did not Israel possess from YHWH an eternal means for remission of sin at HIS alter, and did not Israel have "*everlasting salvation*" prior to the arrival of Jesus? Did not Israel have their own GOD whom they could call on by HIS sacred name? Was not Israel already "*redeemed*" by their GOD YHWH?

And finally, if his message was so important for Israel, why was so much of what he said spoken in parables, riddles and stories and made so difficult for his followers to understand, even then? YHWH said HIS sacrifice offerings will continue forever. Additionally, the prophets clearly state that sacrifice for sin will be continued after the SEED of David reigns, so what did Jesus die for?

Yet one thing should have been easily understood by all if they were paying attention to his words closely. Jesus said to keep the Commandments of GOD if they wanted to live. In this, his message was clear, even if nothing else was. For in this sense, nothing else mattered which was outside of the Law of Moses. In as far as prophesy supposedly concerning Jesus, the Hebrew Bible just does not support this idea, neither Moses nor the Prophets. If anyone spoke of Jesus, their words were not written down for the scriptures do not reflect prophesies regarding Jesus or anyone like him.

THEN WHY – WHAT FOR

Regarding the Jewish people and Israel then, what was the life and the death of Jesus really for 2,000 years ago? What was going on?

For from the time of Jesus who preached the Law of Moses and keeping of the Commandments to Israel, through Paul who jettisoned the Law of Moses and it's Commandments who preached to the Gentiles, and finally to the Gentiles who jettisoned Israel and the Jewish people completely, the message changed radically. From "**YHWH**" the GOD of Israel and keeping HIS Law, to "**Jesus**" the "*god*" of the Gentile Nations without GOD'S Law, a new religion developed and spread across the earth devoid of much of the original message of Jesus and without the foundation or underpinnings of the Law or it's eternal Statutes and Ordinances.

CHAPTER SIX

'COVENANT / TESTAMENT'

The concept of *"Covenant"* in the Hebrew Bible can take several forms. It can be a real contractual agreement between parties, or it can be symbolic.

Ezekiel 16:8-9, (8) Now when I passed by thee, and looked upon thee, and, behold, thy time was the time of love, I spread my skirt over thee, and covered thy nakedness; yea, I swore unto thee, and <u>entered into a Covenant</u> with thee, saith the Lord YHWH, and thou becamest Mine.(9) Then washed I thee with water; yea, I cleansed away thy blood from thee, and I <u>anointed thee</u> with oil.

This is a metaphor of love for Israel by YHWH, yet it is also very real. There are more examples of symbolic or real Covenants such as Malachi 2:14 between man and woman. Above, GOD is speaking of HIS betrothing Israel to HIMSELF. But the idea is that the *bond* or *contract* is binding between the parties. Notice as well, that HE cleansed away the blood and anointed HIS betrothed with oil. In many ways this chapter in Ezekiel sums up YHWH'S feelings as well as HIS relationship with Israel. *"Thou art MINE". 43:1, (1) But now thus saith YHWH that <u>created</u> thee, O Jacob, and He that <u>formed</u> thee, O Israel: Fear not, for I have <u>redeemed</u> thee, I have called thee by thy name, <u>thou art Mine</u>.*

Israel is a people *created* by GOD, *formed* by GOD and *redeemed* by GOD, for GOD HIMSELF. Israel belongs to GOD, and as Pharaoh found out any and all who threaten HIS *treasured possession,* HIS *holy portion,* HIS *inheritance,* will answer to YHWH the GOD of Israel. Israel is eternally covenanted with GOD.

HEBREW BIBLE COVENANTS

"*<u>The Covenant</u> which He made with Abraham, and His <u>Oath</u> unto Isaac; And He established it unto Jacob for a <u>Statute</u>, to Israel for an <u>Everlasting Covenant</u>*"

What is the difference between *"covenant"* and *"testament"*? Is there a difference? What is the origin of the Hebrew word for *"Covenant"*? What did the concept of *"Covenant"* mean to the ancient Israelites, and later to the Jewish people during the time of Jesus? What did it mean to the Gentiles?

In understanding why the overwhelming majority of the Jewish people did not accept what is called by Christians the *"New Testament"*, when referring to Jesus and his message, one must have a working knowledge of what this term meant in ancient Israel. <u>New Testament</u> translates as <u>New Covenant</u>, and in the minds of most Jewish people, the death of Jesus did not constitute a *"New Covenant",* as it was in no way similar to their existing Covenants with YHWH their GOD. For unlike the Gentiles, GOD had already made several eternal Covenants with HIS people Israel.

The word *"Covenant"* of Middle English / Middle French, translates as a formal, solemn binding agreement, a compact between two or more parties which necessitates the performance of some form of an action or actions. It is a pledge, a binding contract between parties.

Between men it can also have the meaning or essence of a *"constitution"* *"treaty"*, *"pledge"* or *"alliance"*. There are several examples of these in the Safer Torah. But between GOD and man, a Covenant takes on a much more serious, solemn and binding eternal air to it. It is much more of an awesome undertaking, usually with severe penalties for breach of contract. The Sinai Covenant between YHWH and Israel is just such a Covenant. A Covenant with GOD is a *holy* contract. This is true when made with a man or a people.

This definition sums up very nicely the Covenant relationship between YHWH and Abraham and between YHWH and Israel. GOD'S Covenants are *"legally"* binding contracts between HIMSELF and between Abraham and Israel, who is Abraham's SEED. For the Covenant YHWH made with Abraham, was made with Abraham's SEED (Genesis 12:7). YHWH was to perform certain actions of the agreement, and Abraham and his SEED Israel, was to perform, per their *"conditions"*, certain actions as part of their agreements. All parties had *"actions"* to perform as their part of the contract. However, Israel had *"penalties"* attached to their contract which they would suffer, when and if they did not perform all of their part of the agreement according to the words of the contract for which they had agreed to with GOD. As will be stated often their *contract* with YHWH is by it's very nature *technical*. It is for this reason that knowing the original and the exact words written in the Gospels is paramount to understanding what happened 2,000 years ago in Israel. The Law deals with technical issues and is specific.

'TESTAMENTUM'

The word *"testament"* of Middle English / Late Latin / Latin, from *"testamentum"* translates as *"covenant with God"*. This translation sends the focus back to the word *"covenant"*.

The Hebrew origin of the word for *"Covenant"* comes from the word *"brit"*, *(Bet-Resh-Yood-Tav)*. It has the meaning of *pact, compact, agreement* or *pledge*. In the Hebrew Bible, a Covenant generally was accompanied by an animal sacrifice, but not always. When a Covenant was made with GOD, it took on a legal and binding status somewhat different than that made between men. The seriousness of such a Covenant with GOD cannot be articulated.

The Covenant YHWH made with Abraham required Abraham to **circumcise** not only himself, but all born in his house or bought. In Hebrew *"Brit Milah"* literally translates as *"Circumcision Covenant"*. When a new born male of Israel is circumcised on his eighth day, this (Brit Milah) is what it is called. The shortened version of this procedure is simply called a *"bris"* (Askenazi pronunciation), literally *"brit"*, meaning *Covenant*. According to the Gospels, on the eighth day after his birth, Jesus was circumcised. Jesus was circumcised <u>into</u> the Covenant. He became like Abraham was, part of the same Covenant GOD YHWH made approximately 1500 years before his own birth, just as were all other circumcised male SEED descendants of Abraham were part of that same Covenant **by birthright**. It was father to son by SEED.

A Covenant is not to be confused with the making of a *"vow"* *(neder)* from *(Nun-Dalet-Resh)*. Nor should it be confused with a *"blessing" (brakah)* from *(Bet-Resh-Coph)*.

A Covenant in the ancient world of Abraham and later with Israel, was a very formal affair compared to other types of agreements between individuals or with GOD, such as a *"vow"*.

With a *"vow"*, the word *"if"* plays a big part in it's understanding. It is *"conditional"*. A "vow", unlike a Covenant, is almost always *"conditional"*. *"If" you will do "X", then I will do "Y."* Or, said another way, *I will do "X" if you will do "Y"*. The story of the birth of the Prophet Samuel in the Book of Samuel (I Samuel 1:1-28), is a good example of a *"vow"*. A barren woman promises to *"lend"* to GOD her son (*if* GOD will give her one), for she had asked for a son, if HE would give her a *"man child"*, a male SEED.

A *"blessing"* on the other hand, is just that. The blessing given from Isaac to Jacob or of Jacob to Ephraim are examples of a blessing. It is a type of *"gift"* in a sense. One is giving and one is receiving. The rather long drawn out stories of Isaac and later Jacob receiving their father's blessing of the *"first born"* over their brothers in Ishmael and Esau respectively, shows the importance of *"blessing"*. At least, in receiving the blessing of the first born son who was to inherit a double portion, it was important. Before Jacob died, the importance of the blessing of the first born, is brought out again with the story of Joseph bringing his two sons Ephraim and Manasseh to Jacob for their blessing. In the story of the Patriarchs, the blessing needed to accompany the son who was first born in order to validate his birthright.

UNILATERAL – BILATERAL - MULTILATERAL

In TaNaKh, there are at least three very distinct types of Covenants. A Covenant can be an act performed by one party as a *"unilateral"* act with little or no obligation by another party. A Covenant can be performed by a mutual *"bilateral"* agreement between two parties. Or a Covenant can be an agreement between two or more *"multilateral"* parties. Usually *"bilateral"* and *"multilateral"* Covenants have specific conditions associated with them which entail penalties when the conditions of the agreement are not kept, are broken or otherwise are violated. A type of *"punishment"* is incurred.

UNILATERAL COVENANT

NOAH

The *"Covenant"* that GOD had made with Noah and his SEED could be called a type of *"unilateral"* Covenant whereby the recipient had no obligation to perform as his part of an agreement. He was mostly a recipient.

GOD destroyed the earth with a flood. HIS *"Covenant"* afterward, was a promise not to do it again. It might be considered a type of unilateral *"one sided"* type of Covenant GOD made. But GOD did require of Noah to abstain from eating and shedding the blood. YHWH does not say that HE *"repented"* for what HE had done, as HE does so often in TaNaKh, although it sounds very similar. HE declares that he will never do it again, *"While the earth remaineth, seed time and harvest, and cold and heat, and summer and winter, and day and night shall not cease"*. GOD commands Noah to abstain from eating and shedding of blood though this command came afterward and adds to the idea of it being more of a unilateral than bilateral oath.

YHWH made a Covenant with Noah, his SEED and *"with every living creature"* that he would not flood the earth again but would set a sign in the clouds to remind HIMSELF. Noah made animal offerings by fire to YHWH.

'THE EVERLASTING COVENANT'

Genesis 9:9-17, (9) 'As for Me, behold, I establish My Covenant with you, and with your SEED after you; (10) and with every living creature that is with you, the fowl, the cattle, and every beast of the earth with you; of all that go out of the ark, even every beast of the earth. (11) And I will establish My Covenant with you; neither shall all flesh be cut off any more by the waters of the flood; neither shall there any more be a flood to destroy the earth.' (12) And God said: 'This is the token of the Covenant which I make between Me and you and every living creature that is with you, for perpetual generations: (13) I have set My bow in the cloud, and it shall be for a token of a Covenant between Me and the earth. (14) And it shall come to pass, when I bring clouds over the earth, and the bow is seen in the cloud, (15) that I will remember My Covenant, which is between Me and you and every living creature of all flesh; and the waters shall no more become a flood to destroy all flesh. (16) And the bow shall be in the cloud; and I will look upon it, that I may remember the Everlasting Covenant between God and every living creature of all flesh that is upon the earth.' (17) And God said unto Noah: 'This is the token of the Covenant which I have established between Me and all flesh that is upon the earth.'

In this Covenant, GOD told Noah of HIS *intent* and *what* HE was doing. HE told Noah *why* HE was doing it. Only after the Covenant is made not to flood the earth again to destroy man, does GOD tell Noah of his own obligation not to shed blood (of man) and eating of blood. Noah is told what not to do, but there are no penalties or threats associated with what he was told, although they may be implied. Noah, for all intent and purposes, is a passive recipient of the Covenant. It is GOD who is making the Covenant by HIMSELF.

GOD had destroyed the earth but for Noah and his sons, and the animals were saved. The rainbow, was the sign of the Covenant that HE made, and it was meant not only to remind HIMSELF never to flood the earth again, but it was also to assure man and all life, when the storms came and the winds blew upon the earth, that GOD was not flooding to destroy all life with a deluge.

This Covenant where GOD made a rainbow, is an exception to most all of the examples of Covenants made in the Hebrew Bible. It is different because it was not so much as an *"agreement"* made between two or more parties in the traditional Covenant, but was more like an eternal promise, made by the force of great authority by only one party. Noah neither agreed to the Covenant nor rejected the Covenant. He had no say so. It was made by GOD, it was done, and that was it. Unlike Abraham who was told what he was to do as his part of the Covenant, Noah is the passive recipient of GOD'S Covenant.

GOD had made an eternal Covenant with Noah and his SEED after him, that he would not flood the earth again to destroy mankind. This everlasting Covenant would be passed on to Noah's SEED long after he was gone. It *was* passed on to Noah's SEED. It was *"eternal"*. All of mankind was beneficiary.

Genesis 9:9,16 (9) 'As for Me, behold, I establish My Covenant with you, and with YOUR SEED after you; ....(16) And the bow shall be in the cloud; and I will look upon it, that I may remember *the <u>Everlasting Covenant</u> between God and every living creature of all flesh that is upon the earth.'*

The eternal, everlasting Covenant which YHWH made with Noah and with his SEED, did not end because GOD later made another Covenant with Noah's SEED in Abraham. GOD'S eternal Covenant with Noah and his SEED was that HE would never destroy the earth again by flood.

The Covenant YHWH later made with Abraham was for Abraham to circumcise his sons and all of the males of his house as his part of the Covenant to inherit all of the land of Canaan and GOD'S blessings. But, the *"rainbow"* Covenant GOD had made with Abraham's forefather Noah remained as well and the promise not to flood the earth because it was an *"everlasting"* Covenant. Because of it's nature, it was a unilateral Covenant.

After the next Covenant was made with Abraham, the rainbow in the sky did not stop being a rainbow in the sky, because Abraham was now circumcised. The *"bow"* (rainbow) in the cloud became part of Abraham's reality through Shem, Noah's son. And as Abraham is of the SEED of Noah, the Covenant of Noah was passed on to Abraham, *"behold, I establish My Covenant with you, and with YOUR SEED after you"*, and likewise was the Covenant of Abraham passed on through Isaac. From SEED to SEED they are passed on.

Likewise, the Covenant of Noah which was passed to Abraham, was also passed on to all of Abraham's sons as well as to all of the SEED of Noah (Japheth and Ham) not of Abraham. As all of mankind upon the earth are descended from Noah, they all benefit from the Covenant YHWH made with their forefather Noah. The Covenant of Noah remains. All of Noah's SEED and all living creatures upon the earth are beneficiaries of this Covenant.

Noah appeared not to have had a reciprocal part in the Covenant. He was told to multiply etc., and was instructed to not eat *"the blood"*, but at first, this does not appear to be part of the Covenant itself (Genesis 9:1-7) which came after the blessing. Multiplying itself would be a natural part of their existence, *"Be fruitful, and multiply, and replenish the earth"*. It was only after GOD speaks to Noah and blesses him and his SONS, that Noah is told that YHWH is establishing HIS Covenant with him.

Only later GOD said to Noah that HE would establish a Covenant with him, *"As for Me, behold, I will establish MY Covenant with you, and with your SEED after you; and with every living creature that is with you...."*(Genesis 9:8-17). So, this Covenant YHWH made, was with Noah and his SEED and all living creatures upon the earth. GOD promises that HE would never again destroy all flesh with a flood as HE had done, *"And I will establish MY Covenant with you; neither shall all flesh be cut off any more by the waters of the flood; neither shall there any more be a flood to destroy the earth"*

With Noah GOD blessed him and his sons above all of the creatures on the face earth and gave him the sign of the *"rainbow"* as the sign of YHWH'S Covenant. Later with Abraham, YHWH gave the land of Canaan to Abraham and his male SEED descendants. And as a sign of this Covenant, as was Abraham circumcised, all of Abraham's male SEED descendants would too be circumcised. The sign of this Covenant between YHWH and Abraham was the *"circumcision"*. In this Covenant with Abraham, YHWH GOD did something as HIS part of their agreement, and Abraham was to do something as his part of the agreement, but with a penalty if not performed. Anyone not circumcised would be ***cut off*** from his own people and by extension, ***YHWH.***

After the Covenant YHWH made with Noah, YHWH <u>blessed</u> Noah and his sons and as part of HIS blessing HE required of him and his SEED to abstain from ***eating*** blood or from ***shedding*** the *blood*, to be fruitful and multiply.

Genesis 9:4-6, (4) <u>*Only flesh with the life thereof, which is the blood thereof, shall ye not eat.*</u> *(5) And surely your blood of your lives will I require; at the hand of every beast will I require it; and at the hand of man, even at the hand of every man's brother,* <u>*will I require the life of man.*</u> *(6)* <u>*Whoso sheddeth man's blood*</u>*, by man shall his blood be shed; for in the image of God made He man.*

An argument could be made that *"will I require the life of man"* is GOD'S penalty for violating his commandment not to eat or shed blood so therefore the blessing and commandment to abstain from eating or shedding blood makes the Covenant a type of *bilateral* not a *unilateral* Covenant. However, it is a weak argument, as YHWH'S Covenant is more of a *unilateral* oath. Even an argument could be made that it was a type of *multilateral* oath to all SEED with an *"inferred"* penalty attached regarding not eating the blood.

With the Noah Covenant all of mankind became part of the eternal Covenant. Not so with the Covenant GOD made later with Abraham and his SEED. This eternal Covenant of Abraham was a Covenant made *only* with the circumcised male SEED descendants of Abraham himself. Herein lies the difference between the first Covenant of Noah, and the second Covenant of Abraham. Whereas, all mankind were heirs of the first Covenant as all were of the SEED of Noah through his three sons, only the *blessed* SEED of Abraham through his circumcised son who received the blessing of the *first born* was heir of the second Covenant of *circumcision,* the *SEED Covenant.*

BILATERAL COVENANT

ABRAHAM

In the story of the Covenant that YHWH made with Abraham, there were two parties to the agreement, but with a caveat. GOD YHWH promised to give to <u>***Abraham and his SEED***</u> all of the land between the River of Egypt and the River Euphrates. That is, GOD is giving to Abraham's SEED all of the land of the Canaanites. So in this sense, a case could be made that the Covenant GOD made with Abraham might also be considered a *"multilateral"* Covenant as Abraham's *"SEED"* is also a party to the Covenant. For the Covenant was made with Abraham's SEED just as it was made with Abraham himself. Therefore, the Covenant of Abraham was made between YHWH, Abraham and Abraham's (collective) SEED not yet born.

Genesis 15:18-21 (18) <u>*In that day YHWH made a Covenant with Abram,*</u> *saying: 'Unto thy SEED* <u>*have I given this land*</u>

The interesting thing about this Covenant is that when speaking to Abraham,   YHWH made the Covenant with Abraham's SEED. Only sometime later does YHWH mention Abraham as part of the Covenant. GOD'S first words were to Abraham's **SEED**. In this scripture, YHWH is equating Abraham and SEED as ONE. The way YHWH'S words read in Hebrew, is that HE made HIS Covenant with Abraham / SEED, as they are one and the same. This scripture is extremely important to remember as SEED dominates TaNaKh.

This is what GOD was doing for Abraham. This is one half of the agreement of their Covenant. Normally, when a Covenant was made, there was a type of *"contract"* made between two or more parties to the agreement, and the agreement made was usually sealed in a ceremony by the spilling of blood. One such example of this is this Covenant made between YHWH and Abraham (Genesis 15). But here, GOD has not asked as yet, anything of Abraham for his part. From the beginning of the twelfth chapter to a third of the way through the seventeenth chapter of Genesis (Genesis 12 thru 17:10), YHWH has been telling Abraham what HE will do for him. Not until Genesis 17:10 does YHWH finally tell Abraham what is *his part* of their Covenant.

'AS FOR THEE'

Genesis 17:9, (9) And God said unto Abraham: 'And as for thee, thou shalt keep My Covenant, thou, and thy SEED after thee throughout their generations. (10) This is My Covenant, which ye shall keep, between Me and you and thy SEED after thee: every male among you shall be Circumcised.

It is "*circumcision*".

The penalty associated with not complying with the Covenant YHWH made with Abraham to circumcise was to be "*cut off*" from his people.

'AN EVERLASTING COVENANT'

Genesis 17:13-14, (13)…........and My Covenant shall be in your flesh for an Everlasting Covenant.(14) And the Uncircumcised male who is not Circumcised in the flesh of his foreskin, that soul shall be cut off from his people; he hath broken My Covenant.'

Today, the sign of this Covenant is still worn in the flesh of all direct male SEED descendants of Abraham in their circumcision. These circumcised male descendants of Abraham are sons of the Covenant, the *"SEED"* spoken of by GOD, "*In that day YHWH made a Covenant with Abram, saying: 'Unto thy SEED have I given this land"*. Together, Israel is the collective "**SEED**".

Genesis 17:11, (11) And ye shall be Circumcised in the flesh of your foreskin; and it shall be a token of a Covenant betwixt Me and YOU.

The *"you"* here is a *"collective"* you, meaning a circumcised Abraham *and* Abraham's individual circumcised SEED which would come after him. Each and every circumcised male SEED descendant of Abraham are as Abraham.

The circumcision in the flesh of the foreskin (itself) of a male SEED descendant of Abraham is his personal sign *of his own Covenant* that he has with YHWH his GOD, the GOD of his forefather Abraham. This Covenant he receives irrespective of who the mother is. She plays no part in the eternal Covenant that exists between YHWH and Abraham's circumcised SEED.

ABRAHAM'S SEED

'TO BE A GOD UNTO THEE AND TO THY SEED'

Genesis 17:7 (7) And I will establish MY Covenant between ME and THEE and THY SEED after thee throughout their generations for an Everlasting Covenant, to be a God unto Thee and to Thy

SEED after thee. ….

ME – THEE – THY SEED

YHWH'S Covenant "*established*" GOD'S Everlasting Covenant between **YHWH, Abraham** and **SEED**. Additionally, YHWH'S Covenant "*established*" YHWH "*to be a GOD*" to **Abraham and SEED**.

The point here, is that the circumcised SEED of Abraham has YHWH as his "*established*" GOD because of who his father is. "YHWH" is the **_official_** "*established*" GOD of every circumcised son of Abraham. He wears the sign of his GOD and HIS GOD'S Covenant, cut into his flesh. Additionally, he has the promise of that Covenant which was made to Abraham as Abraham's heir. Absolutely none of this has anything whatsoever to do with who his mother is, who she isn't, who she might be or who she could be. She is simply not relevant to the Covenant, the Agreement, the Oath or the legally binding Contract which was made between two other parties for which she was not privy to, part of, nor was she responsible for.

YHWH "*established*" HIMSELF as "*GOD*" not only to **Abraham**, but to Abraham's **SEED**, "*Everlasting*", "*Forever*", "*For all eternity*". GOD did not just give Abraham some land in exchange for him circumcising his sons. YHWH GOD **"ESTABLISHED"** Himself as **GOD** _forever_ to Abraham and to Abraham's SEED. YHWH became GOD _for all eternity_ to the SEED of Abraham. For ever and ever, eternally and everlasting, YHWH is GOD.

There were several important Covenants which were made before the giving of the Law at Mount Sinai, the most well known perhaps would be that which is discussed here and referred to as the "*SEED Covenant*" by this author, that YHWH made with the Patriarch Abraham. The reason it is referred to in this way as "*SEED Covenant*" is because of the way that it was made in Hebrew. The SEED Covenant was made between *YHWH and Abraham and* his *SEED*. It is important to understand that there are *more* than just two parties to this Covenant. It is "*multilateral*" in that sense although it is actually a bilateral type of collective Covenant. Abraham and his *SEED* are _one._

For as mentioned earlier, the first time YHWH appeared to Abraham after Abraham arrived in the land of Canaan (Genesis 12:7), YHWH does not even mention Abraham, but speaks *only* of Abraham's **SEED**, "*And YHWH appeared unto Abram, and said: 'Unto thy SEED will I give this land...*". Abraham builds an alter to YHWH who appeared to him and then leaves.

Ever since the day when Abraham circumcised himself, and all of the males in his house into the SEED Covenant of GOD ("*onto thy SEED*"), each and every male of the male SEED descendants of Abraham which was blessed through Isaac and Jacob, becomes a *party* to that Covenant GOD made with Abraham as if they were there. The individual SEED of Abraham possesses physically the "*seal*" of that eternal Covenant cut into his flesh and worn. It is his own "*sign*" that _he too_ is part of a most wonderful Covenant with GOD.

In the sense that the eight day old SEED of Abraham sacrifices some of his flesh and his blood is spilled during the process of his circumcision, the infant has more in common with the Covenant YHWH "*cut*" with Abraham that may be first realized. He becomes, and is, no different than his father Abraham from whence he came. He is SEED of his father and heir to the promise of the Covenant. The *sign* of that Covenant made with YHWH GOD, he *wears* cut into his flesh and worn his entire life, passing it on to the next generation of male descendants of Abraham, "*Covenant Circumcision*".

When a son is circumcised into the Covenant of Abraham, as was Jesus at eight days old, his *"Brit Milah"* or *"Circumcision Covenant"* is cause for great celebration. When Abraham's eight day old male SEED descendant is <u>circumcised into the Covenant</u>, he becomes as was Abraham, an heir to the promise YHWH made with him by Covenant of sacrifice. (Genesis 15:1-21).

In appreciating the significance of the Covenant YHWH made with Abraham and *"thy SEED"*, it must be understood that Abraham's SEED and Abraham are the same. Upon circumcision, Abraham's SEED becomes heir as was Abraham, to the promise made to him and his SEED forever as *"one"*.

ISRAEL

MULTILATERAL COVENANT

When YHWH made HIS Covenant with Israel at Sinai, it was a *"Covenant of Blood"*. It was an *"agreement"* between GOD and *"HIS*" people Israel. Israel *"IS"* the SEED of Abraham. And not too dissimilar from the Priests when (Leviticus 8:22-24) becoming consecrated by the putting of the blood of the sacrifice upon them as they entered into their unique relationship before their GOD as HIS special servants. Israel too, entered into a unique relationship with their GOD YHWH by the sprinkling of the blood upon them at Sinai.

Exodus 24:8, (8) And Moses took the Blood, <u>and sprinkled it on the people</u>, and said: 'Behold the Blood of the Covenant, which YHWH hath made with you In Agreement with all these Words.'

'BLOOD OF THE COVENANT'

The **"Blood of the Covenant"** is important in understanding the severity of this *"agreement"* which YHWH made with Israel. By severity is meant the seriousness of it's legal implications, especially when it has not been kept.

Psalms 50:5-7, (5) <u>'Gather My saints</u> together unto Me; <u>those that have made a Covenant with Me by Sacrifice.</u>' (6) And the heavens declare His righteousness; for God, He is judge. Selah (7) 'Hear, O <u>My people</u>, and I will speak; O Israel, and I will testify against thee: <u>God, thy God, am I.</u>

Israel made a Covenant with YHWH *"by Sacrifice"*. They are GOD'S saints, HIS people who have YHWH as their GOD. But as important, they are HIS.

Psalms 52:11, (11) I will give Thee thanks for ever, because Thou hast done it; and I will wait for Thy name, for it is good, in the presence of <u>Thy Saints.</u>

The Hebrew for *"saints"* is a word which usually translates as *"kind"* and *"good"*, but has other meanings like *"grace"*, *"pious"* and *"godly"*. Israel is often described as YHWH'S *"goodly ones"*, *"pious ones"* and *"godly ones"*. In this Psalm, David speaks of Israel being GOD'S *"godly"* people and that he will wait on ***the Name of YHWH***, in the presence of THY *"godly ones"*.
The emphasis here is on the name of GOD, who is *"YHWH"*.

Zechariah 10:12, (12) And I will strengthen them in YHWH; <u>and they shall walk up and down in His name</u>, saith YHWH.

SINAI COVENANT

The Covenant YHWH made with Israel at Mount Sinai after that of Abraham and the SEED Covenant, was very important. At Mt. Sinai, Moses received the Law of YHWH and explained / offered it to Israel. Israel said, *"And all the people answered together, and said: 'All that YHWH hath spoken we will do.' And Moses reported the words of the people unto YHWH"*.

So Israel agreed to the Covenant of GOD YHWH. But, it was not solidified yet. There would be a *ceremony, sacrifice* and *blood*.

Exodus 24:7, (7) And he took the Book of the Covenant, and READ in the hearing of the people; and they said: 'All that YHWH hath spoken will we do, and obey.' (8) And Moses took the blood, and sprinkled it on the people, and said: 'Behold the Blood of the Covenant, which YHWH hath made with you in agreement with all these words.'

With the Sinai Covenant came *blessings* and *curses*. Those who do not keep YHWH'S Covenant, there are severe penalties which that person will pay.

Leviticus 26:25, (25) And I will bring a sword upon you, that shall execute the Vengeance of the Covenant; and ye shall be gathered together within your cities; and I will send the pestilence among you; and ye shall be delivered into the hand of the enemy.

SIGNS AND COVENANTS

Now we are discussing three Covenants, that of Noah, of Abraham, and now all of Israel at Sinai. So, with the first two Covenant's of Noah and his SEED and Abraham and his SEED, there are two everlasting Covenants. Noah's Covenant is with his SEED which includes all of mankind. And there is the everlasting Covenant with Abraham and with his SEED, which includes only the circumcised male SEED descendants of Abraham through his grandson Jacob. Both Covenants are in full force and neither have been canceled. The rainbow still *rainbows*, and Abraham's sons still *circumcise* their sons into the eternal Covenant with YHWH. Neither rainbows nor circumcisions conflict with one another, but both mutually exist together as part of GOD'S divine plan for his people.

With Noah the sign of the *"rainbow"* was the **sign** of YHWH'S Covenant. With Abraham, YHWH gave the land of Canaan to Abraham and his descendants but required of Abraham something. The sign of this Covenant between YHWH and Abraham was that Abraham was to *"circumcise"* himself and his *sons* as the **sign** of their Covenant. Just as the *rainbow* is the *sign* of the first Covenant, *circumcision* is the *sign* of the second Covenant.

So, the difference between these two Covenants of GOD is that the Covenant of Noah was with all of mankind, and the Covenant with Abraham is **only** with Abraham and Abraham's circumcised male SEED descendants who received his blessing. Here the family tree comes into focus. For much as a young lad may carve his own initials into a tree to be remembered, the Covenant of YHWH is cut into the flesh of Abraham's SEED as a token sign of the eternal Covenant he has with his GOD. However it does not stop with him but is passed on to the next generation as a continuum from generation to generation as each male SEED descendant is circumcised into the Covenant.

With the Covenant of Abraham, the blessing which comes with the Covenant is narrowed even further through his son Issac and not Ishmael, and with Jacob and not Esau. Thus, the blessing and the Covenant of Jacob is passed on to his sons who continue to circumcise their sons into the Covenant of their forefather Abraham. According to scripture, the blessing was given to Joseph and to his son Ephraim. So, the blessing itself can actually be traced through five generations from *father to son* beginning with Abraham and ending with Ephraim. Regardless of who the sons of Jacob married, whether Canaanite, Hittite, Ammorite or Egyptian, the blessing of the Covenant was transferred from father to son no matter who or where the mother came from. For the Covenant was with the "SEED" of Abraham's circumcised male descendants, *not* with the unknown female of whomever they chose to marry.

With each successive Covenant and / or blessing of the Covenant, GOD made a specific agreement with a specific individual and with his SEED. It was done verbally and sometimes verbally with a blood sacrifice. With Abraham it was a Covenant of blood (Genesis 15:8-21), the Covenant was confirmed with both Isaac (Genesis 26:2-6) and with Jacob (Genesis 28:10-15). As the Covenant was the same Covenant, another needed not to have been made, so YHWH "*confirmed*" it by speaking to Isaac and to Jacob after both of them had received his father's "*blessing*".

The original Covenant YHWH made with Abraham was a formal affair. This formal Covenant making would become even more formal with Jacobs sons at Mount Sinai, when Israel accepted the Covenant of Law upon themselves symbolized by the sprinkling of blood. This was the ***Blood of the Covenant***.

JACOB / ISRAEL

Exodus 2:24, (24) And God heard their groaning, and God remembered His Covenant with Abraham, with Isaac, and with Jacob.

While the SEED of Abraham labored as slaves in Egypt, GOD remembered HIS Covenant with Abraham, Isaac and Jacob. Why? HE remembered HIS Covenant because it is an ***eternal*** Covenant with their SEED. Although Israel was living as slaves, they still circumcised their sons and rainbows still appeared in the sky. Covenant's of YHWH GOD are "*everlasting promises*" made by the ONE GOD who is truth. Covenants of YHWH GOD are *eternal oaths* made by the ONE GOD who cannot lie and changes not. "*GOD remembered*".

"*And God heard their groaning*"

GOD used HIS servant Moses to free Israel, but Israel needed HIS Law to live by. For they were no longer a small family, but many. Thus, GOD brought Israel to the foot of Mount Sinai and made yet another Covenant with them. YHWH gave Israel HIS ***"Law"***. Israel accepted GOD'S eternal Law to live by. It was a Law which was forever as was the eternal portion of the sacrifice for the Priests of GOD as well as keeping of the Sabbath eternal.

Numbers 18:19, (19) All the heave-offerings of the holy things, which the sons of Israel offer unto YHWH, have I given thee, and thy SONS and thy daughters with thee, as a due for ever; it is an Everlasting Covenant of salt before YHWH unto thee and to thy SEED with thee.'

Leviticus 24:8, (8) Every Sabbath day he shall set it in order before YHWH continually; it is from

the sons of Israel, an E<u>verlasting Covenant.</u>

The Covenant of Sinai was an everlasting Covenant made with and accepted by all of Israel, where the Priests of YHWH would forever (everlasting) receive their holy portion of the sacrifice (heave-offering) and the Sabbath is GOD'S holy day of rest forever (everlasting) and must be kept.

This was a Covenant made in blood. It was a very formal procedure, as was that YHWH made with Abraham. The SEED of Abraham accepted the Covenant of the Law which YHWH GOD offered to them. They promised to *"do"* and to *"obey"* all of GOD'S words read to them by the servant Moses.

The details of the Law of GOD are written in the Safer Torah. Included within the Safer Torah, is *"circumcision"* as **written** Law. Other practices observed by Abraham such as not eating the blood etc., became **written** Law as well. Therefore, the Covenant made with Noah regarding not eating the blood, or the shedding of blood, as well as the Covenant with Abraham to circumcise his SONS, were both *incorporated* into the **written** Law at Sinai. Before the Law was given at Sinai, not eating or shedding the blood and circumcision were already practiced by the SEED of Abraham, but then it became written Law at Mount Sinai, as it was *"etched in stone"*.

So, now we have three Covenants which are in force. The Covenant YHWH made with Noah and with his SEED, the Covenant YHWH made with Abraham and with his SEED, and now the Covenant YHWH made with all of the SEED of Israel which included the ordinances of the first two Covenants. Only the Covenant made with Noah could be said to apply to the Nations, as all mankind are of his SEED. But neither the Covenant with Abraham and his SEED nor the Covenant with Israel at Sinai apply to the Nations. The Covenant of Law at Sinai was not a Covenant made with the Nations. Neither Moabites, Ammonites, Philistines, Russians, Icelanders nor Mexicans were part of the Covenant YHWH made with Israel, who were circumcised sons of Jacob, son of Isaac, son of Abraham.

So unlike the Covenant of Noah, which was for to all of mankind, the Covenant of Abraham, and later with Israel, was a Covenant made and accepted by *only* them, *with* YHWH as their GOD. The family tree is now much more focused

Psalms 147:19-20, (19) He declareth His <u>word</u> unto <u>Jacob</u>, His <u>Statutes</u> and His O<u>rdinances</u> unto Israel. (20) <u>He hath NOT dealt so with any Nation; and as for His ordinances, they have not known them.</u> Hallelujah.

The rainbows still *"rainbow"*, the circumcisions of foreskins are still made by the *"mohel"* who continue to *"circumcise",* and the *"Law"* of Moses is kept. The Law may not be kept by all of the SEED of Israel the same, or at all by some, but that is an issue between that individual and GOD. Each is judged according to his own sins. But all of Abraham's circumcised male SEED descendants are under GOD'S Law, regardless as to whether they keep HIS Law or there is sacrifice. The Law remains in force and is still in affect.

None of these three Covenants have been annulled, circumvented, replaced or abrogated. The Law of GOD has not been canceled. All three of the Covenants continue in full force. The fact that YHWH was angry with Israel and HE allowed HIS Temple to be destroyed, does not abrogate HIS eternal Covenant with Israel. No more than when HE exiled Judah centuries earlier. GOD'S Covenant at Sinai with Israel, as well as the other Covenants, remain in full force. Whether Israel can keep all of the Statutes and Ordinances of the Law or is able to, the Covenant of Sinai remains in effect and *"forever", "everlasting"* and *"eternal"*are still *"forever","everlasting"* and *"eternal"*.

'COVENANT OF AVRAHAM'

As discussed, in the Covenant of Abraham, Abraham was required to circumcise his male offspring as his part of the Covenant. All of Abraham's sons and those whom he owned of his house were circumcised *"In the selfsame day was Abraham circumcised, and Ishmael his son. And all of the men of his house, those born in the house and those bought with money of a foreigner, were circumcised with him" (Genesis 17:26)*. Thus, Abraham fulfilled his part of the Covenant made by YHWH. There was also a blood sacrifice between YHWH and Abraham seemingly *sealing* their Covenant.

Before YHWH had Moses free Israel from Egypt, HE reminded Moses and Israel of HIS *existing* Covenant with Abraham, Isaac and Jacob, as they were the "*SEED*" of Abraham, Isaac and Jacob. "*SEED*" is extremely important.

Exodus 6:3-4, (3) and I appeared unto Abraham, unto Isaac, and unto Jacob, as God Almighty, but by My name YHWH I made Me not known to them. (4) <u>And I have also established My Covenant with them, to give them the land of Canaan, the land of their sojournings, wherein they sojourned.</u>

The Covenant YHWH made with Abraham and his SEED before they were in Egypt, was in some respects lying "*dormant*", like a SEED placed into the soil waiting for rain so it's secrets can be "*executed*". When YHWH heard their cries <u>HE *remembered* HIS</u> Covenant, It was then, HE "*remembered*".

Exodus 2:23-25, (23) And it came to pass in the course of those many days that the king of Egypt died; and the sons of Israel sighed by reason of the bondage, and they cried, <u>and their cry came up unto God</u> by reason of the bondage. (24) And God heard their groaning, <u>and God remembered His Covenant with Abraham, with Isaac, and with Jacob.</u> (25) And God saw the sons of Israel, and God took <u>cognizance</u> of them.

GOD took *"cognizance"* of them. GOD *<u>recognized</u>* the SEED of Abraham.

It is interesting to note that the Hebrew root translated as *"cognizance"* is the word meaning to "*know*" or to *"have knowledge"* of something. But it can also have the sense of recognizing something (or someone) that is familiar. The sense is that GOD had a familiarity with someone. GOD had familiarity with Israel because Israel was the SEED of Abraham of whom GOD had an eternal Covenant. Thus YHWH remembered HIS Covenant with Abraham when HE heard Abraham's SEED cry. <u>HE recognized Abraham's SEED</u>.

YHWH had made the Covenant with Abraham and his SEED. YHWH, remembered Abraham and his SEED *"In that day YHWH made a Covenant with Abram saying: 'Unto thy SEED have I given this land"*.

ABRAHAM'S COVENANT INCORPORATED

At Sinai, Israel, Abraham's SEED, accepted the offer of Covenant of the Law made by YHWH to them. They *agreed* to keep the Law of Moses.

Deuteronomy 5:24-26, (24) Go thou near, and hear all that YHWH our God may say; and thou shalt speak unto us all that YHWH our God may speak unto thee; and we will hear it and do it.' (25) And YHWH heard the voice of YOUR WORDS, when ye spoke unto me; and YHWH said unto me: 'I have heard the voice of THE WORDS of this people, which they have spoken unto thee; they have well said all that they have spoken. (26) Oh that they had such a heart as this alway, to fear Me, and keep all My Commandments, that it might be well with them, and with their children for ever!

Isaiah 59:21, (21) And as for Me, this is My Covenant with them, saith YHWH; My spirit that is upon thee, and My Words which I have put in thy mouth, shall not depart out of thy mouth, nor out of the mouth of thy SEED, nor out of the mouth of thy SEED'S SEED, saith YHWH, from henceforth and For Ever.

What is YHWH saying by the mouth of the Prophet Isaiah by, "*My words which I have put in thy mouth*"? They are the very words which are on the heart of Israel, and which with their tongue and with their lips they teach to their children. They are the same words which they "*talk of*" when they are sitting, walking, lying down and when they are rising up.

Deuteronomy 6:5-7, (5) And thou shalt love YHWH thy God with all thy heart, and with all thy soul, and with all thy might. (6) And these words, which I command thee this day, shall be upon thy heart; (7) and thou shalt teach them diligently unto thy children, and shalt talk of them when thou sittest in thy house, and when thou walkest by the way, and when thou liest down, and when thou risest up.

The Law of YHWH, HIS Commandments, HIS Statutes and HIS Ordinances were to be on the *hearts*, on the *minds* and on the *lips* of Israel *always*.

This too, was the world in which Jesus lived. It was an environment in which the Law of Moses permeated every aspect of one's existence. What was done or not done and how it was done or not done if it was done at all, was dictated by the Law of Moses.

In understanding the Law given to Israel at Sinai, at no time did YHWH say that HIS Law had a set expiration time or date, or an end time for HIS Torah. Just the opposite exists. For when HIS Safer Torah, and also HIS prophets are read, the reader will see that HIS Law is eternal, HIS priests are to offer sacrifice for Israel's atonement for sins forever, and his *"prince"* King David with all of Israel will keep HIS Law, His Statutes, His Ordinances and HIS Commandments as they are everlasting. This will include the *"nations"* who survive HIS judgment as well. The Law is eternal and is for ever. As regarding Jesus, if the examples of the Covenant's of Noah, Abraham and Israel, and the words of GOD'S prophets are any indication, when the New Covenant with Israel becomes a reality, as the prophets clearly state there will be a *"New Covenant"*, it will be a Covenant which *"absorbs"*, *"includes"* and is *"comprised"* of the eternal Covenants which proceeded it (Jeremiah 31:31-36). The Law lives.

'VENGEANCE OF THE COVENANT'

The *"land"* belongs to GOD. The Land of Israel is the *"land"* which belongs to YHWH as *"holy land"*. Even when Israel sinned and was removed from HIS land which HE gave to Abraham and his SEED as an inheritance, the true owner of the *"land"* is always *"YHWH"*. One might say that YHWH is the *"default"* guardian, owner, and landlord of *"Eretz Israel"*. When Israel sinned against YHWH and GOD sent them into exile, the land reverted back to it's original owner. YHWH *"scattered"* Israel, but HE still owns the land.

Hosea 9:3, (3) <u>They shall not dwell in YHWH'S LAND</u>; but Ephraim shall return to Egypt, and they shall eat unclean food in Assyria.

Even the Law pertaining to each tribe was such, that the land could not be really *"sold"*. It's possession remained amongst it's tribal members and stayed within the tribe in perpetuity, and together with the other tribal lands kept Eretz Israel together as the inheritance of Jacob *"And the land shall not be sold in perpetuity; **for the land is Mine**; for ye are strangers and settlers with Me"* (Leviticus 25:23).

'FOR THE LAND IS MINE'

The *"vengeance of the Covenant"* might punish Israel, but the *"land"* remains the eternal holy possession of YHWH their GOD. Even today, these lands eternally belong to YHWH and Israel HIS inheritance. No Arab, regardless of how hard they lie, murder, cheat, steal and attempt to rewrite history can change the fact that the Land of Israel belongs to YHWH and HIS people.

Leviticus 26:25,. (25) And I will bring a sword upon you, that shall execute <u>the Vengeance of the Covenant;</u>

Leviticus 26:42, (42) then will <u>I remember My Covenant</u> with Jacob, and also <u>My Covenant</u> with Isaac, and also <u>My Covenant</u> with Abraham will I remember; <u>and I will remember The Land.</u>

Deuteronomy 7:9-13, (9) Know therefore that YHWH thy God, He is God; the faithful God, who keepeth <u>Covenant</u> and mercy with them that love Him and keep His commandments to a thousand generations; (10) and repayeth them that hate Him to their face, to destroy them; He will not be slack to him that hateth Him, He will repay him to his face. (11) Thou shalt therefore keep the Commandment, and the Statutes, and the Ordinances, which I command thee this day, to do them. (12) And it shall come to pass, because ye hearken to these ordinances, and keep, and do them, that YHWH thy God shall keep with thee the <u>Covenant</u> and the <u>Mercy</u> which He swore unto thy fathers, (13) and He will <u>love</u> thee, and <u>bless</u> thee, and <u>multiply</u> thee; He will also bless the fruit of thy body and the fruit of thy land, thy corn and thy wine and thine oil, the increase of thy kine and the young of thy flock, in the land which He swore unto thy fathers to give thee.

Isaiah 24:5, (5) The earth also is defiled under the inhabitants thereof; because they have transgressed the Laws, violated the Statute, broken the <u>Everlasting Covenant.</u>

Ezekiel 44:24, (24) And in a controversy they shall stand to judge; according to Mine ordinances shall they judge it; and they shall keep My Laws and My Statutes in all My Appointed Seasons, and they shall hallow My Sabbaths.

SALVATION

Isaiah 45:17, (17) <u>O Israel, that art saved by YHWH with an everlasting salvation;</u> ye shall not be

ashamed nor confounded world without end.

Having studied the *"everlasting Covenants"* between YHWH GOD and man, specifically, between Noah and his SEED, Abraham and his SEED, Isaac and his SEED, Jacob and his SEED, and the Covenant at Sinai with all of Israel, including the Priests and King David, the understanding that these *"eternal Covenants"* are *forever* comes to mind and *remain in force*.

To many Christians as regarding the Law, they believe the death of Jesus ended this Covenant of Israel with YHWH. Therefore, according to their doctrine, the Law was / is no longer relevant. But this is not the case.

NEW COVENANT / TESTAMENT

The Jewish people during the time of Jesus would have known well the story Moses and the giving of the Law. It is the distinction between this episode in the history of Israel at the foot of Mount Sinai when Israel accepted the Law of YHWH, when contrasted with that of the disciples of Jesus after his death preaching repentance and believing on a now, dead messiah, that many Jews would have reflected on. The people were being asked to believe the person who was crucified by the Romans was really their messiah. Few people saw him after his *resurrection.* His followers called this the *"New Covenant"* One can see where this might be a huge problem for many Jews of Israel.

Much later, when this new religion was preached to the Gentiles, they were not looking at accepting this new religion from the same place as the Jewish person was. For a Jew, it was the possibility of blasphemy and sacrilege, believing in a false prophet or false messiah as *"god"*. For Gentile pagans to grasp the simple idea that the son of GOD was sacrificed so he could live, if only he would believe, was quite different. He wasn't really giving up anything. The Jew on the other hand was risking his 1,500 year relation with the one and only GOD YHWH, and being forever cut off from YHWH and his own people. To Gentiles, belief in Jesus had a much different meaning.

It is one thing to be given the hope of eternal life where there may not have been any, but it is quite another story to risk everything for something which at the time seemed so odd, and risky and at variance with all known and practiced understanding of your own religion, GOD and HIS word. Israel had quite allot at risk to abandon the Law as he understood it and *"believe"* all of the things told to him and that he had heard. This is especially true regarding believing in the *"name of Jesus"*. For not everyone saw and heard Jesus while alive, and even far fewer after he was crucified. And even those who did hear him were not always witness to everything he said or did, nor apparently did they agree. There were no *"Gospels"* or Bibles to be read and studied. There were no Christians. But there were 1,500 years of YHWH.

It was difficult enough to be able to see and study the Safer Torah. There were no printing presses. Yet, the Jewish people were asked to believe all of the fantastic things being said either by Jesus or about Jesus, his words and the healing etc. This was 2,000 years ago. It must be kept in mind why so many people were reluctant to *"throw caution to the wind"* and *"believe"*. For the Jew unlike the Gentile, there was just far too much at stake. It must be kept in mind as well, that only a small minority witnessed all of the preaching, and miracles of Jesus. We can sit today and read it all, but 2,000 years ago, most would have been hearsay, passed from one person to another.

The concept of *"Covenant"* is important to remember when the Gospels are read, as most Jewish people had an understanding of the *Covenants* made by their forefathers and what they thought *"constituted"* an actual *"Covenant"*.

It is within this concept of *"Covenant"* of ancient Israel, that the uninitiated reader must take into consideration anytime a person who was born, raised and experienced life in the modern world, attempts to approach the events which surrounded the life and death of Jesus 2,000 years ago.

Jesus was an observant Jew, not as one thinks of the Yiddish speaking Orthodox Jews today who think, dress and act as if they are still living in a snow bound *"shtetl"* in Poland, according to their own *"second oral torah"*. But as a Jew who could still go to the Temple of YHWH, offer his sacrifice and inquire from it's priests about the ***true*** written Law of Moses still taught.

Jesus was a man of *"his"* time, and *"his"* culture, of *"his"* religion and *"his"* world, not the Dark Ages, the Renaissance, not Elizabethan England or the Wild Wild West and not our own time. One can read neither the Hebrew Bible nor the Christian Bible without taking this into account. We live in vastly different times than did Israel and Jesus. His entire world consisted of how far one could walk within two or three days or ride on an ass. There were no *"frequent flier"* miles, company discounts or first class seats.

'A NEW COVENANT'?

DRINKING BLOOD & EATING FLESH

To many Jewish scholars, what transpired between Jesus and his disciples during the Passover Seder (Last Supper), did not constitute a *"Covenant"* in the biblical sense of the term. At least not in so far as the examples of *"Covenant"* making in the Hebrew Bible were concerned. The example of *"Covenants"* already given such as SEED Covenant with Abraham and Sinai Covenant with Israel were to draw a contrast between past *"Covenants"* between GOD and man, and that discussed in the Gospels with Jesus. The Covenants made between YHWH with Noah and all life, between YHWH and Abraham and between YHWH and Israel are vastly different than that example given with Jesus. When did GOD actually make a <u>new</u> Covenant?

Law and Covenant are at issue. In the telling of the Passover Seder where Jesus told his followers that the act of eating the bread and drinking of the wine was the *"new testament"*, it was a different type of *"contract"* being made or offered. For the examples of Covenant that YHWH made with Abraham and with Israel, two parties made an oath. A type of ceremony was performed including the spilling of blood by animal sacrifice sealing their contract. Unlike the *"Covenant"* GOD made with Israel which was a contract where two parties agreed to either do something, or abstain from doing something, Jesus appeared to be speaking of something else entirely.

Haggai 2:5, (5) <u>The word that I Covenanted with you</u> when ye came out of Egypt have <u>I established</u>, and My spirit abideth among you; <u>fear ye not</u>.

Did the acts associated with the Last Supper constitute a real *"Covenant"*, according to known Covenants between GOD and man in the Hebrew Bible? Before, Covenants of GOD were made between a heavenly GOD YHWH and his creation on earth below. YHWH made a Covenant, and man accepted the Covenant. But Jesus was a *man* sitting at the same table with his followers. A man who was baptized for forgiveness of his own *"sins"* by John the Baptist.

With the Last Supper Gospel stories (Matthew 26:17-30; Mark 14:12-25; Luke 22:7-23, John 22:13-17), GOD YHWH is absent. Jesus makes a *"statement"* about a *"new covenant"* and explains regarding his *"blood"* and his *"flesh"*. But there is no clear understanding of a binding *"Covenant"* offered to an identifiable person or persons. Nor is there a clear understanding of how this *"offer"* of Covenant is accepted or a clear sense of the responsibilities or the penalties involved by it's violation. One must *"piece meal"* from the entire four Gospels to get an understanding of what is expected of someone who wants to be part of this *"new covenant"*, and even then it is not clear. Is one to eat *matzah* and drink *wine,* pretending they are flesh and blod of Jesus to be part of the *"new covenant"*? Is one just to be *"baptized"* and by whom? Is one just to *"believe"*? And if so, what exactly is one to believe? That Jesus died for Israel? That Jesus died for the sins of the world? Did Jesus die for Israel and for the sins of the world? If Jesus told his followers to keep the Commandments, why does the world ignore his words?

COVENANT VS TESTAMENT

As with much of the story of Jesus, many of the areas concerning Jesus and the Law seem to be in a gray area where it is difficult to understand exactly what has occurred. Like his parables, even the *"new"* Covenant is not clear.

For example the *"anointing"* of his head with perfume by a prostitute. Was this to pass as a type of *"anointing"* with oil? Was it suppose to have? Was Jesus truly of the *"SEED"* of David? Did Jesus give *"new"* commandments to the existing Commandments of the Law of Moses as with the example given of *"divorce"* and *"swearing"*? Does the crucifixion of Jesus on the remains of a tree by the Romans qualify as a *"sacrifice"* according to any of the many types of sacrificial offerings described in the Law? Does it matter?

Well, yes it does matter. These questions and many other similar questions lead to another gray area type of question. The Christians call the Christian Bible the *"New Testament"*, which is usually translated as *"new covenant"*, and comes from the Latin *"testamentum"* (covenant with GOD) given earlier. In turn, *"testamentum"* has it's origin in the Latin *"testari"* meaning *"witness* and *"will"* which comes from *"testis"*, (also is the male reproductive gland). Recall Abraham and Jacob as part of the oath making process, had the others hand placed under his thigh while swearing in the name of YHWH.

Does the death of Jesus qualify as a *sacrifice* according to the Law of Moses? Jesus was nailed to a tree. Was this unclean place away from the holy Temple of YHWH where Jesus was nailed to a tree acceptable to YHWH? Was the tree with no fire a substitute for an alter? What does the Law say about the place of sacrifice? Was the area around the tree sanctified? Was his blood spilled on the ground a substitute for the sprinkling of sacrificial blood on an alter? Many questions regarding what took place in the life and death of Jesus lead to even more questions, when the Law is considered. Especially, as the Law clearly explains how a sacrificial offering is to be made on GOD'S alter.

If it was a true *"Covenant"*, as part of Christian doctrine, how was it made? To whom was it offered and who accepted it? How was it accepted? What were the obligations of each side of the agreement? How was the agreement to be kept and what were the penalties if one or both sides broke their part of the agreement? Was there any kind of a *"formal"* acceptance or *"rejection"?*

Was there a *"sign"* of this *new Covenant?* If so, what was the sign?

TOKENS AND SIGNS OF COVENANTS

The Covenant sign with Noah was the *"rainbow"*. The Covenant sign with Abraham was *"circumcision"*. The Covenant sign with Israel is *"Passover"* as a remembrance forever that with a strong hand, *"hath YHWH brought thee out of Egypt"*. YHWH ransomed Israel and established HIS Law to live by.

The many examples of *"Covenant"* in the Hebrew Bible gives one a very good idea of what a real biblical *"Covenant"* with GOD entails. In the Hebrew Bible, GOD made the *"offer"* of Covenant and man accepts the Covenant with all of it's stipulations. At Sinai, it was the Statutes and the Ordinances of the Law. What was it with Jesus? What exactly is his Covenant, the *"New Covenant"?*

Zechariah 9:11, (11) As for thee also, <u>because of the Blood of thy Covenant</u> I send forth thy prisoners out of the pit wherein is no water.

It must be understood as well that a true Covenant in the Hebrew Bible is a *"legally binding contract"*. Long before there were legal courts, judges, lawyers and laws, men made agreements between one another with witnesses present if possible. The Covenant made between Abraham and YHWH needed no witnesses. But other examples of Covenants made between men did have witnesses. When Abraham bought the burial Cave of Machpelah to bury Sarah, it was a type of Covenant or at least an Oath with many men present who were witness to the purchase. Whether or not it was a true *"Covenant"*, it reads like poetry, like a court drama as the *"legal"* proceedings are acted out. It truly is a marvel of ancient jurisprudence.

Another example of Covenant making was a *"Covenant"* made between men such as between Abraham and Abimelech over a well of water (Genesis 21:22-34 with an exchange of sheep. Or the Covenant made between Jacob and Laban (Genesis 31:44). In this Covenant they built a pillar of stone as *"witness"* to their agreement, Jacob *"swore"*, and *"sacrifice"* was made.

King David made several Covenants and swears an oath with the House of Saul. David made Covenants with King Saul and with Prince Jonathan that David would not destroy Saul's SEED and would be kind to the House of Saul after him. These Covenants took place over a period of time (I Samuel 20:8,14-17; 20:41-21:1; 23:16-18; 24:21-23; [II Samuel 21:7]).

Covenants made between men were very special, at least those of the Patriarchs and men later of the Kingdom of Israel. Because these *Covenants / oaths* usually entailed *"swearing"*. And swearing was normally always done in the name of one's GOD. And Israel's GOD is *"YHWH"*. In II Samuel 21:7 the oath between David and Jonathan it is called *"YHWH'S oath"*.

A Covenant made between GOD and man was a legal contract with clear stipulations regarding each sides obligations to the agreement. But what was or is the actual *"contract"* or *"agreement"* between Jesus and man? Was the *"contract"* made between Jesus as <u>god</u> and Israel. There does not seem to be an actual agreement made of any kind. It appears to be a type of <u>*presentation*</u>.

By contrast, for several chapters GOD tells Abraham what HE is going to do for Abraham and his SEED. YHWH tells Abraham more than once how HE will give to Abraham and to Abraham's SEED all of the land of Canaan. Only after several times explaining to Abraham what HE was going to do for Abraham and his SEED, does GOD finally tell Abraham what is expected of him. Abraham was told that the Covenant being made with him is a Covenant which requires him to *circumcise.* Acceptance was through circumcising.

So, in the situation with Abraham, YHWH gives Abraham and his SEED the land of Canaan, and Abraham circumcises all of the males of his house, both born and bought with money. There is reciprocal agreement between parties.

That a Covenant with GOD is a legally binding contract is not something to be taken lightly. Whether or not most Christians or Jews for that matter, realize that Israel is still *"under contract"* with GOD dating back to the Covenant at Sinai, and even farther to the Covenant of Abraham, who's Covenant was incorporated into the Sinai Covenant, seems doubtful. Israel is still under *"Covenant"* with YHWH, and remain YHWH'S *"anointed".*

Habakkuk 3:13, (13) Thou art come forth for the deliverance of Thy people, <u>for the deliverance of Thine anointed</u>...;

As many Christians appear to be of the idea that somehow the Covenant GOD made with Israel is no longer in affect, it hinders them from understanding the truth of GOD'S real relationship with HIS *"servant son"* Israel. Believing HIS Covenant is dead would be a mistake. For many years *"replacement theology"* seemed to dominate many denominations. But today there is a movement away from this doctrine whereby GOD has rejected Israel and replaced Israel with the Gentiles who have become the *"new Israel".* There does seem to be a movement amongst Christians today, who realize that Israel is still YHWH'S chosen people. And the support for Israel and the Jewish people amongst many Christians appears to be growing. The idea today appears to be that Israel the Jewish people, and Christians who support them are both heirs to GOD'S mercy. Christianity's only obligation seems to be to *"believe",* but *replacement theology* still persists with many.

Amos 3:1-2, (1) Hear this word that YHWH hath spoken against you, O sons of Israel, against the whole family which I brought up out of the land of Egypt, saying: (2) <u>You only have I known of all the families of the earth; therefore I will visit upon you all your iniquities.</u>

For many Christians, especially in the past when the *"replacement theology"* was still much more in vogue, it was because of Israel's suffering and their travail (along with several well placed prophesies taken out of context) which gave this idea such momentum. But had the Law been studied, it would have become crystal clear that it was precisely because Israel was GOD'S chosen people that their suffering and travail was so **"harsh".** For the Law is alive, especially the Book of Deuteronomy revealing why Israel has suffered so in the past and still suffers today. For Israel is punished <u>*because*</u> of the living*"Law",* not because the Law is dead.

Deuteronomy 14:1, (1) <u>Ye are the children of YHWH your God</u>...

Deuteronomy 8:5, (5) And thou shalt consider in thy heart, that, <u>as a man chasteneth his son, so YHWH thy God chasteneth thee.</u>

One need only to read the Book of Deuteronomy to understand the harshness of GOD'S punishment. Related to this, some of the "*replacement theology*" thinking may have been *"wishful thinking"* on the part of many of the early as well as latter day believers for there was much hatred towards the Jewish people by the Gentiles within Christianity. Especially so after the fourth century C.E., for the animosity did not come from the early Jewish believers.

The Covenant of Abraham as well as the Covenant at Sinai are *"eternal"* Covenants. They are forever. The good news is, that there will be many other _nations_ other than Israel once judgment has been accomplished. But they will exist as individual identifiable nations under the Law, not as the _new Israel_.

One more thing about the Covenant of Sinai YHWH made with Israel. In the Law of the Covenant, YHWH makes sure to explain to Israel what they can expect if they break their part of the agreement. This is what was meant by the word *"harsh"*. Unfortunately, over the centuries, many have interpreted GOD anger with his people as a sign that they can *"pile on"*, and that Israel is no longer GOD'S chosen people and it is alright to kick them while they are down. But all they are truly witnessing is the punishment GOD said HE would give to HIS people Israel for violating their Covenant with YHWH.

And if anyone, Jew or Gentile has any doubt as to the truth of these words of GOD, all one needs to do is to read Deuteronomy 28:1-69 with the blessings and curses of GOD. These explain in gory detail what will happen if Israel breaks their side of the Covenant. GOD does not lie. The Covenant is still in force. YHWH has said that HE will not break HIS Covenant with Israel. This means that it's penalties are still being enforced by YHWH, Israel's GOD.

Many people wrongly assume that because Israel has broken their side of the Covenant, then YHWH has broken HIS side of the agreement. However, this is not the Law, for the Law only says GOD will initiate the penalties for Israel breaking HIS Law. He never said that HE would HIMSELF end the Law or anything like it. Israel's *"penalty"* for not keeping HIS Law was their *"punishment"*. For the idea of GOD ending HIS Covenant comes not from GOD. This idea is contrary to the evidence of HIS punishment and HIS own words. Many forget HIS mercy, compassion and blessings abound for HIS anointed Israel.

When reading the curses especially, all one needs to do is to keep in mind the history of Israel and the Jewish people, especially over the last 2,000 years, to understand that HIS words still resonate. And when the words of HIS Prophets are read in tandem with the Law, one can get a sense of what is truly occurring. The problem in many churches for many years has been that many believers in Jesus only read the bad, but do not read all of the rest regarding GOD'S mercy and love for HIS people and that HE will not break HIS side of the Covenant. The punishment and curse will be carried out by GOD as part of the Covenant, but YHWH has said that HE will not break HIS part of the contract. This last part is very important to understand and to remember. *Grace* and *truth, mercy* and *compassion* did not begin with Jesus. GOD'S promise to Abraham and to Abraham's SEED will become manifest.

BLOOD SACRIFICE & 'SWEET SAVOUR'

What are some true examples of *"sacrifice"* and of *"Covenant"* making in ancient Israel? How do they compare to Jesus and his *"New Covenant"*.

GOD seems to be pacified by certain smells. Time and again the description of YHWH smelling the aroma of the sacrifice to HIM on an alter leaves one with the impression that there is much more going on with these sacrifices than may readily be observed. The story of Noah sacrificing after the flood is just one such example. Aside from the Covenant itself, the sacrifice offering was special and unique.

The actual offering made to GOD possessed an almost magical quality to it all it's own. It's essence was very personal to the most holy GOD YHWH. It was an act of supreme meaning received by GOD at the hand of, and from HIS own creation. It appeased YHWH as nothing else appeared to do, calming HIS anger, soothing HIS wrath, dampening HIS fire and restoring HIS compassion anew towards HIS creation.

Genesis 8:20-21, (20) And Noah builded an altar unto YHWH; and took of every clean beast, and of every clean fowl, and offered burnt-offerings on the altar. (21) <u>And YHWH smelled the sweet savour;</u> and <u>YHWH said in His heart</u>: 'I will not again curse the ground any more for man's sake; for the imagination of man's heart is evil from his youth; neither will I again smite any more every thing living, as I have done.

Presumably, GOD smelled the sweet smell of the sacrifice and repented having destroyed most of the earth. This motif is repeated often. The smell of burning flesh is not normally considered an aroma one would run and fetch one's friend to share. But to YHWH it seems to have a special something about it which appears to trigger a warm feeling of love, compassion and forgiveness. Without going into prophesy about hypocrites and wicked people offering sacrifice, "*compassion*" and "*forgiveness*" is often the emotion evoked from this offering. Often it appears as a kind of "*satiation*" on the part of GOD, and an "*appeasement*" to GOD on the part of man, whereby YHWH is satisfied, appeased by man's offering to HIM as one might feel full after a satisfying meal, *"for a sweet savour unto YHWH"*.

Exodus 29:41, (41) And the other lamb thou shalt offer at dusk, and shalt do thereto according to the meal-offering of the morning, and according to the drink-offering thereof, <u>for a sweet savour, an offering made by fire unto YHWH.</u>

Leviticus 4:31, (31) And all the fat thereof shall he take away, as the fat is taken away from off the sacrifice of peace-offerings; <u>and the priest shall make it smoke upon the altar for a sweet savour unto YHWH;</u> and the priest shall make atonement for him, and he shall be forgiven.

Throughout the Safer Torah regarding sacrifice, time and again an emphasis on GOD smelling the sacrifice is made, "*for a sweet savour, an offering made by fire unto YHWH*". The aroma seemed to signify mans connection to his Father, an unbroken umbilical cord of recognition, a childlike need and dependence which triggers a feeling of love and heavenly compassion from his GOD. As the cry of an infant might trigger the compassion of a mother, YHWH'S compassion seemed to be activated by the smell of sacrificial offerings to HIM by HIS sons and by HIS creation.

Leviticus 6:8, (8) And he shall take up therefrom his handful, of the fine flour of the meal-offering, and of the oil thereof, and all the frankincense which is upon the meal-offering, and shall make the memorial-part thereof <u>smoke upon the altar for a sweet savour unto YHWH.</u>

Unlike the smell of burning flesh, this offering actually sounds like one a person would not mind being down wind of, when offered up upon the alter.

The idea of a *"sweet savour"* or *"sweet fragrance"* is something that is so jam packed with meaning, and so far removed from man's understanding, that it is perhaps one of life's biggest mysteries. A miracle of the secret of heaven.

ALTER PYRE VS TREE OF NAILS

"Sweet Savour" is important as it pertains to the *"sacrifice"* of Jesus. No doubt the death of Jesus is considered a *"sacrifice"* according to the Gospels. However, does it qualify by everything that we know about sacrifice in the Hebrew Bible? In other words, was it a *"kosher"* offering?" For according to the story, YHWH turned *away* from Jesus. According to Jesus GOD had forsaken him. Was the death of Jesus in any way a *"sweet savour"* to YHWH?

Psalms 66:15, (15) I will offer unto Thee burnt-offerings of fatlings, <u>with the sweet smoke</u> of rams; I will offer bullocks with goats. Selah

Did it in any way qualify as a *"sweet fragrance"* which allowed GOD to forgive sin? For by all accounts, GOD turned away from Jesus and by his own words, he was *"forsaken"* by his Father. Does this in anyway mimic a sacrificial offering on HIS alter? Is there anything about his death which is sanctified as with the offerings made upon GOD'S alter before HIS Temple? Does it matter?

There was a time in the history of ancient Israel, that people were allowed to make sacrifice just about anywhere. After the Law was given and Jerusalem was established as the place where YHWH put his name, sacrifice was only allowed on the Temple Mount on YHWH'S alter and forbidden elsewhere.

Leviticus 17:1- 5, (1) And YHWH spoke unto Moses, saying: (2) Speak unto Aaron, and unto his sons, and unto all the sons of Israel, and say unto them: This is the thing which YHWH hath commanded, saying: <u>(3) What man soever there be of the house of Israel, that killeth an ox, or lamb, or goat, in the camp, or that killeth it without the camp, (4) and hath not brought it unto the door of the tent of meeting, to present it as an offering unto YHWH before the tabernacle of YHWH, blood shall be imputed unto that man; he hath shed blood; and that man shall be cut off from among his people.</u> (5) To the end that the sons of Israel may bring their sacrifices, which they sacrifice in the open field, even that they may bring them unto YHWH, unto the door of the tent of meeting, unto the priest, and sacrifice them for sacrifices of peace-offerings unto YHWH.

Deuteronomy 12:5-6, (5) <u>But unto the place which YHWH your God shall choose out of all your tribes to put HIS NAME there, even unto His habitation shall ye seek, and thither thou shalt come; (6) and thither ye shall bring your burnt-offerings,</u> and your sacrifices, and your tithes, and the offering of your hand, and your vows, and your freewill-offerings, and the firstlings of your herd and of your flock;

Was the *"sacrifice"* of Jesus a *"kosher"* sacrifice, not having been on the alter of GOD? Was it acceptable to GOD being at a place not sanctified and cleansed by the priests? Was hanging from a tree not abhorrent to GOD? Was Jesus whole and without *"blemish"*?

Deuteronomy 21:22-23, (22) <u>And if a man have committed a sin</u> worthy of death, and he be put to death, <u>and thou hang him on a tree;</u> (23) his body shall not remain all night upon the tree, but thou shalt surely bury him the same day; <u>for he that is hanged is a reproach unto God;</u> that thou defile not thy land which YHWH thy God giveth thee for an inheritance.

'IS A REPROACH UNTO GOD'

Did GOD turn away from Jesus because Jesus was hanging from a tree? As human sacrifice was abhorrent to GOD from everything we know regarding the Canaanites, the only example we have of what a human sacrifice would entail would be the trial of Abraham with his son Isaac, *"the binding of*

Isaac" (Genesis 22:1-18). We know from the story, that this sacrifice required an *"alter"* presumably built of stone not houghed by man, *"wood"*, something for *"binding"*, a *"knife"* and *"fire"*. And of course, something was needed for the sacrifice. One may add as well, that Isaac was no doubt a young boy free of blemish acceptable to GOD, a young *"sheep"* from HIS *"flock"*. At least in the case of Isaac, a secluded place high upon a hill or mountain was used. It might not be a prerequisite, but an elevated place seems to be the preferred place for sacrifice throughout ancient Israel.

When the *"binding of Isaac"* is compared to the death of Jesus, there is something seriously missing. With the binding of Isaac, we not only have an example of what such an offering would entail, but on a completely different level, it is the sacrifice from a Father of his beloved son. This was what Jesus was to have been (John 3:16). Yet, the death of Jesus was not one on an alter accomplished upon the Temple Mount, nor was it made by fire, sending up a *"sweet savour"* made by smoke to GOD. This death of Jesus was a death of humiliation. It was a horrific agonizing death carried out *not* by Israel's priests, but by an uncircumcised foreign power centered in Rome.

Would a GOD such as YHWH, whose compassion for Abraham, whom HE would not allow to sacrifice his own son, not extend to the son of GOD YHWH himself? In other words, would not the *same compassion* YHWH showed to Abraham not begin with HIMSELF, and spare HIS own son? Should GOD'S mercy for HIS own son be any less than that shown for Isaac? Would a compassionate GOD not be imbued with the very same feeling for HIS own son as HE would be for that of HIS creation? How could a Father do such a thing? This is the question. It says that GOD *"so loved the world"* (John 3:16). But how can this *love* necessitate such an absolute horrific death of one HE so loved? Did not God also cherish the life of HIS own son? Was there no other way to salvage mankind but this? Was such a death necessary?

Matthew 27:46 (46) And about the ninth hour Jesus cried with a loud voice, saying, Eli, Eli, lama sabachthani? that is to say, My God, my God, why hast thou forsaken me?

His last words also seem to fly in the face of the words of GOD that HE would never *"forsake"* Israel. Was Jesus the cornerstone rejected?

I Kings 6:13, (13) in that I will dwell therein among the sons of Israel, and will not forsake My people Israel.'

The agony of Jesus is clear and heart wrenching. The GOD which he spoke of as being *"one"* with, and the *"Father"* which he said he represented, seemingly abandoned him. Jesus was quoting King David (Psalm 22:2).

Again, if everything Jesus said was true, was this suppose to have been the way in which he was to *"go out"*? Was this the example of GOD'S sacrifice of HIS *"only begotten son"* for mankind? Was the blood he spilled from the scourging, the beating and from the crown of thorns, the nails on the cross and the spear from the Roman soldier, the blood sacrificed for mankind? Was GOD somehow appeased by this bloodletting without *fire/smoke,* without a *"sweet savour"* and without an *alter?* Was the named place of the *"Skull"* not just more humiliation, especially when comparing the death of Jesus to a real sacrifice by fire on the alter of GOD in HIS Holy Temple. Did YHWH really forsake him? If so, then does his death count?

If the sad death of Jesus was acceptable to YHWH, it is an example of a humiliating and horrific sacrifice of not only a human being, but of a son of GOD. It is very difficult to understand how this would be pleasing to GOD. *Would not a sacrifice of Jesus by HIS priests on HIS alter with fire and smoke and a sweet savour have made more sense and been more acceptable, if GOD was really sacrificing HIS son?*

With all of the religious issues aside, the life and death saga of Jesus, just on a human level, is truly a sad story. For in it exists all of the ingredients of a personal tragedy of monumental proportions. Jesus seems not to have met but few of the criteria for a sacrificial *"lamb"*. Jesus was called the *"lamb of GOD"*, yet his death appeared to have been anything but a sacrifice offering according to the Law, the Law of which he said that Israel must keep. When his death is compared to the Temple of YHWH, HIS priests, and HIS consecrated alter used during many centuries of sacrificial offerings, and the holiness associated with each square centimeter of ground within it's huge blocks of stone, the death of Jesus was truly a grotesque and despicable act and comes across rather more like a back alley murder than an sacrificial offering to the GOD of Israel. For Jesus was *"sacrificed"* outside the holy santuary of the Temple and it's alter in a place not made *"holy"* by the priests. Was this dark horror of a sacrifice the point of his death?

JESUS AND THE LAW

In the Gospels, when one thinks about or discusses *"the Law"* as are mentioned throughout, what they are really encountering is the Covenant made at Sinai where Israel was sprinkled with the blood of the Covenant, accepting the agreement to obey the *"Law"* of YHWH GOD.

For the *"Law"* even in it's most narrow sense, is the entire Covenant made at Mount Sinai between YHWH and Israel. It is to say, a *"legally binding contract"* between YHWH and Israel. It is the agreement between these two principles sealed with / in blood, which is often being discussed in the Gospels and remains the foundation purpose for the events surrounding the life of Jesus. Between GOD and man is this Covenant made. It cannot be taken lightly by Israel as it is a holy Covenant with YHWH. The Covenant of the Law, is *all* of the Commandments of YHWH GOD which Israel accepted at Sinai. It is these Commandments the Pharisees were so contentious about.

GOD first made a Covenant with Noah and then with Abraham and finally with all of Israel. Using the terminology of the legal justice system, one might say that these Covenants are all running *"concurrently"*. That is, they are all running *"together"*. They are all running together at the same time. One eternal Covenant does not cancel out another eternal Covenant, but all are running together simultaneously. *Rainbows* still rainbow, the *"circumcisers"* still circumcise, and Israel is still under Covenant of the eternal Law of YHWH GOD.

Deuteronomy 4:7-8, (7) For what great nation is there, that hath God so nigh unto them, as YHWH our God is whensoever we call upon Him? (8) And what great nation is there, that hath Statutes and Ordinances so righteous as all this Law, which I set before you this day?

'STATUTES AND ORDINANCES SO RIGHTEOUS'

This leads us back to what Jesus said regarding the Law. What did he say? He said if Israel wanted to *"enter into life"* they must keep the Law, *"but if thou wilt enter into life, keep the Commandments"*. Make no mistake, Jesus was speaking of life *eternal*. The Prophet Moses, Deuteronomy 30:19, *"therefore* **choose life**, *that thou mayest live, thou and thy SEED"*.

What do the "*Commandments*" say? They say not to "*add*" or "*diminish*" from the Commandments of the Law. The Law of YHWH is perfect.

What Commandments was Jesus speaking about? "*And it is easier for heaven and earth to pass, than one tittle of the **LAW** to fail*". *All* of GOD'S Commandments must be kept. None are expendable. None will fail. GOD did not tell Israel to keep a few and not to worry themselves about the rest.

The point is that Jesus said to "*keep the Commandments*". Israel was not given the option to pick and choose which Commandments to keep. Their Covenant with YHWH was that they must keep **all** of the Commandments.

Matthew 5:18, (18) For verily I say unto you, Till heaven and earth pass, <u>one jot or one tittle shall in no wise pass from the law, till all be fulfilled.</u>

Regarding the Law of YHWH and the Covenant HE made with his people Israel, Jesus seems to be in complete agreement with all of the Laws, Statutes, Ordinances in the words of the Covenant at Sinai. Whether the Pharisees, Priests or others agreed with his explanation of the Law is another issue. And whether or not Jesus was correct in his teaching of the Law too, is not the issue. The point is, in so far as the Law of Moses, he said to keep the Commandments given by GOD, that they were "*life*" to Israel as said Moses.

Again, it is important to be consistent. Jesus was a Jew born into the Covenant of YHWH. He is quoted as saying to "*keep the commandments*". Jesus is speaking to fellow Jews, not to Lithuanians, Romanians or Vietnamese. Jesus was a Jew speaking only to a Jewish audience. Whether they agreed with him or disagreed with him is not the point here, it was his own people he was speaking to during his entire life time.

Deuteronomy 4:20, (20) But you hath YHWH taken and brought forth out of the iron furnace, out of Egypt, <u>to be unto Him a People of Inheritance</u>, as ye are this day.

If Jesus knew the Torah as well as he appears to have known it (not it's interpretation), then he was more than a little aware of Israel's unique relationship with their GOD YHWH.

'THAT IT MAY GO WELL WITH THEE'

Deuteronomy 4:37-40, (37) And because He loved thy fathers, <u>and chose their SEED after them</u>, and brought thee out with His presence, with His great power, out of Egypt, (38) to drive out nations from before thee greater and mightier than thou, to bring thee in, to give thee their land for an inheritance, as it is this day; (39) <u>know this day, and lay it to thy heart, that YHWH, He is God in heaven above and upon the earth beneath; there is none else</u>. (40) And thou shalt keep His <u>Statutes</u>, and His <u>Commandments</u>, which I <u>command</u> thee this day, <u>that it may go well with thee</u>, and with thy children after thee, and that thou mayest prolong thy days upon the land, which YHWH thy God giveth thee, for ever.

Jesus would have known all would not go well with Israel if they did not keep GOD'S Commandments, for the truth of GOD'S word and history had already shown this.

Deuteronomy 5:1-3, (1) And Moses called unto all Israel, and said unto them: Hear, O Israel, the <u>Statutes</u> and the <u>Ordinances</u> which I speak in your ears this day, that ye may learn them, and *observe to do them. (2) YHWH our God made a Covenant with us in Horeb. (3) YHWH made not this Covenant with our fathers, but with us, even us, who are all of us here alive this day.*

Deuteronomy 8:11, (11) Beware lest thou forget YHWH thy God, in not keeping His Commandments, and His Ordinances, and His Statutes, which I command thee this day;

Deuteronomy 26:18-19, (18) And YHWH hath avouched thee this day to be His own treasure, as He hath promised thee, and that thou shouldest keep all His Commandments; (19) and to make thee high above all nations that He hath made, in praise, and in name, and in glory; and that thou mayest be a holy people unto YHWH thy God, as He hath spoken.

Jesus would have been aware that Israel was a people who should keep all of *"HIS"* Commandments and who were a *"treasure"* to YHWH their GOD, and were different than all of the other nations. Jesus would know that Israel was a holy people to YHWH their GOD, not counted amongst the nations.

Deuteronomy 27:9, (9) And Moses and the priests the Levites spoke unto all Israel, saying: 'Keep silence, and hear, O Israel; this day thou art become a people unto YHWH thy God.

Deuteronomy 29:12, (12) that He may establish thee this day unto Himself for a people, and that He may be unto thee a God, as He spoke unto thee, and as He swore unto thy fathers, to Abraham, to Isaac, and to Jacob.

Deuteronomy 30:11-13, (11) For this commandment which I command thee this day, it is not too hard for thee, neither is it far off. (12) It is not in heaven, that thou shouldest say: 'Who shall go up for us to heaven, and bring it unto us, and make us to hear it, that we may do it?' (13) Neither is it beyond the sea, that thou shouldest say: 'Who shall go over the sea for us, and bring it unto us, and make us to hear it, that we may do it?' (14) But the word is very nigh unto thee, in thy mouth, and in thy heart, that thou mayest do it.

Israel is the *"established"* people of the living GOD, HIS holy people and HIS inheritance. Likewise, YHWH is the *"established"* living GOD of Israel. It is precisely for this reason that Israel is blessed when keeping HIS Statutes, and by the same token it is because they are HIS people that they are cursed when they do not keep HIS Commandments according to curses associated with breaking HIS Law. For Israel has a *contract* with GOD which is still in affect. It is because Israel *is* GOD'S people that they are punished according to what is written in the Law itself. YHWH'S rod of punishment and Israel's chastisement, is evidence of the enforcement of Law, the **vengeance of the Covenant,** not GOD forsaking HIS people, *"And I will bring a sword upon you, that shall execute the **vengeance of the Covenant**; and ye shall be gathered together within your cities; and I will send the pestilence among you; and ye shall be delivered into the hand of the enemy"* (Leviticus 26:25).

'FOR THAT IS THY LIFE'

Deuteronomy 30:19-20, (19) I call heaven and earth to witness against you this day, that I have set before thee life and death, the blessing and the curse; therefore Choose Life, that thou mayest live, thou and thy SEED; (20) to love YHWH thy God, to hearken to His voice, and to cleave unto Him; for that is thy life, and the length of thy days; that thou mayest dwell in the land which YHWH swore unto thy fathers, to Abraham, to Isaac, and to Jacob, to give them.

Was it this scripture that Jesus had in mind when he said, *"but if thou wilt enter into life, keep the commandments?"* The Prophet Moses said to keep the Commandments of GOD if Israel wanted to live, *"therefore choose life, that thou mayest live"*. How could Israel keep GOD'S Commandments which tells them not to add any or to take away any, if they add or take away any of HIS Commandments by accepting any from Jesus not already in the Law?

Therefore for Israel, to reject GOD'S Commandments is to reject life itself. To keep GOD'S Commandments is to choose to live. Was Jesus just paraphrasing Moses regarding rejecting or choosing "*life*"?

This is the apparent battleground of belief on which Jesus tread. His interpretation and his constant dialogue with the various Jewish authorities was not regarding *if* Israel should keep the Law of YHWH, but on *how* Israel should keep the Law. It was not about not honoring the Covenant which Israel had with it's GOD, but about keeping the Covenant which Israel had with it's GOD. Therefore the disagreements for example with the Pharisees, were disagreements over their interpretation of Ordinances and Statutes of GOD'S Commandments, not whether Israel should keep GOD'S Commandments. It was not a disagreement of whether the Law of GOD, all of his Commandments, all HIS Statutes and HIS Ordinances should be kept. Rather, it was how the Statutes and Ordinances of GOD'S Law should be observed, kept and practiced.

'THAT HE MIGHT MAKE THEE KNOW'

Deuteronomy 8:3, (3) And He afflicted thee, and suffered thee to hunger, and fed thee with manna, which thou knewest not, neither did thy fathers know; THAT HE MIGHT MAKE THEE KNOW that man doth not live by bread only, but by every thing that proceedeth out of the mouth of YHWH doth man live.

Matthew 4:4, (4) But he answered and said, It is written, Man shall not LIVE by bread alone, but by every word that proceedeth out of the mouth of God.

Once again it can be seen, that Jesus was paraphrasing from the Law.

Passover is an "*Ordinance*" of YHWH to be kept forever. It is a Law which will not end according to YHWH.

Exodus 12:17, (17) And ye shall observe the Feast of Unleavened Bread; for in this selfsame day have I brought your hosts out of the land of Egypt; therefore shall ye observe this day throughout your generations by an Ordinance for ever

The Law of YHWH is an eternal Law which will one day be put upon the hearts of Israel and will no longer need to be taught by Israel's priests.

Jeremiah 31:31-34, (31) Behold, the days come, saith YHWH, that I will make a New Covenant with the house of Israel, and with the house of Judah; (32) not according to the Covenant that I made with their fathers in the day that I took them by the hand to bring them out of the land of Egypt; forasmuch as they broke My Covenant, although I was a lord over them, saith YHWH. (33) But this is the Covenant that I will make with the house of Israel after those days, saith YHWH, I will put My Law in their inward parts, and in their heart will I write it; and I will be their God, and they shall be My people; (34) and they shall teach no more every man his neighbour, and every man his brother, saying: 'Know YHWH'; for they shall all know Me, from the least of them unto the greatest of them, saith YHWH; for I will forgive their iniquity, and their sin will I remember no more.

Does this mean that the Law given at Sinai by GOD YHWH to Israel has been canceled, abrogated or abolished? God forbid. It will be written permanently on the heart of Israel so it will no longer need to be taught.

COVENANT – COVENANT - COVENANT

The Covenant of Noah was not canceled out because of the Covenant with Abraham, but continues for all eternity. The Covenant at Sinai did not negate the Covenant of Abraham, rather it incorporated the Covenant of Abraham into written Law. Likewise, the Covenant of Sinai is not negated for it is *eternal,* and will also be incorporated into a New Covenant which YHWH said that HE will write upon the heart of Israel when that time comes.

'A PEOPLE SAVED BY YHWH'

Deuteronomy 33:27-29, (27) The eternal God is a dwelling-place, and underneath are the everlasting arms; and He thrust out the enemy from before thee, and said: 'Destroy.' (28) And Israel dwelleth in safety, the fountain of Jacob alone, in a land of corn and wine; yea, his heavens drop down dew. (29) Happy art thou, O Israel, who is like unto thee? a people SAVED by YHWH, the shield of thy help, and that is the sword of thy excellency! And thine enemies shall dwindle away before thee; and thou shalt tread upon their high places.

The Hebrew root for "*saved*" in this scripture is from the same root as "*salvation*" and is written in the *past tense*. Israel is a people who are saved, delivered and liberated by YHWH *already*! Israel needs to understand and to accept their salvation from YHWH their GOD. It is part of their Covenant.

'FOR EVER' – 'EVERLASTING'

What are we to make of the *"for ever", always, "eternal", "everlasting"* and *"for all generations"* in the Hebrew Bible, for there are many, especially as they relate to "*Covenant*"? For YHWH uses these terms constantly in connection with HIS Covenants and HIS Statutes. Does *"for ever"* and *"everlasting"* stop being '*eternal*' because of man's unbelief, because of his inability to understand, or does man even matter? For when the word of GOD is read with the understanding that it is *HIS* "*for ever*" and it is *HIS* "*everlasting*", the reality of man's irrelevance becomes apparent. In other words beyond even believing, it is GOD'S show, with or without man, *"for ever"* is still *"for ever"*, and *"everlasting"* is still *"everlasting"*. That man is even contemplating this concept at all is due to his creator having created him. Other than this he has no voice in the matter. HE must accept. For it is man who is part of GOD'S narrative, not as most of mankind believe, that GOD is part of their own narrative. It is GOD who created finite man.

YHWH has made man part of the narrative for HIS own purpose, and for HIS own glory. But with or without man, *"for ever"* and *"everlasting"* remain within the sphere of the eternal GOD and are in no way limited because of mans existence. A few examples of *"for ever"* and *"everlasting"* are given.

Genesis 9:16, 17:7,13, 19; Exodus 27:21, 28:43, 30:21; Leviticus 16:29, 31, 17:7, 23:14, 21, 31, 41, 24:3, 8; Numbers 10:8, 15:15, 18:19, 23, 19:10.

There are more. When all are put together and seen as one contiguous unit, a much different picture comes into focus than a people holding onto an old warn out and expired Covenant. But one which is still very much alive.

COVENANT OFFERING

Several examples of *"for ever"* and *"everlasting"* are given from TaNaKh in direct association with the ministry of Jesus and the Law. Some are associated with Abraham and his SEED, with King David and his SEED, and many are associated with the High Priest Aaron and his SEED. As there is a connection between the priesthood and sacrifice, and Jesus is as a sacrifice in Christianity (the lamb of GOD, the blood of the lamb etc.), these scriptures are important. Additionally, as Jesus was given to be of the SEED of David, several of these scriptures have been provided as well .

For as has been mentioned, there is a particularly strong Christian doctrine amongst some strains of Christianity that the Law is dead because of the crucifixion of Jesus. Or another doctrine exists that the Law is still alive for the Jewish people, but *"grace"* exists for Christians. However, for two reasons explained already, *"grace and truth"* are part and parcel to the Law already, and there is but _one_ Law for Israel and _one_ Law for the foreigner. If the nations are to worship YHWH with Israel, as per the prophets, then the nations will worship YHWH according to the Law, as per the prophets.

According to the *"grace"* doctrine, with the sacrificial death of Jesus, his *"offering"*, his *"blood"* forever made *"sacrifice"* according to the Law obsolete, and therefore no longer was offering for sin necessary.

Yet, as regarding Aaron the High Priest and his SEED, they will make *"atonement"*, offering sacrifice before YHWH for the *"sins"* of Israel *forever*. Additionally, there are several other priestly functions related to sacrifice that are *"fore ever"*. The idea here is that _if there were no need for atonement_ to be made for ever for Israel's *"sins"*, then it would not have been made an ***"everlasting statute"*** by Law. But it says something else as well. It seems to be implying that Israel has no need of accepting Jesus as sacrificial atonement for sin, as atonement for their sins will be made *for ever* by Israel's priests. Otherwise an obvious redundancy exists, as it is prophesied the priests will make offerings for Israel's sins *"for ever"*. This puts into serious question the purpose (atonement for sin) of the death of Jesus for Israel.

'EVERLASTING STATUTE'

Leviticus 16:34, (34) And this shall be an <u>Everlasting Statute</u> unto you, to <u>Make Atonement</u> for the sons of Israel because of All <u>Their Sins</u> Once In The Year ....

YHWH made an *"everlasting"* statute that HIS Holy Priests will make atonement for the sins of Israel every year. *Everlasting* is *for ever* and f*or ever* is *eternal* and *eternal* is *unto all generations* and *unto all generations* is *without end* and *without end* is *"everlasting"*. ***It is an Everlasting Statute***.

Regardless whether there is currently HIS Temple or an alter now to perform this offering, there is an everlasting statute which ordains that this offering is to be kept. Just as Israel may have not have been able to keep their part of the Covenant in full, they are still under Covenant with YHWH their GOD to do so. Likewise, the Everlasting Statute regarding the Priests making atonement for Israel is still to be kept, *"in full"*. For it is an *"everlasting statute"*. It is *"perpetual"*.

So the issue of whether or not Jesus was the *"messiah"* is a separate issue than one who died *"to make atonement for the sin of Israel"*. For according to the Law of Moses, it is the Priests of YHWH who must and will make atonement for the sins of Israel, *"because of All <u>Their Sins</u> Once In The Year"*. For had Jesus been able to atone for all of Israel's sins forever, there would not be any more need for the Priests to make sacrificial offerings <u>as a statute for ever for those sins</u>. It would be redundant. And this is the point.

Numbers 25:13, (13) and it shall be unto him, and to his SEED after him, the <u>Covenant of an Everlasting Priesthood</u>; because he was jealous for his God, <u>and made atonement for the sons of Israel.</u>'

Numbers 18:19, (19) All the <u>heave-offerings</u> of the holy things, which the sons of Israel offer unto YHWH, have I given thee, and thy sons and thy daughters with thee<u>, as a due for ever</u>; it is an <u>Everlasting Covenant</u> of salt before YHWH unto thee and to thy SEED with thee.'

Exodus 40:15, (15) And thou shalt anoint them, as thou didst anoint their father, that they may minister unto Me in the <u>priest's office</u>; and their anointing shall be to them for an <u>everlasting priesthood</u> throughout their generations.'

Leviticus 24:8, (8) Every sabbath day he shall set it in order before YHWH continually; it is from the sons of Israel, <u>an Everlasting Covenant</u>

II Chronicles 33:4, (4) And he built altars in the house of YHWH, whereof YHWH said: '<u>In Jerusalem shall My name be for ever.</u>'

II Chronicles 7:16, (16) For now have I chosen and hallowed this house, that My name may be there <u>for ever</u>; and Mine eyes and My heart shall be there <u>perpetually.</u>

Exodus 12:14, 17, 24, And this day shall be unto you for a memorial, and ye shall keep it a feast to YHWH; throughout your generations ye shall keep it a feast by <u>an ordinance for ever.</u> (17) And ye shall observe the feast of unleavened bread; for in this selfsame day have I brought your hosts out of the land of Egypt; <u>therefore shall ye observe this day throughout your generations by an ordinance for ever.</u> (24) And ye shall observe this thing for an ordinance to thee and to thy sons <u>for ever</u>

Exodus 27:21, (21) In the tent of meeting, without the veil which is before the testimony, Aaron and his sons shall set it in order, to burn from <u>evening to morning before YHWH</u>; it shall be a <u>statute for ever</u> throughout <u>their generations</u> on the behalf of the sons of Israel.

Exodus 28:43, (43) And they shall be upon Aaron, and upon his sons, when they go in unto the tent of meeting, or when they come near unto the altar to minister in the holy place; that they bear not iniquity, and die; it shall be <u>a statute for ever unto him and unto his SEED after him.</u>

Exodus 29:28, (28) And it shall be for Aaron and his sons as a <u>due for ever</u> from the sons of Israel; for it is a <u>heave-offering</u>; and it shall be a <u>heave-offering</u> from the sons of Israel of their <u>sacrifices of peace-offerings</u>, even their heave-offering unto YHWH.

Exodus 30:19-21, (19) And Aaron and his sons shall wash their hands and their feet thereat; (20) when they go into the tent of meeting, they shall wash with water, that they die not; or when they come near to the altar to minister, to cause an offering made by fire to smoke unto YHWH; (21) so they shall wash their hands and their feet, that they die not; and it shall be <u>a statute for ever to them</u>, even to him and to his seed <u>throughout their generations.</u>'

Exodus 31:17, (17) <u>It is a sign between Me and the sons of Israel for ever</u>; for in six days YHWH made heaven and earth, and on the seventh day He ceased from work and rested.

Exodus 32:13, (13) Remember Abraham, Isaac, and Israel, Thy servants, to whom Thou didst swear by Thine own self, and saidst unto them: I will multiply your seed as the stars of heaven, and all this land that I have spoken of will I give unto your seed<u>, and they shall inherit it for ever.</u>'

Leviticus 6:15, (15) And the anointed priest that shall be in his stead from among his sons shall <u>offer it,</u> it is a <u>due for ever</u>; it shall be wholly made to smoke unto YHWH.

Leviticus 7:34, (34) For the <u>breast of waving</u> and the <u>thigh of heaving</u> have I taken of the sons of Israel out <u>of their sacrifices of peace-offerings</u>, and have given them unto Aaron the priest and unto his sons as a <u>due for ever</u> from the sons of Israel

Regarding the House of David, YHWH made an *"Everlasting Covenant"*. With the SEED of Jacob through Joseph, YHWH made a promise of everlasting prosperity. Unto Jacob HE reminded him of HIS his eternal Covenant to possess the land and to Abraham who calls on the *"Everlasting GOD"* establishing of HIS *"Everlasting Covenant"*.To Noah YHWH makes HIS *eternal* Covenant not to destroy mankind again with a flood, and to the Levites, David reminds us that they are the ministers of YHWH *for ever*. Israel is reminded of the *Everlasting* Covenant of Abraham and YHWH tells David of HIS *eternal* Covenant with David's SEED. Israel is told to give thanks to YHWH, that HIS mercy endures *forever* and HE tells Moses that *"YHWH"* is HIS name *forever.*

Psalms 89:4, (4) <u>I have made a Covenant</u> with My chosen, I have sworn unto <u>David</u> My servant: (5) <u>For ever</u> will I establish thy SEED, and build up thy throne to <u>all generations</u>.' Selah

The idea behind all of the scriptures is to show how *everlasting*, and *for ever* is not a concept or something in the word of GOD that can be so easily dismissed by man. For whatever the world of Christianity may think of Jesus, according to the Law of YHWH, there are many Covenants, oaths, promises and statues that were made by GOD YHWH to Israel which have no attached expiration date to them. One of these *everlasting for ever* Statutes, Leviticus 16:34 shows, that the Priests are to make atonement for the sins of Israel *fore ever*, *"And this shall be an <u>Everlasting Statute</u> unto you, to <u>Make Atonement</u> for the sons of Israel because of <u>All Their Sins</u> Once In The Year ...."*.

The many Covenants, oaths, promises, Laws, eternal Statutes, Ordinances, Commandments, Precepts and words of YHWH which are eternal and which are for ever and everlasting, did not come to an abrupt halt at the beginning of the Book of Matthew, Chapter one, verse one.

II Samuel 23:5, (5) For is not my house established with God? for an Everlasting Covenant He hath made with me, ordered in all things, and sure; for all my salvation, and all my desire, will he not make it to grow?

Genesis 49:26, (26) The blessings of thy father are mighty beyond the blessings of my progenitors unto the utmost bound of the <u>everlasting</u> hills; they shall be on the head of Joseph, and on the crown of the head of the prince among his brethren.

Genesis 48:4, (4) and said unto me: Behold, I will make thee fruitful, and multiply thee, and I will make of thee a company of peoples; and will give this land to thy SEED after thee for an <u>everlasting possession.</u>

Genesis 21:33, (33) And Abraham planted a tamarisk-tree in Beer-sheba, and called there on the name of YHWH, the <u>Everlasting God</u>.

Genesis 17:7-8, 13, 19, (7) And I will establish <u>My covenant</u> between Me and thee and <u>thy seed</u> after thee throughout their generations for an <u>everlasting covenant</u>, to be a God unto thee and to <u>thy seed</u> after thee. (8) And I will give unto thee, and to <u>thy seed</u> after thee, the land of thy sojournings, all the land of Canaan, for an <u>everlasting possession</u>; and I will be their God.' (13)......<u>must needs be circumcised and My covenant shall be in your flesh for an</u> everlasting covenant.(19) .....and I will establish <u>My covenant</u> with him for an <u>everlasting covenant</u> for <u>his seed</u> after him.

Genesis 9:16, (16) And the bow shall be in the cloud; and I will look upon it, that I may remember the <u>everlasting covenant</u> between God and every living creature of all flesh that is upon the earth.'

I Chronicles 15:1-2, (1) And David made him houses in the city of David; and he prepared a place for the ark of God, and pitched for it a tent. (2) Then David said: 'None ought to carry the ark of God but the Levites; for them hath YHWH chosen to carry the ark of YHWH, and to minister unto Him for ever.'

I Chronicles 16:13-18, (13) O ye SEED of Israel His servant, ye children of Jacob, His chosen ones. (14) He is YHWH our God; His judgments are in all the earth. (15) Remember His Covenant for ever, the word which He commanded to a thousand generations; (16) The Covenant which He made with Abraham, and His oath unto Isaac; (17) And He established it unto Jacob for a statute, to Israel for an Everlasting Covenant; (18) Saying: 'Unto thee will I give the land of Canaan, the lot of your inheritance.'

I Chronicles 17:10-14, ……..Moreover I tell thee that YHWH will build thee a house. (11) And it shall come to pass, when thy days are fulfilled that thou must go to be with thy fathers, that I will set up thy SEED after thee, who shall be of thy sons; and I will establish his kingdom. (12) He shall build Me a house, and I will establish his throne for ever. (13) I will be to him for a father, and he shall be to Me for a son; and I will not take My mercy away from him, as I took it from him that was before thee; (14) but I will settle him in My house and in My kingdom for ever; and his throne shall be established for ever.

I Chronicles 22:10, (10) He shall build a house for My name; and he shall be to Me for a son, and I will be to him for a father; and I will establish the throne of his kingdom over Israel for ever.

I Chronicles 23:13, (13) The sons of Amram: Aaron and Moses; and Aaron was separated, that he should be sanctified as most holy, he and his sons for ever, to offer before YHWH, to minister unto Him, and to bless in His name for ever.

II Chronicles 9:8, (8) Blessed be YHWH thy God, who delighted in thee, to set thee on His throne, to be king for YHWH thy God; because thy God loved Israel, to establish them for ever, therefore made He thee king over them, to do justice and righteousness.'

II Chronicles 13:4-5, (4) And Abijah stood up upon mount Zemaraim, which is in the hill-country of Ephraim, and said: 'Hear me, O Jeroboam and all Israel; (5) ought ye not to know that YHWH, the God of Israel, gave the kingdom over Israel to David for ever, even to him and to his sons by a covenant of salt?

II Chronicles 20:21, (21) And when he had taken counsel with the people, he appointed them that should sing unto YHWH, and praise in the beauty of holiness, as they went out before the army, and say: 'Give thanks unto YHWH, for His mercy endureth for ever.'

Genesis 13:14-15, (14) And YHWH said unto Abram, after that Lot was separated from him: 'Lift up now thine eyes, and look from the place where thou art, northward and southward and eastward and westward; (15) for all the land which thou seest, to thee will I give it, and to thy SEED for ever.

Exodus 3:15, (15) And God said moreover unto Moses: 'Thus shalt thou say unto the sons of Israel: YHWH, the God of your fathers, the God of Abraham, the God of Isaac, and the God of Jacob, hath sent me unto you; this is My name for ever, and this is My memorial unto all generations.

THE PASSOVER OF YHWH

The story of the Last Supper, which was actually the Passover Seder (Pesach), is an interesting story. It is recommended that the entire chapters 12-13 of Exodus are read first regarding Passover so that this will have more relevance regarding Jesus and his words. In Hebrew it is called simply *"YHWH'S*

Passover" (some: *"Passover to YHWH"* [Exodus 12:11]). Passover (Pesach) and the Feast of Unleavened Bread are actually two separate holy days although most Jewish people are unaware of this and celebrate them as if they were the same thing. Passover is an *Eternal Statute.*

In all of the Gospels, the words of Jesus that were said during Passover are the closest thing said by him which one might be called a type of *"official"* doctrine coming from the mouth of Jesus. The story of the Last Passover will be quoted, but before doing so it must be made clear that this was not just a bunch of guys sitting around a table eating *"supper".* For Passover is many things to both GOD YHWH and to Israel HIS people. It is a *"Ordinance".*

Exodus 12:2, (2) 'This month shall be unto you the <u>beginning of months</u>; it shall be <u>the first month of the year to you.</u>

Jesus and his disciples were observing a Commandment from the Torah as an *"ordinance for ever".* It was an Eternal Statute commanded by the Law of Moses to perform this *"ritual feast"* to YHWH, *"Hag L'YHWH".*

Exodus 12:14, (14) And this day shall be unto you for a <u>memorial</u>, and ye shall keep it a F<u>east to YHWH</u>; throughout <u>your generations</u> ye shall keep it <u>a Feast by an Ordinance for ever.</u>

In it's truest sense, a Passover Seder is not a *"meal"* in the traditional sense at all, but a *"ritual feast"* commanded by YHWH to Israel to be performed in commemoration of the Exodus from Egypt and to officially mark the first month of the new year which began with the sighting of the new moon. The purpose was so Israel would never forget their GOD YHWH, their Savior, their Deliverer and Redeemer who saved them from slavery in Egypt and gave them their inheritance,*"redeemed them".* YHWH is Israel's Redeemer.

THE LAST PASSOVER

The Disciples meet with Jesus in an upper room previously prepared. During the Passover Seder, Jesus explains what he calls the *"New Testament"* to them. The story is retold in each of the Gospels of Matthew, Mark, Luke, and John (Matthew 26:17-30; Mark 14:12-25; Luke 22:7-23; John 22:13-17).

Although in John, the details of the washing of the feet are given along with a *"new commandment"* to love each other and other details regarding Judas and teachings which appear to continue until they leave to go to the *"garden".* But the *"new testament"* regarding bread/flesh and wine/blood is not mentioned. This seems a bit odd given the obvious importance of it for his disciples. As the Book of John is more esoteric than the other Gospels, given the symbolism of flesh and blood one would think it would have been explained more in detail given the ethereal nature of this book. Nevertheless, Jesus presents his *"new covenant".*

Matthew 26:26-30, (26) And as they were eating, <u>Jesus took bread</u>, and blessed it, and brake it, and gave it to the disciples, and said, Take,<u> eat; this is my body</u>. (27) And <u>he took the cup</u>, and gave thanks, and gave it to them, saying, <u>Drink</u> ye all of it; (28) <u>For this is my blood</u> of the <u>new testament</u>, which is shed for many <u>for the remission of sins</u>. (29) But I say unto you, I will not drink henceforth of this <u>fruit of the vine</u>, until that day when I drink it new with you in my Father's kingdom. (30). And when they had sung an hymn, they went out into the mount of Olives.

The idea of drinking the *"fruit of the vine"* during Passover is covered extensively elsewhere so it will not be discussed here. As to the *"new testament"*, Jesus is telling his followers that this is a *"covenant"* in addition to that of Moses, even though according to the Law of Moses itself, it states not to add or remove from the Law of Moses (Deuteronomy 13:1, 4:2). So, how can Jesus tell his followers to *"keep the Commandments"*, which state not to add or diminish from the Law of Moses, and also tell them he is giving them a *"new commandment"* and a *"new covenant"* which contradict it? Unless this was only to test them.

It was shown how the Priests of YHWH will forever make sacrifice offerings for the sins of Israel. *Atonement* by the blood sacrifice offering to YHWH is *perpetual*. It may temporarily be interrupted as the Babylonian Exile, but as with the return of the Babylonian Exile, the Temple was rebuilt and sacrifice offerings to YHWH resumed. For the Law is still the Law. For man, 70 years verses 2,000 years may be significant, but to GOD where time is not a condition of existence, they are the same. There will be another Temple.

Leviticus 16:34, (34) And this shall be an Everlasting Statute unto you, to Make Atonement for the sons of Israel because of All Their Sins Once In The Year ….

As the Law makes clear that every man shall die for his own sins, neither Jesus nor any other can *"die"* for the sins of another according to the Law (Deuteronomy 24:16), *"every man shall be put to death for his own sin"*. It is said in a Psalm how costly such a thing is, *"No man can by any means redeem his brother, nor give to God a ransom for him -- For too costly is the redemption of their soul, and must be let alone for ever -- "* (Psalm 49:8-9). Additionally, according to the Law itself only the Priests can make atonement for the sins of Israel other than YHWH HIMELF forgiving Israel's sins. This is part of the eternal Covenant GOD made with Israel.

Having made this statement, it is more than conceivable that a *believer* would respond by saying that Jesus was not a man. Yet Jesus was a man, as he stated many times himself that he was the *"son of man"*. *"Son of man"* usually translates as *"human"* (ben adam)*, or as is common in the Hebrew Bible, *"Man"* or *"mankind"* is *"adam"*. *"Man"* also is *"ish"*. Jesus, being a son of Israel was also a son of GOD, as GOD said of Israel often. So Israel as son of GOD, is also son of man. He is human, but his Father is YHWH.

But it remains that he was still *"human"* and died as humans are apt to do. Whether he was raised or not is another issue. He died as all humans die. How he died without a doubt was not normal, nevertheless he died. And for this, he can be considered a man. Can one man die for another man's sin? Not according to the Law of YHWH.

Which leads back to an earlier question which at the time was more of a rhetorical question. However, it needs to be seriously asked if Jesus died for his own sin? For all men sin and Jesus was still a man. If Jesus died for his own sin, how is belief in him salvation for anyone? This is a new Covenant?

For the Hebrew Bible states clearly that all men sin, and atonement must be made for their sins by the Priest of YHWH (unless YHWH forgives [pardons]). At the same time, we are told that Israel is saved with an everlasting salvation. *"O Israel, that art saved by YHWH with an everlasting salvation"*

Deuteronomy 33:29, (29) Happy art thou, O Israel, who is like unto thee? a people saved by YHWH, the shield of thy help, and that is the sword of thy excellency! And thine enemies shall dwindle away before thee; and thou shalt tread upon their high places.

According to the Law of YHWH, what did Jesus offer Israel that Israel did not already have by Covenant with YHWH their GOD?

CONCLUSION

The words of Jesus are the only words which are considered here regarding the Law and the idea of "*Covenant*". Separating 2,000 years of dogma, doctrine and pagan ritual away from just the words which the Jew Jesus is to have spoken, maybe difficult for many. Regardless, it is only what he said which is important here. When he spoke, there was neither Judaism or Christianity. There was only the religion of Israel centered in the Temple of YHWH in Jerusalem. What came after Jesus must be understood with this in mind. He was a Jewish man of Israel preaching to Jewish people of Israel about a *"new Covenant"* for them to believe. And he was it's center piece.

John 12:50 And I know that HIS Commandment is Life Everlasting: whatsoever I speak therefore, even as the Father said unto me, so I speak.

Yet, as written in the Book of John, Jesus was consistent regarding keeping the Commandments of GOD and Life Everlasting. In this it could be said that Jesus preached to Israel to keep the Law of Moses so they would have life eternal. If Israel has Life Everlasting, what was Jesus offering Israel by his "*covenant*", that was not already possessed by Israel by GOD'S promise?

Compared to the Eternal Covenants YHWH made throughout the Hebrew Bible, both with the Patriarchs, their descendants, and other examples of oath making between men, what is called *"new Covenant"* by the standards already set, leave many unanswered questions. Was the idea of *"new"* covenant an editors alteration? In other words, was this idea added later by Gentile scribes?

Was *to believe* the only criteria of this *new Covenant*? If so, what exactly was one to believe? The presentation made by Jesus during the Last Passover only gives one the idea that he and his followers ate bread with the idea that it was his body which was symbolically being eaten. The same idea for wine when he gave them to drink, that it was his blood that he shed for them. He said to do this in remembrance of *him*. Was this rite to be done during Pesach? If so, why do not the Gentiles who accept this rite as part of Christian doctrine not do it during Passover then, instead during Sunday Mass or at other times? But at the same time, if all were drinking wine during Passover, the *fermented wine* would put them at risk with YHWH GOD by violating this holy day.

Jesus said to keep the Commandments. How could Israel keep the Commandments *and* do anything outside the Commandments of the Law, for one negates the other? Keeping Passover is Law and it cannot be altered.

When was the eating of the bread the drinking of the wine to be done in remembrance of him, was it to be done during Passover? If so, this would be contradicting the very Law itself. For Passover is in remembrance of the redemption by YHWH of Israel from slavery in Egypt, not for the symbolic eating of flesh of Jesus. Unleavened bread is eaten because Israel had to flee Egypt before it could rise or ferment and become "*leavened*" (Exodus12:34, 39; Deuteronomy 16:1-4). So was Jesus attempting to change the very meaning of Passover from Israel fleeing Egypt and having to eat unleavened bread, to eating unleavened bread as a symbol of his flesh? From the *"bread of affliction"* to the *"flesh of Jesus"*? If so, this would be a perversion of Pesach and GOD'S Law.

Deuteronomy 16:3, (3) Thou shalt eat no leavened bread with it; seven days shalt thou eat unleavened bread therewith, even the Bread of Affliction; for in haste didst thou come forth out of the land of Egypt; that thou mayest remember the day when thou camest forth out of the land of Egypt all the days of thy life.

In addition, as already discussed *"wine"* is not part of the Passover *"service"*. Neither is the eating of *"matzah"* to be done as a symbol of a remembrance of eating a mans flesh. For this would be adding / diminishing the meaning of Passover, as fathers were to explain the Exodus from Egypt *not* the flesh of Jesus. The eating of matzah (Bread of Affliction) at Passover and Passover itself was to be remembered as a memorial because it was the haste of Israel's departure from Egypt which was the cause of not having time to make regular *"leavened"* bread for the trip. It was the night YHWH *"passed over"* and delivered Israel and destroyed Egypt. It is to be remembered as YHWH'S Passover for this reason, not as the symbolic flesh of a martyr. This reciting to sons by the father is a Law for Passover.

Exodus 12:25-27, (25) And it shall come to pass, when ye be come to the land which YHWH will give you, according as He hath promised, that ye shall keep this Service. (26) And it shall come to pass, when your sons shall say unto you: What mean ye by this Service? (27) that ye shall say: It is the sacrifice of YHWH'S passover, for that He passed over the houses of the sons of Israel in Egypt, when He smote the Egyptians, and delivered our houses.' And the people bowed the head and worshipped.

It may be of interest to note that the Hebrew uses a root word which comes from *"work"* and *"serve"* *(Ayin-Bet-Dalet)* in referring to Passover. It has the idea of *"labor"* associated with it. Keeping this *"service"* is a type of holy *"service"* to GOD which is Commanded of Israel to perform as an Ordinance from YHWH for ever. Any alteration of this service would be *"adding"*.

What was the exact *"offer"* of the *"new Covenant"*? Exactly when was it made and by whom? If it was made by Jesus, what was said exactly and to whom was it said to? Exactly what were the stipulations of the *"new Covenant"* and the penalties if violated? What were it's terms and conditions? What is to be the reward of the person who believes? What was the responsibility of the *"new Covenant"* person? Was believing all that was necessary or required? Were they told to perform a ritual, a service or meet and do something special together? Could they eat the blood of animals and the flesh of swine? Is the meat and the blood of a monkey acceptable to eat? Why or why not? Were they free to live as they wanted as long as they believed? Were they to keep any of the Laws of Moses or to circumcise, if so, why? Why not? The Law is the Law. You either keep it or you don't, no picking and choosing.

Were the words of Jesus to love one another and to *"follow"* him, all that one needed to know or do? What did *"follow me"* mean? Was just believing that Jesus died for a persons sins all that was needed to have salvation?

The Covenant YHWH made with Noah and his SEED was everlasting. The Covenant YHWH made with Abraham and his SEED was everlasting. The Covenant at Sinai, the giving of the Law, the Priests, atonement for sin and Shabbat were everlasting. The Covenant with King David and his SEED was everlasting. The redemption of Israel as GOD'S inheritance is eternal and everlasting *(Isaiah 43:1)*.

But it is hard to see in Jesus and his words to Israel to whom he spoke, a *"new Covenant"* for Israel or an offer of anything for which Israel did not already have. For Israel is saved with an *"everlasting salvation"* from YHWH. *(Isaiah 45:17)*.

'NEW? TESTAMENT'

When considering the 180 degree change which the Apostle Paul made concerning the words of Jesus, the Law and the Nations, and later when much Gentile pagan worship had been added to what the Jews had originally brought to the table, it was no more a Jewish *"new Covenant"*, but morphed completely into a non Jewish, non Sabbath observant, *"non Covenantal"* religion, not based on any Law from YHWH. It became a religion not based on the Law of Moses, but of the Nations with a Gentile *"god"*.

Contrasted with what Christianity has become, the early church, or at least one major sect of the early Jewish believers called the *"Ebionites"*, kept the Law of Moses and rejected Paul as a heretic and an apostate from the Law. They believed that Jesus was the messiah and interestingly used only one of the Gospels. As only one may have existed when they began, this would explain much. In addition there adherence to the Law of Moses would also explain the very negative attitude and writings towards them by later church officials who were no longer Jewish and kept not the Law.

Apparently the major fault line amongst Jewish believers was in the keeping of the Law. Some believed it only applied to Jewish believers, and other Jewish believers thought it applied to all believers. Some no doubt believed no one needed to keep the Law. Another sect of Jewish believers called the Nazarenes as well as several others are known to have existed. The sect of the Nazarenes were apparently the same Jewish believer sect who tutored Saint Jerome while living in the land of Israel in the fourth century. Some historians believe it was the early name for all Christians.

Additionally, it is known that there exists as well in the rest of the Christian Bible other than the Gospels, some very *"creative editing"*, misquotes and erroneous scripture references to the Hebrew Law and Prophets which have no connection to the narrative in the rest of the Christian Bible. The idea of there being a *"new Covenant"* made by Jesus to the Jewish people of Israel is very, very weak. The idea of a *"covenant"* made by Jesus of any kind with the Nations is weaker still.

Do the words and actions of Jesus translate into a *new Covenant?* As there is no manual to guide us, but the examples given in this chapter of Covenants known to have been made by GOD, those of Noah, Abraham and of Israel, the example story of Jesus is weak. And as the Law of Moses is the only set of instructions for Israel concerning prophets, his life and death make for an incredible story which would seem to be attractive to the nations, but leaves many unanswered questions regarding an actual *"Covenant"* being made with Israel. This is especially true if this *"new'* Covenant was to have replaced the existing Covenant.

Additionally, it is confusing as to whom Jesus was making his *"covenant"* with when speaking to his Jewish followers. For he had said on numerous occasions, that he came for *"Israel"*. And he made a concerted effort to tell his Jewish followers to avoid the Gentiles and go to the *"lost sheep of the House of Israel"*. To whom was this *covenant* made if it was made? If it was being made with the Gentiles (per Paul), why did Jesus tell his disciples to not go to them? If it was made to Israel, what was it? It was discussed by a Jew to other Jews during a Jewish Passover festival. Where do the Gentiles fit into this narrative? They were neither present, partook of the meal, neither were they mentioned at all.

As concerning the Law this is especially troubling, particularly what YHWH said would happen to a prophet who tempted Israel to go after other *"gods"*. In his *"testament"*, Jesus wanted Israel to go after and to follow *"him"* and to believe in *"his"* name. It is very difficult to believe the story as given in the Gospels, when compared to that of GOD YHWH with Noah, or with Abraham, and at the foot of Mt.

Sinai with Israel, and to be convinced that he actually established *"another"* Covenant for Israel in the name of GOD the Father for the sons of Jacob. Moses has the last word on an Eternal Covenant.

*Deuteronomy 4:29-31, (29) **But from thence ye will seek YHWH thy God; and thou shalt find Him, if thou search after Him with all thy heart and with all thy soul.** (30) In thy distress, when all these things are come upon thee, **in the end of days**, thou wilt **return to YHWH** thy God, and hearken unto His voice; (31) for YHWH thy God is a merciful God; He will **not fail** thee, neither destroy thee, **nor forget the Covenant of thy fathers which He Swore unto them.***

Moses is saying several things here. If Israel searches for YHWH with all of their heart and soul, they will find HIM, when they *"return"* and obey HIS voice. YHWH will not forget the Covenant of Abraham, Isaac and Jacob. Neither will HE forget the Covenant at Sinai. *"Return"* means to keep HIS Law. *"End of days"* means exactly that. *"Israel"*, means the circumcised SEED of Abraham. Israel will *"return"* and keep YHWH'S Law, for neither HIS Covenant with Israel's forefathers nor the Covenant of Sinai are dead, *"nor forget the Covenant of thy fathers"*.

Having said this, the ancient Covenants of YHWH with Israel are still very much alive, active and real. And if the precedent of the earlier Covenants YHWH made are any indication, any new Covenant would overlap, become absorbed by or incorporated into a *"new"* Covenant, if made but not end the previous Covenants. Based on this, it is very doubtful that a *"new Covenant"* was made even with the Jewish followers of Jesus who believed there was one. And it is even more doubtful of a *"new Covenant"* having been made with the Gentiles of which Jesus told these same followers to avoid. Although as discussed, if part of GOD'S plan was to use Jesus as a vehicle later for bringing the Nations under the Law, then in a peculiar way they may have more reason for hope than not.

The story in the Gospels does not establish a *"new"* Covenant if the earlier Covenants of GOD made with Noah, Abraham or with Israel are any indication. And if it were new, it would have included the earlier Covenants, based on those same examples and the precedent that had been established. The Law of Moses would not have ended. The nearest to any kind of a **"formal"** offer of Covenant made was of Jesus during Passover. These few words do not appear to have established any kind of a real *"Covenant"* with anyone. There was neither acceptance nor a rejection of a *"Covenant"*.

'BY SACRIFICE'

*Psalms 50:5, (5) 'Gather My Saints together unto Me; **those that have made a Covenant with Me by sacrifice'** .*

CHAPTER SEVEN

YHWH vs JESUS

Exodus 20:1-3, (1) And GOD spoke all these words, saying: (2) <u>I am YHWH thy GOD</u>, who brought thee out of the land of Egypt, out of the house of bondage. (3) <u>Thou shalt have No Other gods before Me.</u>

Yet, according to the Gospels, Jesus is not only called "*Lord and God*", but he tells his "*followers*" time and again to "*follow me*" (Matthew 4:19, 8:22, 9:9, 16:24, 19:21; Mark 2:14, 8:34, 10:21; Luke 5:27, 9:23, 9:59, 18:22; John 1:43, 10:27, 12:26, 13:36, 21:19). YHWH condemns "*prophets*" who lead HIS people Israel astray, to "*follow*" after other "*gods*".

In the Book of John, Jesus is quoted as saying to "*serve*" him and *"My sheep hear my voice, and I know them, and they **follow me**"* (John 10:26-27). But we know from scripture in numerous places that YHWH is Israel's shepherd and Israel is the flock of GOD'S inheritance. Israel is YHWH'S sheep. Was Jesus a false "*god*" or a false "*shepherd*" leading GOD'S sheep astray? YHWH had told Israel to serve <u>only</u> HIM.

Jeremiah 50:6, (6) <u>My people hath been lost sheep: their shepherds have caused them to go astray,</u> they have turned them away on the mountains: they have gone from mountain to hill, they have forgotten their restingplace.

Ezekiel 34:30-31, (30) And they shall know that I YHWH their God am with them, and that they, the <u>House of Israel, are My people</u>, saith the Lord YHWH. (31) <u>And ye My sheep, the sheep of My pasture, are men, and I am your God, saith the Lord YHWH</u>.'

'THE HOUSE OF ISRAEL ARE MY PEOPLE'

To what "*lost sheep*" did Jesus say that he came for (Matthew 15:24)?

Consider it an *"IOU"* if it helps one to understand, but Israel owes an eternal debt to YHWH their GOD for their salvation. It is true, that YHWH had an existing Covenant with Israel, the sons of Abraham. Yet, through GOD'S act of redeeming Israel from Egypt, **Israel became HIS.** YHWH'S "*redemption*" was an act of redeeming Israel to HIMSELF. *"Thou at mine".*

Isaiah 43:1, (1) But now thus saith YHWH that created thee, O Jacob, and He that formed thee, O Israel: Fear not, for I have redeemed thee, I have called thee by thy name, thou art Mine.

The very first commandment of YHWH given to Moses proclaimed HIS name, *"I am YHWH thy GOD".* Not just any *"god"*, but *the* **"GOD"** who brought Israel out from bondage in Egypt. It is immediately followed by commanding Israel that, *"Thou shalt have no other gods before Me".* It is no mere coincidence that YHWH begins exclaiming HIS Commandments by proclaiming HIS holy name. In verse five, HE continues with how *"jealous"* HE is for HIS name.

Jesus made much concerning his own name, similar in a fashion to that of YHWH and HIS own name. So much so, that in many respects it directly competes with that of YHWH and indeed, overshadows or supplants it entirely. At least in the Gospels where he speaks of himself often. This is especially so with regard to salvation. But Israel has a *"Savior"* already in YHWH. Psalm 106 tells Israel of their past, forgetting YHWH their GOD.

Psalms 106:21, (21) They forgot God their Saviour, who had done great things in Egypt;

Who was Israel's *"Savior"* who *"had done great things in Egypt"?* It was *"YHWH"* and no other. HE will not give HIS glory to another. If Israel keeps YHWH'S Law as Jesus himself has said that they should do, then the name of Jesus is and must become something else far less than the importance that he has attached to it, not to speak of the importance many of his followers have given it. For one must ask, who is GOD, but YHWH?

By Law, Israel is to remember that YHWH is their one and only GOD, their redeemer. Israel is to know always that YHWH ransomed them from Egypt.

Micah 6:14, (4) For I brought thee up out of the land of Egypt, and redeemed thee out of the house of bondage, and I sent before thee Moses, Aaron, and Miriam.

Psalms 54:3, 8-9, (3) O God, save me by Thy Name, and right me by Thy might. (8) With a freewill-offering will I sacrifice unto Thee; I will give thanks unto Thy Name, O YHWH, for it is good. (9) For He hath delivered me out of all trouble; and mine eye hath gazed upon mine enemies.

'MY HOLY NAME' vs 'IN MY NAME'

The expression *"what's in a name"* comes to mind.

Isaiah 43:11, (11) I, even <u>I, am YHWH</u>; and <u>beside Me there is no Saviour.</u>

Isaiah 44:6, (6) <u>Thus saith YHWH</u>, the King of Israel, and his <u>Redeemer</u> YHWH of hosts: I am the first, and I am the last, <u>and beside Me there is no God.</u>

Psalms 44:5-6, (5) Thou art my King, O God; command the salvation of Jacob. (6) Through Thee do we push down our adversaries; <u>through Thy Name</u> do we tread them under that rise up against us.

Psalms 44:21-22, (21) <u>If we had forgotten the Name of our God</u>, or spread forth our hands to a strange god; (22) <u>Would not God search this out?</u> For He knoweth the secrets of the heart.

Would YHWH not search it out if Israel were to forget HIS name? Is not YHWH jealous for HIS holy name? Is not YHWH'S very name jealous?

Exodus 34:14-15, (14) For thou shalt bow down to no other god; <u>for YHWH, whose name is Jealous, is a jealous God</u>; (15) lest thou <u>make a Covenant</u> with the inhabitants of the land, and they <u>go astray after their gods</u>, and do <u>Sacrifice</u> unto their gods, and they call thee, and thou eat of <u>their Sacrifice;</u>

Is not the symbolic act of eating the flesh of Jesus and drinking his blood not *"of their sacrifice"*? Is not this symbolism in itself not *"going astray"*?

GOD was angry with Israel. HE wanted to pour out HIS fury on Israel, but HE thought better of it because the nations would see and curse HIS actions, proclaiming that YHWH was not an all mighty GOD. But for the nations who would profane HIS holy name, YHWH would have destroyed Israel. But HE could not, for HIS reputation, honor and HIS glory was at stake.

Ezekiel 20:9, (9) But I wrought <u>for My name's sake, that it should not be profaned</u> in the sight of the nations, among whom they were, in whose sight I made Myself known unto them, so as to bring them forth out of the land of Egypt.

MATZAH AND WINE

Did not Jesus say at the *"Last Passover"*, that he was making with them a *"new Covenant"*. And that they should eat matzah (his flesh) and drink wine (his blood) as part of this *"new Covenant"* in remembrance of his sacrifice? YHWH warned Israel against the Canaanites, not to do as they did, so was this what YHWH was warning Israel against as well? Was Jesus not making a *"Covenant"* with Israel? Did he not tell them to *"follow"* him? Were they not to *"eat"* his <u>flesh</u> and *"drink"* his <u>blood,</u> even if only symbolically?

John 6:53-56, (53) Then Jesus said unto them, Verily, verily, I say unto you, <u>Except ye eat the flesh</u> of the Son of man, and <u>drink his blood</u>, ye have no life in you. (54) Whoso <u>eateth my flesh</u>, and <u>drinketh my blood</u>, hath eternal life; and I will raise him up at the last day. (55) For <u>my flesh is meat</u> indeed, and <u>my blood is drink</u> indeed. (56) <u>He that eateth my flesh, and drinketh my blood, dwelleth in me, and I in him</u>.

A son of Israel must ask himself, how do these word square with the words of YHWH regarding eating of sacrifice to other *"gods"* and making Covenants?

THE NAME OF JESUS

It is the *"name"* of Jesus that is perhaps the biggest sticking point regarding his message. So much of what he is reputed to have said in one fashion or another is connected to *"his name"*. Whether it is salvation, taking away the sins of the world, and eternal life, working miracles, being *"sons of GOD"* or other things for which already exists for Israel through their GOD YHWH, his message appears to directly or indirectly contradict the Law, and challenge the name of his *"YHWH"* as Israel's **only** GOD and Savior.

In a very real sense, Jesus is just offering to Israel that for which they already possess from YHWH such as redemption, salvation, eternal life.

Although as hopefully was brought out earlier, there were serious issues with some of his words and actions, and his interpretation of the Law of Moses, it was his *name* which may have been the most troubling for his contemporaries because of what he said about it. This would be closely followed by his being nailed to the remains of a tree and left to die by a foreign occupying nation.

As the anticipated *"anointed"* savior of Israel awaited by many, his being nailed to the stock of a tree to be left to die, was a bit of a problem for the *"messiah"* of Israel. The people who lived during his life time could not help but have had their doubts when he was taken out in such a fashion. For sure, there was no poll taken of just what the average Israelite was expecting, but it goes without saying that his death, especially the way he died, was not what the majority anticipated in their messiah, especially as written in Isaiah 9:5-6, where *peace, justice* and *righteousness* was prophesied *"for ever"*.

The other half of the name of *"Jesus"* issue, would be the name of *"YHWH"* problem. Perhaps the lack of the name of YHWH might be more accurate.

'THUS SAITH THE LORD YHWH'

Jesus said allot about his own name, but little evidence exists regarding the actual utterance by Jesus of GOD'S holy name itself, nor did he seem to emphasize it in any way. For even if the Greek translation of an original in Hebrew or Aramaic had changed many if not all of the times the actual name of **"YHWH "** had been mentioned by Jesus, if in fact he did, the remains of such an utterance or at least the proforma exclamation that what was being said was from YHWH, should still be detectable. But there is none. This is critical for several reasons. A good example of the *"proforma exclamation"* used throughout TaNaKh by YHWH'S prophets is by the Prophet Ezekiel.

Ezekiel 3:27, (27) **But when I speak with thee,** *I will open thy mouth, and thou shalt say unto them:* **Thus saith the Lord YHWH;** *he that heareth, let him hear, and he that forbeareth, let him forbear; for they are a rebellious house.*

This or a variation is used by **all** of GOD'S prophets, *"Thus saith YHWH"*. Yet, there is no such proclamation in any of the Gospels.

Additionally, everything that Jesus said about himself and / or his own name, had already been said about YHWH and HIS holy name by GOD and by HIS Prophets. If YHWH is Savior, the only holy GOD of Israel who has given eternal salvation to Israel, what is left undone? Is it not redundant, the word of Jesus? Israel would have to believe that YHWH is *not* their only true GOD who has redeemed them and who is their eternal salvation. To think such a thing, is not true. It is the holy name of *YHWH* wherein is Israel's redemption.

Psalms 68:5, (5) <u>Sing unto God, sing praises to His Name</u>; extol Him that rideth upon the skies, <u>whose Name is YH</u>; and exult ye before Him.

NAMES

Names matter. Names matter very much. Names matter very, very much.

Psalms 99:6, (6) Moses and Aaron among His priests, and Samuel among <u>them that call upon His Name, did call upon YHWH</u>, and He answered them.

The names of the main characters in the Hebrew Bible are *very* important just as the SEED of the main characters is *extremely* important. Names in the Hebrew Bible are *extremely* important. Names are so important in fact, that it bears repeating what was just written. "Names in the Hebrew Bible are *extremely* important". They are *extremely* important, *extremely, extremely* so.

Names of places and of people were important, but the name of GOD was especially very important to GOD HIMSELF, and to Israel as their *one* and only GOD, *"Shema Israel, **YHWH** our GOD, **YHWH** is ONE".*

Psalms 50:23, (23) Whoso offereth the sacrifice of thanksgiving honoureth Me; <u>and to him that ordereth his way aright will I show the salvation of God.</u>'

What does the Christian Bible say about the name of *Jesus*, "*Yeshua*", and what does Jesus say himself? And what is the significance of this name relative to Israel? What name is Israel to know and to *"trust in"*? *<u>that know Thy name</u> will put their trust in Thee; for thou, <u>YHWH,</u> hast not forsaken them that seek Thee*

JESUS / MY NAME

John 20:31, (31) But these are written, that ye might believe that Jesus is the Christ, the Son of God; and that believing ye might have <u>life through his name.</u>

According to some estimates, the title *"Elohim"* (the all encompassing collective title of GOD) is written approximately 2600 times, *"Adonai"* (Lord / my Lord) is written 439 times, *"El"* (GOD) is written 238 times and *"YHWH"* (the personal given name of GOD) is written approximately 7,000 (6,828) times in the Hebrew Bible.

In the Christian Bible reference is made to, or about the name of *"Jesus"* (Hebrew *"Yeshua"*) often. It is obviously so important to the message which he preached, that as an orthodox / observant Jew, circumcised on the eighth day of his life into the Covenant of Abraham, and who seemed to be well aware of the words of the Safer Torah, he must have known as well that the giving of any name other than *"YHWH"* was treading on thin ice within the Jewish community. Howbeit, it was precisely his own name which he gave to his people (Israel) telling them that they must believe in his name, meaning in Hebrew *"salvation"*. Jesus said that he was the "*messiah*".

One can ask, was Jesus saying in affect to believe in " *salvation*"? He said to keep the Commandments of GOD. Keeping the Commandments of GOD is salvation for Israel. To Israel, YHWH and HIS Law *is* salvation. It is *life*.

Nevertheless, his own name was used as an important part of the message which he preached and was emphasized considerably, whereas the name of YHWH by all accounts, was not emphasized. Actually, the level of apparent silence concerning the name of YHWH would lead one to think that the name of YHWH was *"d-emphasized"* either through, or by it's omission.

Sometimes, what one does not say, says allot. And in the case of Jesus and the apparent omission of the name of GOD *"YHWH"*, there appears to be a concerted effort, at least within the narrative itself which is available to us, not to emphasize the name of YHWH or as it appears, to not even say the name. Jesus seems to dance around actually uttering the name itself. He mentions *"the name"*, the name *"of the Father"* etc., but there is no actual evidence that every thing he said and did was actually done *in the name of* "*YHWH*". Just the opposite appears to be the case, that everything he said and did was done *in his own name*. And this is the problem regarding names.

At least, it appears this way, but in truth it is hard to tell. If true however, this is very significant given what is known regarding YHWH and what HE has said regarding HIS holy name, and about the importance of HIS own name.

Having said this, in all fairness one can only get an approximate idea of the possible d-emphasis of the name without an original Semitic text to study.

The early Greek translators of the Hebrew Bible usually always translate the proper name of **YHWH** as *"Lord"* or *"the Lord"* into Greek. They appeared to have picked up this bad habit from the Rabbanite Jews although it is not clear exactly when. The literal translation of the Greek into English is *"I am the One being"* (Exodus 3:14) from *"I AM that I AM"*. The proper name of GOD, *"YHWH"* is not used, even 300 years before Jesus. Later English translators just continued this practice. Although even a novice grammarian knows that a proper name does not begin with a *definite article* (the), most translators of the given name of GOD, "*YHWH*" will add the definite article *"the"* in English making "*YHWH*" in Hebrew into *"the YHWH"* which immediately morphs into *"the Lord"* in English when translated. This is especially prevalent with Jewish scholars which is more than likely where Christian scholars acquired it. But they take it even one step farther by not even keeping "*YHWH*" as part of their new creation, but rendering it as "*Lord*". It is the equivalent of adding *"the"* before the name of *"John"*, *"Bob"* or *"Alice"* . Would you call your best friend, *"the John"*?

If the same application is made to *"YHWH"* in the Hebrew without replacing it with *Lord* as they have done, GOD'S holy name would be written as *"the YHWH"*. This appears to have begun with the Greek translation of the Hebrew Bible in the third century BCE who translated "*YHWH*" from Hebrew into *"ho kyrios"* meaning *"the Lord"* ("*Lord*" is one of many titles for GOD, not the name of GOD, "*YHWH*"). The Greeks may have done this out of respect for the Jews. The Greek translators may have just continued this misapplied grammatical confusion as did the later English translators.

At least some of the blame can be attributed to the rabbis who not only forbid the utterance of the name of YHWH, but who quite often will not even write the name of YHWH, but write some made up abbreviation for it.

Isaiah 42:8, (8) I am YHWH, <u>that is My name</u>

Why the Greeks chose to do this instead of translating even a phonetically sounding name of YHWH is not clear. Surely the Greeks were aware that *"YHWH"* was not a title but the name of GOD YHWH, HE said very clearly. But then again, they may have taken their cue from the earlier Jewish translators out of respect or even ignorance. It is understood the reverence for the name etc. However, given the idea that what was being translated was the holy name of GOD HIMSELF, one would think that the act of changing HIS HOLY NAME into one of the many *"titles"* for YHWH would be showing *"less"* respect and less reverence, *"All this word which I command you, that shall ye observe to do; thou shalt not add thereto, nor diminish from it"*.

Jeremiah 16:21, (21) Therefore, behold, I will cause them to know, this once will I cause them to know My hand and My might; <u>and they shall know that My name is YHWH</u>.

When translating the Gospels into Greek from the original Semantic manuscripts, assuming they were Semitic, which would eventually evolve into the codex of the Christian Bible, it is unknown how often and where they translated *"YHWH"* into *"the Lord"*, if this was indeed the case. Only one known example exists, the *"Shema"*. At this point, it does not seem to be known if the name of YHWH even appeared in the original codices of the Gospels which would later become part of the Christian Bible. This is important for it raises several questions concerning how Jesus was referred to. For often, Jesus was referred to himself as *"Lord"*. Was this just the common respectful address of *"lord"* as in *"sir"* or *"mister"*, not meaning *"deity"* by his followers? Or, were they referring to him as *"Lord"* meaning *"GOD"*? It appears from the text in the Gospels that Jesus was referred to as the deity, as GOD, at least some of the time.

Luke 24:34, (34) Saying, <u>The Lord</u> is risen indeed, and hath appeared to Simeon

John: 20:28, (28) And Thomas answered and said unto him, <u>My Lord and my God</u>

 There are more examples, but by these two samples it appears that Jesus was referred to as both *"Lord"* and as *"GOD"*. This is critical because of YHWH being *"one"*. **"Hear O Israel, YHWH our GOD YHWH is One"**

'FOR HIS NAME ALONE IS EXALTED'

Psalm 148:13, (13) Let them praise <u>the Name of YHWH, for His Name Alone is exalted;</u> His glory is above the earth and heaven.

According to David himself, whom Jesus was suppose to be, only the name of **YHWH** is to be exalted! This obviously would exclude the name *"Jesus"*.

'I HAVE MANIFESTED THY NAME UNTO MEN'

In the seventeenth chapter of the Book of John, much is written about how Jesus *"glorified"* GOD (17:4), how Jesus *"kept them in **thy name**"* (17:12), *"I have manifested **thy name** unto men"* (17:6), and *"I have declared unto them **thy name**"* (17:26). He speaks much of He and the Father being *"one"*. Jesus says that his words came from GOD the Father (17:8) stating that his followers *"kept thy word"*

(17:6). Yet, the name "*YHWH*" is never written.

This returns us to the topic of the name *"YHWH"* again and it's absence from the Christian Bible. One is baffled by it's complete non existence and the total lack of any hint of it having been uttered by Jesus during his ministry. To extrapolate, this is true as well of the supposed *"prophetic"* books written after the time of the Gospels such as the Book of Revelations. For a quick comparison between the early Prophets of YHWH and John who is credited with writing the Book of Revelation, provides a stark contrast in authorship. *"Thus saith YHWH"* permeates the words of the ancient prophets of YHWH, but anything comparable is completely missing in the Christian Bible.

'SEARCH THE SCRIPTURES'

In John (John 5:39-47) Jesus speaks of searching the scriptures because it says of Israel they *"think"* they have eternal life. He seems to be saying that Israel does not have eternal life. Yet, this is not so according to GOD'S word."*O Israel, that art saved by YHWH with an **everlasting salvation**; ye shall not be ashamed nor confounded world without end (Isaiah 45:17).*

Psalm 133:3 (3) Like the dew of Hermon, that cometh down upon the mountains of Zion; for there YHWH commanded the blessing, even Life For Ever.

The promise of eternal life existed before Jesus was born. If Israel has *everlasting salvation* and *life* from YHWH, what was the purpose of Jesus? There are many other Hebrew scriptures which attest to the SEED of Abraham having eternal life. Jacob is not now, nor will he ever be forsaken.

Micah 7:18-19, (18) Who is a God like unto Thee, that pardoneth the iniquity, and passeth by the transgression of the remnant of His heritage? He retaineth not His anger for ever, because He delighteth in mercy. (19) He will again have compassion upon us; He will subdue our iniquities; and Thou wilt cast all their sins into the depths of the sea. (20) Thou wilt show faithfulness to Jacob, mercy to Abraham, as Thou hast sworn unto our fathers from the days of old.

But he also says that they (the scriptures) testify of him. Yet, unless one really stretches the meaning of the scriptures and misapply them to the many riddles, proverbs and parables which he spoke, it is very difficult to apply anything he said in the Hebrew scriptures directly to himself. This is especially true because of the incredibly vagueness of much of what he said. But it is equally as true because of the nature of the words written to which he was referencing. His words were riddles and the prophets used metaphors.

In John 5:43 Jesus said that, *"I am come in my Father's name, and ye receive me not: if another shall come in his own name, him ye will receive"*. Yet, Jesus, other than saying that he came in the name of the Father, does not actually *"come"* in the name of the Father *YHWH*, which is never mentioned. Only *his own name* is ever mentioned. It is as if with *"another"*, Jesus is here refering to himself, similar to *"wolf in sheep's clothing"*. In his own name he said to believe. Was *"YHWH"* written but removed by Gentile scribes later? Jesus seems to be describing himself in John 5:43 coming in *"his own name"*.

Psalm 135:13-14 , (13) O YHWH, Thy Name endureth for ever; Thy Memorial, O YHWH, throughout all generations. (14) For YHWH will judge His people, and repent Himself for His servants

Here, the unnamed writer of this Psalm is alluding to Exodus 3:15 where YHWH speaks of HIS NAME "*YHWH*", being remembered a *"memorial"* forever, *"unto all generations"*. Unto all generations means just that, "*all*", *always, forever, eternally* as in *forever* and *forever more.*

Regarding the Law, Jesus alludes to Israel's Covenant with GOD as he states that they have Moses for their accuser. This would include Jesus as well.

John 5:45-47, (45) Do not think that I will accuse you to the Father: there is one that accuseth you, even Moses, in whom ye trust . (46) For had ye believed Moses, ye would have believed me: for he wrote of me. (47) But if ye believe not his writings, how shall ye believe my words?

Jesus seems to be reminding Israel of the Covenant and GOD'S Law which they are responsible for keeping. And it is this Law which judges them. But he seems to be saying as well that in the Law is their salvation, for Moses spoke of "*salvation*" in GOD'S Law. But he also states that Moses wrote of Jesus. Moses gave Israel the Law with all of it's Commandments. Jesus said if Israel wanted to enter eternal life to keep the Commandments. Is Jesus only stating what Israel should already know, that Moses wrote of "*salvation*"? Was Jesus a metaphor for salvation written of in the Law of Moses, that all of Israel must "*keep*"?

John 5:39, (39) Search the scriptures; for in them ye think ye have eternal life; and they are they which testify of me.

In other words was Jesus only reminding Israel of that which already existed in their own Law? That "*salvation*" already exists in the Law?

The word of GOD written by the hand of Moses, takes up the first five books of the Hebrew Bible. These books are referred to collectively as either the Five Books of Moses, Torah, Law, Safer Torah, "Chumesh" and by the Samaritans as the Pentateuch. If one studies these writings for years, they would be hard pressed to find any reference to either Jesus, a person like Jesus or a prophesy regarding a prophet, son of David or messiah who was to be martyred and raised from the dead. Yet, the Gospels say (John 1:45) Moses and the prophets spoke of him. Where did they speak? What was said?

Amos 3:7, (7) For the Lord YHWH will do nothing, but He revealeth His counsel unto His servants the prophets.

As there are a few prophesies in the Safer Torah itself, it must be assumed that Jesus (John 5:39) was referring to them for he said the Moses and the Prophets wrote of him. Even with all of the riddles, proverbs and parables which would allow one to be very liberal with the scriptures, a person would have to be very creative to make any connection between any of the words of Moses or the Prophets and Jesus. One must do either allot of "*assuming*" or creative thinking to stretch the words in the Hebrew Bible of either Moses or the Prophets into prophesy about Jesus. It just is not there.

This leads to an "*outside of the box*" idea that Jesus was speaking not of himself, but of "*salvation*". The "*salvation*" of YHWH as written in the Law of Moses. Just an idea.

DESPOTES

The Greeks used another word "*despotes*", to refer to either "*lord*" or "*master*". It is found once in the Gospels when after Jesus is born and taken to the Temple of YHWH, a man by the name of Simeon proclaims to GOD.

Luke 2:29. (29), <u>Lord</u>, now lettest thou thy servant depart in peace, according to thy word: (30) For mine eyes have seen thy salvation,(31) Which thou hast prepared before the face of all people; (32) A light to lighten the Gentiles, and the glory of thy people Israel.

Simeon apparently does not use the name of *"YHWH"* GOD here, but calls on GOD using *"master"* instead.

Throughout the Christian Bible, the followers of Jesus appear to address Jesus with *"Lord"*, as meaning more than just *"sir", "master"* or *"lord"*. At least according to the oldest Greek translation.

Was the name of *"YHWH"* ever used by Jesus and if so, how was it used? Was Jesus only referred to as *"my lord"* as in *"sir"*. Or did people equate him with YHWH who is GOD as it appears? For the Greeks use the same word for *"lord"* and *"LORD / GOD"* interchangeably in some places when referring to Jesus. Unfortunately, as the oldest known complete translation of the Christian Bible is in Greek, we may never know how many times, or if at all, *"YHWH"* was written or how it was used in the Gospels. For the name of GOD *"YHWH"*, does not appear in the Greek translation of the Gospels. But from the example regarding the disciple Thomas, Jesus himself was referred to as *"Lord and GOD"*. This is extremely problematic for a Jewish person under the Law of YHWH to refer to Jesus or anything or anybody as *"god"*.

SHEMA

But there may be a hint to the answer as to how the Greeks did translate GOD'S holy name in the Christian Bible by a *"quote "* mentioned earlier from Jesus regarding the *"Shema"*, the ancient Jewish prayer taken from the Hebrew Bible. The original Hebrew translation is as follows, followed by the Greek translation of the same passage spoken by Jesus.

Deuteronomy 6:4 (4) Hear, O Israel: <u>YHWH</u> (is) our God, <u>YHWH</u> (is) one.

Mark 12:29 (29) And Jesus answered him, The first of all the commandments is, Hear, O Israel; <u>The Lord</u> our God is one <u>Lord</u>: (usually: "Hear O Israel, the Lord our God, the Lord is One")

Whether Jesus actually said *"YHWH"* or said *"Lord"* is unknown. For as mentioned earlier, even in the Septuagint written 300 years before Jesus, the name of *"YHWH"* was already being translated as *"Lord"* (kyrios). So given this example of translating the known holy name of GOD *"YHWH"* by the Greeks into *"Lord"*, it is safe to say that if Jesus did utter GOD'S holy name, odds are very good that the Greeks would have translated it as *"Lord"* instead of *"YHWH"*. So this leaves the question open.

DEFINITE ARTICLE

As touched on already, a proper name does not begin with *"the"*.

In Hebrew, there is a letter that represents the definite article and is attached to the beginning of a word which translates as *"the"* It *does not exist* with the given name of *"YHWH"*. Of the nearly 7,000 times YHWH is written in the Hebrew Bible only once does this occur, and it is doubtful that it is a correct but is a scribal error. The point is, without the original codices from which the Christian Bible was hammered together, it is uncertain what Jesus may have said regarding *"YHWH"*, or if he said the name of *"YHWH"* at all.

Nevertheless, a quick glance at the scriptures in English regarding *"my name"* indicates that it does not leave much room for even *"my Lord"* even if poorly translated (see examples below). Jesus mentions his *"father"* often, saying how they are the same or are *"one"* etc. But one does not get a sense of the use in any way of the actual name of GOD in so far as giving honor to the *"name"*, only that of the _name_ of Jesus. If this was the case, then it no doubt had to have been a stumbling point for the Jewish population listening to him speak. Likewise even now, when as a Jew and reading his words regarding *"his"* name, a *"red flag"* goes up. It does not *"compute"*.

Psalms 119:55-56, (55) I have remembered <u>Thy name</u>, O YHWH, in the night, and have observed <u>Thy law</u>. (56) This I have had, that I have kept <u>Thy precepts</u>.

This may be difficult for a person not having been born into the Law of Moses to fully appreciate. A huge part of the Law of Moses is the name of YHWH itself. And this is something the Greek translators would not have been sensitive to, especially when contrasted with that of Jesus. It would not be incorrect to say that the foundation of the Law of Moses is the name of YHWH, creator of heaven and earth and the one and only GOD of Israel. The ancient GOD of Israel had a name. It is a name for which HE is very jealous. For Israel, "*YHWH*" is the name of *"deliverance"* and is the *"salvation"* of Abraham and his SEED. It is the *"holy name"* that eternal life for Israel rests on. There is a reason it is the first Commandment given to Moses.

Psalms 38:22, (22) Forsake me not, <u>O YHWH</u>; O my God, be not far from me. (23) Make haste to help me, <u>O Lord, my salvation</u>.

David was a man of faith. Given his incredible life, he was totally dependent of his GOD YHWH for his help and his salvation. "*YHWH*" is the "*name*" for which GOD said that HE is jealous for and that HE would *not* give HIS glory to another. "*YHWH*" is the name that David called on time and time again for his salvation, for help, for comfort and to save him. YHWH is the GOD of David. Ask ones self, how could David call his GOD by the name of his own SEED if Jesus was really his son? Let that sink in for just a moment.

Isaiah 42:8, (8) I am YHWH, that is My Name; and <u>My glory will I not give to another</u>, neither My praise to graven images.

At no place in the Gospels does Jesus refer to his name as being "*holy*". This may be another "*hint*" as to the issue with his name. The name of YHWH is known to be "*holy*", as HE said so often and on many occasions. This is no small matter as reverence for the holy name of YHWH is part of the Law of Moses! For YHWH is the *"HOLY GOD"* of Israel, and HIS name is ONE.

Psalms 111:9-10, (9) He <u>hath sent</u> redemption unto His people; <u>He hath commanded His Covenant for ever; Holy and awful is His name</u>. (10) <u>The fear of YHWH</u> is the beginning of wisdom; a good understanding have all they that do thereafter; <u>His praise endureth for ever</u>.

HIS *"Redemption"* has already been sent, HIS *"Covenant"* is forever, HIS name is "*Holy*" and HIS "*praise*" endures for ever. It must be asked, what did Jesus bring to the table for Israel that did not previously exist?

Fear of YHWH does not just mean to keep HIS Commandments, but to *fear* HIS actual name as well, as HIS name is holy and is to be revered. No substitutes accepted. Where was the praise of HIS name from Jesus?

YHWH has sent *already*, HIS *redemption*, unto HIS people. HIS redemption is in *HIS holy name, "YHWH"*. The Covenant of GOD with Israel is forever. It is not abrogated by man. The Law of YHWH has not ceased. Deliverance for Israel comes in the form of calling on the *"name"* of their GOD YHWH. For Israel, the salvation of YHWH is *"eternal"*. David speaks of YHWH'S deliverance many, many times. It is a constant theme throughout his writings. It is in the name of *"YHWH"*, who is the great deliverer of Israel, that Israel is saved. Likewise, the prophets speak of the deliverance of Israel in the name of YHWH.

Joel 3:5, (5) And it shall come to pass, that <u>whosoever shall call on the Name of YHWH shall be delivered;</u>

Nothing had changed between the time that this prophesy was written by the Prophet Joel for GOD YHWH and the time of Jesus, as YHWH does not change. The reason for the need of these words of Joel when he wrote them, is irrelevant. For the fact remains that it is in the name of YHWH that Israel must seek deliverance. For YHWH the *salvation* of Israel, is still YHWH the *deliverer* of Israel. This requires repeating.

"<u>The salvation</u> of Israel, is still YHWH the <u>deliverer</u> of Israel."

Amos 5:6, (6) Seek YHWH, <u>and live</u> ....

Nahum 1:7, (7) YHWH is good, a stronghold in the day of trouble; and <u>He knoweth them that take refuge in Him.</u>

MOSES AND THE NAME OF GOD

Exodus 3:13-15, (13) And Moses said unto God: 'Behold, when I come unto the children of Israel, and shall say unto them: The God of your fathers hath sent me unto you; and they shall say to me: <u>What is His name?</u> what shall I say unto them?' (14) And God said unto Moses: 'I AM THAT I AM'; and He said: 'Thus shalt thou say unto the children of Israel: I AM hath sent me unto you.' (15) And God said moreover unto Moses: <u>'Thus shalt thou say unto the children of Israel: YHWH, the God of your fathers, the God of Abraham, the God of Isaac, and the God of Jacob, hath sent me unto you; this is My Name for ever, and this is My memorial unto all generations</u>.

Exodus 6:1-3, (1) And YHWH said unto Moses: 'Now shalt thou see what I will do to Pharaoh; for by a strong hand shall he let them go, and by a strong hand shall he drive them out of his land.' (2) And God spoke unto Moses, and said unto him: '<u>I am YHWH</u>; (3) and I appeared unto Abraham, unto Isaac, and unto Jacob, as God Almighty, <u>but by My name YHWH I made Me not known to them</u>

"**YHWH**", is the given name, the proper name, the personal name of GOD.

Was Jesus speaking in the name of *"YHWH"* or was he speaking only in his own name? The available evidence does not indicate that the name of *"YHWH"* was ever mentioned by Jesus. Likewise, as Jesus stated that Moses spoke of him, the only written evidence is that Moses spoke only of *YHWH*.

There was no precedent for what Jesus was saying regarding his own name. It was on many different levels, against everything taught in the Law of Moses. For no other prophet or " *holy*" person no matter what that person did, even raising the dead such as the Prophet Elisha, preached in his own name.

For other observant Jews listening to the words of Jesus then, there must have been an immediate and visceral sense of alarm and caution when Jesus spoke regarding his own name. For a Jew who was founded in the word of GOD, much of what Jesus said must have had an *"other-ness"* quality about it which was extremely foreign to everything which is taught in the Safer Torah. For although Jesus was preaching much of what was written in the Safer Torah, other of his words or actions appeared to stand in stark contrast to to the Law of Moses as understood by the majority of his coreligionists. This was why they were astonished at the words of his *"doctrine"*.

Aside from the many truths Jesus brought to the surface regarding especially the Pharisees, but others as well, it was the *"otherness"* issue of those things which he said that jolted the very foundation of the Law of Moses. And his doctrine of the use of the name of *"Jesus"* would have been just such a jolt.

A few examples of the things which he is reputed to have said regarding his own *"name"*, have been quoted. These examples are taken *only* from the four Gospels. There are more references to his name in the rest of the Christian Bible even more radical. But for this purpose, only the Gospels are quoted.

Matthew 10:22 (22) And ye shall be hated of all men for my name's sake: but he that endureth to the end shall be saved.

Matthew 18:5, 20, (5) And whoso shall receive one such little child in my name receiveth me. (20) For where two or three are gathered together in my name, there am I in the midst of them.

Matthew 19:29, (29) And every one that hath forsaken houses, or brethren, or sisters, or father, or mother, or wife, or children, or lands, for my name's sake, shall receive an hundredfold, and shall inherit everlasting life.

Matthew 24:5, 9 (5) For many shall come in my name, saying, I am Christ; and shall deceive many. (9) Then shall they deliver you up to be afflicted, and shall kill you: and ye shall be hated of all nations for my name's sake.

Mark 9:37, 39, 41 (37) Whosoever shall receive one of such children in my name, receiveth me: and whosoever shall receive me, receiveth not me, but him that sent me. (39) But Jesus said, Forbid him not: for there is no man which shall do a miracle in my name, that can lightly speak evil of me. (41) (41) For whosoever shall give you a cup of water to drink in my name, because ye belong to Christ, verily I say unto you, he shall not lose his reward.

Mark 13:6, 13 (6) For many shall come in my name, saying, I am Christ; and shall deceive many. (13) And ye shall be hated of all men for my name's sake: but he that shall endure unto the end, the same shall be saved.

Mark 16:17, (17) And these signs shall follow them that believe; In my name shall they cast out devils; they shall speak with new tongues;

Luke 9:48 (48) And said unto them, Whosoever shall receive this child in my name receiveth me: and whosoever shall receive me receiveth him that sent me: for he that is least among you all, the same shall be great.

Luke 21:8, 12, 17, (8) And he said, Take heed that ye be not deceived: for many shall come in <u>my name</u>, saying, I am Christ; and the time draweth near: go ye not therefore after them.... (12) But before all these, they shall lay their hands on you, and persecute you, delivering you up to the synagogues, and into prisons, being brought before kings and rulers for <u>my name's</u> sake.... (17) And ye shall be hated of all men for <u>my name's</u> sake.

John 14:13-14, 26 (13) And whatsoever ye shall ask in <u>my name</u>, that will I do, that the Father may be glorified in the Son. (14) If ye shall ask any thing in <u>my name</u>, I will do it. (26) But the Comforter, which is the Holy Ghost, whom the Father will send in <u>my name</u>, he shall teach you all things, and bring all things to your remembrance, whatsoever I have said unto you.

John 15:16, 21, (16) Ye have not chosen me, but I have chosen you, and ordained you, that ye should go and bring forth fruit, and that your fruit should remain: that whatsoever ye shall ask of the Father i<u>n my name</u>, he may give it you. (21) But all these things will they do unto you for <u>my name's</u> sake, because they know not him that sent me.

John 16:23-24, 26 (23) And in that day ye shall ask me nothing. Verily, verily, I say unto you, Whatsoever ye shall ask the Father in <u>my name,</u> he will give it you. (24) Hitherto have ye asked nothing in <u>my name</u>: ask, and ye shall receive, that your joy may be full. (26) At that day ye shall ask in <u>my name</u>: and I say not unto you, that I will pray the Father for you:

What was a Jew living 2,000 years ago to make of this *"name"* Jesus, knowing what they did about the *"name"* of their GOD *"YHWH"* written in their Safer Torah, and the name of YHWH whom their priest blessed them with? For the Hebrew scriptures regarding the name of *"YHWH"* are very specific regarding the name of GOD, and that it is the name by which Israel is to call on GOD, makes their vows and to swear and oath. It is the name of **YHWH** that Israel is to be blessed and must call on, and by no other name.

Again, much later in the world of the Gentiles as the words of Jesus morphed into a full blown religion taken to the four corners of the earth by the Gentile nations, the overwhelming majority of the Jews of Israel remained *"wed"* to their Father, their GOD and their Savior named *"YHWH"*. Even if the Rabbis have caused Israel to forget how to say the name *"YHWH"* the GOD of Israel, it was still YHWH who was their GOD and most Jews were aware.

Psalms 46:11-12, (11) '<u>Let be, and know that I am God</u>; I will be exalted among the nations, I will be exalted in the earth.' (12) YHWH of hosts is with us; the God of Jacob is our high tower. Selah

Jesus appeared to have been asking Israel to basically forget everything that they had been taught and believed in, specifically, that the name of *"YHWH"* was the only name of their GOD, that YHWH redeemed them and it was HE who is their Savior and the source of their salvation.

Jesus was asking Israel to basically throw out all that they have been taught by their forefathers regarding YHWH, and to call to GOD their father in the name of *"Jesus"*. As discussed earlier, many years later when the message of Jesus was preached to the Gentiles, very little of this was known or could have been an issue to them, ie., the *"vengeance of the Covenant"*

Leviticus 26:25,(25) And I will bring a sword upon you, that shall execute the <u>Vengeance of the Covenant;</u> and ye shall be gathered together within your cities; and I will send the pestilence among you; and ye shall be delivered into the hand of the enemy

The nations had no GOD named *"YHWH"* who had threatened to cut them off from both HIMSELF and their own people. They were not of Israel and were not Jews. They needed not to fear GOD'S retribution in the, *Vengeance of the Covenant.* It was easy for the pagan to break their idol if they possessed one, and pick up the message of Jesus. For his message was a compelling one. It was unlike any of the surrounding poly-god type religions of the uncircumcised masses who surrounded Israel at that time. The god *"Ra"* of Egypt may die every night and be reborn every morning, but it is hardly a compelling story. Sacrificing one's children in fire to appease Molech was hardly an appealing story and had it's limitations. The story of Jesus if nothing else, was unique and inviting to the pagan nations, unlike Israel who had a powerful GOD already in *"YHWH"*, and who had done a pretty good job of taking care of Abraham's SEED for approximately 1,500 years prior to Jesus.

DOCTRINE – MIRACLES - NAME

Even if a Jew was to accept all of the doctrine of Jesus, on marriage and divorce, on what is clean to eat, he offered little else to Israel that they did not already possess. If they accepted his idea of eternal life, *"salvation"* (which already existed), of being *"sons of GOD"* (which already existed), heavenly kingdom and that he was a prophet and the messiah as savior, which YHWH already was, there was not much left for him to offer Israel. That he died and was resurrected (life after death was already a belief). That Jesus performed many miracles and works (which had been common in Israel) before Israel and children of GOD, was not so profound. That he turned water into wine, healed lepers, raised people from the dead and returned sight to the blind, there is still the very large issue of *"Lord"* and *"God"* which Thomas articulated so profoundly when he proclaimed the divine status of Jesus.

It is quite allot to accept that Jesus was *"Lord and GOD"*. Given everything which YHWH wrote about HIMSELF and HIS name (and HIS threats), than for any other name or for any other *"god"* to exist other than HE who has been given by name, is truly outside of the Hebrew scriptures. For Thomas was stating quite clearly that Jesus was *"god"*. And as the scriptures indicate, Thomas received no rebuke from Jesus after making such a pronouncement, and Jesus let his words stand unchallenged. This cannot go unnoticed.

John 20:28, (28) And Thomas answered and said unto him, <u>My Lord and my God.</u>

'DO I MAKE KNOWN THAT WHICH SHALL SURELY BE'

Hosea 5:9, (9) Ephraim shall be desolate in the day of rebuke; <u>among the tribes of Israel do I make known that which shall surely be.</u>

YHWH has said that HE sends HIS prophets to make Israel know of what will be. In as far as *"prophesy"* goes regarding a person such as Jesus, it would seem if YHWH really wanted Israel to know what would be concerning <u>HIS</u> messiah, <u>a</u> messiah or <u>the</u> messiah and it was of paramount importance, HE would have had HIS early prophets to say so without the listener of Jesus being confused by his parables and the hearer of Jesus being bewildered by his stories and his doctrine, and the reader about Jesus having to sew together a fabric made from the bits and pieces of words of

GOD'S prophets over the entire TaNaKh consisting of the Safer Torah, the Prophets and the Writings of GOD'S people in order to "*prove*" how Jesus was foretold, and still not have a clear documented example of "*prophesy*".

For as has been shown already, much of what Jesus had to say was vague to say the least. The people listening to him and hearing his words were often confused and could not make out what he was saying. And much of the scriptures purportedly which was to either show something "*fulfilled*" in his regard, or to prove something regarding him, were even more vague, or altogether unconnected or as with the example of Isaiah (Isaiah 42:1-4; Matthew 12:17-21) to be generous, was "*misquoted*". The name of Jesus itself was and still is a major issue, even accepting of everything else he said or did. Belief in his "*name*" as "*god?*" or for other similar related reasons is against all of the Law of YHWH, the very Law that Jesus said to "*keep*". So then was Jesus telling his listeners to disregard him?

YHWH / MY NAME & GOD AND SAVIOR

Psalm 124:8, (8) <u>Our help is in the name of</u> YHWH, who made heaven and earth.

"*Our help is in the name of YHWH*" said King David. David as a youth and as King of Israel was a very GOD fearing man. Not in a traditional sense by today's meaning as it is commonly used. But David had a very close and personal relationship with YHWH unlike anything known today. His life reads like a man who had truly been touched by the hand of GOD. When he was *good* he was very good. When he was *bad*, he was very bad. David was truly a man with flaws and is exposed, "*warts and all*". His sin regarding Uriah was magnified as he was seriously punished by YHWH GOD. But YHWH never forsook David.

Additionally, when David "*numbered*" Israel, he was punished. David's life was a constant roller coaster of ups and downs. From a shepherd boy to being hero and son-in-law to King Saul and having the might of that king come down on him, David was chased, hounded and betrayed from one end of the kingdom to the other even before he became king of Israel himself. But David never lost his faith in YHWH and was more than a little aware of where his own strength lie. It was all he had to sustain him. Even after he became king, within his own family, he was tormented by sibling rivalry and ambition which spelled the death of friends, sons, rape of a daughter and concubines and made him flee from his son Absalom in the face of his people to save his own life. Yet, David never abandoned YHWH, and YHWH never abandoned David. David's unflinching devotion to YHWH is unparallelled.

David was a man of faith. When reading his words, especially Psalms where he poured out his heart to his GOD, one can see a man who had put YHWH and his Law before him completely. Whether he is sad, happy or in fear, his words resonate with an undying awe and love for his GOD YHWH. David knew that it was ***in the name*** of ***"YHWH"*** from ***<u>whence</u>*** his *help*, his *deliverance* and his *salvation* came. And David needed much deliverance.

As the line from Psalm 124:8 attests, David understood well that it was in ***the name of*** "**YHWH**" where mercy rests. YHWH is the GOD of mercy.

YHWH'S NAME

What does YHWH GOD say about HIS own name? YHWH has plenty to say about HIS own holy name. Although it is written nearly 7,000 times, it is made mention of or referred to, perhaps even countless more times.

Isaiah 40:8, (8) The grass withereth, the flower fadeth; but the word of our God shall stand for ever.'

Some of the many things YHWH has to say about his name is that HE is jealous, that he will not give his glory to another and to call on HIS name to be delivered etc., *"thy name"*.

Psalms 124:8, (8) Our help is in the name of YHWH, who made heaven and earth.

Regarding salvation, a previous discussion touched on YHWH as *"Savior"*. The TaNaKh does not say to call to YHWH either *on, through,* or *by,* any other name. It says to call on the name of *"YHWH"*.

Psalms 3:9, (9) Salvation belongeth unto YHWH; Thy blessing be upon Thy people. Selah

King David knew it was his GOD *"YHWH"* who was his *help.*

Psalms 8:10, (10) O YHWH, our Lord, how glorious is Thy Name in all the earth!

Psalms 9:11, (11) And they that know Thy Name will put their trust in Thee; for thou, YHWH, hast not forsaken them that seek Thee.

SAVE – SAVIOR – SALVATION

In the Hebrew Bible, YHWH many, many times refers to HIMSELF as the one who will *"save"* Israel, as being the *"salvation"* of Israel, and as being the *"Savior"* of Israel. Additionally, the Prophets of YHWH and David amongst others, refer to YHWH as *"saving"* them, and as their *"salvation"*. YHWH refers to HIMSELF and is referred to as Israel's *"redeemer",* the one who will *"deliver"* them. The words *"save", "salvation"* and *"savior"* all have the same root. They are all basically the same word from the Hebrew root meaning to *"deliver", "rescue", "save", "victory", "salvation"* and *"deliverance".*

II Samuel 22:2-4, (2) and he said: YHWH is my Rock, and my Fortress, and my Deliverer; (3) The God who is my Rock, in Him I take Refuge; my Shield, and my Horn of Salvation, my High Tower, and my Refuge; my Saviour, Thou Savest me from violence. (4) Praised, I cry, is YHWH, and I am saved from mine enemies.

"THE" Savior of Israel is *"YHWH"*. *"A"* Savior of Israel can be anyone that GOD chooses to use to save HIS people when they cry to HIM. This person may or may not have been *"anointed"* (with anointing oil) as *"a savior"*.

In the same manner that Israel had many *"kings"*, YHWH said that HE is *"KING"* of Israel. Israel had leaders referred to as Israel's *"shepherds"*, David being the chief amongst them, but YHWH is Israel's true *"SHEPHERD"*. Israel inherited the Promised Land, but even afterwords, YHWH proclaims that the *"land"* is HIS land. Likewise, Israel had many *"saviors"* throughout their long existence, nevertheless, it has always been YHWH who is *"the"* SAVIOR of Israel. Bridging the distance between understanding *"a"* and *"the"* is key to knowing the difference between YHWH as *"Savior"*, and Gideon, Sampson, Othniel and Ehud as *"saviors"*.

MESSIAH

From the Hebrew root meaning to *"anoint", smear"* or *"consecrate"*, this word can have meanings other than anointing of Kings, Priests and vessels. but can mean a *"consecrated portion"* such as that set aside for the Priests to eat. Israel is referred to as being YHWH'S *"anointed"*.

Habakkuk 3:13, (13) Thou art come forth for the deliverance of Thy people, for the deliverance of Thine anointed

SAVIOR VS MESSIAH

According to scripture YHWH is Israel's *"Savior"*, but Israel can have a *"savior"* in the person of one chosen by GOD to *"save"* them (see Judges). This person does not need to be *"anointed"* such as the King of Israel or Priest of GOD, but can be someone chosen by GOD to perform HIS will. King David may be an example of a *savior* who was also *anointed*, but someone who was never addressed as such, though he surely earned the title.

Israel is / has been expecting (tradition) a *"savior"* who will also be *"anointed"*. This person is expected to be of the House of David as King David was anointed, not once, not twice, but three times (I Samuel 16:13; II Samuel 2:4; II Samuel 5:3. The Prophet Samuel anointed David when he was still a shepherd boy. The men of Judah in Hebron anointed David King of Judah. And all of Israel anointed David King of Israel in Hebron.

I Samuel 16:1 (1)....fill thy horn with oil, and go, I will send thee to Jesse the Beth-lehemite; for I have provided Me a king among his sons.'

The future *"messiah"* of Israel is anticipated to be a circumcised male SEED descendant of King David who will restore the kingdom and reign as king of Israel. As there is no *"holy anointing oil"* (Exodus 30:22-33), it is assumed that the *"messiah"* therefore will be one of David's male descendants who because of his father having been anointed, is considered *"anointed"* himself.

Then again, the *"mesiach"* may not necessarily have to be anointed with oil, but *"chosen"* to fulfill the task as mesiach, similar to Cyrus.This may or may not be how things unfold. Nevertheless, the hope in a *"messiah"* is real, the *"Savior"* of Israel is GOD YHWH, and the prophets of a restored Kingdom of Israel with David's SEED reigning as king will be. He will bring *"peace"*, *"justice"* and *"righteousness"* according to the Prophets, *"for ever"*.

'CALL ON THE NAME OF YHWH'

The Prophets of GOD speak of HIS name and declare it is YHWH'S name by which one is to take refuge, and is *"delivered"* by.

Amos 5:4, 6, 8, (4) For thus saith YHWH unto the house of Israel: Seek ye Me, and live ....(6) Seek YHWH, and live - ...(8) ......YHWH is His name;

Nahum 1:7, (7) <u>YHWH</u> is good, a stronghold in the day of trouble; and <u>He knoweth them that take refuge in Him.</u>

David knew something these prophets knew. It was the name of *"YHWH"* that David took refuge in from the time he was a shepherd boy to his dying breath as King of Israel. David knew what few others dared to understand. That in the holy name of *"YHWH"* was his help, his salvation, his savior and his refuge. It was not his sword, or his army or his sling stone, but "YHWH". *It was in the name of "YHWH".*

YHWH AS SAVIOR

It was his GOD YHWH in whom David took refuge during time of trouble. It is hard to imagine David taking refuge in any other name.

Psalms 7:2, (2) <u>O YHWH my God, in Thee have I taken REFUGE;</u> SAVE me from all them that pursue me, and DELIVER me

One may ask, *"so what has changed"?* Has GOD'S arm shortened so that HE cannot *save* or *deliver*? Are HIS words any less the truth today than when they were spoken? Has YHWH given HIS *"glory"* to another?

Isaiah 50:2, (2)....Is My hand shortened at all, that it cannot <u>redeem</u>? Or have I no power to <u>deliver</u>?

The words by the Prophet Isaiah (42:8) are extremely important when the name of Jesus is thought of. For YHWH is saying that HIS name, is glorious, and he will not share the glory of HIS name with another. Yet, this seems to be what is happening with the name of *"Jesus"* verses the name of *"YHWH"*.

Isaiah 43:7, (7) Every one that is called by <u>My name</u>, and whom I have created for <u>My glory</u>, I have formed him, yea, I have made him.'

Isaiah 46:13, (13) I bring near My righteousness, it shall not be far off, and <u>My salvation</u> shall not tarry; and I will place <u>salvation</u> in Zion for <u>Israel My glory</u>.

Isaiah 48:10-12, (10) Behold, I have refined thee, but not as silver; I have tried thee in the furnace of affliction. (11) For Mine own sake, for Mine own sake, will I do it; for how should it be profaned? <u>And My glory will I not give to another</u>. (12) Hearken unto Me, O Jacob, and Israel My called: <u>I am He; I am the first, I also am the last</u>

Throughout TaNaKh, YHWH GOD is saying through HIS Prophets, through David and other YHWH fearing people of Israel, that it is *in the name of YHWH* that Israel is delivered, that it is *in the name of YHWH* that Israel lives, and the refuge of Israel is found only *in the name of YHWH*. HE said YHWH is the *first* and the *last* and HE will *not* give HIS glory to another.

Does the truth of GOD'S word fade with time? Is the eternal truth of GOD'S Prophets made to any less affect because of mans disbelief or because the sun has yet revolved around the sun again? Is the holy name of YHWH any less holy, glorious or mighty that Israel should not call on HIS name and be delivered? Does it not say that YHWH is the GOD of mercy, and the GOD of our salvation? Does GOD change, that HIS word no longer has meaning, or that the salvation of YHWH no longer exists? Is not the promised salvation of GOD still with HIS inheritance, that is Israel today?

Malachi 3:6, (6) <u>For I YHWH change not;</u> and ye, O sons of Jacob, are not consumed

Isaiah 62:11, (11) Behold, <u>YHWH</u> hath proclaimed unto the end of the earth: say ye to the daughter of Zion: 'Behold, <u>thy salvation</u> cometh; behold, <u>His</u> reward is with <u>Him</u>, and <u>His</u> recompense before Him.

The salvation of Israel is YHWH, whose reward is with HIM. David, as much as any, perhaps more than most, relied on his faith <u>in the name of YHWH</u> to save him. King David refers to his faith in YHWH and HIS holy name often. There are so many references to the name of "**YHWH**" both by David and others, that it defies all thought to understand today how the remnant of Israel today has forgotten the name of "*YHWH*", and how rabbis have forbidden Israel to pronounce it, if it were still known.

Psalms 119:126, (126) It is time for YHWH to work; <u>they have made void Thy law.</u>

Jeremiah 23:23-27, (23) <u>Am I a God near at hand, saith YHWH, and not a God afar off</u>? (24) Can any hide himself in secret places that I shall not see him? saith YHWH. Do not I fill heaven and earth? saith YHWH. (25) I have heard what the prophets have said, that prophesy lies in My Name, saying: 'I have dreamed, I have dreamed.' (26) How long shall this be? Is it in the heart of the prophets that prophesy lies, and the prophets of the deceit of their own heart? (27) <u>That think to cause My people to forget My Name</u> by their dreams which they tell every man to his neighbour, as their fathers forgot My name for Baal.

The mere fact that rabbis forbade it's use by Jews at all, tells us that it was still in use by the Jewish population, at least up until sometime after the Temple of YHWH was destroyed in 70 CE. It is a *"given"* that the Temple Priests invoked the holy name of YHWH and that the *"rabbis"* would not hardly have been telling the Priests of YHWH not to say HIS name in their blessing to Israel. The rabbis edict not to utter the name of YHWH was directed at the general public only after they became the default religious authority when there were no priests.

Isaiah 29:13-14, (13) And the Lord said: Forasmuch as this people draw near, and with their mouth and with their lips do honour Me, but have removed their heart far from Me, <u>and their fear of Me is a Commandment of men learned by rote;</u>

It is interesting that his particular train of thought continues with YHWH stating what HE will do regarding these *"men who learned by rote"*.

(14) Therefore, behold, I will again do a marvellous work among this people, even a marvellous work and a wonder; <u>and the wisdom of their wise men shall perish</u>, and the prudence of their prudent men shall be hid.

Further research could probably come up with a more precise date of when the rabbis forbid the utterance of the name of "*YHWH*". But in the end it really does not matter. The devastatingly negative effect it has had on the Jewish people has been done. The Greek translation of the Christian Bible does not indicate that Jesus ever used GOD'S holy name. As stated, it is generally translated as *"the Lord"*. But to be fair, as there is no original Semitic Gospel, it may never be known if Jesus praised or gave YHWH the glory due HIS holy name. Indications are however, that he did not use "*YHWH*" if what has come down to us in the Gospels can be trusted. If this is the case, it is significant regarding the issue of Jesus and his own name.

Psalms 44:21-22, (21) <u>If we had forgotten the name of our God</u>, or spread forth our hands to a strange god; (22) <u>Would not God search this out?</u> For He knoweth the secrets of the heart.

II Samuel 22:4, (4) <u>Praised, I cry, is YHWH</u>, and I am <u>saved</u> from mine enemies.

Psalm 44 is from the sons of Korah, and the quote from II Samuel is from King David. Both of these words regarding GOD telling of GOD'S holy name and how it is a name of profoundness. The sons of Korah speak of the "*unforgettable*" name of YHWH. It is the holy name and the GOD of Israel, which if HIS people were to forget, YHWH HIMSELF would search it out. David exclaims that YHWH is his *rock, fortress* and *deliverer*, his *rock, refuge* and *shield*, that YHWH is his *salvation, refuge* and *SAVIOR*. It is by the name of YHWH that David is saved when he cries to GOD. And as the sons of Korah made known, it is not a name which YHWH will let Israel forget. Is Israel any less Israel that they should not call on their GOD YHWH today? And is YHWH any less YHWH today? "*I change not*".

The Prophet Jeremiah wrote how the false prophets attempted to cause Israel to forget YHWH'S holy name. Anyone who attempts to cause Israel to forget GOD'S most holy name is no different, "*That think to cause My people to forget My name*". Whether called "*false prophets*" or "*rabbis*", or by any other name, as the end result is the same, so are they the same.

It goes without saying, if the name of YHWH had no relevance, HIS name would not have been an issue to HIM, nor would it matter to YHWH if Israel forgot HIS holy name. Nor for that matter, would the rabbis forbid it's use. It is GOD'S jealousy for HIS HOLY NAME, and HIS everlasting protection of HIS holy name which HE will not forget. For in Egypt GOD made a "*name*" for HIMSELF. HIS *name* and HIS *glory*, HE will give not give to another. So what were the rabbis really afraid of in forbidding the utterance of ***the name***?

Jeremiah 32:20, (20) who didst set signs and wonders in the land of Egypt, even unto this day, and in Israel and among other men; and madest Thee a Name, as at this day;

The "*name*" which YHWH made for HIMSELF is both HIS "*name*" itself, and HIS "*reputation*". These two things are intimately interwoven and are "*one*". For as the story of the Exodus and later when Joshua led Israel into Canaan show, the "*reputation*" of YHWH including the "*fear*" of YHWH preceded Israel even amongst the uncircumcised.

Joshua 5:1, (1) And it came to pass, when all the kings of the Amorites, that were beyond the Jordan westward, and all the kings of the Canaanites, that were by the sea, heard how that YHWH had dried up the waters of the Jordan from before the sons of Israel, until they were passed over, that their heart melted, neither was there spirit in them any more, because of the sons of Israel.

There should be little doubt that YHWH will reestablish HIS name and with it HIS reputation. And if the prophets are any indication, this time neither the enemies from without nor the enemies from within will cause Israel to forget YHWH'S name again nor forbid it's use. And according the prophets it will be established in such a way that never again will his name ever be forgotten.

'UPON WHOM MY NAME IS CALLED'

The name of "*YHWH*" is **called ON** Israel. They, YHWH and Israel, are together as one people and one GOD. HIS holy name is **called ON** Israel. Additionally, Israel is **called BY** the Name of YHWH.

Isaiah 43:1, 3, 7, (1) But now thus saith YHWH that created thee, O Jacob, and He that formed thee, O Israel: Fear not, for I have redeemed thee, I have called thee by thy name, thou art Mine. …. (3) For I am YHWH thy God, The Holy One of Israel, thy Saviour; ……(7) EVER ONE THAT IS CALLED BY MY NAME, and whom I have created for My glory, I have formed him, yea, I have made him.'

'THE HOLY ONE OF ISRAEL THY SAVIOUR'

The name of YHWH is extremely important because it is *'the name*' which is called **ON** Israel, and Israel who is called **BY** HIS name.

*II Chronicles 7:13-14, (13) If I shut up heaven that there be no rain, or if I command the locust to devour the land, or if I send pestilence among **My people**; (14) **if My people, UPON WHOM MY NAME IS CALLED**, shall humble themselves, and pray, and seek My face, and turn from their evil ways; then will I from heaven, and will **forgive their sin**, and will **heal** their land.*

'MY HOLY NAME'

*Exodus 34:14, (14) For thou shalt bow down to no other god; **for YHWH, whose name is Jealous, is a jealous God**;*

Jesus said to <u>follow</u> and to <u>serve</u> him. Yet he told Satan to serve only GOD. What is going on here? So, Jesus is saying now he is *not one* with the Father?

*John 12:26, (26) 26 If any man **serve me**, let him follow me; and where I am, there shall also **my servant** be: if any man **serve me**, him will my Father honour.*

*Matthew 4:10, (10) Then saith Jesus unto him, Get thee hence, Satan: for it is written, **Thou shalt worship the Lord thy God, and him only shalt thou serve**.*

So, there appears to be another contradiction here as Jesus has told his followers to "*follow*" and to "*serve*" him. Yet, he told Satan to serve only GOD. Was not Jesus called "*God*"? Does not this apply to Jesus as well and to all of Israel? It is with this thought that understanding HIS jealousy for the name, "*YHWH*" must be understood. In Israel, GOD'S reputation is at stake, and it is for this reason that HE continually states throughout TaNaKh, for "*MY name sake*". To make the point, HIS holy name is "*YHWH*" not Jesus.

*Ezekiel 36:21-23, (21) **But I had pity for My Holy Name**, which the house of Israel had profaned among the nations, whither they came. (22) Therefore say unto the house of Israel: Thus saith the Lord YHWH: **I do not this for your sake**, O house of Israel, **but for My Holy Name**, which ye have profaned among the nations, whither ye came. (23) **And I will sanctify My Great Name**, which hath been profaned among the nations, which ye have profaned in the midst of them; **and the nations shall know that I am YHWH, saith the Lord YHWH**, when I shall be sanctified in you before their eyes.*

'MY GREAT NAME'

It can be thought of as "*ego*" or whatever helps one to understand, that it is GOD'S "*great holy*" name that is at stake. And HE will *not* let HIS great name be tarnished by HIS own people or by anyone else.

*Deuteronomy 4:24, (24) For YHWH thy God is a **devouring fire**, a **jealous God**.*

YHWH'S holy *name*, HIS *honor*, HIS *glory*, HIS *reputation*, HIS *word* and *HIS Covenant's* are on the line. YHWH will not and can not let HIS great holy name be sullied. This is why HE continually says that it is through Israel that HE will be *"glorified"*, *"whom I have created for My Glory"*. And this is why HIS mercy will never leave nor depart from the Jewish people, the remnant of Israel. Not just because of HIS promise to Abraham and to David made as an eternal Covenant, but because YHWH'S *"holy name"* is associated with the people of Israel through HIS Covenant. And it is through Israel that the *glory* of YHWH will be manifest, for HIS *glory* is associated with the blessings of GOD upon Israel. HE swore by HIMSLEF.

In case this went by too fast, it will be restated in another way. All YHWH said of Israel must happen as HIS word was given. All of HIS word is associated with the future of Israel. All of the future of Israel is associated with the *glory* of YHWH.

Ezekiel 36:32, (32) <u>Not for your sake do I this</u>, saith the Lord YHWH, <u>be it known unto you</u>; be ashamed and confounded for your ways, O house of Israel.

Ezekiel 36:36, (36)…..I YHWH <u>have spoken</u> it, and I <u>will do</u> it

GOD will not let even Israel tarnish HIS holy name, HIS reputation, or the glory which is HIS name. YHWH will establish HIMSELF, over Israel and rule over them by might of force, for HE is GOD Almighty. **HE is YHWH!**

Ezekiel 20:33, (33) <u>As I live</u>, saith the Lord YHWH, surely with a mighty <u>hand</u>, and with an outstretched <u>arm</u>, and with <u>fury</u> poured out, <u>will I be KING over you</u>;

But this is not all that our GOD YHWH says about Israel in the future. HE declares how Israel will be brought *"into the bond of the Covenant"*.

Ezekiel 20:37, (37) And I will cause you to pass under the rod, <u>and I will bring you into the bond of the Covenant</u>;

The nations too, who will know HIS name, and who will worship HIM, will be brought *"into the bond of the Covenant"*, as there is but one Law for Israel, and one Law for the stranger.

All of the *"GLORY"* of the living GOD YHWH who created the heaven and the earth, the sun and the stars, the mountains and the oceans and all that there is, will manifest itself through HIS people HE created for HIMSELF called *"Israel"*. The GLORY of the living GOD YHWH, HIS Majestic Essence, HIS Might and HIS GLORY will be expressed through a people, HIS people, called *"Israel"*. "*And My Glory will I not give to another."*) *Every one that is called by My name, and <u>whom I have created for My glory</u>, I have formed him, a, I have made him.'*
Psalms 48:11, (11) <u>As is Thy name</u>, O God, so is Thy praise unto the ends of the earth;.........

It will be *by, <u>through</u>* and *<u>in</u>* the circumcised SEED of Abraham whom YHWH will show to the nations of the earth, HIS GLORY.

All of this must be kept in mind when the *"name of Jesus"* as referred to in the Christian Bible, is read or spoken. *Isaiah 49:3, (3) And He said unto me: '<u>Thou art My servant, Israel, in whom I will be glorified.</u>'* It is the name of **YHWH**, which will be glorified *in* Israel. And it is the honor of HIS holy name that HE is protecting. Giving HIS glory to the name *"Jesus"* or to any other would have just the opposite affect. Or put another way, allowing Jesus or any other to steal from HIM the Glory due HIS holy name will not happen. There is not enough room for two names. YHWH is emphatic about HIS name, HE is jealous for HIS holy Name. Indeed, HIS very name is jealous, as HE said in Ezekiel 20:33, *"will I be King over you"*.

Zechariah 14:9, (9) And YHWH shall be King over all the earth; in that day shall YHWH be One, and His name One.

For YHWH is ONE, and HIS NAME is ONE. Given what Jesus is reputed to have said about his own name, excluding the many other things said about his name by others, there is a clear conflict of space and time in the ethereal place of *"holiness"*. The name issue is almost as if it is a challenge to YHWH and HIS holy name. The Law of physics may not apply here, but the idea is the same. Two names cannot occupy the same place at the same time as *one*. If YHWH is One and HIS name is One, where does that leave Jesus?

Isaiah 43:25, (25) I, even I, am He that blotteth out thy transgressions for Mine own sake; and thy sins I will not remember.

YHWH forgives sin for *HIS own name sake*, not because of the self righteousness of Israel. A few more scriptures from the Hebrew Bible regarding the name of YHWH are given, as they are powerful indications of how YHWH feels about HIS own name, it's holiness and meaning as the name of the Almighty GOD who is LORD of all creation, Savior of Israel.

"I, even I, am YHWH; and beside Me there is no Saviour".

This scripture and several others which are similar to it are very difficult to get around. They quite simply cannot be ignored, like Exodus 34:14.

Isaiah 41:4 (4)...........I, YHWH, who am the first, and with the last am the same.

Isaiah 42:8 (8) I am YHWH, that is My name; and My glory will I not give to another,....

Isaiah 43:3, 10-13, 25 For I am YHWH thy God, The Holy One of Israel, thy Saviour; I have given Egypt as thy ransom, Ethiopia and Seba for thee......(10) Ye are My witnesses, saith YHWH, and My Servant whom I have chosen; that ye may know and believe Me, and understand that I am He; before Me there was no God formed, neither shall any be after Me. (11) I, even I, am YHWH; and beside Me there is no Saviour. (12) I have declared, and I have saved, and I have announced, and there was no strange god among you; therefore ye are My witnesses, saith YHWH, and I am God. (13) Yea, since the day was I am He, and there is none that can deliver out of My hand; I will work, and who can reverse it?.......(25) I, even I, am He that blotteth out thy transgressions FOR MINE OWN SAKE; and thy sins I will not remember.

Isaiah 44:6-8, (6) Thus saith YHWH, the King of Israel, and his Redeemer YHWH of hosts: I am the first, and I am the last, and beside Me there is no God.(7) And who, as I, can proclaim -- let him declare it, and set it in order for Me -- since I appointed the ancient people? And the things that are coming, and that shall come to pass, let them declare. (8) Fear ye not, neither be afraid; have I not announced unto thee of old, and declared it? And ye are My witnesses. Is there a God beside Me? Yea, there is no Rock; I know not any.

Isaiah 44:21-22, (21) Remember these things, O Jacob, and Israel, for thou art My Servant; I have formed thee, thou art Mine own servant; O Israel, thou shouldest not forget Me. (22) I have blotted

out, as a thick cloud, thy transgressions, and, as a cloud, thy sins; return unto Me, for I have redeemed thee

Isaiah 45:5, 14-25, (5) I am YHWH, and there is none else, beside Me there is no God

"Only in YHWH, shall one say of Me, is victory and strength"

Although one may see in Christian writings where it is often written that *victory* and *strength* are through Jesus, victory and strength are actually in the name of *"YHWH"*. Regarding Israel, *Salvation* and *deliverance* are in the name of *"YHWH"*. *Life everlasting* is in the name of *"YHWH"*. *Forgiveness of sin* is in the name of *"YHWH"*. *Redemption* is in the name of YHWH.

Isaiah 45:18-19, 21-24, (18) For thus saith YHWH that created the heavens, He is God; that formed the earth and made it, He established it, He created it not a waste, He formed it to be inhabited: I am YHWH, and there is none else. (19) I have not spoken in secret, in a place of the land of darkness; I said not unto the SEED of Jacob: 'Seek ye Me in vain'; I YHWH speak righteousness, I declare things that are right. (21)........ And there is no God else beside Me, a just God and a Saviour; there is none beside Me. (22) Look unto Me, and be ye saved, all the ends of the earth; for I am God, and there is none else. (23) By Myself have I sworn, the word is gone forth from My mouth in righteousness, and shall not come back, that unto Me every knee shall bow, every tongue shall swear. (24) Only in YHWH, shall one say of Me, is victory and strength; even to Him shall men come in confusion, all they that were incensed against Him. (25) In YHWH shall all the SEED of Israel be justified, and shall glory.

Isaiah 46:9, (9) Remember the former things of old: that I am God, and there is none else; I am God, and there is none like Me;

Isaiah 46:13, (13) I bring near My righteousness, it shall not be far off, and My salvation shall not tarry; and I will place salvation in Zion for Israel My glory.

Isaiah 50:10, (10) Who is among you that feareth YHWH, that obeyeth the voice of His servant? though he walketh in darkness, and hath no light, let him trust in the Name of YHWH, and stay upon his God

Isaiah 51:7-8, (7) Hearken unto Me, ye that know righteousness, the people in whose heart is My law; fear ye not the taunt of men, neither be ye dismayed at their revilings. (8) For the moth shall eat them up like a garment, and the worm shall eat them like wool; but My favour shall be for ever, and My salvation unto all generations.

Isaiah 51:15-16, (15) For I am YHWH thy God, who stirreth up the sea, that the waves thereof roar; YHWH of hosts is His Name. (16) And I have put My words in thy mouth, and have covered thee in the shadow of My hand, that I may plant the heavens, and lay the foundations of the earth, and say unto Zion: 'Thou art My people.'

Jeremiah 17:14, (14) Heal me, O YHWH, and I shall be healed; save me, and I shall be saved; for Thou art my praise.

Jeremiah 30:10-11, (10) Therefore fear thou not, O Jacob My Servant, saith YHWH; neither be dismayed, O Israel; for, lo, I will save thee from afar, and thy SEED from the land of their captivity; and Jacob shall again be quiet and at ease, and none shall make him afraid (11) For I am with thee, saith YHWH, to save thee; for I will make a full end of all the nations whither I have scattered thee, but I will not make a full end of thee; for I will correct thee in measure, and will not utterly destroy thee

Hosea 1:7, (7) But I will have compassion upon the house of Judah, and will save them by YHWH their God, and will not save them by bow, nor by sword, nor by battle, nor by horses, nor by horsemen.'

Zephaniah 3:17, (17) YHWH thy God is in the midst of thee, a Mighty One who will save; He will rejoice over thee with joy, He will be silent in His love, He will joy over thee with singing.'

Zechariah 8:7, (7) Thus saith YHWH of hosts: Behold, I will save My people from the east country, and from the west country;

Zechariah 8:13, 13) And it shall come to pass that, as ye were a curse among the nations, O house of Judah and house of Israel, so will I save you, and ye shall be a blessing; fear not, but let your hands be strong.

Zechariah 9:16, (16) And YHWH their God shall save them in that day as the flock of His people; for they shall be as the stones of a crown, glittering over His land.

Zechariah 10:12, (12) And I will strengthen them in YHWH; and they shall walk up and down in His Name, saith YHWH.

Zechariah 12:7, (7) YHWH also shall save the tents of Judah first, that the glory of the house of David and the glory of the inhabitants of Jerusalem be not magnified above Judah.

One may be struck as to why a person of Israel would feel the need to believe in anything but their GOD YHWH. For it was their own corruption which was the issue not the lack of an All Mighty GOD who is both Savior of Israel and their Shepherd to lead them. Israel had and still has salvation. They were just ignorant of HIS word. This was what Jesus chided them about, not knowing the Law. But the prophets of GOD chided them first saying how they die for lack of knowledge, *"My people are destroyed for lack of knowledge"* ie. the Law. The Jewish people did then, and do now, have salvation in their own GOD YHWH and in the Law of Moses.

But perhaps Ezekiel (36:21-24) summed it up best when YHWH stated HE will perform all of HIS word in spite of Israel, *But I had pity for My holy name.* YHWH will not allow Israel to embarrass HIM in front of the nations.

The words of GOD'S Prophets speak of Israel being GOD'S people. They speak of YHWH being Israel's Savior. They speak of GOD being the only GOD. They speak of YHWH as being Israel's King and Israel's Redeemer. They speak of *HIS NAME* being the salvation of Israel. They speak of YHWH saving Israel. They speak of YHWH'S compassion and mercy for Israel. They speak of the SEED of Israel being justified in the NAME of YHWH. They speak of victory and strength only being in the NAME of YHWH. They speak of Israel being justified and shall glory in the NAME of YHWH. They speak of YHWH'S favor being to all generations, *forever* for those in whom is HIS Law. They speak of YHWH who told Israel not to seek HIM (YHWH) in vain. They say that YHWH is the first and the last and only HE is GOD. They speak of Israel as YHWH'S servant and that YHWH will save them. They speak of YHWH blotting out the transgression and sins of Israel. They say that there was only ONE GOD (YHWH) formed, and that there is only ONE Savior (YHWH), besides YHWH there is no Savior. Theyspeak of YHWH being the GOD of Israel, the HOLY ONE of Israel, and the Savior of Israel. *What did Jesus offer that Israel did not have from YHWH?*

"Who is among you that feareth YHWH, that obeyeth the voice of His servant? though he walketh in darkness, and hath no light, let him trust in the Name of YHWH, and stay upon his God"

It is to be remembered that there are two subjects in these scriptures. One is YHWH who is the eternal GOD of Israel, and the other is Israel HIS sons. Israel is bound to YHWH through their Covenant of

Circumcision with Abraham, and his SEED. Additionally, it is the Law of YHWH which binds Israel to their GOD YHWH and who has eternally blessed them.

"Hearken unto Me, ye that know righteousness, the people in whose heart is My law......." (Isaiah 51:7).

"The people whose heart is MY Law". This is pretty heavy stuff. A people in whose heart is the Law of YHWH GOD! Let that soak in for a few minutes. But even more so, the words of Isaiah continue on stating how GOD'S *favor* is for ever with Israel, and that HIS salvation is forever.

Isaiah 51:7-8, (7) Hearken unto Me, ye that know righteousness, the people in whose heart is My Law; fear ye not the taunt of men, neither be ye dismayed at their revilings. (8) For the moth shall eat them up like a garment, and the worm shall eat them like wool; but My Favour shall be for ever, and My Salvation unto all generations

'AND MY SALVATION UNTO ALL GENERATIONS'

There are more scriptures which add even more to this connection, this bond and eternal symbiotic relationship between YHWH GOD and HIS people Israel through HIS Law. When one analyzes all of these words of YHWH and HIS Prophets, there remains scant room for anyone or anything else in the way of a person such as the Jew Jesus. And this is the point. For given all of what YHWH says about HIMSELF and HIS eternal salvation, there is neither a need nor reason for the story told in the Gospels to exist for Israel.

The story in the Gospels would be a limiting factor to the omnificent, omnipotent, omnipresent, and omniscient GOD of Israel. For YHWH is unlimited in HIS greatness. YHWH is GOD Almighty. YHWH can save the world without creating yet the story of sacrificing a son of GOD. All of Israel's son are GOD'S sons, *'Thou art My people'*. Through, and in the Name of YHWH, will many nations be saved, will know the name of YHWH, and will worship only HIM. But it will come through Israel's glory.

Joel 4:16, (16) And YHWH shall roar from Zion, and utter His voice from Jerusalem, and the heavens and the earth shall shake; but YHWH will be a refuge unto His people, and a stronghold to the sons of Israel.

Today, Israel is represented by the Jewish people. These words are not referring to the Uzbek, the Aleutian or to the Swahili. These words of the Prophets of YHWH, as were the words of Jesus himself, were spoken to the people of Israel. Yet according to the Prophets of YHWH, it is through YHWH who is GOD that the nations will be saved. *'Look unto Me, and be ye saved, all the ends of the earth; for I am God, and there is none else. Only in YHWH, shall one say of Me, is victory and strength'*? One may ask, what is *victory* and *strength* for Israel if not the salvation of YHWH their own GOD?

Psalms 96:1-3, (1) O sing unto YHWH a new song; sing unto YHWH, all the earth. (2) Sing unto YHWH, bless His Name; proclaim His Salvation from day to day. (3) Declare His Glory among the nations, His marvellous works among all the peoples.

It is within this context that the words of the Hebrew Bible and the words of Jesus in the Gospels must be understood.

All of the words spoken by the Prophets of GOD quoted above were as true and real to the Jewish people during the time of Jesus as when they were first uttered by YHWH'S Prophets hundreds of years before. And they are as true and real today to the Jewish people as they were when they were first uttered several thousand years ago by YHWH'S Prophets. At least in one sense, some of them may be even more "true" today as the *end of days* approaches. For in the same breath of *"salvation"* is that of *"all the nations"*.

For as many of the Prophets tell it, the prophecies of Israel and Israel's reestablishment as a kingdom with David as it's king will surely come. And according to the Prophets, sacrifice will also be offered again upon the alter. And those of the nations which are left will *"go up"* to celebrate Sukkot every year with Israel and offer sacrifice. One Law, one GOD, one Name.

WHO IS 'YHWH' TO ISRAEL

There is much more scripture and better examples of YHWH and HIS name. There are still a few words from the prophets which resonate. A careful look at just a few of these will indicate a few things which a person not familiar with certain aspects of the Law may not fully appreciate.

But first, to make a few sentences out of several of these quotes to illustrate a point before the Law is looked at. These quotes from several of the previously cited scriptures have been strung together by this author. The Hebrew Bible is full of YHWH GOD'S pronouncements about HIMSELF, about HIS holy name and about what and who Israel is to HIM.

These following scriptures have purposely been taken out of context and arranged in a continuous run-on sentence. It could just have easily been put into a *"bullet"* form. It does not effect their innate truth regarding either GOD YHWH as Israel's Savior, Israel's salvation nor the special place they occupy with YHWH who is their GOD. It is done to make a point. With this in mind, read what is written with the understanding that this is but a very small sample from only one prophet.

Additionally if possible, this should be read as one who lived 2,000 years ago in Israel listening to the words of Jesus and what he said about himself and his own name. For it is within this context that the Jewish people the remnant of Israel, heard his words spoken. It will begin with HIS first Commandment.

*'Thou shalt have no other gods before Me', 'For I am YHWH thy GOD, I, YHWH, who am the first, and with the last am the same. I am **YHWH**, that is **My name**; and My glory will I not give to another,... For I am YHWH thy God, The Holy One of Israel, **thy Saviour**, understand that **I am He**; before Me there was no God formed, neither shall any be after Me.... I, even I, am YHWH; and **beside Me there is no Saviour**, saith YHWH, and I am God, .I, even I, am He that blotteth out thy transgressions for Mine own sake; and thy sins I will not remember. Thus saith YHWH, the King of **Israel**, and his Redeemer YHWH of hosts: I am the first, and I am the last, and **beside Me there is no God** . And ye are My witnesses. Is there a God beside Me? Yea, there is no Rock; I know not any. **I have blotted out**, as a thick cloud, thy transgressions, and, as a cloud, **thy sins**; return unto Me, for I have redeemed thee, I am YHWH, and there is none else, **beside Me there is no God**. O God of **Israel**, the **Saviour**. I am YHWH, and **there is none else**. I have not spoken in secret, in a place of the land of darkness; I said not unto the **SEED of Jacob**: 'Seek ye Me in vain'; I YHWH speak righteousness, I declare things that are right. And there is no God else beside Me, a just God and a Saviour; there is **none beside Me**. Look unto Me, and be ye saved, all the ends of the earth; for I am God, and there is none else. **O Israel, that art saved by YHWH with an Everlasting Salvation. Only in YHWH**, shall one say of Me, is victory and strength, **SEED of Israel** be justified, and shall glory. Remember the former things of old: that **I am God**, and **there is none else**; I am God, and **there is none like Me**, and My salvation shall not tarry; and I will place salvation in Zion **for Israel** My glory, **let him trust in the name of YHWH**, and stay upon his God. Hearken unto Me, ye that know righteousness, the people in whose heart is My law,*

*My favour shall be for ever, and My salvation unto all generations. For I am YHWH thy God, YHWH of hosts is His name, **Thou art My people.**'*

The point to this exercise is to remind the reader that the words of GOD YHWH are in stark contrast to many of the words of Jesus. Or one can say that the words of Jesus stand in stark contrast to the words of GOD YHWH. It is to *"Israel"*, the circumcised male SEED descendants of Abraham through Jacob these words are being directed. It is YHWH who is the Savior, who is the Redeemer, who is Deliverer, and who is the Mighty One of Israel. When Jesus was chiding the Pharisees about not knowing the Law of Moses (or the Prophets or Writings), he may have had these things in mind.

Isaiah 49:26, (26) And I will feed them that oppress thee with their own flesh; and they shall be drunken with their own blood, as with sweet wine; <u>and all flesh shall know that I YHWH am thy Saviour, and thy Redeemer, the Mighty One of Jacob.</u>

'I WILL BE JEALOUS FOR MY HOLY NAME'

In the Hebrew Bible, YHWH said that HIS *"name is jealous"* and that HE is a *"jealous GOD"*. YHWH is *"jealous for MY holy name"*.

There are many mentions of *"HIS HOLY NAME"* in TaNaKh. There are many times HE refers to what HE is doing, HE is doing *"for HIS NAME sake"*. In other words, as HE told Israel countless times, it is not because of you I will do this, but for the sake of "MY HOLY NAME". As YHWH said that HIS very name is *"jealous"*, HIS rage in the end will be tremendous.

Exodus 34:14, (14) For thou shalt bow down to no other god; <u>for YHWH, whose name is Jealous, is a jealous God;</u>

In <u>YHWH: The Name of GOD, The Forgotten GOD of the SEED of Abraham,</u> the importance of **this** name, HIS NAME "***YHWH***", is the subject of the entire book. It is not a book on how to pronounce HIS NAME, but it is a book on the *significance* and the *importance* of HIS NAME.

The holiness of HIS NAME and it's significance to YHWH HIMSELF cannot be overstated. When reading the Hebrew Bible, this should be kept in mind. To be remembered, HIS NAME, "*YHWH*" is written nearly 7,000 times and reference is made to and about HIS name, both by GOD and by Israel, at least that many times if not more. There is a reason for this.

Ezekiel 39:25, (25) Therefore thus saith the Lord YHWH: Now will I bring back the captivity of Jacob, and have compassion upon the whole house of Israel; <u>and I will be jealous for My holy name.</u>

It is this scripture just cited and others like it, which must be remembered with regard to the name of "*Jesus*" when discussed. The jealously of YHWH for HIS own holy name, and HIS relationship with HIS people Israel are one.

Psalms 79:9, (9) Help us, O God of our salvation, <u>for the sake of the glory of Thy Name</u>; and deliver us, and forgive our sins, <u>for Thy Name's sake.</u>

'NOT FOR YOUR SAKE DO I THIS'

Exodus 20:5 (5) thou shalt not bow down unto them, nor serve them; for I YHWH thy God am a jealous God,

The people of Israel had Laws given to them by their GOD YHWH which helped them understand what to do whenever a person of Israel prophesied in the name of YHWH or not. This is why it is so critical to know if Jesus even mentioned or said that his words were the words of "*YHWH*". Jesus said that they are the words of the "*father*". Jesus said that he and the "*father*" were one, but this is not the same. This is not the "*NAME*". This is not "**YHWH**". There is a difference if he uttered not the "*name*" itself and gave glory to it.

So what does the Law of Moses have to say about prophets?

THE NAME OF DELIVERANCE

To whom, and how did Israel call for "*deliverance*"?

Psalms 54:3, (3) O God, savdelivere me by Thy Name, and right me by Thy might.

Psalms 44:6-9, 14-16, (6) Through Thee do we push down our adversaries; through Thy Name do we tread them under that rise up against us. (7) For I trust not in my bow, neither can my sword save me. (8) But Thou hast saved us from our adversaries, and hast put them to shame that hate us. (9) In God have we gloried all the day, and we will give thanks unto Thy Name for ever. Selah.....

Psalms 50:14-15, (14) Offer unto God the sacrifice of thanksgiving; and pay thy vows unto the Most High; (15) And call upon Me in the day of trouble; I Will Deliver Thee, and thou shalt honour Me.'

Who is Israel to call on in their "*day of trouble*", but "*YHWH*" their GOD?

Perhaps David, the shepherd who became king, had at least as much or maybe more understanding of this than any. For David was beset often times both from the enemy without as well as the enemy within. But the enemy from within was often his biggest challenge. This does not touch on the mercy of YHWH shown to David for David's own misdeeds.

'WHOSO IS WISE'

Psalm107, whether it was written by David or Solomon or by one of the Priests, expresses the same sense of awe toward YHWH as David does time and again in his own words. As with many of the Psalms it's subject is *redemption* and *deliverance* by calling on the *name* of "*YHWH*". And it's message is to remember and to give thanks to YHWH for what HE has done for HIS people Israel in their hour of need.

It is a long Psalm, so only portions of it will be given. It begins by reminding Israel of YHWH'S mercy and how HE has redeemed them, and returned them from their exile. It later speaks of Israel calling on "*HIS NAME*" when in trouble and YHWH delivering them. And ultimately it ends reminding Israel that it is "*wise*" for Israel to observe all of these things and "*consider*" all of the "*mercies*" of YHWH their GOD.

Psalms 107:1-3, 6, 43, 'O give thanks unto YHWH, for He is good, <u>for His Mercy endureth for ever.'</u>
(2) So let the Redeemed of YHWH say, whom He hath Redeemed from the hand of the adversary; (3)
And gathered them out of the lands, from the east and from the west, from the north and from the
sea...(6) <u>Then they cried unto YHWH in their trouble</u>, and <u>He Delivered</u> them out of their
distresses...(43) <u>Whoso is wise</u>, let him observe these things, <u>and let them Consider the Mercies of</u>
<u>YHWH.</u>

The motif of most Psalms is the same. This example is one which is worth quoting, specifically
because of the ending verse, "*<u>Whoso is wise</u>, let him observe these things, and let them Consider the*
Mercies of YHWH".

What is it the Psalm wants the *wise* to *observe* and *consider*? It is that it is **YHWH** who is Israel's
redeemer. It is **YHWH'S** name which Israel is to call on for *deliverance*, and that the *mercy* of **YHWH**
is eternal, "*for HIS mercy endureth forever*". The Jewish people today should ___consider___ this. They have
a compassionate GOD who has redeemed them and who will deliver them.

PROPHETS / FALSE PROPHETS

According to Deuteronomy 13 and 18, we know that YHWH puts Israel "*to proof*" by sending them
prophets. That whosoever does not hearken to the prophets words shall GOD require, and prophets who
speak in the name of YHWH which YHWH did not command him shall die. Both John the Baptist and
Jesus died. But, then Israel killed many of their own prophets of whom YHWH sent.

DYING FOR THE SINS OF ANOTHER

According to the basic tenants of most Christian doctrine regarding the life, death and resurrection of
Jesus, Jesus came as the messiah of Israel, but was rejected by Israel. Instead of Jesus being the
messiah of Israel, Jesus was crucified and so became the savior of the nations. If one "*professes belief*"
in "*Jesus*" and is baptized, one is "*saved*".

One question arises here. If Jesus came as the messiah of Israel, and GOD always knew that Israel
would reject him, then Jesus did not become the savior of the world by *default*, but by *design*. In other
words, Jesus was never to have been the "*messiah*" of Israel, given this understanding. For YHWH
knows all, and surely knew according to the Gospels themselves the eventual outcome of his life. So
what does this mean? Was there some kind of grand conspiracy on a colossal scale happening 2,000
years ago?

According to most church doctrine, Jesus was crucified and was resurrected and will return for his
"*church*", ie., those who are saved by being baptized and by their belief in his "*name*". Accordingly,
Jesus died "*once*" for all, shedding his "*blood*" for the sins of mankind, therefore according to this
belief, the "*Law*" is dead and serves no purpose, especially regarding it's sacrificial offerings for sin.
There is no longer any need for the "*Law*", or for the shedding of blood, ie., "*blood sacrifice*". But how
does this basic "*doctrine*" (It is understood there are many different beliefs in Christianity) jibe with the
Law of Moses. Is there precedent regarding such a doctrine?

A few scriptures regarding the giving of life for another are here given from the Christian Bible,
specifically Jesus giving his life for others. There are many more scriptures where Jesus speaks on this

topic. Most are parables or metaphors regarding his own life and death. But basically, the idea of his dying for Israel, is what he was talking about, and how his words and deeds are understood. It is Israel who are the *"sheep"*.

Matthew 20:28, (28) Even as the Son of man came not to be ministered unto, but to minister, <u>and to give his life a ransom for many.</u>

Yet, YHWH has already *"ransomed"* Israel! *"For I am YHWH thy God, The Holy One of Israel, thy Saviour; **I have given Egypt as thy <u>ransom</u>**, Ethiopia and Seba for thee"*(Isaiah 43:3)

John 10:11, 15, 17, 28 (11) I am the good shepherd: te good shepherd <u>giveth his life for the sheep</u>.....(15) As the Father knoweth me, even so know I the Father: <u>and I lay down my life for the sheep</u>....(17) Therefore doth my Father love me, <u>because I lay down my life</u>, that I might take it again....(28) <u>And I give unto them eternal life</u>; and they shall never perish, neither shall any man pluck them out of my hand.

John 15:13, (13) Greater love hath no man than this, <u>that a man lay down his life for his friends.</u>

Jesus states in John 10:28, that it is <u>he</u> who gives eternal life! But something else is being said here. Jesus said he gave his life for *"the sheep"*. The is always <u>Israel</u>. It never represents the *"nations"*. For it must be remembered as well that it was **<u>only</u>** to the *"Lost Sheep of the House of Israel"* that Jesus said he came. If this is so, then his giving his life for the *"sheep"* is referring to him dying for Israel, not the nations, and is consistent with his words.

HUMAN SACRIFICE & THE LAW

The story of the life and death of the Jew called Jesus is very compelling. To be as objective as a person can be as one who is an observant Jew and not a follower of Jesus, there are few other more compelling stories written whether fact or fiction, which is so dramatic. The stories of the Patriarchs, Abraham, Isaac and Jacob with that of Joseph are extremely dramatic. Especially when GOD *"proved"* or tested Abraham with his son Isaac, has more drama and is a superior story in many respects, when the lead up chapters of how Abraham was so determined to have a male heir are added.

Having said this, the saga involving the life and eventual death of the Jew Jesus is a powerful story, else what today is called *"Christianity"* would be no more than a small cult, a brief foot note on the world stage. Yet, it is the largest religion in a world of approximately 6 billion souls, comprised of 2.2 billion people, give or take a few million. That's allot of souls who believe.

The story of Jesus has some of the elements of the stories of the Patriarchs, but in a different way. It has much drama and is very compelling in it's own right. The story of GOD sacrificing his only son for the souls of mankind does not get much better as a story line. If one were trying to write a story to top the one of Jesus, whether one accepts the story of Jesus or not, he would be hard pressed to do so. The story of Jesus when compared to other stories like Greek mythology, the Norse Mythology, Hindu Mythology, or any of the gods of Egypt or any other of the pantheon of *"gods"* in the many fables, myths and sagas concerning *"gods"*, none come close to the story of Jesus. Only the Hebrew Bible stories, according to this writer, are more compelling.

Genesis 22:11, (11) And the angel of YHWH called unto him out of heaven, and said: 'Abraham,

Abraham.' And he said: 'Here am I.' (12) And he said: 'Lay not thy hand upon the lad, neither do thou any thing unto him; for now I know that thou art a God-fearing man, <u>seeing thou hast not withheld thy son, thine only son, from Me.</u>'

If one reads the entire life story of Abraham from the time he left Haran when GOD spoke to him, and them visualizes his putting the wood on Isaac as the two walk up the mountain together where he binds Isaac for offering to GOD, it is a very powerful story. And with the knife to his throat, is stopped by the angle of GOD as he is about to sacrifice the one thing which meant more to him than anything else upon this earth, then a glimmer of understanding may appear. It is more than compelling but a situation beyond ones imagination or ability of comprehension. It is something difficult to fathom, especially given the build up to that point in Abraham's life. Other stories, such as the story and build up to the meeting of Jacob and his estranged brother Esau, or the story of Joseph and his own estranged brothers and their reconciliation in Egypt, is without peer in drama and pathos.

SIN / SACRIFICE

Did Jesus die for his own sin? Was Jesus a man under the Law of YHWH who was without sin? And even if one believes he was without sin, did the Law allow for one man to sacrifice himself for another? For even Jesus did not cast a stone at the adulteress as he was required to do under the Law. He shamed the Pharisees and was left alone with her, but he did not cast a stone. Was Jesus too with sin?

I Kings 8:46, (46) <u>If they sin against Thee -- for there is no man that sinneth not</u> -- and Thou be angry with them,....

John 8:34, (34) Jesus answered them, Verily, verily, I say unto you, <u>Whosoever committeth sin is the servant of sin.</u>

All men sin according to the Law and YHWH provided for Israel Priests to make atonement for their sin. As King Solomon states, *"for there is no man that sinneth not"*. What did Jesus mean by *"Whosoever committeth sin is the servant of sin"*. Jesus was human, baptized by John for his sins. Was Jesus a servant of sin too? Jesus lived and died a human being even if he was special.

Jesus often referred to himself as the *"son of man"*. This is a fairly common expression meaning *"son of adam"*, *"human"*, *"man"*. Jesus was a *"human being"*. As Israel is the son of GOD as HIS first born, and also human with sin, does not this apply to Jesus too? Was this not what Jesus was possibly signaling by continually reminding those who were close to him, that regardless of whatever he was or claimed to be, he was still *"human"*?

Ezekiel 18:4, (4) Behold, all souls are Mine; as the soul of the father, so also the soul of the son is Mine; <u>the soul that sinneth, it shall die.</u>

Was not Jesus making offerings to YHWH upon HIS alter in accordance with the Law of Moses as sacrifice for sin? Did Jesus not keep the Law? If so, then he did as all Jews did regarding the mandatory offering before GOD in HIS Temple. And even more so, the Priests continually made sacrifice for the people of Israel of who Jesus was counted. If no man *"sinneth not"*, did Jesus die for his own sin? How can a lamb with a blemish be acceptable to GOD?

Exodus 12:5, (5) Your lamb shall be without blemish.........

One must ask, did Jesus die because of his own sin against YHWH?

This is not said to be offensive to Christians, but Jesus is being looked at strictly as Jesus the Jew under the Law. For Jesus was under the Law which mandates that offerings are made before YHWH for Israel's sins. And Jesus was part of Israel according to the Law. For contrary to what many may believe, during his entire life time, sacrifice was made for the sins of Jesus, whether it was acknowledged or not in the Gospels. For both individuals brought sacrificial offerings according to the Law, and the Priests offered sacrifice for Israel. The Law he said to keep, still existed during his life time.

The Laws of sacrifice were continual, always and were to be forever according to the Law. The Law of Passover, Exodus, 12:14-24 is "*eternal*". The Law of the Sabbath, Exodus 31:16-17 is "*eternal*". The Law of Yom Kippur, Leviticus 16:29-34 is "*eternal*". The Law of Daily Sacrifice, Exodus 29:38-46 is "*eternal*". The sacrifices for all of Israel also included Jesus as he too was "*Israel*".

Leviticus 16:29-34, (29) And it shall be a <u>STATUTE FOR EVER</u> unto you: in the seventh month, on the tenth day of the month, ye shall afflict your souls, and shall do no manner of work, the home-born, or the stranger that sojourneth among you. (30) <u>For on this day shall Atonement be made for you, to cleanse you; from all your Sins shall ye be clean before YHWH</u>. (31) It is a sabbath of solemn rest unto you, and ye shall afflict your souls; it is a <u>STATUTE FOR EVER</u>. (32) And the priest, who shall be anointed and who shall be consecrated to be priest in his father's stead, shall make the <u>Atonement,</u> and shall put on the linen garments, even the holy garments. (33) And he shall make <u>Atonement</u> for the most holy place, and he shall make <u>Atonement</u> for the tent of meeting and for the altar; and he shall make <u>Atonement</u> for the priests and for all the people of the assembly. (34) <u>And this shall be an EVERLASTING STATUTE unto you, to make Atonement for the sons of Israel because of all their Sins once in the year.</u>' And he did as YHWH commanded Moses.

This "*Everlasting Statute*", this Law pertaining to the Atonement for the sins of Israel begs the question, if the making of Atonement for the sins of Israel is a "*Statute For Ever*", what did Jesus die for?

Atonement was made for all of Israel once a year during Yom Kippur. This "*atonement*" was a special day which was set up and mandated by GOD as a "*perpetual*" offering by the Priests on behalf of Israel for their sins. It is an eternal offering of atonement for Israel. It is a "*statute forever*". This "*statute forever*" part is very difficult to get around. It simply cannot be ignored. The original Hebrew is very strong concerning this.

This statement is being made knowing full well that Christian doctrine denies sacrifice as an obligation because of the death of Jesus. Yet, the very Law with all of it's Commandments which Jesus said must be kept, demand that offerings are to be made "*continually, from generation to generation, forever, always, everlasting, eternally*" for "*sin*". This requirement according to the Commandment of the Law, did not stop because Jesus died. All of the Statutes and Ordinances of the Law will be kept, and that includes the continual "*atonement*" sacrifice offerings made for "*sin*" as per the Law, and as per the word of YHWH by HIS prophets.

Burnt-offering, Sin Offering, Guilt Offering, Meal Offering, Drink Offering, Thanksgiving Offering, Gift Offering, Peace Offering, Freewill Offering, Wave Offering, Heave Offering, and Offering of Consecration did not cease because Jesus died. These offerings temporarily halted because the Temple was destroyed by the Romans approximately 40 years after he died, in the same way that the Temple was destroyed earlier by the Babylonians. But the Law is "*eternal*". And if the return of the Jewish people from Babylonian exile shows anything, it is that the Law of YHWH was still in affect whether during Israel's 70 year exile or not. Today, it is no different. For whether 70 years or 2,000 years, the Law is eternal for Israel, "*And this shall be an **everlasting statute** unto you, to make atonement for the sons of Israel because of all their sins once in the year' ..... ".*

Basically, the Law states that every man will die for his "*own*" sins.

Deuteronomy 24:16, (16) The fathers shall not be put to death for the children, neither shall the children be put to death for the fathers; <u>every man shall be put to death for his own sin.</u>

Jeremiah 31:30, (30) <u>But every one shall die for his own iniquity</u>; every man that eateth the sour grapes, his teeth shall be set on edge.

Ezekiel 33:18-20, (18) When the righteous turneth from his righteousness, and committeth iniquity, he shall even die thereby. (19) And when the wicked turneth from his wickedness, and doeth that which is lawful and right, he shall live thereby. (20) Yet ye say: The way of the Lord is not equal. O house of Israel, <u>I will judge you every one after his ways</u>.'

II Chronicles 25:4, (4) But he put not their children to death, <u>but did according to that which is written in the law in the book of Moses, as YHWH commanded</u>, saying: 'The fathers shall not die for the children, neither shall the children die for the fathers; <u>but every man shall die for his own sin</u>.'

Ezekiel 18:20-21, 30-32, (20) <u>The soul that sinneth, it shall die</u>; the son shall not bear the iniquity of the father with him, neither shall the father bear the iniquity of the son with him; the righteousness of the righteous shall be upon him, and the wickedness of the wicked shall be upon him. (21) But if the wicked <u>turn</u> from all his sins that he hath committed, <u>and keep all My statutes</u>, and do that which is lawful and right, <u>he shall surely live</u>, he shall not die.....(30) <u>Therefore I will judge you, O house of Israel, every one according to his ways, saith the Lord YHWH.</u> Return ye, and turn yourselves from all your transgressions; so shall they not be a stumblingblock of iniquity unto you. (31) Cast away from you all your transgressions, wherein ye have transgressed; and make you a new heart and a new spirit; for why will ye die, O house of Israel? (32) For I have no pleasure in the death of him that dieth, saith the Lord YHWH; <u>wherefore turn yourselves, and live</u>.

Jeremiah 32:17-19, (17) 'Ah Lord YHWH! behold, Thou hast made the heaven and the earth by Thy great power and by Thy outstretched arm; there is nothing too hard for Thee; (18) who showest mercy unto thousands, and recompensest the iniquity of the fathers into the bosom of their children after them; the great, the mighty God, YHWH of hosts is His name; (19) <u>great in counsel, and mighty in work; whose eyes are open upon all the ways of the sons of men, to give every one according to his ways, and according to the fruit of his doings;</u>

The question is, was it possible for Jesus to live his entire life as a human being and never sin once? For the scriptures say that "*all men sin*".

'RANSOM'

In the Book of Psalms 49, a Levite of the sons of Korah states how beyond us it is for man to redeem his brother, "*<u>No man can by any means redeem his brother, nor give to God a ransom for him</u> -- For too costly is the redemption of their soul, and must be let alone for ever –But God will redeem my soul from the power of the nether-world; for He shall receive me. Selah* ". For it is a cost too high for us and must needs be left in the hands of GOD. It is GOD who will redeem our soul. YHWH often reminds Israel that they have been redeemed by HIM. It was YHWH who redeemed Israel from Egypt. YHWH the compassionate and merciful further states that Israel is HIS son, and that Israel is HIS possession, *thou art MINE*. Jesus said that there is no greater love than for a man to give up his life for his brother, " *Greater love hath no man than this, that a man lay down his life for his friends* " (John 15:13). More than one soldier has jumped on a hand grenade to save his fellow soldier, but this is different than dying as "*atonement*" for the "*sin*" of another as Jesus seems to be saying.

If Jesus was making a statement about "*brotherly love*", then this would not be in conflict with the Law. But if dying for the sin of another, it would be.

ISRAEL THE REDEEMED OF GOD

Jeremiah 51:19, (19) The portion of Jacob is not like these; for He is the former of all things, and Israel is the tribe of His inheritance; YHWH of hosts is His name.

Psalms 94:14, (14) For YHWH will not cast off His people, neither will He forsake His inheritance.

Israel is a people redeemed by the hand of GOD.

This is an important concept to remember, for whatever else Israel is, they are the redeemed people of YHWH and are HIS eternal "*inheritance*". They are HIS.

The Law of Moses, if not anticipating such a concept as human sacrifice, which existed in abundance within the surrounding nations during the period of the giving of the Law of Moses, it nevertheless addresses the issue. The people of Canaan practiced child sacrifice which YHWH warned Israel regarding. As a people entering into the land promised to Abraham their father, Israel was being prepared by GOD on how to live in this special land. As it was a "*holy land*" and would "*vomit*" them out if they did not live as a "*holy*" people while in the land. Even still, YHWH realizes Israel is but dust.

Psalms 103:8-18, (8) YHWH is full of Compassion and gracious, slow to anger, and plenteous in Mercy. (9) He will not always contend; neither will He keep His anger for ever. (10) He hath not dealt with us after our sins, nor requited us according to our iniquities. (11) For as the heaven is high above the earth, so great is His Mercy toward them that fear Him. (12) As far as the east is from the west, so far hath He removed our transgressions from us. (13) Like as a father hath Compassion upon his children, so hath YHWH Compassion upon them that fear Him. (14) For He knoweth our frame; He remembereth that we are dust. (15) As for man, his days are as grass; as a flower of the field, so he flourisheth. (16) For the wind passeth over it, and it is gone; and the place thereof knoweth it no more. (17) But the Mercy of YHWH is from everlasting to everlasting upon them that fear Him, and His righteousness unto children's children; (18) To such as keep His Covenant, and to those that remember His precepts to do them.

'CHILDREN OF THE MURDERERS HE PUT NOT TO DEATH'

There is an interesting story where the law pertaining to one being answerable for one's own sins comes into play, "*every man shall be put to death for his own sin*".

In the story of King Amaziah of Judah, there was a situation which he was confronted with shortly after he became king. His father King Joash, was murdered by his own servants in a conspiracy (II Kings 12:21). The temptation to destroy not only the conspirators, but their SEED as well, must have been very powerful as these things were often done. Yet, King Amaziah withheld his hand from breaking the

Law of GOD by not killing their sons. King Amaziah had to believe that GOD'S Law was stronger than any future blood revenge these sons might harbor. King Amaziah kept GOD'S Law.

II Kings 14:5-6, (5) And it came to pass, <u>as soon as the kingdom was established in his hand, that he</u> *<u>slew his servants who had slain the king his father; (6) but the children of the murderers he put not</u>* *<u>to death</u>; according to that which is written in the book of the law of Moses, as YHWH commanded saying: 'The fathers shall not be put to death for the children, nor the children be put to death for the fathers; <u>but every man shall be put to death for his own sin.</u>'*

PROPHESY AND SACRIFICE

Jesus is not mentioned in the Hebrew Bible. *Nazareth* is not mentioned in the Hebrew Bible. Nowhere in any part of the entire Hebrew Bible which Christians call the "Old Testament" is either the town of "*Nazareth*" or "*Jesus*" mentioned by name. And although Jesus makes reference on several occasions to Moses or events which took place and the Prophets writing about him, it is difficult to see the connection. One of the oddest references Jesus makes is regarding Moses and the *"serpent"* discussed earlier.

Neither is the cessation of sacrifice by GOD'S Temple Priests ever mentioned in the Hebrew Bible but for the Prophet Hosea in 3:4-5. Quite the opposite regarding sacrifice is written from the word of YHWH'S Prophets. This in is the future with sacrificial offerings.

Jeremiah 33:17-22, (17) For thus saith YHWH: There shall not be cut off unto David a man to sit upon the throne of the house of Israel; <u>(18) neither shall there be cut off unto the priests the Levites a man</u> *<u>before Me to offer burnt-offerings, and to burn meal-offerings, and to do sacrifice continually.</u> (19) And the word of YHWH came unto Jeremiah, saying: (20) Thus saith YHWH: If ye can break My Covenant with the day, and My Covenant with the night, so that there should not be day and night **in** their season; (21) Then may also My Covenant be broken with David My servant, that he should not have a son to reign upon his throne; <u>and with the Levites the priests, My ministers.</u> (22) As the host of heaven cannot be numbered, neither the sand of the sea measured; so will I multiply the SEED of David My servant, and the Levites that minister unto Me.*

The Prophet Ezekiel in chapters 43-46 in describing the new Temple of YHWH which will be in Jerusalem, describes the future sacrifice offerings by the Priests in detail. This is after the SEED of David is reigning upon his throne and the SEED of Zadok is again High Priest.

FORGIVING THE SIN OF ANOTHER

Jesus was *"forgiving"* people of their sin. This is quite remarkable. He said his followers would be able to forgive also, which is even more remarkable.

Matthew 9:2, 5, 6, (2) And, behold, they brought to him a man sick of the palsy, lying on a bed: and Jesus seeing their faith said unto the sick of the palsy; <u>Son, be of good cheer; thy sins be forgiven</u> *<u>thee.</u> (5) For whether is easier, to say, Thy sins be forgiven thee; or to say, Arise, and walk? (6) But <u>that ye may know that the Son of man hath power on earth to forgive sins,</u> (then saith he to the sick of the palsy,) Arise, take up thy bed, and go unto thine house.*

Forgiving of sins by Jesus was just one of the charges leveled against Jesus, However, there was more to the forgiveness of sins. For Jesus tells his followers that *they too* can forgive sin! At the risk of sounding disrespectful, it sounds almost like a commercial whereby the listener is told, '*and you too, can look 20 years younger by spreading just two mega-glops of this here Youaintseennothinyet beauty aid all over your face'*. After Jesus was resurrected, he came to his disciples and *"breathed on them"* telling them to receive the *"Holy Ghost"*. Then he said this about forgiving sins.

John 20:23, (23) Whose soever sins ye remit, they are remitted unto them; and whose soever sins ye retain, they are retained.

Jesus was telling, or rather giving his disciples authority and / or power to *"forgive sin"*. This is a truly astounding event. Not only did Jesus tell people that there sins were forgiven them by himself, equating himself with GOD, but now he was *"authorizing"* his followers to do the same!

Yet, in Matthew, Jesus told his followers *not* to judge.

Matthew 7:1-2, (1) Judge not, that ye be not judged. (2) For with what judgment ye judge, ye shall be judged: and with what measure ye mete, it shall be measured to you again.

So how is one of his sinful disciples (for we all sin) to get from being a follower, to being like Jesus and forgiving sin as if GOD himself, if Jesus has told him not to judge? For what is forgiving sin, if not judging another's sin?

SON OF MAN / SON OF DAVID / SON OF GOD

Jesus was referred to often as *"son of man"*, most often about himself. This term was common in the Hebrew Bible and was often employed by GOD'S prophets to refer to *"man"."Ben adam"* in Hebrew literally means *"son of Adam"*. There are many examples in the Hebrew Bible such as these listed here, (Numbers 23:19; Isaiah 51:12, 56:2; Jeremiah 49:18, 33, 50:40 51:43; Ezekiel 2:1,3,6,8 3:1 etc.).

Depending on the way it is used, it can simply mean *"man"*, or can have the feel of *"human"* (as in human being) or even *"mortal"* (as in being mortal). This term was used often regarding Jesus. Jesus often referred to himself by this term. Here are several listed, (Matthew 12:8, 32, 40; 13:37, 41; Mark 14:21, 41, 62; Luke 17:22, 24, 26, 30; John 12:23, 34). One might ask what was Jesus thinking whenever he used this term? Was Jesus suppose to have been the son of GOD without sin to die for the sin of others. Or was Jesus with sin as common man? If he was *ben adam*, was he not as man *with* sin? If Jesus was as man with sin, how could he be *"without blemish"*?

Jesus was called *"son of David"* by the people during his ministry. And like being called *"LORD"* and *"GOD"* by Thomas, Jesus did not rebuke the people who referred to him as the *"son of David"*, nor *"LORD"* or *"GOD"*.

And whether he was the *"son of David"* seemed to be of little consequence as someone who was wearing the title of *"messiah, son of man"* and *"Lord and GOD"* was put to death in an unholy place not sanctified by priests.

As Jesus was fairly consistent in his statements concerning himself and the *"Father"* as being *"one"*, his dying the way he did also presents another problem because of the numerous *"titles"* and *"names"* attached to him which he was either called by others or said of himself.

THE INCIDENT IN THE GARDEN

When Jesus was being arrested in the Garden of Gethsemane and Simon Peter drew his sword cutting off an ear of one of the bad guys, after rebuking Peter he stated that but for a prayer to his Father he could receive legions of angels (to save him).

Matthew 26:52-54, (52) Then said Jesus unto him, Put up again thy sword into his place: for all they that take the sword shall perish with the sword. (53) Thinkest thou that I cannot now pray to my Father, and he shall presently give me more than twelve legions of angels? (54) But how then shall the scriptures be fulfilled, that thus it must be?

The reference usually given for verse Matthew 26:54 is Isaiah 53:7, in the *"suffering servant"* chapter which many Christians have adopted as referring to Jesus. Although the scene with Jesus declaring he could have twelve legions of angels as his followers are squaring off against the Priests and Pharisees in the garden, has very little connection to Isaiah 53.

Unlike Matthew 26:52, in John 18:11, Jesus seems to be resigned to his fate, *"Then said Jesus unto Peter, Put up thy sword into the sheath: the cup which my Father hath given me, shall I not drink it"*? This, supposedly said Jesus in referring to his death. Yet, when this is contrasted with his words of agony on the cross he seemed shocked by what was actually happening to him, *"why hast thou forsaken me"*? Did Jesus believe that GOD would repent in the end and allow mankind to perish and not to be saved by his preordained death?

And if they are *"one"*, how could the Father forsake himself and be divided?

Jesus neither asked for help nor for legions of angels, but did ask his Father not to make him go through with the ordeal of his death in his prayer *"And he went a little further, and fell on his face, and prayed, saying, O my Father, if it be possible, let this cup pass from me: nevertheless not as I will, but as thou wilt (Matthew 26:39).* He let his feelings be known that he did not want to go through with it, but acquiesced to the will of his Father and to his fate. Yet in the end, he seemed shocked at the outcome as if somehow he had been surprised and left *"out of the loop"* with the proceedings. Yet, they were _one_.

Additionally, the statement regarding praying for angles, presumably to save him, was never utilized. The point here is that Jesus as both *"man"*, and as *"God"*, by allowing these things to take place according to the scripture, he appears to be killing himself by not intervening on his own behalf to save himself. For at the risk of offending, it is very difficult to follow how someone who is *"GOD"* in the flesh as *"ben adam"*, let himself be crucified without a fight. For if Jesus was truly *"one"* as *"GOD"* how could GOD let GOD die? Even if only in the flesh he died. If they were really *"one"*, then how can there be a *"difference"* between the *"Father"* and the *"son"*? If the *"son"* dies, does not the *"Father"* die with him if they are truly *"one"*? For even Jesus said that to see *"him"* was to see the *"Father"*.

John 14:8-9, (8) Philip saith unto him, Lord, <u>shew us the Father</u>, and it sufficeth us.(9)] Jesus saith unto him, Have I been so long time with you, and yet hast thou not known me, Philip? <u>he that hath seen me hath seen the Father</u>; and how sayest thou then, <u>Shew us the Father</u>?

Philip did not seem too convinced that seeing Jesus was seeing the Father. The many, many statements of Jesus being *"one"*, both in word and in deed with the *"Father"*, if one takes this to mean that there is no difference between the two, that they are truly *"one"*, then how could Jesus die and the Father not be part of his death? Did the Father suffer as well?

Having said this, one is aware that it is talking about *"spirit"* and *"flesh"*. The flesh died, not the spirit. But in the suffering of Jesus, did not his spirit suffer in agony during his travail? Would not the spirit of the Father who was one with the spirit of the son, suffer as well as his son suffered and died such a horrible death? Then there is the question, *'did the spirit die too"?*

John 5:25-26, (25) Verily, verily, I say unto you, The hour is coming, and now is, when the dead shall hear the voice of the Son of God: and they that hear shall live.(26) For as the Father hath life in himself; <u>so hath he given to the Son to have life in himself</u>; (27) <u>And hath given him authority</u> to execute judgment also, <u>because he is the Son of man.</u>

Here, it appears that Jesus has life *"in himself"* seemingly separate from that of his Father. Additionally, it appears that the Father gave Jesus power (authority), separate from his own as well, because Jesus was *"human"*. Was it this last fact of his being *"human"* that allowed him to understand the suffering of man, and which qualified him to *"judge"* mankind?

Yet in the same chapter, he seems to contradict himself stating that he can do nothing *"of mine own"*. Yet, he had just said that he had been given authority to *"execute judgment"* and to *"lay it down"* (his life) and *"take it again"*. If this is so, then he is much more like just a servant than being *"one"* with GOD, and at the same time he said also that he had *"life in himself"* as if totally separated from that of GOD and could do what he wanted with it. These contradict one another.

John 5:30 (30) <u>I can of mine own self do nothing</u>: as I hear, I judge: and my judgment is just; because I seek not mine own will, but the will of the Father which hath sent me.

Then again in John 10:17-18 he said that he was laying down his life and that he could take it back, *"I have power...."*. Well, he has no power at all, if his words are to be understood that he is <u>only</u> a mouth piece for the Father.

John 10:17-18, (17) Therefore doth my Father love me, because I <u>lay down my life, that I might take it again</u>. (18) No man taketh it from me, but I lay it down of myself. <u>I have power to lay it down, and I have power to take it again</u>. This <u>commandment</u> have I received of my Father.

Is this yet, another *"commandment"* added to the Law of Moses? What is it?

John 14:10, (10) Believest thou not that I <u>am in the Father, and the Father in me</u>? the <u>words</u> that I speak unto you I speak not of myself: <u>but the Father</u> that dwelleth in me, he <u>doeth the works.</u>

So is it the Father who does all of the works, telling him what to say, giving him authority to judge and raise himself up from the dead or does he have the power to do so on his own? Jesus prayed for his followers before his arrest.

John 17:21-23, (21) That they all may be <u>one</u>; <u>as thou, Father, art in me, and I in thee</u>, that they also may be <u>one</u> in us: that the world may believe that thou hast sent me. (22)And the glory which thou gavest me I have given them; that they may be <u>one</u>, <u>even as we are one</u>: (23) I in them, and thou in me, that they may be made perfect in <u>one</u>; and that the world may know that thou hast sent me, and hast loved them, as thou hast loved me.

Jesus speaks of his followers being *"one"* with Jesus, as Jesus is *"one"* with the *"Father"*. So eventually, the followers of Jesus, Jesus himself and the Father are all to be one together? So his followers are to be as GOD too? And as Jesus was to have been the son of David, were his followers to have been also? So his followers were to be as GOD, Jesus and David also?

Unless one assumes scripture like Isaiah Chapter 53 is about Jesus, there are no *"prophesies"* that a messiah would come and have to go through the ordeal which Jesus suffered.

Luke 24:26 (26)26 Ought not Christ to have suffered these things, <u>and to enter into his glory</u>?

Exodus 15:18, (18) YHWH shall reign for ever and ever.

If Israel is the glory of YHWH, how is Jesus to enter into *"his"* glory? What glory is that? YHWH said that HE will *not* give HIS glory to another.

BIBLICAL MESSIAH

What are the expectations of Israel for a *"messiah"*? And what was the precedent established which gave Israel their idea of a *"Savior"*?

According to Jewish *"tradition"*, the messiah will be an *"anointed"* SEED of David, who will gather in the scattered SEED of Israel and the *"Jews"*, returning them to Israel. The Third Temple will be *"rebuilt"* and peace will reign. Ezekiel describes the Temple without it's actual construction. There are several other related things according to Jewish (Rabbinic) *"tradition"* which are to occur, but they are not relevant. Presumably, the messiah son of David will reign in power, reestablishing the might and the glory of YHWH LORD of heaven and earth as GOD of Israel. He will bring *righteousness, justice* and *peace* according to the Prophet Isaiah. Some of this has been covered, however, a more in depth look at this idea and the many examples given in TaNaKh are necessary.

We first encounter this phenomena of *"Savior"* in the Book of Judges when Israel had sinned and cried to GOD to *"save"* them. Interestingly, Moses, who arguably *"saved"* Israel by leading them out of Egypt is not referred to in this way, and GOD surely used Moses to *"save"* Israel from Egypt. There is an exceptionally good reason why Moses is not thought of in these terms. Moses is Prophet, YHWH is Savior. YHWH was establishing HIS holy name. YHWH was making a *"name"* for HIMSELF, to Israel and the nations. Additionally, as GOD'S Prophet, Moses made GOD angry by *"trespassing"* against HIM and by not *"sanctifying"* before Israel (Deuteronomy 32:51-52). Moses did something he was not to have done, and he did not make holy to Israel his GOD YHWH by his actions or by his inaction. Moses was *"prophet"*, not *"mesiach"*. Moses was Israel's greatest prophet, but he too was human. Because of his actions, YHWH would not allow Moses enter.

In freeing Israel from bondage in Egypt YHWH, the GOD of Abraham, Isaac and Jacob was establishing HIS *"ownership"* of Israel as HIS own possession, as HIS own people. Israel was to be a free people who were servant to the one and only GOD. There is no contradiction in this. Israel belonged to GOD. And it would be by the example of the Pharaoh of Egypt that *"ownership"* would not only be established, but YHWH established HIMSELF as Israel's GOD and *"Savior"* as well, their *"Deliverer"*. But to establish ownership, *"possession"* must first be established, and for Pharaoh unfortunately, it was he who was used for this task. As shall be seen, Pharaoh thought that these Hebrew slaves belonged to him. But he was profoundly mistaken as *"ownership"* of these people became a battle of wills between GOD and Pharaoh. Israel was *ransomed* by YHWH and *redeemed* to HIM.

Exodus 3:7-8, (7) And YHWH said: 'I have surely seen the affliction of My People that are in Egypt, and have heard their cry by reason of their taskmasters; for I know their pains; (8) and I am come down to Deliver them out of the hand of the Egyptians,.....

YHWH was establishing HIMSELF to a people who had only heard of HIM through stories told and passed down. As slaves they did not know YHWH as their forefathers had. The Patriarchs had long been dead. The freedom, status and prosperity they had once known while Joseph was called *"Zaphenath-paneah"*, the Grand Vizier to Pharaoh, the second most powerful man in all of Egypt they had not experienced. Joseph had been the man who wore the signet ring of Pharaoh and it was hailed before him *"Abrech"* as he rode in the *"second chariot"* behind Pharaoh. No one was as powerful or mighty as was Joseph nor did *"no man lift up his hand or his foot in all the land of Egypt"* without Joseph's approval. This same Joseph who had been given Asenath, daughter of Potiphera priest of On as his wife was now all but just a distant memory. Now, YHWH would establish HIMSELF as Israel's GOD.

Israel went from being in a very high place of status and influence, to being as about as far away and as opposite as they could possibly be. Now, YHWH was reclaiming what was HIS. Moses would be used to do this, but it was YHWH'S show. And it was YHWH who was establishing HIMSELF as Israel's *"Savior"*. And even more so, when it was all over and the dust had settled, Israel would *"know"* that YHWH was their GOD and their *"Savior"*.

Exodus 3:10, (10) Come now therefore, and I will send thee unto Pharaoh, that thou mayest bring forth My people the sons of Israel out of Egypt.'

Isaiah 43:3, (3) For I am YHWH thy God, The Holy One of Israel, thy Saviour; I have given Egypt as thy ransom, Ethiopia and Seba for thee.

In freeing Israel from bondage and bringing Israel to the land which HE had promised, YHWH was not only establishing HIMSELF as Israel's *"Savior"* but also HE established HIMSELF, *"YHWH"* as their GOD, Israel as HIS people, and fulfilled HIS Covenant promise to Abraham. It is in this light why Moses was not referred to as *"Savior"* when so many others were later.

Before the first time that Moses and Aaron appeared before YHWH, they were instructed what to say to Pharaoh. This is very critical for understanding the relationship between GOD and Israel.

Exodus 4:22-23, (22) And thou shalt say unto Pharaoh: <u>Thus saith YHWH: Israel is My Son, My First-Born</u>. (23) And I have said unto thee: <u>Let My Son go, that he may serve Me</u>; and thou hast refused to let him go. Behold, I will slay thy son, thy first-born.' --

FATHER AND SON

YHWH GOD of Israel is Father of Israel, and Israel is HIS first born son.

'THAT HE MAY BE UNTO THEE A GOD'

Deuteronomy 29:12, (12) <u>that He may establish thee this day</u> unto Himself for a People, <u>and that He may be unto thee a God</u>, as He spoke unto thee, and as He swore unto thy fathers, to Abraham, to Isaac, and to Jacob.

'I WILL TAKE YOU TO ME FOR A PEOPLE'

Exodus 6:5-8, (5) And moreover I have heard the groaning of the sons of Israel, whom the Egyptians keep in bondage; and <u>I have remembered My Covenant.</u> (6) Wherefore say unto the Sons of Israel: <u>I am YHWH</u>, and I will bring you out from under the burdens of the Egyptians, and <u>I will Deliver you</u> from their bondage, and <u>I will REDEEM you</u> with an outstretched arm, and with great judgments; (7) <u>and I will take you to Me for a People, and I will be to you a God; and ye shall know that I am YHWH your God, who brought you out from under the burdens of the Egyptians</u>. (8) And I will bring you in unto the land, concerning which I lifted up My hand to give it to Abraham, to Isaac, and to Jacob; and <u>I will give it you</u> for a heritage: <u>I am YHWH</u>.'

'I WILL BE TO YOU A GOD'

As GOD'S first born son, Israel is being "*redeemed*" by his Father YHWH. It is this *redemption* from Egypt by YHWH that Israel is reminded of by their Father YHWH who has established HIMSELF as Israel's GOD in Exodus.

Exodus 13:13-15, (13) And every firstling of an ass thou shalt <u>redeem</u> with a lamb; and if thou wilt not redeem it, then thou shalt break its neck; <u>and all the first-born of man among Thy Sons shalt thou redeem</u>. (14) And it shall be when Thy Son asketh thee in time to come, saying: What is this? that thou shalt say unto him: By strength of hand YHWH brought us out from Egypt, from the house of bondage; (15) and it came to pass, when Pharaoh would hardly let us go that YHWH slew all the firstborn in the land of Egypt, both the first-born of man, and the first-born of beast; therefore I sacrifice to YHWH all that openeth the womb, being males; <u>but all the First-Born of My Sons I redeem.</u>

YHWH *ransomed* Israel to be a people for HIMSELF. Israel is GOD'S *redeemed,* HIS *treasured possession* forever. Israel is GOD'S *first born son*.

Jeremiah 31:11, (11) For YHWH hath <u>ransomed</u> Jacob, and He <u>redeemeth</u> him from the hand of him that is stronger than he.

As a Shepherd who loves HIS flock, YHWH leads HIS redeemed of Israel to HIS holy abode with HIS might. HE led them to HIS holy land.

Exodus 15:13, (13) Thou in Thy love hast led <u>the people that Thou hast redeemed</u>; Thou hast guided them in Thy strength to Thy <u>holy habitation.</u>

The rest of the story of the Exodus need not be told, for there is too much else regarding *"Savior"* which needs to be discussed. The point being made here is that Moses is often thought of as the greatest of GOD'S Prophets, yet as *"savior"* he is not. The idea of *"deliverance"* and being *"saved"* is for Israel's GOD *"YHWH"*. Moses was a devoted servant and Prophet of GOD, but he was not their *"savior"*. For it was freeing Israel from bondage in Egypt which YHWH used to establish HIMSELF as both Israel's GOD *"YHWH"*, and as their *"Savior"*. YHWH *delivered* Israel and *redeemed* them to HIMSELF.

Exodus 13:1-3, (1) And YHWH spoke unto Moses, saying: (2) 'Sanctify unto Me all the First-Born, whatsoever openeth the womb among the Sons of Israel, both of man and of beast, it is Mine.' (3) And Moses said unto the people: '<u>Remember this day</u>, in which ye came out from Egypt, out of the house of bondage; <u>for by strength of hand YHWH brought you out from this place</u>; there shall no leavened bread be eaten.

Long before Moses was born, YHWH had made a Covenant With Abraham's SEED. It was this Covenant which YHWH remembered when HE heard Abraham's SEED cry while as slaves in Egypt. HE heard Israel *"groan"*.

In freeing Israel, YHWH *established* HIMSELF as their GOD forever and as their eternal *"Savior"*. Moses was many things, but he was not to be Israel's *"savior"*. As servant and Prophet of the most HIGH GOD, Moses fulfilled his task to YHWH his King. From the Exodus of Israel from Egypt until today, YHWH the God of Israel established HIMSELF to not only Israel, but to the world as Israel's GOD and Savior. Many may have forgotten, but it want last.

Exodus 10:2, (2) and <u>that thou mayest tell</u> in the ears of Thy Son, and of Thy Son's Son, <u>what I have wrought upon Egypt</u>, and My signs which I have done among them; <u>that ye may know that I am YHWH.</u>'

SAVIORS - JUDGES – PROPHETS

After Joshua led Israel and conquered the *"Promised Land"*, the tribes settled down into each of their allotted inheritance and began to live on the land. YHWH their GOD was their *"King"* as they had no earthly king yet. Israel was to have many ups and downs. While they were being good and keeping GOD'S Commandments all was fine, but when they were bad and not keeping GOD'S Commandments YHWH would allow their neighbors to hold authority over them, kill them, enslave them, tax them and generally make their lives miserable. Each time, Israel would *"groan"* as when in Egypt.

Israel would *"cry"* to YHWH and YHWH would hear their *"cry"*. YHWH would then send to them *a "savior"*. *"A"* *"savior"* would be someone of one of the tribes in whom YHWH would put HIS spirit and who would save them. All would be well for a while until they went back to their old ways and once again YHWH would allow their neighbors to bully and abuse them. They would cry again to

YHWH and YHWH again would hear their cry and send to them *a "savior"*. This repeated itself for several hundred years. Over time, the idea of *a "savior"* was established in the mind of Israel.

SAVIOR

In Hebrew the root letters for *"savior"* is *"Yood-Shin-Ayin"*, and generally has the sense of *"deliver, rescue, salvation, safety* or *welfare"*. It is from this root that the Hebrew name of Jesus derives, *Yeshuah* meaning *"salvation"*.

In the Book of Judges, there are many *"saviors"*. Often they are referred to also as *"Judges"* or as *"Prophets"*, nevertheless they were *"saviors"* called upon to *"save"* Israel. The *"saviors"*, accomplished the tasks of that office more or less the same by delivering Israel from their oppressor, such as Samson from the Philistines or Gideon from the Midianites. They brought Israel back from under the yoke of who ever was abusing them and gave them peace. This *"peace"* usually lasted the equivalent of one generation until all was forgotten and the cycle repeated itself again. Some of Israel's *"saviors"* are listed below.

Judges 3:9, (9) And when the sons of Israel cried unto YHWH, YHWH raised up <u>a saviour</u> to the sons of Israel, who saved them, even <u>Othniel</u> the son of Kenaz, Caleb's younger brother.

Judges 3:15, (15) But when the sons of Israel cried unto YHWH, YHWH raised them up <u>a saviour</u>, <u>Ehud</u> the son of Gera, the Benjamite, ….

Judges 3:31, (31) And after him was <u>Shamgar</u> the son of Anath, who smote of the Philistines six hundred men with an ox-goad; and he also <u>saved Israel</u>.

Judges 4:4, (4) Now Deborah, a prophetess, the wife of Lappidoth, she <u>judged Israel</u> at that time.

Judges 6:11-12, (11) And the angel of YHWH came, and sat under the terebinth which was in Ophrah, that belonged unto Joash the Abiezrite; and his son <u>Gideon</u> was beating out wheat in the winepress, to hide it from the Midianites. (12) And the angel of YHWH appeared unto him, and said unto him: '<u>YHWH is with thee, thou mighty man of valour.</u>'

Judges 10:1, (1) And after Abimelech there arose to <u>save Israel Tola</u> the son of Puah, the son of Dodo,
Judges 10:3, (3) And after him arose <u>Jair</u>, the Gileadite; and he <u>judged Israel</u> twenty and two years.

Judges 12:7, (7) And <u>Jephthah judged Israel</u> six years.

Judges 12:8, (8) And after him <u>Ibzan</u> of Beth-lehem <u>judged Israel</u>.

Judges 12:11, (11) And after him <u>Elon</u> the Zebulunite <u>judged Israel</u>;

Judges 12:13, (13) And after him <u>Abdon</u> the son of Hillel the Pirathonite <u>judged Israel</u>.

Judges 13:24, (24) And the woman bore a son, and called his name <u>Samson</u>; and the child grew, and YHWH blessed him. ……..Judges 15:20, (20) And he <u>judged Israel</u> in the days of the Philistines *twenty years.*

Of these, perhaps Samson and Gideon are the two most famous of Israel's many *"saviors"*. So a *"savior"* could be a person who saved Israel from their enemy in times of oppression. As mentioned, the reader may be thinking that Moses surely met this criteria. This is true, but YHWH had as yet not established HIMSELF in the eyes of Israel as their *"savior"* and *"deliverer"* as their GOD their Father. This first had to be done, and YHWH used Moses to do it. Yet the situation after Israel had received the Law of Moses and lived with YHWH for 40 years in the desert as their GOD, and then going in to possess the land, the situation was considerably different. These *judges / saviors*, "saved", but they were not *the "Savior"*. For this was "**YHWH**".

So, as these stories indicate, a person can be a *"savior"* without being *"anointed"*. Yet, there is one curious example which shall be discussed where a person is called *"anointed"*, acts as a *"savior"* in a very significant way, yet fought no one nor is there any indication that he was ever actually *"anointed"* in any way, nor is he of Israel or ever set foot in Israel.

In general, the *"task"* of the *"savior"* is the *"deliverance"* of the people.

'ANOINTED'

The Hebrew root for *"anointed"* is *"Mem-Shin-Chet"* generally having the meaning of to *"smear, anoint,* or *consecrate"*. This word *"anointed"* is normally used to designate either the King or the High Priest who has had the *"holy oil"* poured on their head. When a noun it is the person himself, such as King David being *"the anointed"* or the High Priest Aaron. Or if a verb, it is the act of *"anointing"* or pouring of the oil.

The King or the High Priest to be, would have the *"holy oil"* poured upon their head as the official act of *"anointing"* (being anointed). For the King, it was often the Prophet of YHWH such as when the Prophet Samuel anointed both Saul and later David. Or when Moses anointed Aaron as High Priest.

'HE IS MY SHEPHERD'

In the Book of Isaiah there is an interesting scripture relating to the story of the Jews returning to Israel to rebuild the Temple of YHWH. The Persian King Cyrus had defeated the Babylonians. GOD used him to allow those exiled to return and to rebuild the Temple, even supplying funds and other services to expedite accomplishing the task.

It is odd because in all of the TaNaKh, no other leader, no matter how kind he was to Israel, was ever called *"MY shepherd"* or *"HIS anointed"*. For even the Pharaoh of Egypt whom Jacob blessed, and who had made Joseph second in all of the land only to himself, did not have such words by GOD called on him. And it was this same Pharaoh who by his actions saved Jacob and his family from famine and allowed them to live in the choice part of Egypt in Goshen, *"in the best of the land"*. By all accounts this Pharaoh was a great king and a *"mensch"* allowing all of his servants, the elders of his own house including all of the elders of Egypt to accompany Joseph and his fathers house as they returned to Canaan to bury Jacob. Yet, this Pharaoh who is never identified, who was so instrumental in the salvation of the 70 souls of Jacob during the famine, was not so honored. Nor did Hiram King of Tyre, friend of both David and Solomon have such praise from YHWH.

It is this author's personal belief that it is because of the reason for the remnant of Israel's return, for the reason that such honor was bestowed upon Cyrus. For Cyrus was not allowing the Jewish exiles to return to reestablish *"Israel"*. He was sending them back to Israel to rebuild the Temple of YHWH which YHWH had put in his heart to do. For it is the Temple of YHWH in Jerusalem, the place where the name of YHWH is called was the reason for their return. The time of their exile was finished. They must return and they must rebuild GOD'S Temple. It would be up to Cyrus King of Persia to see that this was done. Cyrus is often referred to as *"Cyrus the Great"*.

In this capacity, Cyrus acts as a *"shepherd"* and is called *"My Shepherd"* gathering up GOD'S *"elect"* to return to Israel to the fifth Persian province (satrap) called *"Beyond the River"*, *"Abar Nahara"* (phonetically written many different ways) which included as one of it's lands, *"Yehud"* (Judah).

Isaiah 44:28, (28) That saith of Cyrus: 'He is My Shepherd, and shall perform all My pleasure'; even saying of Jerusalem: 'She shall be built'; and to the Temple: 'My foundation shall be laid.'

Isaiah 45:1-5, (1) Thus saith YHWH to His Anointed, to Cyrus, whose right hand I have holden, to subdue nations before him, and to loose the loins of kings; to open the doors before him, and that the gates may not be shut: (2) I will go before thee, and make the crooked places straight; I will break in pieces the doors of brass, and cut in sunder the bars of iron; (3) And I will give thee the treasures of darkness, and hidden riches of secret places, that thou mayest know that I am YHWH, who call thee by thy name, even the God of Israel. (4) For the sake of Jacob My servant, and Israel Mine elect, I have called thee by thy name, I have surnamed thee, though thou hast not known Me. (5) I am YHWH, and there is none else, beside Me there is no God; I have girded thee, though thou hast not known Me;

The return and the rebuilding of the Temple of YHWH was a long drawn out affair. It began with King Cyrus but was continued by Cambyses II, Darius I (Darius the Great), Artaxerxes I through Artaxerxes II. According to scripture, the Second Temple was completed during the reign of Darius II.

Ezra 6:14-16, (14) And the elders of the Jews builded and prospered, through the prophesying of Haggai the prophet and Zechariah the son of Iddo. And they builded and finished it, according to the commandment of the God of Israel, and according to the decree of Cyrus, and Darius, and Artaxerxes king of Persia. (15) And this house was finished on the third day of the month Adar, which was in the sixth year of the reign of Darius the king. (16) And the sons of Israel, the priests and the Levites, and the rest of the children of the captivity, kept the dedication of this house of God with joy.

"Darius the King" referred to by Ezra must refer to Darius II (423-404) son of Artaxerxes by Cosmartidene of Babylon. He was succeeded by Artaxerxes II. The undertaking would have taken many years, so it is not unreasonable to think that it took the better part of 100 years to complete under several kings.

ANOINT - CHRIST - MESSIAH - SALVATION

"Christ" is Greek for *"anointed one"*. So *"Christ"* and *"anointed"* are saying basically the same thing. This would be true with *"messiah"* as well as *"messiah"* means *"anointed"* in Hebrew (*"mesiach"* literally *"anointed one")*. *"Jesus"* means *"salvation"* in Hebrew from a different unrelated root stem.

But anointed can mean several things, not the least of which someone has been *consecrated* to be something or to perform a specific task such as Cyrus.

But this can be for the king to perform the "*task*" of kingship, or the Priest perform the tasks associated with his priestly office. King David often makes mention of his being *"anointed"*. For Cyrus, being called "*HIS Anointed*" seemed to have been more of a title bestowed upon him by GOD YHWH. In this respect, it has the sense of having been "*chosen*" for a special purpose.

Psalms 132: 10,(10) For Thy servant David's sake turn not away the face of Thine Anointed.

The Prophet Isaiah was "*anointed*" to perform just such a task as Prophet of the living GOD.

Isaiah 61:1, (1) The spirit of the Lord YHWH is upon me; <u>because YHWH hath Anointed me to bring good tidings unto the humble</u>; He hath sent me to bind up the broken-hearted, to proclaim liberty to the captives, and the opening of the eyes to them that are bound;

Yet there is another use of the term as with Israel who are GOD'S anointed.

Habakkuk 3:13, (13) Thou art come forth for the deliverance of <u>Thy people</u>, for the deliverance of <u>Thine Anointed</u>;

Psalms 84:9-10, (9) O YHWH God of hosts, hear my prayer; give ear, O God of Jacob. Selah (10) Behold, <u>O God our shield, and look upon the face of Thine Anointed</u>.

The Prophet Habakkuk is speaking about Israel as GOD'S anointed people whom HE is delivering. In the Hebrew scriptures there are several hints of the Prophet who will come before "*YHWH*". Many interpret this as meaning the "*messiah*", son of David. Although that is more an assumption than a prophesy. There is absolutely no doubt but that the SEED of David will sit on the throne of Israel and rule in peace, justice and righteousness. But YHWH is Savior.

Malachi 3:22-24, (22) Remember ye the law of Moses My servant, which I commanded unto him in Horeb for all Israel, even statutes and ordinances. (23) <u>Behold, I will send you Elijah the prophet before the coming of the great and terrible day of YHWH</u>. (24) And he shall turn the heart of the fathers to the children, and the heart of the children to their fathers; lest I come and smite the land with utter destruction.

If one reads carefully, the Prophet Elijah will come before "*YHWH*".

"*Anointed*" can be used in a symbolic way as an allegory for Israel by GOD.

Ezekiel 16:9, (9) Then washed I thee with water; yea, I cleansed away thy blood from thee, and <u>I Anointed thee with oil</u>.

Psalms 105:15, (15) 'Touch not <u>Mine Anointed ones</u>, and do My prophets no harm.'

The Prophet Zechariah speaks of two "*anointed*" ones who stand on each side of the Lord of all the earth as the angel explains what he was seeing.

Zechariah 4:13-14, (13) And he answered me and said: 'Knowest thou not what these are?' And I said: 'No, my lord.' (14) Then said he: '<u>These are the two Anointed ones</u>, that stand by the Lord of the whole earth.'

King David speaks of, or refers to his own anointing often.

Psalms 2:2, (2) The kings of the earth stand up, and the rulers take counsel together, against YHWH, and against His Anointed:

Psalms 18:51, (51) Great salvation giveth He to His king; and showeth mercy to His Anointed, to David and to his SEED, for evermore.

Psalms 20:7 (7) Now know I that YHWH saveth His Anointed; He will answer him from His holy heaven with the mighty acts of His saving right hand.

Psalms 92:11, (11) But my horn hast Thou exalted like the horn of the wild-ox; I am Anointed with rich oil.

Psalms 132:10, 17, (10) For Thy servant David's sake turn not away the face of Thine Anointed. (11) YHWH swore unto David in truth; He will not turn back from it: 'Of the fruit of thy body will I set upon thy throne.......(17) There will I make a horn to shoot up unto David, there have I ordered a lamp for Mine Anointed.

And perhaps the most famous of all of David's Psalms which also speaks of being anointed is *"the 23rd Psalm"*.

Psalms 23:5, 5) Thou preparest a table before me in the presence of mine enemies; Thou hast Anointed my head with oil; my cup runneth over.

King David speaks not only of his anointing as *"King"* but as a metaphor for GOD'S blessings toward him, *"my cup runneth over"*, but also Israel.

Psalms 28:8-9, (8) YHWH is a strength unto them; and He is a stronghold of salvation to His Anointed. (9) Save Thy People, and bless Thine Inheritance; and tend them, and carry them for ever.

Many Psalms were written by Levites and Priests, Asaph, the sons of Korah, Ethan the Ezrahite and King Solomon. These were written about David, the anointed King of GOD. There was never a greater King upon this earth.

Psalms 45:8, (8) Thou hast loved righteousness, and hated wickedness; therefore God, thy God, hath Anointed thee with the oil of gladness above thy fellows.

Psalms 84:10, (10) Behold, O God our shield, and look upon the face of Thine Anointed.

Psalms 89:21. (21) I have found David My servant; with My holy oil have I Anointed him;

The Prophet Daniel too speaks of an anointed prince and other words of prophesy, but not of Israel.

The idea here is that the word *"anointed"* itself can and does have more than one meaning. In as far a an *"anointed"* one coming to save Israel, there is no specific scripture. Only if one takes the anointing of David and extrapolate can one arrive at this conclusion from scripture. There are many allusions to his SEED, a *"shoot"* etc. So what does the Hebrew Bible say about David's SEED? Similarly, the

Prophet Ezekiel mentions a *"horn to shoot"* up unto the house of Israel (Ezekiel 29:21).

Beginning with Isaiah 9:5-6 scriptures speak of a child being born who will sit upon the throne of David. This would have to be David's SEED. Again in Isaiah 11:1-5 it speaks of the the SEED of Jesse being born with the spirit of YHWH, who will be wise and judge with righteousness. He will smite the land and will stand as a banner, a leader for the people. The nations shall seek him and his resting place will be *"glorious"*. The dispersed of Judah *and of* Israel will be gathered.

The Prophet Jeremiah writes of the SEED of David who shall reign as King (Jeremiah 23:5-6) very similar to Isaiah 11:1-5. In 30:9, 21-22 Jeremiah talks of King *"David"* being raised up, Israel's prince who will be their ruler. Again in 33:14-26 Jeremiah writes of the *"shoot of righteousness"* to grow up unto David. Judah will be saved, Jerusalem will be safe, *"For thus saith YHWH: There shall not be cut off unto David a man to sit upon the throne of the house of Israel; neither shall there be cut off unto the priests the Levites a man before Me to offer burnt-offerings, and to burn meal-offerings, and to do sacrifice continually* (Jeremiah 33:17-18). Jeremiah is saying that neither the kings from David's SEED nor the Levites who offer sacrifice will cease.

The Prophet Ezekiel likewise writes of King David being shepherd and prince over Israel (34:23-31). Also, in 37:21-28 the Prophet writes of YHWH gathering Israel and bringing them back to *"their own land"*. Israel will be one nation with one king, *"and MY servant David shall be king over them"*. Here too it speaks of *"for ever"* regarding Israel living in their land for ever in peace and also, **"walk in MINE Ordinances, and observe MY Statutes, and do them"**.

One of the things all of these references to either David or his SEED have in common, is that none of these things have occurred yet. Additionally, none of these references state that David or his SEED is the "meshiach". It is *assumed* to be the case. David or his SEED will reign in *righteousness*, bring *justice* and *peace* to Israel according to the prophets. This has yet to happen. The future regarding the Law, according to all available prophesy, Statutes and Ordinances *will be observed and kept*. According to Ezekiel, it includes the offering of sacrifice. **The Law of sacrificial offering for sin is not dead**.

YHWH said HE would set HIS sanctuary (*"mishkan"*) *"in the midst of them for ever"*. GOD goes on to say that his dwelling place shall be over them and he will be their GOD and they shall be *"MY people"*.

Ezekiel 37:28, (28) And the nations shall know that I am YHWH that sanctify Israel, when My sanctuary shall be in the midst of them for ever.'

Ezekiel 34:23-31, (23) And I will set up one shepherd over them, and he shall feed them, even My servant David; he shall feed them, and he shall be their shepherd. (24) And I YHWH will be their God, and My servant David prince among them; I YHWH have spoken.

In the vision of Ezekiel, there is much said concerning the *"prince"* of YHWH, sacrifice and YHWH'S court. Ezekiel chapters 44-46 speak much of him. Chapter 48 gives the borders of his inheritance.

Psalms 46:11-12, (11) 'Let be, and know that I am God; I will be exalted among the nations, I will be exalted in the earth.' (12) YHWH of hosts is with us; the God of Jacob is our high tower. Selah

It is **YHWH** who will be exalted among the nations, not the name of *"Jesus"*.

So we have much written regarding a future King, the prince of GOD who will one day reign. BUT, is he one and the same as the *"messiah"*? It does not say? YHWH has some very clear things to say regarding this topic. Some have been quoted. But by all appearances, ***the*** *"messiah"* and King David and his SEED do not appear to be one and the same thing. It is possible that they are, but according to scripture, they appear to be two very separate phenomena. It appears that GOD will make ready the throne of David so he can rule. In the end, it really does not matter whether the *messiah* and King David or his SEED are one and the same. For it is the end result which will matter. And it will be glorious. *"I, even I, am YHWH; and beside Me there is no saviour"* (Isaiah 43:11).

EPILOGUE

In discussing the Gospels, we began with the history of Israel leading up to the time of Jesus. In doing so, beginning with Abraham and the Patriarchs, through Israel as slaves in Egypt, the desert wandering and receiving the Law, the conquering of the Land of Canaan, period of Judges and the two Temples of YHWH and Israel's exiles were briefly gone over.

For as has been stated more than once, Jesus did not live in a vacuum. He did not suddenly appear out of no where and for no reason. For according to the Gospels, all things which preceded him were prerequisites for his coming. And it is for this reason that observing the early history of *"the people"* that YHWH has called *"Mine"* is imperative. If the Jewish people were to all suddenly become as Christians, they would be indistinguishable from Gentiles, which is the opposite from who and what Israel is to GOD as HIS holy portion, HIS own inheritance.

Leviticus 20:26, (26) <u>And ye shall be holy unto Me</u>; for I YHWH am holy, and have <u>set you apart</u> from the peoples, <u>that ye should be Mine.</u>

To better understand the world in which Jesus existed during the period he preached, the political, social, cultural and religious world of Jesus lived was looked at. That Israel *"shall be holy"* is an undercurrent in the Gospels. Or perhaps put a different way, it was the *"elephant in the living room"*.

Some of the Laws which the Priests and Pharisees brought up to Jesus were analyzed and assessed from the Law of Moses. A comparison of his words and actions was made against the Law as well as the Prophets. For it was these very Laws which were the issue concerning Jesus. For whether or not Jesus was the awaited *"messiah"* or not hinged on these Laws. It was the understanding or misunderstanding, the application or misapplication and the interpretation or misinterpretation of Law by the Priests which determined his fate according to the Gospels. For it was by the Law of Moses that the Priests determined that Jesus had committed a sin against YHWH which was punishable by death. Jesus was accused of *"blasphemy"* (John 11:47-53).

This is an extremely telling scripture. For not only does the High Priest prophesy that Jesus should die for the Kingdom of Israel but for the *"children of GOD"* who were *scattered* abroad.

This author has maintained all along that Jesus came for scattered Israel as he said himself, the *"lost sheep of the House of Israel"* was his purpose for his coming according to the Gospels. This included all the *"children of GOD"*.

John 11:47-52, *(47) Then gathered the chief priests and the Pharisees a council, and said, What do we? for this man doeth many miracles. (48) If we let him thus alone, all men will believe on him: and the Romans shall come and take away both our place and nation. (49) And one of them, named Caiaphas, being the high priest that same year, said unto them, Ye know nothing at all, (50) Nor consider that it is expedient for us, that one man should die for the people, and that the whole nation perish not.(51) And this spake he not of himself: but being high priest that year, he prophesied that Jesus should die for that nation; (52) And not for that nation only, but that also he should gather together in one the Children of God that were scattered abroad.*

The whole *"nation"* refers to the Jews of Israel which existed when the High Priest spoke these words. The *"children of GOD"* are Israel, wherever they are located. Wherever the SEED of Jacob is scattered, they are the focus of the words of Jesus to be found, and they are the words of prophesy from the High Priest Caiaphas. *"Israel"* was scattered all over the Mediterranean area and beyond. These words of the High Priest and those of Jesus agree. Additional, they are both in agreement with all of the Hebrew Bible which refers to Israel as YHWH'S elect, anointed, sheep, flock, betrothed, treasured, loved and chosen people. Caiaphas's prophesy is of Judah and of scattered Israel. It is not referring to the Nations or to Gentiles but to the SEED of Jacob only.

When GOD was angry with Israel, HE would disassociate HIMSELF from them. Yet, when HE later would repent and would remember HIS love for Israel, HE would remind HIMSELF of HIS own affection.

Hosea 2:1, *(1) Yet the number of the Sons of Israel shall be as the sand of the sea, which cannot be measured nor numbered; and it shall come to pass that, instead of that which was said unto them: 'Ye are not My people', it shall be said unto them: 'Ye are the Sons of the living God.'*

" Thus saith YHWH: Israel is My son, My first-born". Israel, is YHWH GOD'S first born son. *"O fear YHWH, ye His holy ones"* (Psalm 34:10).

During the time of Jesus, there were many Jews and many of *"Israel"* scattered amongst the nations of the former Assyrian and Persian Empires. But especially those provinces of the Roman Empire, but not just the Roman Empire but of the former Greek cities and settlements which existed before them throughout the Mediterranean like the substantial Jewish population of Alexandria, and throughout Asia Minor in the various ancient Greek city states. These *"lost sheep of the House of Israel"* were both free and slave. Additionally, much of the SEED of Israel from the earlier exiles of both the Kingdoms of Israel and of Judah still existed in various stages of being *"lost"*.

Hosea 9:17, *(17) My God will cast them away, because they did not hearken unto Him; and they shall be wanderers among the nations.*

According to the Gospels, the High Priest Caiaphas was prophesying that Jesus would die for the people that the entire *"nation"* not perish. That nation is *"Israel"*. At the time Caiaphas uttered these words, the Jewish people lived in the Kingdom of Israel which had been reestablished during the time of the Maccabees after having defeated the Greeks. The people of that nation are the circumcised male SEED descendants of Abraham through his grandson Jacob, who are collectively called *"Israel"*. The *"children of GOD"* are the descendants of the blessed SEED of Jacob, wherever they were *"scattered abroad"* upon the earth, and in the *"nations"* they were living in. It would be to these nations which

Jesus would send his disciples to preach to scattered *"lost sheep of the House of Israel"*. Jesus did not send his disciples to preach <u>*to*</u> the nations, but ***in*** the nations, ***to*** the *"lost sheep of the House of Israel"*.

This bears repeating. Jesus did not send his disciples to preach <u>*to*</u> the nations, but *"**in**"* the nations, *"**to**"* the lost sheep of Israel, according to the Gospels.

Matthew 10:5-7, (5)These twelve Jesus sent forth, and commanded them, saying, <u>Go not</u> into the way of the <u>Gentiles</u>, and into any city of the <u>Samaritans</u> enter ye <u>not</u>: (6) But go rather to the Lost Sheep of the House of Israel. (7) And as ye go, preach, saying, The kingdom of heaven is at hand.

The overwhelming majority of all of the words of Jesus throughout all four Gospels agree with this scripture and others like it. The one or two scriptures which appear to not agree, are at variance with the majority of all of his words regarding Israel and keeping the Law and do not fit with his teaching. Nor do they agree with the prophesy of Caiaphas or Israel as GOD'S elect.

Of note, in Hebrew what is translated here as *"House"* also means *"sons"* (Bnei Israel/Sons of Jacob). Also, it is interesting to note, that although Jesus told his disciples ***not*** to go *"into any city of the Samaritans"*, they were told to go into the nations to preach to the lost sheep of the House of Israel.

Matthew 24:14 (14) And this gospel of the kingdom shall be <u>preached in all the world for a witness unto all nations</u>; and then shall the end come.

Luke 24:47, (47) And that repentance and remission of sins should be preached in his name <u>among all nations</u>, beginning at Jerusalem.

The point of *"to"* the nations verses to the *lost sheep of Israel* *"in"* the nations has already been made. How one wishes to square some of these other scriptures with what Jesus appeared to be saying, must be made on an individual basis. It is this author's own belief however, that his words were meant for Israel, wherever they were scattered and only later did the Gentile leaders of the new <u>*religion*</u> adopt a different meaning to include the <u>*nations*</u>.

Having said this, his words have had a profound impact on the rest of the world and it is also this author's contention that this was meant to be. The exposure to the world of the words of not only Jesus but of all of the Hebrew Prophets, the Law of Moses and the Writings is no accident. The number one selling book in the world for many, many, years has been and remains the Hebrew and the Christian Bibles together. Exactly what it means one can only guess, but aside from a few Crusades, Pogroms, Inquisitions and other unhealthy experiences for the Jewish people it has had an overall positive civilizing affect on a third of the earth's population (if compared to their previous lifestyle), the consequences of which can be measured. As has been hinted at by this author, it has the fingerprints of GOD upon it. For whatever HIS plan is, there appears to be a connection between the Jewish people and the Gentile believers in Jesus. It remains to be seen what that connection is.

<u>TO</u> *THE NATIONS VS* <u>IN</u> *THE NATIONS*

In Matthew 28:19; Mark 16:15; Luke 24:47 the disciples are being told where to go and what to do. Again, it is this authors contention that they were being instructed to go to all of the nations wherever the *"lost sheep of the House of Israel"* were located and to preach to them. Anything which contradicts this is either a misquote, misunderstanding or a fabrication. Only Matthew appears to contradict the earlier statement of Jesus to avoid the Gentiles, and only Matthew adds the *"Father, Son, Holy Ghost"* idea which does not exist in the other Gospels or anywhere else. It is interesting to note as well that in Matthew 28:20 the last words of Jesus said *"Teaching them to observe all things whatsoever I have <u>commanded</u> you: and, lo, I am with you alway, even unto the end of the world. Amen. "*

What did Jesus *"command"*? Jesus said to *"keep the Commandments"*. Who was given the Commandments to *"keep"*? This can only refer to *"Israel",* the circumcised male SEED descendants of Jacob who had been given the Law.

Jesus, by his own words, instructed his disciples NOT to go to the Gentiles, but to go and preach to the *"lost sheep of the House of Israel"*. The lost sheep of the House of Israel were scattered amongst the nations. The words of Jesus are in agreement with his words spoken when he himself was far from his own people in Tyre and Sidon, which is in Lebanon. The immediate response to a Canaanite woman was anything but cordial. Jesus also appears to have been preaching *"beyond"* the Jordan as well, to the east of Israel.

Matthew 15:24, (24) But he answered and said, I am not sent <u>but</u> unto the <u>Lost Sheep of the House of Israel.</u>

So if anything, Jesus by his own example, appeared to have been preaching far afield from Israel itself. Jesus told his disciples not to go into any city of the Samaritans, yet the Gospels indicate that he went himself *"Then saith the woman of Samaria unto him, How is it that thou, being a Jew, askest drink of me, which am a woman of Samaria? for the Jews have no dealings with the Samaritans"* (John 4:9).

Later in Matthew 28:19 a similar statement is uttered. The King James translates this as *"teach all nations"* which contradicts the words of Jesus while speaking to the Canaanite woman, and the words of Jesus when instructing his own disciples, and the prophesy of the High Priest Caiaphas.

Matthew 28:19, (19) Go ye therefore, and teach all nations, baptizing them in the name of the Father, and of the Son, and of the Holy Ghost:

The idea of *<u>baptizing</u> "in the name of the **Father**, and the **son**, and the **Holy Ghost"*** is new. It is unprecedented in all of Hebrew scripture. The *"mikva"*, from where the idea of *"baptisim"* originated, was well known and was used during ritual purification. However, if these words really are those of Jesus, it was suggesting something completely alien from the Law of Moses.

Whereas a missing *"in"* or *"to"* can make all of the difference in the world when trying to understand a copy of an original which no longer exists, such as we have here, it falls to the reader to make sense of what was being said.

Given the very clear earlier messages of Jesus already cited, this reader understands this scripture to mean the same. For his disciples were being instructed to teach *<u>in</u>* all of the nations, *<u>not to</u>* all of the nations, only to Israel.

There is yet one more scripture which appears to be more in agreement with those scriptures regarding preaching to the *"lost sheep of the House of Israel"*. In Mark, the disciples are instructed to *"publish"* among all nation. Well if they were to find the *"lost sheep of the House of Israel"*, preaching amongst all of the nations would be necessary and would be in sync with finding those of Israel who were *"lost"* or *scattered* throughout the earth.

Mark 13:10, (10) And the gospel must first be published among all nations.

At the time that the High Priest prophesied (John 11:47-52), Jesus was still very much alive. There were no other peoples associated with YHWH GOD. The Samaritans were no longer considered *"Israel"* by the Jews, although their animosity aside, this is GOD'S call not the Jews. There were no Christians. The High Priest is speaking only about *"Israel",* for Israel is the people of YHWH, the *"sons"* of GOD, and the SEED of YHWH that was blessed. The most important line of this scene of the chief priests and Pharisees is verse 52, *"And not for that nation only, but that also he should gather together in one **the children of God** that were scattered abroad".*

These words could in no way refer to the nations / Gentiles as they were not the *"lost"*, nor the *"scattered"* abroad and they were not the *"children of GOD"*. From the perspective of the speaker, *"abroad"* would be outside of Israel, as in Israel, the Children of GOD who were scattered abroad, outside their own holy land.

Deuteronomy 4:20, (20) But you hath YHWH taken and brought forth out of the iron furnace, out of Egypt, to be unto Him a People of Inheritance, as ye are this day.

Deuteronomy 7:6, (6) For thou art a Holy People unto YHWH thy God: YHWH thy God hath Chosen thee to be His own Treasure, out of all peoples that are upon the face of the earth.

According to the *"prophesy"* by the High Priest Caiaphas, Jesus was to die for the *"lost sheep of the House of Israel"*. As he said himself. It was not only for the Jews of his kingdom of Israel where he lived *"the nation"*, but for those scattered SEED of Israel wherever they were. High Priest Caiaphas and the words of Jesus regarding his death, were in perfect harmony.

Jeremiah 31:10, (10) Hear the word of YHWH, O ye nations, and declare it in the isles afar off, and say: 'He that scattered Israel doth gather him, and keep him, as a shepherd doth his flock.'

The only way in which the words attributed to Jesus could be directed at *"Gentiles"*, would be for Gentiles to be of the SEED of both *"Jews"* and *"Israel"* of the blessed SEED of Abraham through his grandson Jacob. Which they are not. Jesus was a Jew, living in a Jewish kingdom called Israel, preaching to Jews about salvation of Israel from their GOD, the GOD of Israel, *"HIS people"*.

Another thing, the people referenced were not people who had yet been preached to by Jesus or his disciples. They were a people who were *already* the *"children of GOD"*.

GOD had been *"scattering"* his people for many centuries by the Arameans, Assyrians, Babylonians, (the Persians allowed them to return) Greeks and Romans. The High Priest was speaking of *two* groups of GOD'S people. Once again, John 11:52 is quoted.

John 11:52, (52) And not for that nation only, but that also he should gather together in one the children of God that were scattered abroad.

The *"Gentiles"* were not scattered abroad either by YHWH or anyone else. This scripture very clearly refers to *"Israel"*. The Prophet Ezekiel speaks of a future time when the two kingdoms will once again be one.

Ezekiel 37:19-22, (19) say into them: Thus saith the Lord YHWH: Behold, I will take the stick of Joseph, which is in the hand of Ephraim, and the tribes of Israel his companions; and I will put them unto him together with the stick of Judah, and make them one stick, and they shall be one in My hand. (20) And the sticks whereon thou writest shall be in thy hand before their eyes. (21) And say unto them: Thus saith the Lord YHWH: Behold, I will take the sons of Israel from among the nations, whither they are gone, and will gather them on every side, and bring them into their own land; (22) and I will make them one nation in the land, upon the mountains of Israel, and one king shall be king to them all; and they shall be no more two nations, neither shall they be divided into two kingdoms any more at all;

When the lines in the Gospel of John 11:52 were spoken, what was called *Israel* under the Roman yoke, consisted primarily of the tribes of Judah, Levi and Benjamin, with a few representatives from the other tribes. But other than these three tribes of what was then called *Israel*, it was the ten *lost* tribes of Israel who were *scattered*, that these words were speaking of, *"And YHWH shall scatter you among the peoples, and ye shall be left few in number among the nations whither YHWH shall lead you away"*(Deuteronomy 4:27). Yet, HE also said that when HE brings them back, HE will heal them and will multiply them so that they cannot be numbered.

Ezekiel 34:6, (6) My Sheep wandered through all the mountains, and upon every high hill, yea, upon all the face of the earth were My Sheep scattered, and there was none that did search or seek.

In verse 11:52 *"that nation"*, referred to *"Israel"* which consisted primarily of Judah, Levi and Benjamin, with *"children of GOD that were scattered abroad"* referred to the rest of Israel's *sheep* that had been *"lost"*, ie, *Israel*.

I Samuel 12:22, (22) For YHWH will not forsake His people for His great name's sake; because it hath pleased YHWH to make you a people unto Himself.

The Prophet Isaiah (Isaiah 43:1-7) tells of returning Israel from the four corners of the Earth, *"Every one that is called by My name"*.

'I WILL SEND MANY FISHERS'

GOD'S prophets speak of a time in the end of days when all of Israel will be returned to Israel. There are several powerful scriptures which cover this topic. As a matter of fact, it is a constant theme throughout many of the prophets, giving detailed visions of times to come. One of the prophets speaks of GOD sifting the earth for Israel in a sieve to gather up Israel again, not loosing one grain (Amos 9:9-15). Another prophet is Jeremiah who writes of GOD sending out *"fishers"* and *"hunters"* who will fish and who will hunt for, find and bring home Israel. The motif is the same. YHWH will gather up the lost and scattered of Israel and restore Israel beyond it's former glory.

Jeremiah 16:14, (14) Therefore, behold, the days come, saith YHWH, that it shall no more be said: 'As YHWH liveth, that brought up the children of Israel out of the land of Egypt,' (15) but: 'As YHWH liveth, that brought up the children of Israel from the land of the north, and from all the countries whither He had driven them'; and I will bring them back into their land that I gave unto their fathers. (16) Behold, I will send for many fishers, saith YHWH, and they shall fish them; and afterward I will send for many hunters, and they shall hunt them from every mountain, and from every hill, and out of the clefts of the rocks.

Is this what Jesus was referring to when he was instructing his followers to go to all of the nations to preach to the lost sheep of the House of Israel?

Matthew 4:18-20, (18) And Jesus, walking by the sea of Galilee, saw two brethren, Simon called Peter, and Andrew his brother, casting a net into the sea: for they were fishers. (19) And he saith unto them, <u>Follow me, and I will make you fishers of men</u>. (20) And they straightway left their nets, and followed him.

YHWH AND 'HIS PEOPLE'

This author does not feel that the original goal of being totally objective has been accomplished. For this, an apology to the reader is in order.

As a non-Christian, it is very difficult to remain object within the onslaught of overwhelming Hebrew Bible scripture regarding the Almighty GOD YHWH, HIS holy name, HIS salvation and that it is *"HE"*, who is Savior.

The overwhelming magnitude of the number of statements made by YHWH and by HIS Prophets as to *who* and *what* *"YHWH"* is to Israel is absolutely astounding. This is especially true with regard to HIS name.

There are so many references *to* YHWH, *about* YHWH and *of* YHWH and HIS eternal bond with the people who make up the circumcised SEED of Abraham, that there is not enough time or place to describe the immensity of it all. The point being, that it is the *"name"* **YHWH** who is GOD and Savior of Israel, and that there is *no other*, which is the message given in all of the Hebrew Bible. This fact of *"name"* is something that YHWH is extremely jealous about. YHWH is jealous for HIS holy name and HIS reputation.

These are not just *"throw away lines"* as one might say with no real meaning, *"The beginning of Thy word is truth; and all Thy righteous ordinance endureth for ever"* (Psalm 119:160). That GOD says that HE is jealous for HIS glorious name in the first place, means that HIS name is special above any and all names. GOD speaks only truth. When YHWH says that HE is jealous for HIS holy name, this is something one can understand to mean that HE will not let HIS name remain without it's *"glory"*. Nor, will YHWH allow HIS glory, *"MY glory"*, to be given to another. The name of *"YHWH"* will not be replaced by another name. HE said this specific thing.

'FOR MINE OWN SAKE, FOR MINE OWN SAKE'

Ezekiel 20:44, (44) And ye shall know that I am YHWH, when I have wrought with you <u>for My Name's sake, not according to your evil ways</u>, nor according to your corrupt doings, O ye house of Israel, saith the Lord YHWH.'

Ezekiel said YHWH, will do as HE has spoken that HE will do, *to* and *for* Israel, <u>*because*</u> of HIS holy name. HIS reputation is at stake. The reputation of HIS very name. For through HIS own prophets, YHWH has proclaimed many times and often what HE will do and what will be done, and what will be. For HIS own sake, *"for MINE own sake"*, HE said. It is HIS holy name, the name of **"YHWH"** for which HE will do as HE has proclaimed.

'BUT I HAD PITY FOR MY HOLY NAME'

Who else will have "*pity*" on the name of YHWH, if not YHWH HIMSELF?

"But I had pity for My holy name, which the house of Israel had profaned among the nations, whither ye came" (Ezekiel 36:21)

YHWH had given HIS "*word*" to Abraham and to Isaac and to Jacob as to what HE would do for them and their SEED after them. It is because of this and the honor of HIS holy name that HE will fulfill all that HE has spoken.

Deuteronomy 9:6, (6) Know therefore that *it is not for thy righteousness* that YHWH thy God giveth thee this good land to possess it; for thou art a stiffnecked people.

YHWH removed the nations of Canaan because of their wickedness and replaced them with Israel. It is not because of the righteousness of Israel for which YHWH will be glorified by Israel, but YHWH will use Israel to glorify HIS holy name. And it is for HIS NAME, the name of "*YHWH*" which HE will demand HIS *honor* and HIS *glory*. HE will not *give* HIS *glory* to anyone else. HIS actions are to **"establish the word which YHWH swore"** to Abraham, Isaac and Jacob. This, HE will do *in spite* of Israel. And perhaps as important, in spite of the nations who try to destroy Israel.

Isaiah 48:11, (11) _For Mine Own Sake, for Mine Own Sake_, will I do it; for how should it be profaned? _And My Glory will I not give to another_.

In some translations, "*My glory*" equals "*My honor*".

It is largely because of the incredible amount of jealousy written into the Hebrew Scripture regarding YHWH and HIS name, which makes the name of "*Jesus*" a problem, because of how often he said it is *his* name one must believe in, not the name of "*YHWH*".

Mark 16:17, (17) And these signs shall follow _them that believe; In my name_ shall they cast out devils; they shall speak with new tongues;

John 14:13-14, (13) And whatsoever ye shall ask _in my name_, that will I do, that the Father may be glorified in the Son. (14) If ye shall ask any thing _in my name_, I will do it.

Believing "*in*" him, believing "*on*" his name, believing his "*word*", believe "*me*", and just to "*believe*", all have the same "*otherness*" quality about them which is vastly different than the words written in the Hebrew Bible, whether it is the Law, the Prophets or the Writings regarding YHWH and HIS name.

John 14:1, (1)Let not your heart be troubled: ye believe in God, believe also in me.

John 20:31, (31) But these are written, that ye might _believe that Jesus is the Christ_, the Son of God; and that believing _ye might have life through his name._

"*Ye might have life through his name*"? What new doctrine is this?

DO THE GOSPELS LIMIT YHWH?

The Gospel story would appear to be a limiting factor to the omnificent, omnipotent, omnipresent, and omniscient Almighty GOD of Israel.

For YHWH is unlimited in HIS greatness. YHWH is GOD Almighty. By this is meant that the Gospels, although the story itself is an incredible example of GOD'S compassion, what is often referred to by Christians as the *"Passion"* is an unnecessary saga, and it is in a way redundant.

There already existed in place a sophisticated apparatus for the exculpation of ones transgressions for Israel, and ultimataly for the sins of the nations. For regarding the future, the Prophets of YHWH speak of the nations knowing HIS name and offering sacrifice to HIM. Sacrifice will still be offered, and those sacrifices will be offered in the name of YHWH. And according to the Prophet Zechariah, the type of sacrifice (*Zyin-Bet-Chet*) will be a *"slaughter sacrifice"*. As vegetables are seldom *"slaughtered"* (unless you are a *"weed whacker"*), the Prophet Zachariah is speaking of animal sacrifice. In addition, the Prophet Ezekiel speaks of the Priest slaughtering sacrifice offerings to make atonement for the sins of Israel. The nations will be taught the Law.

This is important because of the Christian doctrine, animal or blood sacrifice is no longer necessary because of the "*sacrificial*" death of Jesus. Jesus was the (sacrificial) "*lamb*" of GOD which is anchored in church doctrine.

Yet, returning to the idea of redundancy, YHWH can save the world without creating yet the story of sacrificing the son of GOD. The concept itself has a Greek mythological quality to it, something almost alien. All Israel's sons are GOD'S sons, *"I said: Ye are Godlike beings, and all of you Sons of the Most High" (Psalm 82:6)*. Israel is GOD'S redeemed people. HIS *"first born son"*.

According to the Hebrew Bible, YHWH GOD hates child sacrifice. One of the reasons for which GOD destroyed the Canaanite people and gave the land to Israel, was because of their sick practice of child sacrifice, amongst other things (refer back to Deuteronomy 9:4-6), "*for the wickedness of these nations*". He warned Israel many times through HIS Prophets about these bad habits and not to do them. Human sacrifice, especially child sacrifice was repugnant to GOD, *"And ye shall be holy unto Me; for I YHWH am holy, and have set you apart from the peoples, that ye should be Mine"*.

Leviticus 18:24, 30, (24) Defile not ye yourselves in any of these things; for in all these the nations are defiled, which I cast out from before you... (30) Therefore shall ye keep My charge, that ye do not any of these abominable customs, which were done before you, and that ye defile not yourselves therein: I am YHWH your God.

Leviticus 20:23, 26 (23) And ye shall not walk in the customs of the nation, which I am casting out before you; for they did all these things, and therefore I abhorred them. ..(26) And ye shall be holy unto Me; for I YHWH am holy, and have set you apart from the peoples, that ye should be Mine.

There is an example during the time of the southern Kingdom of Judah when a really perverse king had his own son, *"pass through the fire"*. There is no detail given regarding this practice, although it is mentioned several times and was practiced by the former occupants of the land. It is assumed that this son was sacrificed although his name is not given and it is not stated if he was burned up. King Manasseh was so evil that he surpassed the evil that was done in the land before him by the Canaanites, *"Manasseh hath done these abominations, and hath done wickedly above all that the Amorites did, that were before him"* (II Kings).

II Kings 21:6, (6) <u>And he made his son to pass through the fire</u>, and practised soothsaying, and used enchantments, and appointed them that divined by a ghost or a familiar spirit: he wrought much evil in the sight of YHWH, to provoke Him.

"Moreover, Manasseh shed innocent blood very much, till he had filled Jerusalem from one end to another..." (II Kings 21:16).

Aside from the horror of a son passing through the fire, it must be remembered that if King Manasseh really did sacrifice his son, he was sacrificing the SEED of David as well. David's SEED is anointed and blessed by YHWH. One may suspect that GOD'S anger regarding King Manasseh, even long after he was dead, had to do with the fact that he was responsible for David's own SEED, whom YHWH loved, *"pass through the fire"*.

YHWH stated later during the reign of good King Josiah, that for the sin of King Manasseh, HE would still destroy Judah as HE had destroyed Israel.

The idea here is, that just as GOD did not have Abraham sacrifice Isaac, a type of sacrifice which was practiced in the land of Canaan before Israel, HE did not approve of it for Israel in HIS Law forbidding them to imitate the Canaanites whom HE replaced with the SEED of Abraham.

Likewise, the idea that after HIS giving the Law forbidding such Canaanite practices to Israel, and then for GOD to do so HIMSELF and to sacrifice HIS own son in Jesus, seems outrageous as well as contradictory. This is a very powerful idea against the sacrifice by GOD of a son of Israel, HIS own son.

JEALOUS NAME

This returns us to YHWH being *"jealous"* for HIS holy name. In the Hebrew Bible, it is the name of YHWH written so many times that the focus is on. In the Christian Bible, it is the name of Jesus that is the main focus. There is a clear problem here. The Christian Bible appears to be at variance with the Hebrew Bible and the Hebrew Bible's emphasis on the name of *"YHWH"*. The stress on the name *"Jesus"* in the Christian Bible is every bit as profound as the stress on the name of *"YHWH"* is in the Hebrew Bible. There is no clear indication the name of YHWH ever existed in the Christian Bible.

The lack of Christian biblical support for any indication of *"YHWH"*, whose name is *"jealous"*, verses the human sacrifice and emphasis of the name of *"Jesus"*, clearly seems at variance with all that is known of YHWH and HIS Law given to his holy people, jealousy for HIS holy name and HIS *"glory"*.

Another meaning for the Hebrew word used for *"jealous"* is *"zeal"*. The root for *"jealous"* comes from a word which comes from the color produced in the face by deep emotions. Both *"passionate"* and *"zealous"* comes to mind as GOD'S feeling for HIS holy name are expressed. One might say that YHWH is *"zealous"* for HIS holy name. The point is, there does not seem to be room for the name of Jesus within this paradigm. It does not fit, and it conflicts greatly with what YHWH has to say not only about HIS name, but about HIMSELF as well *"For I am YHWH thy God, The Holy One of Israel, thy Saviour;... I, even I, am YHWH; and beside Me there is no Saviour"*.

If there is *"no Savior"* but YHWH, how and where does Jesus or his name fit into GOD'S plan, whether of the SEED of David or not? As if attempting to force two pegs into the same hole at the same time, the two names of YHWH and of Jesus cannot be GOD at once, believed, followed and called on as one.

JESUS THE JEW

At the outset, it was said that *"Jesus was not a Christian"*. Jesus was a **JEW.**

According to the Gospels, Jesus was circumcised into the eternal Covenant of Abraham his forefather. By all accounts, Jesus was an *"Israelite"* born of the tribe of Judah. Jesus the Jew earned his living by working as a carpenter

Jesus practiced the ancient Temple of YHWH religion of Israel. This was before it was destroyed and before secular Jews created their own new religion loosely based on the original ancient Temple of YHWH religion and naming it after their tribe. According to the Gospels, the Jew Jesus was an observant Jewish man who appeared to be well versed in the Safer Torah, the Writings and with GOD'S Prophets.

John 15:10, (10) If ye keep my commandments, ye shall abide in my love; even as <u>I have kept my Father's commandments</u>, and abide in his love.

Jesus lived as a Jew practicing the ancient religion of Israel based only on the Safer Torah and the Temple of YHWH, in a kingdom called *"Israel"* dominated by a foreign power in Rome. During his life time, there were many different religious, political and cultural factions who were to vie for the affections of the people. The main powers were the Temple Priests, the Pharisees, Sadducees and of course the Romans. As has been discussed, there were other groups, but these were the more powerful. Although it must be noted however, that though the *Sicarii* were relatively small in number, these *"zealots"* made a larger impact regarding the attitude of the Romans, than their own numbers reflected.

The ethnicity, religion, culture and people of which Jesus lived were his own Jewish people who actually consisted of peoples of many tribes but were dominated by that of Judah. Jesus was first and foremost a *"Jew"*. He was not part of any other ethnicity, religion culture or people. Jesus was *"Jewish"*.

THE MESSAGE OF JESUS

The message of Jesus as already indicated was for *"Israel"*. This is crucial to understand. He stated that he came for Israel, specifically for the *"lost sheep of the House of Israel"*. Jesus healed people when approached by those who were not of Israel but came as he stated, only for Israel. Caiaphas prophesied it was for scattered *Children of GOD*. Only Israel is ever referenced as such.

Jesus, referring to himself, said that he came **_ONLY_** for Israel. He did not indicate anything different. What is more, he made this understanding about going **only** to the *"lost sheep of the House of Israel"* known to his followers as well. Jesus instructed his disciples to go **_ONLY_** to Israel, those who were the lost sheep of the House of Israel, was his focus, and he wanted this to be the focus of his disciples **also**. He stated to avoid the Gentiles. Again, Jesus's instruction was to go to *"Israel"* to the *scattered* sheep.

Matthew 10:16-23, (16) Behold, I send you forth as sheep in the midst of wolves: be ye therefore wise as serpents, and harmless as doves. (17) But beware of men: for they will deliver you up to the councils, and they will scourge you in <u>their synagogues</u>; (18) And ye shall be brought before governors and kings for my sake, for a testimony against them and <u>the Gentiles</u>. (19) But when they deliver you up, take no thought how or what ye shall speak: for it shall be given you in that same *hour what ye shall speak. (20) For it is not ye that speak, but the Spirit of your Father which speaketh in you. (21) And the brother shall deliver up the brother to death, and the father the child: and the children shall rise up against their parents, and cause them to be put to death. (22) And ye shall be hated of all men for my name's sake: but he that endureth to the end shall be saved. (23) <u>But when they persecute you in this city, flee ye into another: for verily I say unto you, Ye shall not have gone over the cities of Israel, till the Son of man be come.</u>*

This last statement does not make much sense unless it is understood *"the cities of Israel"* represent the cities where Israel is *scattered* within the nations, not within the physical boundary between the Mediterranean and the Jordan. *"Israel"* means the *"people"* or sons of Jacob who are scattered in the nations / Gentiles. He is warning them that their fellow Jews will bring them before *their* own councils, scourge them in *their* synagogues and haul them before the Gentiles, just as was Jesus.*"Go not into the way of the Gentiles"*.

It should be noted as with most of the Gospels, that there is a distinction being made here between *"their"* councils and synagogues and being brought before the Gentiles. If Jesus had sent his followers to the Gentiles, which he didn't, this distinction would not be unnecessary. But as was Jesus brought before the Gentile Romans, so will his followers for preaching to Israel.

*Matthew 10:5-7, (5) <u>These twelve Jesus sent forth</u>, and commanded them, saying, <u>Go **not** into the way of the **Gentiles**</u>, and into any city of the Samaritans enter ye not: (6) But go rather to the <u>lost sheep of the house of Israel.</u> (7) And as ye go, preach, saying, The kingdom of heaven is at hand.*

What was his message to the *'lost sheep'?*

Matthew 19:17 ...... but if thou wilt enter into life, Keep The Commandments.

It appears that the message that *"the kingdom of heaven was at hand"*, goes hand and hand with *"keep the Commandments"*. For it is in keeping the Commandments that makes it possible for *scattered* Israel to *"enter into life"*. It is eternal life and the kingdom of heaven which are being proposed by Jesus. They are being proposed **to** Israel, who must **keep** the their Commandments **already given** to them by YHWH with whom they have an eternal contract. As the High Priest prophesied about scattered Israel.

*John 11:49-52, (49) And one of them, named Caiaphas, being the high priest that same year, said unto them, Ye know nothing at all, (50) Nor consider that it is expedient for us, that one man should die for the people, and that <u>the whole nation</u> perish not. (51) And this spake he not of himself: but being high priest that year, <u>he prophesied that Jesus should die for **that nation**</u>; (52) <u>And not for **that nation** only, but that also he should gather together in one the **children of God** that were **scattered** abroad</u>.*

Caiaphas is referring to *"that nation"* of the Jewish people (called Israel) that existed during his prophesy, and the rest of the scattered *"Children of GOD"* abroad. No other people on planet earth have ever been referred to as the Children of GOD but Israel. Not ever. Caiaphas and Jesus are speaking of the same people, the same thing is the scattered lost sheep of Israel, **not** Gentiles.

So Jesus was sent *only* to the *"lost sheep of the House of Israel"* to preach this message and sent his disciples **only** to the lost sheep of Israel, and his message was that the *"kingdom of heaven was at hand"*, that if a person of Israel wanted to *"enter into life"*, that they must *"keep the Commandments"*.

Why would Jesus come for the *"lost sheep of the House of Israel"*?

To begin with, there was a *"promise"*, an *"oath"*, a *"Covenant"* made with Abraham and with his SEED. Aside from the Law given at Sinai, there was this other personal *"agreement"* existing between GOD YHWH and with Abraham and his **"SEED"**. For prior to the Law given at Sinai, this *"gift"*, to Abraham's SEED was a Covenant agreement between Abraham and YHWH. Abraham was to circumcised his SEED, and YHWH would give his SEED the promised land. *"And YHWH appeared unto Abram, and said: 'Unto thy **SEED** will I give this land"* (Genesis 12:7).

Isaiah 59:21, (21) And as for Me, this is My Covenant with them, saith YHWH; My spirit that is upon thee, and My words which I have put in thy mouth, shall not depart out of thy mouth, nor out of the mouth of thy SEED, nor out of the mouth of thy SEED'S SEED, saith YHWH, from henceforth and for ever.

YHWH goes much more into detail about HIS *"giving"*, for as one would give a present or a gift, so did YHWH give as a *"gift"* the land of Canaan to Abraham. In Genesis 13:14-17; 15:4-5; 15:18-21; 17:1-14; 17:19; 22:15-18 there is much more detail as to GOD'S gift to Abraham. The Covenant YHWH made with Abraham was confirmed with Abraham's SEED Isaac, and with Isaac's SEED Jacob. At Sinai it was confirmed with the SEED of Jacob (Israel), and written into Law. This refers to *"circumcision"* which was the sign of the Covenant YHWH made with Abraham and his SEED.

This *"gift"* of the giving of the land of Canaan is not contingent on the Law given at Sinai. The Sinai Covenant incorporated *"circumcision"* as part of the written Law, but it did not cancel out the Covenant of Abraham. The *"gift"* of the land of Canaan from YHWH exists, with or without the Law. Whether every circumcised male SEED descendant of Abraham may benefit or not from that Covenant is up to YHWH. The rebellion of Korah is a case in point (Numbers 16:1-35). Not all of Abraham's SEED will make it.

Over a period of approximately 1,500 years prior to Jesus, many of the SEED of Israel became lost either through rebellion, exile, slavery, intermarriage or as refugees in foreign lands. Circumcised sons of Israel who married Gentile women and moved away were still part of the Covenant of Abraham. As pedigree was always *"patrilineal"* in ancient Israel, ones genealogy was determined by who one's father was. The emphasis on *"SEED"* in the Hebrew Bible is profound. It is done for a reason. It is there for a reason.

Genesis 9:9, (9) 'As for Me, behold, I establish My Covenant with you, and with your SEED after you;

Isaiah 6:12-13, (12) And YHWH have removed men far away, and the forsaken places be many in the midst of the land. (13) And if there be yet a tenth in it, it shall again be eaten up; as a terebinth, and as an oak, whose stock remaineth, when they cast their leaves, so the HOLY SEED shall be the stock thereof.'

Isaiah 41:8, (8) But thou, Israel, My servant, Jacob whom I have chosen, the SEED of Abraham My friend;

Isaiah 61:9, (9) And their SEED shall be known among the nations, and their offspring among the peoples; all that see them shall acknowledge them, that they are the SEED which YHWH hath blessed.

When YHWH made a Covenant with a man, the SEED of that individual is normally always mentioned in the Covenant. This was true of Abraham, Isaac, Jacob, David and the *"sons"* of Aaron. A mans SEED is important.

Israel is a holy SEED. The motif of *"SEED"* can fill many pages. But this is just one more to emphasize the importance of "SEED" and how it relates to the words of Jesus and to whom his message was meant discussed earlier.

Genesis 13:15-16, (15) for all the land which thou seest, to thee will I give it, and to thy SEED for ever. (16) And I will make thy SEED as the dust of the earth; so that if a man can number the dust of the earth, then shall thy SEED also be numbered.

With these few examples regarding *"SEED"* and many more not given, the idea that Abraham's SEED as being extremely important to the narrative of the entire TaNaKh cannot be over stated. That the SEED of Abraham as being a *"Covenant SEED"*, that Abraham's SEED is a *"chosen"* SEED, that of Abraham's SEED being a *"holy"* SEED and of Abraham's SEED being a *"blessed"* SEED *forever*, only touches on the importance of the *"SEED"* of Abraham through his grandson Jacob who is called *"Israel"*, the *"elect"*.

This takes us back to the message of Jesus as his message was to **this** SEED. The message of Jesus was to the eternally *chosen, holy, blessed, anointed, Covenant SEED* of Abraham, the *"children of GOD"*. It was not to any other SEED but to that of Abraham, through his grandson Jacob. SEED matters, SEED matters much. This is why it is Israel, who are the *"Children of GOD"*.

'ALL THE SEED OF ISRAEL'

Isaiah 45:25, (25) <u>In YHWH shall all the SEED of Israel be justified</u>, and shall glory.

The metaphor used throughout TaNaKh regarding Israel being GOD'S flock, and HIS sheep and YHWH being Israel's shepherd is appropriate as in a very real sense as the shepherd David knew all too well, *"YHWH is my shepherd"*.

*"And they shall know that I YHWH their God am with them, and that they, the **House of Israel**, are My people, saith the Lord YHWH. And ye My sheep, the sheep of My pasture, are men, and I am your God, saith the Lord YHWH"* (Ezekiel 34:30-31).

Matthew 19:17 (17) And he said unto him, Why callest thou me good? there is none good but one, that is, God: but if thou wilt enter into life, <u>keep the Commandments.</u>

For who was given the *"Commandments"* to **"keep"**, but Israel who had been given the Law? It was not given to the Gentiles <u>to keep</u>, neither did Gentiles accept them as a Covenant at Sinai. The offer of Covenant was made only to Abraham and his *"house"*. It was to *"Israel"*, the SEED of Abraham that their GOD YHWH made HIS Covenant and who accepted HIS Law to **keep**. *"Keep"* must be understood more as to *"retain"* something already in your possession. To hold on to what you already have. To embrace what is yours.

Amos 3:2, (2) You only have I known of all the families of the earth; therefore I will visit upon you all your iniquities.

The Prophet Amos speaks of Israel being the only family of the families of the earth that YHWH has known. And it is for this reason that it is Israel, not the Gentiles, who have been **punished** for not *keeping* GOD'S Law.

Ezekiel 6:10-11, (10) <u>And they shall know that I am YHWH; I have not said in vain that I would do this evil unto them.</u> (11) Thus saith the Lord YHWH: Smite with thy hand, and stamp with thy foot, and say: Alas! because of all the evil abominations of the house of Israel; for they shall fall by the sword, by the famine, and by the pestilence

YHWH warned Israel in the Book of Deuteronomy by HIS Prophet Moses of the curse which awaited them if the did not **keep** HIS Commandments or obey HIS Statutes and HIS Ordinances, and broke HIS Laws. Of the many things that HE said that HE would do was that HE would *scatter* them. But, as YHWH is a merciful GOD, YHWH would gather them up again.

Ezekiel 34:11-13, 16, (11) For thus saith the Lord YHWH: Behold, here am I, <u>and I will search for My Sheep, and seek them out</u>. (12) As a Shepherd seeketh out his flock in the day that he is among His Sheep that are separated, <u>so will I seek out My Sheep; and I will deliver them out of all places whither they have been Scattered</u> in the day of clouds and thick darkness. (13) And I will bring them out from the Peoples, and <u>gather</u> them from The Countries, and will bring them into their own land; and I will feed them upon the mountains of Israel, by the streams, and in all the habitable places of the country. ......(16) <u>I will seek that which was Lost</u>, and will bring back that which was driven away,.....

The idea here is, that whether or not Jesus was actually the *"messiah"* of Israel or not, his message was *to* and *for* Israel for whom he said he came.

MESSIAH MESSAGE

According to the scripture, the message of Jesus was a message to Israel. It was as much a message of repentance and to keep GOD'S Law and HIS Commandments as anything. One can debate as to whether he himself kept the Commandments, but what he said was if a person of Israel, his "*target audience*" wanted to enter into eternal life, the Commandments must be kept.

As to whether Jesus was the "*messiah*" of Israel or not the reader will have to define "*messiah*" and decide that for himself. The scriptures seem to indicate that this was not the case for Israel, primarily because of the Law which states that every man will die for his own sins and Jesus did not bring *peace, justice* and *righteousness "for ever"* as the Prophet Isaiah states (Isaiah 9:6).

Deuteronomy 24:16, (16) The fathers shall not be put to death for the children, neither shall the children be put to death for the fathers; <u>every man shall be put to death for his own sin.</u>

Ezekiel 33:20, (20)...... O house of Israel, <u>I will judge you every one after his ways.</u>'

WORSHIPING AND BEING SAVED

In the name of YHWH, according to the Prophets, will all (surviving) nations be saved after judgment and will know the name of "*YHWH*". In the capacity of judging and bringing salvation to the world through Israel whom YHWH will be glorified by, the nations by extension will be judged and know salvation. For it is the salvation of Israel that is the key to the salvation of the nations. The nations will be "*judged*". Both Israel and the nations will understand that it was because of Israel's sins that they were exiled. And it was because of YHWH'S mercy, that Israel was brought back from exile.

And lest people who identify themselves as "Christians" are offended by much of what has been said about the "*nations*" or about "*Gentiles*" (which means "*nations*"), it is this author's thorough belief that GOD'S mercy includes those not born of Abraham's SEED. And that many of the nations will be saved after YHWH judges the nations. How and when all of this will come about is up to GOD. In the future *many nations* will know the name of YHWH, will keep HIS Law, and worship the one and only GOD YHWH.

Amos 9:11-12, (11) In that day will I raise up the tabernacle of David that is fallen, and close up the breaches thereof, and I will raise up his ruins, and I will build it as in the days of old; (12) That they may possess the remnant of Edom, and all the nations, upon whom My Name is called, saith YHWH that doeth this.

HUMAN SACRIFICE

The all encompassing might of YHWH GOD simply does not lend itself to the necessity of sacrificing a son of GOD (all circumcised sons of Israel are sons of GOD), for Israel's sin, when HE already had a sacrificial system in place to do so. The ancient Temple before it was destroyed and the future Temple described by Ezekiel had and will have the means to offer for Israel, sacrifice to YHWH for atonement of sin and will according to GOD'S word.

The prophet Ezekiel prophesied about Israel being brought back to their land because of GOD'S compassion and because of HIS jealousy *"for MY holy name"*. And they will understand *why* they went into captivity as well as *why* they have been brought back to their land and the name of YHWH *who* did it.

Ezekiel 39:25-29, (25) Therefore thus saith the Lord YHWH: Now will I bring back the captivity of Jacob, and have compassion upon the whole house of Israel; and I will be jealous for My holy name. (26) And they shall bear their shame, and all their breach of faith which they have committed against Me, when they shall dwell safely in their land, and none shall make them afraid; (27) when I have brought them back from the peoples, and gathered them out of their enemies' lands, and am sanctified in them in the sight of many nations. (28) And they shall know that I am YHWH their God, in that I caused them to go into captivity among the nations, and have gathered them unto their own land; and I will leave none of them any more there; (29) neither will I hide My face any more from them; for I have poured out My spirit upon the House of Israel, saith the Lord YHWH.'

JESUS AND THE LAW - THE COMMANDMENTS

What was the attitude of Jesus toward the Law? Jesus said if *"Israel"* wanted to enter into eternal life, *they* must keep the Commandments. As only Israel had the Law to keep, it was to Israel he spoke.

Jesus at times appeared to contradict the Law by either adding to the Law or diminishing from the Law. But then again, this goes back to whether he kept all of the Laws himself and how this bears on his message. His message remained to keep the Commandments. Whether or not he was perfect in keeping the Law himself is not at issue. It is his words regarding Israel keeping the Commandments that are important, as they were what he left.

'HIS COMMANDMENT IS LIFE EVERLASTING'

John 12:50, (50) And I know that HIS Commandment is Life Everlasting: whatsoever I speak therefore, even as the Father said unto me, so I speak.

Matthew 19:17, (17) And he said unto him, Why callest thou me good? there is none good but one, that is, God: but if thou wilt enter into life, keep the commandments.
Matthew 5:18, (18) For verily I say unto you, Till heaven and earth pass, one jot or one tittle shall in no wise pass from the law, till all be fulfilled.

As of this writing, heaven and earth have not passed away. The Law lives.

So here, Jesus is saying that the Commandments of GOD *are* life everlasting, to *keep* the Commandments of GOD to enter life, and *all* of the Law will be fulfilled. What else is there to say? Subtract all else from that which is GOD'S Commandments, and what you have left is the Law of Moses!

SALVATION / REEDEMED

This is a very heavy scripture. It is in the past tense and proclaims in Hebrew something which is already an established fact. There are also many, many scripture regarding Israel being "*redeemed*". Not that YHWH will redeem Israel, but as something that is an established fact already. It has happened.

Isaiah 45:17, (17) O Israel, that art Saved by YHWH with an Everlasting Salvation; ye shall not be ashamed nor confounded world without end.

Exodus 15:13, (13) Thou in Thy love hast led the people that Thou hast Redeemed; Thou hast guided them in Thy strength to Thy holy habitation

Isaiah 43:1, (1) But now thus saith YHWH that created thee, O Jacob, and He that formed thee, O Israel: Fear not, for I have Redeemed thee, I have called thee by thy name, thou art Mine.

There are several scriptures in the Hebrew Bible which are saying that Israel's salvation exists by nature of who they are as the SEED of the Covenant.

Micah 7:7, (7) 'But as for me, I will look unto YHWH; I will wait for the God of My Salvation; my God will hear me.

YHWH has said many times, that it is HE, "*YHWH*" who is "*Savior*" of Israel. For in the name of YHWH, as HE has said, Israel shall be delivered.

Hosea 13:4, (4) Yet I am YHWH thy God from the land of Egypt; and thou knowest no God but Me, and beside Me there is no Saviour.

If Israel is already *saved* and *redeemed*, other than reminding Israel to keep the Commandments by possibly tempting them, what could Jesus offer Israel? For to accept the premise that Israel needed "*saving*" or needed to be "*redeemed*" from their sins, is a supposition which wold equate Israel as being no different than the nations. And this simply is not accurate.

Amos 3:2, (2) You only have I known of all the families of the earth; therefore I will visit upon you all your iniquities.

SINS

As far as the east is from the west, so far hath He removed our transgressions from us (Psalm 103:12).

Isaiah 43:25, (25) I, even I, am He that blotteth out thy transgressions for Mine own sake; and thy sins I will not remember.

Zechariah 13:1, (1) In that day there shall be a fountain opened to the house of David and to the inhabitants of Jerusalem, for purification and for sprinkling.

Who hath the power to show mercy and to forgive sin but YHWH? Many times, YHWH has said how HE will show compassion of HIS people, and forgive their sin. The Prophet Micah sums it up nicely with GOD'S words of mercy towards HIS people Israel.

Micah 7:18-20, (18) Who is a God like unto Thee, that pardoneth the iniquity, and passeth by the transgression of the remnant of His heritage? He retaineth not His anger for ever, because He delighteth in Mercy. (19) He will again have Compassion upon us; He will subdue our iniquities; and Thou wilt cast all their sins into the depths of the sea. (20) Thou wilt show Faithfulness to Jacob, Mercy to Abraham, as Thou hast sworn unto our fathers from the days of old.

There are many scriptures where GOD is angry with HIS people Israel. And make no mistake about it, Israel belongs to GOD. But there are also many scriptures where HE speaks of compassion and showing HIS mercy. When YHWH blessed Abraham and his SEED, Isaac and his SEED and Jacob and his SEED after him, YHWH'S blessing was an *eternal* blessing. "*And I will bless them that bless thee, and him that curseth thee will I curse; and in thee shall all the families of the earth be blessed.(Genesis 12:3).* Even those who dared to curse Israel would themselves be cursed as was Balaam.

Numbers 22:12, (12) And God said unto Balaam: 'Thou shalt not go with them; thou shalt not curse the people; for they are blessed.'

Being of the *SEED* of Abraham, being *blessed* and being of *Israel* was a status which separated Israel out from the nations forever. The down side was being cursed by GOD HIMSELF, when HIS Commandments were broken. Nevertheless, Israel remains separate from the nations in a unique way.

Psalms 135:4, (4) For YHWH hath chosen Jacob unto Himself, and Israel for His own treasure.

Israel is not counted with the other nations, but remains in a category all unto themselves. Israel is the servant of the living GOD. "*But thou, Israel, My servant, Jacob whom I have chosen, the SEED of Abraham My friend*". For YHWH hath said that Israel is a people that HE *created, formed* and "*redeemed*" to be HIS *treasure*, HIS *inheritance*, as HIS holy *people* and as HIS *servant.* GOD said that Israel, HE set "*apart*".

For these and other reasons, not the least of which is that Israel is under Covenant with YHWH GOD, Israel is not counted with the other nations. They are punished for their sins separately. They are punished for their sin against their GOD more severely because of the Law of Moses which they agreed to keep by Covenant with GOD.

The nations are *not* under Covenant with YHWH, therefore they cannot break their agreement with GOD or "*keep*" the Commandments, as Jesus spoke of. Whatever sins Gentiles commit and for whatever reason they are punished, it is not for breaking the Law of YHWH. It is in this light that the statement is made, that Israel is not "*reckoned*" with the Nations. They are a people who dwell alone, a solitary existence. Nations are judged separately.

Israel is not lumped together with the Uncircumcised Nations as Paul would have one believe, but are separate, as GOD has done, a holy people to HIM.

Numbers 23:9, (9) For from the top of the rocks I see him, and from the hills I behold him: lo, it is a people that shall dwell alone, <u>and shall not be reckoned among the nations.</u>

Micah 7:14, (14) Tend Thy people with Thy staff, the flock of Thy heritage, <u>that dwell solitarily,</u> as a forest in the midst of the fruitful field; let them feed in Bashan and Gilead, as in the days of old.

Hosea 8:1-2, (1) Set the horn to thy mouth. As a vulture he cometh against the house of YHWH; because they have <u>transgressed My Covenant,</u> and trespassed against <u>My Law.</u> (2) Will they cry unto Me: <u>'My God, we Israel know Thee'?</u>

Additionally, it is in this light that the ministry of Jesus should be viewed. Jesus preached and taught regarding the Law of YHWH. That Israel needed to keep GOD'S Law. If Israel wanted to *"enter life"*, they must *"keep the Commandments"*. Christians ignore YHWH'S Law that Jesus preached yet many claim to be *"Israel"*, the *"new Israel"*, or other. This is said to make a point. If Jesus was speaking to the Gentiles as many believe, then he was telling them to *keep* the Law and all of it's Commandments.

Another point must be made regarding the *"need"* to sacrifice anyone, *"man"* or *"son of GOD-man"* when YHWH already had an eternal system in place. The same system of sacrifice offering which existed while Jesus was still alive and which existed for the next generation after his death and will again.

KNOWING YHWH'S NAME

The following is an incredible piece of prophesy concerning the future of the Nations. For according to the prophesy, the Nations of the earth, by GOD'S might, will eventually come to realize that only **"YHWH"** is GOD.

Jeremiah 16:19-21, (19) O YHWH, my <u>strength,</u> and my <u>stronghold,</u> and my <u>refuge,</u> in the day of affliction, <u>unto Thee shall the nations come from the ends of the earth,</u> and shall say: 'Our fathers have inherited nought but lies, vanity and things wherein there is no profit.' (20) Shall a man make unto himself gods, and they are no gods? (21) Therefore, behold, I will cause them to know, this once will <u>I cause them to know</u> My <u>hand</u> and My <u>might</u>; <u>and</u> <u>they shall know that My Name is YHWH.</u>

It is *not* the name of *"**Jesus**"* that the nations will know according to the Bible which Jesus himself taught from, but the name of **"YHWH"**. And *deliverance, salvation* and *eternal life* will come from calling on the name of YHWH. YHWH is the ***Savior*** of Israel and the name the Nations will know.

Isaiah 43:3, 11, (3) For I am YHWH thy God, The Holy One of Israel, thy Saviour; ......(11) I, even I, am <u>YHWH; and beside Me there is no Saviour.</u>

This is pretty startling. Israel is to call on the name of YHWH for deliverance and that YHWH is the Savior of Israel. YHWH is Israel's salvation. This goes against the doctrine of most Christian belief in the name of *"Jesus"*.

Psalms 50:1, 5, 14-15, (1) God, God, YHWH, hath spoken, and called the earth from the rising of the sun unto the going down thereof.........(5) <u>'Gather My saints together unto Me; those that have made a Covenant with Me by Sacrifice.'</u> ....(14) Offer unto God the sacrifice of thanksgiving; and pay thy vows unto the Most High; (15) <u>And call upon Me</u> in the day of trouble; <u>I will deliver thee, and thou shalt honour Me.'</u>

YHWH'S Prophets say that the Nations will worship HIM and all will know HIS name. In the Book of Jeremiah, Jeremiah speaks of the future, as does the Prophet Ezekiel and others of the Levites offering up burnt offerings to YHWH forever. The Prophet Isaiah speaks of a time when Egypt will offer sacrifice to YHWH, (Isaiah 19:19-21).

It goes without saying, that this event has hardly taken place yet. When it does happen, it want go *"un-missed"* by the rest of the world nations. But something else is happening here as well. Egypt is still Egypt. Egypt as will other Nations, will come to know the salvation of YHWH and HIS name. But they will *not* "*be*" Israel, but will retain their own identity as separate Nations. YHWH hints as much in another scripture.

Isaiah 19:23-25, (23) <u>*In that day*</u> *shall there be a highway out of Egypt to Assyria, and the Assyrian shall come into Egypt, and the Egyptian into Assyria; and the* <u>*Egyptians shall worship with the Assyrians.*</u> *(24) In that day shall Israel be the third with Egypt and with Assyria, a blessing in the midst of the earth; (25) for that YHWH of hosts hath blessed him, saying:* <u>*'Blessed be Egypt My people and Assyria the work of My hands, and Israel Mine inheritance.'*</u>

These words written by GOD'S prophets are extremely important for several reasons. First, it shows the mercy of GOD. It gives the names of at least two nations who will be saved by GOD and indicates what they mean to HIM. Lastly, it indicates that the Nations who are saved do not "*become*" Israel. They are "*saved*" as separate identifiable nations. Egypt remains "*Egypt*", Assyria remains "*Assyria*". And Israel remains "*Israel*". Being saved, in other words, does not automatically mean that one "*becomes*" Israel.

'EGYPTIANS SHALL KNOW YHWH IN THAT DAY'

Knowing *"YHWH'S name"* is closely tied in with the idea of *judgment.* GOD will judge the nations. And as the man said, *"it want be pretty"*. Words like an *"overflowing shower"*, *"great hailstones"*, *"fire and brimstone", GOD'S wrath* are mentioned. YHWH speaks much of the judgment of the Nations. The Nations will come to *"know"* the GOD of Israel, and the *"name"* by which HE is called. That is, those Nations who survive HIS wrath will.

Ezekiel 38:23 (23) Thus will I <u>*magnify*</u> *Myself, and* <u>*sanctify*</u> *Myself,* <u>*and I will make Myself KNOWN in the eyes of many Nations; and they shall KNOW that I am YHWH.*</u>

YHWH will *magnify* HIMSELF, *sanctify* HIMSELF and will *glorifed* in Israel. The gist of this is that the Nations will come to know the Name of "*YHWH*". It does not appear that all Nations will survive. But those who do survive will worship the name of "*YHWH*". The name of "*Jesus*" is not mentioned by the prophets as the name which shall be known by either Israel or the Nations. The prophets declare it is the name **"YHWH"**. It does not take a genius to understand that YHWH wants the world to know HIS holy name and that it is HE alone who is GOD. Why? Because HE is jealous for HIS holy name. How can a Jew who knows his GOD and HIS Law miss this?

SACRIFICE OFFERING

A person might ask the Christian why the need for continual sacrifice by GOD'S priests if Jesus was *sacrificed once for all* mankind? For it is said that Jesus shed his blood once for sins. According to basic Christian doctrine, because of his "*blood*" sacrifice, there is no more need for blood "*sacrifice*", therefore the "*Law*" is dead and no longer viable, necessary or in affect. Accordingly, sacrificial offering of the Law of Moses has become *redundant*.

However, as the Gospels themselves have indicated, even Jesus said for Israel to keep the Law, all of it. Whether the Pharisees or Priests thought that Jesus did or did not keep the Law himself is immaterial. Aside from whatever else that he preached, he said to keep the "*Commandments*". This may come as a huge surprise to many Christians, but calling on the *name of YHWH* and *sacrificial offerings* are a big part of keeping the Commandments. The name of Jesus is not part of the Law. Even Jesus did not say to keep just some of the Commandments for this would be breaking the Law itself. All of the Law of YHWH is to be kept. You cannot be just "*a little bit pregnant*".

And if one is wondering, well what about the Jews? Don't worry, the Jews are paying a heavy price for their sins, and not being able to sacrifice to YHWH for them. But this will not always be the case as said by the prophets.

Deuteronomy 8:5 (5) And thou shalt consider in thy heart, that, as a man chasteneth his son, so YHWH thy God chasteneth thee.

And who is *thee,* but Israel, the son of GOD, Israel "*the Children of GOD*".

The Jewish people are still under the Law. Regardless as to whether they can keep all of it or not. But there is one other thing. YHWH is merciful to HIS people Israel whose sons, being circumcised into the Covenant of Abraham, are still part of it's blessing as well. And on whom HIS compassion abides.

PROPHETS - PROPHECIES - OFFERINGS

In ancient Israel, there are many different types of "*offerings*" made to YHWH. Depending on the reason for the offering, it could be one of many types of offering. Whether it was for a commanded offering or an offering of the free will of man, these offerings were special to YHWH GOD.

Some of the types of offerings are a *burnt offering, meal offering, peace offering, sin offering, guilt offering, thanksgiving offering, gift offering, free will offering, wave offering, heave offering, consecration offering,* and a *drink offering*.

Making an offering to YHWH took many different forms. They did not always entail the spilling of blood, as in the meal offering. They could be in the form of an animal sacrifice, or an animal and vegetable sacrifice. They could be large or small, commanded or free will, specific and special.

This scripture in Isaiah (Isaiah 19:19-21) deals with a ***future*** time which has not yet occurred. The Hebrew root used for "*sacrifice*" in Isaiah 19:21 *(Zyin-Bet-Chet),* is one of "*slaughter sacrifice*". It is not just "*sacrifice*" but a type of "*sacrifice*" which requires "*slaughter*". The same form of this word is used in Isaiah 34:6 referring to the "*sacrifice*" of nations by the wrath of GOD. This is a sacrifice of "*flesh*". The nations will pay with their "*hide*".

The other Hebrew word used for "*offering*" is *(Mem-Nun-Chet-Heh)* and means "*gift*", "*tribute*" or "*offering*". When alone, "*minchah*" can be either an animal or grain / meal offering but appears to be used by itself more often as "*meal offering*" (Amos 5:22). However, the word "*zevach*" is separate from "*minchah*" which has an "*and*" *(Vav)* attached to it which indicates that it is not a phrase for one type of offering, but two separate offerings. One which requires "*slaughtering*", and the other which does not, "*meal*".

So, it appears that the Prophet Isaiah is referring to a *future* animal sacrifice offering and a meal offering. A meal or grain offering can be offered as well, but the Hebrew reads that a "*slaughter sacrifice*" offering is to be made. If it were *only* for a grain offering or meal offering etc., it would not include the word for "*slaughter sacrifice*" as neither grain nor meal is slaughtered. If this is the case, then Egypt and other Nations will be offering animal sacrifices to YHWH in the future. And these call for the spilling of blood.

Generally, when referring to a meal offering, the term "*karban mincha* is used, but not always.

Another example of *future* sacrifice is with the Levites who will be offering sacrifice to GOD. The Prophet Jeremiah speaks of a time when the Throne of David will be restored and the Levites will again offer sacrifice **continually.** The literal translation of *continually* is "*all the days*".

Jeremiah 33:17-18, (17) For thus saith YHWH: There shall not be cut off unto David a man to sit upon the throne of the house of Israel; (18) neither shall there be cut off unto the priests the Levites a man before Me to offer <u>burnt-offerings</u>, and to burn <u>meal-offerings</u>, and to do <u>sacrifice continually</u>.

The Hebrew word used for "*burnt-offering*" is "*olah*" (*Ayin-Lamed-Vav-Heh*) meaning whole burnt offering (beast or fowl). It is used differently than either of the other two words and refers to animal sacrifice.

According to the Prophet Jeremiah, Levites will offer both burnt animal and meal sacrifice offerings to YHWH *forever*. And this will be during a time when the throne of David is restored (Ezekiel Chapters 34-37. This has not occurred as of this writing. This puts into question the "*sacrifice*" of Jesus as sacrifice will continue. The Laws concerning sacrifice "*for atonement for Israel's sins*" will not end for they are eternal according to Leviticus 16:34, as "*an Everlasting Statute unto you*". YHWH'S priests will always offer sacrifice offerings for atonement for the sins of Israel, as it is <u>eternal</u>.

Given that Christians accept the Hebrew Bible, it is difficult to understand how so many of the scriptures regarding future sacrifice offerings by Israel's priests for their sin have been either ignored or have not been noticed.

JESUS AND THE LAW

According to Christian doctrine, there is no need for the "*Law*", which signifies the need for sacrifice. For when Jesus was crucified and sacrificed his "*blood*", both sacrifice and the Law which commands it, were finished.

Yet, YHWH'S Prophets indicate that this is surely not the case, that the Law is not dead.

Micah 4:1-2, (1) <u>But in the end of days it shall come to pass</u>, that the mountain of YHWH'S house shall be established as the top of the mountains, and it shall be exalted above the hills; and peoples shall flow unto it. (2) And <u>many Nations</u> shall go and say: 'Come ye, and let us go up to the *mountain of YHWH, and to the house of the God of Jacob; and He will <u>teach</u> us of His <u>ways</u>, and we will walk in His <u>paths</u>'; for out of Zion shall go forth the Law, and the Word of YHWH from Jerusalem.*

In the future, Israel will *have* GOD'S Law written on their hearts according to the prophets (Jeremiah 31:31-34), but according to the prophets (Micah 4:2), the Nations will be *taught* GOD'S Law. The Nations will be taught the *"ways"* of YHWH and the *"paths"* of YHWH. They will be taught the *"word"* and the Law of YHWH. There is *one* Law for Israel and the stranger.

Exodus 24:3, (3) And Moses came and told the people all the <u>Words of YHWH</u>, and all the Ordinances; and all the people answered with one voice, and said: '<u>All the Words</u> which the Lord hath spoken will we do.'

Psalms 25:4-5, (4) Show me <u>Thy ways</u>, O YHWH; teach me <u>Thy Paths</u>. (5) Guide me in <u>Thy Truth</u>, and <u>Teach me</u>; for Thou art the God of my Salvation; for Thee do I wait all the day.

Psalms 25:10, (10) <u>All the Paths</u> of YHWH are Mercy and Truth unto such <u>as keep His Covenant and His Testimonies.</u>

Psalms 119:35, (35) Make me to tread in the P<u>ath</u> of Thy C<u>ommandments</u>; for therein do I delight.

The *"path"* of YHWH, the *"ways"* of YHWH and the *"word"* of YHWH are HIS *Commandments,* HIS *Statutes* and HIS *Ordinances,* to keep them and to live by them. This is HIS Law which the Nations will be taught to keep and to live by. This, apparently Jesus was aware of as he told his own followers.

'BUT AS FOR ME'

Joel 1:14, 19, (14) Sanctify ye a fast, call a solemn assembly, gather the elders and all the inhabitants of the land unto the house of YHWH your God, <u>and cry unto YHWH</u>....(19) <u>Unto Thee, O YHWH, do I cry</u>;...

Joel 2:27, (27) And ye shall know that I am in the midst of Israel, <u>and that I am YHWH your God, and there is none else</u>; and My people shall never be ashamed.

The words of Joshua may be instructive here. For before Joshua died, as did Moses before Moses died, Joshua admonished Israel one last time. For Joshua had been with Moses and had been a leader since his youth and then the leader of Israel himself after Moses died. Having spent his formative years with Moses and Aaron and then leading Israel in battle to conquer their promised land, he warned Israel one last time. For surely as did Moses before him, Joshua knew their weakness and feared, as YHWH had warned them.

In the last days of the life of Moses, Moses recited the blessing and the curse before Israel. It is quite extensive, located in the last few chapters of Deuteronomy. Afterward, YHWH called Moses and Joshua into the *"Tent of Meeting"* before Moses died, to give Moses his last instructions. YHWH spoke of Israel going astray, *"And YHWH said unto Moses: 'Behold, thou art about to sleep with thy fathers; <u>and this people will rise up, and go astray</u> after the foreign gods of the land, whither they go to be among them, and will forsake Me, and break My Covenant which I have made with them"*. So both

Moses and Joshua were aware of the future stumbling of Israel and warned Israel of what they would be facing.

Before he died, Joshua spoke similar words to Israel as a warning to them and ends by saying that as for he and his house, they would serve YHWH.

The ministry of Jesus must be understood within this context as well. For it was not only the time in which Jesus lived which must be taken into consideration, but the 1,500 years or so which preceded it. For Israel was a very ancient people. As has been said several times, Jesus was not born and did not die unconnected to Israel's history but was part of it. Where and how he lived, what the circumstances and situation of his surroundings were during his time must be understood to appreciate his words, those of the Priests, the Pharisees and others.

Jesus was a circumcised male SEED descendant of Abraham living amongst a people who lived under the Law of Moses. And when weighing the words of Jesus against the words of *"YHWH"* as the Deliver and Savior of Israel and the *holiness of HIS name,* it is in understanding this context, that the these words of Moses and Joshua spoken to Israel must be read and applied.

Deuteronomy 10:12-13, (12) And now, Israel, what doth YHWH thy God require of thee, but to fear YHWH thy God, to walk in all His ways, and to love Him, and to serve YHWH thy God with all thy heart and with all thy soul; (13) to keep for thy good the Commandments of YHWH, and His Statutes, which I command thee this day?

Deuteronomy 4:39, (39) know this day, and lay it to thy heart, that YHWH, He is God in heaven above and upon the earth beneath; there is none else.

Joshua 24:15, (15) And if it seem evil unto you to serve YHWH, choose you this day whom ye will serve; whether the gods which your fathers served that were beyond the River, or the gods of the Amorites, in whose land ye dwell; but as for me and my house, we will serve YHWH.'

WALK - FEAR – KEEP – HEARKEN – SERVE - CLEAVE

Deuteronomy 13:5, (5) After YHWH your God shall ye walk, and Him shall ye fear, and His Commandments shall ye keep, and unto His voice shall ye hearken, and Him shall ye serve, and unto Him shall ye cleave.

How can one walk after YHWH and follow Jesus? How can one serve YHWH and serve Jesus? How can one have YHWH GOD, and call on Jesus? How can one believe in YHWH and on Jesus?

HOPE AND MYSTERY

There is absolutely no doubt that the life story of Jesus the Jew has given literally millions of people hope over the centuries. And this writer in no way is attempting to diminish that hope. For the worlds 2.2 million believers in Jesus, the hope in his words are the hope of eternal life. That this story even exists is amazing. For in a short three year period of time, his life and his words transformed the world. *But as for Israel*, he did not qualify as *messiah*. Yet, these numbers of Christians alone must not obscure how he was viewed 2,000 years ago by his people living under the Law of Moses. For today there are many followers of another religion based on the words of a guy who hallucinated in a cave, words of hate and death. Yet he has many followers also, spewing his hate and death especially towards GOD'S "*elect*".

The fact that Jesus was a circumcised Jew of a people known as "*Israel*", who worshiped the ONE GOD called "*YHWH*", should not be over looked. Whether or not Jesus acknowledged YHWH by name or not we may not be able to know definitely. One thing is for certain, Jesus taught Israel to keep the Commandments of YHWH and his influence on the world is incalculable even if that part of his message was later forgotten by his followers. His earliest followers apparently kept the Commandments according to history.

Even the Romans stopped feeding Christians to the lions and adopted Christianity. Emperor Constantine converted to Christianity and thus demoted himself and all future Emperors of Rome forever from being a "*god*" to being just a man. And by doing so, recognizing that there really was a GOD, the GOD of the Jews. The same GOD of a stiff necked people on the far side of the Mediterranean whom the Romans had previously subjugated, and to whom the carrying out of the death sentence of Jesus fell. That Rome would eventually adopt as a religion one whose leader they scourged and nailed to the remains of a tree, and whose followers they had tried to destroy is profound in itself. Though by accepting Jesus they also managed somehow to elevate Mary to being the *"mother of GOD"* as part of their new religion.

And although it is true that Constantine was no friend of the Jews, the slow civilizing (some will disagree) affect that the words of not only Jesus, but of David and the rest of GOD'S Prophets would eventually have on the world, though not perfect, was quite an improvement over their former state.

That one man born as a lowly Jew in a far away Kingdom of Israel, had so much influence on the world, is truly without merit. In western civilization, only one other person had such a broad impact. And that is Moses. For today's ***Judaeo-Christian*** ethical and moral principals are founded on the Laws of the Hebrew Bible. The very foundation of the laws of Western Society themselves have their basis in the Law brought down from Mount Sinai from YHWH GOD by Moses and the very Commandments Jesus said for Israel to keep.

Having said this, it was to "*Israel*" that the Jew Jesus said he came for. And it was to the *"lost sheep of the House of Israel"* that he preached. It was also to the *"lost sheep of the House of Israel"* that Jesus sent his disciples to preach in the Nations where they were scattered. And for the first couple of centuries or so after his death, the majority of the believers were Jews.

However this was soon to change as the Apostle Paul appeared and delivered a radically different message to the Gentile world. Paul's message was seemingly different than that which the Jew Jesus preached to Israel and what his immediate followers understood at that time. Paul and the disciples of Jesus who were with him, had a difference of opinion, even during Paul's life time regarding the Law and the Gentiles. There was disagreement.

However, unlike Paul, Jesus had been speaking primarily to a circumcised Jewish audience who were already born with the Law.

GOD'S PLAN

It may well be that GOD has a few more surprises up HIS sleeve. It would not be in any way too shocking if *"the end"*, when it comes, will be nothing like most of the people who try to predict such things have written.

Somehow it seems as well, that the Christian population, not all, will play a very important part in what transpires during what might be Israel's darkest hour, before or during the time of judgment. For those who truly bless, and support Israel and the Jewish people will in no way be ignored by YHWH GOD. In the same way that those people, whoever they are and whatever they call themselves, who hate the SEED of Jacob, will not be forgotten or ignored, *"Cursed be every one that curseth thee, and blessed be every one that blesseth thee"*.

Growing up in the US, more than once has this author heard from various Jewish people and have read from several Jewish writers, that many Jews consider Jesus as a Prophet. The interesting thing about these people is that they are not *"believers"*. They are not *"messianic"*. They do not consider him as the *"messiah"*, but that his words were too powerful to ignore, and that in some undefined way, his words were prophetic for the Jewish people.

As this is being written, the world is being drawn up into more or less two opposing camps. As every day goes by, this is becoming more and more apparent to anyone who is bothering to take notice.

Genesis 27:29, (29) Let peoples serve thee, and nations bow down to thee. Be lord over thy brethren, and let thy mother's sons bow down to thee. <u>Cursed be every one that curseth thee, and blessed be every one that blesseth thee.</u>

Christians may play a future part with Israel. Islam is attempting to create a world Caliphate. A one world religion. Similar to what was once the goal of Communism. However, unlike Communism which was at least *"rational"*, Many Muslims believe they must either go ahead and defeat the "infidel", or for the more radical branch, bring on an apocalypse so the the 12th Imam, (the Mahdi) will reappear and establish the Caliphate. Their first priority is to destroy Israel. The Christian West and others will come later. Although the destruction of the Christian populations in the Middle East has already been going on for decades, few speak of this. As of this writing, the only real acknowledged and vocal allies Israel and the Jewish people have are the hundreds of thousands, if not millions of Christians who support them. They call themselves *"Christian Zionists"*. Their support often far exceeds that of liberal Jews and is a true testimony to their faith and the power of the word of GOD, as their understanding of who Israel really is comes from the Hebrew Bible. They get their faith from their belief in Jesus and from Hebrew scripture. They seem to understand that Israel is still GOD'S chosen people.

How this will all play out in the total scheme of things is known only to GOD. But one thing seems to be for certain. The future of Israel and the Jewish people today, appears to be somehow linked with Christian supporters who love and stand by them. To the chagrin of many Jewish people, Jews seem to be more and more inextricably linked as participants with true Christian followers of Jesus in YHWH'S plan for HIS *inheritance*. This may not be so apparent outside of Israel, but from within Israel's borders, things are much clearer than on the outside. It is especially apparent as the hate of Islam gathers it's clouds together to annihilate Abraham's blessed SEED.

Zechariah 8:22-23, (22) <u>Yea, many peoples and mighty Nations shall come to seek YHWH of hosts in Jerusalem, and to entreat the favour of YHWH.</u> (23) Thus saith YHWH of hosts: In those days it shall come to pass, that ten men shall take hold, <u>out of all the languages of the Nations</u>, shall even *take hold of the skirt of him that is a Jew, saying: We will go with you, for we have heard that God is with you.'*

But there is also a very powerful strain of *"christians"* who support Arab and Islamic hatred of Israel and the Jewish people, especially from Europe and from within the Middle East.

WOLVES AND SHEEP

This book attempted to look at Jesus not as 99.9% of the world sees him, but as the Jews of Israel did 2,000 years ago who were born under the *Law*. How was Jesus perceived by his own *"family"*, his *"house"*, his *"clan"*, his *"tribe"*, and his *"people"* Israel. How did his words measure up against the *"Law?*

Jesus was often referred to as the *"lamb of God"*. As in a sacrificial lamb for mankind, Jesus is often portrayed in this light. As the narrative of the Gospels tells the story of a man who was a son of God, who was sent to save Israel, Jesus is seen as a helpless figure who was very much as a sacrificial lamb readied for the alter and who was destined to die. But was he?

Matthew 7:15, (15) Beware of false prophets, which come to you in sheep's clothing, but inwardly they are ravening wolves.

According to many instances in the Gospels, Jesus was a commanding presence, who when he spoke, the people were in awe of him. Even the Pharisees were stuck by the authority by which he spoke and were often left speechless after having a confrontation with him. This is significant when one remembers how these people spent most all of their waking hours studying and discussing the Law between themselves. The rabbis may not have had all of the correct answers or may have been blinded by their own *"traditions"*, but they were not shy when it came to voicing their opinion. But often as not, when they were before Jesus, they were *"dumb struck"* and unable to speak for Jesus spoke with such authority as to put them to silence.

Matthew 22:34, 46, (34) But when the Pharisees had heard that <u>he had put the Sadducees to silence,</u> they were gathered together......(46) And no man was able to answer him a word, neither durst any man from that day forth ask him any more question.

Matthew 7:28-29, (28) And it came to pass, when Jesus had finished these sayings, the people were <u>astonished</u> at his doctrine: (29) <u>For he taught them as one having authority</u>, not as the scribes.

Matthew 21:23, (23) And when he was come into the Temple, the chief priests and the elders of the people came unto him as he was teaching, and said, <u>By what authority</u> doest thou these things? Who gave thee <u>this authority?</u>

When Jesus was betrayed and arrested, the scene described in the Gospel of John, was one of the secret arrest of an innocent man in the darkness of night by a body of conspirators too fearful of the people to do so in the light of day. They are portrayed as little more than a body of degenerates who were too guilt stricken of conscience to confront Jesus in open daylight, but by stealth, arrested him in such a manner that there would be few, if any witnesses. Going to the place where Jesus and his followers often met and prayed, the *"band"* of men came with lanterns, torches and weapons. But when they had finally cornered their prey, they fell down in fright.

John 18:3-6, (3) Judas then, having received a band of men and officers from the Chief Priests and Pharisees, cometh forth thither with lanterns and torches and weapons. (4) Jesus therefore, <u>knowing all things</u> that should come upon him, went forth, and said unto them, Whom seek ye? (5) They answered him, Jesus of Nazareth. Jesus saith unto them, <u>I am he</u>. And Judas also, which betrayed him, stood with them. (6) As soon as he had said unto them, <u>I am he</u>: <u>they went backward, and fell to the ground.</u>

The point is that Jesus who is often portrayed as a helpless victim in the sense that his death was a fate which was ordained by GOD, was actually a strong person who knew the Law and spoke with authority, and was a man who apparently people were in awe of and who put fear into the hearts of men.

Jesus was no *"wallflower"* but a person of deep conviction and was very self assured, who did not lack any self confidence when before Israel or any of it's self styled leaders. There may be no better example of this than the story of Jesus cleansing the Temple and teaching daily in the Temple (Luke 19:45-48; Matthew 21:12-13; Mark 11:15-19; John 2:13-16) with the most educated Jews of his day. His words seem to echo Jeremiah 7:11. According to John 18:19-21, after Jesus was arrested and brought before the High Priest, he chided them for the way that they arrested him, telling them, *"I spake openly to the world; I ever taught in the synagogue, and in the Temple, whither the Jews always resort; and in secret have I said nothing"*.

Matthew 26:55, (55) Are ye come out as against a thief with swords and staves for to take me? I sat daily with you teaching in the Temple, and ye laid no hand on me.

When speaking before the people in general, the Sadducee, Pharisee, Scribes, Priests or even the Romans just before his death, he did not lack any self assurance and was consistent throughout with his message and his ministry.

The fate of Jesus at no time, up until near the end of his life, seemed to be out of control or beyond his ability to change. By this is meant that he was smart enough to know that the final outcome could have been different had he responded differently to the Priests of whom he stood before. For it was a sure death sentence which he faced if he did not recant some of his words spoken. There was no contrition and no sense of a humble carpenter before the High Priest of YHWH, but a man who said to them everything that was sure to get their ire and a sentence of death as they had even warned him. He showed no less fear before Pilate. He was very consistent in this regard. For the two most powerful people, Caiaphas and Pilate (Annas, former High Priest and er-in-law to Caiaphas should be included) he had to deal with, and whom might possibly keep him from sure death, he was unyielding.

'THAT PROPHET'

The suspicion exists that Jesus was the ultimate *"plant"* by GOD to test Israel cannot be ignored. For YHWH had said that HE would *"try"* Israel, *"to know if they kept HIS Law"*. In other words, YHWH had warned Israel that false prophets would come to *"prove"* them to know if they really loved him with all of their *heart* and *soul*. Yet, at the same time, his death may have served a greater purpose.

If GOD was going to *"try"* Israel, what better way to do this or a better time to do such a thing, than when Israel was about as bad off as they had ever been. As was stated at the beginning of this book, there may not have ever been a more corrupt and hopeless time in the long history of Israel than during the time of Jesus. It is said, that a *"person / people who believes in nothing, will believe anything"*. Perhaps many had lost their faith in GOD. If Jesus was a false prophet, he was a very good one who performed his task by really testing Abraham's descendants as well as possibly laying groundwork for the future. Sort of a *"two-fer"* accomplished. That is, if that was the plan.

Whatever GOD'S plan, it involves HIS gathering and restoring of HIS people Israel It is only regarding Israel, the Law and where and how Jesus fits into the life and culture of an ancient religion based on the name of YHWH their GOD that brings these forces together. YHWH had said that HE would *"prove"* Israel to see if they really loved HIM with all of their *heart* and *soul*. One of the ways that HE said HE would do this, is with false prophets. The main point here is, that at the time of Jesus, there was no such thing as Christianity. Jesus was a Jew living under the Law of his forefathers. What happened 2,000 years ago in the small Kingdom of Israel and with it's Jewish people, concerned only them and their relationship with their GOD YHWH.

Nevertheless, there seems to be a mystery concerning the affect that he had on the rest of the world that is too profound to be either ignored nor is accidental. His (and Paul's) *"doctrine"* seemed at times to be a variance with the Law, yet Israel was to keep the Law *and* he gave hope to the Nations.

Was the message of Jesus given to Israel to *"keep the Commandments"* GOD'S way for telling them to *"return"*. And was not the message of Jesus possibly GOD'S way of preparing the Nations to know *YHWH and HIS Law*?

Malachi 1:11, (11) For from the rising of the sun even unto the going down of the same <u>My Name is great among the Nations</u>; and in every place offerings are presented unto My Name, even pure oblations; for <u>My Name is great among the Nations, saith YHWH</u> of hosts.

These words by the Prophet Malachi were words of shame to Israel who had become corrupt and were making offerings to YHWH in vain. The Prophet reminds Israel of their offering blind, lame and contemptible offerings to their GOD. It is not inconceivable that many of the surrounding people not of Israel, sacrificed to the mighty GOD of Israel *"YHWH"* whom they had heard about from their own hills in their own Nations, much as Israel had sacrificed to foreign *"gods"* of other Nations themselves.

YHWH often uses the nations to shame Israel for Israel's own misconduct.

Isaiah 2:2-3, (2) And it shall come to pass <u>in the end of days</u>, that the mountain of YHWH'S house shall be established as the top of the mountains, and shall be exalted above the hills; <u>and all Nations shall flow unto it</u>. (3) And many peoples shall go and say: '<u>Come ye, and let us go up to the mountain of YHWH, to the house of the God of Jacob; and He will teach us of His Ways, and we will walk in His paths.</u>' For out of Zion shall go forth <u>the Law</u>, and the word of YHWH from Jerusalem.

RIDDLES - PROVERBS - PARABLES

One thing is for sure, Jesus was a very intelligent SEED of Abraham. If GOD did *"plant"* Jesus to tempt HIS own people, HE could not have chosen a better way to do so. For the fact that Jesus spoke so much in riddles, proverbs and parables made it almost impossible to define much of what he was actually saying. It was very evident even back 2,000 years ago that the people were clearly frustrated by the way that he spoke. They had a difficult time pinning him down on certain issues and understanding what he was saying half of the time, especially regarding the Law. Even his own followers could not keep up with his way of teaching much of the time during his ministry.

Given the issue of a translation from an ancient Semitic language from 2,000 years ago regarding a very technical document such as the Law of Moses, then the riddles, proverbs and parables become an even larger obstacle in understanding the truth.

Was the sending of Jesus to Israel somehow calculated on the part of GOD? Was Jesus the very thing that Jesus *himself* warned his followers (Matthew 7:15-20) to guard against? Was Jesus a *"wolf in sheep's clothing"* (to Israel)? Was Jesus warning his followers by hinting about himself? Was Jesus *"the lamb of GOD"*, or was he something else to the Jewish people? As if to say that his entire life and death was a huge conspiracy by GOD to tempt his own people. If this was the case, it would have been the greatest conspiracy of all time. In addition, was the creation of the world's Christian population as an outcome of Israel's rejection of Jesus by design? It appears more and more that Israel was suppose to reject Jesus and for the nations to accept. But if so, what was the purpose? Was it somehow to lay the groundwork for future help for Israel? Was it to prepare those of the Nations to know the name of "YHWH" and to be taught the Law, as per the prophets?

For truly, there is no drama or passion even close to that told of the life and death of Jesus as a religious figure in all of the worlds other religions combined. For whether one believes or not, it is a remarkable story and links Jews and Christians who truly fear GOD, in a way which only GOD understands. For it must be appreciated that if there were no Jews, there would have been no Jewish Jesus. And if there had not been a Jewish Jesus, there would be no Christians. Today there would not be several million Christian *"Zionist"* supporters of Israel. Was this by design? To this author, there are no such thing as accidents or coincidents. There is a reason for all things. But just how this develops may determine the fate of many Christians as their real true support for Israel is tried, tested and authenticated by GOD.

'SIGNS AND WONDERS'

Jesus had said that if they could not believe his words, then at least believe because of his *"works"*. Works, miracles, signs and wonders were warned against. GOD said to Israel in so many words, not to be fooled by *"signs"* and *"wonders"* (Deuteronomy 13:1-6). For HE wants to know that Israel really loves HIM or not, *"for **YHWH your God** putteth you to PROOF, to know **whether ye do love YHWH your God** with all your heart and with all your soul. **After YHWH your God** shall ye walk, and **Him** shall ye fear, and **His** commandments shall ye keep, and unto **His** voice shall ye hearken, and **Him** shall ye serve, and unto **Him** shall ye cleave."*

It is after YHWH, the GOD of Israel, and only after YHWH the GOD of Israel that Israel is to walk, to fear, to keep Commandments, to hearken, to serve and to cleave.

To many of the Christian faith, the name of *"Jesus"* is synonymous with *"GOD"*. Jesus is worshiped *as* GOD, or Jesus *is* thought of as *being* GOD. Likewise, according to Christian doctrine, it is the name of Jesus wherein salvation is found. This is a huge problem according to the Hebrew scriptures regarding YHWH and his holy name. In **_YHWH: The Name of GOD, The Forgotten GOD of the SEED of Abraham,_** importance of HIS holy name and that there is no other name under heaven for Israel HIS people is explored. According to the word of GOD YHWH, there is no other name for the GOD of

Israel, or for the salvation of Israel. It is HE alone *"YHWH"*, who is the author and finisher of Israel HIS people. It is *"YHWH"* who is *"Savior"*.

John 14 continues where Jesus said to ask anything in *"his"* name (John 14:1-14). The beginning of the chapter had begun with a statement about believing in *"God"* so believe in *"me"*, apparently equating himself with *"God"*, later *"his name"* referring to Jesus (John 14:13-14). It would seem with all of the times that Jesus had to tell or remind his listeners who he was, that John the Baptist had not done his job very well before his head was taken from him.

The name of **"YHWH"** and the name of **"Jesus"**, are two different names.

Zechariah 10:12, (12) And I will strengthen them in <u>YHWH</u>; <u>and they shall walk up and down in His Name</u>, saith <u>YHWH</u>.

Zechariah 13:9, (9)........<u>They shall call on My Name</u>, and I will answer them; I will say: 'It is My people', and they shall say: '<u>YHWH is my God.</u>'

In the many words of the Prophets of YHWH, it is the name of *"YHWH"* that all of the Nations will <u>know</u>, will <u>bow</u> down to, and will give <u>praise</u> to. With regard to the *"works"* of Jesus, in telling his doubters at one point, if they could not bring themselves to be convinced that he was the *"messiah"* because of his words, then at least be persuaded by what they saw in the things that he did. This is very telling. As if his own words did not matter. If in the end, their acceptence did not have to be any deeper than what they could see and hear with their senses, what does that say about his message?

YHWH had warned against, even *"signs"* and *"wonders"*, *"thou shalt not hearken"*. Anything which remotely would lead Israel away from the path of YHWH their GOD was something they were to ignore. Signs and wonders alone were not enough, neither any doctrine which gave not YHWH HIS honor or did not keep HIS Law. This is especially relevant when the issue of *"name"* comes up. Again, there is no evidence that the name of YHWH was ever uttered by Jesus. None of the Prophets of YHWH prophesied without proclaiming the words as the words from YHWH, **"by name"**. That is, they uttered HIS name, **YHWH**, as the author of their words, *"thus saith YHWH"*.

Jesus had much to say about the Father, about being *"one"*, about the Father's words, the Father's Commandments etc., but he never said that magic name which gives authority to his words spoken. Even if Jesus had said the name of GOD which is *"YHWH"*, his doctrine then becomes the remaining issue still unresolved. Was Jesus *"adding"* or *"diminishing"* from the Law?

'THAT PROPHET'

There is evidence that many of Israel not only were suspicious that Jesus may have been sent to *"try"* them, but it was apparently known and expected that YHWH would *"tempt"* Israel with false prophets as YHWH clearly had said that HE would as illustrated by questions put to John the Baptist and to Jesus.

The Hebrew used in Deuteronomy 13:4 and translated as *"proof"*, comes from the root *(Nun-Samech-Heh)* meaning *test* or *try,* and can have the meaning to *tempt* or *prove* something or someone. Why did GOD say that HE would do this? It was to *prove* Israel, to *test* HIS people and to *"try"* and *"tempt"* them *"to know whether ye do love YHWH your God with all your heart and with all your soul."* This was, and still is very important to GOD.

It was true then, when those words were written by GOD 'S Prophet Moses, and remains true now, of supreme importance to YHWH that YHWH'S holy inheritance love him with all of their heart and soul, *"willingly"*. It is important that Israel obey and fear GOD, but it is more important for Israel to love their GOD YHWH because they choose to love HIM.

YHWH continues by telling what Israel is to do with *that prophet* (*Ha-Navi Ha-Hoo*) who tempts Israel to follow other gods . *"That Prophet"* is to be put to death, *"And THAT PROPHET, or that dreamer of dreams, shall be put to death"*. Was Jesus tempting Israel to follow him? Did Jesus die for *tempting*?
Was his death *not* a death for others sins but for his own sins by the Law?

This same expression (that prophet) is used again in Ezekiel regarding a *"prophet"* whom YHWH has *"enticed"*. This particular phrase regarding a prophet is not used when referring to one of GOD'S *"good"* prophets. It is used when referring to a false prophet or a good prophet *"gone rogue"*. ***"The Prophet"*** in Ezekiel 14:9 is a good Prophet of YHWH. ***"That Prophet"*** is the same prophet *after* he was enticed by GOD and became bad. It is a subtle difference, but a significant difference nevertheless. The Hebrew Bible is fairly consistent in this usage.

Ezekiel 14:9, (9) And when The Prophet is enticed and speaketh a word, I YHWH have enticed That Prophet, and I will stretch out My hand upon him, and will destroy him from the midst of My people Israel.

The scripture from Ezekiel, is a *"good"* Prophet, *"the prophet"* who has been *"enticed"* by GOD to utter prophecy not from GOD. Once enticed, *"the"* Prophet now becomes *"that prophet"*. This is the same wording used in Deuteronomy 13:6 referring to a bad prophet. Was this what was meant when John was asked who he was? Were the people asking John the Baptist (John 1:25) if he was *"that"* prophet being neither the *"messiah"* or the Prophet Elijah, but one who was sent to *"prove"* them?

John 1:19-21, (19) And this is the record of John, when the Jews sent priests and Levites from Jerusalem to ask him, Who art thou? (20) And he confessed, and denied not; but confessed, I am not the Christ. (21) And they asked him, What then? Art thou Elias? And he saith, I am not. Art thou that prophet? And he answered, No.

There is an odd story of a *"man of God"*, a prophet, who in I Kings 13:1-32 is accused by YHWH of rebellion, that he *"rebelled against the word of YHWH"*. It is the story of someone who as a man of GOD, had gone against the word of YHWH which was given to him. YHWH had him slain by a lion. So a prophet can *"overstep"* as in this case. For YHWH had a good prophet tempted by a false prophet. This is not the only example of such a thing, but perhaps the most telling. Even a prophet must be careful of being tempted.

That Israel was aware of this possibility of being tempted is hinted at regarding some discussion regarding John the Baptist. For the people asked him, as they would later with Jesus, who he was. Their question is possibly more important than the answer. For they asked John the Baptist if he was the *"messiah"* (Christ, Savior, the anointed one), or if he was *"Elias"* (Elijah the Prophet who was to come before the day of YHWH), or was he *"that Prophet"*. The people were asking for an answer to one of three possibilities, *"messiah"*,or (the *"good"* prophet) *"Elijah"*, or *"other"*, ie. (***"that prophet"***).

Well, if John the Baptist was neither the long awaited *"messiah"*, nor was he the Prophet *"Elijah"*, they were definitely speaking of something or someone else. By all appearances, they were in a strange way asking him if he were *"that Prophet"*, one who would come to tempt Israel, if in deed *"that"* prophet meant a tempter. Which on the face of it, would have received a lie as an answer if he really were a false prophet, else a truthful answer would have been defeating the purpose of his being there in the first place. *"That prophet"* alludes to a *"false prophet"* to *"try"* Israel.

It would be a little like asking someone if that person were lying to them, or would they lie to them. If they were a liar, they would of course say *"no"*, so what is the point of asking if the questioner believes that the possibility exists of being deceived? Nevertheless, John the Baptist was asked if he were *"that prophet"*. He denied that he was the messiah and the Prophet Elijah, yet Jesus said that John the Baptist (Matthew 17:11-13) was Elijah. Regarding John the Baptist, when Israel asked who he was, John the Baptist denied that he was the Prophet Elijah as well as the others questions put to him.

John 1:20-21, (20) And he confessed and denied not; but confessed, <u>I am not the Christ</u>. (21) And they asked him, What hen? <u>Art thou Elijah?</u> And he saith, <u>I am not</u>. Art thou <u>that prophet</u>? And he answered, <u>no</u>.

John 1:25, (25) And they asked him, and said unto him, Why baptizest thou then, if thou be not <u>that Christ</u>, nor <u>Elias</u>, neither <u>That Prophet</u>?

Jesus said plainly referring to John the Baptist that he <u>was</u> Elijah.

Matthew 11:14 (14) And if ye will receive it, this is Elijah , which was for to come.

This term (that prophet) is used again referring to Jesus, however it seems to be possibly taken as the opposite in meaning. When Jesus was making miracles of bread and fish, the men proclaimed that this was proof the Jesus was *"that prophet"* that would come, unless of course they were accusing Jesus of being a false prophet *because* of his miracles. This too, is a distinct possibility. But also, they seem to be saying that Jesus was possibly *"Elijah"* for he was expected and many already believed that Jesus might be him. But looking at the other side, if they were accusing Jesus, they were saying that his miracles were only proof of his deceiving the people because of his doctrine being so different. As with many things concerning Jesus, it is difficult to tell. What exactly was meant by *"that"* prophet is not clear.

But many Christian Bibles will refer to Deuteronomy 18:15-22 which is not referring to Elijah and appears to be GOD stating how he will raise up to Israel a Prophet from their own people when one is needed. This was done by GOD many times and often. The entire Book of Judges consists of such *"messiahs"*, *"prophets"*, *"seers"* and *"judges"* who *"delivered"* Israel.

Returning to Deuteronomy 13:1-6, it goes on to state that that Prophet shall speak *in the name* of *"YHWH"*. As already covered, it is not known if the name of *"YHWH"* was ever uttered by Jesus or John for that matter. Knowing this is critical, for the prophet who speaks words *presumptuously* in YHWH'S name which YHWH did not give to speak, or speak words in the name of other *gods* **shall die**. Jesus seemed to speak most of the time in *his own name*.

John 6:14 (14) then those men, when they had seen the miracle that Jesus did, said, This is of a truth, <u>That Prophet</u> that should come into the world

They may have been doubters accusing Jesus of being a *"tempter",* although for many apparently persuaded by what they had seen, they threw caution to the wind and followed Jesus, believing in *"his name"* based seemingly just on their senses seeing miracles rather than the Law. For it was knowing the Law and keeping it that YHWH was speaking of. *For the Law itself would protect them from being fooled by the very miracles of such a false prophet.*

Again, most seemed to take these miracles as a positive sign, although it is unclear what exactly was meant other than they seemed to look on Jesus as at least a prophet, and perhaps a specific prophet. It may be instructive to see what Jesus had to say about false prophets himself.

Matthew 7:15-20, (15) Beware of false prophets, which come to you in sheep's clothing, but inwardly they are ravening wolves. (16) Ye shall know them by their fruits. Do men gather grapes of thorns, or figs of thistles? (17) Even so, every good tree bringeth forth good fruit; but a corrupt tree bringeth forth evil fruit. (18) A good tree cannot bring forth evil fruit, neither can a corrupt tree bring forth good fruit. (19) Every tree that bringeth forth not good fruit is hewn down, and cast into the fire. (20) Wherefore by their fruits ye shall know them.

Jesus was speaking of *"true prophets"* of YHWH verses *"false prophets"*. If one determines the *"fruits"* of the Apostle Paul (based loosely on the words of Jesus), as being the faith of the Nations of the the world, then an argument could possibly be made that the words of Jesus bore much fruit. As it is difficult to argue against the existence of 2.2 billion Christians in the world, even though throughout history they have not always lived up to his words.

However regarding Israel, if one measures the amount of *"fruit"* produced by the number of believers of the *"lost sheep of the House of Israel"*, another picture comes into focus. For as has been thoroughly discussed already, Jesus said that he came *"but"* (only) for the *"lost sheep of the House of Israel"*, and instructed his disciples not to preach to the Nations but to *"Israel"*. So the question then arises concerning Israel and it's lost sheep, did Jesus as prophet bear much fruit? Where are the sheep? How does one measure such a thing?

'THE JEWS'

One may be struck in reading the Christian Bible, that most of the time whenever the *"Jews"* are mentioned, it has an air about it that is *"foreign"*. In other words, it often has the feel not as a Jewish people writing about themselves, but of another people far removed from the *"Jews"* writing about them, *"the Jews"*. As a Jewish person it screams to this author on every page.

The wording of the scriptures when referring to *"the Jews"*, reads not as a people who speaks of itself, but as a foreign people speaking of an *"other"* people. Depending on the translation of course, at least the English reads not as a Jewish people relating a story about itself to itself, but as a story told by someone else about *"the Jews"*, as a voyeur does through another's window.

If a person's family name was *"Jews"*, they would not continue to refer to themselves as *"the Jews"* to their own family. They would not repetitiously repeat *"the Jews"* did this, or *"the Jews"* did that. A person speaking about his own people would hardly keep referring to them by their name in such a fashion. There would be no need to do so, as your audience and your topic were one and the same.

They might say *"the people were angry"*. They would hardly say, *"the Jews were angry"*. To always feel the need to constantly refer to your own people as *"the Jews"* would not be done and is odd on the face of it. It would only be written in such a fashion if the writer was not Jewish. For after all, the original writers of the Gospels by all accounts, were Jewish and were writing about events which took place in Israel regarding their own people.

By most historical accounts, for approximately the first two hundred years, the majority of *"believers"* were Jewish, although no one really knows for sure how long they remained in the majority. Even if it were only for the first hundred years, it would not make much difference. The point is however, it is very doubtful that the original Gospels were written down by non Jews, in whatever language it was written. Yet, they all read as such. Having said this it becomes even more suspicious why then what has come down to us today called the *"Gospels"*, refers to *"the Jews"* as if they were describing or distancing themselves from some unclean vermin. Many of the scriptures that have written *"the Jews"*, have a very distinct *"them"* and *"us"* feel to it.

It must be said that for years when studying the Gospels the feeling of strong discomfort existed with no understanding as to why. Then one day it struck like a bolt of lightening. The writers are writing in the third person. They are speaking not only from another place but as a different people. It is consistent throughout all four of the Gospels as if an editor went through all of them and made this alteration. The vantage point of the original Jewish writers writing about his own people and events, changed to reflect that of an alien people.

By way of illustration, if an American is either telling a story or writing about events having taken place somewhere in America, that person would tell the story but would not keep stating over and over again each time either an individual is mentioned or that the people in the story were *"American"*. If you are an American talking to your fellow Americans about another American (a news report is a good example), you would not state the people in the story you were describing as being *"American"*. At least not unless the writer was possibly not an American himself, and / or was writing possibly to, or for a non American audience. All of the Gospels reads like this.

Yet, other than a few obvious exceptions which were made to draw a distinction between individuals or groups (for example between *"the Jews"* and the Samaritans, or when the Romans are mentioned) most, if not all of the scriptures were written as if the life and times of Jesus was observed by an alien from either another planet, or at least someone who is not Jewish. For most of the references made concerning *"the Jews"* appear to have been written by an observer, someone from other than the Jewish people.

However, there are other possible explanations which might help explain this phenomenon. It could be the translation. This seems highly doubtful though given the way some of the text reads. It could be just a writing style, which too, does not seem very plausible. There does appear another, more sinister cause for this and it has much more to do with anti-Jewish doctrine by some of the early church fathers after the new *"religion"* was no longer thought of as just another Jewish sect, and the Gentiles became the dominate force with the new religion now becoming the religion of the *"Nations"*.

As shown already, some of the early writers of the Gospels were not above changing the words of Hebrew Prophets to fit their doctrine (Isaiah 42:1-4 vs. Matthew 12:17-21), so we already know that possibly inserting words or changing or redacting older texts is not out of the question. In this example, verse 12:21 of Matthew was rewritten from Isaiah 42:4 *"And the isles shall wait for his teaching"*, to *"And in his name shall the Gentiles trust"*, we know that Gentile *"agenda"* did exist. As was discussed earlier, there is no way the Hebrew or Aramaic could possibly be interpreted, mistranslated or accidentally written like this. It was a deliberate changing of the text by the writer of the Gospel of Matthew or was later redacted and altered to fit a particular doctrine by early church scribes. According to the Greek text, it apparently began with them and has survived until now in other translations.

If one wanted to make a significant difference in the Gospels without exerting to much mental effort, it would not be all that difficult to change for example, nothing but *"the people"* in the four Gospels to *"the Jews"*. It may not be possible to know if this was done or not, but by the simple act of changing *"the people"* to *"the Jews"*, it would have significantly changed the texture and feel of the stories as *"the Jews"* take on a more ominous air of evil about them each time those words are either read or uttered. They have an accumulative negative affect on both the reader and listener.

Additionally, the obvious bias of the writer changes what was an insular story of a people relating a part of their own history about themselves to themselves, into what then becomes a chronicle of *"us"* and *"them"*, where *"the Jews"* take on more of a *"boogie man"* type of persona rather than a people writing about a part of it's own history about one of it's own sons.

'GOD'S SABBATH'

As the belief in Jesus and the hope of salvation spread to the Nations far beyond the land of Israel, eventually all of the Jewish believers became a distinct minority, and then eventually just an invisible historical footnote. Those Jews of the SEED of Israel who began as believers in Jesus from it's inception, eventually died out, and their offspring became absorbed into the great mass of believers of what would become an entirely new religion of the Gentiles, shed of any legal underpinnings related to the Law of Moses.

"Christianity" fast evolved into a world religion. After the Council of Nicaea in 325 was convened by the Roman Emperor Constantine, the codification of church doctrine and most of the non Jewish practices of the new religion became etched into stone. A good place to look for when or where the Gentiles began redacting original Jewish writings would be around this time.

According to many historians, Constantine was not interested in the Jewish origins of the new religion and was not overly friendly towards the Jewish people in general, who to him were responsible for killing the son of God. Many of his feelings were eventually reflected in some of the early church doctrine which has remained largely intact until this day. For what else could explain the jettison by the believers in YHWH the GOD of Israel and of YHWH'S *"Sabbath"* day of rest and other Jewish practices to the point that most all of any connection to the origin of their new religion from Israel no longer exists and has been obliterated. Early church doctrine distanced itself from any and all roots associated with Israel, the Jewish people or the Law of Moses but for the bear minimum needed as a base to prop up their new religion. They put the Jewish people in as negative a light as possible in their rewriting the Gospels which fell into their hand. This was no mere accident.

As the new faith grew, changed and morphed into what would eventually become an unrecognizable religion completely devoid of any of the original Jewish or Israelite vestiges of Covenant or Law, much of the wording within the Christian Bible itself took on an appearance reflective of that change. In much of the writings, when referring to *"the Jews"*, the obvious dichotomy between the author and the Jewish subjects in the story is observable, and indeed can be felt. The reader is obliged to assume the vantage point of the writer as he reads through the Gospels, much as a voyeur observing out of morbid curiosity the sufferings of another. There is a sense of detached bemusement from the words used describing the curious people, *"the Jews"*.

Whether the original words of the Gospels were written as they have come down to us today, which seems highly unlikely or they were altered by some enterprising young monk along the way may never be known. But one thing seems fairly certain, the words referring to *"the Jews"* in the Gospels as they stand now do not reflect a person who identified himself as being Jewish but reflects the mentality, position and vantage point of someone who was and is completely outside the Jewish historical narrative.

'THE JEWS, THE JEWS, THE JEWS'

Matthew 28:15, (15) So they took the money, and did as they were taught: and this saying is commonly reported among the Jews until this day.

Mark 7:3, (3) For the Pharisees, and all the Jews, except they wash their hands oft, eat not, holding the tradition of the elders. (Mark 7:1-23)

Luke 7:3, (3) And when he heard of Jesus, he sent unto him the elders of the Jews, beseeching him that he would come and heal his servant.

In these scriptures, why was it necessary when referring to the people to identify them as *"Jews"*? Would a common *"saying"* be said *"until this day"* not need to be identified? Would not *"the Pharisees, and all the people"* make more sense? And would it not be obvious who the *"elders"* were by the writer, if that writer was Jewish? If he was a Jewish writer, why would he continually feel the need to say *"the Jews"* unless he was not a Jew?

Luke 23:37, (37) And saying, If thou be the king of the Jews, save thyself.

Luke 23:51 (51) The same had not consented to the counsel and deed of them;) he was of Arimathæa, a city of the Jews: who also himself waited for the kingdom of God.

John 1:19, (19) And this is the record of John, when the Jews sent priests and Levites from Jerusalem to ask him, Who art thou?

Even a group of unruly bystanders would simply ask, *"If thou art king, save thyself"*. In the third example, would not a simple statement that Priests and Levites were sent from Jerusalem to inquire, have been sufficient? Who else would have sent the priests and Levites and why the need to say *"the Jews"*?

John 2:6, (6) And there were set there six waterpots of stone, after the manner of the purifying of the Jews, containing two or three firkins apiece

Who else would have needed pots for purification? Why would the writer, if Jewish, feel the need to associate the water pots for purification with *"the Jews"*? Who was this writer and who was he writing for, the Klingons?

John 2:13, (13) And the Jews' Passover was at hand, and Jesus went up to Jerusalem,

Unless there was some phantom people in Israel who were celebrating Passover in Jerusalem, what other people could *"Passover"* possibly be referring to but the Jewish people! Of course it was *"the*

Jews Passover". The writer of this verse surely gives himself away as being foreign to the proceedings of Jewish observance by his repeated reference to *"the Jews"*. As has been mentioned, even though the Samaritans still existed, they lived in the north of the country in *"Samaria"*. The Samaritans too observed Passover, but unless they or anyone else are specifically mentioned in the Gospels the Jews are always the subject people in the narrative. Additionally, the Samaritans would never have been allowed into Jerusalem to celebrate nor would they want to as they did not recognize Jerusalem as the place where YHWH put HIS holy name. So why did the writer feel the need to identify the Jews celebrating Passover in Jerusalem, unless the writer himself is someone else other than a Jew who felt the need to point this out?

John 11:55 (55) And <u>the Jews</u>' Passover was nigh at hand: and many went out of the country up to Jerusalem before the Passover, to purify themselves.

The people were not *"the Jews"*. The people were the people in the story who were Jewish. The writer constantly identifies himself by his use of this expression as someone who is not one of *"the Jews"* in the story nor is apparently related to them in any way, but an outside observer who is writing about *"them"*. *"And the Jews Passover"* was nigh at hand who were going up to Jerusalem. To who else would Passover have been *"nigh at hand"*? As just noted, with the exception of when others are brought into the story and identified as such, there was no one but *"the Jews"* associated with Passover and Jerusalem? Certainly when referring to Passover being celebrated, identifying the celebrants as *"the Jews"* is not only redundant but downright suspicious. Even the Samaritans who celebrate Passover only on Mt. Gerizim are only mentioned when they are there for a reason, such as the woman at the well. Otherwise the entire story of the Gospels is always a story of *"the Jews"*.

John 2:18, (18) Then answered <u>the Jews</u> and said unto him, What sign shewest thou unto us, seeing that thou doest these things?

John 2:20, (20) Then said <u>the Jews</u>, Forty and six years was this temple in building, and wilt thou rear it up in three days?

"Then answered / said the people" would have made much more sense as the entire scene involved only Jesus and Jews in the Temple in Jerusalem. Why would the writer feel the need to identify the people as *"the Jews"*?

John 3:1, (1) There was a man of the Pharisees, named Nicodemus, a ruler of <u>the Jews</u>:

What other people but the Jewish people would a Pharisee be a ruler of? Had one of the Pharisees gone out into the desert unbeknownst to the rest of his crowd, and gathered a group of Bedouin tribesmen to brainwash? Of course the *"Pharisee"* Nicodemus was a ruler of the Jews. Or perhaps the writer was concerned that the reader might mistaken Nicodemus for the leader of a motorcycle gang? He could just as easily have said that the Pharisee Nicodemus was a leader amongst the people or even of the Pharisees.

John 3:25, (25) Then there arose a question between some of John's disciples and <u>the Jews</u> about purifying.

Once again, at a place where *"the people"* would have been the obvious choice for a Jewish writer, the term *"the Jews"* is used instead. Unless John the Baptist had become the secret leader of a legion of Roman soldiers, the question between his disciples who were *"Jews"* and the *"Jews"* who were *Jews*" was a question amongst "*Jews*", and most assuredly a question of the same people. *"A question arose amongst the people"* would have been more than sufficient in telling this story. The odd thing about the story is the awkward distance the writer is attempting to put between *"John's disciples"* and the "*Jews*". Think about this. They are all Jews! There are a dozen ways one can draw a distinction between the followers of John and those who were not. Yet the writer in remaining consistent continues to identify *"the people"* as *"the Jews"*. Apparently, there are *"John's Jews"*, and then there are *"the Jews Jews"*. One is reminded of "*clean*" and "*unclean*" when this is read.

John 4:9 (9) Then said the woman of Samaria unto him, How is it that thou, being a Jew, askest drink of me, which am a woman of Samaria? For the Jews have no dealings with the Samaritans

John 4:22, (22) Ye worship ye know not what; we know what we worship; for salvation is of the Jews

Within these two scriptures is a good example where a distinction *was* necessary and is appropriate. Jesus the Jew was speaking to the non Jewish Samaritan woman. When this example is contrasted with the example just cited earlier regarding John the Baptist, it makes that of John the Baptist and his disciples concerning the reference of *"the Jews"* sound forced and silly.

John 5:1, (1) After this there was a feast of the Jews; and Jesus went up to Jerusalem.

What other people in the story of the Gospels were there but the Jews of Israel? And who would have been celebrating a feast in Jerusalem but *"the Jews"*, especially if it were one of the three feasts according to the Law which require Israel's males to appear in Jerusalem before their GOD YHWH? As already discussed, the Samaritans do not recognize Jerusalem as the holy city of YHWH where HE chose to put HIS name nor do they accept it is as the place of HIS holy Temple. Indeed, they would not have been welcomed in Jerusalem. The writer is very clearly not speaking of them. If the writer was Jewish from this time period, he would surely have been aware of this. But even more importantly, he would not have felt the need to identify the people going up to Jerusalem to celebrate this feast as "*the Jews*".

John 5:10, (10) The Jews therefore said unto him that was cured, It is the Sabbath day: it is not lawful for thee to carry thy bed.

John 5:15-16, 18, (15) The man departed, and told the Jews that it was Jesus, which had made him whole.(16) And therefore did the Jews persecute Jesus, and sought to slay him, because he had done these things on the Sabbath day.....(18) Therefore the Jews sought the more to kill him, because he not only had broken the Sabbath, but said also that God was his Father, making himself equal with God.

Two thousand years ago, what other people on the planet knew what the Sabbath was or observed it but the Samaritans and the Jews. And we are not altogether that sure of what the Samaritans were doing on Shabbat. Again, *"the people"* here would have been the obvious choice in the telling of this episode. Other than specific groups of people like the Priests or the Pharisees etc., who are identified whenever they are involved, to constantly explain to the reader that these people are *"the Jews"* is without question an act of alien redundancy.

John 6:4, (4) And the Passover, a feast of the Jews, was nigh

Given the repeated identification of Passover as being a feast of *"the Jews"*, it becomes all too obvious that the writer is someone who is **not** one of the participants in the feast of *"the Jews"*, but is an outsider who is describing a people who is celebrating this feast time for an audience who does not celebrate Passover. He is not a *"member of the tribe"*. There is no other way of explaining the consistent identification of the people as being *"the Jews"*.

In other words, who ever this person is who is doing the writing, he is someone who is describing an event which is foreign to himself. One other strong possibility exists, that the writer has taken the original document telling of these events written from the perspective of a native born participant, a *"Jewish scribe"*, and changed it completely from a first person observer into a story for an audience not acquainted with Jewish feast days.

Additionally, as has been stated as well, the constant reference to *"the Jews"* in this manner throughout the four Gospels, has a very negative overall affect on the reader. By the time the reader finishes reading the last Gospel, *"the Jews"* have taken on a sinister roll far in excess of what actually took place in the drama. Something else the non Jewish reader must take into consideration, that this entire story took place in a very small kingdom entirely amongst it's own people. It had nothing whatsoever to do with the other Nations nor were there any Gentiles involved. Other than a couple of Romans or a Samaritan here and there, the only real players were all Jewish and only specifically identified as Pharisees, Sadducees or Priests when appropriate. Jesus was a Jew with a Jewish message for a Jewish people. There were no Christians to be offended as yet, for there was no such thing as a Christian. The followers of Jesus were **not** Christians but were *"the Jews"*.

Something else, as each of the four Gospels was supposedly written by a different person, the consistency in use of the term *"the Jews"* in the manner in which it is used throughout each Gospel is all the more suspicious when one really thinks about it. It has all of the ear markings of later editors, most likely the same editor, giving prominence to the Jewish people when none was needed, called for or warranted.

*John 6:41,41 **The Jews** then murmured at him, because he said, I am the bread which came down from heaven*

*John 6:52, (52) **The Jews** therefore strove among themselves, saying, How can this man give us his flesh to eat?*

*John 7:1-2, (1) After these things Jesus walked in Galilee: for he would not walk in Jewry, because **the Jews** sought to kill him (2) Now **the Jews'** Feast of Tabernacles was at hand.*

"The people, the people, the people" murmured, strove and sought, not *"the Jews"*! Of course, the *"feast of Tabernacles"* was the feast, they all were celebrating. Why not write, *'The Jews sought to kill the Jew'*?

*Matthew 10:18, (18) And ye shall be brought before governors and kings for my sake, for a testimony against them and **the Gentiles.***

Again, when it was necessary to distinguish between groups, it was done. However, the writers of the Gospels almost always distinguish *"the Jews"* even when they are the <u>only</u> people in the story and when it is not only not necessary, but downright strange when it is done.

Again, unless a group of people is singled out for distinction, the story in the Gospels is *always* about *"the Jews"*. It is the celebration of *"Sukkot"* (Booths) which is being talked about here. Why the writer feels the need here to tell the reader that *"tabernacles"* is *"the Jews"* feast is just plain weird. It sounds almost as if the writer himself is from Mars or from some distant planet, who clandestinely was visiting Mecca and trying to describe the stoning of Satan experience during the annual Hadj to his fellow green buddies back home.

John 7:11, 13, 15, 35, (11) Then the Jews sought him at the feast, and said, Where is he? (13) Howbeit no man spake openly of him for fear of the Jews. (15) And the Jews marvelled, saying, How knoweth this man letters, having never learned? (35) Then said the Jews among themselves, Whither will he go, that we shall not find him? will he go unto the dispersed among the Gentiles, and teach the Gentiles?

John 8:22, 48, 52, 57, (22) Then said the Jews, Will he kill himself? because he saith, Whither I go, ye cannot come. (48) Then answered the Jews, and said unto him, Say we not well that thou art a Samaritan, and hast a devil? (52) Then said the Jews unto him, Now we know that thou hast a devil. Abraham is dead, and the prophets; and thou sayest, If a man keep my saying, he shall never taste of death. (57 Then said the Jews unto him, Thou art not yet fifty years old, and hast thou seen Abraham?

In these two examples, at least some of the participants being spoken of needed to be identified as they mention the Gentiles, and the Samaritans. Calling Jesus a *"Samaritan"* was a strong insult as the Samaritans were no longer considered as being of Israel. Although some of the other usage of *"the Jews"* is still questionable. As Jesus was speaking with his people during the feast in the first example, identifying them as *"the Jews"* still has that *"alien"* quality about it. John 8:22, 48, 52 and 57 could all have been *"Then said / answered the people"* without screaming out their ethnicity.

John 9:18, 22, (18) But the Jews did not believe concerning him, that he had been blind, and received his sight, until they called the parents of him that had received his sight.(22) These words spake his parents, because they feared the Jews: for the Jews had agreed already, that if any man did confess that he was Christ, he should be put out of the synagogue.

Once again we have here, *"the Jews"* fearing *"the Jews"*. As if to say, *'because these Jews feared the Jews, for the Jews had agreed already....'*.

John 10:19, 24, 31, (19) There was a division therefore again among the Jews for these sayings.(24) Then came the Jews round about him, and said unto him, How long dost thou make us to doubt? If thou be the Christ, tell us plainly.(31) Then the Jews took up stones again to stone him.(33) The Jews answered him, saying, For a good work we stone thee not; but for blasphemy; and because that thou, being a man, makest thyself God.

Apparently here, we have *"the Jews"* who were speaking to *"the Jews"*. What an oddity, the Jews speaking to the Jews!

John 11:8, 19, 31, 33, 36, 45, 53-55, (8) His disciples say unto him, Master, the Jews of late sought to stone thee; and goest thou thither again? (19) And many of the Jews came to Martha and Mary, to comfort them concerning their brother. (31) The Jews then which were with her in the house, and comforted her, when they saw Mary, that she rose up hastily and went out, followed her, saying, She goeth unto the grave to weep there. (33 When Jesus therefore saw her weeping, and the Jews also weeping which came with her, he groaned in the spirit, and was troubled,(36) Then said the Jews,

Behold how he loved him! (45) Then many of the Jews which came to Mary, and had seen the things which Jesus did, believed on him.(53) Then from that day forth they took counsel together for to put him to death. (54) Jesus therefore walked no more openly among the Jews; but went thence unto a country near to the wilderness, into a city called Ephraim, and there continued with his disciples. (55) And the Jews' Passover was nigh at hand: and many went out of the country up to Jerusalem before the passover, to purify themselves.

Think about this for just a moment and realize just how non nonsensical this statement from John 7:13 really is, *" Howbeit no man spake openly of him for fear of the Jews"*. Now as all of the players in this scene are Jews, what the writer is actually saying is that, *'Howbeit no Jew of the Jews spake openly of the Jew for fear of the Jews' of the Jews.*

The length this writer of the Gospel of John, or these writers of all of the Gospels have gone to, to draw a distinction between those Jews who followed Jesus from those Jews who did not follow Jesus is stark. Even as with John the Baptist in the earlier example, when all of the people in the scene are *"the Jews"*, the writer remains addicted to his drug of identifying the people as *"the Jews"*, seemingly unable to get enough for his *"fix"*. Obviously, what is really being said here, is that there are the *"good Jew Jews"* and then there are the *"bad Jew Jews"*. The way it is written, it is anti-Semitic in nature. The constant reference to *the Jews* in such a fashion is deliberate, calculated and has the same pen. There is no other explanation.

It seems that the obvious proclivity toward this particular slant was more than likely done by non Jews after the original Gospel was completed. In other words, these constant reminders of *"the Jews"* appear to be more likely the work of a later period than by John the Jew. For John the Jew would hardly have felt the need to keep reminding his Jewish audience that they were Jewish or that Passover was a Jewish feast, or other less subtle reminders. If John the Jew did write the Gospel of John, then his words were later altered. This could be said for all four of the original writers of the Gospels whoever they were, and whatever language they were written in. They were changed.

John 12:9, 11, (9) Much people of the Jews therefore knew that he was there: and they came not for Jesus' sake only, but that they might see Lazarus also, whom he had raised from the dead. (11) Because that by reason of him many of the Jews went away, and believed on Jesus.

John 13:33, (33) Little children, yet a little while I am with you. Ye shall seek me: and as I said unto the Jews, Whither I go, ye cannot come

Now the writer even has Jesus the Jew referring to his own people as if they had just arrived from some far away galaxy totally disconnected from himself, *"and as I said unto the Jews"*. This example actually borders on the strange. It is similar to the earlier example of John the Baptist. What Jesus was actually saying was that as he was speaking to *"the Jews"*, he told *"the Jews"* that he had told other *"the Jews"*, *"Whither I go, ye cannot come..."*. But, as it is written by the author (or editor), it is as if somehow Jesus was magically not of *"the Jews"* himself, but somehow different.

Perhaps more so than most any other scripture, the writer, scribe, redactor or author of these words in John 13:33 is allowing his true prejudice to surface. Here he clearly is attempting to make a *"distinction"* between the *"good"* Jews (the followers of Jesus), and the *"bad"* Jews (the apparent reference to the Pharisaic Jews in John 8:21) who will die in their collective sins. This theme is constant throughout the Gospels and leads this writer to conclude that at some point in the evolution of these religious writings, they underwent a significant theological cleansing, establishing the official attitudinal dogma, doctrine and prejudice towards the Jewish people. It is quite evident.

John 18:12, 14, 20, 31, 33, 36, 38, 39, (12) Then the band and the captain and officers of the Jews took Jesus, and bound him, (14) Now Caiaphas was he, which gave counsel to the Jews, that it was expedient that one man should die for the people.(20) Jesus answered him, I spake openly to the world; I ever taught in the synagogue, and in the Temple, whither the Jews always resort; and in secret have I said nothing. (31) Then said Pilate unto them, Take ye him, and judge him according to your law. The Jews therefore said unto him, It is not lawful for us to put any man to death: (33) Then Pilate entered into the judgment hall again, and called Jesus, and said unto him, Art thou the King of the Jews? (36) Jesus answered, My kingdom is not of this world: if my kingdom were of this world, then would my servants fight, that I should not be delivered to the Jews: but now is my kingdom not from hence. (38) Pilate saith unto him, What is truth? And when he had said this, he went out again unto the Jews, and saith unto them, I find in him no fault at all. (39) But ye have a custom, that I should release unto you one at the Passover: will ye therefore that I release unto you the King of the Jews?

The essence of these writings leaves one with the feeling that Jesus had somehow undergone a transformation from being a *"Jew"* into being something which was not a *"Jew"*, and who was standing amidst an alien crowd of on lookers who were drooling on each other over his blood.

John 18:12, 14, 20, is a scene where they are all Jews and only Jews. Jesus and his followers, and the band of Priests who have come to arrest him are all in the garden together. Yet, three times, the author of these words felt the craving need to identify either the Priests or their band of merry arresting men as *"the Jews"*, even having Jesus refer to his fellow countrymen as *"the Jews"*. Who else would these Priests or their men have been but *"the Jews"*?

For the writer who is detailing this scene on paper to feel the need to identify those who bound Jesus as *"the Jews"*, or that the High Priest Caiaphas was he who *"gave counsel to the Jews"* borders on an insult. That is, unless again the writer in scratching down his notes, was planning to sell his writings to a tabloid and needed to explain to the potential readers that it is *"the Jews"* who *"resort"* in the *"synagogue"* and in the *"Temple"*. Even the Romans, Greeks and Idumaeans knew that *"the Jews"* spent time in the synagogue and in the Temple. When you really stop to think what these writers of the Gospels are doing, it becomes truly bazaar. Whoever they are, it is painfully obvious that they are not writing about themselves and their own people but someone else. They were not Jewish!

This only becomes important if one is to believe that the Gospels were truly written by the Jewish followers of Jesus who witnessed these events. When in fact, the evidence points to the Gospels as being written by persons not only not Jewish, but unfamiliar with either Jewish culture or the Temple religion of Israel. We may never know who wrote the bulk of these words, but what seems certain is that much of it is alien from Israel and the Jewish people, and destroys much of it's credibility.

John 19:3, 7, 12, 14, 19-22, 31, 38, 40, 42, (3) And said, Hail, King of the Jews! and they smote him with their hands. (7) The Jews answered him, We have a law, and by our law he ought to die, because he made himself the Son of God. (12) And from thenceforth Pilate sought to release him: but the Jews cried out, saying, If thou let this man go, thou art not Cæsar's friend: whosoever maketh himself a king speaketh against Cæsar. (14) And it was the preparation of the Passover, and about the sixth hour: and he saith unto the Jews, Behold your King! (19) And Pilate wrote a title, and put it on the cross. And the writing was, JESUS OF NAZARETH THE KING OF THE JEWS. (20) This title then read many of the Jews: for the place where Jesus was crucified was nigh to the city: and it was written in Hebrew, and Greek, and Latin. (21) Then said the Chief Priests of the Jews to Pilate, Write not, The King of the Jews; but that he said, I am King of the Jews. (22) Pilate answered, What I have written I have written. (31) The Jews therefore, because it was the preparation, that the bodies should not remain upon the cross on the sabbath day, (for that sabbath day was an high day,) besought Pilate that their legs might be broken, and that they might be taken away. (38) And after this Joseph of Arimathæa, being a disciple of Jesus, but secretly for fear of the Jews, besought Pilate that he might take away the body of Jesus: and Pilate gave him leave. He came therefore, and took the body of Jesus.(40) Then took they the body of Jesus, and wound it in linen clothes with the spices, as the manner of the Jews is to bury. (42 There laid they Jesus therefore because of the Jews' preparation day; for the sepulchre was nigh at hand.

*"Then said the Chief Priest **of the Jews** to Pilate"* Ask yourself what Jewish scribe or other writing about these events would think to add *"of the Jews"* when speaking of the High Priest? Why would the High Priest of Israel need to ever be identified as being of *"the Jews"?* Only a person who was significantly far removed from these events specifically and the Jewish people in general would feel the need or think to insert such words. "*For fear of the Jews"* seems to be a popular catch phrase in the Gospels as it is written often. A person could start having nightmares if he reads this too often.

John 20:19, (19) Then the same day at evening, being the first day of the week, when the doors were shut where the disciples were assembled for fear of the Jews, came Jesus and stood in the midst, and saith unto them, Peace be unto you.

Here is another very good example of the writer, whomever he was, was attempting to draw a distinction between *"the disciples"* and *"the Jews"* again when they were all very clearly *"the Jews"*. Like the previous example cited, this as good an example as any of the many scriptures which use the term *"the Jews"*, shows why it was employed from the beginning. It was used to make *"the Jews"* as a separate entity. A Jewish person could develop a "*complex"* with so much negative insinuation. They were somehow the *"bad regular Jews"* as oppose to the *"good disciple Jews"*. As if both the idea of *"bad"* and *"Jew"* had been somehow cleansed from his followers because of what the disciples believed. For they too were "*Jews"*. But the stigma of "*bad*" and "*Jew"* remaind on "*the Jews"* who did not believe.

According to the scripture just quoted, somehow the Jewish disciples of Jesus miraculously are identified not as Jews but only as "*disciples"*, but the non disciple Jews are identified as *"the Jews"*. So just as Jesus has *abra-ka-dabra* morphed into a non Jewish type of Gentile *'god'*, his followers too have lost their own Jewishness, even while still alive.

So, something else is occurring by the use of *"the Jews"* over many, many times to describe the stories in the Gospels. For they, the Jewish disciples, were in fear of *"the Jews"*. Once again, *"the Jews"* were afraid of *"the Jews"*. I hope they got some help. After a while, the impression that comes about after repeatedly reading these identifiers, is as if that somehow Jesus himself has morphed into someone who is not related to all of these very bad people, *"the Jews"*. And from John 11:55, apparently neither are his disciples. Jesus has magically become non Jewish and his disciples have somehow become non Jewish as well. Jesus has magically become something who is "*other*", outside of the Covenant of YHWH and the Law, but one with the "*nations*". He has now become the non Jewish Gentile "*god*".

This would explain the possessiveness by many Christians who either are not aware that Jesus was a Jew, have forgotten that Jesus was a Jew, deny that Jesus was a Jew, or who feel very uncomfortable with the fact that Jesus was a Jew. Many Christians are extremely protective of what they perceive as the non Jewishness of their *"Savior"*. And if they believe as do most Jews do in a resurrection and that there is life after death, then in their religion *the second coming*, they will be shocked, for he is still a Jew and will return as such. They will be in for quite a surprise. Many Christians are unaware that Jesus was and still is a Jew, and that Jesus is not, nor was he ever a *"Christian"*.

So, just as many Gentiles, especially in the West do not regard the Jewishness of Jesus, something even more bazaar has occurred amongst many or most of the Arab Christians who have proclaimed that Jesus was not of Israel nor was he Jewish, but Jesus was a *"Palestinian"*!

'THE JEWS'

Finally, as most scholars accept that all or most of the original Gospels were first penned by Jewish followers of Jesus in what ever language they were written, these many examples of *"the Jews"* very clearly indicate that these same original Gospels underwent a significant transformation by later scribes **not** of the Jewish people. These later scribes clearly had an agenda and their constant reference to *"the Jews"* is without a doubt a mechanism by which was used to distance the believer and prejudice the believer in the negative.

'O YE SEED OF ABRAHAM'

Psalm 105: (6) O ye SEED of Abraham His servant, ye children of Jacob, His chosen ones. (7) He is YHWH our God; His judgments are in all the earth. (8) He hath remembered His Covenant for ever, the word which He Commanded to a thousand generations; (9) The Covenant which He made with Abraham, and His Oath unto Isaac; (10) And He established it unto Jacob for a Statute, to Israel for an Everlasting Covenant; (11) Saying: 'Unto thee will I give the land of Canaan, the lot of your inheritance.

The SEED of Abraham is quite literal. As is the SEED of Isaac and the SEED of Jacob. It is the same SEED. It is not some ethereal cosmic symbolic spiritual place where holy dudes hang out. It is the actual SEED of Abraham on this earth, which YHWH made a Covenant with when YHWH made HIS Covenant with Abraham *"And YHWH appeared unto Abram, and said: 'Unto thy SEED will I give this land'; ...."* (Genesis 12:7).

The Covenant made by GOD YHWH with Abraham and his *"SEED"* is an *"Eternal Covenant"*. Eternity is a concept which man has a very difficult time grasping, so he limits it so as to make it more manageable. But with GOD, *"for ever"* means *"for ever"*. And *"Everlasting Covenant"* means *"Everlasting Covenant"* and *"eternal"* means *"eternal"*, *"to all generations"* means *"to all generations"* and *"always"* means *"always.* These are God's words. HE speaks of eternity from the place of eternity.

The more one studies the many religions, most, but not all of them have their own variation of *"replacement theology"*. Whether Christianity or Islam or offshoots of these two main religions, it becomes more obvious why GOD saw fit to emphasize "SEED", pedigree and genealogy in the Hebrew scriptures and why for so many centuries these same religions have attempted (and some still do) to destroy that SEED. For as long as the *"SEED"* exists, the story of these other religions as *"god's"* people have huge holes in them. Destroying any *"witnesses"* then becomes imperative, an essential ingredient in their narrative whether with the sword or by the pen. Leave no witnesses

'HIS SEED SHALL ENDURE FOR EVER'

Psalm 89:16-37, (16) Happy is the people that know the joyful shout; they walk, O <u>YHWH</u>, in the light of <u>Thy countenance</u>. (17) In <u>Thy name</u> do they rejoice all the day; and through <u>Thy righteousness</u> are they exalted. (18) For <u>Thou</u> art the <u>glory</u> of their <u>strength</u>; and in <u>Thy favour</u> our horn is exalted. (19) For of <u>YHWH</u> is our <u>shield</u>; and the Holy One of Israel is our <u>king</u>. (20) Then Thou spokest in vision to <u>Thy godly ones</u>, and saidst: 'I have laid help upon one that is mighty; I have exalted one chosen out of the people. (21) <u>I have found David My servant; with My holy oil have I anointed him; (22) With whom My hand shall be established; Mine arm also shall strengthen him.</u> (23) The enemy shall not exact from him; nor the son of wickedness afflict him. (24) And I will beat to pieces his adversaries before him, and smite them that hate him. (25) <u>But My faithfulness and My mercy shall be with him; and through My Name shall his horn be exalted.</u> (26) I will set his hand also on the sea, and his right hand on the rivers. (27) He shall call unto Me: Thou art my Father, my God, and the rock of my salvation. (28) <u>I also will appoint him first-born</u>, the highest of the kings of the earth. (29) <u>For ever will I keep for him My Mercy, and My Covenant shall stand fast with him.</u> (30) <u>His SEED also will I make to endure for ever</u>, and his throne as the days of heaven. (31) If his children forsake My law, and walk not in Mine ordinances; (32) If they profane My Statutes, and keep not My Commandments; (33) Then will I visit their transgression with the rod, and their iniquity with strokes. (34) <u>But My Mercy will I not break off from him</u>, nor will I be false to My faithfulness. (35) My Covenant will I not profane, nor alter that which is gone out of My lips. (36) <u>Once have I sworn by My Holiness</u>: Surely I will not be false unto David; (37) <u>His SEED shall endure for ever</u>, and his throne as the sun before Me. (38) It shall be established for ever as the moon; and be stedfast as the witness in sky.' Selah

It is important to note, what YHWH has said pertaining to what HE would do if *"his children forsakes MY Law"*. The Law does not end as many are want to think. But the terms and conditions of the Law, it's *"penalties"* are applied and come into effect. The *"small print"* becomes the *"big print"* as Israel is punished for their transgressions with the rod of GOD'S wrath. But the compassion and the mercy of YHWH HE will **not** remove from the SEED of David nor from Israel, as HE has sworn, 'Once have I sworn by My Holiness'.

'THROUGH MY NAME SHALL HIS HORN BE EXALTED'

It says that it is through the name of **"YHWH"** that David will be exalted. If Jesus was the anointed SEED of David, then it would be in the name of *"YHWH"* that he would have been established. It would not be in any other name. It would not be the name of *"Jesus"*. YHWH will exalt David's horn, for HE has sworn in HIS *"holiness"*. Lest there is any doubt, the SEED of David is established as YHWH has sworn, and the *"horn"* of David will be exalted through the name of *"**YHWH**"* (Psalm 89:25). This scripture alone throws a huge monkey wrench into the entire story of Jesus. For the life and death of Jesus hinges on his own name. But it is the name of YHWH that will exalt David.

The Covenant YHWH made with David, is a Covenant including his SEED. The Covenant YHWH made with David too, is a Covenant which YHWH has said he will not break. When it comes to David's SEED, *"endure"* or *"last"* forever, may well be a problem for some Christian doctrine as Jesus is not known to have left any *"SEED"* himself. As with Abraham and his SEED, the Covenant YHWH made with David and his SEED is *"fore ever"*. And *"for ever"* means *"for ever"*.

Psalms 48:15, (15) For such is God, our God, <u>for ever and ever</u>; He will guide us <u>eternally.</u>

The reason why this is important, as has been stated several times already concerning the Law itself, is that it is *"technical"*. The issue of *"SEED"* is both biological and technical. For the scripture indicates that it is the *"SEED"* of David that will sit upon his throne. YHWH has sworn! Jesus has not sat on David's throne as yet bringing *"righteousness, "justice"* and *"peace", "forever"* per the prophets. It is a very physical, earthly, *"biological"* entity. A very strong argument can be made *against* a non-biological human form coming with the clouds, qualifying as David's SEED. David's SEED is not only a *"biological"* reality, but the Covenant YHWH made with it is *"technical"* as in the word of GOD. YHWH has sworn in HIS *"holiness"* makes his promise to David every bit as technical as the Law with all of it's Statutes and Ordinances as it too is the word of GOD.

EPILOGUE OF EPILOGUE

JESUS THE JEW

As stated several times, Jesus was a circumcised Jewish man born into the Law of Moses during the most corrupt time in Israel's long history. He preached to Israel, his people. He stated that he came *"but"* for the *"lost sheep of the House of Israel"* and he told his followers to avoid the Gentiles and preach to the *"lost sheep of the House of Israel"* in all the Nations.

JESUS AND THE LAW

Jesus preached that Israel needed to keep all of the Commandments if they wanted to *"enter life"*. He was very consistent concerning this. Some of his own ideas are questionable, nevertheless he said that the Commandments must be kept by Israel. Israel was the target audience of Jesus. It was only to Israel, GOD'S elect, that he came, according to his own words. Unto Israel he sent his followers. Keeping the Law of Moses was the message.

That Jesus seemed at times to be *"adding"* or *"diminishing"* from the Law, which was then and still is now an issue, does not detract from his overall message regarding Israel keeping the Commandments. Even then, the people asked what *"new doctrine"* was this that he was preaching. The examples given of the Law concerning fornication where an *adulteress* was caught in the act, or the Law concerning *swearing* are two good examples. His teaching on these subjects did not appear to be in line with the Law of Moses.

JESUS AND THE PROPHETS

Many times in the Gospels, mention is made of *"fulfilled"* words of the prophets and other similar expressions. However, most all of the references given are of Hebrew scriptures completely unrelated to what was happening in the narrative or is entirely misquoted. In some cases the circumstance, and the *"fulfilled"* words of a Prophet are so vague that they could be made to apply to almost anything, anyone, or any situation. And as was shown, some of the Hebrew scriptures were rewritten to *"fit"* the story of who Jesus was suppose to be as was Isaiah 42. Or the bad translation of the original Hebrew word such as with *"young woman"* and *"virgin"* as was shown, steadily weakened the story, only detracting and adding nothing to it's believability.

'MESSIAH'

According to the words from YHWH, YHWH alone is Israel's "*Meshiach*". And that HE will send the Prophet Isaiah before HE comes.

JESUS

According to Jesus's own words, he came not to bring peace, but a "*sword*". Further, he stated he came to bring "*fire*" and "*division*" (father against son).

'SEED OF DAVID'

According to many of the prophetic writings regarding the "*SEED of David*", a reign of "*peace*", "*justice*" and "*righteousness*" will exist and it will continue. This did not come with Jesus, he brought "*division*".

KING DAVID / JESUS

The conflicting genealogy of King David, with that given of the two genealogies of Jesus in the books of Matthew and Luke, only weakens the story. When one compares the genealogy of King David in the Hebrew Bible along side that of Jesus given in Matthew and that given in Luke, the three genealogies not only do not match, but one of them appears to have a considerable more number of additional generations than the other two which aside from not matching, adds several hundreds of years to the pedigree.

One of the many sons of the SEED of David listed as part of the pedigree of Jesus, SEED was cursed by GOD (Jechoniah/Coniah/Jehoiachin son of Jehoiachim), to never occupy the throne of David (Jeremiah 22:24-30).

The other issue is regarding the "*SEED*" of David. Even if assuming Jesus was of the SEED of David, it ended with him. So, whoever David's SEED is who will one day sit upon his throne again, it will be from David's SEED which still exists here on earth. Else by definition, it is not SEED. As already explained, unless Jesus had offspring that no one was aware of, his own SEED ended with him. The name of YHWH will exalt the SEED of David.

In addition, returning to the "*virgin*" birth idea for a moment, if this were actually true, Jesus would **not** have been of the SEED of David to begin with. If Jesus had not the SEED of Joseph his own father, who according to his "*genealogy*" was of the SEED of David, then being a "*son of David*" was not possible for Jesus. Jesus may have been a son of GOD, but not of David.

On an even more detailed level, if Jesus was of "*virgin birth*" as the Gospels claim, then he not only does not have the Y-DNA from the SEED of his father Joseph and therefore not of David, but he would not have any Y-DNA at all, as Y-DNA only is passed down by the male. He would have received only an X chromosome from his mother. Her mitochondrial DNA (mt-DNA) which is only passed down from the female, even this would not have been of any of the Matriarchs as their X chromosome _ceased_. His mother's X chromosome would have been of an unknown origin as were most all of the sons of Jacob. It is doubtful as well that any human could exist with only half the number of chromosomes needed to be a viable being.

What is meant by _"ceased"_ is that unlike the Patriarchs, none of the Matriarchs had daughters to pass on their genes but for Leah the mother of Dinah, who had no children of her own according to scripture. Jacob's sons married and fathered children by the surrounding women of the land of Canaan. The gene pool of Israel began largely through these women. Of Simeon and possibly Levi and by all accounts Judah, their wives were Canaanite. Of Joseph, his wife was Egyptian. Several of the older brothers it appears may have married Hivite women taken from Shechem after the slaughter of all the males. The point is, that Jesus, _if really of virgin birth_, received none of Abraham, Isaac or Jacob's genes and therefore he could not be the _"son of David"_ on either side of his gene pool, neither from father or mother, not male or female.

SACRIFICE OFFERING

According to the Law, each man shall die for his own sins. Further, one person cannot die for the sins of another. According to the Law and prophets, priests of YHWH will eternally sacrifice to atone for Israel's sins. Therefore, Jesus could not have died for Israel as an eternal sacrifice offering for sin.

'ARE ONE'

Jesus said many times in various ways how he and the Father are one, how their words are one and how he does the work of his Father. How _seeing him was seeing the Father_ and how he does the will of the Father. Yet, were they?

John 10:30, (30) I and my Father are one.

GOD has a name HE said is **"YHWH"** and that HE is to be remembered by this name, called by this name, and Israel is to swear by this name. YHWH said that HE is **"One"**. HE said that **"Only"** HE is GOD. HE said that **"Only"** HE is **"Savior"**, redeemer, deliverer of Israel as their GOD. HIS name _alone_ is exalted.

Whether Jesus claimed to be the son of God, God's twin brother or God's second cousin twice removed, there are still _two_ entities to deal with and to try to make into _one_ without a seam. There remain two very separate and identifiably distinct _names_. Anyway you choose to look at it, in spite of what Jesus is reputed to have said, there are two distinct names and two distinct bodies of words which are different and are at variance. The theory of objects, space and time dictate that _"two different objects cannot occupy the same place at the same time"_. Or alternatively, _"an object cannot be in two different places at the same time"_. It is understood that these axioms may not apply to GOD who is omnipresent. Nevertheless, one would still have to accept that Jesus was God in order to believe he was _"YHWH"_. In addition, only one name is to be _exalted_ according to GOD. That name is **"YHWH"**. So, unless YHWH has an identical twin, there is going to be a problem for Christians trying to fit Jesus into the place of YHWH GOD.

To believe all of the words of Jesus, forces one into believing something that according to the word of

GOD does not exist, cannot exist and will not exist. For the thing which always separated Israel and it's GOD from all other nations was that of YHWH'S unique "*oneness*".

It is very difficult to square the words of Jesus against those of YHWH GOD without allot of fancy footwork and explanation in attempting to make fit an obvious conflict and contradiction between the two. It is very difficult to get around these and other words from the most holy GOD YHWH. Some may be able to, but not this author. These are two very distinct entities, not one.

YHWH AND LORD

The Christian religion uses much scripture from the Hebrew Bible to bolster their case for Jesus. Perhaps the most beautiful Psalm ever translated into English is one of them. One of the beauties of the King James Bible is the Old English. It is a beautiful language when both read quietly or when read out loud. The twenty third Psalm written by King David can be recited by many Christians. Yet, there is a profound misunderstanding of David's words precisely because of the poor translation of the name of GOD, *"YHWH"*. Unknown to most Christians who know and love this Psalm of David, and who are able to recite it word for word in English, they are profoundly misquoting it by using *"Lord"* and not "YHWH" the Hebrew name of GOD as it is originally written.

This Psalm begins and ends proclaiming the name of YHWH, but by the English translation, the reader would never be aware of this. The Hebrew of Psalm 23:1 reads in most English translations as follows.

Psalm 23:1, (1) The <u>Lord</u> is my shepherd, I shall not want"

Psalm 23:6, (6) Surely goodness and mercy shall follow me all the days of my life; and I shall dwell in the house of the <u>Lord</u> for ever.

As most all English translations of Hebrew scriptures translate the name of GOD *"YHWH"* as *"Lord"* and Christians relate to Jesus as *"Lord"*, many if not most think of Jesus when reading this Psalm. Indeed, most think that it speaks of Jesus. Yet, this entire Psalm is about YHWH, not Jesus. Else, David would have been calling his own SEED GOD, if Jesus really was of his SEED. Then David would be as GOD also? Would David have been praying to himself? And what of YHWH who is GOD? Where did HE go?

If Christians want to read this ancient Hebrew Psalm written by a Jewish King of Israel and apply it to themselves with Jesus as *"Lord"*, that is fine. As long as they are aware that they have it wrong. The Greeks wrongly mistranslated the Hebrew name of GOD *"YHWH"* (name) as *"Lord"* (title). Psalm 23 is not refering to *a* Lord, or *the* Lord, but to **YHWH GOD**, *"I am YHWH, that is My name; and My glory will I not give to another"*.

The original Hebrew translation renders the following.

Psalm 23:1, (1) <u>YHWH</u> is my shepherd, I shall not want"

Psalm 23:6, (6) Surely goodness and mercy shall follow me all the days of my life; and I shall dwell in the house of <u>YHWH</u> for ever.

It must be recalled that David worshiped the one and only GOD *"YHWH"*. Names matter.

HOPE

Jesus seems to take a very dim view on those who will actually *"enter life"*.

Matthew 7:14, (14) Because strait is the gate, and narrow is the way, which leadeth unto life, and few there be that find it.

So does this mean that the Nations (Gentiles) have no hope. GOD forbid!

On the contrary. Many Nations will be judged and come to <u>know</u> the name of YHWH, for YHWH is the GOD of Salvation. They will live by HIS Law as HIS prophets have declared. And the name of YHWH they will be exalted.

The Nations (Gentiles) <u>*will*</u> be judged and many will come to know the name of **"YHWH"**, the GOD of Israel. But that judgment will be made by YHWH and the Nations will come to know the *"Law"*. There is quite allot of prophesy concerning the judgment of the nations and most of it has to do with GOD'S wrath, fire and brimstone, and the Nations knowing YHWH'S name. However, those nations or peoples who survive, according to the Prophets of YHWH, will be joined as individual Nations under the same Law with Israel in the worship of YHWH. Egypt and Assyria are but two named.

Zephaniah 3:8-9, (8) Therefore wait ye for Me, saith YHWH, until the day that I rise up to the prey; for <u>My determination is to gather the nations,</u> that I may assemble the kingdoms, to pour upon them Mine indignation, even all My fierce anger; <u>for all the earth shall be devoured with the fire of My jealousy.</u> (9) For then will I turn to the peoples a pure language, <u>that they may all call upon the name of YHWH,</u> to serve Him with <u>one consent.</u>

How will they serve HIM with *"one consent"*? As the Prophet Malachi and Isaiah write, the nations will be *taught* GOD'S holy <u>name</u> and YHWH'S <u>Law.</u>
They who remain will serve *"YHWH"* with *one heart* and *one language.*

There was a reason why Israel was *"for a light of the nations"*. Even Jesus said that *"salvation is of the Jews"* when speaking with the Samaritan woman at the well. For what is called the "*Jews*" by Jesus, is the *remnant* of Israel, the *"light of the nations"* and Judah is the *"sceptre"* of YHWH.

Isaiah 42:6, (6) I YHWH have called thee in righteousness, and have taken hold of thy hand, and kept thee, and set thee for a Covenant of the people, <u>for a light of the Nations;</u>

Psalms 60:9, (9) Gilead is mine, and Manasseh is mine; Ephraim also is the defence of my head; <u>Judah is my sceptre.</u>

For aside from the personal story of a people, it is the "*Law*" which GOD YHWH *blessed* Israel with that was given to not only Israel, but eventually the world. It will be this Law which will be on the hearts of Israel and all of the Nations will learn and will serve YHWH with Israel, *"with one consent"*.

Deuteronomy 6:5, (5) And thou shalt love YHWH thy God with all thy heart, and with all thy soul, and with all thy might. (6) And these words, which I command thee this day, <u>shall be upon thy heart</u>; (7)and thou <u>shalt teach</u> diligently unto thy children.....

In the beginning, it was incumbent upon Israel to teach it and to put it upon their own heart. However, though the Law will be on Israel's heart in the future, there will be no need to *"teach"* as YHWH will write HIS Law on Israel's heart in a New Covenant, HIMSELF. It appears however, that the Nations will be taught the Law as they come to know YHWH (Isaiah 2:1-3).

Jeremiah 31:31-34, (31) <u>Behold, the days come, saith YHWH, that I will make a New Covenant with the house of Israel, and with the house of Judah</u>; (32) not according to the Covenant that I made with their fathers in the day that I took them by the hand to bring them out of the land of Egypt; forasmuch as they broke My Covenant, although I was a lord over them, saith YHWH. (33) <u>But this is the Covenant that I will make with the house of Israel after those days, saith YHWH, I will put My Law in their inward parts, and in their heart will I write it</u>; and I will be their God, and they shall be My people; (34) and they <u>shall teach no more</u> every man his neighbour, and every man his brother, saying: 'Know YHWH'; for they shall all know Me, from the least of them unto the greatest of them, saith YHWH; for I will forgive their iniquity, and their sin will I remember no more.

For there is one Law for the *"homeborn"* and the *"stranger"*.

Exodus 12:49, (49) <u>One law</u> shall be to him that is <u>homeborn</u>, and unto the <u>stranger</u> that sojourneth among you.'

Numbers 15:15-16, (15) As for the congregation, there shall be <u>one Statute</u> both for you, and for the <u>stranger</u> that sojourneth with you, <u>a Statute for ever</u> throughout your generations; as ye are, so shall the <u>stranger</u> be <u>before YHWH</u>. (16) <u>One Law</u> and <u>one Ordinance</u> shall be both for you, and for the <u>stranger</u> that sojourneth with you.

QUESTIONS

There appears to be at least two issues regarding the story of Jesus. There is *"Israel"* and there is the *"nations"*. Jesus said he came for Israel. His entire ministry was *to*, *for* and *about Israel*. But Israel, by it's own GOD YHWH, and HIS existing Covenants with Israel, did not require such a sacrifice as is given in the story of Jesus. Without repeating all of the scriptures regarding who and what Israel was and is to GOD YHWH as HIS redeemed first born son and how Israel has eternal salvation, the death of Jesus was unnecessary.

This brings us to the *"nations"*. Was Jesus somehow GOD'S way of preparing the Nations for YHWH'S Law? Are the *true* followers of Jesus the beginning of the salvation of the Nations? Was the purpose of Jesus to somehow ready the Nations for HIS Law? Are they being prepared to receive the **Law** of YHWH ? Are the true believers of Nations in preparation for the acceptance of HIS Law, His Ordinances and Statutes from Zion? For according to the prophets, all the Nations will keep HIS Law. Was Jesus to only *"prove"* Israel, but the Gentiles mistakenly made a religion out of his martyrdom? Will there be many Gentiles who survive GOD'S judgment?

Isaiah 2:1-3, (1) The word that Isaiah the son of Amoz saw concerning Judah and Jerusalem. (2) And it shall come to pass in the <u>end of days</u>, that the mountain of YHWH'S house shall be established as the top of the mountains, and shall be exalted above the hills; <u>and all Nations shall flow unto it</u>. (3) And <u>many peoples</u> shall go and say: 'Come ye, and let us go up to the mountain of

YHWH, to the house of the God of Jacob; and He will teach us of His ways, and we will walk in His paths.' For out of Zion shall go forth the Law, and the Word of YHWH from Jerusalem.

Here again, the prophets speak of the *Law*.

LONG LIVE THE LAW

The "*Law*" not only is not dead, but it will no longer need to be taught to Israel for the Law of the New Covenant of YHWH will be "*put*" by YHWH HIMSELF, into Israel's "*inward parts*". Israel may have broken their part of the Covenant, but the Law did not cease being the Law because Israel was not able to uphold their part of the agreement. Israel was punished.

Ezekiel 39:23, (23) And the Nations shall know that the House of Israel went into captivity for their iniquity, because they broke faith with Me, and I hid My face from them;....

The discernible actions of GOD'S "*penalties*" associated with Israel for not keeping their part of the Covenant is proof GOD said that HE would keep HIS Covenant with Israel, and if nothing else HIS scattering and punishment of Israel is the sure sign of the truth of HIS Covenant and that it is still "*in force*". But HE also said HE would gather Israel and return their "*captivity*".

Lamentations 3:22-24 (22) Surely YHWH'S mercies are not consumed, surely His compassions fail not.(23) They are new every morning; great is Thy faithfulness. (24) 'YHWH is my portion', saith my soul; 'Therefore will I hope in Him.'

Neither did GOD'S compassion for HIS people Israel cease, for HE knows that Israel is but "*flesh*". YHWH'S compassion is reborn each day and fails not, and HIS mercies are not consumed for HIS people. This is often ignored by many too quick to rush to judgment, wanting to write off Israel.

Lamentations 3:31-32, (31) For the Lord will not cast off for ever. (32) For though He cause grief, yet will He have compassion according to the multitude of His mercies.

The "*baby was not thrown out with the bath water*". Neither YHWH'S love and affection for "*Israel*" nor the "*Law*" has ceased, ended, or been forgotten. Neither has Israel been forsaken. The salvation of YHWH is an everlasting salvation to Israel. The Nations will learn to fear the name of YHWH.

Isaiah 54:7-8, (7) For a small moment have I forsaken thee; but with great compassion will I gather thee. (8) In a little wrath I hid My face from thee for a moment; but with everlasting kindness will I have compassion on thee, saith YHWH thy Redeemer.

WHAT WILL BECOME OF THE NATIONS

"as ye are, so shall the stranger be before YHWH" (Numbers 15:15)

There are many scriptures which tell of the nations being joined along with Israel as individual Nations worshiping YHWH. How this will come about exactly is only hinted at, but some of the things we do know are written by the Prophets of YHWH for our benefit. There are several things which the Prophets speak of which are certain. One of these things is of YHWH gathering Israel and returning them back to their inheritance in the Land of Israel from the four corners of the earth. But it also speaks of the Nations gathering against Israel. We know that there will be a *"judgment"*. It appears that it will be an extremely violent *"judgment"* with much fire involved during the wrath of GOD. Many people will perish, and many *"nations"* will be no more. But of the Nations which will remain after YHWH has judged them, they will be taught the Law and will worship YHWH with Israel.

Aside from the many people who will perish, from scripture we know that not all of the Nations will remain as such either, as some *"nations"* will no longer exist by the name which they are called and shall be no more. There are many prophesies concerning this. These many scriptures will not be cited, but the reader is encouraged to search the scriptures of the Prophets of YHWH themselves. Zechariah is but one (Zechariah 14:16-21).

Zechariah 14:16, (16) And it shall come to pass, that every one that is left of all the Nations that came against Jerusalem shall go up from year to year to worship the King, YHWH of hosts, and to keep the Feast of Tabernacles.

Here, the *"King"* and *"YHWH"* of hosts appear to be the same and will be worshiped by not only Israel, but by the *"nations"* such as Egypt and Assyria so named. One day David will reign as king, but ultimately it is YHWH who is *"King"*, as ultimately it is YHWH who is *"Savior"*. *"Long live the King"*

How the name of *"Jesus"* would fit in with this would be a problem. For there are many such scriptures which speak of YHWH as Savior, King, Lord, and how it is that HIS name, *"YHWH"* will be worshiped, exalted, praised and known by the *"nations"*. It leaves no room for another name or for HIS *"glory"* to be given to another but that of **"YHWH"** alone is to be glorified.

The coming of Egypt to Jerusalem to give their offering (Zechariah 14:18) obviously has not occurred as yet. There are many such scriptures which tell of a time in the future which has not occurred. The day when Egypt brings their offerings to Jerusalem to celebrate Sukkot, something truly marvelous will have occurred. YHWH speaks of sending Egypt a *"savior"* if they call to HIM in need. In addition, Egypt is still Egypt, as a proud nation of it's own.

Isaiah 19:20-21, (20) And it shall be for a sign and for a witness unto YHWH of hosts in the land of Egypt; for they shall cry unto YHWH because of the oppressors, and He will send them a saviour, and a defender, who will deliver them. (21) And YHWH shall make Himself known to Egypt, and the Egyptians shall know YHWH in that day; yea, they shall worship with sacrifice and offering, and shall vow a vow unto YHWH, and shall perform it.

Interesting enough, there are already thousands of Christians representing many countries from around the world who support Israel and have been coming to Jerusalem for years and celebrating Sukkot (Zechariah 14:16; Feast of Tabernacles). It is a big event in Jerusalem and one which is truly beautiful to see and also viewed with much amusement by many secular Israelis and others who are unaware of this prophesy.

Zechariah 14:19, (19) This shall be the punishment of Egypt, and the punishment of all the Nations that go not up to keep the Feast of Tabernacles.

The surviving peoples of the Nations who have been judged and have been joined as Nations with Israel to worship YHWH, will offer sacrifice and come to Jerusalem during the feast of Sukkot (Feast of Tabernacles). We also know that *"Yom Kippur"*, the (Day of Atonement) will continue as well as *"Pesach"* (Passover), and *"Shuvot"* (Feast of Weeks), and *"Yom T'ruah"* (Day of Shouting / Horn

Blowing). We know from TaNaKh that there will be a new heaven and a new earth. And we know the Law is kept by "**all**".

The Law of YHWH is neither dead nor will it be forgotten, but will be kept by all who worship GOD. As the Law is eternal, it's Commandments will be kept. The Nations that remain will keep YHWH'S Law. Israel and the Nations together will keep the Law of Moses.

How do we know many of the things pertaining to the *"nations"*, who will survive? We know this from specific scriptures given as well as we know that there is but *"one"* Law for Israel and *"one"* Law for the *"sojourner"*. And as the Law is eternal, the Nations will stand before GOD in HIS Law. Any and all Nations will take on the blessing of the Law, or perish.

This pretty much sums it up. For the Nations which survive YHWH'S judgment, they will be taught the Law of YHWH and will live according to it's Statutes and Ordinances. As Israel lives by the Law, so too the Nations.

AUTHORSHIP

There is a *"thread"* of consistency which exists throughout the Gospels which are in sync with many prophesies by YHWH'S Prophets concerning Israel HIS people, but not Jesus. These speak not of the many scriptures given as *prophesies* supposedly which were either *"fulfilled"*, or speak of Jesus. Nor are they speaking of the *"interpretation"* of many such scriptures by Christian theologians over several centuries. Rather, they speak instead of the special place of Israel with GOD YHWH, and their place in the world.

They speak of the eternal Covenant's which YHWH has with Israel and what HE said about Israel as HIS servant, HIS inheritance, HIS anointed, HIS special treasure and HIS holy portion. For HE said that Israel is *"MINE"*.

They speak of YHWH making an eternal *"Covenant"* with Abraham, which was confirmed with Isaac and established with Jacob and acknowledged throughout all of TaNaKh that Israel is GOD'S own people. They show the eternal Covenant YHWH made with Israel at Mount Sinai, with the SEED of Aaron as High Priest, the Tribe of Levi YHWH'S ministers, and the SEED of David who will sit upon the throne of Israel forever. The Gospels remind the reader of all of these things in accordance with keeping the Law. If one looks.

There is far, far, too much scripture and / or prophesy regarding these Covenants, oaths, and promises to discuss here. And Jesus preaching to Israel to keep the Commandments in no way contradicts these eternal agreements.

Additionally, Jesus sending his followers to all the Nations to preach to the *"lost sheep of the House of Israel"* and to keep *"the Commandments"* is also in keeping with the Law and does not contradict it in any way.

Given this, it is highly suspicious of the scriptures which do *"appear"* in any way to contradict these things. It is suspected that other than just poor translation of some of the text itself, some of the original text, whatever it may have originally said in any language, has purposely been *"redacted"*.

Also, issues such as *"father, son, and holy ghost"* is a concept not part of the Hebrew scriptures or the Law and is totally alien. Some of the words of Jesus regarding giving a *"new commandment"*, as well as the words associated with him on the Law itself, such as divorce and swearing are troubling.

But perhaps more than anything is the lack of evidence or of the respect, honor, praise and holiness of the name of *"YHWH"* in the Gospels. On top of this are the many scriptures of the followers of Jesus referring to him as *"LORD"*, apparently not in the respectful manner of *"lord"* as *"sir"*, but as *"GOD"*, as Thomas confessed. That there is no evidence that Jesus corrected his followers from blurting out such things is extremely problematic.

Some of these issues can possibly be explained away through bad translation, as well as the authors not being sensitive to the Law, and therefore were careless in their choice of words. Other explanations may have much more to do with *non* Jewish theological *"doctrine"* or *"agenda"* propagated by it's new adherents as the believers in Jesus became more and more Gentile, and less and less Jewish. As this happened, almost every hint of the Law of Moses or the Jewish origin of what eventually became *"Christianity"* disappeared. And where the *"people"* were transformed into *"the Jews"*.

The most profound change in this cleansing of anything Jewish in the new religion being firmly established by the Gentile world after Jesus, most likely occurred around the time of the Council of Nicaea in 325. Or more precisely to the point, when most of these non Jewish changes became established theological doctrine by the *"nations"*. Honoring of GOD'S Sabbath, HIS holy days, circumcision, not eating blood or unclean animals were all forgotten.

The first Council of Nicaea was convened by the Roman Emperor Constantine sometime after the emperor adopted the *"Christian"* religion. The purpose of the council was to establish an agreed upon *"doctrine"* of the new faith and establishing canon law of the new faith. The details of this council are not as important as in knowing that they substantially deviated from the Law of Moses in most all areas previously known and practiced by the Jewish believers in Jesus and the religion of Israel. But more importantly, it deviated from belief in the <u>GOD of Israel called *YHWH*</u> and HIS Sabbath.

To say that the Law of Moses, and the Prophets became *"subservient"* to the will of the *"church"* leaders of this new, and now Gentile religion would be an understatement. Given his new found *"faith"* in Jesus, Constantine did not look on his Jewish subjects favorably and with time, many anti-Jewish, anti-Judaism laws and measures were enacted which severely constrained the Jewish population throughout the empire. Constantine's negative attitude towards the Jewish people may account for the constant negative slant in the Gospels regarding **"the Jews"**. The Gentile take on a purely Jewish saga, or said another way, a family affair concerning the people of Israel with one of it's own sons, changed into a religion of Nations completely bereft of any and all things associated with Israel, the Jewish people, Law, their holy religion or their GOD YHWH. Gentiles created for themselves a new world religion.

For much as the rabbis created their own religion loosely based on the Law of Moses with their own second *"torah"* (oral law), the Gentiles too created their own religion loosely based on what was the religion of Israel, founded on the Law of Moses and created their own religious books and doctrine.

The question is, how much of the original Gospels were changed to fit the prejudices, the bias and the anti-Jewish leanings of it's church leaders, from what was first written? Given the negative tone of the Gospels towards the Jewish people, if the Gospels were originally written by Jews, then they were severely altered by others to cast the Jewish people into a very negative light.

ONCE MORE 'THE JEWS'

If the original Gospels were written in Hebrew or Aramaic or even in Greek by a Jewish believer, then they have been heavily redacted by someone who was not Jewish. Anyone who reads these four books cannot help but be struck by how far removed the author of each of the four Gospels is from the people, culture and religion of the subject people who are being written about or the situation being described. Nor from reading the Gospels does one get a sense that there is any feeling of kinship with the characters in the story by the person who is wielding the pen. He is far removed from the people and events taking place, though in theory, he was there and witnessed the events he wrote about. Instead, he is an alien voyeur peeking at the pain of another.

Whatever the ethnicity or religion of the original writers of the Gospels were, it differed from that which is reflected in the Gospels that have come down to us and which exists today. For as has been discussed in detail, the constant use of the term *"the Jews"* to identify what would be considered obvious and unnecessary when one is writing about ones own people, culture and religion, and unnecessary when Jesus was speaking with either the Priests, Scribes or Pharisees, makes one curious as to who penned the final draft of the Gospels. It is even more painfully obvious when the Gospel speaks of any one of the several major holy days of Israel as a feast of *"the Jews"*, making it all too clear that the person writing was not only not Jewish, but did not appear to be all together that familiar with the religion or the holy days of Israel and constantly felt compelled to remind his like minded foreign readers as well.

The Gospels may not have begun as such but they ended up becoming as they are, as a very provocative accusation / indictment against the Jewish people.

Most of the Gospels read as someone who is far removed from the events taking place amongst the Jewish people, speaking almost as if an anthropologist was describing an aboriginal people in some remote distant island or an astronaut describing creatures discovered on a far away planet who possessed strange customs alien from the norm of humanity on earth.

In other words, it does not in any sense of the word feel like a Jewish person describing events amongst his own people, but rather someone entirely from outside the social, cultural, and religious sphere of which he is writing about. What is equally as important is the very negative attitude of the writer. Yet, the authors of the Gospels were to have *"witnessed"* the words and events dscribed in the Gospels, and would have been *"Jewish"* by most accounts.

Or, the possibility exists that the Gospels if originally written from the perspective of a Jewish person, writing about his own people, his own culture and religion, but whose words were later heavily redacted to reflect someone who was not only not Jewish, but as someone who purposely misrepresented the Jewish people as an almost foreign demonized alien entity, in an extremely negative light. This possibility is the stronger. No Jewish person would constantly keep referring to his own Jewish people as *"the Jews"*.

For as a Jewish person reading many of these repetitious occasions which constantly refer to *"the Jews "*, it becomes after a while tedious, almost burdensome and painfully obvious of how negative the constant bombardment of this phrase *"the Jews"* is after having many, many encounters with it. And it becomes painfully obvious too that it is no accident that they exist, nor why they are there. If the authors of the Gospels wanted to create a *"villain"* in the story of Jesus, then they could not have done more to prejudice the reader against the Jewish people than the explicit number of times and the manner in which they constantly refer to *"the Jews"*. Especially, when it was not only not necessary because of the narrative, but because as stated, the majority of all of the people in the stories in all four Gospels were Jewish people. *Jews were constantly in fear because of Jews.*

The constant need to remind the reader in referring to *"the Jews"* has another affect as well in *creating* in Jesus a man who was somehow anything but *"Jewish"*. The same affect is accomplished on his followers by repeatedly disassociating them from *"the Jews"*. As if to say that there are the disciples of Jesus, and then there are *"the Jews"*. As if to remove Jesus and his followers from the taint of these people, they are constantly referred to the reader in such a subtle manner, to remind the reader that they are the *"other"*.

One sees in *"the Jews"* a type of *"villain"* from the way that the people of Jesus are portrayed, so too, the very person of Jesus slowly takes on the persona of someone who is not a Jew. But Jesus the Jew was, and is a *"Jew"*. He was not Christian or Gentile. His followers and detractors were both Jews.

As a Jewish person reading some of these words which refer to *"the Jews"* by the writer of the Gospels, when it is painfully clear that all of the people in the scene are only Jews, whether they are Scribes, Pharisees or Priests, it has a very negative *"otherness"* foreign quality about it which is extremely powerful and hard to shake off. When the scene is discussing the feast of *"the Jews"*, one cannot help but ask, who was the author of such words? Was there a Greek or a Roman hiding in a tree for three years taking notes?

No people writing about itself, would feel the need to constantly identify itself, about itself, to itself. Yet, the authors of the Gospels obviously feel a constant and strong compulsion to draw the readers attention to these seemingly curious people *"the Jews"*, and consistency identify them as such at every opportunity when this should never be necessary. The author who constantly refers to the *"followers"* or the *"disciples"* of Jesus in the same scene of Jewish people, in juxtaposition to those who were also standing there but who were not believers as *"the Jews"*, says quite allot about the author. They were all Jews! Additionally, by their obvious slanted approach to the story telling, Jesus takes on more and more of an air of someone who is somehow not *"Jewish"* but managed to transcend his ethnicity and was cleansed of his own *Jewishness*. Until today he has become the Gentile GOD.

It is personally troubling for several reasons, not the least of which is that it sends up red flags and brings to mind the example given earlier regarding the obvious *"creative"* writing by the author (or editor) of the Book of Matthew. It may be recalled that an entire line of scripture from the Prophet Isaiah 42 had been changed and completely rewritten to reflect Christian doctrine. This was no accident. Neither is the constant reminder of *"the Jews"* in the story.

There are other examples for which should make a Jewish person cautious in accepting all of what was written in the Gospels as being the *"gospel"*. This is especially true as the texts which eventually ended up being the *"Gospels"* went through many hands and many years of human development before they reached their final status. They may have begun *Jewish,* but ended *unJewish.*

ALL IN ONE JESUS

According to the Gospels, if all of what is said about Jesus, concerning Jesus regarding Jesus or relating to Jesus is understood, then he is an all encompassing being, and Thomas in calling him *"god"* was reflecting this.

The Gospels equate Jesus the son as being one with YHWH the Father. Jesus the son of man, is equated as the same as GOD in heaven. The Gospels equate the words of Jesus as being the words of the Father. The Gospels equate the teachings of Jesus as being the teachings of the Father. The Gospels teach that the words of Jesus are the words of the Father. The Gospels teach that the will of Jesus is the will of GOD the Father.

The Gospels call Jesus *"Lord"* and *"God"*.

The Gospels teach that Jesus is a type of priest. The Gospels teach that Jesus is *"king"*. The Gospels teach that Jesus is the *"savior"*. The Gospels teach that Jesus was the *"messiah"*. The Gospels teach that Jesus is the son of David. The Gospels teach that Jesus was born without SEED of man, but was born of GOD by a virgin woman. The Gospels teach that Jesus is the suffering servant. The Gospels teach that Jesus was a martyr, a sacrificial offering (karbon) to GOD for sin. The Gospels teach that Jesus is the lamb of GOD. The Gospels teach that Jesus is the rock. The Gospels teach that Jesus is both man and GOD.

The Gospels teach that by one's belief in the name of Jesus he can have eternal life. The Gospels teach that Jesus can forgive sin. The Gospels teach that the believer in Jesus has the authority as well to forgive sin (John 20:23). (Did this mean that his followers could all walk around as if God, and forgive the sins of the world?). The Gospels teach that Jesus can make a person a son of GOD. The Gospels teach that Jesus died for the sins of the world. The Gospels teach that Jesus brought division and a sword to his people, not peace. The Gospels teach that Jesus was a prophet. According to the Gospels it is taught that *"grace* and *truth"* came by Jesus. The Gospels teach that John the Baptist baptized Jesus for the remission of his sins. The Gospels teach to pray in the name of the Father, the son and the holy spirit and to ask for things in the name of Jesus.

The Gospels teach that Jesus said to *"keep the Commandments"* of GOD if one wanted to enter into life. The Gospels teach that not one *"jot"* or one *"tittle"* would not be accomplished of the Law. The Gospels teach that Jesus came **but** to *"the lost sheep of the House of Israel"*. The Gospels teach that Jesus sent his disciples out to the nations to preach to *"the lost sheep of the House of Israel"*. Yet, David said it is YHWH who is GOD and the Rock?

Psalm 18:32, (32) For who is God, save YHWH? And who is a Rock, except our God?

For a Jewish person, that person must ask himself if all of these things (and others) add up to himself as a circumcised Jewish male, forsaking his own GOD YHWH, and believing in any other name but his own GOD **"YHWH"**. Whether he knows how to pronounce the name is less important than knowing that it is only "YHWH" who is his GOD. For none of the things stated, are things which Israel, the sons of GOD do not already either possess, or that their GOD YHWH has not already done or will do for them, or are things which are not part of the Covenant of Abraham or the Covenant of Sinai. Israel is already the *"son of GOD"*. Was Jesus going to allow them to become something that they already were? Had Israel known their own Law, they would surely have known that what he said already existed, for Israel is the first born son of GOD. Did Israel know their own Law? By Jesus, no.

GOD states that HE is very jealous for HIS holy name, and that HE will take pity on HIS holy name. HE states that HE alone is GOD and Savior and that there is no other. YHWH states that it is HE who is the Rock and Salvation of Israel. HIS Law is eternal and HIS salvation for Israel is eternal. YHWH states that it will be through HIS name, **"YHWH"** that David will be exalted.

So who and what was Jesus to *"Israel"*. And who and what was Jesus to the *"nations"*. These are two vastly different questions.

ISRAEL

As Jesus said to Israel to <u>keep the Commandments</u> of the Law, then whatever else he was or was not, only pertain to the Law and it's Commandments. Israel already had it's GOD YHWH. Their GOD YHWH already provides salvation as their Savior. Israel had priests who sacrificed for their sin.

All things not of GOD'S Law, should be discounted immediately based on the Law itself, including any words of Jesus which are not in agreement with the Law which he himself said to keep. If it is not Lawful, don't do it.

In three years, Jesus said much that was true concerning the Law of Moses. But he also said many other things which were questionable. By telling Israel to keep the Commandments, he was also telling them that all that was *not* commanded in the Law of Moses to ignore. For both keeping and not keeping the Commandments was not possible. In keeping the Law, all else is not Law.

A hypothetical analogy might be that YHWH told Israel to keep only the blue and white cords being given to them. Then for the next three years, Israel is given red, yellow, blue, green, orange, purple, white and brown cords of thread. All they needed was two things. First, they needed to know what was the *"Law of threads"* told to them by GOD, then second, to separate out and keep only the blue and white cords. For example, anything not blue or white is to be discounted. Keeping the Commandments of GOD are the same. Jesus told the rabbis, if they had known the Law of Moses, then they would know if what he said was his doctrine or not. By telling Israel to keep the Law, he was saying that any *doctrine* related to himself *not* in the Law of Moses was not something they needed to be concerned with and could be discounted.

Isaiah 43:11, (11) I, even I, am YHWH; and beside Me there is no Saviour.

For Israel, there is no other GOD or Savior but **YHWH**. Was Jesus a prophet telling Israel to repent and to keep the Commandments? Was he to try Israel?

As the Law in the Safer Torah states was Jesus a prophet sent by GOD to *"proof"* (Deuteronomy 13:1-19; 18:15-22) Israel as HE said HE would surely do?

It is within this context from the Jewish perspective of the Law that his story in the Gospels is viewed. According to the Law, each man shall die for his own sin, *"The fathers shall not be put to death for the children, neither shall the children be put to death for the fathers; <u>every man shall be put to death for his own sin"</u> (Deuteronomy 24:16).*

YHWH has provided a mechanism for the atonement of sin for Israel. It is eternal and as the Prophets of YHWH write, this atonement for sin by sacrificial offering will continue in the future and for all eternity. In the mean time, Israel must keep the Law. Not having a Temple for now, does not let Israel *"off the hook"* in as far as keeping GOD'S Law is concerned. For it was their own sin which brought about this situation. It still must be kept. According to the prophets, Israel is heard and has salvation in

YHWH, but they must keep GOD'S Law and *humble* themselves before HIM.

'TO KEEP FOR THY GOOD'

Deuteronomy 10:12-13, (12) And now, Israel, <u>what doth YHWH thy God require of thee</u>, but to <u>fear</u> YHWH thy God, to <u>walk</u> in all His ways, and to <u>love</u> Him, and to <u>serve</u> YHWH thy God with <u>all</u> thy <u>heart</u> and with all thy <u>soul</u>; (13) <u>to keep for thy good</u> the Commandments of YHWH, and His Statutes, which I Command thee this day?

YHWH says here that keeping HIS Commandments is *"for thy good"*.

NATIONS

As stated concerning Israel, as Jesus said to keep the Commandments of the Law, then whatever else he was or was not hinges on the other words and actions he said and did as they pertain to the Law and it's Commandments. If Jesus was a prophet come to try Israel, then his story has more credibility. If he came to prepare the Nations for accepting the Commandments of the Law, then his story makes more sense as well.

Israel rejected Jesus as their *"messiah"* as they had a *"messiah"* in the name of **"YHWH"**. If by his life and death, the nations have been given hope and have been exposed to the GOD of Israel and HIS Commandments as part of a plan, then a conspiracy of universal proportions has been accomplished in regard to the salvation of the Nations, *"Saith the Lord YHWH who gathereth the dispersed of Israel: yet I will gather others to him, beside those of him that are gathered."* (Isaiah 56:8). Is this what HE meant?

For whether Israel accepted Jesus is beside the point, when the affect of his message is viewed in this context. Was this all part of the plan of YHWH? As YHWH is a merciful GOD, showing mercy to Gentiles would be a testament.

According to the prophets, all Nations will know HIS name, and they will live according to HIS Law. Israel was right to *"cleave"* to YHWH. It is Law.

For his universal message of compassion is a message which the Nations must apply when dealing with each other and with Israel, if they want YHWH the Father of Israel to be merciful with them. For it is written that YHWH will show mercy on those who show mercy *"With the merciful Thou dost show Thyself merciful"* (II Samuel 22:26). Is not Israel the anointed flock of GOD, HIS inheritance, yet the Jewish people are hated by many Christians? And what did YHWH say to Abraham? *"And I will make of thee a great nation, and I will bless thee, and make thy name great; and be thou a blessing. And I will bless them that bless thee, <u>and him that curseth thee will I curse</u>; and in thee shall <u>all the families of the earth be blessed"</u>* (Genesis 12:2-3).

Psalms 77:21, (21) Thou didst lead <u>Thy people like a flock</u>, by the hand of Moses and Aaron.

Can the Christian who believes in Jesus, hate Israel and the Jewish people, the family of Jesus? And at the same time, profess his love for their GOD and expect GOD'S mercy? Can the follower of Jesus not know that the people of Israel are GOD'S own people, and whom they must support if they are to be of the Nations who will know YHWH GOD? Can a man say he loves GOD, yet hate GOD'S son? For Israel is YHWH'S first born son (Exodus 4:22) .

LAW / NATIONS

Only the Safer Torah / Law of Moses can unite Jews and the Nations, whatever their belief. This is especially so for Christians who profess Jesus.

If one believes that Jesus was a prophet, then his prophesy was about keeping the Law of GOD. There is only one Law. As there is but one Law for Israel and one Law for the stranger, then symbolically only the circumcised will be able to partake of GOD'S Passover and only those of the Nations who keep the Law of GOD will be accepted and counted as Nations along side of Israel.

As circumcision is a token sign of the Covenant between YHWH GOD and Israel, keeping GOD'S Commandments by the Nations too, allows them to partake of the Passover Meal, as no uncircumcised person may eat of it (Exodus 12:47-51), even as a memorial. None of the Nations who do not keep GOD'S Law will be accepted with Israel. There is one Law for the *homeborn* and one Law for the *sojourner*. One Law for them both. Israel, Egypt, Assyria, and the Nations.

Exodus 12:49, (49) One law shall be to him that is homeborn, and unto the stranger that sojourneth among you.'

If Christians accept the words of Jesus that he spoke to Israel, then they must understand that only in keeping the Commandments of YHWH, GOD of Israel, will his words have any real meaning for them. Do the Nations truly believe that YHWH would accept anything less from them than to keep HIS Law, if this is what is expected of Israel HIS first born son? As the Law for Israel is an eternal blessing, it is no less so for the Nations who must accept it.

As head of the family of Nations Israel will have the Law of YHWH *"I will put MY Law in their inward parts"* (Jeremiah 31:33). The Nations too will live by this Law. They have no choice in the matter. There will not be one Law for Israel and another (or no) Law for the Nations. The Law and the Prophets are very clear on this. There is one Law for Israel and one Law for the stranger.

ABOUT ISRAEL

What did Jesus offer Israel that Israel did not already possess in YHWH their GOD? According to the Law, no man can die for the sin of another, keeping the Law was his message to Israel.

Amos 3:2 (2) You only have I known of all the families of the earth; therefore I will visit upon you all your iniquities.

Deuteronomy 14:2, (2) For thou art a holy people unto YHWH thy God, and YHWH hath chosen thee to be His own treasure out of all peoples that are upon the face of the earth.

Jeremiah 2:3, (3) Israel is YHWH'S hallowed portion, His first-fruits of the increase; all that devour him shall be held guilty, evil shall come upon them, saith YHWH.

There is a curse on Israel when they do not keep GOD'S Law. But too, there is a blessing when the Law is kept. How could Jesus die for the sins of Israel?

Because Jesus seems to have made a concerted effort, according to the Gospels, to remind Israel of their unique status with their GOD by preaching to them and telling them to keep HIS Commandments, Jesus was reminding Israel of what a blessing they had received and a great nation that they were. Israel, represented today mostly by the Jewish people, must understand that the "*Law*" is a blessing, not a curse. It is only because of the rabbis who have made the Law *"as if"* it was a curse, by how far they have perverted it, that makes keeping the Law appear so daunting. But it is not so. The Law of YHWH is easy, simple, wonderful and beautiful to keep, *"For this Commandment which I command thee this day, it is not too hard for thee, neither is it far off".* The Law of YHWH was a _blessing_ given to Israel above and beyond all of the Nations upon the earth. Only Israel was _blessed_ with such a gift. The Law is a _blessing_, *"to keep for thy good".*

The Law and the prophets make very clear that atonement for the sins of Israel are to be made by YHWH'S priests as an Eternal Statute, and that one man cannot die for another man. Each man shall die for his own sins. The Law makes very clear, that GOD YHWH is ONE and HIS name is ONE. There is no other name but **YHWH**.

'FOOD FOR THOUGHT'

There are at least two outstanding issues regarding Jesus which cry out. The first is that Jesus came for Israel *not* the nations and his message was *to* Israel to *"keep the Commandments".* Nothing outside of the Commandments of the Law matter for they are *not* legally binding. So any and all things said by Jesus outside the Law of Moses to Israel are moot. Additionally, aside from Jesus coming to the *"lost sheep of the House of Israel"* it would seem, Jesus was sent to put to *"proof"* Israel, to see if they knew the Law and loved their GOD YHWH with all of their heart and soul, and with all of their might. This is at least a possibility, as the evidence seems to support it.

Accordingly, Jesus spoke with much authority and was very knowledgeable in the Law and the Prophets. If he was a False Prophet sent by YHWH to *"proof"* Israel, he was very affective. For in the process he spawned a new religion based in large part on his death and the hope it has given to millions.

The second issue connected to the first, is the 2.2 billion Christians which exist today. The numbers alone are staggering, but then there are also 1.5 billion Muslims, most of which want to destroy Israel and kill all the Jews. So numbers alone are no clear indication of either having or knowing the truth. What was the connection between the ministry of Jesus and the Jewish people then and what is it today? For a very serious segment of Christian Zionists who accept the truth of the Hebrew Bible, yet accept Jesus as their Savior exists. What does this mean? Was the life and death of Jesus and the Gentile rejection of the Law of Moses in some way GOD'S plan of preparing the _Nations_ for the acceptance of YHWH and HIS Law, the very Law the Nations rejected? For the Law is eternal. Israel may have rejected Jesus as their messiah, but the Gentiles rejected GOD'S eternal Law, including HIS Sabbath in it's entirety.

According to HIS Law, there is one Law for Israel and one Law for the sojourner. According to the prophets, the _Nations_ will know YHWH'S name, worship YHWH and live according to HIS Law. According to the Prophet Ezekiel, the burnt sacrifice offering for sin will continue in the new Temple of YHWH. Are the _Nations_ who truly love GOD and HIS people Israel, and who have been prepared by HIM with the words of King David, the Prophets, the Law of Moses, the Writings and the Christian Bible, the people who will survive GOD'S judgment to live in HIS kingdom as the words of the Prophets have said, who will be keeping the Law? There are no accidents in history.

One other thing touched on earlier. If Jesus was a False Prophet sent to Israel to test and to try them, and Israel ultimately rejected Jesus as their messiah, then the Christian religion itself is based primarily on a rejected False Prophet and a rejected False Messiah of Israel, not on a *"new covenant"* made with Israel or with any other nation or people.

A careful reading of the *"last supper"*in the Gospels itself, shows the words of Jesus are words with Israel. If one reads and studies just the words of Jesus throughout all of the Gospels, the consistent part, a truly objective person will not see in his words to Israel anything but words to Israel, not to the world. This is true of the Gospels in general and of the *"last supper"* specifically.

The Christian religion then appears to be largely based on the words of the later followers of Jesus, not on the words of Jesus himself. Given the apparent heavy handed changes, alterations, editing, redacting, misquotes and bad translations in the four Gospels, it becomes extremely difficult to accept anything written at face value regarding the words in the Gospels or a *new testament*. And if a new testament was made at all, according to the *"last supper"* narrative, it was made with Israel not with anyone else.

The words of Jesus were words spoken _to_, _for_, _about_ and _regarding_ hmself and the _Jews_ at the table. They were words spoken to his Jewish followers and were words exclusive of anyone else not there that night or under the Law of Moses about himself and his relationship to them. The thrust of his message as well, seemed to be associated with the annual Passover meal itself, not on a later man made religious rite created by the Gentiles regarding drinking wine and eating wafers. It is doubtful that without Paul and others, there would be any such religion as Christianity today based on Jesus.

'AND WHAT GREAT NATION IS THERE'

Deuteronomy 4:5-8, (5) Behold, I have taught you Statutes and Ordinances, even as YHWH my God commanded me, that ye should do so in the midst of the land whither ye go in to possess it. (6) Observe therefore and do them; for this is your wisdom and your understanding in the sight of the peoples, that, when they hear all these Statutes, shall say: 'Surely this Great Nation is a wise and understanding people.' (7) For what Great Nation is there, that hath God so nigh unto them, as YHWH our God is whensoever we call upon Him? (8) And what Great Nation is there, that hath Statutes and Ordinances so righteous as all this LAW, which I set before you this day?

The giving of the Law to Israel was _GOD'S blessing_ to HIS people Israel.

Do not the peoples of the nations have some justification (excluding anti-Semites) in their amazement (and perhaps disgust) of such a blessed people such as Israel truly is, who by their own actions (the majority) continue to refuse to live by the blessing of the Law that YHWH has given to them to live by, *"to keep for thy good"*, and thus continue to suffer as a result?

The Law is a blessing, and is a gift from the living GOD YHWH to Israel. It is incumbent for every Jewish person who draws a breath provided by courtesy of their GOD YHWH, to keep and obey HIS Commandments *that HE gave especially to them*. What could Jesus offer Israel?

CONCLUSION

Jesus said to *"search the scriptures"*. Perhaps he said this knowing that it would not be done. In John 5:39-40 he speaks of *"eternal life"* written in the holy scriptures referring to himself. Yet, Israel has eternal life, *"For YHWH taketh pleasure in HIS people; HE adorneth the humble with salvation"* (Psalms 149:4). As for sin, David has these words of wisdom.

" Also unto Thee, O YHWH, belongeth mercy; for Thou renderest to every man according to his work" (Psalm 62:13).

rs for sine Jesus, then statements of *"everlasting salvation"* by GOD to Israel were h 45:17).
According to the Law of Moses, one man cannot die for the sins of another man. Each man shall die for his own sins Deuteronomy 24:16, *"The fathers shall not be put to death for the children, neither shall the children be put to death for the fathers; every man shall be put to death for his own sin"*. If one wishes to argue that Jesus was not a man, this is their prerogative, however it does not address the issue of *"every man shall be put to death for his own sin"*. That individual must *"own up"* before GOD for the own sins that he did. Additionally, according to the Prophets, the Priests will continue to make atonement for the sins of Israel as a Statute forever, Leviticus 16:34, *"And this shall be an Everlasting Statute unto you, to make Atonement for the sons of Israel because of all their Sins once in the year"*. So, if Jesus died for Israel, what need would GOD YHWH have for HIS Priests to continue to make atonement for Israel's sins? Israel has eternal salvation, (Isaiah 45:17) *O Israel, that art saved by YHWH with an Everlasting Salvation"*. Israel is a *"redeemed"* people, YHWH'S first born son according to HIS own words and the words of HIS Prophets.

According to the Prophets, only *"YHWH"* is Israel's *"Savior"* Isaiah 43:11 *"I, even I, am YHWH; and beside Me there is no Saviour"*. In addition, being *"savior"* or *"messiah"* and dying for sin are two separate issues. According to the Law of Moses, Jesus could not die for another, and YHWH is Savior. This leaves very little room for Jesus as either an offering for sin, or as a messiah.

Jesus said that he came not to bring peace, but *"fire"* and a *"sword"*. HE said he came to bring *"division"* (Luke 12:49-51; Matthew 10:34-39). Yet, one of the many prophesies regarding the future SEED of David speaks of him bringing *"peace, "justice"* and *"righteousness"* (Isaiah 9:5-6) when he comes. Not only did the very words of Jesus contradict the words of the Prophet Isaiah, but according to the Prophet Isaiah, once his reign begins, it will be *"henceforth and forever"*. Well, the *"henceforth and forever"* reign of the SEED of David bringing *peace, justice* and *righteousness* has not manifested itself as yet. However, the *"fire, sword* and *division"* spoken of by Jesus is still with us.

Isaiah 45:24-25, (24) Only in YHWH, shall one say of Me, is victory and strength; even to Him shall men come in confusion, all they that were incensed against Him. (25) In YHWH shall all the SEED of Israel be justified, and shall glory.

According to TaNaKh, YHWH has known only Israel, of all the nations of the earth and only the name of YHWH is exalted Psalm 148:13, *"Let them praise the name of YHWH, for His name alone is exalted; His glory is above the earth and heaven"*. Only Israel has YHWH known of all the nations of the earth, *Amos 3:2, "You only have I known of all the families of the earth; therefore I will visit upon you all your iniquities"*. It is difficult to reconcile the idea of the name of "YHWH" as the only exalted GOD, along with the utterance of any other *"name"*, regardless of what that name may be or it's origin.

The Gospels say that *"the Law"* came from Moses, but *"grace and truth"* came from Jesus (John 1:17). But the Law of Moses is the foundation of grace and truth for all eternity. This could not have been articulated any better than as written by King David himself. *Grace* and *truth* abound for those who keep the **testimonies** of YHWH'S Covenant.

Psalm 25:10, (10) All the paths of YHWH are <u>mercy</u> and <u>truth</u> unto such as <u>keep</u> His Covenant and His Testimonies

The Law of YHWH is mercy and truth. The word of GOD is truth and YHWH is the GOD of mercy, *"unto such as **KEEP** HIS Covenant and HIS Testimonies"*. How could Jesus bring or give something for which Israel already possessed from their GOD YHWH? Indeed, but for the grace of GOD, all of mankind would have been destroyed.

Genesis 6:8, (8) But Noah found <u>grace</u> in the eyes of YHWH.

Psalms 84:12, (12) For YHWH God is a Sun and a Shield; <u>YHWH giveth Grace and Glory</u>; no good thing will He withhold from them that walk uprightly.

Because Jesus had said that he came for the *"lost sheep of the House of Israel"* and he told Israel to keep the Commandments to *"enter into life"* (Matthew 19:17), anything else he may have said which was outside of the Commandments of the Law are of no concern with regard to Israel and what they should do. In other words, by definition, by Israel keeping the Commandments of the Law, nothing else matters and is of none affect. Life Eternal is not something Jesus could have offered to Israel, as it already existed for them through *keeping* the Commandments of the Law of YHWH.

The Commandments of the Law of YHWH are a blessing to Israel and the Jewish people. It is a gift from GOD Almighty. Think about this for just a moment. The creator of all existence made man and gave him HIS Law to live by so that man might live by it and to have eternal life. It is *HIS Name* which Israel is to worship, to adore, to call to, pray to and to make their plea. HIS name is **"YHWH"**.

Exodus 20:1-3, (1) And GOD spoke all these words, saying: (2) <u>I am YHWH thy GOD</u>, who brought thee out of the land of Egypt, out of the house of bondage. (3) <u>Thou shalt have no other gods before Me.</u>

Israel is to call only on the name of YHWH when in need of help, and for their own salvation. Calling on <u>any other name</u>, or following *after <u>anyone</u>* or *<u>anything</u>* (*god*) else is foreign to the words of YHWH, the Law and the Prophets of the ancient religion of Israel. This includes the *"name"* of Jesus.

It is the name of **"YHWH"** by which Israel is **"delivered"** and it is the name of **"YHWH"** to which Israel must ask for the **"forgiveness of sins"**.

"O Israel, that art saved by YHWH with an Everlasting Salvation".

What did David have to say about YHWH'S salvation, eternal life from the LORD his GOD? For GOD'S promise to David was for ever and ever.

Psalms 21:1-5, (1) For the Leader. A Psalm of David. (2) <u>O YHWH</u>, in Thy strength the king rejoiceth; <u>and in Thy salvation how greatly doth he exult!</u> (3) Thou hast given him his heart's desire, and the request of his lips Thou hast not withholden. Selah (4) For Thou meetest him with choicest *blessings; Thou settest a crown of fine gold on his head. (5) He asked Life of Thee, Thou gavest it him; even length of days for ever and ever.*

It was to YHWH that David prayed, it was from YHWH David was delivered and received salvation, and it was from YHWH that David asked and received life for *"ever and ever"*. A person must ask, why would GOD sacrifice his *"only begotten son"* for something which already existed for Israel?

ISRAEL TAKE NOTICE

"And what great nation is there, that hath Statutes and Ordinances so righteous as all this LAW, which I set before you this day?"

Matthew 19:16-17, (16) And, behold, one came and said unto him, Good Master, what good thing shall I do, that I may have eternal life? (17) And he said unto him, Why callest thou me good? there is none good but one, that is, God: but if thou wilt enter into life, Keep the Commandments.

Matthew 5:17-20, (17) Think not that I am come to destroy the Law, or the Prophets: I am not come to destroy, but to fulfil. (18) For verily I say unto you, Till heaven and earth pass, one jot or one tittle shall in no wise pass from the Law, till all be fulfilled.(19) Whosoever therefore shall break one of these least Commandments, and shall teach men so, he shall be called the least in the kingdom of heaven: but whosoever shall DO and TEACH them, the same shall be called great in the kingdom of . (20) For I say unto you, That except your righteousness shall exceedthe righteousness of the scribes and Pharisees, ye shall in no case enter into the kingdom of heaven.

If Jesus preached to Israel to *"do"* and to *"teach"* and to *"keep the Commandments"*, then *"keep the Commandments"* is what his followers should have done. According to Jesus, his life was to *"fulfill"* the Law. If this was so, then he was expressing what all Israel is to do by the Covenant which they have with their GOD YHWH. So then nothing else he either said or did, that was either implied, appeared to contradict, was understood or misunderstood that was outside of the Law should be relevant. In order for Israel to *"keep"* the Commandments of GOD, then nothing else said by Jesus which is not part of the Commandments of GOD and in HIS Law, should be of concern. So by definition, all things outside of the Law become unlawful according to the words spoken by Jesus himself and need not be done.

If keeping GOD'S Law was what Israel was to do, then anything which is not part of GOD'S Law and HIS Commandments is by definition, *"outside"* the Commandments, the Statutes and Ordinances of the Law of YHWH, and therefore is *"unlawful"* to Israel. If it is *not* *"legal"* according to the Law, then it is *"illegal"* according to the Law. *"But if thou wilt enter into Life, keep the Commandments".*

If one removes all of what Jesus said or did that is not according to the Statutes and Ordinances of the Law, and everything and anything that is not GOD'S Commandments in HIS written Safer Torah, then all that will be left is the holy path, *"Ha Derech Ha Chodesh"* to enter into *"life"*. For Jesus may have been correct when he said that the Pharisees could not tell his doctrine, if it was from GOD, because they did not know their own Law. For only by Israel truly living GOD'S Law and thereby knowing GOD'S Law can the truth or untruth of the words of Jesus be understood and the truth can be separated from lie. Keep the Law, ignore the rest. The Law of Moses is GOD'S *"Holy Path"* to life eternal.

But if one does not "*know*" GOD'S Law, which is truth, then removing and separating out the rest of the words of Jesus or anyone else becomes much more difficult. The Jewish people then and now who do not truly "*know*" the Law of Moses as written only in the Safer Torah, cannot separate out the words of Jesus (or other man made "*oral*" laws) to see what lies beneath. He spoke to Israel of keeping the Law of their forefathers to enter into life. That was his message to Israel. If he was a prophet sent to put Israel to the *proof*, the rest could be considered "*smoke and mirrors*". But many could not see the truth for lack of knowledge. They may have been blinded by their own ignorance of the Law of Moses, the confusion of the so called "*oral law*" of the rabbis, and the "*smoke*" of the *miracles* of Jesus, "*My people are destroyed for lack of knowledge*". What is knowledge but the fear of GOD, and keeping the Commandments of HIS Law?

.

The Commandments are the Law! Keeping the Law is entering Life. Choose Life. Keep the Commandments of YHWH'S Law and live.

Leviticus 18:5, (5) Ye shall therefore <u>keep</u> My statutes, and Mine ordinances, <u>which if a man do</u>, he shall <u>live</u> by them: I am YHWH.

The final words will come from the Prophet Moses, the greatest prophet of GOD. YHWH gave Moses the task of leading Israel out of bondage and delivering to them the Law which HE had prepared for them to "*live*" by when they entered the land promised to them. Shortly before his death, Moses admonished Israel to keep YHWH'S Commandments, and to choose "*life*" by keeping GOD'S Law. This is the same <u>message</u> Jesus had <u>for life</u>. He said almost the same thing in the Book of John. "*And I know that HIS Commandment is life*". What part of this is to difficult to understand?

Jesus said that GOD'S Commandments are eternal life!

John 12:50, (50) <u>And I know that HIS Commandment is Life Everlasting</u>: whatsoever I speak therefore, even <u>as the Father said unto me</u>, so I speak.

To the Jewish people, Jesus said keeping GOD'S Commandments is "*Eternal Life*". If the Commandments of GOD are Life Everlasting, then, "*end of story*". Other than reminding Israel to "*keep*" the Commandments of GOD, what else could he offer? What else did he offer? Again in 10:25-28, Jesus seems to be saying the same thing when he was asked,"*what must I do to receive eternal life?*". Keeping GOD'S Law is included with loving YHWH with all one's heart and soul, he was saying obey and keep GOD'S Commandments. They are inseparable.

It is in this light that those words of Jesus the Jew should be understood about keeping GOD'S Commandments,"*But if thou wilt enter into **Life**, keep the Commandments. And Moses, "*Therefore choose **Life** that thou mayest **Live***". Moses and Jesus, two sons of Israel, were speaking about keeping the Law. Both equate keeping the Commandments of GOD with "*life*" in order to *live*. Keeping GOD'S Commandments is the *blessing* of life itself. It is good.

Just before he died, Moses reminded Israel to keep YHWH'S Commandments, HIS Statutes, and Ordinances so they would "*live*". He told them this just before they entered into Canaan to take possession of their inheritance, for he had been told by YHWH they would go astray one day. To obey YHWH and to choose "***LIFE***" was his message. As if a fork in the road being put before the sojourner to choose which way to go, GOD gave to Israel a choice between life and death. It was the choice for each individual SEED of Abraham which way he would choose. It remains the same choice for Israel this day. The fork in the road and the choice to be made still exists for all of the sons of Jacob.

In a sense, these words to Israel before entering the Promised Land by Moses is a metaphor for all of ones life, including ones eternal existence as each of Jacob's sons makes his way across life's stage, choosing what to do and how it should be done. According to the Law of GOD, or not. Which leads us back to the words of King David again, *"For Thou renderest to every man according to his work".*

"I call heaven and earth to witness against you this day, that I have set before thee life and death, the blessing and the curse; therefore choose life, that thou mayest <u>live</u>, thou and thy SEED"

Deuteronomy 30:1-20 (1) <u>And it shall come to pass, when all these things are come upon thee, the blessing and the curse, which I have set before thee, and thou shalt bethink thyself among all the nations, whither YHWH thy God hath driven thee, (2) and shalt return unto YHWH thy God,</u> and hearken to His voice according to all that I command thee this day, thou and thy children, with <u>all</u> thy <u>heart,</u> and with all thy <u>soul;</u> (3) that then YHWH thy God will turn thy captivity, and have compassion upon thee, and will return and gather thee from all the peoples, whither YHWH thy God hath scattered thee. (4) If any of thine that are dispersed be in the uttermost parts of heaven, from thence will YHWH thy God gather thee, and from thence will He fetch thee. (5) And YHWH thy God will bring thee into the land which thy fathers possessed, and thou shalt possess it; and He will do thee good, and multiply thee above thy fathers. (6) <u>And YHWH thy God will circumcise thy heart,</u> and the <u>heart</u> of thy <u>SEED,</u> to love YHWH thy GOD with all thy <u>heart,</u> and with all thy <u>soul,</u> <u>that thou mayest LIVE.</u> (7) And YHWH thy God will put all these curses upon thine enemies, and on them that hate thee, that persecuted thee. (8) And thou shalt return and hearken to the voice of YHWH, <u>and do all His Commandments which I command thee this day.</u> (9) And YHWH thy GOD will make thee over-abundant in all the work of thy hand, in the fruit of thy body, and in the fruit of thy cattle, and in the fruit of thy land, for good; for YHWH will again rejoice over thee for good, as HE rejoiced over thy fathers; (10) if thou shalt hearken to the voice of YHWH thy God, <u>to keep HIS Commandments and HIS Statutes which are written in this BOOK of the LAW;</u> if thou turn unto YHWH thy GOD with all thy <u>heart,</u> and with all thy <u>soul.</u> (11) <u>For this Commandment which I command thee this day, it is not too hard for thee, neither is it far off.</u> (12) It is not in heaven, that thou shouldest say: 'Who shall go up for us to heaven, and bring it unto us, and make us to hear it, that we may do it?' (13) Neither is it beyond the sea, that thou shouldest say: 'Who shall go over the sea for us, and bring it unto us, and make us to hear it, that we may do it?' (14) <u>But the word is very nigh unto thee, in thy mouth, and in thy heart, that thou mayest do it.</u> (15) See, I have set before thee this day <u>LIFE</u> and <u>good,</u> and death and evil, (16) in that I command thee this day to love YHWH thy GOD, to walk in His ways, and to <u>keep HIS Commandments</u> and HIS <u>Statutes</u> and HIS <u>Ordinances;</u> <u>then thou shalt LIVE</u> and multiply, and YHWH thy GOD shall bless thee in the land whither thou goest in to possess it. (17) But if thy heart turn away, and thou wilt not hear, but shalt be drawn away, and worship other gods, and serve them; (18) I declare unto you this day, that ye shall surely perish; ye shall not prolong your days upon the land, whither thou passest over the Jordan to go in to possess it. (19) I call heaven and earth to witness against you this day, <u>THAT I HAVE SET BEFORE THEE LIFE AND DEATH,</u> the blessing and the curse; <u>THEREFORE CHOOSE LIFE, THAT THOU MAYEST LIVE,</u> thou and thy <u>SEED;</u> (20) to <u>love</u> YHWH thy GOD, to <u>hearken</u> to His voice, and to <u>cleave FOR THAT IS THY LIFE,</u> and the length of thy days; that thou mayest dwell in the land which YHWH swore unto thy fathers, to Abraham, to Isaac, and to Jacob, to give them.

The words of Moses are as true and relevant to Israel and the Jewish people today as when he first spoke them. Make not the mistake of thinking GOD'S word is diminished with age. Age only applies to man. Neither YHWH nor HIS word changes with time, *"For I YHWH change not.."*. For Israel, the Law of YHWH and HIS Commandments is Life Eternal. *"Therefore, choose life, that thou mayest live"*.

If a son of Israel accepted everything Jesus said about himself, then he would have to accept that there are two *"gods"* with two different names, one being *"YHWH"* and the other being *"Jesus"*. These two different names are hard to reconcile as <u>one</u>, and to place into <u>one</u> existence as the same being. GOD has ONE name and HE is ONE. That person should know that there is only one GOD , HE is *ONE* and HIS name is *ONE*. It is **"YHWH"**. *Only* the name of **"YHWH"** will be exalted, *"Let them praise the name of* **YHWH***, <u>for His name alone is exalted;</u> His glory is above the earth and heaven "*.

'FOR THAT IS THY LIFE'

It was said from the outset, that the approach of this book was to view Jesus through the eyes of the Jewish population. For the Jewish person then and now. To see Jesus as Israel may have while living under the Law as Jesus was himself, *not* as the nations, the Gentiles see him. To see Jesus as a fellow Jew. Jesus the Jew, told Israel his people, to keep the **Commandments of YHWH** there GOD if they want to enter into *"life"*. For the Jewish person, this means keeping the Law of Moses. As Moses the greatest Prophet of GOD stated, *"For that is* <u>*thy*</u> **life**". For Israel and the Jewish people, keep the Law.

Isaiah 2:5, (5) O house of Jacob, come ye, and let us walk in the light of YHWH.

”For <u>that</u> is thy life”

5480012R00203

Printed in Great Britain
by Amazon.co.uk, Ltd.,
Marston Gate.